CHAUCER'S
DREAM POETRY

LONGMAN ANNOTATED TEXTS

GENERAL EDITORS
Charlotte Brewer, *Hertford College, Oxford*
H. R. Woudhuysen, *University College London*
Daniel Karlin, *University College London*

PUBLISHED TITLES
Michael Mason, *Lyrical Ballads*
Alexandra Barratt, *Women's Writing in Middle English*
Tim Armstrong, *Thomas Hardy: Selected Poems*
René Weis, *King Lear: A Parallel Text Edition*
James Sambrook, *William Cowper: The Task and Selected Other Poems*
Joseph Phelan, *Clough: Selected Poems*
Douglas Brooks-Davies, *Edmund Spenser: Selected Shorter Poems*
Priscilla Bawcutt, *William Dunbar: Selected Poems*
Randall Martin, *Women Writers in Renaissance England*
Helen Ostovich, *Ben Jonson: Four Comedies*
Helen Phillips and Nick Havely, *Chaucer's Dream Poetry*

CHAUCER'S DREAM POETRY

EDITED BY

HELEN PHILLIPS and NICK HAVELY

Longman

LONDON AND NEW YORK

Addison Wesley Longman
Edinburgh Gate
Harlow, Essex CM20 2JE, England
and Associated Companies throughout the world.

*Published in the United States of America
by Addison Wesley Longman Inc., New York.*

First published 1997

ISBN 0 582 04012 4   CSD
ISBN 0 582 04011 6   PPR

British Library Cataloguing-in-Publication Data

A catalogue record of this book is
available from the British Library

Library of Congress Cataloging-in-Publication Data

Chaucer, Geoffrey, d.   1400.
    Chaucer's dream poetry : edited by Helen Phillips and Nick Havely.
        p.   cm.
    Includes bibliographical references (p.   ).
    ISBN 0–582–04011–6 (pbk.). –– ISBN 0–582–04012–4 (hard)
    1. Dreams––Poetry.   2. Civilization, Medieval––14th century-
–Poetry.   I. Phillips, Helen.   II. Havely, Nick.   III. Title.
PR1852.P45   1997
821′.1––DC21   96-54627
                                                          CIP

Set by 33 in Sabon 9½/12 pt
Produced by Longman Singapore Publishers (Pte) Ltd.
Printed in Singapore

329645

CONTENTS

PREFACE AND
ACKNOWLEDGEMENTS

This is a collaborative edition, rather than a jointly edited volume. Helen Phillips wrote the General Introduction and was responsible for the sections on the *Book of the Duchess*, the *Prologue* to the *Legend of Good Women*, and the *Legend of Dido* from the *Legend of Good Women*, while Nick Havely was responsible for the sections on the *Parliament of Fowls* and the *House of Fame*. Though we worked closely together as editors in planning the volume, we have taken separate responsibility for (and in some respects different approaches to) the individual critical introductions, the editing and notes to our five texts. Bearing in mind that students may have a particular interest in one of the poems, we have tried to make the five sections useful and coherent in their own right.

We do not include the whole of the *Legend of Good Women*, partly for practical reasons, but also because, in what appears to be Chaucer's later version (the so-called G version), only the *Prologue* is presented as a dream. The text of the *Legend of Good Women* used as the basis for the edition here is that of Cambridge University manuscript Gg.4.27, with the G version of the *Prologue*. This edition includes the G Prologue and one of the legends of 'good women': that of Dido, whose story is also – in an interestingly different way – told in the *House of Fame*.

We should like to thank Charlotte Brewer, the General Editor, Longman Annotated Texts, and Elizabeth Mann, Judith Bamber and Pat Root of Addison Wesley Longman for all their advice, encouragement and patience throughout the process of producing this book. We would like to thank Katy Coutts for her incomparable copy-editing. We also owe particular thanks to A.S.G. Edwards and Stephen Knight who each read substantial sections of our material in the final stages of the project and gave generously of their time, their help and advice. In addition, we are grateful for help of many different kinds to the following people: Kate Belsey, Jacques Berthoud, Julia Boffey, Alison McHardy, Alastair Minnis, Bernard O'Donoghue, Cicely Palser Havely, Morgan Kavanagh, Felicity

Riddy, Graeme Segal, Roger Sewell and David Wallace. We are grateful to the Department of English Studies, the University of Nottingham, and the Department of English, York University, for giving us research-leave to complete the book. And finally we would like to thank each other.

Helen Phillips
Nick Havely

ABBREVIATIONS

The following abbreviations are used throughout:

AA	Ovid, *Ars Amatoria*
A & A	Chaucer, *Anelida and Arcite*
Acts	The Acts of the Apostles
Astr	Chaucer, *Treatise on the Astrolabe*
Aen.	Virgil, *Aeneid*
An M	*Annuale Medievale*
BD	Chaucer, *Book of the Duchess*
BIHR	*Bulletin of the Institute of Historical Research*
BL	British Library
Boece	Chaucer's translation of Boethius's *De Consolatione Philosophiae*
CA	Gower, *Confessio Amantis*
CFMA	Classiques français du Moyen Age
ch.	chapter
Ch	Chaucer
Chau R	*Chaucer Review*
Chr.	The Book(s) of Chronicles
CL	*Comparative Literature*
Cl Prol	Chaucer, Prologue to the *Clerk's Tale*
Cl T	Chaucer, the *Clerk's Tale*
Comp d'Am	Chaucer, *Complaynt d'Amours*
Compl Mars	Chaucer, *Complaint of Mars*
Cons.	Boethius, *De Consolatione Philosophiae*
Conv.	Dante, *Il Convivio*
Cor.	Epistles of Paul to the Corinthians
CT	Chaucer, the *Canterbury Tales*
CUL	Cambridge University Library
CY Prol	Chaucer, the *Prologue* to the *Canon's Yeoman's Tale*
Dan.	The Book of Daniel
De propr rer	Bartholomaeus Anglicus, *De proprietatibus rerum*
Dec.	Boccaccio, *Decameron*

DVE	Dante, *De Vulgari Eloquentia*
EC	*Essays in Criticism*
EETS	Early English Text Society
EHR	*English Historical Review*
ELH	*Journal of English Literary History*
ELN	*English Language Notes*
E & S	*Essays and Studies*
E S	*English Studies*
E St	*Englische Studien*
Ex.	The Book of Exodus
Ezek.	Ezekiel
Fkl T	Chaucer, the *Franklin's Tale*
Fr.	French
Fri T	Chaucer, the *Friar's Tale*
Gen.	Genesis
Geneal	Boccaccio, *Genealogiae Deorum Gentilium*
Gen Prol	Chaucer, the *General Prologue* to the *Canterbury Tales*
Gk	Greek
Heath	H.F. Heath (ed.), *The Works of Geoffrey Chaucer*, London, 1898
Heb.	The Letter to the Hebrews
Her.	Ovid, *Heroides*
HF	Chaucer, the *House of Fame*
Inf.	Dante, *Inferno*
Isa.	The Book of Isaiah
JEGP	*Journal of English and Germanic Philology*
Jer.	The Book of Jeremiah
JMRS	*Journal of Medieval and Renaissance Studies*
Kn T	Chaucer, the *Knight's Tale*
Lam.	The Book of Lamentations
Lat.	Latin
LGW	Chaucer, the *Legend of Good Women*
LGWD	Chaucer, the *Legend of Dido* in *LGW* (used only in the Glossary and Index of Names)
LGWP	Chaucer, the *Prologue* to the *Legend of Good Women* (used only in the Glossary and Index of Names)
M Ae	*Medium Aevum*
Manc T	Chaucer, the *Manciple's Tale*
Matt.	Gospel according to St Matthew
ME	Middle English
MED	*Middle English Dictionary*

Med St	*Mediaeval Studies*
Merch T	Chaucer, the *Merchant's Tale*
Met.	Ovid, *Metamorphoses*
METh	*Medieval English Theatre*
Mil T	Chaucer, the *Miller's Tale*
Mk T	Chaucer, the *Monk's Tale*
MLR	*Modern Language Review*
MLT	Chaucer, the *Man of Law's Tale*
MLT Prol	Chaucer, the *Prologue* to the *Man of Law's Tale*
MLN	*Modern Language Notes*
MLQ	*Modern Language Quarterly*
MP	*Modern Philology*
MS, MSS	manuscript(s)
NM	*Neuphilologische Mitteilungen*
NPT	Chaucer, the *Nun's Priest's Tale*
OCD	*Oxford Classical Dictionary*
OE	Old English
OED	*Oxford English Dictionary*
OF	Old French
OT	Old Testament
par.	paragraph
Par.	Dante, *Paradiso*
PardT	Chaucer, the *Pardoner's Tale*
Pars T	Chaucer, the *Parson's Tale*
PF	Chaucer, the *Parliament of Fowls*
Phys T	Chaucer, the *Physician's Tale*
PL	*Patrologia cursus completus, Series latina*, ed. J.-P. Migne, Paris, 1841–79
PMLA	*Publications of the Modern Language Association*
Poetica J	*Poetica* (Tokyo)
PPl	Langland, *Piers Plowman*
Purg.	Dante, *Purgatorio*
repr.	reprinted
RES	*Review of English Studies*
Rev.	The Revelation of St John the Divine
rev.	revised
Riv.	*The Riverside Chaucer*, gen. ed. L.D. Benson, Oxford, 1987
Rob.	F.N. Robinson (ed.), *The Complete Works of Geoffrey Chaucer*, Oxford, 1957
Rom R	*Romanic Review*
RR	Guillaume de Lorris and Jean de Meun, *Le Roman de la*

	Rose (line references are to the edn of F. Lecoy, Paris, 1965–70)
Rv T	Chaucer, the *Reeve's Tale*
S & A	*Sources and Analogues of Chaucer's 'Canterbury Tales'*, eds W.F. Bryan and G. Dempster, Chicago, 1941, repr. New York, 1958
SAC	*Studies in the Age of Chaucer*
Sam.	The Book(s) of Samuel
SATF	Société des Anciens Textes Français
Shipm–Pri link	Chaucer, link between the *Shipman's* and *Prioress's Tales*
Shipm T	Chaucer, the *Shipman's Tale*
Sk.	W.W. Skeat (ed.), *The Complete Works of Geoffrey Chaucer* vol. III, Oxford, 1900
SN	*Studia neophilologica*
SN T	Chaucer, the *Second Nun's Tale*
SP	*Studies in Philology*
Spec	*Speculum*
Sq T	Chaucer, the *Squire's Tale*
STC	*Short Title Catalogue of Books Printed in England, Scotland and Ireland and of English Books Printed Abroad*, rev. edn, London, 1976–7
S Th	Aquinas, *Summa theologiae*
Sum Prol	Chaucer, the *Prologue* to the *Summoner's Tale*
Sum T	Chaucer, the *Summoner's Tale*
TC	Chaucer, *Troilus and Criseyde*
Tes.	Boccaccio, *Teseida*
Theb.	Statius, *Thebaid*
Thop	Chaucer, the *Tale of Sir Thopas*
TLF	Textes littéraires français
Trad.	*Traditio*
tr.	translation, translated by
TSLL	*Texas Studies in Literature and Language*
UTQ	*University of Toronto Quarterly*
VC	Gower, *Vox Clamantis*
WB Prol	Chaucer, the *Prologue* to the *Wife of Bath's Tale*
WB T	Chaucer, the *Wife of Bath's Tale*
YES	*Yearbook of English Studies*
<	derives from

CHRONOLOGY

1327	Edward III becomes king.
1337	The Hundred Years War between England and France begins.
c. 1342	Chaucer born in London.
1348–9	The Black Death.
1351	Statute of Labourers: attempt to restrict wages to pre-Black Death levels.
1357	Chaucer enters royal service as page in household of Countess of Ulster.
1359, also 1368, 1370, 1376, 1377	Chaucer in France on military and various royal missions.
1366	Chaucer in Spain, probably on government business. Possible date of marriage to Phillipa Pan, in service of Queen and later of Constanza, Duchess of Lancaster.
1367	Chaucer enters King's service.
1368	Death of Blanche, Duchess of Lancaster.
1369–75	Bertrand du Guesclin's successful campaign against England's territories in France.
1371	John of Gaunt marries Constanza of Castile.
1372–3	Chaucer in Genoa and Florence.
1374	Chaucer appointed Controller of Customs.
Before 1375?	The *Book of the Duchess*.
1375	Death of Boccaccio.
1377	Richard II becomes king, aged 10.
1378	Chaucer's second Italian journey: in Lombardy to negotiate with Bernardo Visconti.
Late 1370s or early 1380s	The *House of Fame*.
1377, 1379, 1381	Poll taxes.

1380	Death of French king Charles V, after period in which war with France was very unsuccessful from the English point of view.
1381	The Great Rising (also known as the Peasants' Revolt).
1382	Richard II marries Anne of Bohemia.
	Many of Wycliff's ideas condemned as heretical.
Early 1380s?	The *Parliament of Fowls*.
1380s to 1400	Chaucer working on the *Canterbury Tales*.
1385	Chaucer appointed Justice of the Peace in Kent.
c. 1385	*Troilus and Criseyde*, Chaucer's translation of Boethius.
1386	Chaucer Member of Parliament.
Late 1380s	*Legend of Good Women* (with F version of the *Prologue*).
1388	'Merciless Parliament' and appellant lords attack Richard II's favourites and style of rule, execute some of his supporters.
1389	Richard regains power from opponents in Parliament and the appellant lords.
	Chaucer appointed Clerk of the King's Works.
1393	Richard quarrels with City of London. Lavish pageant of reconciliation after their appeasement of the king.
1394	Death of Queen Anne of Bohemia.
1396	Richard II marries Isabelle of France.
	Measures to curb growth of Wycliffism.
1397–9	Richard II's 'tyranny': exile or execution of several of the king's opponents and critics.
	Henry Bolingbroke (John of Gaunt's son, future King Henry IV) sent into exile.
c. 1397?	G version of *Prologue* to the *Legend of Good Women*.
1399	Bolingbroke invades England.
	Deposition and murder of Richard II.
	Henry IV becomes king.
	Henry reconfirms Chaucer's grants, his income from royal service.
1400	Death of Chaucer, possibly on 25 October.

GENERAL
INTRODUCTION

———

CHAUCER AND DREAM POETRY

Chaucer wrote four dream poems, narratives framed by the fiction of a dream: the *Book of the Duchess* (*BD*) (after 1368), *House of Fame* (*HF*) (late 1370s or early 1380s), *Parliament of Fowls* (*PF*) (perhaps early 1380s) and the *Prologue* to the *Legend of Good Women* (*LGW*), written after about 1385, which exists in two forms. The suggested dating is very tentative. The *Prologue* to the *Legend*, which mentions writings by Chaucer including *HF*, *BD*, *PF* and *Troilus and Criseyde*, must be later than the other dream poems. On Chaucer's life and the historical context of his writing generally, see Pearsall 1992 and Dillon 1993.

No literary genre, with the possible exception of the romance, was more popular than the dream narrative with medieval writers, and none was employed with more versatility and creativity.[1] This must be to a great extent because of the opportunities it offered not only for variety of subject but also for sophistication of structure: for playing with different frames and narrative levels within the same work. It is easy in dream poems to move between narrative and lyric, or between narrative and debate or didactic speeches, and dreams readily accommodate both allegorically and realistically conceived characters and landscapes.

Dream literature began as a religious and philosophical genre, and even when medieval writers use it for satire or amusing and amorous subjects, it carries still the potential for serious purpose and enlightenment, which makes it particularly amenable for parody and satire, as well as for the complex shifts of tone and levels of seriousness characteristic of Chaucer's writing. When Guillaume de Lorris's *Roman de la Rose* (c. 1225) set the fashion for using the dream frame for writing about love, it conveyed also the assumption that sexual love was a serious subject for literature, worthy of intelligent and even philosophical scrutiny.

Love is the central theme of all Chaucer's dream poems. In all of them it is presented interrogatively, in relation to experiences and concepts which render it disturbing and problematic: love and death in *BD*, love and the record which books make of the human experience of the past in *HF* and *LGW*, and love considered, in *PF*, in relation to a cosmic, eternal and divine design, which is represented both by the figure of Nature and

3

by Cicero's vision of the harmonious realm of eternity. Chaucer was a courtier and a royal civil servant.[2] Though nothing certain is known of the precise circumstances of the composition of the four poems – whether they were aristocratic commissions, or how far they contain topical references – they all appear to be in some sense literature of the court. Issues perhaps arising from their role within court culture are discussed in relation to the individual texts on pp. 43–5 (BD), 225–8 (PF) and 294–9 (LGW). Chaucer in all his writings is a poet of complexity, multiple viewpoints and denial of closure. Life at court may, as Patterson suggests,[3] have encouraged writing with these qualities because its imposition on its arts of 'an absolutist idealism' (its myths of chivalric love and honour) conflicts with other elements of the writer's experience of the court: heterogeneity, self-interest and fear – to say nothing of the anxieties of life and the multivalences of language itself. Whatever the causes, the text in these four poems is often a record of emotional pain, and narrative becomes in them a landscape entered by a tentative, deferential, indecisive observer, easily bullied by those he encounters.

Unlike many of the French poems that were their chief models, Chaucer's dream poems do not end with a hope for comfort or solutions to the problems they raise, and they either finish inconclusively (BD, PF) or are unfinished (HF, LGW). They may well have been designed for performance to an audience and for discussion, which might encourage a multifaceted, open-ended approach to their subjects; but it is also characteristic of Chaucer's writing throughout his career to produce texts full of contradictory impulses and often radical discordances whose presence is half-veiled from us by a humorous and elegant surface and undogmatic manner.

Ancient dream narratives and dream theories

Many ancient dream narratives present messages from God or the gods. Examples include Joseph's and Pharaoh's dreams (Gen. 37, 41), the visions in the Book of Daniel, and the messages sent by gods to humans during sleep in Homer's *Iliad* and *Odyssey*. The Homeric concept of the dream itself as a divine messenger is reflected in Ovid's tale of Ceyx and Alcyone in the *Metamorphoses* Book XI (a source for BD), where, at Juno's command, Somnus, the god of Sleep, sends Morpheus, one of the thousand dreams who are his sons, to take a message to the sleeping Alcyone.[4]

Many classical, Jewish and early Christian dream narratives describe journeys to the next world, revealing to a mortal those heavenly truths not normally accessible to human knowledge. Examples include the Book of

Ezekiel and the third-century *Apocalypse of St Paul*. They belong to a wider category of literary journeys to supernatural realms, not all of which are presented as dreams, which includes Odysseus's journey to the world of the dead in Book X of the *Odyssey* and Aeneas's descent to the Underworld in the *Aeneid*, Book VI. The Book of Revelation (the Apocalypse), the last book of the Bible, is a vision of heaven, full of mysterious allegorical and symbolic figures and animals. This tradition of the otherworld journey continued into medieval literature, gaining fresh impetus from the developing doctrine of purgatory, which gave rise to narratives where the living received messages from the dead, warning them to repent or asking for prayers to aid their own progress through the cleansing process of purgatory.[5]

Perhaps as a legacy both of the ancient practice of professional dream interpreters and priests explaining dreams, and also of the classical literary device of dreams as messengers or advice given by a god, medieval dream poems often contain a dream guide or teacher, a figure of supernatural authority. One of the most influential dream narratives was Cicero's *Somnium Scipionis* ('Dream of Scipio'), c. 55 BC. It is an important element in *PF*. In it Scipio Africanus the Younger has a conversation about his grandfather, Scipio Africanus the Elder, and subsequently dreams that his grandfather takes him on a journey to the heavens. He foretells his grandson's future, teaches Scipio that the soul is heavenly and immortal, and shows him the harmony of the cosmos and how tiny the earth is when seen from the vantage-point of heaven. Chaucer includes a summary of it in *PF*, where Scipio is the dream guide – but to a garden of love.

Somnium Scipionis puts human destiny in the largest and highest possible context: the eternal realm of the cosmos, and presents the human soul as an entity which rightly belongs in heaven rather than on earth. It has a dualist world-view, despising the world of the body and passions as a prison to the immortal soul. Chaucer provocatively placed his retelling of it before the dream section of his *PF*, which is a survey not of a spiritual realm but of the bewildering contradictions of sexual bodily passion on earth: the contrasted powers of Venus and Nature, the tensions between romantic idealism and the humdrum necessity of reproduction, and the enigma of desire as the cause of both death and fruitfulness.

Most cultures have believed that dreams, or at least certain dreams, had significance, and the Middle Ages inherited from antiquity writings which offered theories about the nature of dreams or guides to interpretation, and added further 'dream books' to them, including the popular *Somniale Danielis*.[6] Among the most important writers on the nature and significance of dreams are Aristotle, Cicero, Calcidius, Macrobius, Augustine, Gregory the Great, and Vincent of Beauvais. Calcidius and Macrobius both discussed dreams in the course of writing commentaries on other works: Calcidius's *Commentary on Plato's Timaeus*, and Macrobius's *Commentary on the Dream of Scipio*. Macrobius's study, c. 400, is concerned not only with dreams but with other issues, including cosmology, philosophy and the role and value of fiction itself.[7]

Classical and medieval dream theory is an interesting topic in its own right, but, in fact, medieval dream poetry has about as much – or as little – relationship to it as modern theories about aggression have to do with the essential strengths of the detective story.[8] Yet, since Chaucer mentions Macrobius (*BD*, l. 284; *PF*, l. 111) and in some minor ways draws on what he said about dreams, it is necessary to understand his classifications. Like earlier writers on dreams, Macrobius divides dreams into categories. Two types of dream lack prophetic significance: the *insomnium* and the *visum* (or *phantasma*). The *insomnium* results from physical causes or mental distress, or merely mirrors the preoccupations of waking life. The *visum* is a dream of confused and confusing spectres or shapes rushing through the mind, on the borderline between waking and sleeping. Dreams which offer reliable knowledge of the future are divided into the *visio*, a visual presentation of future events, the *oraculum*, where an authority figure reveals the future, and the *somnium*, which presents truths in a symbolic, enigmatic form. In practice, perhaps inevitably, writers often make creative use of dream experiences that dream theory would classify as insignificant. Though theorists dismissed as meaningless those dreams that reflected daytime preoccupations, poets often represent just such a reflection, as in the dream repetition of waking activities in *PF*, lines 99–105, and *LGW*, lines 104–6. When Chaucer and contemporary poets make references to the traditional dream classifications, or other items of dream lore, these tend to belong to the surface of the work. Their poetry does explore the theme of dreaming with profundity and subtlety, but not by turning outward to medieval dream theory; instead, they challenge readers to ponder what a fictional dream means in relation to other internal elements in a particular text. Froissart, for example, in the *Espinette amoureuse* and *Joli buisson de jeunesse*, uses a dream as part of a set of parallels, which may include inset stories, lyrics, and other symbols of representation like a mirror or allegorical edifice, to raise questions about different kinds of representation and the relation of emotional experience to outward, social life. When Langland in *Piers Plowman* questions whether one should take dreams seriously (citing the oft-quoted advice *Somnia ne cures*, 'Pay no attention to dreams'), he puts dreams, together with writing poetry, into problematic relationship to the Christian's duty of active love and work.[9] There is, in fact, always an element of literary game when poets raise questions about the seriousness or interpretation of their dreams, as Chaucer does in *BD* when he says that not even Macrobius or Joseph could interpret his dream: the author has created the dream, together with whatever degree of intelligibility or opacity it offers to the reader, whereas real dreams, despite their deep resemblances to poetic images, are involuntary.

Visionary writings and literary dreams

Dream poetry overlaps with, yet is discernibly distinct from, mystical literature. Most dream poems are consciously literary. The genre is usually not really about dreams or visions as subjects; rather, the fictional device of the dream is a form which facilitates manipulation of a variety of literary structures: frames, juxtapositions, allegory, shifts between narrative levels, and so on. Indeed, literature and fiction themselves become a major subject for late medieval dream poems. Dream poems make the worlds inside and outside the dream frame seem significantly distinct. Mystical visions, in contrast, are presented as a direct knowledge of God's truth, the divine reality suddenly present within everyday, waking reality, and breaking any distinction between them. Ezekiel, typically, conveys such a moment with words like, 'Then I looked and beheld ...', or 'The spirit lifted me up and brought me to the east gate of the Lord's house ...', or 'The word of the Lord came unto me, saying ...' (opening verses of Ezek. 10, 11, 12). The great medieval mystics, like Bernard of Clairvaux, Hildegard of Bingen, Julian of Norwich, Walter Hilton, offer their writings as God-given revelations of truth, and rarely describe these truths as coming in sleep. With some early medieval narratives it is true that it is sometimes difficult to decide whether the author intended them to be read as truth or fiction, and that continues to be true in particular of revelations of purgatory. Many fictional dream poems which are not presented as visionary reality, including *Piers Plowman*, nevertheless explore the subjects of truth and falsehood, and of what kind of truth fictions can have. These are also central themes of secular texts, including Machaut's *Voir Dit* and Chaucer's *HF* and *LGW*. Macrobius's *Commentary on the Dream of Scipio* itself discussed the value of fictional writings as well as the typology of dreams.

Some of the most profound literary visions never explicitly describe their narrative as a dream: these include Boethius's *Consolation of*

Philosophy, a work that had enormous influence on Chaucer's writing and thought, and Dante's *Divine Comedy* (c. 1310).[10] The *Divine Comedy*, with its three-fold vision of *Inferno, Purgatorio ad Paradiso*, is the greatest Christian version of the literary journey to the next world.

Medieval dream narratives

Dream fiction is a genre which encourages the mingling of concepts and styles that belong to different disciplines. For example, in the *Complaint of Nature* of Alain de Lille (c. 1125–1203), we find scholastic and theological speculation infused in the heady romance of luxuriant poetic description, and a vision which examines temporal matters – sex, desire, marriage and homosexuality – in relation to philosophical theories about Creation and cosmic harmony. The narrator is granted a vision of Nature herself, the representative of God the Creator in the living world, presiding over what should be (if it were not for human wilfulness and disorderliness in the conduct of sexual affairs) the harmonious and sacred processes of life and reproduction. Chaucer says in *PF*, lines 316–18, that his own figure of Nature is based on Alain's Nature.

As the tradition of philosophical and religious visions grew and flourished, so poets, scholars, theologians and humorists developed the dream genre for an extraordinary variety of subjects, political, satirical, devout and didactic. The third book of the *Lamentations of Matheolus* (c. 1295) is a satirical dream vision of a heaven where married men – whose sufferings on earth are so terrible – are placed above the saints and martyrs of paradise as reward for what they have endured. Paradoxically, this anti-feminist vision may have influenced the *Prologue* to Chaucer's *Legend* (Phillips 1995a). The Latin dream poem *Gregory's Garden* (after 1280) resembles *HF*; it is a dream journey with an eagle as guide, which considers the place of human music in the divine plan.[11] The *Songe du Vergier* (1378), a French version of a long Latin treatise about major political and legal issues, especially the power of king and pope, employs a form previously associated with debates about questions of love, a dialogue – set within a dream frame – between a cleric and a knight. Two English alliterative examples, *Winner and Waster* and the *Parliament of the Three Ages*, are debates about ranks and relationships in society; many dream poems use the dream to frame debate or allegory. The melancholy mental turmoil attributed to many dream poem narrators before their dream is a device which suggests unresolved problems and provides a contrast with the ensuing order and clarity of debate or personification allegory within the dream frame. The dream often marks out an area for analysis or portrayal of abstract issues. We see that often when dreams are interpolated into longer narratives, like the dream of Fortune which comes to Arthur in the *Alliterative Morte Arthure*. Dreams within romances may be used to indicate emotional truths or warn about the future, often to a character at a point of crisis, and they sometimes evince more interest in the nature and psychology of dreaming as such than does dream poetry.[12]

Framed narratives, of which the narrative enclosed by a dream is only one type, became increasingly common in fifteenth- and sixteenth-century France, England and Scotland. An interesting development is the popularity of dreams for prologues and prefaces, for example in three of the prologues to Douglas's translation of the *Aeneid*, his *Eneados* (1513). This reveals the extent to which in late medieval literature the dream has become a figure for poetic inspiration or composition, an implication encouraged by the practice of both Chaucer and his French contemporaries.

The popularity of the modern critical term 'dream poem' obscures the fact that the dream is only one of many framing devices: others are the garden, the palace, the temple, the island, or an initial statement that the author rode out, or wandered in solitary melancholy.[13] A statement that the narrator walked or rode out is as common as the statement that she or he dreamed, as preface to a revelation. Several different frames may be used one inside the other. The special popularity of the garden as a narrative frame is due to the most famous medieval dream poem, the *Roman de la Rose*.

The *Roman de la Rose*

The *Roman de la Rose* is two linked works: Guillaume de Lorris began it around 1225 but left it unfinished, and it was continued and completed by Jean de Meun between 1269 and 1278. In de Lorris's *Rose* the narrator says that he fell asleep and dreamt a marvellous dream, which afterwards came true. In this dream he goes for a walk in May and comes to a walled garden. It is this second framing device, the garden rather than the dream, that provides this text's most significant division between what lies inside and what lies outside the frame. Outside the garden are representations of a decidedly puzzling combination of states: Hate, Wickedness, Ill-breeding, Covetousness, Avarice, Envy, Sorrow, Old Age, Hypocrisy and Poverty. Admitted through a gate opened by Idleness, the narrator enters a garden owned by Pleasure, where the God of Love is found. Inside, dancing a *carole*, is another and contrasting group, made up of Happiness, Beauty, Wealth, Liberality, Generosity, Courtesy, Idleness and Youth.

Clearly these contrasts are challenging readers to try to define what it is that is presented inside the garden frame: a world of rich, well-born, attractive and generous-hearted young people, where sexual desire proves irresistible. The contradictions in human love are presented through two antithetical authority figures: the God of Love, who wounds the dreamer and demands his total submission, and Lady Reason, who admonishes him to reject such enslavement to passion. As with many later dream poems, the scenes invite the reader to judge as well as read. The *Rose* offers a variety of speakers, each claiming authority. Which, if any, correspond to the moral standpoint of the author? How, too, do we assess its contradictory spatial symbolism, an Eden-like garden ruled by Pleasure and a cruel God of Love? The space enclosed by the garden wall is both a total, self-sufficient world and a partial world, for most of the serious elements of life are left outside it. The *Rose* created a precedent for challengingly ambiguous mixtures of register and literary allusion. Its narrator-dreamer often seems wilful and naive: we cannot rely on him always to see clearly or judge wisely on our behalf.

The continuation by Jean de Meun increased the poem's complexity and potentiality for ironic readings. De Meun's narrative is both more comic and more philosophical, more sensual, even bawdy, and more intellectual. It provides a popular summary of contemporary ideas on many topics: Nature, the planets, fortune, free will, and so on, presented through the speeches of the personifications and enriched with examples and short anecdotes from classical history and literature. At its close the dreamer achieves his goal of sexual intercourse, described with a relish for the body and its sensual needs, and also in an unreverential and unreticent language used for sexual matters elsewhere in the work, which shocked many medieval readers. *En route* to this conclusion, much of de Meun's narrative is filled with cynical and anti-feminist speeches: an Old Bawd tells of the tricks and deceptions of women (ll. 12710–14516), the Jealous Husband attacks women (ll. 8426–9390), Nature and Genius ('Reproduction') talk of the necessary role of sex in a world where Atropos – death – has power. De Meun, who had translated Boethius's *Consolation of Philosophy* into French, includes a long passage about Fortune (ll. 5812–6870) which was an important source for *BD*.

The *Rose* is so complex a work that readers have always been divided over whether it is for or against love, whether it is written from a moral or amoral standpoint, and whether it should be read ironically or not. It was extremely influential and it also generated opposition (see Badel 1980). The sections which caused most offence are in the de Meun continuation, especially the misogynist and libertine speeches mentioned above. One later defence of women, the *Vray disant advocate des dames*, c. 1500, says misogynists have two books hidden in their closets: the *Lamentations* of Matheolus and the *Rose* (and, like Chaucer's *Legend*, ll. 280–1, it contrasts the reliable evidence of historians – Orosius and Valerius Maximus – for woman's virtue).[14] The *Roman de la Rose* also inspired virtuous parody, like Guillaume de Deguileville's *Pèlerinage de vie humaine* (c. 1332). Deguileville, a Cistercian monk, composed this as an anti-*Rose*, a dream allegory about progress towards salvation rather than towards sexual satisfaction.[15] Chaucer's *Legend* belongs, ostensibly at least, to this tradition of presenting the *Rose* as a work insulting to women, against which other works must be written as a redress. At the beginning of the fifteenth century, Christine de Pizan inaugurated the *Querelle de la Rose*, a literary debate about the poem: on one side, she and Jean Gerson, Chancellor of the University of Paris, condemned its immorality and misogyny; on the other, Pierre and Gontier Col, and Jean de Montreuil, attempted to rebut the criticism.[16]

The *Rose* inspired a whole school of imitators, and in the fourteenth century poets like Machaut and Froissart produced a great flowering of dream poems and framed narratives, which take the legacy of the *Rose* in new directions (see pp. 38–43). Their *dits amoureux* centre on the theme of love, but love becomes the occasion for many other themes: death, Fortune, and literature itself. They experiment with ever-increasing sophistication with the role of the dreamer-narrator and with poetic structures that move between lyric and narrative.[17]

The narrators of dream narratives

Dream narratives have first-person narrators. In a culture where literature was still composed with the assumption that it might be performed aloud, that tends to cast the narration, the narrating voice, more as a speaker who is the presenter of the fiction to a reader in the role of listening audience than is usual in later culture where books assume silent reading as the norm – though late medieval dream poems also play increasingly often with the motif of the book itself as one of the frames: see p. 15. Discussion of Chaucer's probable real-life audience includes Strohm 1983 and Dillon 1993: 25–43, but his poems also construct fictional audiences (who are described as hearing, *HF*, ll. 109–10, or reading, *PF*, ll. 678–9).[18] *LGW* frequently constructs a female audience: the narrator addresses women in *Dido*, lines 1254–65, and warns his audience to trust no man except him in the *Legend of Phyllis*, lines 2559–61.

Some first-person narrators are protagonists in the dream fiction, others observers. As Boitani (1982: 188–9) points out, dream poems make specially creative use of those shifts in narrative level which Gérard Genette distinguished as homodiegetic/heterodiegetic and extradiegetic/intradiegetic.[19] Genette does not discuss medieval dream poems, and in fact their spectator-narrators usually cross his neat divides: they are simultaneously homodiegetic and intradiegetic – narrators and also characters within the internal, framed, dream story. But they are also present in sections of the narrative outside the dream: in Genette's terminology these are extradiegetic and heterodiegetic narrative positions. Whereas the narrator of the *Rose* and of some later dream narratives is himself the protagonist of the central action, many texts give their first-person narrators a curiously semi-detached role in relation to events in the story, as primarily observers, or recipients, of didactic speeches. Late medieval poets may employ virtuoso devices to foreground this ambiguity in the narrator, half representative of the author, half character. The narrators of Dunbar's *Twa mariit Wemen and the Wedo* and Chartier's *Belle dame sans merci* hide in order to overhear the dialogues that form the main subject; the narrator of the *Chevalier des Dames* is magically invisible. Chaucer's dreamer merely overhears the knight in *BD*, and then, like the narrator in several poems by Machaut and Froissart, makes himself respectfully known to the noble, lamenting lover and becomes the companion of his woe: the poet's composition in these cases comes to figure as the possession of the patron, with the narrator functioning as an aid or channel for self-expression (see pp. 39–41). Spearing 1993 associates the external standpoint of such spectator-narrators in relation to erotic subject-matter with Freud's theory of voyeurism and the theories of the exploitative 'male gaze' pioneered by Berger, Mulvey and Kaplan, and that view seems just in many cases, though Chaucer's tendency to make his narrators spectators rather than protagonists seems to be primarily a dramatization of a diegetic level. Probably all three factors are present in many love visions. Chaucer's preferred methods of creating a narrator who is half-external to the story are to present him as a puzzled, inadequate or unassertive figure, too old or unsuitable for love.

Many dreamer-narrators are accorded attributes at moments in the text which encourage us to identify them with their authors: William Langland's dreamer in *Piers Plowman* is called Will, for example, and the *HF* eagle addresses the dreamer as 'Geffrey' (l. 729) and refers to him as a poet (ll. 620–5) whose daily work involves 'rekynynges' (l. 654) – clearly suggesting Chaucer's work as Controller of Customs between 1374 and 1386. Such details set up an ambiguous sense of how the fictional speaker relates to the real-life author: clearly the rather naive dreamer to whom fantastic episodes are shown is presented as a version of their creator. Reacting against earlier twentieth-century critics who had too readily assumed that such narrators provided autobiographical evidence about the author, two highly influential studies – Spitzer 1946 and Kane 1965 – explored the ways in which there is also a literary game and an element of dramatic 'persona' in such representations of the narrator, who is ignorant in ways the real author could not be.[20] Many critics subsequently adopted a belief that dream poem narrators were often fully dramatized characters, quite separate from the real-life author – as if medieval writers were inventing the kind of fictional, unreliable narrators presented in Victorian novels like Collins's *The Moonstone*. In fact, although medieval narrators, like many other figures in medieval fiction, may be given at times attributes of 'personality' and moments of psychologically individualized speech and behaviour, there is rarely anything like a thoroughgoing attempt to create the illusion of consistent character, in the fashion that is one of the chief artifices and glories of the Victorian novel. Both the naive assumption that the narrator represents the author and the seductive critical construct of the persona offer us too simple a view of the narrative voice, exaggerating the reader's sense of authorial control over the reading experience and therefore tending to stifle critical investigation into the discordances and multivalencies in these, as in all, literary texts. Belief in a consistently fictionalized narrative persona often goes with a belief in widespread irony in these poems: both these approaches can have the effect of obscuring the complexity of these texts and detaching them from critical interpretation (on this issue in *LGW*, see the introduction to that poem in this volume). Critical currents in recent years have worked against rigid adherence to the cult of the persona, recognizing that the narrative voice in all texts is a complex creation of the text, going beyond simple dichotomies like 'author' *versus* 'fictional character'. The narrator – especially the narrator of a dream poem, who advances through an experience which came to him from some source external to his own active control and whose role is, above all, to see and hear – is, after all, more the surrogate of the reader, gradually experiencing the narrative, and the critic attempting to interpret it, than of its author writing it. Rather than seeing the first-person narrator as a unified character, critics now stress the 'polyphonic' nature of the narrative voice in writers like de Meun, Machaut and Chaucer, evoking at different times in the text a variety of roles in relation to the narrative: author, hero, listener/recipient of the text, lover filled with desire, courtly retainer serving a prince or patron, translator or redactor, scribe or compiler.[21]

All dreamer-narrators have a tendency to seem stupid to some extent, for the encounter between dreamer and dream, or dreamer and authority figure, is a structure which splits the didactic enterprise in two, into the learning function and the teaching function. Chaucer's dreamers often combine an element of naivety with other attributes perhaps inspired by Machaut's handling of dream narrators. Guillaume de Machaut (d. 1377), the greatest fourteenth-century composer of music, was also an important poet. He was a *clerc*, employed as personal assistant and private secretary to several French princes. (We are actually very ignorant about what might have been the precise *economic* implications of any of the poetry written by Machaut, Chaucer and other courtiers and royal servants and administrators: though critics sometimes talk as if John of Gaunt or Anne of Bohemia were Chaucer's patrons, there is no evidence that they were, or what exactly that would mean for the composition of the poetry if it were so.) Machaut's narrators are presented sometimes as lovers uncertain of success, or as courteous, affectionate and respectful companions to lovelorn nobles and ladies, eager to help and sensitive to melancholy.[22] At times his dreamer is also the poet, and in some later works an ageing poet.

Chaucer developed these devices in new ways. His dreamer is physically passive: he gets to the central subject of his text by wandering after a puppy in *BD*, by being picked up by an eagle in *HF*, by being shoved unceremoniously in through a gate, at which he himself was hesitating, in *PF*, and by accepting condemnation of his own poems and instructions for his future compositions in *LGW*. He displays uncertainty: he is bewildered by love at the beginning of *PF*, bewildered by his own state of mind at the beginning of *BD*, and bemused by the end of it. His dream guide in *PF* describes him as one who is unaffected by words addressed to lovers (ll. 158–61), and in *LGW* he is called old (l. 262). Like the narrator of the *Canterbury Tales*, he is not in charge of events and is dominated or criticized by his own characters: by the eagle in *HF* and by the God of Love in *LGW*. In *BD*, *HF* and *LGW* he is presented as a writer, but in the first of these he is puzzled by the experience he will write up and in the second he is said to lack a subject (ll. 641–81); in the *Legend* his subject is dictated to him as a punishment for previous faults as a writer. In the *Legend* his passivity takes the additional form of a claim to be only a translator of other men's compositions and the servant of patrons, lacking creative intention of his own.[23] Apart from Machaut and Froissart, another contemporary from whom Chaucer may have learnt the advantages of a passive narrator is Deguileville: his pilgrim-dreamer is also a timid figure, often making mistakes and often violently bullied and attacked by other characters. Though the religious allegory differs from Chaucer's love visions in many ways, it seems to have been known to him (the green stone wall around the garden in *PF* is a detail that may come from de Deguileville's *Pèlerinage*).

Self-conscious fictions

Dream narratives often present the text within the dream as if it is raw material in need of interpretation: they invite the reader to complete the process of understanding or judgement. Significantly, many late-medieval dream poems have open-ended conclusions. In some, like Machaut's *Fonteinne Amoureuse* and *BD*, the narrator announces an intention to write down what he has seen or heard. Such texts are 'self-creating fictions', works which purport to tell how they themselves came to be written.[24] The *LGW Prologue* develops this strategem further: the individual legends which follow it within the text are said to be the writings that are to be composed as a result of the dream. Similarly, in the unfinished *HF* the dream journey is presented as a quest to find subject-matter for subsequent composition.

Chaucer's narrators express a preference for books over other amuse-ments (*BD*, ll. 47–51; *HF*, l. 657; *LGW*, ll. 30–4), and the God of Love describes the *Legend* dreamer as a man with a vast library, by contempor-ary standards, of sixty books (l. 273). This bookish narrator is one of the motifs in the dream poems that raises the issue of the relationship of books to experience, and also of the relationship of Chaucer's own narratives to earlier authors' books, especially classical authors like Ovid and Virgil, to which they so often refer – and from which they can so radically depart (see the introduction to the *Legend of Dido* below).

Another structure that focuses attention on this issue of books and experience is the retelling of an old story prefaced to the dream: Ovid's tale of Ceyx and Alcione in *BD*, Cicero's *Somnium Scipionis* in *PF* and Virgil's story of Dido, the first element of the dream in *HF*. It has several possible precedents, including de Deguileville's reference to reading the *Roman de la Rose* before the dream in his *Pèlerinage de vie humaine*. Chaucer seems to be the first author to retell a preliminary story at length, and set up provocatively puzzling links and contrasts between its content and the dream 'experience' juxtaposed to it. Several fifteenth-century French and English dream poems took up and developed, often with great inventive-ness and self-reflexive sophistication, this framing device of the book (see next section).[25]

Late-medieval poets seem less interested in fictional dreams as mirrors of real-life dreaming than as mirrors of the imagination, consciousness and literary composition. The dream, in its interiority, individuality and inventiveness, and with its ancient guarantees of serious meaning, is an apt figure for the poet's mind, or for the reader's submersion in the experience of fiction. Like the experiences of writing or reading, the narrator-dreamer crosses a threshold from one conscious realm to another, whether that transition be through crossing into dream, walking into a landscape, or entering a building or enclosed garden, and – like the relationship of a narrative to its subject – the dreamer-narrator is both outside and present in the events he presents. As Kermode said,[26] fiction satisfies our hunger 'for ends and crises', a desire for 'closure'; and the dream, with its sudden onset and an ending which is often marked in medieval texts by a shock, a bell or a noise, is a form which, more than most, dramatizes that myth of closure. Chaucer's dream poems, either literally unfinished or ending with a teasing sense of inconclusiveness, foreground the fictive 'sense of an ending' by both holding out the expectation of, and failing to provide, a decisive conclusion to the problems – of death and love and literary truth – they raise.[27]

Many dream narratives, including Chaucer's, are structures which explore the roles and relationships of narrator and narration, of literary composition and its sources, whether in experience or in past literature. All Chaucer's dreamers, except in *PF*, are also writers. The most consciously literary and self-reflexive poem is *HF*, and there have been many narratological and poststructuralist critical studies of it.[28] Its text-decorated temple of Venus, followed by a desert of sand (ll. 119–495), seem clearly images of the poet's pre-compositional state – whatever else they signify. The bemusing and sceptical style in which it introduces ostensibly authoritative material – like theories about dreams' significance (ll. 1–118), language (ll. 675–864) and 'fame' (the record literature makes of experience) – seem designed to dislodge any naive certainties readers may have about the relationship of literature to truth.

Embedded stories, intertextual narrative

The device of the dream frame and the constant presence of the 'I' narrator give dream poems an overt unity, yet these poems, like many *dits amoureux*, employ structures which present a series of juxtaposed but quasi-discrete narratives rather than an immediately coherent linear plot. In *BD*, for instance, we have an episode read in a book, an episode which is a long reminiscence of the past, a description of the narrator's melancholy, a description of a hunt, and so on. Some are told by the narrator, some come from other minds – from the knight or the author of the book of 'fables' read in bed. The knight's narrative belongs to an earlier time than the dreamer's narrative, and so is an analepsis or retrospective embedded story. Narratives and literary references are embedded in Chaucer's primary narratives by a variety of fictional devices: for example, by buildings with stories depicted on them, as in *HF* (ll. 140–479) and *BD* (ll. 322–34), and by briefer, ekphrastic images like the statues on the pillars which are memorials to literature, in *HF* (ll. 1419–1512).[29] Short, interpolated and self-contained narratives and references like these are a favourite method by which dream poems (like some romances) create a many-layered, intertextual structure.

The effect of such structures in Chaucer's poems is not mere book-ishness. To know the source of a reference is not to read its meaning in Chaucer's text. Reminiscences of other books, and of moments and scenes in other books, are not just inert decoration. They certainly do invite the reader's memory of an earlier literary experience, but the effect may be either to evoke that earlier literary experience with the associations it originally had, thus adding its power to Chaucer's own text, or to evoke it while changing its associations and meaning, or even to use it ironically in a way diametrically opposed to its original significance. Intertextual references, so common in these poems, whether they are in lists of names, brief summaries or longer descriptions, invite the reader to draw simul-taneously on two types of signification: the memory of what import the reference had in a prior text, and the meanings given by its new context and the new author's wording.

A clear example would be the list of lovers in *PF* (ll. 288–94). Sixteen names are painted on one side of Venus's temple. They are all from classical narrative or medieval courtly romance (in the case of figures like Paris, Achilles or Helen, they were known from both). Though each name may have recalled its own separate literary echoes for readers – for these are well-known characters – a reader might also have been familiar with them as groups: five of the names also occur in Boccaccio's *Teseida*, seven appear in Hell in Dante's *Inferno*.[30] But recalling the Boccaccio or Dante passages will not tell us how to read Chaucer's list, for Boccaccio's context was neutral – these figures exemplify Venus's power – and Dante's was condemnatory: they are punished for the sin of lust. Chaucer's passage, however, gives its readers explicitly a theme which unifies his own group of figures: line 294 says they are those who loved and died in misery. Their full meaning also involves the group's new context within Chaucer's poem: their place in relation to his temple of Venus and the larger significant patterns of *PF*, such as the contrasts set up by the juxtaposition of Venus and Nature, or the presentation of love's contradictory nature in the two inscriptions (ll. 127–40) and the opening stanzas.

Narratives which use embedding and intertextual references as frequently and creatively as these poems make the reader take an unusually
active role in the completion of meaning. Self-contained ekphrastic
passages challenge the reader to seek for relevance between the inserted
reference and the surrounding narrative, perhaps particularly when
fictionally represented as portrayed on separate objects, like walls, shields,
robes, inscriptions or books. Why, for example, is it the *Romance of the
Rose* and the story of Troy that are depicted on walls and windows in *BD*
(ll. 322–34)? With what import does Chaucer echo Boethius in *PF* (ll.
90–1) or in *HF* (ll. 972–8)? Contexts, wording and stylistic register
provide guides to how to assess them, but even they rarely provide a full
interpretation. Chaucer's descriptions and his use of classical allusions are
often richly ambiguous – as the often conflicting critical interpretations of
these four poems illustrate.

Coda

Dreams have always fascinated people; in life and literature they present
enigmas and a challenge to find meaning, and the device of the fictional
dream proved one of the most inventive of poetic structures.[31] Whereas
many ancient and medieval dream theorists believed dreams could provide
knowledge from beyond the normal scope of human information, to
twentieth-century psychologists dreams may seem valuable because they
offer access to knowledge coming from inside the dreamer.[32] The literary
uses of sleep and dream did not cease with the Middle Ages. Dream poetry
in the late-medieval mode continued to flourish at least to the end of the
sixteenth century, and the dream frame went on being used – often for
satire, serious and even for bawdy works – through the seventeenth
century, which is the century of *Pilgrim's Progress*; but it was Romantic
and Victorian writers who returned to the genre with the same inventive-
ness and aesthetic and philosophical intensity we find in the medieval
period. *Kubla Khan*, Keats's *Fall of Hyperion*, the *Belle Dame sans Merci*,
Dante Gabriel Rossetti's *The Orchard Pit* and William Morris's *News
from Nowhere* are not particularly like medieval dream visions, either in
subject or narrative techniques, but their differences, as well as their
imaginative power, and the strands of reminiscence and allusion which
connect them to their predecessors, bear witness to the extraordinary
resources of the genre.

Helen Phillips

1. See Spearing 1976.
2. See Pearsall 1992: 34–68, 96–102, 128–35, 178–214.
3. In Aers 1992: 28–30.
4. Greek and Latin authors often depict dreams as messengers; the dreams
    are sometimes servants who attend the god, waiting to be sent with
    messages to humans. Some gods come themselves as dream-messengers:
    Athene and Hermes, for example, in Homer appear at the head of the
    sleeper's bed, sometimes taking the disguise of the form of a human friend,
    and reveal information or advice to the dreamer.
5. See Le Goff 1984. There is a good short account in Spearing 1976:
    14–16.
6. See Fischer 1978; Peden 1985; Minnis 1995: 36–55; also Kruger 1992,
    an interesting but selective account which, unfortunately, begins its study
    only with late antiquity.
7. See Stahl's 1952 translation and introduction. The discussion of dreams
    is in ch. III. Macrobius was one of the channels through which Platonic and
    Neoplatonic ideas reached medieval readers.
8. Minnis 1995: 51–3, however, offers the illuminating suggestion that
    Chaucer uses the theory in *BD* that waking melancholy leads to dreams of
    black things. This, admittedly, does show a creative exploitation of dream
    theory by the poet to forge an implicit structural link between frame
    narrative and core in that poem.
9. Langland ed. Schmidt 1978: Bk VII, l. 150; see observations in Minnis
    1995: 46–7.
10. Such narratives, however, mark with some other device the narrator's
    entry into a realm where he appears to be granted insights unavailable to
    him on earth: for example, the arrival of Lady Philosophia in Boethius and
    the motif of the journey to the Inferno in the *Divine Comedy*.
11. Edition: Rigg 1966. Rigg 1993: 306 suggests it was influenced by *HF*;
    it seems to me the influence might also have been in the opposite
    direction.
12. Examples include the dreams in *TC* III, ll. 911–31, V, ll. 246–80,
    1233–43, and Arthur's dreams in Layamon's *Brut*, ll. 12750–93,
    13977–14034. Fischer 1978 explores this role for dreams, particularly in
    German courtly romance and epic.
13. See Davidoff 1988 generally on framed narratives.
14. Attributed to Jean Marot (d. 1523). See Montaiglon 1855–78 vol. X:
    225–68, at 258.
15. De Deguileville wrote a second version of the *Pèlerinage* about 1350. His
    view of *RR* was ambiguous: more positive in the first version, more
    condemnatory in the second.

16.   See for the texts Hicks 1977 and Baird & Kane 1978, and the excellent survey in Hill 1993.

17.   See Poirion 1965; Brownlee 1984; Huot 1987.

18.   On the importance of both the implied audience and the wider networks of readers and listeners, outside the court and its civil servants, see Riddy 1993: 104–27, and the discussion in Minnis 1995: 19–35.

19.   See Genette 1980. *Extradiegetic*: external, authorial narration; *intra-diegetic*: narration of story enclosed within the extradiegetic narration; *heterodiegetic*: narration by narrator who is not a character; *homodiegetic*: narration by a narrator who is also a character involved in the story. See also Calin 1974.

20.   This is built on the construct of the dramatized narrator in Kittredge 1915b, an integral part of his Bradley-like interpretation of Ch's writings as above all the dramatization of personality.

21.   Huot 1987: 64; see also Brown 1995: 197–211.

22.   See Brownlee 1984, Cerquiglini 1985 and Brown 1995: 197–246 on the complexity of late medieval authors' presentation of first-person narrators.

23.   These motifs also appear in the *Complaint of Venus* (see Phillips 1993b).

24.   Kellman 1976.

25.   A French example, the *Livre de l'amoureuse alliance*, has Ovid's *Art of Love* as prefatory book, while particularly ingenious are the *Chevalier des Dames* (the dreamer wakes to find the book he is planning to write about the dream lying next to him, already completed), Douglas's prologues to his *Eneados* (half-way through the translation, Prologue VII, he describes himself, in fiction, continuing his half-written book), and Henryson's *Testament of Cresseid* (the narrator summarizes Ch's *Troilus*, then fiction-ally picks up another book – which is his own, ensuing, narrative).

26.   Kermode 1967: 55.

27.   See Bridges 1984; McGerr 1989; Burrow 1991.

28.   See the list of critical studies in Kruger 1992: 118 n. 3, and also Spearing 1976: 73–89 and Miller 1982. Postmodernist readings of the dream poems became standard in the 1980s: e.g. Sklute 1984: 35–47; Russell 1988: 139–74; Edwards 1989; Minnis 1995: 216–27. The writer who comes closest to a Romantic or modern use of dream-like fictions, which are not explicitly dreams and express psychological truth or wish-fulfilment, is Marie de France.

29.   *Ekphrasis* or *ecphrasis* is an ancient rhetorical term, used for a conventional description of a person or place imported into a text. More generally, it can mean a short, self-contained and detachable description or reference, reminiscent of an earlier text, embedded in a later text: see Dubois 1983: 5–6; Kurman 1974; Delany 1994: 21–4.

30. *Tes*. VII, l. 62; *Inf*. V, ll. 52–69. See the notes in this edition to *PF*, ll. 288–94.
31. See the anthologies by Almansi & Beguin 1986, Wolff 1952 and Brook 1983 for dream narratives of various periods and cultures.
32. Many classical writers, including Hippocrates, Galen and Aristotle, emphasized links between dreams and mental or bodily states; the real contrast with modern attitudes is less in the move towards wholesale belief in somatic causes than in the importance psychoanalysis attributes to structures of personality and emotion, and the decline in belief in divine agency or prophecy.

NOTES ON LANGUAGE AND METRE

On Chaucer's language generally, see Davis 1974, Elliott 1974, Burnley 1989. Smith 1995 provides an excellent short account. The following are notes on some features which may cause particular problems for readers unfamiliar with ME.

It is important to remember that the surviving MSS give us the grammatical forms and spellings of scribes. Some may be closer to Chaucer's own forms than others. Chaucer's English was that of late fourteenth-century London, where the dominant dialect was that of the East Midlands.

Variant forms

Spellings and forms, even of the same word in the same manuscript, vary.

(1) Past participles sometimes appear with the prefix *i-, y-*: e.g. *imakede*, 'made' (this prefix is not, however, restricted to past participles). Infinitives may have an *-n* or *-en* inflection: 'to doon' (*BD*, l. 374; compare the infinitive without this inflection, 'to ryde', *BD*, l. 371).

(2) The unstressed syllables of inflections, e.g. the noun plural *-es* and the preterite verb *-ed*, may appear with *e, i* or *y* as the vowel. Thus we find 'baladis, roundelys and vyrelayes' (*LGW*, l. 411) for the three plural nouns 'balades, roundels and virelayes'. We find *imakede*, 'made', *grevyd*, 'grieved'. In these inflectional syllables the letters *e, i, y* probably all represent the *schwa* sound [ə], like the second vowel in 'button'.

(3) ME often distinguished between singular and plural verb forms. The plural inflection, when it is used, in Chaucer's East Midlands dialect, is *-en, -yn, -n*: e.g. 'they wentyn' (*LGW*, l. 199); 'Hyr women ... broughten hir' (*BD*, ll. 124–5), but plural verbs without this inflection were already common, e.g. 'these goddys lay' (*BD*, l. 166). (Note that infinitives may have an *-n* inflection too, as explained above: e.g. 'to doon', *BD*, l. 374.) There are also plural imperatives (commands) with the inflection *-eth, -ith, -yth*: e.g. 'Awaketh' (*BD*, l. 183); 'Awake', two lines earlier, illustrates the singular imperative.

Thou/thee and *Ye/you*

ME uses *thou*, *thee* as the singular form and *ye*, *you* as the plural. *Thou* and *ye* are used for the subject, *thee* and *you* for the object and indirect object. In addition, the grammatically plural forms *ye* and *you* are used, when addressing one person, to express respect. We find that the dreamer uses *ye/you* respectfully to the knight, whereas the knight addresses the dreamer as *thou/thee*, creating a sense that he is socially more humble. The God of Love and the eagle use the familiar *thou* and *thee* to the dreamers in *LGW* and *HF*, but the God of Love and Alceste, equal in rank, use *ye* and *you* to each other. *Thou* and *thee* can sound either affectionate or condescending, depending on the context. They are often used between friends, lovers and spouses, but in cases where lovers are very dignified figures, like Seys and Alcyone, even at highly emotional moments Chaucer often depicts them keeping to the more elevated *ye* and *you*. *Thou* and *thee* are used in prayers and in poetic addresses, like the *LGW balade*.

Since *thee* is sometimes spelled *the*, it can be confusing. In the marginal glosses we have sometimes translated this as 'thee' rather than giving the normal modern equivalent, 'you', to make this clear.

Impersonal verbs

These are verbs like 'It pleases me', where the subject is an impersonal 'it', which in ME may or may not be expressed (the 'me' in such a sentence is an indirect object: literally, 'it is pleasing *to me*'). ME had more impersonal verbs than modern English does. They include:

    liste(n)/lyste(n)/leste(n), 'please': e.g. *hym liste*, 'it pleased him'
    mette(n), 'dream': e.g. *me mette*, lit. 'a dream came to me', 'I dreamed'
    think(n), 'seem': e.g. *hire thoughte*, 'it seemed to her'

Oaths and emphatic phrases

It is a feature of ME style that writers often add almost meaningless phrases which are equivalent to 'certainly', 'doubtless', or 'indeed'. Some are assertions of the truth of what is being said: *withouten les*, 'without a lie'; *soth to seyn*, 'to tell the truth'; *I dar wel sayn*, 'I dare to say'; *withoute drede*, 'without fear'. Others are mild oaths: *as have I joye, as God me save, as helpe me God*, etc. Some phrases also comment on the pace of the narrative: e.g. *to tellen shortely*.

Stress

Some words, especially foreign words and names, have variable stress: *Eneas* usually has the main stress on the first syllable, but it can be on the second. Two-syllable words, especially if of French origin, may have stress on either syllable: e.g. *Dido, Fortune* are found with both stress-patterns. Examples where the metre suggests stress on the second syllable are:

> Hyde Jonathas, al thy frendelý manére   *LGW*, l. 205

> Nought have agilt ne don to Love trespás   *LGW*, l. 453

Here *manere* and *trespas* are of French origin, but *frendely* is English.

Metre

During the ME period, some inflections died out and others became optional, like the *-n* inflections described above. During Chaucer's lifetime, some inflections which were disappearing were represented by a final *-e*, which could be pronounced. The fifteenth-century scribes of our MSS do not necessarily present this *-e* as a spelling, even in lines where the metre suggests it was probably pronounced by Chaucer, and they freely add *-e* to the spelling of words where it was probably not pronounced. In many lines it is pretty obvious whether an *-e* needs to be pronounced or not – for example:

> How that I lyve, for day ne nyghte
> I may nat slepé wel nigh noght   *BD*, ll. 2–3

Chaucer's metre is, however, a flexible and expressive iambic one: there is not necessarily a single 'right' way to interpret the pattern of stress in a line. As with later iambic pentameter verse in English, there is often a creative tension between strict metrical expectations and the natural speech rhythms and emphasis of the statement. His verse also includes metrical variations like a strong initial stress or an extra 'feminine' syllable at the end of a line:

> Yévyn credénce, in every skylful wyse
> And trowyn on these olde aprovede stóryis   *LGWP*, ll. 20–1

BD and *HF* are in rhyming couplets with four stresses to a line, an iambic tetrameter. *LGW* is in iambic pentameter couplets, which Chaucer seems to have pioneered for English literature. *PF* uses a stanza of seven iambic pentameter lines, rhyming *ababbcc*, also Chaucer's invention, which is usually called 'rhyme royal'. There are several lyric forms interpolated into three of the narratives:

roundel: this form uses only two rhymes. It begins with a refrain which is repeated at the end of the stanza(s): see notes to *PF*, ll. 680–7.

balade: like the roundel, a French lyric form with a refrain. *Balades* come in many forms, but Chaucer's *balade* in *LGW* ll. 203–23 is fairly typical, with its three stanzas, rhyming *ababbcc*, and the use of the last line as the refrain. Chaucer brought *balades* and roundels into English literature.

BD contains two short lyrics which are not in any of the fixed forms, like the roundel or *balade*: they are ll. 475–86 and 1171–6. See *LGW*, ll. 410–11 for Chaucer's claim that he had written many roundels, *balades* and virelays in honour of love (a virelay is another French form with a refrain, which is also the first line; it has three four-line stanzas, with a two-line refrain that is repeated at the beginning and end of each stanza).

THE
DREAM POEMS

———

THE *BOOK OF THE DUCHESS*

INTRODUCTION

The *Book of the Duchess* (*BD*) is believed to have been written in honour of Blanche, Duchess of Lancaster, who died in 1368.[1] She was born between 1340 and 1347, the younger daughter of Henry, first Duke of Lancaster (d. 1361) and co-heiress to the vast Lancaster estates. In 1359 she married Edward III's son, John of Gaunt, Earl of Richmond. After Blanche's only sister's death in 1362, he inherited, in right of his wife, the whole of 'the largest inheritance in England after the crown'.[2] He subsequently became Duke of Lancaster. Blanche had five children of whom three, including the future Henry IV, survived.

The chief link between the poem and the Duchess is word-play. The poem praises a woman called 'White', presumably an anglicization of Blanche. Line 1318 plays on the names 'Blanche' ('white') and 'Lancaster' ('longe castel': 'Loncaster'/'Loncastre' are common ME forms of the name):

A longe castel with wallys white,

and line 1319 on 'John' and 'Richmond' ('riche hille', reflecting the etymology of 'Richmond' from Norman French: *riche mont*, 'rich hill'):

Be Seynt John, on a riche hille.[3]

The poem was probably written between late 1368 and 1372, when the earldom of Richmond was returned to the Duke of Brittany, John de Montfort. Gaunt married Constance of Castile in 1371 and, though there is no reason to assume that Constance, herself a great lady and heiress, would object to a memorial to the great lady and heiress who had been her predecessor as Duchess, remarriage might make the suicidal misery of the knight in the poem less appropriate.[4] Hardman 1994 suggests, with some plausibility, that the poem might have been written for a memorial in the mid-1370s.

The poem has some of the qualities of an elegy. Elegies take many forms. Elegies for an individual typically contain two elements: praise and mourning. Praise is present in *BD*, above all, in the description of White (ll. 805–1296), which forms the poem's artistic and psychological centre. Mourning is expressed in the text surrounding this description in a number of different ways: most obviously in the sorrow of the knight in black and of two parallel figures, Alcyone (ll. 76–214) and the narrator (ll. 1–43). Loss is symbolized in the chess allegory, where Fortune has taken the queen (ll. 618–709), and in the hunters' loss of the hart (ll. 380–6, 1311–13).

We might expect an elegy also to offer some form of religious or philosophical consolation. There is no explicit Christian consolation in Chaucer's poem, though some critics believe elements in the text implicitly point to a Christian message.[5] Philosophical arguments are present, however, in the dreamer's replies to the knight (ll. 714–41), urging him to resist suicidal despair and despise Fortune.[6] Yet these arguments are rejected by the knight (ll. 742–4), and when at line 1309 he makes a clear statement of his sorrow, 'She ys ded', the dreamer offers no further arguments but only pity: 'Be God, hyt ys routhe' (l. 1310). Arguments similar to the dreamer's are put into the mouth of Ceyx, who urges his bereaved wife to accept the fact of his death and cease from mourning (ll. 201–11), but here too the message is not accepted. Alcyone continues to grieve and dies.

Chaucer is using the fictional dream, a genre often associated in medieval literature, from the *Roman de la Rose* onwards, with unrequited desire for a beautiful lady, for a poem of mourning and commemoration, to express love and longing for a lady who is unobtainable because she is dead. It is not uncommon for elegy-writers to use a genre which elevates, beautifies and distances their subject: for example, many elegies, including Milton's *Lycidas* (1638) and Boccaccio's *Olympia* (c. 1355), had used the pastoral. Other fourteenth-century examples which use the dream frame include *Pearl* (c. 1390) and two poems in French: the *Songe vert* (c. 1394?), a poem possibly indebted to *BD*, written in French, perhaps in England after the death of Richard II's queen, Anne of Bohemia; and Jean de la Mote's *Li regret Guillaume* (c. 1339), in memory of Guillaume, count of Hainault, and dedicated to Guillaume's daughter Philippa, Edward III's queen.[7] *Li regret* may have been one of Chaucer's inspirations. The dream genre, combined with the tradition in medieval love poetry of using the language of suffering and death to express desire, enable Chaucer both to transmute death into a yearning for an ideal, and to present comfort in a dream. The process can be seen as representing the art of the poem itself – which means that it can be read as either more or less authoritative as each reader decides. At the same time, the use of these poetic forms also enables Chaucer to restate the fact of death at line 1309 with sudden nakedness, as if the veil of poetic imagery, which had briefly made it beautiful and remote, has been swept aside.

It is an infinitely tactful structure, and one which works by indirectness: by juxtaposition, symbols, parallels and contrasts.[8] Because the structure is a set of frames – book, dream, hunt, the knight's story, etc. – one inside the other, it is possible to read one episode as a context for another and draw connections between what is said, about mourning or comfort, in one episode and in others. This design makes the embedded narrative, describing White and the lovers' perfect union of hearts, into both the climax of the linear sequence of episodes, and also the centre of the set of frames.[9] These frames contain elements of lament, consolation and acceptance.

The colour-symbolism of a knight in black and a lady White obviously represents mourning for a woman called Blanche, and it is central to the chess allegory, but this contrast of dark and light is also one of many dualities in the structure: dullness and brightness, lifelessness and energy, sickness and healing, loss and love, and – to quote the narrator – 'joy or sorwe' (l. 10). Ellis 1995 suggests the poem remains balanced, without resolution, between mourning and consolation: two contradictory impulses which he sees fortuitously embodied in two alternative titles which remained current until the nineteenth century, 'the Deeth of Blaunche the Duchesse' (expressing mourning) and the 'Book of the Duchess' (expressing the celebratory, consolatory aspect). We could, however, see instead the dualities running through the poem as ultimately offering the possibility of consolation, since for each of the mournful images – sickness and despair, the black knight's lamentation, the life-threatening sleeplessness of the narrator and Alcyone, and so on – there are subsequent images which are recuperative opposites. Thus sleep comes after sleeplessness, a dream of beauty and morning follows the anxious lethargy of the narrator and Alcyone, there is brightness, energy and natural renewal after the life-denying 'siknesse' and despair of both of them, and arguments against Fortune's power rebut the knight's expressions of hopelessness.

Like Chaucer's other dream poems, but in its own characteristically subdued and unexplicit fashion, the work poses – but is it soothingly or problematically? – the relationship of literature to painful emotional reality. Several moments suggest the comfort that art can offer the bereaved, while disconcertingly revealing the ultimate inadequacy of words to assuage the real-life pain. The work's literary images – images of a noble lover singing of unrequited love, the knight's song, which the dreamer seems able to misunderstand, images of Fortune and chess (again capable of misinterpretation), and the lyrical speeches in which the beloved past is celebrated and temporarily recreated – all these serve simultaneously both to beautify and to dissemble the fact of mutability.[10] The knight's general impatience towards whatever comfort the ignorant if well-meaning dreamer tries to propose conveys indirectly a sense of the impossibility of any consolations which could simply erase such sorrow. Similarly, the puzzlement and the asking of questions that characterize the narrator convey to the reader almost imperceptibly a sense that the poem will not simply hand us an authoritative answer.

Though none of the three sorrowing characters, the melancholy narrator, Alcyone and the knight, finds comfort, the poem offers its reader – if the reader chooses to accept – a message of consolation, though that consolation takes the form of acceptance of the inevitability of earthly mutability. This theme of acceptance is, in fact, associated with each of the three sorrowing figures. First, the sleepless narrator says at line 42, 'That wyl not be mote nede be lefte'; then Ceyx urges: 'Let be your sorweful lyfe, / For in your sorwe there lyth no rede ... To lytel while oure blisse lasteth' (ll. 202–3, 211). The third expression of this theme of acceptance of loss occurs in association with the figure of the knight, but it is placed just outside his dialogue with the dreamer: at lines 1309–10 the knight states that the lady is dead and the dreamer expresses pity. Then suddenly we switch to the framing narrative of the hunt, with this statement:

> And with that worde ryght anoon
> They gan to strake forth. Al was doon
> For that tyme the herte huntynge.   (ll. 1311–13)

This third statement of an acceptance of loss is not obtruded into the section of the poem presenting the knight's mourning, but is juxtaposed to it and left there for the reader who so chooses to apply it to the state of mourning, as dream and narrative end.[11]

The dreamer learns early on (at l. 483) that the knight's lady has died, but seems subsequently not to have understood this. Some critics in the past saw in this a deliberate dramatization of the narrator as a stupid character.[12] Others have believed it depicts a pretence that he does not understand, to encourage the knight into 'talking it over' therapeutically.[13] Morse (1981: 205) sensibly dismisses such 'persona' readings as over-literal; what appears to be the fictional dreamer's slowness in understanding is one of the devices by which the poem creates, for the reader, an experience of understanding: 'here, as in other dream poems, there is a distinction between what is learned in the poem and what is learned from it'. The dreamer's questions also contribute to a submerged *Ubi sunt* question which runs through the dialogue and culminates in his enquiry (the blindness of which is foregrounded by the reader's prior knowledge of its inappropriateness): 'Where is she now?' (l. 1298).

The description of White, lines 759–1309

This memorial to beauty, goodness and happiness is in what are instantly recognizable as conventional terms: the Duchess is represented not by any realistic assessment of her life, or her importance to the wealth and power of John of Gaunt and their children, nor by a description of her personality and appearance that gives the impression of a naturalistic portrait of an individual, but by idealized statements which frequently repeat lines from descriptions of beloved women in poems by contemporary French poets (see below). This reliance on art rather than nature gives the portrait a fixity, and a dissociation from individual reality, which could have produced merely an aesthetic cliché in another writer's hand, but which here create an image of perfection, an icon of beauty, goodness and graciousness (see Margherita 1994: 82–99 and the excellent ideological-rhetorical analysis in Allen 1992).

Building on the associations of the name 'White', Chaucer evokes a beauty that is flawless and superlative, whether in a throat that is smooth without blemish, a face in whose look there is never an unpleasant expression, or a sociability that is never undignified. She is like the sun among the planets, the chief example of Nature's creation, the source of light for others, and the 'chefe meroure' among ten thousand. She is described through some terms often associated with the Virgin Mary (e.g. 'tower of ivory', l. 946, 'Phoenix', ll. 982–3, 'the dwelling-place of Truth himself', ll. 1003–5), and the lovers' union is etherealized by being presented as a union of hearts, without physical consummation.[14]

There is, of course, no reason why conventional images may not represent qualities which actually were those of a real-life woman – for example charity, good humour, self-control, and so on – just as accurately, even more accurately, than a description in naturalistic style. From a feminist viewpoint what is diminishing about the figure is less the transmutation of living individuality into a generalized ideal than the relatively narrow range of qualities chosen for praise of a dead woman: beauty, pleasantness, goodness, self-command, and wisdom in personal interactions, though these are also idealized aristocratic social functions.

White is praised for beauty but even more for character: dignity and benevolence, kindness but a kindness that is always wisely directed towards deserving cases, attractiveness without flirtatiousness, a capacity for making those around her enjoy themselves, but ruled in everything by 'mesure', the great classical and medieval virtue of moderation (ll. 859–82). Almost every quality she possesses is qualified by some controlling restraint and self-mastery. This is a portrait of a young noblewoman who has learned the difficult and even contradictory arts of perfectly well-bred behaviour in a woman. It evokes all the secular qualities considered most desirable in a woman: high position, intelligence, attractiveness, pleasantness, purity and kindness, and each is presented as made even more impressive by its qualifications: a wide intelligence that is always inclined towards goodness; radiant attractiveness that is entirely without those 'nakkes smale', the little games by which lesser mortals play with their admirers of the other sex; love for others that is benevolent and fraternal (interestingly, Reason, in the passage from the *Rose* mentioned on p. 10, praises that kind of love as a force resistant to Fortune's blows, higher and less subject to mutability than romantic passion).

Ceyx and Alcyone, lines 47–269

BD may be the first dream poem to preface the dream with a reference to reading a book whose content proves to be relevant to the subject of the dream. Here the story of Alcyone provides a royal female figure to be a counterpart to the bereaved lover in the narrator's dream which follows, and her husband's message in *her* dream parallels the arguments against suicide in the narrator's dream.[15] Like the legends in the *Legend of Good Women* (*LGW*), it retells a classical story about a tragic woman.[16] Ovid's tale of Ceyx and Alcyone is in *Metamorphoses* Book XI, lines 410–748. Much of Ovid's narrative is devoted to the adventures and sorrows of Ceyx (ll. 410–572): travelling to consult an oracle, his ship breaks up in a storm and, thinking all the time of his beloved Alcyone, Ceyx drowns. Chaucer rapidly summarizes all this, to concentrate on two episodes that interest him and provide analogies to other elements in his own work: the anguish of the bereaved spouse Alycone and the benevolent dream sent by the gods. Ovid's tale ends, like all those in the *Metamorphoses*, with a transformation: Alcyone finds her husband's drowned body and, as she runs into the sea towards it, the gods turn both of them into the devoted Halcyon birds, who mate and raise their family in specially peaceful days each winter. Chaucer omits that, and also alters the message the dream brings to the sorrowing spouse. Ovid's Ceyx tells his wife, 'I am dead! Do not cherish in vain your hopes about me' (l. 662), but goes on to request: 'Rise up, give me your tears, put on mourning clothes and do not send me unwept down to lifeless Tartarus' (ll. 669–70). In contrast, Chaucer's Seys asks Alcyone to desist from fruitless sorrow and gently tries to persuade her to accept that the fact of his mortality is reason for her to see that no earthly joy lasts. The differences seem to indicate that Chaucer saw the Ovidian tale not only as the source of parallel sorrow, but also as an opportunity to voice a certain kind of consolation: that which comes from a recognition that all earthly joy, including a beloved person, has to be subject to transience.

As the notes on the poem show, some details of Chaucer's treatment of Ceyx, Alcyone and Morpheus may have been influenced by other works: the cave of sleep in Statius's *Thebaid*, Book X, lines 79–136, and passages by Machaut and Froissart. Chaucer probably also knew some of the so-called 'moralizations' of Ovid, medieval allegorical interpretations of the *Metamorphoses* which presented them as fables about Christian doctrine: the most important are the French *Ovide moralisé* and the Latin *Ovidius moralizatus*. There is no certain evidence that they influenced Chaucer's poem, though some critics have suggested that he intended his readers to recall either Ovid's metamorphosis or the moralizations and to deduce, from these missing elements, a message about the afterlife.[17] Cooper 1988 shows how implausible are theories based on implied metamorphosis, and Le Fèvre's *Livre de Leësce*, lines 2647–2707, expresses what seems to have been a common contemporary view when he ridicules and condemns the role of pagan deities and metamorphoses in Ovid.

The figures of the poem, the lady, the knight and the dreamer, are not the Duke and Duchess of Lancaster and Geoffrey Chaucer, however much their situations may at times parallel those of real historical individuals.[18] They are more general figures, representing sorrow and honour. The narrator's initial distress, whatever we may like to imagine as its unspoken cause, contributes towards the expression of the same sorrow as the knight's lament and Alcyone's despair. The theme of death is diffused through the poem, not just associated with the figure of White: it appears in the death-threatening melancholy of lines 1–24, the 'dedely slepynge soun' of the rivers by the cave of Sleep, the deathly misery of the rejected lover (ll. 1181–1278). Similarly, motifs of joy and new life recur at different points throughout the poem – in the dream morning and the remembered 'gladnesse' of the lady, for example.

Hansen (1992: 68–74) believes the poem presents a 'proper gender difference' between a wife's response to bereavement (she should die, like Alcyone) and a husband's (he must re-enter life). The parallels between the mourning figures seem, however, more prominent in the poem's structure and meaning than their differences, including gender differences – and it is a man, Seys, who bids his wife not to succumb to grief, whereas the narrator ends by leaving the knight to remain in his sense of loss.[19] For Hansen, the work first 'feminizes' its grieving male characters and then restores traditional gender differences when White has been 'fixed' into idealized literary stereotype and Alcyone is dead (p. 73). It negates and nullifies its female figures. This reading, like all those that try to get behind the hypnotic beauty and *gentillesse* of the work, is valuable, but is it completely fair either to the role of Alcyone's inconsolable despair in the structure of the poem or to the iconic, memorial style of the evocation of White?

Chaucer's attitude to suicide – it seems often to be women's suicide – is, like most things in his poetry, subject to contradictory interpretations. In *BD* the totality of Alcyone's misery, leading to death, is treated with respect, as apparently are the deaths of the heroines of *LGW*, but in lines 724–41 the suicides of Dido and other heroines (offered as parallels to the suicidal despair of the male knight) are treated as offences against religion and good sense. Interpretation of the unsympathetic judgement on these suicides is complicated, however, because they are reactions to set-backs in love, not the death of a spouse, so are not exact parallels.[20] In a way, the contradictory presentation of suicide in *BD* seems to pinpoint the poem's acceptance of two opposed certainties: the absolute fact of earthly mutability and the absolute fact of personal subjective consciousness. A mighty tension between these two will make Chaucer's later *Troilus and Criseyde* one of the philosophically most profound poems in European love literature.

Fortune

The discussion between the knight and the dreamer about Fortune (ll. 618–741) contains echoes of poems by Machaut (see notes and below) and also of a famous passage in the *Roman de la Rose* (ll. 5288–6870), where Reason teaches that the wise person should not value anything that is in the power of Fortune, because she represents the deceptive pleasures of this world and those who trust her or become too attached to the mutable goods she gives will only be made miserable by their inevitable loss.

The ultimate source of these ideas is the *Consolation of Philosophy* by the sixth-century philosopher Boethius, a much-read work during the Middle Ages which both Jean de Meun and Chaucer translated. It is a dialogue in which Lady Philosophy, through a series of philosophical arguments, gradually persuades Boethius to abandon his unhappiness over reverses of Fortune in this world and see both that Fortune's favours are unreliable and that true happiness lies only in the unchanging realities of the mind and spirit. Philosophy diagnoses Boethius at the beginning of their debate as suffering from an illness that she can heal, and as being blinded by his tears.[21] This famous dialogue is the origin of a type of medieval work in which an unhappy human is persuaded, by philosophical arguments offered by a figure of supernatural authority, to be consoled for earthly sorrows. An example of this genre, called by modern critics a *consolatio*, is the ME *Pearl*. At times the dialogue between the dreamer and the knight in *BD* seems as if it is going to turn into a *consolatio*, but, as we have seen, the knight never accepts the dreamer's arguments. It is typical of the poem's unstereotypical approach to human emotion and grief that the arguments about Fortune are offered briefly in the middle of the work, not integrated into a conclusion.

The hunt, lines 344–86, 1311–13

Hunting was an aristocratic pastime, and this hunt, associated impressively with the Emperor Octavian, contributes to the poem's courtly ambience. It is part of the new atmosphere of energy and delight once the dream begins and it gets the narrative moving forward, towards the encounter with the man in black. Hunting in medieval literature is often a metaphor for love; Wimsatt 1968: 39–48 and Thiébaux 1974 give examples of allegories of desire as a hunt. Chaucer's hunt is clearly to be read literally, not allegorically, but some symbolism seems to be present, especially in lines 1311–17. Hunts were also quite often associated with death in medieval poetry. Common in both poetry and art were scenes where one or more hunters, often aristocratic or royal, get cut off from the rest of the group and encounter mutability in some form. In *Somer Soneday* the narrator, out hunting, wanders from his companions and has a vision of Fortune and her wheel.[22] In the most widespread version of the tradition, found in art and literature, three kings meet three dead kings who warn them of their own mortality and the importance of heavenly rather than worldly priorities.[23] There is, in delicate, fugitive fashion, a reminiscence of this pattern in Chaucer's poem when the narrator gets detached from the hunters in a wood and finds a solitary figure who is the embodiment of sorrow and bereavement. Knight 1986: 11–13 discusses illuminatingly the way in which, in Chaucer's handling of this structure, there is, however, also a decisive shift inwards, from feudal and public experience to private experience, which is then, in the course of the dialogue, modulated into the 'resocialization' of the knight into his aristocratic identity, just as the presentation of Blanche moves towards the creation of a 'poetic monument'.

The poem is full of the technical language and detail of hunting.[24] John of Gaunt loved hunting, and the scenes might have appealed particularly to him; perhaps when Chaucer mentions Octavian's 'mayster hunte' (l. 375), he is visualizing the Duke's much respected Master of Game, Walter Urswick.[25] The dream day begins, as such a hunt would begin in reality, with hunt servants locating a hart, hidden in the wood, for their master to hunt out later, rather as the man in black is found deep in a secluded part of the forest, to be verbally probed and pursued by the dreamer's questions.

Dits amoureux and the inheritance of the *Roman de la Rose*

As a legacy of the Norman Conquest, French was still used in England in the fourteenth century as a spoken and written vernacular, especially by the upper classes. Legal, administrative, learned and literary writing in French was common. Wills and inventories of book collections show, among people who had books, ownership (and presumably therefore readership) of French books as well as Latin and English works. English people still sometimes composed works in French: Blanche's father wrote the *Livre de seyntz medicines*, an allegory about sins. Chaucer wrote *BD* in English, yet in style and structure it belongs in many ways with a group of works by some of his French contemporaries, the so-called *dits amoureux* composed by Guillaume de Machaut, Jean Froissart and Oton de Graunson. This achievement, of creating a genuinely new, English equivalent to the style and manner of the French *dit* and *balade*, is one of Chaucer's great contributions to English and English literature.

Modern critics often use the terms *dit amoureux* ('lay of love') or *love aunter* ('love adventure') for a type of medium-length narrative poem fashionable in French from the thirteenth century, and in English from the fourteenth century, until the late sixteenth century. *Dits amoureux* are a development from the *Roman de la Rose* (see pp. 9–11). They are framed narratives using a variety of fictional frames, of which the dream is only one. Apart from the dream, other ways by which they create a sense of a cut-off place, an arena for the expression of the central theme, include entry into a garden, a solitary walk into a beautiful landscape, or an island, palace or castle. *Dits* often have at their centre debates, or lovers' *complaintes* (laments). Sometimes, particularly in the later medieval period, they describe winter scenes or wilderness settings, but more often they begin in May, and, as in the *Rose*, the landscape is paradisal, supremely beautiful, immune from the irregularities, imperfections and change of real-life landscapes, with perfectly temperate weather or eternal spingtime, flowers and trees, birdsong of an angelic beauty, and overall a sense of rest and joy for the burdened soul of the narrator – who typically opens the poem by describing his own melancholy.[26] *Dits*, like the *Rose*, treat love and its sorrows, separations and anxieties, as serious matters, and subjects of overwhelming concern to *gentil* minds. Didactic or quasi-philosophical material is frequently introduced. Sometimes there are allegorical figures, but there is rarely sustained allegorical action, and some *dits* entirely lack allegory. Both Machaut and Froissart embed in their narratives retellings of classical stories, often drawn from Ovid, which provide parallels to the situations of the protagonists or hold out hope of consolation.

Dits frequently combine narrative and lyric (see Boffey 1993). In some the narrative becomes a showcase for the lyrics embedded in it. The narrator's own love-experiences may be the central subject, but often he is the observer of another's woe. Surprisingly frequently he overhears a lover lamenting, and the central part of a *dit* typically provides either consolation or a lesson to alleviate melancholy, whether it is the narrator or someone else who is the unhappy lover. In depicting a first-person narrator who converses with a sorrowful lover and tries to offer comfort, Chaucer is drawing on a motif in contemporary French love narratives that was potentially particularly suitable for a poem about bereavement; in several *dits amoureux*, including Machaut's *Fonteinne amoureuse* and Froissart's *Dit dou bleu chevalier* (both c. 1360), a sympathetic companion, having overheard an aristocratic lover lamenting his separation from his lady, is able to help the lover feel some degree of comfort and assurance of faithful love, even though the lovers will remain separated.[27]

Since Chaucer's poem is indebted in structure and many individual passages to a group of *dits* by French contemporaries, I list here some of these sources and analogues, with a brief guide to their content (see notes to the poem for specific parallels).

The most influential was perhaps Guillaume de Machaut's *Fonteinne amoureuse* ('Fountain of Love', c. 1360). It seems to have been written for Jean, duc de Berri, whose name appears anagrammatically in the text, at the time when he faced separation from his wife by having to travel to England as a political hostage. The poem tells how the narrator, unable to sleep, overhears from the next bedroom a long lyric lament by a lover who faces separation from a lady to whom he has never told his love; he recounts the story of Ceyx and Alcyone and asks Morpheus to visit his beloved in a dream and tell her he loves her. The narrator writes down the overheard lament, and next morning meets the lover, a young noble whose manner fills him with admiration. He offers his affection and service and they tell each other of their loves. Resting by the 'Fountain of Love' in a beautiful park, a shared dream comes to them, in which Venus tells the classical legend of the marriage of Peleas and Thetis, and the Apple of Discord, and then the noble lover's lady reassures him that she reciprocates his love. They exchange rings and the dream ends. The narrator accompanies the noble to the port from which he sets sail.

Clearly an inspiration for the insertion of the tale of Ceyx and Alcyone in *BD*, the *Fonteinne* illustrates many typical features of *dits amoureux* found in Chaucer's poem, like the overheard lament and the companionable but deferential relationship between the narrator and a noble lover. The same figure of the sympathetic, respectful, eavesdropping narrator had appeared in Machaut's *Jugement du roy de Behaigne* ('Judgement of the King of Bohemia', c. 1346). Here, on a spring morning whose description directly influenced *BD* (ll. 339–43, 393–401), the narrator wanders out, following the song of a bird, and overhears a lady and knight lamenting their respective sorrows. They debate which kind of sorrow is worse: bereavement or unfaithfulness by the beloved. Many passages influenced Chaucer: the lady apologizes that she was so deep in melancholy thoughts that she did not initially notice the knight's greeting, and he begs her to reveal her sorrow in the hope he can somehow alleviate it; the lady's description of her perfect union, now tragically ended by death, inspired parts of Chaucer's knight's memories; and the description of White draws on the lover's description of his lady. The hidden narrator then comes forward and the lady's puppy, running up to him, provides an excuse to introduce himself. At his suggestion the lovers ask the King of Bohemia (a real person, Machaut's patron at the time the poem was written) to adjudicate, and his judgement is that the nobleman's sorrow, caused by unfaithfulness, will last for ever, whereas the lady, whose perfect union has ended in bereavement, has a less painful sorrow and eventually will be comforted and love again. (Machaut subsequently wrote *Le jugement dou roy de Navarre*, a retraction composed after complaints from women readers, in which the debate is re-opened and the King of Navarre judges that the sorrow of bereavement is the greater.)

Machaut's *Remède de Fortune* ('Remedy for Fortune', 1342) contains many inset lyrics. A despairing lover complains against Fortune, but in a dream Hope comforts him. It influenced Chaucer's allegories of chess and Fortune, and also some lines in the description of White.

Jean Froissart's *Dit dou bleu chevalier* ('Lay of the Blue Knight', c. 1360?) may have influenced Chaucer.[28] The narrator walks out to enjoy the spring morning and overhears a knight dressed in blue, the colour of fidelity, lamenting Fortune's cruelty and his separation from his lady. The narrator's arguments about despising Fortune and trusting in faithful love help to console the lover, and the narrator agrees to write an account of their meeting so that the lady will know of her lover's devotion. Froissart's *Paradis d'Amours* ('Paradise of Love', 1362–9?) influenced the opening and closing sections of *BD* and some details in the prayer to Morpheus. It begins with a melancholy and sleepless narrator. He prays to Morpheus and in the ensuing dream Pleasure, Love and Hope console him and take him to his lady, who accepts him. Waking, he ponders on his dream, finding it amazing, and thanks Morpheus for the gift of the dream and Orpheus for teaching him the art of poetry. Froissart, Queen Philippa's secretary from 1362 to 1367, must have been known to Chaucer. Several of Froissart's other *dits amoureux*, including the *Espinette amoureuse* (c. 1370) and *Joli buisson de jeunesse* (c. 1372), deal with a lover separated from a woman he admires, and in them the most that is offered in the way of comfort or hope in the narrative is brief and inconclusive encounters, either in reality or dream. Froissart's *dits*, like Machaut's, notably the *Fonteinne amoureuse*, have structures that pose questions about the relationship of literary composition to real-life emotion.

What Chaucer learnt from the complex structures of *dits amoureux*, with their frames and inset lyrics and narratives, and their subtle handling of the roles of narrator and unhappy lover (who may be one and the same person or two figures – often a poet and a prince – in dialogue), is more significant than individual verbal borrowings.[29] We must never make the mistake of assuming that finding a source tells us the significance of a line or a passage. There are, for example, echoes in Chaucer's lines 1–24 of the opening of Froissart's *Paradis d'Amours* (ll. 1–12), which also has a melancholy, insomniac narrator. But he tells us his state is due to love. We should not import this explanation into Chaucer's passage, which strikingly does *not* say its narrator's melancholy is due to love, though this has been a common interpretation. Chaucer uses the motif of an insomniac narrator to introduce his reader into an undefined distress and puzzlement – states which will recur throughout the poem. He also adds, in lines 16–21, the new subjects of Nature and Nature's abhorrence of deathlike despair, which will be two of its major consolatory themes. Thus the Froissartian motifs of sorrow and sleeplessness have become different images with new significance, not only because Chaucer has added and taken away meanings, but because they have meaning in relation to later parts of Chaucer's new structure and not in their retrospective relationship to their counterparts in Froissart's earlier text.

The *dits* by Machaut and Froissart, with other sources and analogues, are translated in Windeatt 1982. Wimsatt 1968 and 1991 traces the history of *dits amoureux* before Chaucer. For all their light touch and their decorative and fantastic scenes and figures, the *dits amoureux* offer profound and sophisticated explorations of subjective consciousness and passionate obsession, and of poetic identity – the multivalent role of the first-person narrator in relationship to author, audience, fictional protagonist and patron.[30]

Chaucer's dream poems belong with the great medieval French *dits amoureux*. They are not mere imitations: they invented their own kind of narrative, marked by typically Chaucerian elements like humour, an intense concern with the relationship between modern writing and classical *auctores*, and with a more widely questioning exploration of the nature of love than we find in even the most ambitious French *dit*. They created a new English courtly style, adept not only at moving between lyric and narrative but at working in the sort of *lyrical narrative* that characterizes the French *dits*, as lucid and flowing as French models yet making poetry out of the cadences and idioms of spoken English, and accommodating realistic dialogue – a style that is frequently found in the *Canterbury Tales*.

It was lauded and eagerly adopted by many contemporaries and successors. This was one of Chaucer's great legacies to English literature, and to the growing confidence of writers in England: he created for English a style comparable to the subtlety of Ovid and Virgil, and to the manner of the French *dit amoureux* and *formes fixes* lyric. When his medieval admirers praise him for refining and 'illumining' a 'rude' English vernacular, they mean this style, born in the dream poems. Modern critics may feel their praise ignores the prior existence of English narrative styles in the metrical and alliterative romances, but though the English metrical romances achieved clarity and narrative variety, it was without a range of grandeur, flexibility of reference or any invocation of learned European tradition, or exploitation of the potential of a long line; and although the alliterative tradition could command grandeur as well as vivid description, its archaic, regional diction (and perhaps also the semantic approximations endemic to alliterative technique) must inevitably and permanently have limited its range, especially in the South and the court. To judge from the school of 'Chaucerian' poetry which Chaucer's dream poems engendered for a century or more in England and Scotland, they represented a stylistic and structural innovation of immense creative potential for late medieval and Tudor literature. Chaucer's courtly style, like that of Machaut and Froissart, acclimatizes classical references to a vernacular.

The Latinate 'aureate style' with which many of his fifteenth-century disciples paid tribute to his influence witnesses (however oddly to modern readers' taste) to their appreciation of this assimilation of reference and diction. Chaucer's own judiciousness about when and where and how densely to place words of French and Latin origins – many of which still had a more learned or exotic air than modern readers immediately realize – amid familiar words is unrivalled among English poets. He can create a courtly French or Ovidian Latin manner in English without simply piling up French or Latin words. Something of the delight with which readers appreciated his elegantly natural and expressive style can be seen in the characteristics of the English styles that Hoccleve and Charles d'Orléans adopted for their own translations from French. The colloquialisms introduced into Hoccleve's translation of Christine de Pizan's *Epistle of Cupid*, and the echoes of Chaucer's dream poems added to Charles's English translations of his own French lyrics, seem tributes to Chaucer's invention of an English courtly style, and attempts to imitate its cadences.

A court poem?

BD is in many ways an embodiment of the courtly: the characters, their setting and activities (hunting, dancing, writing love lyrics) and their emotions are *courtois*. It is a fictional world from which what is low, commonplace or even practical has been virtually excluded, to convey a vision of the priorities of aristocratic myth: love, honour and beauty. The technicalities of busy huntsmen, preparing everything before the aristo-crats set out (see notes to ll. 355–79), the servant's hand, ready in the middle of the night to 'reach' the narrator a book (l. 47), and the 'felowe' who is there right at hand, ready to answer a question (l. 366), are tiny interruptions of this which deftly suggest, by their sudden, surprising presence and their usual invisibility, the constant attendance of servants in aristocratic households.[31] The text reflects the lifestyle of the palaces with which Chaucer was familiar, and it also projects an ideal, as the art of those palaces did: a vision of elegance and love.[32] The bedchambers in lines 250–60 and 321–36 resemble the real luxury of royal residences like Shene or John of Gaunt's palace of the Savoy, with their sumptuous decorations, striped, silken bed-covers and tapestries.[33] Richard II owned a set of tapestries of Octavian and others depicting Fortune, the God of Love, and scenes from the romances of Greece and Alexander, and when we look generally at subjects of tapestries belonging to English and French princes we see how Chaucer's poem and the visual art of the courts invoke a similar selection of themes and references: the *Roman de la Rose*, the romances of Troy, Greece and Rome, hunting, lovers, and so on.[34] Like the walls and windows described in lines 321–2, 332–4, expensive interiors of the period had painted walls and glass depicting scenes from literature.[35] Chaucer's subjects evoke contemporary aristocratic self-images. In choosing scenes from the Trojan War and the *Roman de la Rose*, Chaucer prefaces his dream narrative with potent literary representations of love and war, the two chief elements in the chivalric myth. Moreover, to a contemporary reader Troy was known largely from the *romans d'antiquité* like the *Roman de Troie, Roman d'Éneas* and other adaptations of classical subjects to medieval idiom (we can tell Chaucer has the *Roman de Troie* in mind because he includes Medea and Jason, the first episode in that romance, among the characters of his 'story of Troy'). The heroes of Greece, Thebes and Troy functioned as antique patterns for medieval knighthood, depicted in adventures of love and war very like Arthurian romances. Patterson 1991: 233 says: 'within the social environment within which Chaucer wrote, classical history, whatever its sources, had become a form of knowledge that was marked as aristocratic ... with the writing of the *romans d'antiquité* and the Alexander romances ... medieval chivalry began fully to appropriate antiquity to its own ideological needs', a process he sees accelerating from the late twelfth century to the fourteenth.[36] Most royal families claimed antique Greek or Trojan ancestry, the English royal family cultivated the myth of Britain as a land created by Trojans: Caroline Barron suggests that the fashion for calling London 'New Troy' was popular with the court party, not the city leaders.[37] Chaucer's choice of Troy for the painted glass is appropriate not only because, in conjunction here with the *Roman de la Rose*, it recalls literary love stories: of Paris, Achilles, Jason, Lavinia, and so on, the love stories of princes; not only because it paints a revered classical group of princes old and young, like the English royal court circa 1370; but most of all because it frames the ensuing narrative of an intensely *courtois* but predominantly swooning and melancholy lover with images of knights who were the imaginary *fons et origo* of contemporary aristocrats' self-image as fighters: *Ector, Achilles, Jason*, etc. Like the Emperor Octavian's hunt and all the references to *Outremer, Turkye, Ynde, Macedoyne, Alysaundre, Pruyse* and *Walakye* scattered through the ensuing dream, these ensure that enough of the more warlike elements of chivalric myth and contemporary warfare get into the dream about the man in black. Later, in lines 1060–74 and 1118–23, where Chaucer's rhetoric presents the lover's devotion in terms of the greatest of names from chivalric romances – *Alysaunder, Cartage, Ector, Achilles, Rowland and Olyvere*, etc. – we can see him doing this very directly: bringing the associations of this literary myth of antique chivalric honour (prowess, magnificence and *trouthe*) into his rhetorical presentation of the man's passions.

As with his Troilus, Chaucer spends minimum time indicating the knightly status of a male figure whose sorrows clearly engage his interest far more, but he does ensure that input, almost imperceptibly, into the text. Without the hunt and these images of chivalric wars old and new, the dream of the man in black would be less princely (as we readily see by comparing him with his descendant and imitation, the otherwise very similar black-and-white knight in Lydgate's *Complaint of a Lover's Life*).[38] Emotionally prostrate, devoted lovers like Chaucer's knight and Troilus are often dubbed 'feminized' heroes, but if the attribution to men of debilitating devotion to passion and swooning is a device that makes them like women, it was a device that had been going on for a very long time, at least from Chrétien's Lancelot and some of Marie de France's heroes in the twelfth century.[39] In fact, the creation of medieval aristocratic masculinity sometimes depends less on an absence of emotional extremes than on their presence in combination with this invocation of a purportedly changeless and ahistorical chivalric prowess. It is interesting to compare *BD* and *LGW*, two poems separated by at least fifteen years, both concerned with aristocratic love tragedies. *LGW* makes its subject ignoble princes as well as noble love: perhaps the intervening writing of *Troilus* revealed the cracks and inconsistencies in the apparently simple myth of knightly, masculine 'love-longing'.[40] Patterson 1991: 237–43 suggests also a political disillusion by the time of the *Legend* with the myth of the *gentil* that cloaks power.[41]

Criticism of the 1980s and 1990s has foregrounded political and gender issues. The poem is undoubtedly a flattering offering to a prince, all the more effective for being unobtrusive. It presents its female figures in contradictory ways: with Alcyone the implication seems to be that emotional experience will be the same for man or woman; in White the female seems emotionally Other, the object of desire who does not feel desire. The real duchess is absent, absent through death and represented in the text by a figure exemplifying the eternally absent object of desire: it is not her *Book*, yet the structures that create a sense of beauty, desire and *gentillesse* praise her and offer consolation for her loss. *BD* raises questions of how, if at all, literature can express or comfort real-life sorrow: we have a narrator who turns writer; a knight who composes songs; a past dream which will become a future poem. Sleep, dream and words are presented as healing experiences, and the verbal recreation of the past proves so powerful that the listener cries 'Where is she now?' The relationship of words and literature to experience will also be a recurrent preoccupation of Chaucer's other three dream poems. This text is also deeply concerned with the processes of mental perception and understanding, from initial images to full understanding. The poem begins with an expression of puzzlement and ends with an expression of wonder. Its narrator's understanding often clearly falls short of the full meaning of what he sees. At its close, the statement – the text – is still, according to the fiction, to be written. It is a structure which, in all these ways, foregrounds the interpretative role of each reader. The poem presents its audience with the images – images of death and renewal, of comfort and despair – but it deferentially declines to provide their interpretation.

We are introduced to just such a situation with the opening lines, 1–24, where the speaker's mind is filled with 'ymagynacioun' and 'fantasies' – the *imagines* and *phantasmata* which in medieval theories of perception and cognition were a preliminary stage, material on which the interpretative reason, *ratio*, would later get to work. I suggest the poem's reader functions as that interpretative faculty.[42] Since the text's first reader may be supposed to be a mourner, that role is no mere metaphysical or deconstructive exercise. In Chaucer's poetry, love and suffering, his two most constant subjects, pose for us eternally the conflict between an undeniable recognition of earthly mutability and the irreducible fact of subjective emotions.

Helen Phillips

1.   See Palmer 1974; Ferris 1983.
2.   Goodman 1992: 33.
3.   St John is John of Lancaster's saint; the Richmond in question is Richmond in Yorkshire. Blanche was Countess of Richmond.
4.   Schless 1985 suggested that the work might have been written later than 1371, because 'kyng' (l. 1314) might refer to Gaunt's new title of King of Castile, claimed after he married Constance. A later date is certainly possible, though 'kynge' might simply be reinforcing the chess allegory. See note on the eight-year illness, ll. 30–43. *MLT Prol* (l. 57) says Ch wrote 'of Ceys and Alcione' in his youth: if this is *BD*, he would probably be between 23 and 28 at the time of the Duchess's death.
5.   E.g. Robertson 1965: 169–95.
6.   *BD* can be seen as an anti-suicide poem. That is probably not because it was combating real-life suicidal feelings, but rather on philosophical grounds, to show that an immutable grief would be against Nature's (and therefore the Creator's) purpose for living beings. Christian doctrine opposes suicide. This anti-suicide strand in the poem contrasts with the

apparent celebration in *LGW* of women who chose death when faced either with sexual dishonour or loss of the man they loved.

7. *Songe vert* may predate *BD*: see Rosenthal 1933, Seaton 1950 and Crane 1993 for different suggestions for its date; Jean (Jehan) de la Mote, *Li Regret Guillaume*, ed. Scheler 1882.

8. On the structure, see Stevenson 1988.

9. On this structure, see Phillips 1981.

10. Many critics have explored the role of poetry, and the contrast of art and life, in the poem, among them Stevens 1966, Edwards 1989 and Butterfield 1991.

11. See Phillips 1981.

12. For example, Bronson 1952, Gardner 1977: 8, 32; Green 1979: 220 sees it as creating an ironical narrator.

13. Clemen 1963: 50; Whitman 1969.

14. For a Freudian interpretation of White, see Ellman 1984. Calin 1994: 276–89 integrates psychological criticism with a perceptive account of how Ch naturalizes French courtly modes into English.

15. See Martin 1983.

16. And the *MLT Prol* (l. 57) mentions it together with his list of Ch's legends from *LGW*.

17. Robertson 1962 and Delasanta 1969 suggest a Christian consolation based on the implication of a metamorphosis. On the possible influence of moralized Ovids, see Wimsatt 1967a.

18. The difference between the knight's age and John of Gaunt's illustrates this point.

19. In Jehan de la Mote's *Regret Guillaume*, Count William of Hainault is mourned by 30 ladies representing *his* virtues, and their laments seem designed to express the sorrow of any relative or subject of Guillaume, regardless of sex. There are many other precedents for poets using female figures, like Niobe, as objective correlatives to experiences by a member of the opposite sex. Though it may be true that these tend predominantly to be on one side, since female figures are more often exploited as figurations of male or abstract qualities, there are counter examples, like male Absalon and Jonathas compared to a woman's beauty and friendliness in the *LGW balade*.

20. Note, however, that the *Regret Guillaume* includes (ll. 900–10) a female mourner who compares her woe at the Count's death to the misery of Dido at Aeneas's desertion of her. Medieval poets (for example, in the judgement given in Machaut's *Behaigne*) often treat loss of love with as much respect, disconcerting to modern sensibilities, as bereavement. (See Wimsatt 1993: 57 for an allegorical reading of this.)

21. *Cons.* I, pr. 1, ll. 29–30, pr. 2, ll. 17–18.

22.   In Turville-Petre 1989: 140–7. The vision appears during a tired rest or reverie; it is not explicitly labelled a dream.

23.   In ibid.: 148–57.

24.   See the notes on the poem and also Rooney 1987 and 1993, and Orme 1992.

25.   On Gaunt's love of hunting and on Urswick, see Goodman 1992: 358–9.

26.   On the history of landscape descriptions, including paradisal landscapes, see Pearsall & Salter 1973.

27.   See Crane 1993.

28.   See ibid.

29.   See David 1993 on Ch's handling of the theme of the narrator as the companion to a noble lover, where he interestingly links the allusions to books.

30.   The advances by critics of French *dits*, including Poirion, Brownlee, Huot, Calin and Cerquiglini, have paved the way for increased awareness not only of the profundities of Ch's dream poems but of many hitherto somewhat neglected later 'Chaucerian' works.

31.   See Knight 1986: 10–15, and 10–11 also on the evocation of 'feudal' obligation threaded through the text in the scenes before the narrator reaches the knight.

32.   See Sherborne 1994: 171–94 and Given-Wilson 1986 for financial, administrative and political aspects of the operation and culture of the royal court.

33.   See Phillips 1993a: 6–8, 29, and the royal inventories in Nicolas 1845: 37, 51, 57, 77–9; Armitage-Smith 1904: 422–3, 426–7; Wood 1965: 394–401.

34.   Thomson 1906: 86–7, 99–100, 158–65 (on tapestries belonging to Edward III's sons, see 62–3, 74, 117–18); Philip, Duke of Burgundy and the Count of Blois both owned tapestries of Octavian and the Sibyl, see David 1947: 91–2.

35.   Wood 1965: 394–40; Le Couter 1978: 64, 88, 100, 135–6. Courtly narratives also describe such decorative schemes: Dido and Aeneas in *HF*, scenes from the *Roman de Troie* on the fountain in the *Fonteinne amoureuse*.

36.   Green 1980: 135–7; Patterson 1991: 90–9, 155–64, 231–6.

37.   Paper given at *The Myth of Troy* conference, Nottingham University, 5 May 1994.

38.   Ch neatly encapsulates this triple vision of the aristocratic male as (crusading) soldier in foreign wars, lover and huntsman in the first three figures of his *General Prologue*, the knight, his son and his yeoman.

39. Hansen 1992 provides one of the most thought-provoking treatments of 'feminization' in relation to Ch.

40. Knight 1986: 64 sums up briefly a similar view.

41. This disillusionment may, however, have had also directly topical political incentives; see p. 395 on the possible influence of Richard II's slide into tyranny in the late 1390s on the G Prologue to *LGW*.

42. Edwards 1989, in contrast to the view presented here, reads the poem almost exclusively as about literature. Thus he insistently translates *mynde* as 'mind' rather than 'memory', and sees Ch's *ymagynacioun* as closer to a Coleridgean concept of the poetic imagination.

THE *BOOK OF THE DUCHESS*

	I have grete wonder, be this lyghte,	
	How that I lyve, for day ne nyghte	*how I live*
	I may nat slepe wel nygh noght:	*cannot*
	I have so many an ydel thoght,	*meaningless*
5	Purely for defaulte of slepe,	*entirely; lack*
	That, by my trouthe, I take no kepe	*pay no attention*
	Of noothinge – how hyt cometh or gooth,	*comes or goes*
	Ne me nys nothynge leve nor looth.	*good or bad*
	Al is ylyche goode to me,	*equally*
10	Joy or sorowe, wherso hyt be;	*may be*
	For I have felynge in nothynge,	*no sense of anything*
	But as yt were a mased thynge,	*dazed*
	Alway in poynt to falle adoun.	*on the point of*

Title: in two MSS and Retraction to *CT*; *LGW*, l. 406 calls it *the deth of Blaunche the Duchesse*, Thynne *The Dream of Chaucer*.

1–24. *PF* also begins with a bewildered narrator: see ll. 4–14. *BD*, ll. 1–3, 14–15, 22–4 resemble *Paradis d'Amours*, ll. 1–12 (in Froissart, *Poésies*, ed. Scheler 1870–72: I, 1–52). Though medieval poets often link sickness and melancholy to love, and Froissart's narrator is explicitly suffering for love, Ch is unspecific: to read lovesickness into these lines would be to impoverish their suggestiveness. Later dream poetry often uses this initiatory motif of un-focused anxiety: see p. 9. Burnley 1986a discusses the terminology of perception here and elsewhere in *BD*.

1. *be this lyghte*: 'by this daylight', i.e. by the sun. An apt first line, introducing the non-authoritative, wondering narrator and prefiguring light/dark pattern-ing; it contains already potential images of hope: new dawn, enlightenment, even divine light.

8. *leve nor looth*: 'good nor bad', lit. 'beloved or hated'; this is emotional incapacity, not just intellectual dullness, cf. l. 10.

10. *wherso*: 'wherever', or more probably 'whichever': *wher* can be a form of *whether*, which can mean 'which'.

11. *felynge*: a multivalent term, referring to both intellectual and emotional/sensual apprehension, 'sensation' or 'understanding' (cf. *PF*, l. 4). It is a word sometimes associated with theories of perception; Burnley 1979: 105–6, 162–4 shows that *felyng* may mean the preliminary capacity to apprehend sense-data, but it is also used by Ch (e.g. *TC* II, l. 19) for the sympathetic understanding that is born of *gentil* sensitivity.

	For sorwful ymagynacioun	
15	Ys alway hooly in my mynde.	*completely*
	And wel ye woote, agaynes Kynde	*know; Nature*
	Hyt were to lyven in thys wyse,	*live; manner*
	For Nature wolde nat suffyse	*refuses to allow*
	To noon erthely creature	*to any; being*
20	Nat longe tyme to endure	*survive*
	Withoute slepe, and be in sorwe.	
	And I ne may, ne nyght ne morwe,	*cannot*
	Slepe, and thys melancolye	
	And drede I have for to dye:	

14. *ymagynacioun*: 'mental images'; cf. l. 28, *fantasies*: 'vague pictures in the mind'. Both terms belong to the technical vocabulary of medieval theories of perception and cognition: they are the mental imaging of things (formed from sense impressions from the outside world) prior to full recognition or understanding by the intellect. See *S Th*, Ia 79:8; *Cons.* V, pr. 4; Burnley 1979: 102–15; and p. 46. *S Th*, Ia 78:4 calls *imaginatio* and *phantasia* 'the same thing ... a treasure-store of forms received through the senses'. Philosophers used *phantasmata* for the images, *phantasia* or *imaginatio* for the mental faculty that conserves them. Macrobius, *Comm. on Dream of Scipio*, tr. Stahl 1952: 3, used *phantasma* for meaningless (non-prophetic) apparitions passing through the mind between waking and sleep.

16–26. Introduces the themes of Nature and death. Already the text, delicately foreshadowing the knight's suicidal melancholy, puts forward the idea that excessive mourning and life-denying lethargy are against Nature, and therefore against God's design (see note to l. 56). Nature is a personification or a supernatural power, representing God's creative energy and design. Alain de Lille and *RR* (ll. 15861ff.) present Nature as God's 'vicar' (representative), or a craftsman eternally forming creatures according to the design for each species (cf. *BD*, ll. 908–12).

16. *agaynes Kynde*: 'against Nature': Nature opposes Death and life-threatening attitudes, e.g. *RR*, ll. 15847–974; cf. Machaut, *Complainte I*, ll. 16–21, Phillips 1993a: 178–9: 'Love, you have been so hard on me ... I see no hope of recovery, and I believe it is against Nature to endure like this'.

23–4. Sleep is linked to death here as physical healing, prefiguring the intellectual consolation which sleep – and the dream poem – will offer for death and melancholy. Cf. Machaut, *Jugement dou roy de Navarre*, ll. 109–12 (in *Oeuvres*, ed. Hoepffner 1908–21) for the narrator's melancholy. Minnis 1995: 51–3 comments that dream books often link melancholy (caused by excess of black bile in the body) to dreams of black things.

25	Defaulte of slepe and hevynesse	*depression*
	Hath [slain] my spirite of quyknesse,	*liveliness*
	That I have loste al lustyhede;	*so that; cheerfulness*
	Suche fantasies ben in myn hede,	*are*
	So I not what is best too doo.	*do not know*
30	But men myght axe me why soo	
	[I may not slepe and what me is.	*is the matter*
	But nathelesse, who aske this	*anyone who asked*
	Leseth his askyng trewly.	*is wasting his question*
	Myselven can not tel why	
35	The sothe, but trewly as I gesse,	*for certain*
	I holde it be a sicknesse	*to be*
	That I have suffred this eyght yere.	*these; years*
	And yet my boote is never the nere,	*remedy; nearer*
	For there is phisycien but one	*only one*
40	That may me heale. But that is done:	*who can; over*
	Passe we over untyl efte;	*later*
	That wyl not be mote nede be lefte.	*what; must needs be*
	Our first mater is good to kepe.	*theme*
	So whan I sawe I might not slepe	*could*
45	Tyl nowe late this other nyght,	*after a long time*
	Upon my bedde I sate upright	
	And bade one reche me a booke,	*someone hand me*
	A romaunce, and he it me toke,	*fetched for me*
	To rede and drive the nyght away;	*while away*
50	For me thought it better play	*it seemed to me*
	Than play eyther at chesse or tables.	*board games*

31–96. Thynne's 1532 edition is the only source for these lines; see Notes on the Text, pp. 108–9.

36, 39. *sicknesse*; *phisycien*: these may suggest lovesickness, but their precise reference is left undefined.

37. *eyght yere*: French *dits* sometimes use such time expressions with an indefinite sense: cf. Machaut, *Jugement dou roy de Behaigne*, ll. 125–6 (in *Oeuvres*, ed. Hoepffner 1908–21: I, 57–135): 'For seven or eight years my heart has been Love's servant'. It may have had a topical meaning now lost. Eight years after Blanche's death would be 1376.

48. *romaunce*: a loose term, originally a narrative in French (which fits Machaut's *Fonteinne amoureuse* rather than *Met.* – but this is a fictional book). See note to l. 52.

51. *tables*: used for a range of board games including medieval backgammon.

And in this boke were written fables
That clerkes had in olde tyme,   *learned men*
And other poetes, put in ryme
55   To rede and for to be in mynde,   *memory*
Whyle men loved the lawe of Kynde.   *as long as*
This boke ne spake but of suche thynges,   *nothing else but*
Of quenes lyves and of kynges,
And many other thinges smale.
60   Amonge al this I fonde a tale
That me thought a wonder thyng.   *which seemed*
This was the tale: there was a kyng
That hyght Seys and had a wyfe,   *was called*
The best that myght beare lyfe,   *could exist*
65   And this quene hyght Alcyone.   *was called*

---

52. *fables*: 'stories', especially fictions rather than historical accounts (cf. Isidore
     of Seville, *Etymologies*, 1.74.5); Le Fèvre, *Leësce*, ll. 2692–2742, calls Ovid's
     Metamorphoses 'fables' because they are pagan and mythical rather than
     history.
53–5. On books as preservers of the experience of the past and the 'key of
     remembrance', cf. *LGW*, ll. 17–26. See David 1993: 7–9 on the penumbra of
     associations that can hover round Ch's use of 'old'.
55. *mynde*: 'memory'; cf. *LGW*, ll. 17–34.
56. The law of Nature (*Kynde*) is the moral order as known to humans through
     their indwelling powers of conscience and reason. As *PF* illustrates, writers
     like Alain de Lille (who names the virtues associated with Nature as Chastity,
     Temperance, Generosity and Humility, in *The Plaint of Nature*, tr. Sheridan
     1980: 8) portrayed Nature as executing a benevolent Creator's harmonious,
     orderly design, presiding over bountiful fertility in the natural world and
     virtuous human love. Here Ch suggests a Golden Age when humans still
     naturally and happily acted according to moral principles and order. *Met.* I,
     ll. 80–150 begin with humanity's decline from the Golden Age (see note to
     ll. 402–9). *PF*, l. 78 calls lechers *brekers of the lawe*.
58. Royalty is a recurrent motif: see e.g. ll. 60–269, 282, 286, 1314, 1327, though
     Met. does indeed contain many kings and queens.
59. *other thinges smale*: does not sound comic in ME: 'other, less grand, topics'.
62–214. See pp. 34–6 for the story of Ceyx and Alcyone, also *Met.* IX,
     ll. 410–750, and Machaut, *Fonteinne amoureuse*, ll. 542–698 (in *Oeuvres*,
     ed. Hoepffner 1908–21: III, 143–244).
65. *Alcyone* (also *Alchione*): wife of *Seys* (*Ceyx*), king of Trachis.

So it befyl, therafter sone,
This kyng wol wenden over see.   *desired to travel*
To tellen shortly, whan that he   *to be brief*
Was in the see thus in this wyse,   *in this way*
70   Suche a tempest gan to ryse
That brake her maste and made it fal,   *their*
And clefte her shyp and dreynt hem al,   *split; drowned them*
That never was founde (as it telles)   *the tale relates*
Borde ne man ne nothyng elles.   *plank or man*
75   Right thus this kyng Seys loste his lyfe.
       Nowe for to speke of Alcyone his wyfe:
This lady, that was lefte at home,   *who was left*
Hath wonder that the kyng ne come
Home, for it was a longe terme.
80   Anon her herte began to [erme]   *immediately; grieve*
And, for that her thought evermo   *because it seemed to her*
It was not wele: her thought so.   *it seemed to her*
She longed so after the kyng,   *yearned so much for*
That certes it were a pytous thyng   *indeed; would be*
85   To tel her hertely sorouful lyfe   *deeply*
That she had, this noble wyfe,
For him, alas, she loved alderbest.   *above anything*
Anon she sent bothe eest and west   *sent messengers*
To seke him, but they founde nought.   *nothing*
90   'Alas,' quod she, 'that I was wrought!   *created*

66. 'So it happened, soon after that'.
73–4. *telles*: northern form (for rhyme?), instead of Ch's usual East Midland
form, *telleth*. Ovid *does* tell of Ceyx's body being found; maybe Ch
remembered *Ovidius Moralizatus*, l. 160, which says that not one of them
remained. Ovid's ship's timbers, to which Ceyx and others cling (ll. 559–62),
may underlie the fleeting image *borde ne man*.
76. There are too many syllables; if *speke* were a two-syllable inflected infinitive
speken perhaps *Alcyone* got incorporated from a marginal gloss. *Alas* (l. 87)
may be similar.
79. *longe terme*: 'fully the final time for his return'; *longe*: adv. 'by a long time'.
80–1. Is the text confused here? Thynne's *yerne* is probably an error for *erme*,
which was obsolete by his time (the rhyme *terme/erme* occurs in *PardT* VI,
ll. 311–12); *her thought*: perhaps an error for a verb like *he dwelte* ('delayed').

And wher my lorde, my love, be deed?
Certes I nyl never eate breed –
I make a vowe to my god here –
But I mowe of my lorde here.'   *unless I may hear*
95   Suche sorowe this lady to her toke
That trewly I that made this boke]   *who composed*
Had suche pittee and suche rowthe   *compassion*
To rede hir sorwe that, by my trowthe,   *in all sincerity*
I ferde the worse al the morwe   *was distressed by it*
100   Aftir, to thenken on hir sorwe.
       So whan this lady koude here noo worde,   *hear*
That no man myght fynde hir lorde,   *could*
Ful ofte she swouned and sayed 'Alas!'   *swooned*
For sorwe ful nygh woode she was.   *very nearly mad*
105   Ne she koude no rede but oon,
But doune on knees she sate anoon
And wepte, that pittee was to here: *so that; hear*
'A, mercy, swete lady dere!'
Quod she [to] Juno, hir goddesse,
110   'Helpe me out of thys distresse
And yeve me grace my lord to se   *give*
Soone, or wete wherso he be,   *know where he may be*
Or how he fareth, or in what wise,   *in what fashion*
And I shal make yowe sacrifise,
115   And hooly youres become I shal
With good wille: body, hert and al.

91. *wher*: 'whether'; used in the sense 'could it be that…?' *My lorde* (and *my lady*): the upper classes used such third-person forms when referring to a spouse.
92. 'I certainly refuse to eat bread ever again'; *nyl* (*ne* + *wol*) = do not want, refuse.
95. 'This lady gave herself up to such sorrow'.
97. MS Fairfax 16 text (F) resumes here.
99. *ferde*: lit. 'travelled', but used vaguely for experiencing any situation (e.g. *fareth*, l. 113).
105. 'Nor could she think of any solution but one'; *koude* = 'know'; *rede* = 'advice' or 'plan'.
109. *Juno*: the Roman goddess concerned especially with women and childbirth.
111, 118. *grace*: mercy, a merciful gift.
115. 'And I shall become completely your servant'.

	And but thow wilte this, lady swete,	
	Sende me grace to slepe and mete	*to dream*
	In my slepe some certeyn sweven,	*a trustworthy dream*
120	Wherthorgh that I may knowe even	*can know truly*
	Whethir my lorde be quyke or ded.'	*alive*
	With that worde she henge doun the hed	*down*
	And felle aswowne, a[s] colde as ston.	*in a faint*
	Hyr women kaught hir up anoon	*immediately*
125	And broghten hir in bed al naked.	
	And she, forweped and forwaked,	
	Was wery, and thus the ded slepe	
	Fil on hir or she tooke kepe,	
	Throgh Juno that had herde hir bone,	*request*
130	That made hir to slepe sone.	*who caused*
	For as she prayede ryght so was done	
	In dede. For Juno ryght anone	*in reality*
	Called thus hir messagere	
	To doo hir erande, and he come nere.	*approached closer*
135	Whan he was come she bad hym thus,	*asked*
	'Go bet,' quod Juno, 'to Morpheus	
	Thou knowest hym wel: the God of Slepe.	
	Now understonde wel and take kepe.	*pay attention*
	Sey thus on my halfe, that he	*behalf*

117. 'And, if you will grant only this, benevolent lady'.
125. *al naked*: 'undressed' rather than 'nude' (though medieval people seem often to have slept naked).
126. *For-* is an intensifying prefix: 'worn out with weeping and with lying awake'.
127–8. 'Was weary, and thus the dead sleep fell on her before she was conscious'. Note the themes of death and sleep, of consciousness and loss of mental clarity, and of sleep as comfort for sorrow.
134. In *Met.* IX, l. 585 and other sources and analogues, the messenger is female, the goddess Iris; some *Ovidius Moralizatus* MSS have a male messenger (see Martin 1972: 172).
136. 'Go as quickly as you can ...'. In *Met.* IX, ll. 633–79, Morpheus is not the god of sleep but a dream, one of the many sons (dreams) of Somnus, the god of sleep. Ovid's motif of the dream flying to Seys, entering his body and bringing a message to Alcyone reflects the classical idea of dreams as divine messengers, who may adopt the form of a person (see p. 5).

140	Go faste into the Grete Se,	
	And byd hym that on al thynge	*above all*
	That he take up Seys body the kynge,	*should take up*
	That lyeth ful pale and nothynge rody.	*not red at all*
	B[i]d hym crepe into the body	
145	And doo hit goon to Alchione	*cause it to go*
	The quene, ther she lyeth allone,	*where*
	And shewe hir shortly, hit ys no nay,	
	How hit was dreynt thys other day.	*drowned*
	And do the body speke ryght soo,	*make*
150	Ryght as hyt was woned to doo,	*wont*
	The whiles that hit was alyve.	*during the time when*
	Goo now faste and hye the blyve!'	
	This messager toke leve and went	*took his leave*
	Upon hys wey, and never ne stent	*ceased*
155	Til he come to the derke valey	*came*
	That stant betwex roches twey,	*stands*
	Ther never yet grew corne ne gras,	*where*
	Ne tre, ne noght that oughte was,	*was anything at all*
	Beste ne man ne noght elles,	*not animal nor man*
160	Save ther were a fewe welles	*except that*
	Came rennynge fro the clyffes adoun,	*which came; down*
	That made a dedely slepynge soun,	*sound*

140. 'Should go straightaway to the Mediterranean'. In ll. 140 and 142 *go* and *take* are subjunctives: 'should go', 'should take'.

142. *Seys*: a possessive/genitive form, lit. 'Ceyx's body the king'. Since the 16th century constructions like 'Ceyx the king's body' have been used for such group genitives.

145. *Alchione*: the spelling reflects medieval Latin pronunciation.

147. 'And show her straightaway, without any possibility of doubt'.

152. *hye the blyve*: lit. 'haste thee quickly'.

155–71. The cave, darkness, rock and silence have counterparts in *Met.* IX, ll. 591–614. Ch adds *helle pitte*, l. 171, perhaps because Virgil's underworld (*Aen.* VI, ll. 273–84) includes sleep and dreams (ll. 278, 283, 893–6). *Met.* XI, l. 603 places Lethe, the river of the Underworld, in the Cave of Sleep (ME *helle* can denote the classical underworld, as well as Hell).

155–6. Machaut, *Fonteinne amoureuse*, ll. 590–5, has a valley between two mountains.

157–8. The barrenness is also in the Cave of Sleep passage in *Theb.* X, ll. 98–9.

160–2. Cf. *Met.* XI, ll. 60–4; *Ovide moralisé*, ll. 3449–55.

And ronnen doun ryght by a cave   *they ran down*
That was under a rokke ygrave,   *hollowed out*
165   Amydde the valey wonder depe.   *amazingly deep*
There these goddys lay and slepe,   *where; slept*
Morpheus and Eclympasteyre,
That was the God of Slepes eyre,   *heir*
That slepe and did noon other werke.   *who slept; no*
170   This cave was also as derke   *just as*
As helle pitte, overal aboute.   *everywhere about*
They had good leyser for to route,   *opportunity; snore*
To envye who myght slepe beste.
Some henge her chyn upon hir breste   *hung their chins; their*
175   And slept upryght, hir hed yhedde,   *hidden*
And some lay naked in her bedde   *their bed*
And slepe whiles the dayes laste.   *as long as*
This messager come fleynge faste   *flying rapidly*
And cried 'O how! awake anoon!'
180   Hit was for noght: there herde hym non.

163–5. Shannon 1929: 6–7, 330 suggests that *rokke* arises from a scribal error in MSS of *Met*. XI, l. 591, but *Theb*. X, ll. 86–7 has *subterque cavis grave rupibus antrum*, 'under the hollow recesses of a deep cave in rocks', and 'rocks and boulders' at l. 97, which might also have influenced 'cave ... ygrave', as well as fitting Ch's notably barren landscape.

165. 'In the middle of a valley, amazingly deep'.

167. *Met*. IX, ll. 633–43 says Somnus, the god of sleep, has a thousand sons (i.e. dreams) and names three: Morpheus, Icelos and Phantasos. *Eclympasteyre*: Froissart calls Morpheus the god of sleep, and invents 'Enclimpostair', his son (*Paradis d'Amours*, ll. 15–28); see Wimsatt 1993: 190–1. Cartier 1964, a full and funny account of speculation on this name's origin, suggests *enclin-postere*, 'lean-back'.

171. Cf. *Met*. XI, ll. 594–6; *Theb*. X, ll. 115–17, 119. None of the analogues refers to Hell. See Spencer 1927 and the note on *LGW*, l. 502.

173. 'To rival each other as to who slept most soundly'.

175. They slept propped up (i.e. from the waist); cf. the description of Somnus, 'so that his chin touched his chest' (*Fonteinne amoureuse*, l. 607): their heads are hidden because they are slumped forward on their chests.

177. *whiles the dayes laste*: 'right through the days', lit. 'as long as the days lasted'.

179. 'And shouted "Hey! Wake up now!"'

180. 'It was all for nothing: no-one there heard him.'

'Awake!' quod he, 'Whoo ys lythe there?'
And blew his horne ryght in here eere,   *their ear*
And cried 'Awaketh!' wonder hye.   *amazingly loudly*
    This God of Slepe with hys on ye
185   Caste up and axed 'Who clepeth there?'   *Who calls*
'Hyt am I,' quod this messagere.   *It is I*
'Juno bad thow shuldest goon . . .' –   *requested*
And tolde hym what he shulde doon,   *must do*
As I have tolde yow heretofore   *already*
190   (Hyt ys no nede reherse hyt more).   *to repeat*
And went hys wey whan he had sayede.   *spoken*
    Anoon this God of Slepe abrayede   *pulled himself up*
Out of hys slepe and gan to goon
And dyd as he had bede hym doon: *asked him to do*
195   Tooke up the dreynt body sone   *immediately*
And bare hyt forth to Alchione,   *carried*
His wife the quene, ther as she lay,   *where she lay*
Ryght even a quarter before day.
And stood ryght at h[er] beddys fete
200   And called hir, ryght as she hete
By name, and sayede, 'My swete wyfe,
Awake! Let be your sorwful lyfe,
For in your sorwe there lyth no rede.
For certes, swete, I am but dede:
205   Ye shul me never on lyve yse.   *see me alive*

181.   *Whoo ys lythe there?*: 'who is it who is lying there?'
182–3.   The messenger gets similarly aggressive in *Theb*. X, ll. 132–3. Only Ch has
    the horn, foreshadowing the one that wakes his dreamer (ll. 344–56) and
    the bell (ll. 1322–4).
184–5.   *with hys on ye / Caste up*: 'with one of his eyes he looked up'; this
    resembles Machaut, *Fonteinne amoureuse*, l. 632.
198.   'Just exactly a quarter before daybreak'. Dreams just before dawn were
    believed to be reliable: see note to *HF*, ll. 3–11.
200–1.   'Exactly as she was called by name'. Wimsatt 1967b: 237–8 suggests a
    parallel with *Aen*. II, ll. 771–84, where Aeneas's dead wife Creusa appears
    to him urging him to cease pointless mourning for her.
202–4.   'Awake, put aside your sorrowful life, for no solution lies in your misery,
    for in truth, sweetheart, I am simply dead'.

	But, good swete hert, that ye	*I ask that you*
	Bury my body, for suche a tyde	*at such a time*
	Ye mowe hyt fynde the see besyde.	*may find it*
	And farewel, swete, my worldes blysse:	
210	I pray God youre sorwe lysse.	*may comfort*
	To lytel while oure blysse lasteth.'	*too short a time*
	With that hir eyen up she casteth,	
	And sawe noght. 'Allas!' quod she for sorwe,	*nothing; sorrow*
	And deyede within the thridde morwe.	*within three days*
215	But what she sayede more in that swowe	*further; swoon*
	I may not telle yow as nowe;	*cannot recount; now*
	Hyt were to longe for to dwelle.	
	My first matere I wil yow telle,	*I wish to narrate*
	Wherfore I have tolde this thynge	*why*
220	Of Alchione and Seys the kynge.	
	For thus moche dar I say welle:	*can say confidently*
	I had be dolven everydelle	
	And ded, ryght thorgh defaulte of slepe,	
	Yif I ne had redde and take kepe	*if I had not*
225	Of this tale next before.	*just before*
	And [I] wol telle yow wherfore:	
	For I ne myght, for bote ne bale,	*good or ill*
	Slepe or I had redde thys tale	*before*
	Of this dreynte Seys the kynge,	*drowned*
230	And of the goddis of slepynge.	
	Whan I had redde thys tale wel	
	And overloked hyt everydel,	*thoroughly*
	Me thoght wonder yf hit were so,	*it seemed to me*
	For I had never herde speke or tho	*before then*

206. *that*: often used, as here, to introduce a subjunctive and create a gentle imperative; see Elliott 1974: 89.
209. 'And farewell, sweetheart, my happiness in this world'.
210–11. A poignantly concise combination of a Boethian doctrine about earthly emotions (l. 211) with a prayer for comfort (l. 210); cf. *TC* V, ll. 1748–50.
217. 'It would make too long a delay'.
222–3. 'I would have been completely buried and dead, just for lack of sleep'. Ll. 222–5 reinforce the theme of literature and dream as comforts for death-like sorrow.
226. 'And I wish to tell you why'.
232. 'And looked through it from beginning to end'.

235   Of noo goddis that koude make

       Men to slepe, ne for to wake,   *and not lie awake*

       For I ne knewe never god but oon.   *no god but one*

       And in my game I sayede anoon   *frivolity*

       (And yet me lyst ryght evel to pley):

240   'Rather then that Y shulde dey   *die*

       Thorgh defaulte of slepynge thus,

       I wolde yive thilke Morpheus,   *would like to; that same*

       Or hys goddesse dame Juno,   *lady*

       Or some wight ellis, I ne roght who,

245   To make me slepe and have some reste,

       I wil yive hym the alderbeste   *very best of all*

       Yifte that ever he abode hys lyve.

       And here on warde, ryght now as blyve,

       Yif he wol make me slepe a lyte,   *If he agrees to*

250   Of downe of pure dowves white   *pure white doves*

237. Perhaps this is the motif of the ignorant narrator again, but it may reflect a recognition of the pre-Christian nature of Ovid's *fables*, something stressed in Le Fèvre's *Leësce*, ll. 2692–742.

239. 'And yet it was not in the least my desire to be frivolous'.

242–64. Ch's poetic conceit of offerings to the god of sleep, including things like soft bedding which in reality do encourage sleep, imitates Froissart praying for sleep to Morpheus and offering a ring to Juno (see next note), and Machaut's offer of soporific aids to sleep, 'a wreath of poppy and pillow of falcon feathers', *Fonteinne amoureuse*, ll. 250–69. Ch's lines are echoed in Sidney's *Astrophil and Stella*, sonnet 39.

244. 'Or someone else, I do not care who'. Froissart, *Paradis d'Amours*, ll. 13–21, describes the narrator praying specifically to Morpheus, Juno and *Oleus* (Aeolus, god of the winds, Alcyone's father). Ch adds the motif of the ignorant narrator.

246. *alderbeste*: 'best of all'.

247. 'Gift he ever experienced in all his life'.

248. 'And here as a pledge, right now immediately'; *on warde* = 'as a gift given as a pledge' or 'into his keeping' (or perhaps 'straightaway', although that sense is not otherwise found in ME).

	I wil yif hym a feder bedde,	
	Rayed with golde and ryght wel cledde	*striped; draped*
	In fyne blak satyn de Owtermere,	
	And many a pelowe, and every bere	*pillowcase*
255	Of clothe of Reynes, to slepe softe;	*Rennes linen*
	Hym thar not nede to turnen ofte.	*will not need*
	And I wol yive hym al that fallys	*befits*
	To a chambre, and al hys hallys	*bedroom*
	I wol do peynte with pure golde,	*have painted*
260	And tapite hem, ful many folde	
	Of oo sute. This shal he have,	
	Yf I wiste where were hys cave,	*knew*
	Yf he kan make me slepe sone,	
	As did the goddesse quene Alchione.	*as the goddess did for*
265	And thus this ylke god Morpheus	*this same*
	May wynne of me moo fees thus	*earn from; payments*
	Than ever he wanne. And to Juno,	*gained*
	That ys hys goddesse, I shal soo do:	
	I trow that she shal holde hir payede.'	
270	I hadde unneth that worde ysayede,	*scarcely; said*
	Ryght thus [as] I have tolde hyt yow,	
	That sodeynly, I nyste how,	*do not know*
	Suche a luste anoon me tooke	*desire straightaway*
	To slepe, that ryght upon my booke	
275	Y fil aslepe, and therwith evene	*exactly at that point*

251–5. Similarly luxurious bedding and hangings appear in contemporary documents, e.g. John of Gaunt's will refers to fine linen from Rennes in Brittany, striped and embroidered silken covers and curtains (among them sets in cloth of gold and embroidered black velvet set): see Nicolas 1845: esp. 37, 51, 57, 77–9; Armitage-Smith 1904: Appendix I, esp. 422–3; Sherborne 1994: 171–94.

251. feather bed: like a duvet, but it usually went under the sleeper, over the mattress.

253. *de Owtermere*: the Middle East (French, lit. 'from beyond the [Mediterranean] sea'), source of many luxuries, including fine textiles.

258. *chambre*: private room; *hallys*: public rooms. On tapestries in real life often given as gifts between princes and nobles, see p. 43.

259. ME *do* often means 'cause' or 'cause to be done'.

260–1. 'And have them hung with tapestries, in very many sections, all of one set'.

269. 'I trust she will consider herself sufficiently rewarded'.

	Me mette so ynly swete a swevene,	*deeply sweet a dream*
	So wonderful, that never yitte	*yet*
	Y trow no man had the wytte	
	To konne wel my sweven rede;	
280	No, not Joseph, withoute drede,	*without doubt*
	Of Egipte, he that red so	*interpreted*
	The kynges metynge Pharao,	*king Pharaoh's dream*
	No more than koude the lest of us;	*the least*
	Ne nat skarsly Macrobeus,	*nor; even*
285	He that wrote al th'avysyoun	*vision*
	That he mette, kynge Scipioun,	*that he dreamed*
	The noble man the Affrikan –	
	[Suche marvayles fortuned than –]	*wonders happened*
	I trowe, arede my dremes even	
290	Loo thus hyt was: thys was my sweven.	*dream*
	Me thoght thus: that hyt was May,	*it seemed to me*
	And in the dawnynge I lay –	*dawning*
	Me mette thus – in my bed al naked,	*I dreamed thus*
	And loked forth; for I was waked	
295	With smale foules a grete hepe,	*crowd*
	That had affrayed me out of my slepe,	*startled*

278–9. 'I believe no-one had the cleverness to know how to interpret my dream correctly': an incitement to the reader.

280. Joseph, abducted from his Jewish family to Egypt, rose to power and favour partly because of his skill in interpreting Pharaoh's and his officials' dreams, Gen. 40–1.

282. Another group genitive.

284–5. The 'Dream of Scipio' is in Book 6 of Cicero's *De re publica*. Ch may be echoing *RR*, ll. 9–10, which calls Macrobius the author of the vision of *roi Scypion*, whereas in fact he wrote the Commentary on it and Scipio Africanus (185/4–129 BC) was a Roman general. See pp. 5, 220–1.

288. This line is found only in Th (see 'Notes on the text', pp. 108–9).

289. 'I think, interpret my dreams exactly'.

291–2. The dream in *RR* also begins in May with the dreamer waking and listening to birds and then getting up, ll. 45–102.

295–320. Pleasure in birdsong often draws the narrators of dream poems out from houses to walk through a landscape – where the main part of the narrative takes place. The chief source is *RR*, ll. 67–107 (cf. also *BD*, ll. 653–6), and Ch's example further encouraged the motif in 15th-century English works.

	Thorgh noyse and swettenesse of her songe.	*their*
	And, a[s] me mette, they sate amonge	*as I dreamed it*
	Upon my chambre roofe wythoute,	*outside*
300	Upon the tyles overal aboute,	*all around*
	And songe, everych in hys wyse,	*every one; style*
	The moste solempne servise	*magnificent*
	By noote that ever man, Y trowe,	*in singing*
	Had herde. For some of hem songe lowe,	
305	Some high, and al of oon acorde.	*in complete harmony*
	To telle shortly, att oo worde,	*in one word*
	Was never h[e]rde so swete a steven,	*voice*
	But hyt had be a thynge of heven,	*been*
	So mery a soune, so swete entewnes	*sound*
310	That certes, for the toune of Tewnes	*Tunis*
	I nolde but I had herde hem synge.	
	For al my chambre gan to rynge	
	Thorgh syngynge of her armonye.	*their harmony*
	For instrument nor melodye	
315	Was nowhere herde yet halfe so swete,	
	Nor of acorde halfe so mete.	
	For ther was noon of hem that feyned	
	To synge, for eche of hem hym peyned	*made great effort*
	To fynde out mery crafty notys;	
320	They ne spared not her throtys.	

302–8. The conceit of birds' singing as a religious service is common: e.g. *RR*, ll. 658–62.

309. *entewnes*: chanted melodies (?); *entuned*, in *Gen Prol*, l. 123, refers to the skilled art of chanting religious services.

310. *Tewnes*: Tunis, a N. African city, of great wealth, culture and political importance from the 13th century on. It was besieged unsuccessfully by the crusading French king Louis IX in 1270.

311. *nolde but I had herde*: 'I would not have wanted to have missed hearing it'.

315–16. 'Had ever been heard before now half so sweet, nor half so united in harmony'.

317. 'For there was not one of them who did not put all his effort whole-heartedly'.

319. 'To invent beautiful, skilful notes'.

	And, soothe to seyn, my chambre was	*truth to tell*
	Ful wel depeynted; and with glas	
	Were al the wyndowes wel yglasyd	*finely glazed*
	Ful clere, and nat an hoole ycrasyd,	*very clear; cracked*
325	That to beholde hyt was grete joye.	*so that*
	For holy al the story of Troye	*completely*
	Was in the glasynge ywroght thus,	*fashioned*
	Of Ector and of kynge Priamus,	
	Of Achilles and of kynge Lamedoun,	
330	And eke of Medea and of Jasoun,	
	Of Paris, Eleyne, and of Lavyne.	

321–2. Walls painted with scenes or ornament were common (Wood 1965: 394–401). Poets often write of walls and other parts of buildings covered with scenes, and texts, from well-known narratives (Wimsatt 1968: 63–4). *depeynted*: 'decorated with paintings'.

324. The smooth clarity of the glass is a sign of high quality. We are in a world of perfection and brightness, prefiguring the description of a flawless woman.

325–44. This motif of windows in a bedroom introduces pleasure both from the natural world – coming to the narrator from outside – and from literature: the heroic and amorous world of the medieval romances of Troy, and the love allegory of *RR*. Glass was still a rare luxury in secular buildings, and painted scenes and inscriptions occurred in both life and literature. On the medieval romances of Troy and ideological associations, see pp. 44–5. The references to Troy and *RR* suggest love, like the Maytime and birdsong, and, like the hunting, elegant aristocratic life. *Priamus*: Priam, king of Troy; *Ector, Paris*: Trojan princes, Hector, the foremost Trojan warrior, and Paris were sons of Priam; *Lamedoun*: Laomedon, Priam's father, king of the first city built at Troy; *Eleyne*: Helen, the Greek queen whose elopement with Paris caused the war between the Greeks and the Trojans; *Medea*: a princess of Colchis who used her skill in magic to enable Jason to win the Golden Fleece; their story is the first episode of *Roman de Troie*, but their love ended tragically: see *BD*, ll. 726–7, *HF*, ll. 401, 1271, *LGW*, ll. 1580–1650, and also *Met*. VII, ll. 1–158, 162–296; *Achilles*: the foremost Greek warrior, whose tragic love for the Trojan Polyxena is a major episode in the *Roman de Troie* (ll. 17489–18472, 21838–22500); *Lavyne*: Lavinia, the Latian princess whose love for Aeneas dominates the later parts of the *Roman d'Éneas*. For medieval readers of romance these names were associated with love as much as with warfare or classical learning.

329. Hypermetric; *and of kynge* is perhaps added by error from l. 328.

And alle the wallys with colouris fyne
Were peynted, bothe text and glose,
[Of] al the Romaunce of the Rose.
335   My wyndowes were shette echon   *shut; each one*
And throgh the glas the sone shon   *sun*
Upon my bed with bryght bemys,   *beams*
With many glade gilde stremys.   *happy gilded*
And eke the welken was so faire: *also; sky*
340   Blew, bryght, clere was the ayre,
And ful atempre forsothe hyt was;   *perfectly mild truly*
For nother to colde nor hoote yt was,   *neither*
Ne in al the walkene was a clowde.   *the whole sky*
And as I lay thus, wonder lowde   *amazingly*
345   Me thoght I herde an hunte blowe
T'assay hys horne, and for to knowe
Whether hyt were clere or horse of soune.   *it was; hoarse*
And I herde goynge, bothe up and doune,
Men, hors, houndes, and other thynge,   *things*
350   And al men speke of huntynge,   *talking*
How they wolde slee the hert with strengthe,   *intended to*
And how the hert had upon lengthe
So moche embosed – Y not now what.   *don't know*
Anoonryght, whan I herde that,   *immediately*
355   How that they wolde on huntynge goon,   *wanted to go*
I was ryght glad, and up anoon   *very; straightaway*

332–4. *glose*: 'explanation' (lit. a commentary accompanying the basic text of a narrative). Ch often uses it as a rhyme for the *Romance of the Rose*. No bedroom walls could hold the whole *text* of RR; possibly *text* means pictures telling the story and *glose* explanatory inscriptions.

345–7. 'It seemed to me I heard a hunter blow to test his horn and to find out whether it was clear or hoarse in its sound'.

348–53. Ch organizes material here so that what the dreamer hears (at first confused bustle, then gradually clearer information) precedes his active entry into the scene (see Phillips 1981).

353–4. *embosed*: 'fled into the wood': deer hide as deep as possible in woodland during the day; *so moche* stands for a vague recall of an overheard estimate of the animal's position.

355. *huntynge*: a noun, not the present participle: 'on the hunt'. It was the huntsmen's task to locate a suitable animal first thing in the morning before the nobles began hunting (Rooney 1993: 50).

Tooke my hors and forthe I went.
    Out of my chambre, I never stent
    Til I come to the felde withoute.   *open country outside*
360   Ther overtoke Y a grete route   *crowd*
    Of huntes and eke of foresterys,   *huntsmen; foresters*
    With ma[n]y relayes and lymerys,
    And hyed hem to the forest faste,   *they hurried*
    And [I] with hem. So at the laste   *them*
365   I asked oon, ladde a lymere,
    'Say, felowe, whoo shal hunte here?'
    Quod I, and he answered ageyn,   *replied back to me*
    'Syr, th'emperour Octovyen,'

357–8. Kittredge 1915b: 68–9 thought Ch said the dreamer rode out of his bedroom and intended a dream-like absurdity. This explanation is unnecessary: l. 358 surely begins a new sentence – outside the house. 'Once having left my bedroom I never stopped.'

361. *huntes, foresterys*: the foresters' main job was protecting their lord's game preserves; they often joined the huntsmen to assist with the hunt.

362. 'With many packs of hounds and stalking dogs'. Lymers were dogs trained to be on a lead and track game by smell, stalking them silently and, when the hunt began, starting them from their day-time hiding-places. *Tretyse of Huntynge* (Rooney 1987: 50–2) describes hunting with a lymer.

365. 'I asked one, who led a lymer'.

366. '"Tell me, friend, who is due to hunt here?"' Terms of address like *felowe* here (originally 'companion'), indicating the relative status of speaker and addressee, are almost unknown in Pres. Eng. Rooney 1987: 87–8 shows the French equivalent, 'amy', used in hunting calls. ME *schal* often = 'must' or 'is to be'.

368. *emperour Octovyen*: a puzzling reference. Is it a flatteringly imperial symbol of Edward III or John of Gaunt (who claimed the throne of Castile after 1371)? Is it the hero of medieval Octavian romances, whose story has nothing in common with this poem, or – more probably – the Emperor Augustus, also called Octavian (27 BC – AD 14), nephew of Julius Caesar, famed in medieval literature for wealth (to which Machaut refers, *Behaigne*, l. 421) and for a revelation by the Sibyl of Christ's birth? Vincent of Beauvais praises Octavian extravagantly in *Speculum Historiale* VI, 43–8, and the 14th-century Holy Roman Emperors used the figure of Octavian/ Augustus in their art and propaganda. See p. 43 on Octavian in English royal tapestry, also Phillips 1981 and Scott-McNab 1988. Are the knight, the king (l. 1314) and Octavian one fictional person or several, or multiple

	Quod he, 'and ys here fast by.'	*he is close by here*
370	'A Goddys halfe, in goode tyme!' quod I,	
	'Go we faste!' and gan to ryde.	*let's go fast*
	Whan we came to the forest syde,	
	Every man didde ryght anoon	*absolutely promptly*
	As to huntynge fille to doon.	
375	The mayster hunte anoon fote-hote	*coming up hot-foot*
	With a grete horne blewe thre mote.	
	At the uncoupylynge of hys houndys.	
	Withynne a while the herte founde ys,	
	Ihalowed and rechased faste	
380	Longe tyme. And so, at the laste,	*for a long time*
	This hert rused and staale away	
	Fro alle the houndes a prevy way.	*secret*
	The houndes had overshette hym alle	
	And were upon a defaulte yfalle.	
385	Therwyth the hunte, wonder faste,	*hunter, amazingly*

representations of one real-life royal mourner?

370. The dreamer's eagerness to join Octavian's hunt, like his approbation of the knight's affability later, can be seen as a slightly deferential consciousness running through *BD* at times (see Strohm 1989: 50–5). It is also one of the devices for creating a forward impetus, even though the direction the poem is going to take remains unclear to the reader.

374. 'Everything that was necessary to be done for a hunt.'

375–6. *Mayster hunte*: the chief huntsman after Octavian (see Scott-McNab 1988: 185–6); *mote*: notes on the horn or bugle. Sk.'s n. cites Twiti, *Art de venerie* (c. 1320): three motes call together the unleashed hounds; they also 'warne the gentelys that the herte is sene', l. 46. On calls and shouts, see Rooney 1987: 86–8.

377. The hounds have been on leashes in pairs and now they are unleashed for the hunt.

379. *Ihalowed*: 'chased with shouts' (of 'halloo', which originally urged on the hounds to chase the quarry); *rechased*: 'chased back', 'headed back'.

381–2. *rused*: 'doubled back', 'eluded'; *staale away, prevy way*: potentially there is a metaphor here of the hart/sweetheart slipping, through death, out of the possession of the lover (ME *herte* often = 'sweetheart'), and also of the melancholy individual becoming separate from the social group, as in *Three Dead Kings* (Turville-Petre 1989: 148–57).

384. *a defaulte*: 'a failure'; the hounds are in error (Scott-McNab 1988: 191–2).

385. 'At that the hunter with amazing force'.

	Blewe a forleygne at the laste.	*as the conclusion*
	I was go walked fro my tree,	*gone walking away from*
	And as I went ther came by mee	*close to me*
	A whelpe, that fauned me as I stoode,	*puppy*
390	That hadde yfolowed and koude no goode.	
	Hyt come, and crepte to me as lowe	*crouched*
	Ryght as hyt had me yknowe,	*just as if; known*
	Hylde doun hys hede and joyned hys erys,	*its head; its ears*
	And leyde al smothe doun hys herys.	*down its hairs*
395	I wolde have kaught hyt, and anoon	*wanted to have*
	Hyt fled and was fro me goon.	
	And I hym folwed, and hyt forthe went,	*went ahead*
	Doune by a floury grene went,	*path*
	Ful thikke of gras, ful softe and swete,	
400	With flourys fele, faire under fete;	*many flowers*
	And litel used, hyt semed thus.	

386. *forleygne*: a horn call signalling recall, to bring back hunter or hounds who have run on and become separated from the rest of the hunt (Scott-McNab 1988: 192–5). The theme of separation again.

387. *was go walked*: 'had gone on, walking'. *my tree*: the dreamer seems to have taken up his position to assist the hunt (a 'tryst') at a tree.

388–401. A little unused path like this often leads dream poem narrators to a secluded place where they learn something, or meet their lady or a lover: cf. *RR*, ll. 714–20, *Behaigne*, ll. 43–53, etc. (see Wimsatt 1968: 20–1).

389. Is there a Pres. Eng. word for *fauned*, the actions pet animals go through when they want to be stroked? Cf. Machaut, *Behaigne*, ll. 25–44, where the dreamer follows a bird and comes upon sorrowing lovers; closer is the friendly lion, like 'a little dog', in his *Dit dou Lyon*, ll. 288–432 (in *Oeuvres*, ed. Hoepffner 1908–21: II, 159–237), who lets itself be stroked and 'joined its ears' with pleasure at it. The lion leads the narrator to a pavilion where he sees his lady.

390. 'Which had followed and had no idea what to do'. A parallel to the narrator, and also to the reader, ignorant and uninformed about the import of the scenes and images.

395. 'I wanted to have caught it, and straightway'.

395–7. Again the motif of forward movement without clear purpose or enlightenment.

For both Flora and Zephirus,
They two that make floures growe,
Had made her dwellynge ther, I trowe.   *their; believe*
405   For hit was on to beholde   *to look at*
As thogh th'erthe envye wolde   *wanted to compete*
To be gayer than the heven,   *lovelier*
To have moo floures swche seven,
As in the walkene sterris bee.
410   Hyt had forgete the povertee
That wynter thorgh hys colde morwes   *its cold mornings*
Had made hyt suffre, and his sorwes.
All was forgeten. And that was sene,   *clear to see*
For al the woode was waxen grene;   *grown*
415   Swetnesse of dewe had made hyt waxe.
Hyt ys no nede eke for to axe   *also to ask*
Where there were many grene greves   *whether; groves*
[Of] thikke trees, so ful of leves.
And every tree stoode by hymselve   *itself*
420   Fro other wel tene fete [or] twelve.   *from the next*
So grete trees, so huge of strengthe,
[Of] fourty, fifty, fedme lengthe,   *fathoms' height*
Clene withoute bowgh or stikke,   *sheer*
With croppes [brode] and eke as thikke.   *tops; just as thick*
425   They were nat an ynche asonder,   *inch apart*
That hit was shadewe overal under.   *so that; everywhere*
And many an herte and many an hynde,   *hart; hind*
Was both before me and behynde,   *in front of me*

402–9. *Flora*: the classical goddess of flowers; *Zephirus*: the west wind of Spring;
in myth he married Chloris ('green') who then became Flora ('flowery') and
brought forth spring flowers (Ovid, *Fasti* V). On the paradisal landscape,
see p. 39. *RR*, ll. 8373–403 describes an eternal spring, with Flora and
Zephirus, in an Ovidian Golden Age of innocence, when lovers were faithful
and chaste and the earth was without war or labour.

408–9. 'To have more flowers, seven times over, than there are stars in the sky'.

410–15. Spring's forgetting of Winter's poverty echoes *RR*, ll. 53–8. The theme of
recuperation.

411, 412. ME *hys* = 'its' as well as 'his'.

415. *dewe*: popularly believed to aid fertility; see Woolf 1968: 286–7.

417–26. The regularity and abundance of the forest, in a pre-Romantic culture,
symbolize perfection; the almost symmetrical trees echo *RR*, ll. 1363–84.

	Of founes, sowres, bukkes, does,	
430	Was ful the woode, and many roes.	
	And many sqwirels that sete	*who sat*
	Ful high upon the trees and ete,	*ate*
	And in hir maner made festys.	*in their fashion*
	Shortly, hyt was so ful of bestys	*to sum up; animals*
435	That thogh Argus, the noble counter,	*mathematician*
	Sete to rekene in hys counter,	*abacus (?)*
	And rekene with his figuris ten	*add up*
	(For by tho figuris mowe al ken,	
	Yf they be crafty, rekene and noumbre,	*add up and enumerate*
440	And tel of everythinge the noumbre)	*count up to*
	Yet shulde he fayle to rekene evene	
	The wondres me mette in my swevene.	*I dreamed; dream*
	But forth they romed, ryght wonder faste	
	Doune the woode, so at the laste	*at last*
445	I was war of a man in blak,	*became aware*
	That sete and had [y]turned his bak	*turned*
	To an ooke, an huge tree.	
	'Lorde,' thogh[t] I, 'Who may that be?	*Who can*

429. These are all fallow deer: *fawns*: up to one year; *sowres*: four-year-olds; *bukkes*: adult males; *does*: adult females.

430. *roes*: female roe-deer.

435. *Argus*: Mohammed ibn Músá, surnamed Al-Khowárizmí, a 9th-century Arab mathematician whose book on algebra (Latin name *Liber algorismus*) introduced Arabic numerals and decimals to Europe. The French form of his surname, *Algus*, appears as Argus in *RR*, l. 12760, perhaps confused with Argus, the hundred-eyed watchman of Greek mythology.

436. *counter*: usually a room where accounts are done, but perhaps it means an abacus here.

437–40. *figuris ten*: the Arabic numerals; l. 439 perhaps refers to the fact that they provide a clearer system of easily distinguished digits for each number than the Roman system. The point Ch is making is that Arabic numbers can present extremely large numbers, whereas the Greek and Roman systems could not do this.

438. *mowe*: 'may'; *ken*: (Sk.'s n.) perhaps a Kentish dialect form of *kin*, in the sense 'mankind'.

441. 'Even then he would be bound to fail to count precisely'.

443. *they* refers to the many deer. 'But they roamed on ahead, quite amazingly quickly'.

	What ayleth hym, to sitten here?'	
450	Anoonryght I went nere.	*immediately*; *nearer*
	Than founde I sitte even upryght	*sitting straight upright*
	A wonder wel-farynge knyght,	
	By the maner me thoght soo:	
	Of good mochel and ryght yonge therto,	*good build*; *also*
455	Of the age of foure and twenty yere,	*twenty-four*
	Upon hys berde but lytel here.	*hair*
	And he was clothed al in blake.	
	I stalked even unto hys bake,	*right up to*
	And ther I stoode, as stille as ought,	*still as anything*
460	That, soth to saye, he sawe me nought;	*saw me not at all*
	Forwhy he henge hys hede adoune,	*down*
	And with a dedely sorwful soune	
	He made of ryme X vers or twelfe	*composed*; *ten lines*
	Of a compleynt, to hymselfe:	*lament*
465	The moste pitee, the moste rowthe	*pitiful*; *affecting*
	That ever I herde. For, by my trowthe,	
	Hit was gret wonder that Nature	
	Myght suffre any creature	*could permit*; *being*
	To have suche sorwe and be not ded.	
470	Ful petuose pale and nothynge red,	
	He sayed a lay, a maner songe,	*poem*; *sort of*
	Withoute noote, withoute songe,	*music*
	And was thys, for ful wel I kan	
	Reherse hyt: ryght thus hyt began:	*repeat*
475	'I have of sorwe so grete wone	
	That joy gete I never none,	

452. *wel-farynge*: 'handsome', with the senses also of 'robust' and 'flourishing'.

455–6. This reference to the knight's age is a mystery. John of Gaunt was 28 when Blanche died and would be older whenever the poem was written (Ch had been between 23 and 28, Blanche herself between 21 and 28). Possibly another numeral got changed to xxiv in scribal transmission. The sparse hair on the chin is probably a general sign of youth – it is used loosely for a man in his twenties, or a youthful fashion for little or no beard. See David 1993: 8 on the knight as a figure representing both youth and sorrow.

464. *compleynte*: 'lament'. On the lyrics, see Hardman 1993, Butterfield 1991.

470. 'Quite pitifully pale and not red at all.'

475. *wone*: lit. 'habitation', can also mean 'habit': 'I have such a vast habitation of sorrow'.

Now that I see my lady bryght,
Which I have loved with al my myght,
Is fro me ded and ys agoon,
480 [And thus in sorowe lefte me alone.]
Allas, Dethe, what ayleth the,
That thou noldest have taken me,
Whan thou toke my lady swete
That was so faire, so fresh, so fre,
485 So goode that men may wel se
Of al goodenesse she had no mete.'   *equal*
      Whan he had made thus his complaynt,   *lament*
Hys sorwful hert gan faste faynt,   *rapidly to fail*
And his spiritis wexen dede.   *grew dead*
490 The bloode was fled, for pure drede,   *fear*
Doune to hys hert to make hym warme –
For wel hyt feled the hert had harme –   *had sustained injury*
To wete eke why hyt was adrad,   *to know also*
By Kynde, and for to make hyt glad.   *in order to*
495 For hit ys membre principal   *principal organ*
Of the body. And that made al
Hys hewe chaunge and wexe grene   *complexion; go pale*
And pale, for ther noo bloode ys sene   *seen*
In no maner [l]ym of hys.   *no part whatsoever*
500   Anoon therwith, whan Y sawgh this,   *immediately at that*
He ferde thus evel, there he sete,
I went and stoode ryght at his fete
And grette hym. But he spake noght,   *greeted; not at all*
But argued with his oune thoght,   *debated*
505 And in hys wytte disputed faste,   *mind; urgently*
Why and how hys lyfe myght laste;   *could continue*
Hym thought hys sorwes were so smerte   *agonizing*

---

480. This line is found only in Th. It is possibly spurious.
481–2. 'Alas, Death, what ails you [thee], that you did not want to take me too?'.
484. 'Who was so beautiful, lively and gracious'.
489. *spiritis* were believed to be highly refined vapours, created by the blood in
the liver, carrying life and vigour through the body's organs.
494. Nature sends blood to the heart to restore warmth and cheerfulness and find
out what is wrong with it. Note Nature's urge to heal and concern to fight
death and misery; cf. ll. 16–21.
501. 'That he was in such a bad state, as he sat there'.

	And lay so colde upon hys herte.	
	So throgh hys sorwe and hevy thoght	*depressed*
510	Made hym that he herde me noght,	*not at all*
	For he had wel nygh loste hys mynde,	*almost*
	Thogh Pan, that men clepe God of Kynde,	*call*
	Were for hys sorwes never so wrothe.	*might be; angry*
	But at the last, to sayn ryght sothe,	*to say*
515	He was war of me, how Y stoode	*aware*
	Before hym, and did of myn hoode,	*took off*
	And had ygret hym, as I best koude,	*greeted*
	Debonayrly and nothyng lowde.	*courteously; not at all*
	He sayde 'I prey the, be not wrothe:	*angry*
520	I herde the not, to seyn the sothe.	*heard thee; truth*
	Ne I sawgh the not, syr, trewly.'	*did not see you*
	'A, good sir, no fors,' quod Y,	*it is unimportant*
	'I am ryght sory yif I have oughte	*at all*
	Destroubled yow out of your thoughte.	*disturbed*
525	Foryive me yif I have mystake.'	*done wrong*
	'Yis. Th'amendys is lyght to make,'	
	Quod he, 'For ther lyeth noon therto:	
	There ys nothynge myssayde nor do.'	*said or done amiss*
	Loo, how goodely spake thys knyghte,	*lo; well*
530	As hit had be another wyghte!	
	He made hyt nouther towgh ne queynte.	
	And I sawe that, and gan m'aqueynte	*to get to know*

512–13. Again Nature opposes life-threatening misery. *Pan*: originally an Arcadian god of shepherds; since *pan* (Greek) = 'all', in late classical times he became a universal god (see Isidore of Seville, *Etymologies* IX; *Met.* I, ll. 699, 705, etc.).

517. 'And had addressed him as well as I knew how'.

519. Difference in status is indicated by the knight's second-person singular pronouns (*thow, the(e)*, etc.), used to close friends or social inferiors, and the dreamer's use of the formal and respectful second-person plural pronouns (*ye, you*, etc.). See David 1976: 10; Strohm 1989: 52.

526–7. 'The recompense is easily made: for none is required'.

530. 'As if it were a different person' (than the one previously overcome with grief). Note the dreamer's deferential admiration.

531. 'He did not make it either difficult or complicated'.

	With hym, and fonde hym so tretable,	
	Ryght wonder skylful and resonable,	*discerning*
535	As me thoght, for al hys bale,	*suffering*
	Anoonryght I gan fynde a tale	
	To hym, to loke wher I myght oughte	*whether; at all*
	Have more knowynge of hys thoughte.	
	'Sir,' quod I, 'this game is doon.	*sport; finished*
540	I holde that this hert be goon.	*consider; is gone*
	These huntes konne hym nowher see.'	*hunters*
	'Y do no fors therof,' quod he,	*take no interest*
	'My thought ys theron never a dele.'	*not a bit*
	'Be oure Lorde,' quod I, 'Y trow yow wele:	
545	Ryght so me thenketh by youre chere.	*your face*
	But sir, oo thyng – wol ye here?	
	Me thynketh in grete sorowe I yow see.	
	But certys sir, yif that yee	*certainly; if you*
	Wolde ought discure me youre woo	*at all reveal*
550	I wolde, as wys, God helpe me soo,	
	Amende hyt yif I kan or may.	
	Ye mowe preve hyt be assay,	
	For, by my trouthe, to make yow hool	*well*
	I wol do alle my power hool.	*devote; entire ability*
555	And telleth me of your sorwes smerte;	*tell me; painful*
	Paraventure hyt may ease your herte,	*perhaps; can*
	That semeth ful seke under your syde.'	*very sick*
	With that he loked on me asyde	*sideways*
	As who sayth 'Nay, that wol not be'.	*like one who*
560	'Graunt mercy, goode frende,' quod he,	*many thanks*

533. *tretable*: 'responsive', 'reasonable'. On *cortois* manners and speech, see
   Burnley 1986b, Redwine 1988, Saul 1992.

536. 'Straightaway I tried to find a way of talking'.

544. '"By our Lord," I said, "I completely believe you."'

546. 'But sir, one thing – would you be willing to listen to me?'

548–57. In Ovid's *Tristia* V, ll. 59–60, Alcyone found comfort by lamenting her
   misfortunes.

550–2. 'I would like, certainly, if God may be my helper, to amend if I know how
   to and am able. You can prove it by experience'.

553–4. *hool ... hool*: 'rime riche', rhymes between identical-sounding words with
   different meanings or grammatical functions, was considered an ornament
   in medieval poetry.

'I thanke the that thow woldest soo,	*desire that*
But hyt may never the rather be doo.	
No man may my sorwe glade,	*make glad*
That maketh my hewe to fal and fade	*colour; diminish*
565 And hath myn understondynge lorne,	*lost*
That me ys woo that I was borne.	*I am miserable*
May noght make my sorwes slyde,	*nothing can; go away*
Nought al the remedyes of Ovyde.	
Ne Orpheus, god of melodye,	
570 Ne Dedalus with his playes slye;	*subtle devices*
Ne hele me may noo phisicien,	
Noght Ypocras ne Galyen.	
Me ys woo that I lyve oures twelve.	*hours*
But whooso wol assay hymselve	*test for himself*

562. 'But it cannot be done, even so'.

568. Ovid's *Remedia Amoris* ('Remedies for Love') contains, in mock-serious vein, instructions for curing oneself of the pains of love.

569. *Orpheus*: the legendary musician whose music had such power that it could charm trees and animals and won his dead wife back from Hades (*Met.* X–XI). Sk.'s n. cites *Met.* X, ll. 40–4: Orpheus's harp halted briefly the tortures of the damned, including Sisyphus, Ixion, Tantalus and Tityrus. *Gregory's Garden* (see p. 8) mentions Orpheus and Tubal as inventors of music. Ch is probably also implicitly recalling *Cons.* III, met. 12, about how the enlightened soul can rise above sorrow and earthly ties, but Orpheus and souls clinging to worldly desires cannot ascend from Hades. These Hades references, as symbols of the mind obsessed with emotion, which cannot ascend, recur in *TC*, ll. 463–76.

570. *Dedalus*: the theme of ascending above earthly concerns again; Daedalus used magic machinery to fly out of prison in Crete, *Met.* VIII, ll. 183–263.

571–2. In *RR*, ll. 15927–30, Nature says Death catches its victims despite physicians, naming among the great doctors Hippocrates (*Ypocras*, c. 460–c. 377 BC) and Galen (AD 129–c. 200), the most famous doctors of antiquity and the founders of European medicine. The theme of healing again; cf. ll. 1–24, 553–7.

574–6. These lines are slightly reminiscent of the medieval 'reproaches' of Christ from the cross, a set of statements, drawn from the OT, asking humanity to *see* his suffering and feel pity, including 'O you all who pass by ... observe and see if there is any sorrow like mine' (Lam. 1:12), which is used in Good Friday liturgy and echoed widely in literature, including texts where Christ is presented symbolically as a lover-knight (Woolf 1968: 32–47; Gray 1972:

575	Whether his hert kan have pitee	
	Of any sorwe lat hym see me:	
	Y, wrechch that deth hath made al naked	*stripped bare*
	Of al [the] blysse that ever was maked,	
	Yworthe worste of al wyghtys,	*become*
580	That hate my dayes and my nyghtys.	
	My lyfe, my lustes, be me loothe,	*pleasures; hateful*
	For al welfare and I be wroothe;	*contentment; are in conflict*
	The pure deth ys so ful my foo	
	That I wolde deye: hyt wol not soo.	
585	For whan I folwe hyt hit wol flee;	*wants to flee*
	I wolde have hym, hyt nyl nat me.	*does not want*
	This ys my peyne, wythoute rede,	*without solution*
	Alway deynge and be not dede;	*dying; not to be*
	That Thesiphus that lyeth in helle	
590	May not of more sorwe telle.	
	And whoso wiste alle, be my trouthe,	*whoever knew; by*
	My sorwe, but he had rowthe	*unless; compassion*
	And pitee of my sorwes smerte,	*painful*
	That man hath a fendely herte	*fiendlike*
595	For whoso seeth me firste on morwe	
	May seyn he hath mette with sorwe:	
	For Y am sorwe and sorwe ys Y.	
	Allas, and I wol tel the why:	
	My so[ng] ys turned to pleynynge,	*lamenting*
600	And al my lawghtre to wepynge,	
	My glade thoghtys to hevynesse;	*misery*
	In travayle ys myn ydelnesse	

140–45). Cf. *Songe vert*, ll. 195–9: 'There is no man so cruel that he would not feel any pity if he saw the very deep sorrow I suffer night and day.'

583–4. 'Death itself is so completely my enemy that I want to die: it refuses it'. Cf. *Songe vert*, ll. 176–7, '[Death] was unwilling to come near me, nor would it allow me to come to him'.

589. *Thesiphus*: variant forms in the MSS and Th suggest that Ch or a scribe confused the names Tityus and Sisyphus. Tityus was punished in Hades by being stretched out while vultures gnawed his liver, Sisyphus by eternally pushing a marble block uphill, only to see it roll back (*Met*. IV, ll. 457–60).

599–617. This resembles a similar list of joys turned to sorrows, by a bereaved lady, overheard by the narrator, in Machaut, *Behaigne*, ll. 177–87.

602. 'My leisure is turned into dismal labour'.

	And eke my reste; my wele ys woo,	*well-being*
	My goode ys harme, and evermoo	*evermore*
605	In wrathe ys turned my pleynge	*into anger; cheerfulness*
	And my delyte into sorwynge.	
	Myn hele ys turned into sekenesse,	*health*
	In drede ys al my sykernesse,	*into fear; security*
	To derke ys turned al my lyghte.	
610	My wytte ys foly, my day ys nyghte,	*intelligence*
	My love ys hate, my slepe wakynge,	*insomnia*
	My merthe and meles ys fastynge,	*sociability*
	My countenaunce ys nycete	
	And al abawed, whereso I be.	*quite disconcerted*
615	My pees in pledynge and in werre:	
	Allas, how myght I fare werre?	*be worse*
	My boldenesse ys turned to shame.	
	For fals Fortune hath pleyde a game	
	Atte the chesse with me, allas the while!	*alas the time*
620	The trayteresse fals and ful of gyle,	
	That al behoteth and nothyng halte;	*promises; holds to*

613. 'My self-command is silliness'.
615. 'My peace has declined into arguments and conflicts'.
617. 'My confidence is turned to embarrassment'. ME does not always distinguish the purely psychological experiences of feeling confident, embarrassed or shy from the moral attributes of boldness or shame.
618–739. *Fortune* (see pp. 36–7) was a popular late classical deity who became in medieval literature a personification of mutability, a power operating in the sublunary world and subject to God. Many elements in this passage, like Fortune's wheel, her treachery and her double appearance, are motifs whose main source is *Cons.*; they are found widely in Ch and other medieval literature, e.g. *Fortune, TC* I, ll. 835–53. For the paradoxes of Fortune's traditional character, see Patch 1927: 55–7; Kittredge 1915a: 10–14. Ch's closest sources are: Machaut, *Remède de Fortune*, ll. 921–3, 1138–91 (in *Oeuvres*, ed. Hoepffner 1908–21: II, 1–157); *RR* for games allegories (ll. 6527–30, 6619–6726), filth strewn over with flowers (ll. 8878–83), cheating (ll. 6825–32) and stabbing in the back while flattering at the front (ll. 6713–16). Traditional epithets for Fortune often parallel misogynist attacks on women.
619. *allas the while*: an idiom lamenting the time when a sad event happened.

	She gethe upryght and yet she halte,	*upright; hobbles*
	That baggeth foule and loketh faire,	
	The dispitouse debonaire	
625	That skorneth many a creature.	*who scorns*
	An ydole of fals portrayture	
	Ys she, for she wol sone wrien.	*turn away*
	She is the mo[n]stres hed ywrien,	*covered over*
	As fylthe over-ystrawed with flouris.	*like; strewn over*
630	Hir moste worshippe and hir flour ys	*honour; triumph*
	To lyen, for that ys hyr nature:	*lie*
	Withoute feythe, lawe or mesure.	*fidelity; moderation*
	She ys fals and ever lawghynge	*always*
	With one yghe and that other wepynge.	*the other*
635	That ys broght up she sette al doun.	*down*
	I lykne hyr to the scorpioun	*compare*
	That ys a fals flaterynge beste:	*animal*
	For with his hede he maketh feste,	*is gracious*
	But al amydde hys flaterynge	*its*
640	With hys tayle hyt wol stynge	*its*
	And envenyme. And so wol she.	*poison*

622. Cf. Machaut, *Remède de Fortune*, l. 1167: 'One foot going straight, the other crooked'.

623–4. 'She squints horribly and looks nice, the contemptuous gracious one'.

626. 'A misleadingly depicted idol'. Wimsatt 1968: 159 compares Machaut motet 8.7–9, 'Une ydole ... de fausse pourtraiture'.

628–33. Fortune is a 'monster enveloped in happiness, full of misery'; cf. Machaut's *balade* 188.13–14, echoing *Cons.* 2, pr. 1, ll. 6–8. Imagery of harlotry and face-painting is common in Fortune literature. There is an underlying 'whited sepulchre' metaphor here (Matt. 23: 27). See also *RR*, ll. 8877–8912, and Wimsatt 1979: 119–31.

633–4. '[Fortune] laughs with one eye, cries with the other', Machaut, *Remède de Fortune*, l. 1162.

635. 'Whatever is carried up she sets down'. Artists often depicted Fortune's wheel with four figures around its circumference: carrying one person up, bringing another to the highest point, where they sit enthroned, and also – by the same process – bringing a third figure down, and finally dropping at the bottom a fourth figure, tumbling to misery, loss of power or prosperity, and the grave.

636–41. See Rev. 9:10 for scorpions' 'stings in their tails', also Machaut, Latin motet IX, ll. 45–8.

	She ys th'envyouse charite	*jealous benevolence*
	That ys ay fals and semeth wele:	*always; good*
	So turneth she hyr fals whele	
645	Aboute. For hyt ys nothynge stable.	*not at all*
	Now by the fire, now at table,	
	F[ul] many oon hath she thus yblent.	*many a one; blinded*
	She ys pley of enchauntement,	*trick*
	That semeth oon and ys not soo.	*one thing*
650	The fals thefe! What hath she doo,	*done*
	Trowest thou? By oure Lorde, I wol the sey:	*do you think*
	At the chesse with me she gan to pley,	
	With hir fals draughtes dyvers;	*various moves*
	She staale on me and toke my fers.	*queen*
655	And whan I sawgh my fers away,	*lost*
	Allas, I kouthe no lenger play,	*I could*
	But seyde, "Farewel, swete, ywys,	*darling; indeed*
	And farewel al that ever ther ys."	
	Therwith Fortune seyde "Chek here!"	*Check here*
660	And "Mate!" in the myd poynt of the chekkere,	*chessboard*

642. '[Fortune] is the envious charity', Machaut, *Remède de Fortune*, l. 1138.

646–8. *pley of enchauntement*: a phrase from Machaut, *Behaigne*, ll. 1072–8, like the reference to fire and table (fickleness flits 'now here, now there, at fire or table') which Ch transforms to describe Fortune's victims, deceived as they sit at fire and table: the traditional scene for feasting in Winter Labours of the Month. The motif of Death removing men from their feasting recurs in the *Ubi Sunt* tradition: cf. 'Where beth they biforen, us weren', Davies 1963: 57, 7–12, also Tristram 1976: 112–21.

649. To 'seem one' is to appear to be sincere, without duplicity.

651–745. See Connolly 1994. On other chess allegories, see Murray 1913: 396–402, 421–8, 515–35, 559–61. On the medieval game and the allegedly unimportant role of the *fers* or 'queen' before the 15th century, see Cooley 1948, French 1949, Connolly 1994. *Athalus* III (l. 663), Philometer, King of Pergamos (mentioned in *RR*, ll. 6661–3), is one of the reputed inventors of chess.

659. 'She enjoys the games so much, she says as she vanquishes one "Check and mate!"', Machaut, *Remède de Fortune*, ll. 1190–1.

660–1. Cf. *RR*, ll. 6622–5 for the image of death as check with a *pawn errant*, a 'mating pawn'. Fortune was sometimes depicted as half white, half black (Patch 1927: 43). 'Check mate' comes from the Arabic *Shah ma'at*, 'The king is dead', and ME *mat(e)* often means 'bereft of liveliness'.

With a poune errante, allas!
Ful craftier to pley she was
Than Athalus, that made the game   *invented*
First of the chesse – so was hys name.
665 But God wolde I had oones or twyes   *would to God*
    Ykoude and knowe the jeupardyes   *mastered; known*
    That kowde the Greke Pictagoras!   *knew*
    I shulde have pleyde the bet at ches   *all the better*
    And kept my fers the bet therby.   *better because of it*
670 And thogh wherto? For trewly   *to what end*
    I holde that wysshe nat worthe a stree: *consider; straw*
    Hyt had be never the bet for me,   *would have been*
    For Fortune kan so many a wyle   *knows*
    Ther be but fewe kan hir begile.   *know how to*
675 And eke she ys the lasse to blame: *the less*
    Myselfe I wolde have do the same,   *done*
    Before God, [had] I be as she;   *in her position*
    She oght the more excused be.   *the more readily*
    For this I say yet more therto: *on that subject*
680 Had I be God, and myghte have do   *have executed*
    My wille whan she my fers kaught,   *my will; captured*
    I wolde have drawe the same draught,   *taken; piece*
    For, also wys God yive me reste,
    I dar wel swere [s]he tooke the beste.   *affirm confidently*
685 But throgh that draught I have lorne   *move; lost*
    My blysse – allas, that I was borne –
    For evermore, Y trowe trewly.   *believe*
    For al my wille, my luste holly
    Ys turned. But yet what to doone?
690 Be oure Lorde, hyt ys to deye soone.   *by; straightaway*
    For nothynge I leve hyt noght,   *I trust in nothing*
    But lyve and deye ryght in this thoght.   *as I think this*
    For there nys planete in firmament,   *is no*
    Ne in ayre ne in erthe noon element,   *nor no element*

666–7. *jeupardye* (Fr. *jeu parti*) = an equally balanced contest, a dilemma or
    danger, and (as here) a chess problem; see French 1949. It is unclear why the
    Greek mathematician Pythagoras (*Pictagoras*) should be linked to chess
    problems (usually attrib. to Xerxes and Philometer, see Murray 1913: 751).
688–9. 'Against all my desire, my happiness has been reversed. But what can I do
    now?'

82   The *Book of the Duchess*

695	That they ne yive me a yifte echon	*gift each one*
	Of wepynge, whan I am allon.	
	For whan that I avise me wel	*think it over*
	And bethenke me everydel	*consider all of it*
	How that ther lyeth in rekenynge	
700	Inne my sorwe for nothynge,	
	And how ther levyth noo gladnesse	*lives*
	May glad me of my distresse,	*cheer me out of*
	And how I have loste suffisance,	*contentment*
	And therto I have no plesance,	*in addition*
705	Than may I say I have ryght noght.	*then can; absolutely nothing*
	And whan al this falleth in my thoght,	*comes into*
	Allas, than am I overcome.	*then*
	For that ys doon ys not to come.	*what; will not return*
	I have more sorowe than Tantale.'	
710	And whan I herde hym tel thys tale,	*say this*
	Th[u]s pitously, as I yow telle,	
	Unnethe myght Y lenger duelle:	*scarcely; wait*
	Hyt dyd myn hert so moche woo.	
	'A, goode sir,' quod I, 'Say not soo.	
715	Have some pitee on your nature	
	That formed yow to creature.	*as a creature*
	Remembre yow of Socrates,	*remember about*
	For he ne counted nat thre strees	*reckoned; straws*
	Of noght that Fortune koude doo.'	*for anything*
720	'No,' quod he, 'I kan not soo.'	

699–700. 'How, as regards sorrow, there is nothing left still on account', i.e. still to be paid as sorrow's due.

709. *Tantale*: Tantalus, tormented in Hades by unquenchable thirst, was surrounded by water which receded when he tried to drink (*Met.* IV, l. 458, X, l. 41; *Cons.* III, met. 12; *RR*, l. 19250).

715–25. A compact sequence of arguments against suicide: the knight should remember his created human nature which (because it was created by God with a soul and destiny in the next world) makes suicide and despair sins. *Nature* here means both his creation as a human and Nature as an instrument of God.

717–18. *Socrates*: a Greek philosopher, often praised in medieval literature for his indifference to Death and Fortune; in *RR*, ll. 5815–5820 Reason bids the dreamer not to 'give a plum' for Fortune's wheel, like Socrates, who was quite unmoved by joy and sorrow alike.

	'Why so, good syr? Yis parde,' quod Y,	*yes, indeed*
	'Ne [say] noght soo, for trewly	*do not say so*
	Thogh ye had loste the ferses twelve,	*even though*
	And ye for sorwe mordred yourselve,	*if*
725	Ye sholde be dampned in this cas –	*in such a situation*
	By as goode ryght as Medea was,	*with as correct justice*
	That slowgh hir children for Jasoun.	*who slew*
	And Phillis also, for Demophoun,	*because of Demophon*
	Henge hirselfe so, weylaway,	*alas*
730	For he had broke his terme day	*agreed return day*
	To come to hir. Another rage	*madness*
	Had Dydo, the quene eke of Cartage,	*also*
	That slough hirselfe for Eneas	*because*
	Was fals: which a foole she was!	*what*
735	And Ecquo died for Narcisus	*because*
	Nolde nat love hir, and ryght thus	*refused to love*
	Hath many another foly doon.	*committed folly*
	And for Dalida died Sampsoun,	
	That slough hymselfe with a piler.	*slew*
740	But ther is no man alyve hére	
	Wolde for a fers make this woo.'	

723. *ferses twelve*: the exact meaning of this is unclear, though the general import is obvious. Perhaps 'even if you lost twelve ferses', omitting *the* as probably scribal error (Cooley 1948). *Fers* could = 'pawn'; see Murray 1913: 482–90 on the 'Courrier' game, where there are twelve pawns.

725. The Church has always forbidden suicide, e.g. Augustine, *City of God* I, par. 20. *Inf.* XIII puts suicides, those who are violent against themselves, in the seventh circle of Hell.

726–39. Dido, Phyllis and Medea in *RR*, ll. 13144–13234, are examples of women ruined by men, and *LGW* celebrates their fidelity; but here they represent the madness of excessive emotion, leading to the sin of suicide. *Medea*, Queen of Colchis, angry at Jason's desertion, slew their two children; Dido, Queen of Carthage in N. Africa, killed herself when Aeneas left her to pursue his destiny of founding Rome; Phyllis killed herself when Demophon was late returning for their wedding; Echo, enchanted by Juno so that she could only repeat others' words, pined away with unrequited love for Narcissus, until only her voice remained (*Met.* III, ll. 380–99); and the OT hero Samson, betrayed by Delilah into the hands of his enemies, the Philistines, pulled down the pillars of their temple, killing himself and them (Judges 16).

'Why so?' quod he, 'hyt ys nat soo.
Thou woste ful lytel what thou menyst: *know*; *are saying*
I have loste more than thow wenyst.'   *suppose*
745   'Loo, [how] that may be,' quod Y,   *how that can*
'Good sir, telle me al hooly: *completely*
In what wyse, how, why, and wherfore   *and for what reason*
That ye have thus youre blysse lore.'   *lost*
'Blythely,' quod he, 'come sytte adoon;   *gladly*; *down*
750   I telle hyt the up a condicioun   *thee on a condition*
That thou shalt hooly with al thy wytte   *must wholly*; *mind*
Doo thyn entent to herkene hitte.'   *give your attention*
'Yis syr.' 'Swere thy trouthe therto.'   *oath to that*
'Gladly.' 'Do thanne holde here[t]o.'   *hold to that*
755   'I shal ryght blythely, so God me save,   *very gladly*
Hooly with al the witte I have   *completely*; *mind*
Here yow, as wel as I kan.'   *listen to*
'A Goddys halfe!' quod he, and began.   *Amen!*
          'Syr,' quod he, 'sith firste I kouthe   *since*; *knew how*
760   Have any maner wytte, fro youthe,
Or kyndely understondynge,   *natural comprehension*
To comprehende in anythynge   *grasp at all*
What love was, in myn oune wytte,   *understanding*
Dredeles I have ever yitte   *assuredly*; *all this time*
765   Be tributarye and yive rente   *vassal*; *given tribute*
To Love, hooly, with goode entente,
And throgh plesaunce become his thralle   *delight*; *bondsman*
With good wille: body, hert and alle.
Al this I putte in his servage   *service*

745. A list of questions like this was common both as a rhetorical device and as
a scheme for organizing sermons, confessions, and other material. The
commonest list, 'Who, what, where, by what means, why, in what manner,
when?' derives from Cicero's definition of the questions that must be
answered in a plausible narrative (*On Invention* I, 21–8; Cicero, *De
Inventione*, ed. Hubbell 1968). Ll. 746–68 help to focus the reader's
concentration.
760. 'To possess any kind of understanding, from youth on'.
766. 'To Love, completely, with whole-hearted sincerity'. The immediate source
of this metaphor of *homage* to the God of Love is Machaut, *Behaigne*,
ll. 125–32, but imagery of passion as feudal vassalage was ubiquitous,
fuelled particularly by *RR*, ll. 1880–2040.

770	As to my lorde, and did homage.	
	And ful devoutely I prayed hym to	*to him*
	He shulde besette myn hert so	*place; my heart*
	That hyt plesance to hym were,	*would be pleasing*
	And worshippe to my lady dere.	*honour*
775	And this was longe, and many a yere	*long ago*
	Or that myn herte was set owhere,	*before; anywhere*
	That I did thus and nyste why;	*did not know*
	I trowe hit came me kyndely.	*to me naturally*
	Peraventure I was thereto moste able	
780	As a white walle or a table,	*like; tablet*
	For hit ys redy to cachche and take	*take; receive*
	Al that men wil theryn make,	*wish to compose on it*
	Whethirso men wil portrey or peynt,	*whether; want to draw*
	Be the werkes never so queynt.	*designs; complicated*
785	And thilke tyme I ferde ryght so:	*acted like that*
	I was able to have lerned tho,	*capable; then*
	And to have k[o]nde as wel or better,	*studied*
	Paraunter other arte or letre,	*perhaps; study*
	But, for love came firste in my thoght,	*because*
790	Therfore I forgate hyt noght.	
	I ches love to my first crafte,	*as; skill*
	Therfore hit ys with me lafte;	*has remained*
	Forwhy I toke hyt of so yonge age	*because; acquired*
	That malyce hadde my corage	*heart*
795	Nat that tyme turned to nothynge,	*not yet; worthlessness*

779. 'Perhaps I was particularly receptive to it'.

780–96. Themes of whiteness and of the mind and processes of perception and cognition again; cf. ll. 1–15, 28–9. Aristotle's idea of the mind as *tabula rasa* (a tablet cleaned ready for writing) was known to medieval writers; Ch might also have met it in *AA* I, l. 437. He uses here the equivalent medieval image of walls and wooden *tables*, used like modern canvases, whitewashed for painting or drawing to be put on them (Wood 1965: 395). He is elaborating, so that it becomes an image of the mind and its impressions, the metaphor of the white table in *Remède de Fortune*, ll. 23–30, where it refers to the state of moral innocence in young people. Ch moves on to that idea, with overtones of original sin, in ll. 794–6, where understanding (*knowlachynge*, suggesting the Tree of Knowledge) becomes provocatively the operation of evil (*malyce*) potentially threatening the permanence of emotional impressions.

	Thorgh to mochel knowlachynge.	*too much knowledge*
	For that tyme Yowthe, my maistresse,	*governess*
	Governed me in ydelnesse.	
	For hyt was in my first youthe	*earliest*
800	And thoo ful lytel goode Y couthe,	
	For al my werkes were flyttynge	*activities; ephemeral*
	That tyme, and al my thoght varyinge;	*changeable*
	Al were to me ylyche goode	*all things; equally*
	That I knewe thoo; but thus it stoode	*then; it was*
805	Hit happed that I came on a day	*chanced; one day*
	Into a place ther that I say	*where I saw*
	Trewly the fayrest companye	
	Off ladyes that evere man with ye	*anyone; eye*
	Had seen togedres in oo place.	*one*
810	Shal I clepe hyt happe other grace	*call it; or*
	That broght me there? Nay, but Fortune,	
	That ys to lyen ful comune,	
	The fals trayteresse pervers	*antagonistic*
	(God wolde I koude clepe hir wers!),	
815	For now she worcheth me ful woo.	

798. An allegorical oxymoron: a governess who insists on idleness. The personification Idleness lets the young lover/dreamer into the garden of Delight in
RR, ll. 532–620.

800. *kan/couthe goode*: an idiom meaning 'know/knew what to do', cf. l. 390,
but in this context the ideas of both knowledge and goodness regain their
full senses.

805–9. On reminiscences of the much imitated scene where the dreamer sees the
elegant companions of Delight, dancing a *carole*, in *RR*, ll. 725–1288, see
pp. 9–10; cf. also Machaut, *Dit dou Vergier*, ll. 157–8 (in *Oeuvres*, ed.
Hoepffner 1908–21).

810–12. *happe*: 'chance'; *grace*: 'divine providence'; cf. *TC* I, l. 896. L. 810
sounds positive, 811–12 turn bitter. Perhaps Ch is reformulating the
commonplace that God's gifts to man divide into gifts of Nature, gifts of
grace and gifts of Fortune (Patch 1927: 65–8).

812. 'Who gives herself utterly promiscuously to lying'. *Comune* perhaps means
both 'frequently' and 'like a common woman', a prostitute: a conventional
image for Fortune.

815. 'For now she causes me total unhappiness'. Similar anger against Fate for
ever bringing lovers together, when faced with parting, is put into the mouth
of the real-life Joan of Kent by the Chandos Herald in his *Life of the Black*

	And I wol tel sone why soo.	
	Amonge these ladyes thus echon,	*every one of them*
	Soth to seyn, Y sawgh oon	*to say truth*
	That was lyke noon of the route,	*crowd*
820	For I dar swere withoute doute	*beyond doubt*
	That, as the somerys sone bryghte	
	Ys fairer, clerer and hath more lyghte	
	Than any other planete in hevene,	
	The moone or the sterres sevene,	
825	For al the worlde, so had she	*truly*
	Surmountede hem al, of beaute	*in beauty*
	Of maner, and of comelynesse,	*loveliness*
	Of stature and of wel sette gladnesse,	
	Of godelyhede and so wel besey:	*virtue; fine-looking*
830	Shortly, what shal Y [more] sey?	
	By God and by [his] halwes twelve,	*saints*
	Hyt was my swete, ryght al hirselve!	*entirely her own self*
	She had so stedfaste countenaunce,	*trustworthy manner*
	So noble porte and meyntenaunce.	*bearing; behaviour*
835	And Love, that had wel herd my boone,	*request*
	Had espyed me thus soone,	*spied me out*
	That she ful sone in my thoght,	*immediately*
	As helpe me God, so was ykaught	*caught*
	So sodenly, that I ne toke	
840	No maner counseyl but at hir loke	
	[And] at myn he[r]t; forwhy hir eyen	*because*
	So gladly, I trow, myn hert seyen,	*believe; saw*
	That purely tho myn oune thoght	*then*
	Seyde hit were beter serve hir for noght	*would be; to serve*
845	Than with another to be wel.	*to be successful*
	And hyt was sothe, for everedel	*in every way*

Prince (ed. R. Barber, London, 1979, p. 111).

824. *sterres sevene*: the Pleiades.

844. In view of the vast inheritance the real Gaunt gained from marrying Blanche of Lancaster, this particular transmutation into the literary language of love might strike a cynical reader as grossly ingenuous, but *serve hir for noght* probably means 'love without hope of reciprocation', a medieval definition of 'true love' and the ideal of true *amicitia*; see Burnley 1979: 137.

I wil anoonryght telle the why: *straightaway; thee*
I sawgh hyr daunce so comelely,   *beautifully*
Carole and synge so swetly,   *dance carols*
850   Lawghe and pley so womanly,   *be happy*
And loke so debonairly,   *graciously*
So goodely speke and so frendly,
That certes Y trowe that evermore   *for evermore*
Nas seyne so blysful a tresore.   *was never seen*
855   For every heer on hir hede,
Soth to seyne, hyt was not rede,
Ne nouther yelowe ne broune hyt nas:
Me thoghte most lyke [gold] hyt was.
And which eyen my lady hadde!   *what eyes*
860   Debonair, goode, glade and sadde,   *gracious; sensible*
Symple, of goode mochel, noght to wyde.   *sincere; size*
Therto hir looke nas not asyde,
Not overt[h]wert, but besette so wele
Hyt drewh and tooke up eveydele
865   Al that on hir gan beholde.   *looked at her*
Hir eyen semed anoon she wolde

847–960. The physical description of White, in terms, details and ordering of content, is very close to *Behaigne*, ll. 281–322, 356–83. The description of a lady whose virtues inspired the dreamer to love and virtue in *Remède de Fortune*, ll. 197–266, contributed to the praise of mind and character, Ch stressing, even more than the *Remède*, qualities like lack of affectation, kindness, self-command and rational moderation.

849. A *carole* was a ring-dance, the dancers moving round hand in hand while a refrain was sung, then standing still for each stanza. It was a court fashion throughout the 14th century (not specially associated with Christmas). In the 15th century *carole* begins to be used for the lyrics (of distinctive verse-form) to which the dances were performed.

859. Eyes, and a woman's look – whether she is consciously *looking at* the admirer or not – receive much attention in medieval descriptions of beauty; cf. *RR*, ll. 1536–1880; *TC* I, ll. 295–305, 325.

863. *overthwert*: askance, with a critical look.

864. 'It attracted and completely captivated'.

866–7. 'Her eyes gave the impression she would instantly be merciful'. *Mercy* in medieval love literature usually means the lady's acceptance of the man's love, usually presented as nothing more substantial than her recognition of him as her 'servant' (e.g. *TC* III, ll. 92–182). By analogy with a military

	Have mercy – foolys wenden soo –	
	But hyt was never the rather doo.	*not so, for all that*
	Hyt nas no countrefeted thynge;	*affectation*
870	Hyt was hir oune pure lokynge,	*pure gaze*
	That the goddesse dame Nature	
	Had made hem opene by mesure,	
	And cloos; for, were she never so glad,	
	Hyr lokynge was not foly sprad,	*foolishly wide*
875	Ne wildely, though that she pleyde.	*were having fun*
	But ever me thoght hir eyen seyde	
	"Be God, my wrathe ys al foryive."	*By God; forgiven*
	Therwith hir lyste so wel to lyve	*enjoyed living*
	That dulnesse was of hir adrad.	*scared*
880	She nas to sobre ne to glad;	*too*
	In alle thynges more mesure	
	Had never, I trow, creature.	*any creature*
	But many oon with hire loke she hert,	*glance; wounded*
	And that sate hyr ful lytel at hert,	*entered her mind*
885	For she kn[e]we nothynge of her thoght;	*their thoughts*
	[But whether she knewe or knewe it nought,]	
	Algate she ne rought of hem a stree.	*anyway; reckon; straw*
	To gete hyr love noo nerre was he	*nearer*

captive begging mercy, and with Christian praying for God's mercy, a gift freely given out of divine beneficence and not deserved by the humble suppliant, a man's desire is often expressed as a prayer for mercy in medieval literature. Here, as in ll. 876–8, 885, 891–2, 1017–33, the knight insists that his lady had a friendly manner, and gives a glimpse of what it might be to be loved by her, without loss of dignity and virtue, or encouraging flirtatiousness.

872. 'Had made them open with perfect moderation'.

877. Behind the *wrathe*, against potential lovers, which White's manner suggests she will not show, lies the traditional metaphor of *daunger* (*RR*, ll. 2904–3778). OF *daunger* originally meant 'jurisdiction'/'power to punish'; it can mean a woman's lack of interest in a wooer's suit. The portrait presents White as unresponsive to masculine desire, with *wrathe* always a possibility (ll. 883–90, 1151, 1190, 1251). Her attitude is ladylike, rational, stable, with perhaps also the motif of instinctive female chastity adumbrated also in *Kn T*, with Emelye's devotion to Diana, and *PF*, with the female eagle's reluctance to serve Venus or Cupid.

886. This line is only in Th.

	That woned at home tha[n] he in Ynde:	*lived; India*
890	The formest was alway behynde.	*first; at the back*
	But good folke over al other	*above all others*
	She loved, as man may do hys brother.	
	Of whiche love she was wounder large	*amazingly generous*
	In skilful placis that bere charge.	
895	But which a visage had she thertoo!	*face; also*
	Allas, myn hert ys wonder woo	*amazingly miserable*
	That I ne kan discryven hyt;	
	Me lakketh both Englyssh and wit	*words and cleverness*
	For to undo hyt at the fulle.	*reveal it*
900	And eke my spiritis be so dulle	*natural abilities*
	So grete a thynge for to devyse;	*achieve*
	I have no witte that kan suffise	*be adequate*
	To comprehende hir beaute.	*fully survey*
	But thus moche dar I sayn, that she	*say confidently*
905	Was white, rody, fressh, and lyvely hewed,	
	And every day hir beaute newed	*was new again*
	And negh hir face was alderbest.	
	For certys Nature had swich lest	*took such pleasure*

890–4. Her principles when assessing other people: she valued people according to character, not rank, and was discerning in disbursing considerable charity.

890. Echoes 'many that are first shall be last', Matt. 19:30.

894. 'In well-judged situations that merited her attention'.

897–9. 'That I do not know how to describe it; both language and ability are lacking in me to reveal it adequately'.

905. 'Was white, rosy, fresh and delightfully complexioned'.

906–7. 'Every day ... her face was nearly best of all' makes little sense in the context of otherwise extreme praise of her beauty. It is probably based on *Remède de Fortune*, ll. 1629–36, where the lady 'increases in beauty from day to day without a break' and 'increases and abounds [in good qualities] more than any other lady in the world'. The simplest solution is to take *negh* as scribal error for *newe*, 'anew'.

908–12. Images of Nature or God as artisan are often associated with descriptions of female beauty: the idea of Nature as craftswoman, producing creatures in each species from the ideal pattern or form of that species, is ancient (Economou 1972: 19–27). *moustre* (l. 912): 'pattern'. Whereas Machaut (*Behaigne*, ll. 384–426) says Nature will never make her like again, Ch turns White into this 'platonic idea', unique and raised beyond ordinary human

	To make that faire that trewly she	*in forming; lovely one*
910	Was hir chefe patrone of beaute,	*pattern for beauty*
	And chefe ensample of al hir werke	*exemplar; handiwork*
	And moustre. For be hyt never so derke	*pattern*
	Me thynkyth I se hir evermoo.	
	And yet moreover, thogh al thoo	*those*
915	That ever levede were now alyve,	*lived*
	Ne sholde ha founde to diskryve	
	Yn al hir face a wikked sygne,	*bad sign*
	For hit was sad, symple and benygne.	*sober; sincere*
	And which a goodely softe speche	
920	Had that swete, my lyves leche:	*doctor of life*
	So frendely and so wel ygrounded,	*grounded*
	Up al resoun so wel yfounded,	*on complete reason*
	And so tretable to al goode	*inclined*
	That I dar swere wel, by the Roode,	*Cross*
925	Of eloquence was never founde	
	So swete a sownynge facounde,	
	Ne trewer tonged ne skorned lasse,	*less likely to mock*
	Ne bet koude hele, that by the masse	*that could heal*
	I durste swere – thogh the Pape hit songe –	*Pope; sang*
930	That ther was never yet throgh hir tonge	
	Man ne woman gretely harmed.	
	As for hi[r] was al harme hyd,	*injury invisible*
	Ne lasse flaterynge in hir word,	
	That purely hir symple recorde	*plain statement*
935	Was founde as trewe as any bonde	*reliable*
	Or trouthe of any mannys honde.	*pledge*

nature, as also in ll. 974, 982.

916. 'No-one would have been able to have discerned'.

919–38. A series of points about her virtues as a speaker: her speech was gentle, always based on reason, eloquent, not denigrating people, not flattering them, making trustworthy statements, and not grumbling.

923–4. 'And so inclined to all that is good that I give my word, by the Cross'.

926. Meaning unclear. Probably *facounde* = noun, *sownynge* = adjective: 'such sweet-sounding eloquence' (alternatively *facounde* = adjective, *sownynge* = noun: 'such a sweet, eloquent voice').

930. Meaning unclear: perhaps scribal corruption. Maybe 'to her all evil [or all offence against her?] was invisible', i.e. she saw the best in people. That conflicts with ll. 996–8.

Ne chyde she koude never a dele:
That knoweth al the worlde ful wele.
But swiche a fairenesse of a nekke   *such beauty*
940   Had that swete that boon nor brekke
Nas ther non seen that myssatte:
Hyt was white, smothe, streght and pure flatte,   *quite smooth*
Wythouten hole or canel boon,
As be semynge had she noon.   *so that apparently*
945   Hyr throte, as I have now memoyre,   *memory*
Semed a rounde toure of yvoyre,   *ivory*
Of goode gretenesse and noght to grete.
And goode faire White she hete.   *was called*
That was my lady name ryghte.   *lady's; rightly*
950   She was bothe faire and bryghte;
She had not hir name wronge.
Ryght faire shuldres and body longe   *tall*
She had, and armes; every lyth   *limb*
Fattyssh, flesshy, not grete therwith.   *rounded; plump*
955   Ryght white handes and nayles rede,
Rounde brestes, and of good brede   *width*
Hyr hippes were; a streight flat bakke.
I knewe on hir noon other lakke,   *no blemish*
That al hir lymmes nere pure sywynge,
960   In as ferre as I had knowynge.
Therto she koude so wel pley   *be amusing*
Whan that hir lyst, that I dar sey   *it pleased her*

939–60. These physical details and their order follow *Behaigne* closely (e.g.
fattyssh = grasset) apart from two added motifs of whiteness (presumably
both word-plays on 'Blanche': on the name White, ll. 948–51, and the *toure
of yvoyre*, l. 946).

940–1. 'Had that lovely one, that there was neither bone nor blemish to be seen
that marred it'.

943. 'Without hollow or collar-bone'.

946. Word-play on 'Blanche' could explain this image. Wimsatt 1967a suggests
association with Mary; the image, from *Song of Songs* 7:4, 'thy neck is a
tower of ivory', was used in Marian literature.

958. A compressed phrase: 'other' probably refers to other parts of her body, cf.
Behaigne, ll. 380–3, 'I knew no further blemish elsewhere'.

959. 'Which would make her limbs anything but just as beautiful' (lit. 'completely matching').

That she was lyke to torche bryght,
That every man may take of lyght   *take light from*
965   Ynogh, and hyt hathe never the lesse.   *in plenty*
Of maner and of comlynesse
Ryght so ferde my lady dere:
For every wight of hir manere   *everybody; from*
Myght cachche ynogh yif that he wolde,   *if he wished*
970   Yif he had eyen hir to beholde.   *eyes to see her*
For I dar swere wel, yif that she   *swear confidently*
Had amonge ten thousande be,   *been*
She wolde have be at the lest   *at least*
A chefe meroure of al the fest,   *mirror*
975   Thogh they had stonde in a rowe   *stood*
To mennes eyen koude have knowe.
For wherso men had pleyed or wakyd   *wherever; stayed awake*
Me thoght the felysshyppe as naked,   *company; denuded*
Withouten hir – that sawgh I oones –
980   As a corowne withoute stones.   *precious stones*
Trewly she was to myn eye
The soleyne Fenix of Arabye;   *unique*

963–5. Light imagery again. Sk.'s n. cites examples of this image, including *RR*,
ll. 7380–2 (in a very different context).

966.   'In her manner and her beauty'.

972.   Echoes *Song of Songs* 5:9–10 (referring to a male beloved): 'What is thy
beloved more than another beloved, O thou fairest among women? What is
thy beloved more than another beloved, that thou dost so charge us? My
beloved is white and ruddy, the chiefest among ten thousand.'

974.   A complex image that continues the imagery of light; mirrors were also
associated with feminine beauty; medieval mirrors were often finely decorated luxury items; *mirror* and Lat. *speculum* were also used in the sense
'epitome', 'summary of everything'.

976.   'To the eyes of people with the knowledge to judge' (the similarity to beauty
contests makes this a difficult image for modern readers, but see note to
l. 972).

982.   The phoenix was a mythical Arabian bird. Only one existed at a time, the
new phoenix rising out of the pyre of the previous one (*Met.* XV,
ll. 392–407; *RR*, ll. 15947–75). Here the phoenix is a symbol of the lady's
bright beauty and uniqueness to a lover's eyes, but in devotional literature
the phoenix is an allegory of the resurrection, and is also used of Mary's
unique purity as virgin mother (Wimsatt 1967a). The image could stem

For ther levyth nevir but oon,	lives; *but one*
Ne swich as she ne knowe I noon.	*such as she*
985 To speke of godenesse, trewly she	
Had as moche debonairyete	*kindness*
As ever had Hester in the Bible,	
And more, yif more were possyble.	
And, sothe to seyn, therwythalle	*at the same time*
990 She had a wytte so generalle,	*intelligence; wide*
So hoole enclyned to alle goode,	*wholly devoted*
That al hir wytte was set, by the Rode,	*mind was inclined*
Withoute malyce upon gladnesse.	*evil; happiness*
And therto I sawgh never yet a lesse	*anyone less*
995 Harmeful than she was in doynge.	
I sey nat that she ne had knowynge	*had not knowledge*
What harme was, or elles she	*what evil was*
Had koude no good, so thenketh me.	
And trewly, for to speke of trouthe,	*integrity*
1000 But she had hadde hyt hadde be routhe.	
Therof she had so moche hyr dele	*Of that; portion*

from an originally anti-feminist comparison, transformed into praise: *RR*, ll. 8657–8, following Walter Map's *In Rufinum*, says a good woman is rarer than a phoenix.

986–7. *debonairyete*: 'generosity', 'gentleness'. Associated like *fre* and *gentil* especially with the well-born, it also often conveys 'meekness', a quality attributed to *Hester*, Queen Esther, the Jewish wife of Ahasuerus and the heroine of the apocryphal Book of Esther who saved her people from persecution. On the complex late 14th-century concept of ideal queenship, combining meekness, authority and intercession, associated with Hester and with contemporary queens, see Strohm 1992: 94–9.

994–5. 'And in that I never saw anyone in whose actions there was less harm'.

996–8. 'Chaucer plays with the notion of definition by contraries' here: Burnley 1979: 240 n. 11. The distinction between innocence and ignorance is common (Matt. 10:16); Sk.'s n. cites *Aen.* I, l. 630, where Dido says that through not being ignorant of injuries herself, she can help others.

998.   'Would not have known how to do right, as it seems to me'.

999–1005. ME *trouthe* = 'faithfulness', and more generally 'goodness', 'integrity'. It was also beginning to gain the modern sense of 'certainty' or 'reality'. Here it seems, as in *PPl* I, V, VII, to mean divine goodness personified or God (God is truth, John 14:6).

1000.   'It would have been a tragedy [lit. 'pity'] if she had not had that'.

(And I dar seyn and swere hyt wele)
That Trouthe hymselfe, over al and alle,
Had chose hys maner principalle   *main residence*
1005 In hir, that was his restynge place.   *who was*
Therto she hadde the moste grace   *greatest gift*
To have stedefaste perseveraunce,
And esy atempry governaunce,   *pleasant calm control*
That ever I knewe or wyste yitte,   *or learned of yet*
1010 So pure suffraunt was hir wytte.   *completely receptive*
And resoun gladly she understoode.
Hyt folowed wel she koude goode:
She used gladly to do wel.
These were hir maners everydel.   *in all things*
1015 Therwith she loved so wel ryght,   *besides; justice*
She wronge do wolde to no wyght.   *intended harm*
No wyght myght doo hir noo shame;   *dishonour her*
She loved so wel hir oune name   *reputation*
Hyr lust to holde no wyght in honde;   *dominate no-one*
1020 Ne, be thou siker, she wolde not fonde   *be sure of this; try*
To holde no wyght in balaunce,   *in uncertainty*
By halfe worde ne by countenaunce   *hint; her manner*
(But yif men wolde upon hir lye).   *unless people wanted to lie*
Ne sende men into Walakye,

1002–3. 'And I can say confidently and swear utterly that Truth himself, of all and
every place'. Truth is personified as a medieval king with many estates, one
of which he chooses as chief residence. Mary is often described as a place
where God had taken his dwelling-place, e.g. Ch's *ABC*, ll. 9–14.

1024–6. Places on the borders of 14th-century Christendom subject to campaigns
or crusades: where Turkish, Saracen and Mongol expansion was bringing
conflict between Islam and the West. They were distant, dangerous
countries to which – in literature if not in life – an imperious lady might
be imagined to send her lover to prove his prowess; many heroes of
romance, like Godfrey of Boulogne, were Christian crusaders against
Islam. *Walakye*: Wallachia, territory of the Vlachs, and Moldavia, west of
the Black Sea, became independent principalities in the 14th century, but
Balkan Christians came under Ottoman Turkish domination and in
1368–9 Louis I of Hungary campaigned, vainly, against Wallachian
independence. Ottoman power encroached from the south and it became
an Ottoman vassal-state; *Pruyse*: Prussia, still regarded as crusading
territory. The Teutonic Knights, a crusading order, campaigned against the

1025	To Pruyse and into Tartarye,	
	To Alysaundre, ne into Turkye,	
	And byd hym faste anoon that he	*directly command him*
	Goo hoodeles to the Drye Se	*hoodless*
	And come home by the Carrenare,	
1030	And sey "Sir, be now ryght ware	*take good care*
	That I may of yow here seyn	*can hear said*
	Worshyppe or that ye come ageyn".	*praise; before*
	She ne used no suche knakkes smale.	*little games*
	But wherfore that Y tel my tale?	*why do I*
1035	Ryght on thys same, as I have seyde,	*on this woman*
	Was hooly al my love leyde;	*set*
	For certes she was, that swete wife,	*certainly; woman*
	My suffisaunce, my luste, my lyfe,	*contentment; joy*
	Myn happe, myn hele and al my blysse,	*fortune; health*
1040	My worldys welfare and my goddesse,	*worldly happiness*
	And I hooly hires, and everydel.'	*wholly; completely*
	'By oure [Lord],' quod I, 'Y trowe	
	you wel:	*believe; entirely*
	Hardely your love was wel besette:	*certainly; placed*
	I not how ye myght have doo bette.'	*done better*
1045	'Bette? Ne no wyght so wele!' quod he.	*no-one*

pagan Prussians in the 13th century and controlled the area in the 14th century. Blanche's father, Henry of Lancaster, went on an expedition to Prussia in 1352; *Tartarye*: the Ta(r)tars, a Turkish-speaking Mongol people, were being pushed back by Christian powers during the 14th century from much of eastern Europe into S. Russia, east and north of the Black Sea. Ch may be thinking more generally of the increasing power and conquests of the Second Mongol Empire under Tamerlane (1336–1405); *Turkye*: used loosely for Ottoman Turkish territory: Ottoman Turks were gaining control of Anatolia and Byzantine Christian territory west of the Dardanelles and advancing into modern Bulgaria and Russia.

1028–9. *Drye Se*: the Gobi Desert in Mongolia, west of *Carrenare* (Kara-Nor, the 'Black Lake'): places on the trade route to China, opened up by the Mongols (see Lowes 1905–6). Whereas ll. 1024–6 suggest the lover being sent on a crusade, ll. 1028–9 perhaps suggest routes to the most remote place he might be sent to fetch something for his lady.

1036. 'My love was wholly devoted'.

1038. On *suffisaunce* and ideas of freedom from worldliness associated with it in Ch's poetry, see Burnley 1979: 89.

'Y trowe hyt wel sir,' quod I, 'parde.'   *I credit it; indeed*
'Nay, leve hyt wel.' 'Sire, so do I: *believe; I do so*
I leve yow wel that trewly   *believe*
Yow thoghte that she was the best,   *it seemed to you*
1050 And to beholde the alderfayrest,   *loveliest of all*
Whosoo had loked hir with your eyen.'   *if anyone*
'With myn? Nay, al that hir seyen   *who saw*
Seyde and swore hyt was soo.
And thogh they ne hadde, I wolde thoo   *even if; then*
1055 Have loved best my lady free,   *noble*
Thogh I had hadde al the beaute   *even if*
That ever had Alcipyades,
And al the strengthe of Ercules,
And therto had the worthynesse   *also; prowess*
1060 Of Alysaunder and al the rychesse   *wealth*

1056–72. On such lists of figures representing virtues, see Phillips 1995a. *Alcipyades*: a type of beauty, Alcibiades was an Athenian general, playboy and politician famous for beauty (and debauchery); *RR*, l. 8913 says that his body, outwardly so beautiful, was ugly inside; *Ercules*: Hercules, the legendary classical hero famed for strength; *Alysaunder*: Alexander the Great of Macedon (356–323 BC): his empire extended from Greece to N. India; in the Middle Ages he was a hero of legend and romance; *Ector*, *Achilles*, *Polyxena*: see note to ll. 328–9; Hector and Alexander were two of the medieval 'Nine Worthies', famous warriers of old; *Antylegyus*: Antilochus was killed with Achilles; *Mynerva*: (Athene), the classical goddess of wisdom. Dares Phrygius's *De excidio Troiae historia* (see l. 1070) was a major early source for medieval knowledge of Troy, though Ch was probably remembering accounts in later versions, like the *Roman de Troie* or Guido delle Colonne's *Historia Destructionis Troiae*.

1060–3. Cities famed for wealth: *Babylon*, in modern Iraq, was the centre, from 1900 BC on, of an empire of fabled wealth (Vincent of Beauvais, *Speculum historiale* III, 12). The Babylonian emperor took the Jews into captivity from 586 BC. Because the Scarlet Woman of Rev. 17 is the 'Whore of Babylon', Babylon became a medieval image of luxury and vice; *Macedonia*, in N. Greece, was famed for two great kings: Philip II, who became king of all Greece in 338 BC, and Alexander the Great; *Nineveh*, in modern Iraq, was the capital of the Assyrian empire from the 9th to the 7th centuries BC, which was destroyed by the Babylonians; the story from the Book of Jonah of how God threatened to punish it for wickedness is the subject of a 14th-century poem, *Patience*; *Carthage* was a Phoenician city,

	That ever was in Babyloyne,	
	In Cartage or in Macedoyne,	
	Or in Rome, or in Nynyve,	
	And [ther]to also hardy be	*been just as brave*
1065	As was Ector, so have I joye,	
	That Achilles slough at Troye	*whom*
	(And therfore was he slayn alsoo	
	In a temple, for bothe twoo	
	Were slayne: he and Antylegyus,	
1070	And so seyth Dares Frygius,	
	For love of Polyxena);	
	Or ben as wis as Mynerva,	
	I wolde ever, withoute drede,	*without doubt*
	Have loved hir for I most nede.	*needs must*
1075	Nede? Nay, trewly, I gabbe nowe:	*talk nonsense*
	Noght nede. And I wol telle howe.	*not need at all*
	For of goode wille myn hert hyt wolde,	*wanted it*
	And eke to love her I was holde	*bound*
	As for the fairest and the beste.	
1080	She was as good, so have I reste,	*as I hope for peace*
	As ever was Penolopee of Grece,	
	Or as the noble wife Lucrece,	
	That was the best – he telleth thus	*who was the best*
	The Romayne Tytus Lyvyus.	*Roman*
1085	She was as good – and nothynge lyke	

founded c. 750 BC on the N. African coast. Ancient historians record Dido as its founder; it rivalled Rome and was destroyed by Scipio Africanus the Younger in 146 BC.

1081–2. Penelope was the loyal wife of Odysseus (Ulysses); in Homer's *Odyssey* she resisted remarriage during the ten years he took to return from the ten-year-long Trojan War. Like Lucretia, she is often cited as the ideal wife: see *Her.* I; Jerome, *Against Jovinian* I, col. 45; Claudian, *Praise of Serena*, ll. 25–8; *RR*, ll. 8573–30. *Lucrece*: Lucretia, the Roman wife who killed herself rather than live dishonoured after being raped by Sextus Tarquinius; this is the first story of Livy's *History* (= *Tytus Lyvyus*).

1085. *nothynge lyke* is puzzling: 'not at all like them'? Though both women were exemplary faithful wives, one was raped and the other was left waiting ten years for her husband's return (as she complains in *Her.* I). Perhaps Ch was discouraging too close identification of White and her lover with these stories in every detail; the resemblance is in the fidelity and wifely honour.

	(Thogh hir stories be autentyke).	*authentic*
	Algate she was as trewe as she.	*at least; faithful*
	But wherfore that I telle the?	*why do I*
	Whan I firste my lady say	*saw*
1090	I was ryght yonge, sothe to say,	*very young*
	And ful grete nede I hadde to lerne.	
	Whan my herte wolde yerne	*longed eagerly*
	To love hyt was a grete empryse;	*great undertaking*
	But as my wytte koude beste suffise,	*was able to achieve it*
1095	After my yonge childely wytte,	*immature mind*
	Withoute drede I besette hytte	*certainly; set*
	To love hir in my beste wyse,	*the best way I could*
	To do hir worshippe and the servise	*honour*
	That I koude thoo, be my trouthe,	*knew how to; by*
1100	Withoute feynynge outher slouthe.	*feigning or*
	For wonder feyne I wolde hir se,	*amazingly eagerly*
	So mochel hyt amended me,	*much; aided*
	That whan I sawgh hir first amorwe	*in the morning*
	I was war[ys]shed of al my sorwe	*healed*
1105	Of al day after, til hyt were eve:	*for all the day*
	Me thoght nothyng myghte me greve,	*could grieve me*
	Were my sorwes never so smerte.	*painful*
	And yet she sytte so [in] myn herte	*still; sits*
	That, by my trouthe, Y nolde noght	*would not want*
1110	For al thys worlde, oute of my thoght	
	Leve my lady. Noo, trewly.'	*let my lady go*
	'Now, by my trouthe, sir,' quod I,	
	'Me thynketh ye have suche a chaunce	
	As shryfte wythoute repentaunce.'	
1115	'Repentaunce? Nay, fy!' quod he,	

1113–14. 'It seems to me you have the kind of good fortune that brings absolution without repentance': perhaps 'happiness without paying for it'. Perhaps the narrator observes that the knight has little chance of being 'cured' of his sorrow since he shows no desire to modify his attitude towards earthly happiness? See Diekstra 1981: 224.

1115. '"Repentance? No, do not say such a thing!" he said'. *Fy* often indicates that something should not be said.

'Shulde Y now repente me   *should I repent*
To love? Nay, certis, than were I wel   *I would be totally*
Wers than was Achetofel   *worse*
Or Anthenor – so have I joye –   *as I may have joy*
1120   The traytor that betraysed Troye,   *who betrayed*
Or the fals Genelloun,
He that purchased the tresoun
Of Rowlande and of Olyvere.
Nay, while I am alyve here,   *as long as I live*
1125   I nyl foryete hir nevermoo.'   *forget; for eternity*
'Now, good syr,' quod I thoo,   *then*
'Ye han wel tolde me herebefore,   *have; before now*
Hyt ys no nede reherse [it] more,   *to repeat it*
How ye sawgh hir firste, and where.
1130   But wolde ye tel me the manere
To hire which was your first speche?   *first words*
Therof I wolde yow beseche.   *for that; beg*
And how she knewe first your thoght,
Whether ye loved hir or noght.   *about whether*
1135   And telleth me eke what ye have lore,   *tell; also; lost*
I herde yow telle herebefore.'   *that I heard*
'Yee,' seyde [he], 'Thow nost what thou menyst.   *do not know*
I have lost more than thou wenyst.'   *realize*
'What losse ys that?' quod I thoo,   *then*
1140   'Nyl she not love yow? Ys hyt soo?   *does she not wish to*
Or have ye oght doon amys,   *done anything wrong*
That she hathe lefte yow: ys hyt this?   *so that*
For Goddys love, telle me alle.'
'Before God,' quod he, 'And I shalle:

1116.   *repente* had a sense of 'regret', 'change mind', esp. about love (cf. *LGW*, l. 133), as well as its religious meaning. The knight's chain of thought leads him on to betrayals. But there is also a sense of the confessional in the dialogue, and perhaps revelation of a need to modify emotional fixation.

1118–23.   A list of famous traitors. Achitophel incited Absalom to rebel against his father King David (2 Sam. 15–17); Antenor betrayed Troy to save his life (*Roman de Troie*, ll. 24387–824; delle Colonna, *Historia*, ll. 218–21); Ganelon betrayed Roland and Oliver in the OF epic, the *Song of Roland*.

1122.   'He who brought about the betrayal'.

1135–6.   As in l. 365, a relative pronoun is omitted, replaced by a 'contact clause'.

1145	I say ryght, as I have seyde:	*just*
	On hir was al my love leyde	*all my love was hers*
	And yet she nyste hyt nat, never a del,	*did not know; not a bit*
	Noght longe tyme: leve hyt wel.	*believe it well*
	For [be] ryght siker, I durste noght	*be quite certain*
1150	For al this worlde tel hir my thoght.	*for anything*
	Ne I wolde have wraththed hir, trewly,	*angered*
	For wostow why? She was lady	*do you know*
	Of the body: she had the hert,	
	And who hath that may not astert.	*whoever; be ousted*
1155	But for to kepe me fro ydelnesse	
	Trewly I did my besynesse	
	To make songes, as I best koude,	*knew*
	And ofte tyme I songe hem loude,	*them aloud*
	And made songes th[u]s a grete dele;	*great number*
1160	Althogh I koude not make so wele	*compose*
	Songes, [ne] knowe the arte alle,	*nor*
	As koude Lamekys sone Tuballe,	
	That founde out firste the art of songe;	*discovered*
	For as hys brothres hamers ronge	*rang*

1152–3. Cf. *RR*, ll. 1994–5. *lady*, l. 1152, and *hir knyght*, l. 1179, are used in feudal senses: 'liege-lady' or 'commander' and 'her vassal'.

1154. *astert*: usually 'escape'. *Riv.* translates: 'and if anyone has that a man may not escape'. *May astert* can mean 'fail' (*MED*, senses 3, 5). Alternatively, *not* may be a corruption of *nought*, 'nothing', and l. 1154 could mean 'and nothing eludes the power of the person who has that', which fits *RR*, ll. 1996–7, a possible source for ll. 1152–4. Cf. *CA* I, l. 2805 for similar phrasing.

1155–7. Lovers in medieval literature, esp. *dits amoureux*, often compose lyrics; cf. *Remède de Fortune*, ll. 357–680, where the lady shows no awareness of his love and he composes songs, but having read her one he retreats in embarrassment and despair.

1162–78. Lamech's sons Jubal, 'father of those who sing to the harp and organ', and Tubalcain, a smith, were sometimes confused by medieval authors (see Gen. 4:20–22). The story about the anvil was told, about Pythagoras, by Macrobius, *Commentary* II.1. Sk.'s n. says Ch's phrasing resembles Higden, *Polychronicon* III ch. 3:ii. *Aurora*: a 12th-century Lat. verse rendering of the Bible by Peter of Riga (ed. P.E. Beichner, Notre Dame, 1965), which mentions Jubal and Pythagoras as discoverers of musical intervals; see Beichner 1954, Young 1937.

1165	Upon hys anvelet up and doon,	*anvil*
	Therof he tooke the first soon.	*from that; sound*
	But Grekes seyn Pictagoras	*say*
	That he the first fynder was	*discoverer*
	Of the arte: Aurora telleth soo.	
1170	But therof no fors of hem twoo!	*at all events*
	Algatis songes thus I made	*at all events*
	Of my felynge, myn hert to glade.	*make cheerful*
	And loo, th[i]s was altherfirst –	*very first*
	I not wher hyt were the [werst]:	*do not know*
1175	"Lorde hyt maketh myn herte lyght,	
	Whan I thenke on that swete wyght	*being*
	That is so semely on to see.	*to look at*
	And wisshe to God hit myght so bee.	*could so be*
	That she wolde holde me for hir knyght,	*retain*
1180	My lady that is so faire and bryght."	
	Now have I tolde the, sothe to say,	*thee*
	My first songe. Upon a day	
	I bethoght me what woo	*thought to myself*
	And sorwe that I suffred thoo	*then*
1185	For hir, and yet she wyst hyt noght,	*knew nothing of it*
	Ne tel hir durst I nat my thoght.	*I dared not tell*
	"Allas," thoght I, "Y kan no rede,	*know no solution*
	And but I telle hir I am but dede;	*unless*
	And yif I telle hyr, to sey ryght sothe,	*to tell the truth*
1190	I am adred she wol be wrothe.	*afraid*
	Allas, what shal I thanne doo?"	*then*
	In this debate I was so woo	*inner debate*
	Me thoght myn hert brast atweyne.	*broke apart*
	So at the last, sothe to sayne,	*to say the truth*
1195	I bethoght me that Nature	*thought that*
	Ne formed never in creature	
	So moche beaute, trewly,	

1170. 'But it does not matter about those two!'
1183–1272. *Behaigne*, ll. 427–880 describes a similarly unconfident lover; Hope
     tells him such beauty cannot exist without pity; his lady rejects his halting
     confession of love, declares she is not responsible for his misery; her eyes
     seem to promise love, and after a long time she grants him 'the noble gift
     of her sweet mercy', cf. *BD*, ll. 1195–8. (This lady later proves false.)
1196. 'Never formed, in any created being'.

And bounte, wythoute mercy.   *goodness*
In hope of that, my tale I tolde
1200   With sorwe, as that I never sholde;
For nedys, and mawgree my hede,   *despite myself*
I most have tolde hir, or be dede.   *I had to tell*
I not wel how that I beganne   *do not know*
(Ful evel reherse hyt I kan),
1205   And eke, as helpe me God withalle,   *also*
I trowe hyt was in the dismalle
That was the ten woundes of Egipte,
For many a worde I overskipte   *missed out*
In my tale for pure fere,   *speech; sheer fear*
1210   Lest my wordys myssette were.   *badly designed*
With sorweful herte and woundes dede,   *deadly*
Softe, and quakynge for pure drede   *softly*
And shame, and styntynge in my tale   *halting; speech*
For ferde, and myn hewe al pale,   *fear; complexion*
1215   Ful ofte I wexe bothe pale and rede.   *became*
Bowynge to hir I heng the hede:
I durste nat ones loke hir on,   *even once*
For witte, maner and al was goon.   *mind, savoir faire*
I seyde "Mercy", and no more.
1220   Hyt nas no game: hyt sate me sore.   *affected; painfully*
      So at the laste, sothe to seyne,   *tell the truth*
Whan that myn hert was come ageyne,   *had returned*
To telle shortely al my speche,
With hool herte I gan hir beseche   *all my heart*
1225   That she wolde be my lady swete,
And swore and gan hir hertely hete   *to promise sincerely*
Ever to be stedfast and trewe,
And love hir alwey fresshly newe,
And never other lady have,
1230   And al hir worshippe for to save,   *honour; defend*
As I best koude. I swore hir this:

1200. 'With sorrow, as one who was hopeless of succeeding'. The loose, parenthetic sentence structure of ll. 1200–20 mimics his hesitations.
1206. *dismalle*: 'unlucky days', when activities will go wrong, from Lat. *dies mali*, 'evil days'. They were linked to the plagues of Egypt (Ex. 9, 12), because plague struck the first-born on the 12th day of the month (Ex. 12: 1).
1207, 1211. *woundes*: plagues (Lat. *plaga* means 'wound' as well as 'plague').

'For youres is alle that ever ther ys
For evermore, myn herte swete,   *sweetheart*
And never to false yow (but I mete)   *unless I dream*
1235   I nyl, as wysse God helpe me so."   *I resolve; surely*
    And whan I had my tale ydoo,   *finished my speech*
God wote, she acounted nat a stree   *reckoned; straw*
Of al my tale, so thoght me.   *for all I said*
To telle shortly, ryght as hyt ys,
1240   Trewly hire answere hyt was this.
I kan not now wel counterfete   *reproduce*
Hyr wordys, but this was the grete   *essence*
Of hir answere: she sayde "Nay".
Alle outerly. Allas that day!   *quite utterly*
1245   The sorowe I suffred, and the woo:
That trewly Cassandra, that soo
Bewayled the distruccioun   *lamented*
Of Troy and of Ilyoun,
Had never swich sorwe as I thoo.   *then*
1250   I durst no more say thertoo   *dared; about it*
For pure fere, but stale away.   *sheer fear; stole*
    And thus I lyved ful many a day,
That trewly I hadde no nede   *had no need*
Ferther than my beddes hede,   *bed's head*
1255   Never a day, to seche sorwe;   *search to find*
I fonde hyt redy every morwe,
Forwhy I loved hyr in no gere.   *passing fashion*
So hit befel, another yere,   *happened*
I thoughte ones I wolde fonde   *attempt*
1260   To do hir knowe and u[n]derstonde   *cause her to*
My woo, and she wel understode

1234.   'Never to be false to you consciously' (lit. 'unless I am dreaming'): *but I mete* has this sense because of the doctrine that one is not responsible for sins committed in dreams.

1246.   *Cassandra*: a Trojan princess and prophetess whose prophecies were doomed never to be believed. Ch is recalling her powerful lament in Guido de Columnis, ed. Griffin 1936, *Historia*, 79. 242–3 (Phillips 1995a).

1248.   *Ilyoun*: Ilium, the central citadel of Troy.

1257.   *gere* usually = 'apparel', 'customs', 'equipment'. The adjective *geery* often = 'changeable', 'capricious', cf. *Kn T* I, l. 1536; this is an unusual example of that sense for the noun.

	That I ne wilned nothynge but gode	*willed*
	And worshippe, and to kepe hir name	*honour; preserve*
	Over alle thynges and dred hir shame,	*guard against*
1265	And was so besy hyr to serve,	*diligent*
	And pitee were I shulde sterve,	*would be; die*
	Syth that I wilned noon harme ywys.	*no harm indeed*
	So whan my lady knewe al thys,	
	My lady yaf me al hooly	*gave; entirely*
1270	The noble yifte of hir mercy,	*gift*
	Savynge hir worshippe, by al weyes,	*keeping safe*
	(Dredles I mene noon other weyes).	*without question*
	And therwith she yaf me a rynge.	*gave*
	I trowe hyt was the first thynge.	*believe*
1275	But yif myn hert was iwaxe	*if; grown*
	Gladde that is no nede to axe!	*ask*
	As helpe me God, I was as blyve	*rapidly*
	Reysed as fro dethe to lyve;	*raised; life*
	Of al happes the alderbeste,	*fortunes; best*
1280	The gladdest and the most at reste.	*peaceful*
	For trewly that swete wyght,	*creature*
	Whan I had wrong and she [the] ryght,	*was wrong*
	She wolde alway so goodely	
	Foryeve me so debonairely;	*graciously*
1285	In al my yowthe, in al chaunce,	*eventualities*
	She tooke me in hir governaunce.	*under her direction*
	Therwyth she was alway so trewe,	*faithful*
	Our joye was ever ylyche newe;	*the same anew*
	Oure hertys werne so evene a payre	*were; evenly matched*

1263. Given that in real life Blanche was the heiress to a great name and estate, some sense of her status may come through the poetic motif of the lover's 'service' to his lady here.

1270–3. The lover's desire is often presented as service in medieval love poetry, and the woman's acceptance as acceptance of him as her servant; cf. *TC* III, ll. 92–210. Other *dits amoureux* envisage a similarly platonic climax, e.g. Machaut, *Remède de Fortune*, ll. 4072–82, where it is the giving of a ring. Machaut's *Fonteinne amoureuse* presents the patron's real-life marriage as unconsummated, and unspoken, love for a lady who, the lover believes, knows nothing of it.

1289–95. Conveys emotional union, the perfect climax of the knight's narrative: a poetic parallel to real-life marriage?

1290	That never nas that oon contra[yr]e	*one of them*
	To that other, for noo woo.	*to the other*
	Forsothe ylyche they suffred thoo	*identically*
	Oo blysse and eke oo sorwe bothe;	*also one*
	Ylyche they were bothe glad and wrothe.	*identically*
1295	Al was us oon, withoute were.	*one to us; conflict*
	And thus we lyved ful many a yere,	
	So wel I kan nat telle how.'	*describe*
	'Sir,' quod I, 'Where [is] she now?'	
	'Now?' quod he, and stynte anoon.	*stopped immediately*
1300	Therwith he waxe as dede as stoon	*stone*
	And seyde, 'Allas that I was bore!	*born*
	That was the losse that herebefore	*earlier*
	I tolde the, that I hadde lorne.	*what; lost*
	Bethenke how I seyde herebeforne	*think*
1305	"Thow wost ful lytel what thow menyst.	*thou knowest*
	I have lost more than thow wenyst".	*more than you realize*
	God wote, allas, ryght that was she!'	*God knows*
	'Allas, sir, how? What may that be?'	
	'She ys ded.' 'Nay!' 'Yis, be my trouthe.'	*I give you my word*
1310	'Is that youre losse? Be God, hyt ys routhe.'	*By*
	And with that worde ryght anoon	*immediately*
	They gan to strake forth. Al was doon,	
	For that tyme, the herte huntynge.	*hart hunting*
	With that me thoght that this kynge	*it seemed to me*

1298. The climax of a submerged *Ubi sunt* theme running through the text (*Ubi sunt*, 'Where are ...?, was a traditional motif for stressing the transience of earthly life). See Phillips 1981.

1308–10. Dialogue like this without discourse markers ('he said', etc.) or their equivalents is rare in medieval narrative and is associated with extreme emotion.

1312. *strake forth*: 'made the horn-cry to abandon the hunt'. The huntsmen cease when the king decides to finish, whether the hart has been slain or not; see Emerson 1922: 135–7.

1313. *herte huntynge*: in the context it seems impossible not to read a pun on 'heart' here, and also a suggestion that the hunt earlier could be read symbolically as well as literally. *Herte* often means 'sweetheart' in ME. For a variety of interpretations of the *hert-huntynge*, see Grennen 1964: 131–9; Thiébaux 1974: 115–27.

1314. *kynge*: see p. 46 n. 4 and the note on l. 368.

1315	Gan homewarde for to ryde,	
	Unto a place was there besyde,	*near there*
	Which was from us but a lyte:	*little*
	A longe castel with wallys white,	
	Be Seynt John, on a ryche hille,	*By*
1320	As me mette; but thus hyt fille	*I dreamed; befell*
	Ryght thus me mette, as I yow telle,	
	That in the castell ther was a belle,	
	As hyt hadde smyte oures twelve.	*which seemed; struck*
	Therwyth I awooke myselve	*at that*
1325	And fonde me lyinge in my bedde,	*myself*
	And the booke that I hadde redde,	
	Of Alchione and Seys the kynge,	
	And of the goddys of slepynge:	
	I fond hyt in myn honde ful evene.	*right there*
1330	Thoght I, 'Thys ys so queynt a swevene	*curious; dream*
	That I wol, be processe of tyme,	*in process*
	Fonde to put this swevene in ryme	*attempt to write*
	As I kan best, and that anoon.'	*as well as I know*
	This was my swevene; now hit ys doon.	

Explicit the Boke of the Duchesse.

1318. *longe castel*: the form *Loncastre* was common for 'Lancaster' (*Lan-/Lon-* has nothing to do with 'long' but comes from the name of the river Lune, probably from Celtic *slán*, 'healthy'); see p. 29.

1319. Probably a reference to John of Gaunt's name and title (see p. 29). A reference to St John, the author of the Book of Revelation, would also be not inappropriate for a dream poem (cf. Joseph and *Scipioun* in ll. 280 and 286). For the theory that a specific reference to St John's vision of the New Jerusalem is intended, see Huppé & Robertson 1963: 91–9.

1322. *belle*: since this rings 'oures twelve' it cannot be a funeral bell, like that at the end of *Songe vert*; Sk.'s n. suggests a clock striking midnight.

1329. *in myn honde ful evene*: 'right there in my hand'. Froissart's narrator renews his sense of his physical surroundings on waking by touching his bed (*Paradis d'Amours*, ll. 1689–92). The return to the situation at the beginning of the work in ll. 1311–34 is, as Burrow 1971: 64–9 points out, a frequent device at the end of late 14th-century works. For the concentric nest of framing devices in *BD*, see Phillips 1981, Davidoff 1988.

NOTES ON THE TEXT

Sources

There are four extant authorities for the text of the poem:

T Oxford Bodleian Library MS Tanner 346; mid-15th century, perhaps before 1450 (Robinson 1980: xix). *BD* is on fols 102–119^v. It lacks ll. 31–96, 288, 480, 886, 1257 and 1283. T also contains *PF* and *LGW* and several 'Chaucerian' texts, including Hoccleve's *Letter of Cupid*, Lydgate's *Temple of Glas* and *Complaint of the Black Knight*.

F Oxford Bodleian Library MS Fairfax 16; mid-15th century (Norton-Smith 1979: ix–xii). *BD* is on fols 130–47^v. The MS lacks ll. 31–96, 288 and 886 with spaces left for them, and 480 without a space. A 16th-century hand, usually assumed to be that of John Stowe, the Tudor historian and antiquary who published an edition of Chaucer in 1561, wrote in ll. 288 and 886. A 17th-century hand inserted ll. 31–96, probably from Stowe's 1561 text, an imperfect descendant of Th (see below) (Dickerson 1968: 56–8). It contains seven other poems by Chaucer, including *HF*, *LGW* and *PF*, and several Chaucerian texts, including *Epistle of Cupid* and *Temple of Glas*.

B Oxford Bodleian Library MS Bodley 638; after 1450–75 (Robinson 1980: xii) or 1475–1500 (Seymour 1995: 4). *BD* is on fols 110^v–41. The text is very close to that of F and they are probably from a common exemplar. It lacks ll. 24–96. A leaf has been lost before fol. 111, which probably contained ll. 24–30 and then a space like that in F. Ll. 288 and 886 are omitted and spaces left; ll. 480 and 791–2 are omitted without any spaces. It contains a similar range of material to F, including *BD*, *PF*, *LGW* and Lydgate's *Temple of Glas*.

Th Thynne's edition, *The Workes of Geffray Chaucer*, 1532. Th is the only source for ll. 31–96, 288, 477 and 886. It includes *HF*, *PF* and *LGW* as well as most of Chaucer's extant works and many Chaucerian texts.

Apart from the presence of ll. 31–96 in Th, there are no major differences between the four texts. F and B are probably derived from a common ancestor; T is close to them but also shares features with Th (Phillips 1986). As the notes below show, Th sometimes has a better reading than the MSS. Ll. 31–96 may have been lost from the MSS simply through a missing leaf in a common ancestor, though if Chaucer did write a separate work about Ceyx and Alcyone, as *LGW* possibly suggests, the task of integrating such a work into a longer *Book of the Duchess* may have resulted in the survival of a text in which the opening of the Alcyone episode was not neatly linked to the opening of *BD*. It is also possible that ll. 31–96 are spurious. On the text and this problem in particular, see Dickerson 1968; Blake 1981, 1986; Phillips 1986, 1993a: 62–75; Seymour 1995: 1–3; Minnis 1995: 79–80.

On titles for the poem, see Ellis 1995. F and B have the *Booke of the Duchesse*, Th has *The dreame of Chaucer*, T has *Chaucer's Dream* in a 16th-century hand that added other titles. The text in this edition is based on F, apart from lines found only in Th. Unless otherwise indicated, emendations are based on T, B and Th. *Abbreviations*: scribes do not use abbreviations completely systematically and it is impossible to expand them sensibly with complete consistency. Where they have been expanded here it has been with regard to the necessity of readability in a text of this kind. B is not cited separately unless its reading has significance for this text.

Selected textual notes

13. *adoun*] *adovun.*
19. *erthely*] *ertherli.*
22. *ne*[2]] *no* F.
26. *slain*] T, Th; F omits.
31–96. Only in Th. Added in a 17th-century hand in F.
35. *sothe*] *southe.*
80. *erme*] most eds; *yerne* Th.
100. *Aftir*] *And aftir* F.
109. *to*] Th; F, T omit.
123. *as*[1]] Th; *and* rest.
144. *Bid*] *Bud* F.
182. *erre*] *heere* F.
199. *her*] Th; *hys* rest.
215. *swowe*] *sorowe* F.
226. *I*] F omits.
271. *as*] F omits.
281. *he*] *ho* F.
288. Th; the rest omit; added in F in a 17th-century hand.
291. Enlarged initial capital *M.*
298 *as*] Th; *al* rest.
307. *herde*] *harde* F.
319. *mery*] T, B; *of mery* F; *many* Th.
334. *Of*[1]] *And* MSS, Th.
362. *many*] *may* F.
364. *I*] Th; the rest omit.
418. *Of*[1]] F.   *trees*] *of trees* F.
420. *or*] Th; *fro other* rest.
422. *Of*] *Or* F.
424. *brode*] Th; *bothe* rest.
446. *yturned*] Th, T; *turned* F, B.
448. *thoght*] *thogh* F.
475. *so*] *of so* F.

480. Th only; line omitted in MSS.
484–6. In order 486, 484, 485 Th.
499. *lym*] *hym* F.
509. *sorwe*] *sorwes* F.
512. *clepe*] *clepe the* F.
578. *the*] Th, T; F omits.
584. *wol*] *wolde* F.
599. *song*] Skeat and most eds; *sorowe* MSS, Th.
607. *sekenesse*] *sekernesse* F.
622. *she*²] Th; *she is* F, T.
627. *wrien*] Th; *varien* rest.
628. *monstres*] *mowstres* F.
647. *Ful*] Th; *For* MSS.   *she thus*] *thus she* F.
670. *thogh*] *thoght* F.
677. *had*] *as* F.
684. *she*] Th; *he* MSS.
711. *Thus*] *This* F.
722. *say*] Th; MSS omit.
745. *Loo, how that may*] *loo she that may* MSS; *Howe that may* Th.
754. *hereto*] Th; *here lo* MSS.
774–6. T's order is 775, 776, 774.
787. *konde*] *kende* F; *conde* T, B, Th.
828. *wel*] Th, T; *so wel* F.
830. *more*] Th; MSS omit.
831. *his*] F omits.
841. *And*] Th, B; *But* F, T.   *hert*] *hest* F.
854. *so*] *so a* F.
858. *gold*] F omits.
863. *overthwert*] *overtwert* F.
885. *knewe*] *knowe* F.
886. Th; T, B omit; added in a 17th-century hand in F.
889. *than*] T, Th; *that* F.
905. In F a 16th-century hand adds *blanche* in margin.
932. *hir*] *hit* F.
942. In F a 16th-century hand adds *blanche* in the margin.
949. In F a 16th-century hand adds *blanche* in the margin (referring to l. 948).
1025–6. Placed after 1042 in T.
1028. *to*] Skeat and some eds; *into* MSS, Th.
1042. *Lord* added in later hand in F.
1064. *therto*] Th; *to* MSS.   *also hardy*] T, Th, most eds; *also as hardy* F, B.
1104. *warysshed*] Th; *warshed* MSS.
1108. *in*] F omits.
1128. *reherse*] B; *to reherse* rest.   *it*²] F omits.

1137. *seyde he*] T; *he seyde* F; *sayd* Th.
1149. *be ryght*] *ryght be* F.
1155. *fro*] *so fro* F.
1161. *ne*] T, Th; *the* F; *to* B.
1173. *this*] Th; *thus* MSS.
1174. *werst*] Th; *first* MSS.
1223. *al*] *at* F.
1282. *the*] F omits.
1290. *contrayre*] *contrarye* F.
1298. *is*] omitted in F, added in a later hand; *she ys dede* added by a 16th-century hand in margin.

THE *HOUSE OF FAME*

INTRODUCTION

Date, verse, language and dreams

The *House of Fame* (*HF*) is twice acknowledged by Chaucer as his own work: in the list of his early work in the *Prologue* to the *Legend of Good Women* (l. 405 in this volume), and among the 'translacions and enditynges of worldly vanitees' which are mentioned at the end of the *Canterbury Tales* (I, l. 1086). The poem was also quite well known in its time. In the mid-1380s Thomas Usk paraphrased the narrator's and Dido's condemnation of male treachery (ll. 269–361) in his *Testament of Love* (II, ch. 3), and early in the fifteenth century Lydgate's *Temple of Glas* (which appears in all the manuscripts containing *HF*) contains a number of parallels and allusions.[1] Usk's allusions indicate that *HF* was in circulation by about 1385, and the allusion to *rekenynges* (l. 653), if it refers literally to Chaucer's book-keeping as Controller of customs, may mean that Book II at least was not begun before 1374.[2] The poem's interests, for instance in Boethius and the Troy story, might suggest a time of writing quite close to that of the *Boece* translation and the *Troilus* (i.e. the late 1370s or early 1380s), but attempts to date it more precisely (whether in relation to royal marriage negotiations or Chaucer's Italian journeys of 1372–3 and 1378) are at best speculative and at worst self-contradictory.[3]

The poem's metre also makes it likely (though not certain) to have been composed before the *Parliament of Fowls* (*PF*). The four-stress couplet, which was used in the *Book of the Duchess* (*BD*) and appears here for the last time in Chaucer's work, had been long established in Middle English verse. It had been the metre of earlier long vernacular poems such as the *Owl and the Nightingale* and romances such as *Sir Orfeo*, and was the chosen form of the major English work by Chaucer's contemporary, John Gower: the *Confessio Amantis*. A regular pattern of eight syllables to a line for this kind of verse appears to have been established quite early in Middle English poetry, but much of the vigour of *HF*'s verse is due to its frequent departures from this norm and from regular 'iambic' stress patterns, especially in Books II and III.[4]

HF shows consciousness of metre, including its own lack of a syllable or two (ll. 1096–8), and of language as well. The wordy eagle in Book II appropriately spends a good deal of time drawing attention to the very nature of *speche* and *langage* (e.g. ll. 761–863, 1025–31 and 1068–83), and his own vocabulary covers a wide range, from oaths, proverbs and colloquialisms to specialized terms from the art of poetry (ll. 622–3) and academic disputation (ll. 725–8, 871).[5] The extent to which introduction of what the eagle calls *termes of philosophie* is part of the poem's wider agenda is hard to assess. It has been claimed that *HF* introduces fifty-seven 'new' words from French, Italian or Latin, but it has also been pointed out that the significance of such borrowings 'varies infinitely', and that we need to know, for instance, 'the associations and status of every word, and whether specific applications of it would seem to contemporary hearers in any way out of the ordinary'.[6]

The definition of terms becomes an issue in *HF* almost from the very start. It is not just the causes and effects of dreams that are uncertain (ll. 2–5), but the very words used to describe them (*avision, revelacion, dreme, swevene, fantome, oracles*) seem confusing in their variety and, in several cases, unstable in their meanings. Even the old Anglo-Saxon word for 'dream', *swevene*, seems to have some particular application in line 9 that differs from its generic significance in line 3; and *avision* (ll. 7 and 40) has at least three meanings in *HF*. Already, then, in its first few lines the poem's terminology seems to be reflecting a stance on the narrator's part that has been characterized as 'neutral', 'offhand' or even 'slippery'.[7] Thus, by the time that the narrative of the dream itself begins on that specific but enigmatic 'tenth day of December' (l. 111), it has become apparent that this poem's view of visions is itself highly problematic and self-questioning.

Love and lies: from Dido to Yseult

Initially, *HF* looks like a love vision. Like *BD*, it addresses the subject of love and loss early on, and like *PF* it makes the first edifice in its landscape the temple of Venus. Venus is also the first 'figure' to appear in the dream (ll. 130–9), arising from the sea, as in myth and mythography,[8] adorned with rose-garland and doves, as in the *Knight's Tale* and the main manuscript of *HF*, and attended by her somewhat dysfunctional family (reckless Cupid and gloomy Vulcan).

The reworking of *Aeneid*, which occupies most of Book I, can be seen as, in some respects, the triumph of Venus – beginning with a quotation (of sorts) from Virgil's epic, but also acknowledging a further important source and emphasis by referring the reader to Ovid (l. 379), who is later in the poem to be exalted as 'Venus clerk' (l. 1487). Venus herself is invoked several times by the narrator, who seems, at this stage of the poem, to be her devotee (ll. 213, 465–7, 518–19), and it is not until the appearance of Jupiter's bird, the eagle, in Book II that her presence and influence in the poem begin to wane. In Book I, her glamorous appearance as a huntress (ll. 228–30) is initially allowed even to upstage the entrance of the book's most vividly portrayed human figure, Dido, who is much more plainly introduced as a queen subject to Venus's power.[9]

Dido, however, through her 'complaint' about Aeneas's desertion (ll. 300–61), finds a voice that gives her some affinity with the betrayed speaker in *Anelida and Arcite*, as well as to the Dido of the *Legend of Good Women*.[10] In this respect she differs considerably from the quiet (or totally silent) female figures in *BD* ('White') and *PF* (the female eagle). Dido's attitude towards Aeneas in *HF* is still characterized as to some extent 'foolish' (*nyce*, ll. 276, 287), as it is in *BD* (l. 734). But the text of Book I, as it moves from the Virgilian to the Ovidian version of events, accords her some power to 'write herself', even though the narrator is not allowed to relay 'all the words that she spoke', or 'what she wrote before she died' (ll. 376, 380), and the portrayal of how Dido was *yshamed* by Aeneas prompts the poem's first references not only to *Fame* (as Rumour, ll. 349–50) but also to *bokes* (l. 385).

The initial uses of the word *boke* in *HF*, like the example of Dido's love, implicitly address a problem that the poem will explore further. In its second occurrence the word refers to an authoritative witness to a woman's fidelity and trust (Ariadne's for Theseus, l. 426).[11] Yet only three lines later (l. 430) *the booke* is just as emphatically invoked to justify Aeneas's betrayal of Dido. These two closely adjacent instances seem, perhaps disturbingly, to emphasize the medium's capacity both to convey and celebrate 'truth' in love, whilst at more or less the same time compounding and perpetuating falsehood. *Fals and soth compouned* is a phrase that is twice used in the poem to describe the *tydynges* that come to be the object of the dreamer's quest (ll. 1029, 2108). It could also, as Chaucer's text shows, apply in several ways to the enterprises in which dreamers, storytellers and makers of books themselves are engaged. Even the illustrious Homer, on his column in Fame's hall, can be accused by a rival of having *made lyes* (l. 1477).

Fiction, storytelling and dreams are, of course, all 'lies' of a sort, but some kinds of lie are, as medieval critics from Augustine onwards recognized, more defensible than others.[12] In a defence of poetry completed not more than a decade before *HF*, Boccaccio had developed further the concept of what Dante had termed 'veiling truth with a beautiful lie',[13] confidently dismissing the notion that poetic inventions might be considered 'void and empty' and arguing that most fictions, from the *Aeneid* to the fireside folk-tale, can be found to convey some kind or degree of meaning 'hidden beneath the superficial veil of myth'.[14] Whether *HF* ultimately shares Boccaccio's degree of confidence in the validity of the poetic enterprise is open to question in this and other respects; but in a variety of ways – the handling of Aeneas's betrayal of Dido, the dreamer's forlorn quest for 'tidings of love', the difficulty of disentangling true report from falsehood, and the unanswered accusation that Homer 'just made things up' – Chaucer's text shows an implicit awareness of the problems.

A few more specific passages from *HF* may provide material for further discussion of these problems. In the invocation to Book II, for instance, the appeal to Venus for *favor* (ll. 518–19) could be compared with that in *PF*, lines 113–19, and strongly suggests that some aspect of love is to be the continuing subject of the poem. Yet how does this hopeful prayer relate to the fearful plea for protection against 'illusion' that the dreamer in the desert has just expressed (ll. 492–5), or to the bewildering multiplicity of *tydynges / Of Loves folke* with which he is about to be confronted (ll. 674–99)?

It might be argued that from this point on love, true or false, becomes merely one aspect of the poem's concern with the subject of multiplicity itself. By the time the dreamer has disembarked at the House of Fame after the eagle's lecture-tour in Book II he has been (albeit reluctantly) drawn back to the 'first principles' of sound and speech behind the *tydynges* (ll. 729–852), reminded of his role and craft as writer (ll. 853–63, 1000–10), and warned through several dire examples (the myths of Icarus and Phaëthon) of the dangers of taking on more than one can manage.[15] When he reaches Fame's hall in Book III Venus is mentioned again, for the last time and at some distance, as the inspirer of her *clerk*, Ovid (l. 1487); by this time, however, it seems that love poetry has become but one of the many forms of writing with which *HF* is concerned.

Yet connections between love and fiction continue to be suggested quite late in the poem. The sixth and seventh groups of Fame's petitioners (ll. 1727–1810) are those who have been idle all their lives and yet seek *gret renoun*, particularly as lovers (ll. 1739–62). For these (and there seems no reason to distinguish between the claims of the two groups), love is itself a fiction, a 'void and empty invention' – to use Boccaccio's words (see above, n. 14) or (to use their own) the *name* rather than the *body* (ll. 1759–61). Fame's response to these two groups is characteristically inconsistent: she instantly colludes with the fiction in the first case

(l. 1763) and savagely demolishes it in the second (ll. 1776–99). Her conclusion is particularly pertinent here, when, to the losers in this lottery, she scathingly suggests they would like people to think that *bele Isawde* (Yseult) herself could not refuse them her love (ll. 1796–7). Yseult, the mistress of Tristan, is to appear again, along with Dido, among the great lovers depicted on the wall of Venus's temple in *PF* (ll. 289–90). She was one of the most prominent heroines of medieval romance, and Fame's mocking allusion here may imply that these clients' fantasies have themselves been shaped by the reading of romantic fiction. Does the irony here perhaps also extend to those who collude with such fantasies by writing *bokes, songes or ditees* in honour of Venus and Cupid, yet are left behind in the actual 'dance' of love?[16]

Poets, pilgrimages and quests: Boccaccio, Petrarch, Dante, Alanus of Lille, Boethius

Boccaccio's ideas about poetry (quoted in the previous section) provide a context if not a source for *HF*'s poetics. His own poetry, particularly the *Filostrato* and the *Teseida*, forms a significant part of the range of Italian literature with which Chaucer was becoming familiar during the 1370s. Another of Boccaccio's early poems, the *Amorosa Visione*, invokes Venus at the start of its second canto and leads the dreamer into the 'great hall' of worldly Glory (canto IV), where the attendant poets include Virgil, Homer, Lucan, Ovid and Statius (V); and it reverts on a number of occasions to the situation and complaints of betrayed women, including Dido. Common tradition and the influence of Ovid's *Heroides* accounts for much of the resemblance between this and *HF*, but it seems clear nonetheless that the two works share a similar poetic agenda.[17]

There are also some parallels between *HF* and the three sections on Fame in the *Trionfi* by Boccaccio's friend and contemporary, Petrarch. In one version of the latter work a couple of authors are shown (as in Chaucer's hall of Fame) in dispute over the true version of the Troy story.[18] Chaucer could well, during his second visit to Italy in 1378, have come into contact with further evidence of the Petrarchan cult of fame, in the form of the frescoes at Padua that had been commissioned in the late 1360s and were based on one of Petrarch's Latin works, *De viris illustribus* ('Of Famous Men').[19]

Neither Petrarch nor Boccaccio is actually named in *HF*. Dante, however, is: he makes his first appearance in the poem (and in English) as an authority on Hell, alongside Virgil and Claudian towards the end of Book I (l. 450). The passage that runs from this appearance to the eagle's swoop upon the dreamer contains much that represents a new departure, both for 'Geffrey' and for Chaucer. Amongst other things, it reflects the diversity of *HF*'s responses to this Italian poet. For Dante's presence within this passage (ll. 450–592) takes three distinct (if related) forms. Initially, he appears beside the two classical writers in a position that reflects his status as a modern *auctor*: the only vernacular writer, apart from Petrarch, to whom Chaucer ever gives the title of *poete*.[20] Secondly, Dante's poem is a main source for Chaucer's narrative at this point, although one that gets significantly altered in the 'translation' process. The eagle that sweeps up the pilgrim in *Purgatorio* IX, lines 19–33, is part of the pilgrim's dream, not a 'real' figure in the poem, and apart from its golden feathers and 'terrible descent like lightning' it is not realized in detail; whereas in *HF* the monstrous bird is encountered close at hand as a *grym* reality with 'paws', 'sharp nails' and 'strong claws' (ll. 541–6). And thirdly, both the narrator's invocation and the dreamer's speech in this passage on occasion actually recall Dante's, particularly the mixture of confidence and doubt that characterizes poet and pilgrim in the second canto of *Inferno*.[21]

The narrator's invocation to Book II of *HF* also finds Chaucer's first verbal allusions to Dante coinciding with his first appeal to the poetic Muses. Invocations to the Muses are quite commonplace in classical and medieval Latin, but for the vernacular poets of the fourteenth century they represent a new and quite audacious assertion of purpose and status. It seems quite likely that Chaucer is following Dante's example in being the first poet in his vernacular to invoke the Muses.[22] This feature of *HF* can be seen as part of a larger agenda here as well as in other poems of this period in Chaucer's writing, especially *Anelida*, *PF* and *Troilus & Criseyde*.[23] For, through following Dante's precedent and at times appropriating Dante's invocatory language, Chaucer positions his own poetic enterprise in relation to the *Commedia*'s announcements of new departures in vernacular writing. *HF* is itself, both seriously and comically, all about beginnings and new departures – not only in the invocation to Book II, but also in the appeal to Apollo at the opening of Book III.

The invocation to Book III of *HF* is tonally an odd mixture, and its oddness could be taken to epitomize the poem's stance with regard to the *Commedia*. Together with some quite close echoes of Dante's ambitious, laurel-seeking invocation to Apollo at the opening of *Paradiso* (for instance, in ll. 1101, 1103 and 1109), there is also some distinctly un-Dantean disclaiming of skill (ll. 1094–1100) – an unsettling combination, which resembles in some respects the way in which Chaucer is to invite comparison between his 'boat' and Dante's in the proem to Book II of *Troilus*. The seriousness with which Chaucer in such passages regards Dante's *craft* as

model or precedent has been given varying degrees of emphasis by modern
critics, but most of them seem to find in his response to the *Commedia* in *HF*
a measure of ambition combined with some degree of tentativeness or
scepticism.[24]

One of the many ways in which Chaucer here differs significantly from
Dante is the representation of pilgrimage. Through his evocations of the idea
of pilgrimage in *Purgatorio* and *Paradiso* Dante affirms both the energy and
direction of a personal vision (as in *Purg.* IX, ll. 16–18, or *Par.* I, l. 51) and a
sense of communal purpose (as in *Purg.* II, l. 63, or XIII, ll. 94–6). Chaucer in
HF also alludes to pilgrimage quite frequently, but his most positive view of it
is reflected in the eagle's oath (ll. 885–6), where *seynt Jame* is rhymed with
game in a way that perhaps signals a genial alternative to the arduous
journey to Compostella. Otherwise the attitude is merely neutral
(ll. 1928–30), cryptic (l. 117) or outrightly satirical, as in the final association of pilgrims with falsehood in lines 2122–4.[25] This last instance finds
Chaucer rather more in tune with Langland than with Dante. The B-text of
Piers Plowman is thought to have been written 'between about 1377 and
1379',[26] and is hence very close to the probable time of *HF*'s composition. In
its Prologue (ll. 46–52) Langland shows pilgrims going to Compostella or
Rome 'with many wise tales' and gaining licence therafter to lie for the rest of
their lives. His description of their speech as 'tempred to lye / Moore than to
seye sooth' comes very close to Chaucer's representation of the mixture of
truth and falsehood in his House of Rumour and in particular to *HF*'s
representation of pilgrims bearing bagfuls of lies *entremedled* ('mingled')
with tydynges (ll. 2123–4).

Other forms and traditions of journey and quest are also explicitly
invoked by Chaucer in *HF*. One important example – and one that
indicates a significant strand in Chaucer's reading and thinking during the
composition of both *HF* and *PF* – is the long (c. 4,500-line) medieval
Latin poem by Alanus of Lille, the *Anticlaudianus* (dated 1181–4). The
Anticlaudianus is mentioned by name (along with its main source, the
late-classical *De nuptiis Philologiae et Mercurii* of Martianus Capella) as
one of the authorities on the nature of *hevens region* in Book II of *HF*
(ll. 985–6), just as Dante was named in Book I as an *auctour* on the
subject of Hell. Chaucer was clearly influenced to some degree by
Alanus's rather ponderous account of Prudence's quest for the soul of the
perfect man in Books IV–VI of the *Anticlaudianus*. He may well have been
particularly interested in the way that Alanus's spirits or 'wandering
citizens' of the sphere of air (Chaucer's *citezeyns* and *eyryssh bestes* in *HF*,
ll. 929–34 and 964–9) are said to confound truth with falsehood.[27] In
conveying the fears and misgivings of his more reluctant voyager here (*HF*,

ll. 979 and 1015–16), Chaucer may also have had in mind the opening of Book V of the *Anticlaudianus*, which shows Prudence in a similarly troubled and bedazzled state and even (like Phaëton) having some difficulty controlling the horses of her space-chariot.[28] The eventual outcomes are in distinct and perhaps (on Chaucer's part) deliberate contrast. At the end of Book IX of Alanus's poem, the triumph of the New Man in the battle against the Vices brings the return of a golden age in which he, unaffected by lust, pride or the entanglements of deception (*fraudis … error*), authoritatively 'guides the earthly kingdom with the reins of law'.[29] In Book III of *HF*, on the other hand, an atmosphere of expanding and intensifying confusion precedes and accompanies the final appearance of Chaucer's *man of grete auctorite*.

Both Alanus and Chaucer were affected in their representation of celestial journey and quest by developments in Boethius's *Consolation of Philosophy*. The passage Chaucer chooses to quote just after naming Boethius (ll. 972–8) is significant from this point of view: it comes from the speech in the fourth Book of the *Consolation* (IV, met. 1) in which the Philosophy of Chaucer's translation, like the eagle, promises to equip her pupil's thought with 'swifte fetheris that surmounten the heighte of the hevene' and enable him (like Phaëton?) to join 'his weies with the sonne'. Boethius is also a precedent for the distrust of earthly glory and fame, as well as one of the sources for *HF*'s description of Fame herself and possibly also the Muses that stand around her throne.[30] There are many other thematic and verbal parallels between Boethius's *Consolation* and *HF*, especially in Book II of the poem,[31] and, given the commonly accepted dating of the *Boece* translation in the late 1370s or early 1380s, it is quite possible that Chaucer was working on the two texts at about the same time. The eagle's *swifte fetheris* and *swift thoght* ultimately bring his captive audience to a kind of destination and vision that is very different from the one Lady Philosophy promises: that of 'the worschipful lyght [or] dredefulle clerenesse of God … the schynynge juge of thinges, stable in hymself' (*Boece* IV, met. 1, ll. 27–32). But the journey they encompass in Book II could be seen in some quite literal senses as a 'translation', a 'carrying over' of the dreamer and writer from one world to another.

Further translations: from 'grete clerkys' to 'jugelours' and beyond

'In the end *all* poetry' (according to one Romantic poet and critic) 'is translation' – yet of these four dream poems *HF* is the one that, in several senses, is more of a translation than the others.[32] To say this is not to attempt to rouse again the hoary old question of whether *HF* is the *Daunte in Ynglissh* with which Lydgate later, and rather enigmatically, credited Chaucer[33] – but rather to suggest that the poem could usefully be seen in relation to the various translation projects of its author and its time.

As a poem of the late 1370s or early 1380s, *HF* comes early in a period when the question of translation and vernacular literacy was, in England at any rate, becoming increasingly politicized.[34] The debate focused with particular sharpness upon the issue of translating the Bible and other sacred texts, as is demonstrated, for example, by the 1387 *Dialogue between a Lord and a Clerk* (which is itself a translation) by the Oxford scholar John Trevisa.[35] Trevisa also translated, somewhat later than *HF*, a Latin encylopaedic work that Chaucer, too, appears to draw upon in both *HF* and *PF*: Bartholomaeus Anglicus, *De proprietatibus rerum* ('On the Properties of Things'), for a variety of subjects, from the harmony of the spheres to the behaviour of magnetized iron.[36]

Among Chaucer's own translation projects, one (the version of Boethius) has already been mentioned; another was his reworking of the Troy story that was to culminate in *Troilus*. Evidence of this reworking is apparent at several points in *HF*. In Book I, for instance, the account of Aeneas's journey begins with a description of the fall of Troy (ll. 151–92) in which Chaucer gives more detailed attention to Virgil's text than he does anywhere else in the poem. The 'matter of Troy' and its conflicting versions becomes a subject of the poem's concern again in Book III (ll. 1464–80), where the disagreement between Homer and his anonymous critic (ll. 1475–80) sets the tone for the review of 'alle these clerkes'. Whether or not the 'Lollius' mentioned here (l. 1468) is to be identified with the Boccaccio whose version of the tragic Trojan love story in *Filostrato* is the main source for the *Troilus*, his presence is one more declaration of interest on Chaucer's part in questions of truth and falsehood relating to Troy.[37]

Of the *clerkes* identified in the hall of Fame, the one whose influence on *HF* itself is most pervasive is 'Venus clerk, Ovide'. Even the most avowedly Virgilian part of Chaucer's poem (Book I) presents the story of Dido increasingly and, in the end, explicitly through Ovid's version (*Heroides* VII, to which the reader is referred in ll. 379–80). Ovid's *Metamorphoses* is the very first (and perhaps the very last) classical text to be drawn upon in *HF*.[38] His identification as *Venus clerk* (l. 1487) reflects his status as a love poet and myth-maker who was influential on other major texts and writers that Chaucer knew (such as the *RR*, Dante, Gower), and whose work was the subject of a substantial commentary tradition (e.g. the *Ovide moralisé*) to which *HF* is also indebted.[39] A number of the formative myths in *HF* (such as those of Morpheus, Ganymede, Daedalus and Phaëthon) have all or part of their genesis in Ovid's *Metamorphoses*, and his description of the House of Rumour (*Met.* XII, ll. 39–63) has been seen as 'the embryo of Chaucer's poem'.[40] In going back to the first principles of its subject – to Creation itself and the origins of change – *HF* has also been thought to be formally 'the closest of Chaucer's poems to the *Metamorphoses*'.[41] And Chaucer's enigmatic *man of grete auctorite* who appears and instantly disappears at the end of *HF* could himself be partially descended from Ovid's equally anonymous *novus auctor* (*Met.* XII, l. 58), as a typical contributor to the mingling of truth and falsehood in the ever-turning mill of Rumour.

Among the more modern *grete clerkys* who may have contributed to *HF*'s learned scepticism are biblical commentators such as the Dominican, Robert Holcot (d. 1349(?));[42] the various logicians and grammarians who set the agenda for the discussion of language in the fourteenth century;[43] and adventurous speculative scientists of the 1370s and 1380s, such as the Parisian masters, Nicole Oresme (d. 1382) and Henry of Langenstein (d. 1397).[44] But the poem seems concerned not only with 'translating' the ideas of illustrious *clerkes* in the arts and sciences. It is also interested in the techniques of anonymous craftsmen, from masons to lead-smelters and gun-masters,[45] and in the skills of performers, from Orpheus to Colle the *tregetour*.

Orpheus, as he appears on the façade of Fame's castle (ll. 1201–3), indeed shows a pre-eminent degree of *craft* as a performer, but he is, in Chaucer's text, far from being the divine poet-theologian that he is, for example, in Boccaccio's mythography.[46] His harping, superlative as it is, places him among the motley crowd of *mynstralles* and *gestiours* (ll. 1197–1200), and he heads a line of performers that include *jugelours* and other kinds of illusionists (ll. 1259–81). The verb *pleyen* itself is used here in a way that seems to link Orpheus's music to the weird conjuring tricks of 'Colle tregetoure' (ll. 1201, 1259, 1279), and, like other features of this passage, it seems to imply not a celebration of illustrious 'craft' (let alone *art poetical*), but rather an interest in various (and sometimes nefarious) performing skills.

'Lousy jugglers', as the fastidious devil in the *Friar's Tale* calls them, continue to occupy the borderlands between fiction and deception in Chaucer's later writing.[47] Their presence at this stage in *HF* contributes significantly to the poem's 'hybrid' nature, as a work that mingles writing and oral culture, the learned and the *lewed*, *grete clerkys* and *mynstralles*, the perfume of roses and the fumes from the lead-furnace, the illustrious and the grotesque.

Elements of the grotesque are increasingly in evidence in the final book of *HF*. The figure of the ape – traditionally associated both with art and with folly – appears at several points here (ll. 1189, 1212 and 1806).[48] The final group of Fame's clients erupts into the already rather shambolic proceedings as a gang of fools (ll. 1823–41). And the poem's final location, the hectic and ramshackle House of Rumour, appears to be entirely dominated by grotesque images, sounds and activities – by multiple *entrees* and manifold *gyges, chirkynges, rounynges* and *jangles*. This last scene of the poem was probably what a later seventeenth-century critic had in mind when he compared London to the poets' 'House of Fame', as 'a City where all the noises and businesses in the World do meet'.[49] It also appears to have inspired Pope in *The Temple of Fame* (1711) to imitate Chaucer by evoking 'Projectors, Quacks and Lawyers' in a way that prefigures the urban follies of the *Dunciad*.[50]

The appearance of 'fools' and the references to folly, laughter and 'play' in the closing stages of *HF* (ll. 1805–10, 1823–41, 1972, 2018, 2133) perhaps strengthen the case for associating this December dream with 'winter foolery'.[51] The poem's final scenes reflect the difficulty of distinguishing not only between truth and falsehood but also between wisdom and folly, and its lack of formal closure has even been taken as a sign of an 'open', 'infinite' (rather than incomplete) structure.[52] Whatever, though, may be thought of the vision's 'conclusion in which nothing is concluded', it looks from this standpoint in the quest as if the answer to the eagle's earlier rhetorical question about giving a fool control over a journey (ll. 957–9) may not be quite so simple as it first appeared.

Nick Havely

1. For the Lydgate parallels see *Temple of Glas*, ed. J. Schick (1891), EETS (e.s.) LX, ll. 6–7, 19, 36, 39, 53, 58–9, 144, 533–5, 706, 1303–5. See also Lydgate's *Fall of Princes*, ed. H. Bergen (1924), EETS (e.s.) CXXIII, Book VI, ll. 108–19.

2. For documents about Chaucer's appointment and work as Controller of the wool custom, see Crow & Olson 1966: 148–9.

3. For examples of such theories, see Howard 1987: 257–9 and Fisher 1977: 564.

4. See, for example, ll. 872, 896–903, 1425, 1515, 1623, 2044, 2053, and for discussion of this kind of metre, Smithers 1983.

5. On oaths, etc., see Elliott 1974: 244–7, 267, 372; and on the vocabulary of logic and disputation, see Burnley 1989: 162–4.

6. Brewer in Brewer 1966: 27, against Davis in Brewer 1974: 73. The Davis essay is an excellent brief survey of Chaucer's English; for a fuller account see Burnley 1989.

7. Eldredge 1970: 110; Miller 1986: 188; Peden 1985: 68.

8. See note on ll. 130–9.

9. Contrast the introduction of Dido in *LGW*, ll. 1035–43.

10. *A&A* is generally thought to be quite close to *HF* in the time of its composition (see *Riv.*, p. 991) and in some of its other features (Clemen 1963: 197–203).

11. It is not certain, however, what actual *boke* Ch had in mind here, since Ovid (*Her.* X) does not tell the whole story as far as Ariadne's desertion is concerned. See the note on ll. 405–26, below.

12. For a summary of medieval theory in this area and quotation of Augustine's distinction between 'fictitious' and 'mendacious' feigning, see Minnis & Scott 1991: 209–11.

13. Dante thus defines the 'allegorical sense' of texts in *Conv.* II, ll. 1, 3; for a translation see Minnis & Scott 1991: 396.

14. *Geneal* XIV, ch. 10, tr. Osgood 1956: 52–4.

15. On the 'theme of poetic discretion' in *HF*, see Simpson 1986.

16. See the eagle's earlier characterization of 'Geoffrey' as writer in *HF*, ll. 615–40 and 666–8. The persona in Chaucer's *balade* 'To Rosemounde' (*Riv.*, p. 649) is described (self-mockingly?) as 'trewe Tristam the secounde' (l. 20).

17. For the argument that Chaucer and Boccaccio were both, early in their careers, 'grappling with remarkably similar problems' and struggling 'to accommodate the influence of Dante within a French-derived dream poem format', see Wallace in Boitani 1983: 145 and Wallace 1985: 6.

18. See Bennett 1968: 109–10 and Boitani 1984: 122–3.

19. These frescoes (obliterated in 1779) were in the Sala dei Giganti of the Reggia Carrarese at Padua and had been commissioned by Petrarch's friend, Francesco il Vecchio da Carrara; see Plant 1987: 181–8. On the cult of fame in fourteenth-century Italy, see Boitani 1984: 73–131.

20. On the meanings of the term, see Olson 1979: 272–90 and Brownlee 1984: 7, 220–1. For its application to Dante, see *WB T*, l. 1125 and *Mk T*, ll. 2460–1; and to Petrarch, *Cl Prol*, l. 31.

21. See especially *HF*, ll. 523–8 & n., 588 & n.

22. For Dante's usage, see the *Grande Dizionario della lingua italiana*, *s.v. Musa*[1], senses 1, 3 & 4. For Chaucer's, see *MED*, *Muse* n. a–d. The earliest recorded uses of the word in English are probably those in *HF*, l. 1399 and Ch's *Boece* translation, e.g. I, met. 1, l. 4; pr. 1, l. 44.

23. See also, e.g.: *A & A*, ll. 15–20; *PF*, ll. 85–7, 127–40; *TC* II, ll. 1–7.

24.   See, for instance: Bennett in Boitani 1983: 107; Boitani in Boitani 1983: 120; *Riv.*, p. 348. On the contrasts within the invocation to Book III of *HF,* see Gellrich 1985: 179; Wallace in Boitani & Mann 1986: 23; Russell 1988: 191. Recent approaches to *HF* that emphasize the sceptical features of its reading of the *Commedia* are Ellis 1988: 282–4; Taylor 1989: ch. 1, esp. 39; Kiser 1991: ch. 2, esp. 32, 40.

25.   For further references to pilgrimage in *HF,* see the note on ll. 115–18, below. On pilgrimage generally at this time, see Hall 1965 and Sumption 1975.

26.   A.V.C. Schmidt, in Langland, ed. Schmidt 1978: xvi.

27.   Alanus of Lille, *Anticlaudianus*, ed. Bossuat 1955: IV, l. 284; tr. Sheridan 1973: 128.

28.   *Anticlaudianus*, ed. Bossuat 1955: V, ll. 1–82; tr. Sheridan 1973: 138–9.

29.   *Anticlaudianus*, ed. Bossuat 1955: IX, ll. 387–90; tr. Sheridan 1973: 215–16.

30.   For the Boethian view of fame, see, e.g., *Cons.* II, pr. 7, which may be alluded to in *HF,* l. 907; also Koonce 1966: 23–32; Bennett 1968: 110–12; Boitani 1984: 46–7. On the sources of *HF*'s description of Fame and the varying interpretations of the Muses' song, see the notes on ll. 1360–94 and 1395–1406, below.

31.   See, for instance, the notes on ll. 730–6, 754–6, 761–822, 784, 907 and 972–8 below.

32.   The quotation is from a letter by Friedrich Novalis (1772–1801) to A.W. Schlegel on 30 Nov. 1797, as cited and translated in S. Prawer, *Comparative Literary Studies* (London, 1973), p. 86 (for the original see *Novalis, Briefe und Dokumente*, ed. E. Wasmuth (Heidelberg, 1954), pp. 367–8).

33.   Lydgate's phrase is in the Prologue to *The Fall of Princes*, ed. H. Bergen (1924), EETS (e.s.) CXXI, Book I, l. 302.

34.   For a helpful brief survey of the situation, see Coleman 1981: 35–43.

35.   For an edition of Trevisa's *Dialogue*, see Burrow & Turville-Petre 1996. On Trevisa's career, see Coleman 1981: 40–1, and more fully D.C. Fowler, *John Trevisa* (Aldershot and Ashfield, VT, 1993). For a later, more polemical text on the subject of biblical translation, see C. Bühler, 'A Lollard Tract on Translating the Bible into English', *M Ae* VII (1938), pp. 167–83.

36.   The modern edition of Trevisa's translation is by Seymour (see under 'Bartholomaeus Anglicus' in Bibliography). For examples of Chaucer's possible use of Bartholomaeus, see the notes on *HF,* ll. 21–2 and 29–30, and *PF,* ll. 57–63 and 148–51.

37.   See the note on ll. 1464–74, below. Troilus himself is mentioned among the victims of Venus in *PF,* l. 291.

38.   See the notes on ll. 66–76 and 2158, below.

39. On *HF* and the *Ovide moralisé*, see Delany 1968.
40. Bennett 1968: 72; see also the note on ll. 711–24, below.
41. Fyler 1979: 24. For further discussion of Chaucer and Ovid, see both Fyler 1979: esp. 23–64, and Cooper in Martindale 1988: 71–88.
42. For Holcot's discussion of Fame, see Boitani 1984: 141–9, and on his career and work in general, see Smalley 1960: 133–202.
43. On linguistic theory in and around *HF*, see Delany 1972: ch. 2; Boitani 1984: 212–15; Irvine 1985: 850–76.
44. On Oresme, see Delany 1972: 20–1 and Kruger 1992: 140–9; and for a lucid account of Henry of Langenstein's ideas, especially in his *Lectures on Genesis* (1386–93), see Steneck 1976.
45. On masonry and architectural terms in *HF*, see Braswell 1981. On medieval technology in general, the most relevant surveys are in White 1962 and Gimpel 1988.
46. See *Geneal* XIV, l. 8, tr. Osgood 1956: 44–6.
47. See *Fri T*, ll. 1467–8; *Sq T*, ll. 217–19; *Fkl T*, ll. 1139–51.
48. On these aspects of 'ape lore', see Janson 1952: 201–2 and 287–94.
49. Thomas Sprat, *History of the Royal Society* (1667), p. 42.
50. Pope, *Temple of Fame*, ll. 458–65. A relevant study of the grotesque in relation to 'low' urban locations (although it makes no specific reference to *HF*) is P. Stallybrass and A. White, *The Politics and Poetics of Transgression* (London, 1986), esp. the discussion of marketplace and fair, pp. 27–44.
51. See Billington in Williams 1979: 40–2.
52. Thus, for example, Boitani 1984: 208. For arguments against this view and suggestions that the ending may simply have been lost in the process of textual transmission, see Blake 1984: 66; Edwards 1989: 82; and Burrow 1991: 37.

THE *HOUSE OF FAME*

[BOOK 1]

	God turne us every dreme to goode!	
	For hyt is wonder, be the Roode,	*Cross*
	To my wytte, what causeth swevenes	*thinking; dreams*
	Eyther on morwes or on evenes,	
5	And why th'effecte folweth of some	
	And of some hit shal never come;	
	Why that is an avision	
	And why this a revelacion,	
	Why this a dreme, why that a swevene,	
10	And noght to every man lyche evene –	
	Why this a fantome, why these oracles,	
	I not – but who so of these meracles	*don't know; whoever*
	The causes knoweth bet then I	*better than*
	Devyne he, for I certenly	
15	Ne kan hem noght, ne never thinke	*don't understand*
	To besely my wytte to swinke	
	To knowe of hir signifiaunce	
	The gendres, neyther the distaunce	
	Of tymes of hem ne the causis,	
20	Or why this more then that cause is –	
	As, yf folkys complexions	

1–2. For other appeals to divine power, see below, ll. 57–8, 97. Invocation of the Cross (*Roode*, ll. 2, 57) may also recall the practice of placing a cross at the start of a piece of writing (see Barr 1993: 213).

3–11. Dreams near dawn (ll. 4–6) were thought to be more trustworthy than those occurring early in the night; cf. Dante, *Inf.* XXVI, l. 7, and Kruger 1992: 72. Various types of dream are referred to here: *avision* (l. 7, 'precognitive dream'); *fantome* (l. 11, 'delusion'); and *oracles* (l. 11, 'revelatory dreams'). On medieval classifications of dreams, see Lewis 1964: 63–4; Kruger 1992: 17–82.

5. 'And why some come true'.

16. 'To overburden my brain'.

17–18. *of hir signifiaunce / The gendres*: 'the classification of their meanings'.

21–2. *complexions ... reflexions*: the belief that some dreams presented images reflecting the dreamer's temperament (*complexion*) is also expressed in *NPT*, ll. 2926–36, and in Bartholomaeus Anglicus, *On the Properties of Things*, ed.

	Make hem dreme of reflexions –	
	Or elles thus, as other sayn:	
	For to grete feblenesse of her brayn,	*As a result of*
25	By abstinence or by sekenesse,	
	Prison, stewe or grete distresse –	*confinement*
	Or ellis by dysordynaunce	*disturbance*
	Of naturell acustumaunce,	*habits*
	That some man is to curiouse	
30	In studye, or melancolyouse –	
	Or thus: so inly ful of drede	
	That no man may hym bote bede;	*offer remedy*
	Or ellis that devocion	*prayer*
	Of some and contemplacion	*On the part of*
35	Causeth suche dremes ofte;	
	Or that the cruelle lyfe unsofte	
	Whiche these ilke lovers leden,	
	That hopen over muche or dreden –	
	That purely her impressions	*their reactions*
40	Causeth hem avisions;	*Cause them (to have)*
	Or yf that spirites have the myght	
	To make folke to dreme anyght –	
	Or yf the soule, of propre kynde,	
	Be so parfit as men fynde	
45	That yt forwote that ys to come,	*foreknows what*
	And that hyt warneth al and some	

Seymour 1975: I, 336–7.

28. 'Of one's usual way of life'.

29–30. On dreams engendered by mental preoccupations, see also *PF*, ll. 99–108, and Bartholomaeus, *Properties*, ed. Seymour 1975: I, 336 (ll. 31–2) and 338 (l. 4).

39–40. *Impressions* are emotional reactions; *avisions* here (contrast l. 7 above) seem to be the kind of dreams that merely reflect the preoccupations of waking life.

41–8. On dreams caused by *spirites*, see Kruger 1992: 43–53. The belief that the soul can attain divinely 'perfect' vision in sleep (ll. 43–5) is also expressed by Dante in *Purg.* IX, ll. 16–18, and *Conv.* II, chs 8, 13.

43. *of propre kynde*: 'through its very nature'.

44. *fynde*: 'learn through experience'.

45. *forwote that*: 'knows beforehand what'.

Of everiche of her aventures
Be avisions or be figures –
But that oure flessh ne hath no myght   *Except that*
50   To understonde hyt aryght,
For hyt is warned to derkly.
But why the cause is noght wot I.
Well worth of this thyng grete clerkys
That trete of this and other werkes –
55   For I of noon oppinion
Nyl as now make mensyon,   *Shall not*
But oonly that the holy Roode
Turne us every dreme to goode!
For never, sith that I was borne,   *since*
60   Ne no man elles me beforne
Mette, I trowe stedfastly,   *Dreamt*
So wonderful a dreme as I
The tenthe day, now, of Decembre –
The which, as I kan now remembre,
65   I wol yow tel everydele.   *in full*
        But at my gynnynge, trusteth wele,   *opening*
I wol make invocacion

48. *be figures*: 'through symbols' (*MED figure* n. 3(a)).

51. 'Because it [the body, "flesh"] is warned too obscurely'. Cf. St Paul in 1 Cor. 13:12.

53–4. 'Good luck to those men of great learning who discuss this and other matters'. Authorities on this subject would, in Ch's 'book', probably include Chalcidius, Macrobius, Augustine and Gregory the Great; see Lewis 1964: 63–4; Kruger 1992: 58–9, 61; Introduction, above, p. 121 and nn. 42, 44.

63. The date is repeated at l. 111 below. It could be evidence for the year or occasion of the poem's composition (see Bevington 1961: 292; Leyerle 1971: 249–51), or an ironic departure from the spring-time conventions of love-vision (Bethurum 1959: 514; Miller 1986: 51), or a kind of Joycean ploy to puzzle the professors (see Gellrich 1985: 181; Pearsall 1992: 113). Other winter dates for dream visions are in Machaut, *Jugement dou Roy de Navarre* (9 Nov.) and Froissart, *Le Joli Buisson de Jonece* (30 Nov.).

66–76. Cf. the description of Somnus, Morpheus and the dark land of the Cimmerians in Ovid, *Met.* XI, ll. 592–649, and the adaptation of the passage by Ch in *BD*, ll. 153–91. *Invocacion* (l. 67) is the earliest use of the word recorded in the *MED*. This is the first passage in *HF* to be given marginal glosses in the manuscripts (see Notes on the Text).

	With special devocion	
	Unto the god of slepe anoon,	*at once*
70	That duelleth in a cave of stoon	
	Upon a streme that cometh fro Lete –	*Lethe*
	That is a floode of helle unswete –	
	Besyde a folke men clepeth Cymerie;	*Cimmerians*
	There slepeth ay this god unmerie	*always; gloomy*
75	With his slepy thousande sones,	
	That alwey for to slepe hir wone is.	
	And to this god that I of rede	*speak of*
	Prey I that he wolde me spede	*help me*
	My swevene for to telle aryght,	*correctly*
80	Yf every dreme stonde in his myght.	*control*
	And he that mover is of al	*originator*
	That is and was and ever shal,	*shall be*
	So yive hem ioy that hyt here	*hear it*
	Of alle that they dreme to yere,	*this year*
85	And for to stonde al in grace	
	Of her loves, or in what place	
	That hem were levest for to stonde,	
	And shelde hem fro poverte and shonde	*harm*
	And fro unhappe and eche disese;	*accident*
90	And sende hem alle that may hem plese	
	That take hit wele and skorne hyt noght,	*understand*
	Ne hyt mysdeme in her thoght	*Nor; despise it*
	Thorgh maliciouse entencion.	*antagonism*
	And who so, thorgh presumpcion	*arrogance*
95	Or hate or skorne, or thorgh envye,	
	Dispite or jape or vilanye,	
	Mysdeme hyt, pray I Ihesus God	*Christ*
	That – dreme he barefote, dreme he shod –	

71–2. 'Lethe, which is a bitter river of Hell'. Cf. Claudian, *De raptu Proserpinae* I, l. 282 (Pratt 1947: 423 & n. 31).

76. 'Whose way of life it is to sleep all the time'.

81. Reflects the Aristotelian view of God as 'unmoved mover'; cf. *Kn T*, l. 3004, and *Boece* III, met. 9, ll. 5–7.

85–6. *stonde al in grace / Of*: 'find success in'.

96. *dispite ... jape ... vilanye*: 'spite ... frivolity ... boorishness'.

98. The line could refer simply to dreaming in bed or out, but it might also be an ironic allusion to the academic reputation of the 'barefoot' friars.

	That every harme that any man	
100	Hath had syth the worlde began	
	Befalle hym therof or he sterve,	
	And graunte he mote hit ful deserve!	*may; fully*
	Loo, with suche a conclusion	*result*
	As had of his avision	
105	Cresus that was kynge of Lyde,	*Croesus; Lydia*
	That high upon a gebet dide,	
	This prayer shal he have of me –	
	I am no bet in charyte.	
	Now herkeneth, as I have yow seyde,	
110	What that I met or I abreyde.	*before; awoke*
	Of Decembre the tenthe day,	
	Whan hit was nyght, to slepe I lay	
	Ryght ther as I was wonte to done	*Just where; used*
	And fille on slepe wonder sone,	
115	As he that wery was forgoo	*was tired out*
	On pilgrymage myles two	
	To the corseynt Leonarde,	
	To make lythe of that was harde.	
	But, as I slept, me mette I was	
120	Withyn a temple ymade of glas,	

101. *therof*: 'because of this [despising the dream]'; *or he sterve*: 'before he dies'.

105. Croesus, king of Lydia (c. 560–546 BC) was believed to have foreseen his death in a dream. See *RR*, tr. Horgan 1994: 99–101; *Mk T*, ll. 2727–60; *NPT*, ll. 3138–40.

108. 'This is the full extent of my goodwill'.

109. The same 'oral narrative' formula recurs at the start of the poem's second Book (l. 509). Similar phrases are frequent at the start of romances (e.g. *Sir Orfeo*, l. 23). On this kind of address to a listening audience, see Burrow 1982: 50–5.

115–18. The first of several allusions to pilgrimage in the poem (cf. ll. 885, 1131, 1183, 2122–3).

117. *corseynt*: saint (whose body is the object of pilgrimage).

118. 'To smooth out (make easy) what was difficult'. The problem to be 'smoothed out' may have something to do with St Leonard's role as protector and deliverer of prisoners (cf. above, l. 26, and Sumption 1975: 158, 174).

120. Bennett (1968: 11) thinks the *glas* of the temple may signify 'love's insubstantiality'. A poem by Lydgate that was much influenced by *HF* is called *The Temple of Glas*.

	In which ther were moo ymages	*more images*
	Of golde, stondynge in sondry stages,	*various levels*
	And moo ryche tabernacles	*canopied niches*
	And, with perré, moo pynacles	*gemstones*
125	And moo curiouse portreytures	*fine carvings*
	And queynt maner of figures	*intricate kinds*
	Of olde werk then I sawgh ever.	
	For certeynly, I nyste never	*had no idea*
	Wher that I was, but wel wyste I	*knew*
130	Hyt was of Venus, redely,	*obviously*
	The temple, for in portreytoure	
	I sawgh anoonryght hir figure,	*at once*
	Naked, fletynge in a see,	*floating*
	And also, on hir hede, pardee,	*indeed*
135	Hir rose garlonde white and rede	
	And hir combe to kembe hyr hede,	*to comb*
	Hir dowves and Daun Cupido,	*doves; Lord Cupid*
	Hir blynde sone, and Vulcano,	
	That in his face was ful broune.	
140	But as I romed up and doune	
	I fonde that on a walle ther was	
	Thus writen on a table of bras:	*plate*
	'I wol now say, yif I kan,	
	The armes and also the man	
145	That first came, thorgh his destanee,	
	Fugityfe of Troy contree,	

122–7. On Ch's use of architectural terms (e.g. *stages, pynacles, tabernacles*) here and elsewhere in *HF*, see Braswell 1981: 102–8.

130–9. On Venus's association with the sea and its metaphorical implications, see Fulgentius, tr. Whitbread 1971: 66; and for the use of *fleten* in the context of erotic *blisse*, cf. *TC* III, l. 1221. An image of the sea-borne Venus is also portrayed with rose-garland, doves and blind Cupid in the temple in *Kn T*, ll. 1955–66. For a detailed discussion of the iconography, see Twycross 1972: esp. 6–14, 70–93, 86–8. The inclusion of *Vulcano* (Vulcan), Venus's husband, here is an ironic touch, alluding to the myth of his discovery of Venus's adultery with Mars (cf. *Kn T*, ll. 2383–92); his *broune* ('dark') face recalls the description of him in *RR*, ll. 13834–8, as 'ugly' and 'sooty from his forge' (tr. Horgan 1994: 213).

143–8. A distorted rendering of Virgil, *Aen*. I, ll. 1–3; see Pearsall 1992: 114 and Edwards 1986.

In Itayle with ful moche pyne,   *great difficulty*
Unto the strondes of Lavyne ...'   *shores; Lavinium*
And tho began the story anoon
150   As I shal telle yow echon.   *you all*
First sawgh I the destruction
Of Troy throgh the Greke Synon,
With his fals forswerynge,
And his chere and his lesynge
155   Made the hors broght in to Troye,
Thorgh which Troyens lost al her joye.
And after this was grave, allas,   *engraved*
How Ilyon assayled was   *Ilium*
And wonne, and Kynge Priam yslayne
160   And Polite his sone, certayne,   *Polites*
Dispitously of Daun Pirrus.   *Cruelly by*
And, next that, sawgh I how Venus,
Whan that she sawgh the castel brende,   *was burning*
Downe fro the hevene gan descende

149–50. Unlike Virgil, Ch begins the story with an account of the fall of Troy (cf. *Aen.* II). His version then describes Aeneas's voyage to Carthage (*Aen.* I) and love affair with Dido and concludes (below, ll. 433–67) with a very brief summary of *Aen.* V–XII. On his treatment as a way of 'medievalizing' the *Aeneid*, see Hall 1963: 148–59.

151. *sawgh I*: similar phrases describe the narrator's 'reading' of the story in ll. 162, 174, 193, etc. (see Miller 1986: 51; Kolvé 1984: 41–2). A precedent for rendering the fall of Troy in visual form is Virgil, *Aen.* I, ll. 446–93; cf. *LGW*, ll. 1023–9 and Carruthers 1987: 186–7.

152–6. The story of the wooden horse and Sinon's trickery is told in *Aen.* II, ll. 13–249. Ch's summary here contains the first references to deception in *HF* (*fals forswerynge, chere, lesynge*), and his portrayal may well have been affected by the 'artfulness' of Virgil's Sinon in *Aen.* II, ll. 77–194. Cf. also Dante, *Inf.* XXX, esp. ll. 112–15, and Alanus, *De Planctu Naturae*, tr. Sheridan 1980: 217.

153–4. '(Who) with his false perjury, feigned friendship and lies'.

155. *Made the hors broght*: 'caused the [wooden] horse to be brought'. For the syntax here, see Mustanoja 1960: 605–6 and *Kn T*, l. 1913, *MLT*, l. 171 and *Cl T*, l. 1098.

159–73. Cf. *Aen.* II, ll. 526–58 (on the Greek warrior Pyrrhus's killing of Priam, King of Troy, and Polites, his son), ll. 588–620 (Venus's appearance) and ll. 717–20 (the rescue of Anchises).

165	And bad hir sone Eneas flee,	*Aeneas*
	And how he fled and how that he	*how he*
	Escaped was from al the pres	*mêlée*
	And tooke his fader Anchises	
	And bare hym on hys bakke away,	*carried*
170	Cryinge 'Allas' and 'Welaway' –	*Woe*
	The whiche Anchises in hys honde	*This; hands*
	Bare the goddes of the londe,	*images (of gods)*
	Thilke that unbrende were.	*Those; not burnt*
	And I saugh next in al thys fere	*in this group*
175	How Creusa, Daun Eneas wife,	
	Which that he lovede as hys lyfe,	*Whom*
	And hir yonge sone Julo	*Julus*
	And eke Askanius also	
	Fledden eke with drery chere	
180	That hyt was pitee for to here;	*to hear*
	And in a forest as they wente,	
	At a turnynge of a wente,	*path*
	How Creusa was yloste, allas,	
	That dede (not I how) she was;	
185	How he hir soughte, and how hir goste	*ghost*
	Bad hym to flee the Grekes oste	*army*
	And seyde he most unto Itayle,	*must go*
	As was hys destanye sauns faille;	*without doubt*
	That hyt was pitee for to here,	
190	When hir spirite gan appere,	*appeared*
	The wordes that she to hym seyde	
	And for to kepe hir sone hym preyde.	*keep safe; son*
	Ther sawgh I grave eke how he,	
	Hys fader eke and his meynee,	*also; followers*
195	With hys shippes gan to saylle	
	Towardes the contree of Itaylle	
	As streight as that they myghte goo.	

177. *Julus* was originally another name for Ascanius, not a separate person (as Ch appears to have thought).
179. *drery chere*: 'sorrowful faces'.
181–92. In *Aen.* II, l. 739, Aeneas says that Creusa may have strayed from the path or fallen through exhaustion. She reappears as a prophetic ghost in *Aen.* II, ll. 772–94.
184. 'And so died, I know not how'.

	Ther saugh I the, crwel Junoo,	*you (thee)*
	That art Daun Jupiters wife,	
200	That hast yhated al thy lyfe	
	Alle the Troianyssh bloode,	*Trojan race*
	Renne and crye as thou were woode	
	On Eolus the god of wyndes	*To Aeolus*
	To blowe, oute of alle kyndes,	
205	So lowde that he shulde drenche	*drown*
	Lorde and lady, grome and wenche	*boy and girl*
	Of al the Troian nacion	
	Withoute any savacion.	
	Ther saugh I suche tempeste aryse	
210	That euery herte myght agryse	*be terrified*
	To see hyt peynted on the walle.	
	Ther saugh I graven eke withalle,	*alongside*
	Venus, how ye, my lady dere,	
	Wepynge with ful woful chere,	*expression*
215	Prayen Jupiter an hye	*above*
	To save and kepe that navye	*preserve*
	Of the Troian Eneas,	
	Syth that he hir sone was.	*Since*
	Ther saugh I Joves Venus kysse	*Jupiter*
220	And graunted of the tempest lysse.	
	Ther saw I how the tempest stent,	*ceased*
	And how with alle pyne he went	*with much trouble*
	And prevely toke arryvage	

198–211. The narrative here turns to events described at the start of *Aen.* I, where 'cruel Juno', the goddess hostile to Troy (l. 4), summons Aeolus to raise a storm and sink the Trojan fleet (ll. 8–123).

199. *That art*: '(You) who are'.

202. 'Run wild and cry, as if you were mad'.

204. *oute of alle kyndes*: 'in a wild, disorderly way'.

208. 'Without anyone being spared'(*MED savacioun* n. 1(b)).

212–20. Ch here conflates two episodes from *Aen.* I (ll. 124–56 and 227–96). By making Venus appear more responsible for the calming of the storm, he gives her role more prominence; see Rand 1926: 222; Kittredge 1915b: 78.

220. *of the tempest lysse*: 'relief from the tempest'.

221–38. Cf. *Aen.* I, ll. 157–222 and 305–401. Aeneas later reproaches Venus for teasing him with 'illusions' (ll. 407–8).

223. 'And secretly came ashore'.

	In the contree of Cartage;	*Carthage*
225	And on the morwe how that he	*the next day*
	And a knyghte highte Achate	*called Achates*
	Metten with Venus that day,	
	Goynge in a queynt array	
	As she had ben an hunteresse,	*As if*
230	With wynde blowynge upon hir tresse;	*hair*
	How Eneas gan hym to pleyne,	
	Whan that he knewe hir, of his peyne,	
	And how his shippes dreynte were,	*sunk*
	Or elles lost, he nyste where;	*knew not*
235	How she gan hym comforte thoo	
	And bad hym to Cartage goo,	*told*
	And ther he shulde his folke fynde	
	That in the see were lefte behynde.	
	And, shortly of this thyng to pace,	
240	She made Eneas so in grace	
	Of Dido, quene of that contree,	
	That, shortly for to tellen, she	
	Became hys love and lete hym doo	
	Al that weddynge longeth too.	
245	What shulde I speke more queynte,	*more delicately*
	Or peyne me my wordes peynte,	
	To speke of love? – hyt wol not be;	

228. *queynt array*: 'elegant costume' (cf. *Aen.* I, ll. 314–20).

231–2. 'How Aeneas, when he recognized her, began to bewail his misfortunes'.

239. 'And, to touch only briefly on this subject'. For other 'abbreviating formulae' in Ch's treatment of the story at this stage, cf. ll. 242, 245–8, 251–2 (see also Miller 1986: 56).

240–1. *so in grace / Of*: 'so favoured by'.

241–4. On Dido in the Middle Ages, see Lord 1969 and Desmond 1994. The allusion to *weddynge* (l. 244) perhaps recalls *Aen.* IV, l. 172 ('she calls it marriage').

244. 'Everything that has to do with marriage'.

245. *more queynte*: 'in a more elaborate way'.

246. 'Or strive to find fine expressions'. The image of 'painted words' perhaps alludes to the traditional 'colours' (ornaments) of rhetoric (see below, l. 859) and may also derive in part from the visualizing of Virgil's text here (cf. *peynted* in l. 211).

I kan not of that faculte.
And eke to telle the manere
250   How they aqueynteden in fere –   *came together*
Hyt were a longe processe to telle,   *story*
And ouer longe for yow to dwelle.   *spend time on*
          Ther sawgh I grave how Eneas
Tolde Dido euery caas   *event*
255   That hym was tyd upon the see,   *befell him*
And after grave was how shee
Made of hym, shortly, at oo worde,   *to be brief*
Hyr lyfe, hir love, hir luste, hir lorde –   *beloved; delight*
And did hym al the reverence
260   And leyde on hym al dispence
That any woman myght do,
Wenynge hyt had al be so
As he hir swore, and herby demed   *she thus judged*
That he was good, for he suche semed.
265   Allas, what harme doth apparence   *outward show*
Whan hit is fals in existence!   *in reality*
For he to hir a traytour was,
Wherfore she slowe hir selfe, allas.   *killed*
          Loo, how a woman doth amys   *goes wrong*
270   To love hym that unknowen ys;
For, be Cryste, lo, thus yt fareth: *so it goes*
Hyt is not al golde that glareth.   *glitters*
For, also browke I wel myn hede,

248.   'I do not have that kind of learning'.
253–5. Aeneas's narrative of his voyage occupies most of *Aen.* III. Cf. the
         eagerness of Dido to hear the story of Troy in *LGW*, ll. 1150–5.
256–7. 'Then it was shown how she / Made him ...'
260.   *leyde ... dispence*: 'spent (all the) money'.
264.   On Aeneas's outward appearance, see also *LGW*, ll. 1066–74.
267.   The main medieval adaptations of the *Aeneid* do not represent Aeneas as
         'traitor', but he has this reputation in a number of other works (e.g. *RR*, l.
         13162, tr. Horgan 1994: 203); cf. *LGW*, ll. 927, 1236f. and 1328. For other
         references to him as seducer, see Clemen 1963: 84.
272.   For the proverb, see Whiting 1968: G 282, and for other proverbial phrases
         see below, ll. 290–1, 351–2, 361, 681, 698, 957–9, 1147, 1257–8, 1783–5,
         1810, 2078–80, 2140.
273.   *browke*: 'may I keep, use'.

	Ther may be, under godelyhede	*fair appearance*
275	Kevered, many a shrewde vice.	*disguised; wicked*
	Therfore be no wyght so nyce	*person; naïve*
	To take a love oonly for chere	*just on looks*
	Or for speche or for frendly manere.	
	For this shal every woman fynde –	
280	That some man, of his pure kynde,	
	Wol shewen outwarde the fayrest	
	Tyl he have caught that what him lest,	
	And than wol he causes fynde	
	And sweren how that she ys unkynde	
285	Or fals, or prevy double was.	
	Alle this sey I be Eneas	
	And Dido and hir nyce lest	*foolish desire*
	That loved al to sone a gest.	*stranger*
	Therfore I wol seye a proverbe:	
290	That he that fully knoweth th'erbe	*the herb*
	May safly ley hyt to his yë,	*apply; eye*
	Withoute drede, this ys no lye.	*Without doubt*
	But let us speke of Eneas,	
	How he betrayed hir, allas,	
295	And lefte hir ful unkyndely.	
	So, when she saw, al utterly,	
	That he wolde hir of trouthe fayle	
	And wende fro hir to Itayle,	
	She gan to wringe hir hondes two.	
300	'Allas,' quod she, 'what me ys wo!	
	Allas, is every man thus trewe,	

280. On falsehood as the *kynde of man*, cf. *A & A*, l. 149, and *LGW*, ll. 2447–51 (where Demophon is said by *nature* to inherit his father Theseus's tendency to treachery).
282. 'Until he has got what he wanted'.
285. *prevy double was*: 'was secretly two-timing'. Arcite accuses Anelida of *doublenesse* (to cover his own *traitorie*) in *A & A*, ll. 155–61.
287. *nyce*: cf. above, l. 276, and the reference to Dido as *fool* in *BD*, l. 734. In *LGW* the adjective used of Dido and trusting women is the slightly (but significantly) different *sely* (ll. 1157, 1237, 1254, 1336).
296. *al utterly*: 'quite plainly'.
297. 'That he was going to break his promise to her'.
300. *what me ys wo*: 'how wretched I am'.

	That every yere wolde have a newe –	*a new lover*
	Yf hit so longe tyme dure –	
	Or elles three, peraventure?	*perhaps*
305	As thus: of on he wolde have fame	*through one*
	In magnyfyinge of hys name,	*To make famous*
	An other for frendshippe, seyth he –	
	And yet ther shal the thride be	
	That shal be take for delyte,	
310	Loo, or for synguler profite.'	
	In suche wordes gan to pleyne	*lament*
	Dydo of hir grete peyne,	*because of*
	As me mette, redely –	
	Non other auctour alegge I.	
315	'Allas,' quod she, 'my swete hert,	
	Have pitee on my sorwes smert	*bitter grief*
	And slee mee not – goo noght awey.	
	O woful Dido, weleaway!'	*alas*
	Quod she to hir selfe thoo.	*then*
320	'O Eneas, what wol ye doo?	
	O, that your love ne your bonde	
	That ye have sworne with your ryght honde,	
	Ne my crewel deth,' quod she,	
	'May holde yow stille here with me –	

303. 'If it lasts even that long [i.e. a year]'.
305. *fame*: the first occurrence of the word as a common noun in *HF*. For the others see the Glossary, and for Fame personified see the Index of Names.
306. *name*: the word occurs with higher frequency in *HF* than in any other of Ch's works, partly because it provides a rhyme with *fame* (particularly in Bk III).
310. *synguler profite*: 'his own special advantage'.
313. 'As I dreamt, for sure'. This takes the place of phrases like *sawgh I grave* (l. 253).
314. 'I will cite no other source'. The line seems to suggest that the dream has achieved a certain authority of its own. The noun *auctour* is not used elsewhere in *HF*, and Miller (1986: 58) argues that this is 'the most forceful statement we have yet had of authorial independence'.
321–4. Aeneas's breaking of his pledge is intermittently mentioned in the later part of *Aen.* IV (ll. 305, 366, 373, 421, 597), but his faithlessness is emphasized much more in Ovid, *Her.* VII, ll. 5–6, 8–9, 17–18, 30, 67f. and 81f.

325	O haveth of my deth pitee!	*have*
	Iwys, my dere hert, ye	*Truly*
	Knowen ful wel that never yit,	
	As ferforth as I had wytte,	
	Agylte [I] yowe in thoght ne dede.	*Have I wronged*
330	O, have ye men suche godelyhede	
	In speche, and never a dele of trouthe?	*jot; sincerity*
	Allas, that ever hadde routhe	*pity*
	Any woman on any man!	
	Now see I wel and telle kan,	
335	We wrechched wymmen konne noon arte,	
	For certeyne, for the more parte,	*in most cases*
	Thus we be served, euerychone.	*treated; all of us*
	How sore that ye men konne groone –	
	Anoon, as we have yow receyved,	
340	Certeynly we ben disceyved.	*are*
	For, though youre love laste a seson,	
	Wayte upon the conclusyon	*Look for*
	And eke how that ye determynen,	*end up*
	And for the more part dyffynen.	
345	O, weleaway that I was borne!	*alas*
	For thorgh yow is my name lorne	*good name lost*
	And al myn actes red and songe	*deeds related*

325. Cf. *Aen.* IV, l. 318. For another appeal by Dido to Aeneas's *pite*, see *LGW*, ll. 1311–24; cf. also *A & A*, l. 337.

326–9. Cf. Anelida's rebuke in *A & A*, ll. 256–63.

328. 'As far as I was able'.

332–3. *routhe*: Dido's pity for Aeneas is mentioned in *Aen.* I, ll. 303–4, 597, 628–30, and IV, ll. 373–5. Cf. also *LGW*, ll. 1078–81, 1237, 1257; and for a male lover's appeal for the lady's *routhe*, see *PF*, l. 427.

335. *konne noon arte*: 'have no craft, sophistication'. In the early books of *Aen.* 'craft' (*ars*) is attributed to Sinon (II, ll. 106, 152, 195) and Venus (I, l. 657). In *LGW* (ll. 1257, 1266, 1286) guile is more explicitly imputed to Aeneas.

338. *How sore that*: 'however desperately'.

339. *receyved*: 'accepted (as lover)'.

342. *conclusyon*: 'outcome'. This and *determynen* and *dyffynen* are academic terms; see Burnley 1989: 164.

344. *dyffynen*: 'turn out in the end' (*MED diffinen* v. 2(a)).

346–8. Cf. *Aen.* IV, ll. 321–3. Dido in *LGW* (l. 1361) also laments her loss of *name*; cf. Criseyde in *TC* V, ll. 1058–62.

	Over al thys londe, on every tonge.	
	'O wikke Fame! – for ther nys	*wicked*
350	No thinge so swifte, lo, as she is.	
	O, sothe ys, every thinge ys wyste,	
	Though hit be kevered with the myste.	*shrouded in*
	Eke, though I myght dure ever,	*live for ever*
	That I have do rekever I never,	
355	That I ne shal be seyde, allas,	
	Yshamed be thourgh Eneas –	
	And that I shal thus juged be:	
	"Loo, ryght as she hath now, she	
	Wol doo efte sones, hardely" –	
360	Thus seyth the peple prevely.	*among themselves*
	But that is do is not to done.'	
	But al hir compleynt ne al hir moone,	*lamentation*
	Certeyn, avayleth hir not a stre.	*straw*
	And, when she wiste sothely he	
365	Was forthe unto his shippes goon,	
	She in to hir chambre wente anoon	
	And called on hir suster Anne	*Anna*
	And gan hir to compleyne thanne,	*to lament*
	And seyde that she cause was	*was the reason*
370	That she first loved, allas,	
	And thus counseylled hir thertoo.	
	But, what! when this was seyde and doo,	*well!; done*

349–50. The first appearance of personified *Fame* in *HF*. The description is based on that of *Fama* ('Rumour') in *Aen.* IV, l. 174, which is quoted in the margin by two of the manuscripts of *HF* (F and B, see Notes on the Text, p. 216).

351. *ys wyste*: 'becomes known'.

352. *myste*: 'secrecy (mist)'.

354. 'I shall never make good what I have done'.

356. 'To have been shamed by Aeneas'.

359. 'She'll surely do again'.

361. 'But what is done is not to be done (again)'.

362–3. Cf. *LGW*, l. 1325.

364–74. Summarizes *Aen.* IV, ll. 397–705. Cf. *LGW*, ll. 1325–51, where the verbs *avayleth*, *compleyned* and *rof* also recur.

371. 'And had persuaded her to do so'. In Virgil, Dido's regrets about taking Anna's advice (here ll. 369–71) are expressed indirectly in a soliloquy (*Aen.* IV, ll. 548–9).

	She rofe hir selfe to the herte	*stabbed*
	And dyed thorgh the wounde smerte.	*grievous wound*
375	And al the maner how she dyede	
	And al the wordes that she seyde –	
	Who so to knowe hit hath purpos,	*intends*
	Rede Virgile in *Eneydos*	*the* Aeneid
	Or the epistile of Ovyde,	*epistle*; *Ovid*
380	What that she wrote er that she dyde.	*(For) what*; *before*
	And, ner hyt were to longe t'endyte,	
	Be God, I wolde hyt here write.	
	But, weleaway! – the harme, the routhe	*mischief*
	That hath betyd for suche untrouthe,	
385	As men may ofte in bokes rede	
	And al day se hyt yet in dede –	*in action*
	That for to thynken hyt a tene is.	
	Loo, Demophon, duke of Athenys,	
	How he forswore hym ful falsly	*broke his word*
390	And traysed Phillis wikkidly –	*betrayed*
	That kynges doghtre was of Trace –	
	And falsly gan hys terme pace.	
	And when she wiste that he was fals,	
	She henge hir selfe ryght be the hals,	*hanged*; *by the neck*
395	For he had doo hir suche untrouthe –	*been so disloyal*

378. The first occasion on which Virgil is named by Ch.
379. Refers to the seventh epistle of Ovid's *Heroides* (letters mostly by famous women to absent lovers). The same phrase (*epistel of Ovyde*) is used of *Heroides* in general as a text about *trewe wyves* in *LGW*, ll. 305–6.
381. 'And were it not that it would be too long a story to tell'.
384. 'That has followed upon such disloyalty'.
385. *bokes*: the first three instances of the word in *HF* occur close together (here, and ll. 426, 429).
387. 'Which is distressing to think about'.
388–426. The examples of male treachery derive chiefly from *Her.* (II, III, V, VI, IX, X and XII) and from *RR*, ll. 13143–234 (tr. Horgan 1994: 203–4), which lists Phyllis, Oenone and Medea as other victims, following Dido. Cf. also the list of traitors in *BD*, ll. 725–34 (see David 1960: 337) and the reappearance of most of the same figures (Dido, Aeneas, Jason, Hypsipyle, Medea, Theseus, Ariadne, Phaedra, Phyllis, Demophon) in *LGW*.
391. 'Who was the daughter of the king of Thrace'.
392. *his terme pace*: 'passed the time set [for his return]'.

142   The *House of Fame*

> Loo, was not this a woo and routhe?
> Eke, lo, how fals and reccheles   *uncaring*
> Was to Breseyda Achilles   *Briseis*
> And Paris to Enone   *Oenone*
400 And Jason to Isiphile   *Hypsipyle*
> And efte Jason to Medea   *later*
> And Ercules to Dyanira,   *Hercules; Deianira*
> For he left hir for Yole –   *Iole*
> That made hym cache his deth, parde.   *indeed*
405 How fals eke was he, Theseus,
> That, as the story telleth us,
> How he betrayed Adriane –   *Ariadne*
> The devel be hys soules bane!   *destroy his soul*
> For – had he lawghed, had he loured –   *frowned*
410 He moste have be devoured,   *would surely have*
> Yf Adriane ne had ybe;
> And, for she had of him pite,   *because*
> She made hym fro the dethe escape;
> And he made hir a ful fals jape,   *played; trick*
415 For aftir this, withyn a while,
> He lefte hir slepynge in an ile,   *island*
> Deserte, allone, ryght in the se,   *Abandoned*
> And stale away and lete hir be,   *stole; left her*
> And tooke hir suster Phedra thoo   *Phaedra*
420 With him and gan to shippe goo.
> And yet he had yswore to here   *her*
> On all that ever he myght swere
> That, so she saved hym hys lyfe,   *if*

397–404. Brief examples of women betrayed by mythical heroes: Briseis (see *Her.* III, *MLT*, ll. 70–1); Oenone (*Her.* V, *TC* I, ll. 562–65); Hypsipyle (*Her.* VI, *LGW*, ll. 1396–1579); Medea (*Her.* XII, *Kn T*, l. 1944, *CA* V, ll. 3227–4222). Deianira unintentionally poisoned Hercules because of his love for Iole (see *Her.* IX, *Met.* IX, ll. 134–272, *Mk T*, 2095–2142).

404. 'That indeed was what caused his death'.

405–26. Ariadne, the Cretan princess, fell in love with Theseus, the Athenian hero, and enabled him to find his way out of the Labyrinth (see below, l. 1921) after killing the Minotaur. She fled with him but was abandoned on the island of Naxos (see *Her.* X, *Met.* VIII, ll. 172–6, *LGW*, ll. 1886–2227; also Frank 1972: 111–13 and Doob 1990: 317).

409. 'For, whatever he had done [lit.: "had he laughed or frowned"]'.

	He wolde have take hir to hys wife –	*taken*; *as*
425	For she desired no thinge ellis,	
	In certeyne, the booke tellis.	*For sure*
	But – to excusen Eneas	
	Fullyche of al his trespas –	
	The booke seyth Mercuri, sauns fayle,	*no doubt*
430	Bad hym goo in to Itayle	
	And leve Auffrikes regioun	*the land of Africa*
	And Dido and hir faire toun.	
	Thoo sawgh I grave how that to Itayle	
	Daun Eneas is goon to sayle,	
435	And how the tempest al began	
	And how he lost hys steris-man,	*helmsman*
	Which that the stere, or he toke kepe,	
	Smote over borde, loo, as he slepe.	
	And also sawgh I how Cybile	*the Sibyl*
440	And Eneas, besyde an yle,	*near an island*
	To helle went, for to see	
	His fader, Anchyses the free;	*noble Anchises*
	How he ther fonde Palinurus	*found*
	And Dido and eke Deiphebus,	
445	And every turment, eke, in helle	
	Saugh he, which is longe to telle –	

426. *tellis*: for the pres. 3 sg. form here (*-s* as opposed to Ch's usual *-(e)th*), cf. below, l. 1908. Such forms also appear in *BD*, ll. 73 and 257, although Ch later abandons them (see Elliott 1974: 21 and Burnley 1989: 127).

429. Mercury is traditionally represented as messenger of the gods (cf. *Aen.* IV, ll. 222–78, and *Kn T*, ll. 1384–92).

433–8. Summarizes the account of Aeneas's voyage to Italy in *Aen.* V. With *Thoo sawgh I grave* (l. 433) the narrator returns to 'his original pose as transcriber' (Miller 1986: 61); see above, l. 151. The helmsman lost by Aeneas was Palinurus (see below, l. 443, and *Aen.* V, ll. 835–71 and VI, ll. 347–62); Grennen (1984: 256–7) suggests that his fate reflects the 'poor governance theme' in *HF* and compares ll. 957–9.

437. 'Whom the rudder, before he was aware of it'.

439–46. Summarizes *Aen.* VI: Aeneas's journey to the underworld (guided by the Sibyl), where he meets again Palinurus, Dido, Deiphebus (his brother) and Anchises.

	Which, who so willeth for to knowe,	*wishes*
	He moste rede many a rowe	*line (of verse)*
	On Virgile or on Claudian	
450	Or Daunte, that hit tellen kan.	*Dante*
	Tho saugh I grave al the aryvayle	*landing*
	That Eneas had in Itayle	
	And with kynge Latyne hys tretee	*dealings*
	And alle the batayles that hee	
455	Was at hym selfe and eke hys knyghtis,	
	Or he had al ywonne hys ryghtis;	*Before*
	And how he Turnus reft his lyfe	*deprived Turnus of*
	And wanne Lavyna to his wife,	*won Lavinia as*
	And alle the mervelouse signals	*portents*
460	Of the goddys celestials;	*heavenly gods*
	How, mawgree Juno, Eneas –	*in spite of*
	For al hir sleight and hir compas –	*plots; contrivances*
	Acheved alle his aventure,	*quest*
	For Jupiter tooke of hym cure,	*care*
465	At the prayer of Venus,	*Because of*
	The whiche, I prey, alwey save us	*Who*
	And us ay of oure sorwes lyghte.	
	When I had seen al this syghte	
	In this noble temple thus,	
470	'A, lorde,' thought I, 'that madest us!	

447–50. The references are to Virgil in *Aen.* VI, the *De raptu Proserpinae* of Claudius Claudianus (d. c. AD 404), especially II, ll. 330–50, and Dante's *Inferno*. Claudian, like Virgil, appears later in the Hall of Fame (below, ll. 1507–12); on Ch's knowledge of his work, see Pratt 1947. The reference to Dante is the first in Ch's work and the first known appearance of his name in English.

451–60. Summarizes *Aen.* VI–XII, which include Aeneas's negotiations with King Latinus of Latium and his defeat of the Italian hero Turnus who was his rival for Lavinia, daughter of Latinus. The *mervelouse signals* referred to may be those in *Aen.* XII, ll. 244–56 and 843–86.

462. 'For all her plots and contrivances'.

467. 'And always relieve our suffering'.

470. For similar invocations see below, ll. 584, 646, 970. The image of God as craftsman was widespread in the Middle Ages; see Curtius 1953: 544–6. On the relationship between divine and human 'craft', see Lynch 1988: 14; and for late 14th-century views of God's 'workmanship', see Steneck 1976: 29.

	Yet sawgh I never such noblesse	*excellence*
	Of ymages, ne suche richesse	
	As I saugh grave in this chirche!	
	But not wote I whoo did hem wirche,	*made them*
475	Ne where I am, ne in what contree.	
	But now wol I goo oute and see,	
	Ryght at the wiket, yf I kan	*side-gate*
	See owghwhere any stiryng man	
	That may me telle where I am.'	
480	When I oute at the dores came,	
	I faste aboute me behelde;	*gazed intently*
	Then sawgh I but a large felde	*just*
	As fer as that I myghte see,	*far*
	Withouten toune or house or tree	*dwellings*
485	Or bussh or gras or eryd londe,	*ploughed*
	For al the felde nas but sonde,	*was just sand*
	As smale as man may se yet lye	*fine; still see lying*
	In the desert of Lybye.	*Libya*
	Ne I no maner creature	*kind of being*
490	That ys yformed be Nature	*created by*
	Ne sawgh, me to rede or wisse.	*advise; direct (me)*
	'O Criste,' thought I, 'that art in blysse –	

473. *chirche*: use of this term to describe Venus's temple may seem slightly comical, but the word is occasionally used in ME of non-Christian places of worship (see *MED chirche* n. 2).
478. 'See anyone about anywhere'.
482–8. Ch's field of sand has become a playpit for a wide range of interpretations. For some it reflects desolation attendant upon the love represented by Venus's temple (see Koonce 1966: 126; Bennett 1968: 47), or various kinds of creative failure or disenchantment (Clemen 1963: 89; Fichte 1980: 71–2). To others it suggests 'new spaciousness', 'new potential' or the kind of profusion that is imaged through *greynes ... of sondes* later (l. 691); (e.g. Delany 1972: 58; Miller 1986: 61–2, 190; Fyler 1979: 41). Cf. the *hille of sonde* on which Patience sits outside Venus's temple in *PF*, l. 243.
489–91. 'Nor could I see any kind of ... to advise or guide me'.
490. The first reference to Nature in *HF* (cf. below, ll. 1366, 2039). On Nature as craftsman, see Economou 1972: 19–27; and cf. above, l. 470 & n.
492–5. Cf. above, l. 11 & n. On the range of meanings of *fantoume*, see Delany 1972: 58–68; and on *illusion* as a deceptive dream caused by demonic action, see Kruger 1992: 45, 47 (on *inlusio*, the Latin term).

Fro fantoume and illusion   *apparitions; deceptions*
Me save!' and with devocion
495   Myn eyen to the hevene I caste.   *eyes; raised*
Thoo was I war, at the laste,   *aware*
That, faste be the sonne, as hye   *close to; high*
As kenne myght I with myn yë,
Me thought I sawgh an egle sore –   *soaring*
500   But that hit semed moche more   *much larger*
Then I had any egle seyne.
But this as soothe as deth, certeyne: *this (is) as true*
Hyt was of golde and shone so bryght
That never saugh man suche a sight,
505   But yf the heven hadd i-wonne   *Unless; gained*
Alle new of gold another sonne –   *A bright new golden sun*
So shon the egles fethres bryght,
And somwhat dounward gan hyt lyght.   *descend*

[BOOK 2]

Now herkeneth, every maner man
510   That Englissh understonde kan
And listeneth, of my dreme to lere,
For now at erste shul ye here   *only now*
So sely an avisyon   *marvellous dream*
That Isaye ne Cipion   *Isaiah; Scipio*
515   Ne kynge Nabugodonosor,   *Nebuchadnezzar*

498.   *kenne*: 'make out, follow'; *yë*: 'eye'.
499.   Possible sources for Ch's eagle include astronomy and the bestiaries; Ovid
       (*Met.* X, ll. 155–61), Boethius (*Cons.* IV, met. 1, ll. 1–6), Dante (*Purg.* IX,
       ll. 13–33) and imagery in medieval churches (see Leyerle 1971: 2514).
       Delany 1972: 69 cites a number of biblical texts: Ex. 19:4; Job 39:27; Jer.
       48:40; Ezek. 17:3.
509–12. For the address to listeners, cf. above, l. 109 & n.
511.   'And listen, so that you may learn from my dream'.
514–17. Cf. *BD*, ll. 276–89, where Joseph's interpretation of Pharaoh's dreams
       (Gen. 41:1–36) and Macrobius's version of the dream of Scipio are also
       mentioned (as again in *PF*, ll. 29ff.). Scipio (l. 514) is also cited as a visionary
       (below, ll. 916–18). For the visions and dreams of Isaiah, Nebuchadnezzar
       and Turnus, see Isa. 1:1, Dan. 2:1–45, *Aen.* VII, ll. 413–59 and IX, ll. 1–24.
       Elcanor may be Elkanah, father of the prophet Samuel; see 1 Sam. 1–2.

	Pharoo, Turnus ne Elcanor	*Pharaoh*
	Ne metten suche a dreme as this.	*did not dream*
	Now faire blisfull, O Cipris,	*Venus*
	So be my favor at this tyme,	*be my helper*
520	And ye, me to endite and ryme	
	Helpeth, that on Parnaso duelle	*Mount Parnassus*
	Be Elicon, the clere welle.	
	O Thought, that wrote al that I mette	
	And in the tresorye hyt shette	*enclosed it*
525	Of my brayn, now shal men se	
	Yf any vertu in the be	
	To tellen al my dreme aryght –	
	Now kythe thyn engyne and myght!	*show*
	This Egle, of whiche I have yow tolde,	
530	That shone with fethres as of golde,	*as if*
	Which that so hye gan to sore,	
	I gan beholde more and more,	
	To se the beaute and the wonder.	
	But never was ther dynt of thonder,	*clap*
535	Ne that thynge that men calle foudre,	*thunderbolt*

518–19. *Cipris* (from Cyprus) is a name for Venus (mother and protector of Aeneas). She is also invoked as a kind of Muse in *PF*, ll. 113–19.

520–2. This is the first invocation of the Muses in Ch's work and probably the first in vernacular English poetry (see Boitani 1984: 203–4; Hardman 1986: 478–94; Taylor & Bordier 1992: 219, 223), and they appear again in ll. 1395–1406. The confusion here of Helicon (the Muses' mountain) with Hippocrene (their well) could derive from several sources, e.g. Boccaccio (*Tes*. XI, l. 63), or contemporary French lyric (see Wimsatt 1982: 20–1, 52–5, 60).

523–8. Based on *Inf*. II, ll. 7–9, where the aid of the Muses and poetic invention is invoked and the memory is called upon to show its highest powers (*nobilitate*). Ch's appeal to *Thought* (l. 523) may be stressing 'the considerative powers of the mind', rather than 'memory' (Schless 1984: 51). The notion of the brain as a *tresorye* (l. 524) may derive from *Par*. I, l. 11, although this image was a common trope for the memory (see Carruthers 1990: 84, 113, 160–1 and pl. 25). *Vertu* ('high capacity', l. 526) may recall *virtù* in *Inf*. II, l. 11, and *engyne* ('skill', l. 528) parallels *ingegno* in *Inf*. II, l. 7.

530. Cf. Dante, *Purg*. IX, l. 20.

535. Cf. the eagle as like or bearing thunder in *Purg*. IX, l. 29 and *Met*. X, l. 158.

	That smote some tyme a toure to poudre	
	And in his swift comynge brende,	
	That so swithe gan descende	*rapidly*
	As this foule when hyt behelde	*bird*
540	That I arowme was in the felde.	*was out there*
	And with hys grym pawes stronge,	*talons*
	Withyn hys sharpe nayles longe,	
	Me, fleynge in a swappe he hente	
	And with hys sours ayene up wente,	*again*
545	Me caryeng in his clawes starke	*strong talons*
	As lyghtly as I were a larke –	*easily*
	How high I can not telle yow,	
	For I came up y nyste how,	*I knew not*
	For so astonyed and asweved	*stunned; dazed*
550	Was every vertu in my heved,	*faculty; head*
	What with his sours and with my drede.	*swooping*
	And al my felynge gan to dede,	
	Forwhi hit was to grete affray.	*too; (a) shock*
	Thus I longe in hys clawes lay,	
555	Til at the last he to me spake	
	In mannes vois and seyde 'Awake,	
	And be not agaste so, for shame!'	*so fearful*
	And called me by my name.	
	And, for I shulde the bet abreyde,	
560	Me mette 'Awake' to me he seyde	
	Ryght in the same vois and stevene	*tone of voice*
	That useth oon I koude nevene.	

537. 'And blazed during its swift descent'.

543. 'Flying, in a single swoop, he grabbed me'.

544. *with hys sours*: 'in the same movement'.

545–6. On the implications of the image for the 'feminizing' of the dreamer at this stage, see Hansen (1992: 101–2), who compares the description of Criseyde as *sely larke* in *TC* III, l. 1191.

552. 'And all my senses were stunned'.

556. *mannes* here could mean both 'human' (as opposed to avian) and 'masculine' (cf. *TC* III, l. 1126, and *NPT*, l. 2920).

559. 'So as to rouse me more quickly'.

562. 'That someone I could mention uses'. Some (e.g. David 1960: 337) have suggested this person might be Ch's wife or servant. The base MS for the poem (F) indicates some scribal interest in the question (see Notes on the

And with that vois, soth for to seyne,   *truth to tell*
My mynde came to me ageyne,
565 For hit was goodely seyde to me –   *spoken gently*
So nas hit never wonte to be.
And herewithalle I gan to stere   *at once; stir*
And he me in his fete to bere,
Til that he felt that I had hete   *was warm again*
570 And felte eke tho myn herte bete.
And thoo gan he me to disporte   *cheer me up*
And with wordes to comforte,
And sayede twyes: 'Seynt Mary,   *twice*
Thou art noyouse for to cary!   *difficult to*
575 And nothynge nedeth it, pardee –   *there's no need*
For, also wis God helpe me,
As thou noon harme shalt have of this –
And this caas that betydde the is   *has befallen you*
Is for thy lore and for thy prowe.
580 Let see – darst thou yet loke nowe?   *See here*
Be ful assured, boldely,
I am thy frende!' And therwith I
Gan for to wondren in my mynde:
'O God,' thought I, 'that madest kynde –
585 Shal I noon other weyes dye?   *in no other way*
Wher Joves wol me stellefye?   *Is Jove going to*
Or what thinge may this sygnifye?
I neyther am Ennok ne Elye,   *Enoch; Elijah*

Text, ll. 561–2).

573. St Mary is the first of several saints by whom the eagle swears (possibly with an ironic allusion to the Assumption of the Virgin?). On oaths and colloquialisms in the poem and in the eagle's speech, see Elliott 1974: 244–7, 267, 372.

579. 'Is meant to teach and benefit you'.

584. *kynde*: 'the universe'. On God as creator in *HF* see above, l. 470 & n., and below, ll. 646, 970–1.

586. *stellefye* ('turn into a constellation') is the first recorded use of the verb (cf. below, l. 1002, and *LGW*, l. 513).

588. The patriarch Enoch and the prophet Elijah were believed to have gone directly to Paradise (see Gen. 5:24 and 2 Kings 2:11) and are frequently linked as fast-track redeemed souls. But the structure and context of the line also clearly recall Dante's *Io non Enëa, io non Paulo sono* ('I am not

Ne Romulus, ne Ganymede
590 That was ybore up, as men rede,   *carried*
    To hevene with Daun Jupiter   *by Lord*
    And made the goddys botiller.'   *cupbearer*
    Loo, this was thoo my fantasye.   *delusion*
    But he that bare me gan espye   *perceived*
595 That I so thought, and seyde this:
    'Thou demest of thy selfe amys,   *are wrong about*
    For Joves ys not theraboute –   *does not mean*
    I dar wel put the out of doute –   *assure you*
    To make of the, as yet, a sterre.   *star*
600 But, er I bere the moche ferre,   *before; much further*
    I wol the telle what I am
    And whider thou shalt and why I cam   *where you're going*
    To do thys, so that thou take
    Goode herte, and not for fere quake.'   *tremble with fear*
605 'Gladly,' quod I. 'Now, wel,' quod he.
    'First – I that in my fete have the,
    Of which thou haste a fere and wonder,   *are in fear*
    Am dwellynge with the god of thonder
    Whiche that men callen Jupiter,   *Whom*
610 That dooth me fleen ful ofte fer   *makes me fly*
    To do al hys comaundement,
    And for this cause he hath me sent
    To the. Now herke be thy trouthe: *listen; upon your honour*
    Certeyn, he hath of the routhe,   *is sorry for you*

Aeneas, not St Paul') in *Inf*. II, l. 32 – thus extending the comic parallel
between Dante's pilgrim and Chaucer's dreamer. Cf. other allusions to *Inf.*
II above, ll. 523–8 & n.

589–92. On Romulus's ascent to heaven, see *Met*. XIV, ll. 805–28, and on the
abduction of the boy Ganymede (by Jupiter's eagle) see *Met*. X, ll. 155–61,
and Dante, *Purg*. IX, ll. 22–4. *botiller* (l. 592) might have reminded the
poem's original audience that Ch's father had been the king's deputy butler
(Spearing 1976: 80).

605. *Now, wel*: 'all right then'.

606–11. On the eagle's association with Jupiter, see, e.g., Ovid, *Met*. X, ll.
155–61, and Virgil, *Aen*. I, l. 394, etc.

614–19. Other references to Cupid are at ll. 137, 668 and 1489–90. On the
narrator's devotion to Venus, see above, ll. 213, 465–7, 518–19, and the
initial setting for the vision itself (the temple of Venus in Book I).

615 That thou so longe, trewly,
     Hast served so ententyfly   *devotedly*
     Hys blynde nevewe, Cupido,   *nephew*
     And faire Venus also,
     Withoute guerdon ever yitte.
620 And never the lesse hast set thy witte –   *applied your skill*
     Al though that in thy hede ful lyte is –
     To make bokes, songes or ditees,   *poems*
     In ryme or elles in cadence,
     As thou best canst, in reverence   *in honour*
625 Of Love and of hys servantes eke
     That have hys servyse soght and seke –   *Who have sought*
     And peynest the to preyse hys arte,   *take pains; craft*
     Al though thou haddest never parte.
     Wherfore – also God me blesse –
630 Joves halt hyt grete humblesse   *considers it*
     And vertu eke, that thou wolt make   *merit*
     A-nyghte ful ofte thyn hede to ake   *By night*
     In thy studye, so thou writest,   *writing so hard*
     And ever mo of Love enditest   *(you) write*
635 In honour of hym and in preysynges,
     And in his folkes furtherynges –
     And in hir matere al devisest
     And noght him nor his folke dispisest,

619. 'For no reward right up till now'.
621. 'Although there's little enough of that in your head'.
622. The first explicit indication that the dreamer is a writer.
623. *cadence* may mean 'rhythm', and the passage could thus (like ll. 1094–1100
      below, and *MLT Intro*, ll. 47–8) refer ironically to Ch's technical compe-
      tence. Gower uses the word similarly in *CA* IV, l. 2414, where it is also
      contrasted to *rime*, as an aspect of *metre*.
627. 'And you take pains to honour his [Love's] craft'. Cf. the references to love
      as *arte* or *craft* in *BD*, ll. 785–91 and *PF*, ll. 1–4; also the more disreputable
      meanings of both terms, above, l. 335, and in *PF*, ll. 220–2.
628. The dreamer's lack of direct 'involvement' *(parte)* in love is emphasized
      more fully below, ll. 639–70. Cf. the disclaimers in *PF*, l. 8 and *TC* I, ll.
      15–18, and the comments of another of the dreamer's guides (Scipio) in *PF*,
      ll. 158–61.
636. 'And in aid of his followers'.
637. 'And make them [lovers] the subject of all your work'.

152   The *House of Fame*

	Al though thou maiste goo in the daunce	*may be counted*
640	Of hem that hym lyst not avaunce.	*he won't help*
	'Wherfore, as I seyde, ywis,	*indeed*
	Jupiter considereth this	
	And also, *beau sir*, other thynges –	*dear sir*
	That is, that thou hast no tydynges	*news*
645	Of Loves folke, yf they be glade,	*followers; happy*
	Ne of noght elles that God made –	*Nor; anything else*
	And noght oonly fro fer contree	*distant lands*
	That ther no tydynge cometh to thee,	
	But of thy verray neyghbors	*very own*
650	That duelle almoste at thy dors	
	Thou herist neyther that ne this;	*nothing at all*
	For when thy labour doon al ys	*is completed*
	And hast ymade rekenynges,	*accounts*
	Instid of reste and newe thynges,	
655	Thou goost home to thy house anoon,	*at once*
	And, also dombe as any stoon,	*as dumb*
	Thou sittest at another booke	
	Tyl fully dasewyd ys thy looke	
	And lyvest thus as an heremyte,	
660	Al-though thyn abstynence ys lyte.	*is negligible*
	'And therfore Joves, thorgh hys grace,	*Jupiter*
	Wol that I bere the to a place	*Wishes me to*
	Which that hight the House of Fame,	*Which is called*
	To do the some disport and game,	*give you; fun*
665	In some recompensacion	*As; reward*

639–40. For love as a kind of 'dance', cf. *TC* I, ll. 517–18, II, ll. 1106–7, and III, l. 695; also *Gen Prol*, l. 476, *Phys T*, l. 79.

643. '*beau sir*': a courtly form of address, also used in the Chaucerian translation of *RR* (l. 800).

648. 'Does no news reach you'.

653. *rekenynges* may refer to Ch's work as Controller of the wool custom in the Port of London (1374–86), for which he was obliged to keep accounts in his own hand (see Crow & Olson 1966: 148–9; *Riv.*, p. xvi).

656–7. These lines are often taken as evidence of Ch's 'advanced degree of literacy' (thus Burrow 1982: 53). But their value as evidence about 'silent reading' should not be overstressed; the eagle here seems less concerned with Geoffrey's literacy than with his anti-social bookishness.

658. 'Till your eyes look all bleary'.

	Of labour and devocion	*For (the)*
	That thou hast had, loo, causeles	
	To Cupido the rechcheles.	*uncaring*
	And thus this god, thorgh his merite,	*[i.e. Jupiter]*
670	Wol with some maner thinge the quyte,	*Wishes; to reward you*
	So that thou wolt be of goode chere;	*So long as; spirits*
	For, trust wel that thou shalt here,	
	When we be come there I seye,	
	Mo wonder thynges, dar I leye,	*I guarantee*
675	Of Loves folke – moo tydynges	
	(Both sothe sawes and leysinges)	*true sayings; lies*
	And moo loves newe begonne	
	And longe yserved loves wonne,	
	And moo loves casuelly	
680	That betyde, no man wote why,	
	But as a blynde man stert an hare,	*flushes out*
	And more jolytee and fare	*happiness; well-being*
	While that they fynde love of stele,	*(firm as) steel*
	As thinketh hem, and overal wele –	*seems to them; entirely fine*
685	Mo discordes, moo jelousies,	*More disagreements*
	Mo murmures and moo novelries,	*fickleness*
	And moo dissymulacions	*deceptions*
	And feyned reparacions	*fake reconciliations*
	And moo berdys in two oures,	
690	Withoute rasour or sisoures	

669–70. Cf. below, ll. 2007–9, and the reward for diligent reading promised by
Scipio in *PF*, ll. 109–12. Goffin 1943: 41–2 compares *LGW*, ll. 482–4,
noting that 'here, as in the *Legend*, the "quiting" takes the form of new
poetic material'.

672–98. For a similarly exhaustive list of *tydynges*, cf. below, ll. 1961–76 & n.,
and on 'cornucopic lists' in *HF* see Ruffolo 1993: 325–41. The later stages
of this one tend to stress instability and betrayal in a fairly colloquial tone;
for instance, the phrase 'to make [i.e. trim] someone's beard' (ll. 689–91)
refers especially to sexual deception, and Tkacz (1983: 129–30) compares
WB Prol, l. 361. The mixing of truth with falsehood (l. 676) recurs below
in the House of Rumour (ll. 2088–2109); cf. Ovid, *Met.* IX, ll. 138–9, and
Met. XII, ll. 53–5.

673. *there I seye*: 'to the place I am speaking of'.

678. 'And (more) long-deserved loves gained'.

679–80. *casuelly / That betyde*: 'that happen by chance'.

Ymade, then greynes be of sondes –   *than there grains; sand*
And eke moo holdynge in hondes   *stringing along*
And also moo renoveilaunces   *renewals*
Of olde forleten aqueyntaunces,   *long-lost*
695 Mo love-dayes and acordes
Then on instrumentes be acordes,
And eke of loves moo eschaunges   *changing*
Then ever cornes were in graunges.   *grains; barns*
Unnethe maistow trowen this?'
700 Quod he. 'Noo, helpe me God so wys!'   *in his wisdom*
Quod I. 'Noo? Why?' quod he. 'For hyt   *Because it*
Were impossible to my witte,   *Would be; mind*
Though that Fame had al the pies   *informers*
In al a realme and al the spies,   *kingdom*
705 How that yet he shulde here al this
Or they espie hyt.' 'O yis, yis!'   *detect; yes (emphatic)*
Quod he to me, 'that kan I preve   *prove*
Be reson worthy for to leve,
So that thou yeve thyn advertence   *If you concentrate*
710 To understonde my sentence.   *argument*
        'First shalt thou here where she dwelleth:
And, so thyn oune boke hyt tellith,   *as your own*
Hir paleys stant, as I shal sey,   *palace stands*

695. 'More meetings for reconciliation and settlements'. On *love-dayes*, cf. *Gen Prol*, l. 258. The rhyme here and in l. 696 involves two meanings of *acorde*: (1) 'settlement'; (2) 'harmony', 'harmonic interval' (cf. *PF*, l. 197 and *NPT*, l. 2879).

699. 'Can you ever believe this?'

703. For this meaning of *pie* ('magpie'), cf. *TC* III, l. 527.

705. *he*: this is the reading of all witnesses except Caxton. In his dazed and confused state of mind (ll. 545–6) the dreamer could well be identifying Fame as 'he', by association with the masculine figures of the eagle and Jupiter who seem to be currently in control of his fate.

708. 'With convincing arguments'.

711–24. This is the first occasion in *HF* when Ch draws upon the account of the house of *Fama* ('Rumour') in Ovid's *Metamorphoses* (XII, ll. 39–63), which is the dreamer's *owne boke* to which the eagle refers (l. 712). Other passages based on the Ovidian description are below, ll. 843–7, 1029, 1034–41, 1948–58 and 2060–75 (see also Bennett 1968: 71–3; Delany 1968: 257; and Cooper in Martindale 1988: 71).

	Ryght even in myddes of the wey	*Exactly midway*
715	Betwexen hevene and erthe and see –	
	That, what so ever in al these three	
	Is spoken, either privé or aperte,	*privately or publicly*
	The aire therto ys so overte	*round there; receptive*
	And stant eke in so juste a place	
720	That every soune mot to hyt pace,	*has to reach it*
	Or what so cometh fro any tonge –	*whatever*
	Be hyt rouned, red or songe,	*whispered, spoken*
	Or spoke in suerté or in drede –	*confidently; doubtfully*
	Certeyn hyt most thider nede.	*has to go there*
725	'Now herkene wel, forwhy I wille	*because*
	Tellen the a propre skille,	
	And worthe a demonstracion	
	In myn ymagynacion:	
	'Geffrey, thou wost ryght wel this –	*know very well*
730	That every kyndely thynge that is	*thing in Nature*
	Hath a kyndely stede ther he	*proper place where*
	May best in hyt conserved be;	
	Unto whiche place every thynge,	
	Thorgh his kyndely enclynynge,	*natural inclination*
735	Moveth for to come to	
	Whan that hyt is awey therfro.	*from there*

719. 'And it [the palace] stands in so suitable a place'.

726–8. 'Present you with a logical argument, and one that, in my opinion, is worth putting to the proof'. *Ymaginacion* occurs only here in *HF* and is used in the generalized sense of 'way of thinking, opinion'.

729. The only occasion in Ch's work where his first name is mentioned, although he is named in *MLT Intro*, l. 47 (as *Chaucer*) and in a number of manuscript rubrics. Cf. the naming of the authors of *RR* in ll. 10496 and 10535 (tr. Horgan 1994: 162), and of Dante in *Purg.* XXX, l. 55. See also *Conv.* I, ch. 2, 2–3 (where the rhetoricians are said to have forbidden speaking of oneself without due occasion), and Curtius 1953: 515–18.

730–6. The notion of a natural disposition or propensity (*kyndely enclynynge*) in created things is ultimately Aristotelian (see Crombie 1969: I, 90–1). See also Augustine, *City of God* XI, par. 28; *Boece* III, met. 9, ll. 36–8 and pr. 12, ll. 88–96 (where Ch's translation also uses the term *enclynyng*), and Lewis 1964: 92–4. For a concise general account of the Aristotelian physics of motion in the Middle Ages, see Grant 1977: ch. 4.

732. *conserved be*: 'be preserved'.

As thus: loo, thou maist alday se   *can always see*
That any thinge that hevy be,   *is heavy*
As stoon or lede or thynge of wight,   *Such as; weight*
740   And, bere hyt never so hye on hight –   *if you lift; high up*
Lat goo thyn hande, hit falleth doun.
Ryght so sey I be fire or soun   *I say about; sound*
Or smoke, or other thynges lyght:
Alway they seke upwarde on hight   *move upwards*
745   While eche of hem is at his large –   *unimpeded*
Lyght thinge upwarde, and
    dounwarde charge.   *heavy things downward*
And, for this cause, maistow see   *reason*
That every ryver to the see
Enclyned ys to goo by kynde,   *Tends naturally*
750   And by these skilles, as I fynde,   *for these reasons*
Hath fyssh duellynge in floode and see,   *Fish live; rivers*
And treës eke in erthe bee.
Thus every thinge, by thys reson,
Hath his propre mansyon   *its; place*
755   To which it seketh to repaire,
As there hit shuld not apaire.
Loo, this sentence ys knowen kouthe   *theory; well-known*
Of every philosophres mouthe –   *From*
As Aristotile and Daun Platon   *Aristotle; Plato*
760   And other clerkys, many oon.   *many other scholars*

737–46. The concept of 'natural motion' in heavy and light objects is formulated in Aristotle's *Physics* VIII, ch. 4. On consequent medieval theory of gravity and levity as 'qualities that reside within bodies', see Crombie 1969: I, 90–2; Steneck 1976: 76–8; and Grant 1977: 38–9.

754–6. Cf. *Boece* III, pr. 11, ll. 97–106.

755. *seketh to repaire*: 'tries to return'.

756. 'So that it may be preserved [may not deteriorate] there' (see Notes on the Text).

759. For examples of Aristotelianism in *HF*, see above, ll. 730–6 & n., 737–46 & n., and below, l. 775 & n. Plato was influential chiefly through Calcidius's Latin version of the *Timaeus*; see Crombie 1969: I, 34, 45–50 and Grennen 1984: 237–62.

'And, to confirme my reasoun,   *proposition*
Thou wost wel this: that spech is soun,   *know; sound*
Or elles no man myght hyt here.
Now, herke what y wol the lere: *will teach you*
765   Soune ys noght but eyre ybroken,   *broken air*
And every spech that ys yspoken –
Lowde or pryvee, foule or faire –   *quietly*
In his substaunce ys but aire;   *In its substance*
For, as flaumbe ys but lyghted smoke,   *(a) flame*
770   Ryght soo soune ys aire ybroke.
But this may be in many wyse,   *different ways*
Of which I wil the twoo devyse: *show you two*
As soune that cometh of pipe or harpe –   *Such as; from*
For, whan a pipe is blowen sharpe,   *loudly*
775   The aire ys twyst with violence   *twisted*
And rent – loo, thys is my sentence;   *torn; opinion*
Eke, whan men harpe strynges smyte –   *strike*
Whether hyt be moche or lyte –   *hard or gently*
Loo, with the stroke the ayre tobreketh,   *shatters*
780   And right so breketh it whan men speketh.   *people speak*
'Thus wostow wel what thinge is speche;   *you (now) know*
Now, hennesforth y wol the teche   *straight away*
How every speche or noyse or soun,
Thurgh hys multiplicacioun,
785   Thogh hyt were piped of a mouse,   *squeaked by*

761–822. This speech about speech is probably influenced by medieval commentaries on late-Latin grammarians (see Irvine 1985). On the notion of sound as 'broken air' (ll. 765, 770, 780), see ibid.: esp. 854–5 and 862–3; *Riv.* also compares Boethius, *De Musica* I, l. 3, and Vincent of Beauvais, *Speculum naturale* IV, l. 14: 'sound is a striking [*percussio*] of the air which does not fade until heard'. Irvine 1985: 864 points out that the notion of speech as 'itself essentially air' (l. 768) is a travesty of the contemporary grammatical commentaries which argued that 'a percussion of air is the *cause* of a spoken utterance and not its substance'.

775.   This seems to reflect the Aristotelian distinction between *natural* motion (as of a stone falling to the ground) and *violent* or *unnatural* motion (as of a stone thrown into the air); see Grant 1977: 36.

784.   *multiplicacioun*: 'expansion, amplification'. Ch uses this idea to characterize the transmission of sound again in ll. 801 and 820. His interest in it may well have been further stimulated by *Cons.* III, pr. 11, ll. 16–73.

	Mote nede come to Fames house.	*necessarily*
	I preve hyt thus (take hede now)	
	By experience – for yf that thow	*if you*
	Throwe on water now a stoon,	
790	Wel wost thou, hyt wol make anoon	*at once make*
	A litel roundell, as a sercle –	
	Peraventure brode as a covercle –	
	And ryght anoon thow shalt see wel,	
	That sercle wol cause another whele	*make another circle*
795	And that the thridde, and so forth, brother,	*a third (circle)*
	Every sercle causynge other,	
	Wydder than hym self was.	*Broader; itself*
	And thus, fro roundel to compas,	
	Eche aboute other goynge,	
800	Causeth of othres sterynge,	
	And multiplyinge ever moo,	
	Til that hyt be so fer ygoo	
	That hyt at bothe brynkes bee.	
	Although thou mayst hyt not ysee	*cannot see it*
805	Above, hyt gooth yet alle wey under,	
	Al though thou thenke hyt a grete wonder.	
	And who so seyth of trouthe I varye,	
	Bid hym proven the contrarye.	*Tell him to*
	And ryght thus, every worde, ywys,	*just so; indeed*
810	That lowde or pryvee yspoken ys	
	Moveth first an ayre a-boute,	
	And of thys movynge, out of doute,	*by this movement*
	Another ayre anoon ys meved.	*is at once moved*
	As I have of the watir preved –	
815	That every cercle causeth other –	
	Ryght so of ayre, my leve brother:	*dear*

791–2. 'A small circular ripple, perhaps the size of a cup's lid'. The everyday image from *experience* (l. 788) was also, as Skeat pointed out, used to describe sound in Boethius, *De Musica* I, l. 14 (*PL* LXIII, col. 1179).

798–803. 'And thus, from the central ripple to the circumference, each (circle) encircling another sets another one in motion; and the process repeats itself constantly until it reaches both banks'.

805. 'On the surface, it still moves constantly beneath'.

807. *of trouthe I varye*: 'that I am diverging from the truth'.

811. 'Sets in motion a (circle of) air'.

	Everych ayre other stereth	*moves another*
	More and more, and speche upbereth,	*carries speech up*
	Or voys or noyse or worde or soun,	
820	Ay through multiplicacioun,	*Continually*
	Til hyt be atte House of Fame –	*arrives at the*
	Take hyt in ernest or in game.	*seriously; lightly*
	'Now have I tolde, yf thou have mynde,	*remember*
	How speche or soun, of pure kynde,	*by nature*
825	Enclyned ys upwarde to meve	
	(This, maystow fele, wel I preve)	*you may think*
	And that som styde, ywys,	
	That every thynge enclyned to ys	
	Hath his kyndelych stede.	
830	That sheweth hyt, withouten drede,	
	That kyndely, the mansion	
	Of every speche, of every soun,	
	Be hyt eyther foule or faire,	
	Hath hys kynde place in ayre.	*proper, true*
835	And, syn that every thynge that is	*since*
	Out of hys kynde place, ywys,	*proper, true*
	Moveth thidder for to goo,	*to go there*
	Yif hyt awey be therfroo	*is removed thence*
	(As I have before preved the) –	
840	Hyt seweth, every soun, parde,	
	Moveth kyndely to pace	*naturally to go*
	Al up in to his kyndely place;	
	And this place of which I telle,	
	Ther as Fame lyst to duelle,	*Where; pleases*
845	Ys set amyddys of these three:	*placed midway*
	Heven, erthe and eke the see	
	As most conservatyf the soun.	

824–52. The terms *kyndelych stede* (l. 829) and *kynde(ly) place* (l. 834, 836, 842) refer back to the opening stage of the eagle's argument (above, ll. 730–6).

827–9. 'And indeed that the condition to which each thing is disposed has its due location somewhere' (see ll. 729–36).

830–1. 'That is clearly demonstrated by (the fact) that naturally the destination'.

840. 'It follows that each sound, indeed'.

847. 'As the place that best preserves sound'.

	Than ys this the conclusyon:	
	That every speche of every man,	
850	As y the telle first began,	*to tell you*
	Moveth up on high, to pace	
	Kyndely to Fames place.	
	'Telle me this, feythfully:	*sincerely*
	Have y not preved thus symply,	
855	Withouten any subtilite	
	Of speche, or grete prolixite	*excess*
	Of termes of philosophie,	
	Of figures of poetrie,	*poetic symbols*
	Or colours of rethorike?	*rhetorical figures*
860	Pardee, hit ought the to lyke –	*to please you*
	For harde langage and hard matere	*subject-matter*
	Ys encombrouse for to here	*tedious*
	Attones – wost thou not wel this?'	*Together*
	And y answered and seyde 'Yis.'	*Yes (emphatic)*
865	'A ha!' quod he, 'lo, so I can	
	Lewdely to a lewde man	*Plainly; plain*
	Speke, and shew hym suche skiles	*proofs*
	That he may shake hem be the biles –	*beaks*
	So palpable they shulden be!	*will be*
870	But telle me this, now pray y the –	*I beg you*

848. *conclusyon* here means 'inference', whilst in l. 871 below it has the wider
sense of 'doctrine' or 'argument'. On terms like this, see above, note on
l. 342.

858–9. Ch's first use of the word *poetrie*. For other meanings and related terms,
see below, ll. 1001, 1095, 1478, 1483, 1499, and *BD*, l. 54. *Figures of
poetrie* are poetic forms of expression (such as metaphor or hyperbole) and
are thus closely related to *colours* ('ornaments') *of rethorike*. Cf. *Cl Prol*, l.
16, *Sq T*, l. 39, *Fkl T*, ll. 723–6 and Usk, *Testament of Love*, Prol., l. 3. On
the eagle and rhetoric, see also Teager 1932, and for theory on the
relationship between poetry and rhetoric in the period, see Minnis & Scott
1991: 308–11 and Boccaccio, tr. Osgood 1956: 39–42.

861–3. On the notion of matching style to audience, cf. Ch's own concern about
addressing *curious* style and *hard* concepts to his young son in *Astr Prol*, ll.
45–6. See also Pandarus's tactics in *TC* II, ll. 267–73, and the value Ch's
contemporary Usk places on *rude wordes and boystous* in the *Testament of
Love*, Prol., l. 7 (cf. Burnley 1989: 199).

How thenketh the my conclusyon?' *What do you think of*
'... A goode persuasion,'   *convincing case*
Quod I, 'hyt is, and lyke to be   *likely*
Ryght so as thou hast preved me.' *Exactly as*
875 'Be God,' quod he, 'and as I leve,   *I believe*
Thou shalt have yet, or hit be eve, *before evening*
Of every word of thys sentence   *argument*
A preve by experience
And with thyn eres heren wel,
880 Toppe and taylle and everydel,
That every word that spoken ys   *is said*
Cometh in to Fames house, ywys,
As I have seyde – what wiltow more?' *do you want*
  And with this word upper to sore *to soar upward*
885 He gan, and seyde 'Be Seynt Jame – *James*
Now wil we speke al of game!   *just for fun*
How farest thou?' quod he to me.   *are you doing*
'Wel,' quod I. 'Now see,' quod he,
'By thy trouthe, yonde adoune,   *down over there*
890 Wher that thou knowest any toune *(To see) whether*
Or hous, or any other thinge.
And whan thou hast of ought knowynge, *recognize anything*
Looke that thou warne me,   *Be sure; inform*
And y anoon shal telle the
895 How fer that thou art now therfro.' *far; from it*
  And y adoun to loken thoo
And behelde feldes and playnes,   *fields; plains*
And now hilles and now montaynes,
Now valeys, now forestes,

871. *conclusyon*: 'argument' (*MED conclusioun* n. 4). See note on l. 848, above.
872. *persuasion*: 'case, convincing argument'; Ch's only use of the term (see Delany 1972: 75; Grennen 1984: 243–4).
880. 'From start to finish, in all details'.
885. On the eagle's oaths, see above, l. 573 & n. St James's shrine at Santiago in Galicia was one of the main pilgrimage destinations, so the oath has some appropriateness in the context of the present journey.
888. *Wel*: for other equally terse responses on the dreamer's part, see above, l. 864, and below, l. 913.
896. 'And then I began to look down'.

900	And now unnethes grete bestes,	*with difficulty*
	Now ryveres, now citees,	
	Now tounes and now grete trees,	
	Now shippes seyllynge in the see.	*sailing*
	But thus sone, in a while, he	*just as quickly*
905	Was flowen fro the grounde so hye	
	That al the worlde, as to myn yë,	*in my sight*
	No more semed than a prikke,	*pin-prick*
	Or elles was the aire so thikke	*thick, dense*
	That y ne myght not discerne.	*see clearly*
910	With that he spake to me as yerne	*at once*
	And seide: 'Seyst thou eny to[un],	*Can you see any*
	Or ought thow knowest yonde [a]doun?'	
	I seide: 'Nay.' 'No wonder nys,'	*That's no wonder*
	Quod he, 'for half so high as this	
915	Nas Alisandre Macedo,	*Alexander the Great*
	Ne the kynge, Daun Cipio,	*Lord Scipio*
	That saw in dreme, at poynt devys,	*entirely*
	Helle and erthe and paradys –	

907. The emphasis on the smallness of the earth when seen from this height derives in part from another vision, the *Somnium Scipionis* of Cicero, later commented upon by the Neoplatonist philosopher Macrobius (tr. Stahl 1952: 69–77). Scipio is explicitly named by Ch in this context (below, l. 916); see Bennett 1968: 82–3. The description of the earth as a 'dot' (*punctum*) several times in *Cons*. II, pr. 7, is also likely to have been influential, since Ch was translating it at the time and it occurs in the context of Lady Philosophy's discussion of earthly glory (cf. Fyler 1979: 56).

915. According to medieval sources such as the French *Roman d'Alexandre*, Alexander the Great's attempt to ascend to heaven took place during his march on Babylon and his encounters with the wonders of the East (see Bennett 1968: 87, 169). On the associations of Alexander with vainglory in this and other ventures, see Delany 1972: 81–2, Stevenson 1978: 16 & n. 17, and the *Alexandreis*, tr. Pritchard 1986: 230–1 (where the king's final speech is a bid to displace Jupiter). For illustrations of his flying-machines, see Ross 1971.

916–18. Scipio was not a 'king', but he is given this title also in *BD*, l. 286 and *RR*, l. 10 (and the Chaucerian translation). His vision is described more fully in *PF*, ll. 29–84; see also above, l. 907 & n.

	Ne eke the wrechch, Dedalus,	*unhappy Daedalus*
920	Ne his child, nyse Ykarus	*foolish Icarus*
	That fleegh so hye that the hete	*flew*
	Hys wynges malte, and he fyll wete	*melted; plunged*
	In myd the see and ther he dreynt –	*Straight into; drowned*
	For whom was maked moch compleynt.	*made great lament*
925	'Now turne upward,' quod he, 'thy face	
	And beholde this large place,	
	This eyre, but loke thou ne be	*sphere of air*
	Adrad of hem that thou shalt se.	*Afraid; those (spirits)*
	For in this region, certeyn,	
930	Duelleth many a citezeyn	*inhabitant*
	Of which that speketh Daun Plato –	*Lord Plato speaks*
	These ben eyryssh bestes, lo.'	*demons of the air*
	And so saw y all that meynee	*company*
	Booth goon and also flee.	*walking; flying*
935	'Now,' quod he thoo, 'cast up thyn yë.	*then; raise your eyes*

919–24. Daedalus's legendary skill as craftsman is also mentioned in *BD*, l. 570, and its application to the building of Minos's Labyrinth in Crete is alluded to below (ll. 1920–3). His construction of wings, flight from Crete and the fall of his son Icarus are described in *Met.* VIII, ll. 183–235. See also *Inf.* XVII, ll. 106–11 (linking Icarus with Phaëthon), XXIX, l. 116, and *Par.* VIII, ll. 125–6. Simpson (1986: 11–12) cites Bersuire (14th-century commentator on Ovid), who identifies Icarus with pride and incompetence. In l. 919 the adopted reading (*wrechch*) suggests that Ch was influenced by Ovid's description of Daedalus as an unhappy father ('pater infelix') cursing his craft after the death of Icarus (*Met.* VIII, ll. 231 and 234). But the variant reading (in P, Cx (see Notes on the Text)) of *wryght* ('craftsman') is an interesting possibility, since Daedalus's skill is also emphasized by Ovid (*Met.* VIII, ll. 159, 201, and IX, ll. 741–3).

922. 'Melted his wings and he plunged'.

930–4. The *eyryssh bestes* (l. 932 and below, l. 965) correspond to the demons of the air in Plato (*Timaeus*, see above, l. 759 and n.). But the description of them as 'citizens' (l. 930) and their association with various meteorological phenomena in ll. 965–9 probably owes more to the account of Prudence's ascent into the heavens in Alanus of Lille's *Anticlaudianus* (tr. Sheridan 1973: 126–7, 129–30), which is named below (l. 986).

934. 'Both walking and flying as well'.

Se yonder, loo, the Galoxie,   *Galaxy*
Whiche men clepeth the Melky Weye,   *people call*
For hit ys white, and some, parfeye,   *for sure*
Kallen hyt Watlynge Strete,   *Watling Street*
940   That ones was ybrent wyth hete   *scorched*
Whan the sonnes sonne the rede,
That hight Pheton, wolde lede
Algate hys Fader carte and gye.
          'The carte hors gonne wel espye
945   That he coude no governaunce
And gonne for to lepe and launce   *buck and rear*
And bere hym, now up now doun,
Til that he sey the Scorpioun,
Whiche that in heven a sygne is yit.   *is still a sign*
950   And he for ferde lost hys wyt   *through fear*
Of that, and lat the reynes gon   *let go the reins*
Of his hors, and they anoon   *at once*
Gonne up to mounten and doun
          descende,   *climb up; plunge down*
Til both the eyre and erthe brende –   *were on fire*
955   Til Jupiter, loo, atte laste,
Hym slowe and fer fro the cart cast.   *struck him dead*

936–9. Cf. *PF*, ll. 55–6. The *OED* (under *Watling-street* 2) notes that 'the Milky
    Way received other popular names from famous highways, especially
    pilgrimage routes'. Dante in *Conv.* II, ch. xiv, refers to the popular belief
    identifying it with 'St James's Way'.

940–59. Ovid's vivid version of the disastrous story of Phaëthon spans two books
    in the *Metamorphoses* (I, l. 750–II, l. 400). Ch's concern with *governaunce*
    here (ll. 945, 958) may be influenced by the advice given to Phaëthon and
    Icarus by their fathers (Apollo and Daedalus) in *Met.* II, l. 137 and VIII, l.
    206, and by Dante's emphasis on the incompetence of both travellers (*Purg.*
    IV, l. 72; *Par.* XXXI, ll. 124–5; *Inf.* XVII, l. 111). Simpson (1986: 11)
    compares the identification of Phaëthon with pride and folly in the *Ovide
    moralisé* II, ll. 688–97. Cf. above, ll. 919–24 & n.

941. 'When the son of the fiery (god of the) Sun'.

942–3. *wolde lede / Algate ... and gye*: 'tried wilfully to control and drive (his
    father's chariot)'. *Carte* here and *carte hors* in l. 944 seem to be neutral (not
    ironic or bathetic) terms (see *MED cart* n. 2 & 3).

944. *carte hors*: 'horses drawing the chariot'.

945. 'That he did not know how to steer'.

	'Loo, ys it not a mochil myschaunce	*great mistake*
	To lat a fool han governaunce	*have control*
	Of thing that he can not demeyne?'	*(a) thing; manage*
960	And with this word, sothe for to seyne,	*truth to tell*
	He gan upper alwey for to sore	*ever higher*
	And gladded me ay more and more,	
	So feythfully to me spake he.	*convincingly*
	Tho gan y to loken under me	
965	And behelde the ayerissh bestes,	
	Cloudes, mystes and tempestes,	
	Snowes, hayles, reynes, wyndes	
	And th'engendrynge in hir kyndes	
	All the wey thrugh whiche I came.	
970	'O God,' quod y, 'that made Adame –	
	Moche ys thy myght and thy noblesse!'	*Great*
	And thoo thought y upon Boesse	*Boethius*
	That writ: 'A thought may flee so hye	
	Wyth fetheres of philosophye	
975	To passen everyche element.	
	And whan he hath so fer ywent,	*gone so far*
	Than may be seen behynde hys bake	
	Clowde and erthe' and alle that y of spake.	*I mentioned*
	Thoo gan y wexen in a were	*get worried*
980	And seyde: 'Y wote wel y am here,	*know well that*
	But wher in body or in gost	*whether; spirit*
	I not, ywys, but, God, thou wost!'	*do not know*
	For more clere entendement	*explanation*
	Nas me never yit ysent.	

965-9. See above, ll. 930-4 & n. and the passages from *Anticlaudianus* cited there. On the Aristotelian scientific theory behind the description, see Crombie 1969: I, 110-11 and Steneck 1976: 81, 84-6.

968. 'And the source of their natural properties'.

970-1. There may be an echo here of the tribute to God's power as shown in the earth and heavens at the opening of Psalm 8. On God as creator in *HF*, cf. above, l. 470 & n.

973-8. The quotation is from *Cons.* IV, met. 1. Stevenson (1978: 24) notes that Ch here omits the clause that he translates in *Boece* (IV, met. 1, l. 4) as: 'it despiseth the hateful erthes'.

975. 'That it passes beyond each of the elements'.

980-2. Parodies 2 Cor. 12:2-3. Cf. above, l. 51 & n.

985	And than thought y on Marcian	*Martianus Capella*
	And eke on *Anteclaudian*,	Anticlaudianus
	That sooth was her descripsion	
	Of alle the hevenis region,	
	As fer as that y sey the preve,	*saw; evidence*
990	Therfore y kan hem now beleve.	

With that this Egle began to crye:
'Lat be,' quod he, 'thy fantasye!   *Stop; imagining things*
Wiltow lere of sterres aught?'   *learn; anything*
'Nay, certenly,' quod y, 'ryght naught.'   *nothing at all*
995   'And why?' 'For y am now to olde.'   *too old*
'Elles I wolde the have tolde,'
Quod he, 'the sterres names, lo,
And al the hevens sygnes therto,   *as well*
And which they ben.' 'No fors,' quod y.   *No matter*
1000   'Yis, pardee,' quod he, 'wostow why?   *do you know*
For when thou redest poetrie,   *myths*
How goddes gonne stellifye
Briddes, fisshe, best, or him or here –   *beast, man or woman*
As the Ravene or eyther Bere,   *Raven; Bear*
1005   Or Arionis harp fyne,   *Arion's; excellent*
Castor, Pollex or Delphyne,   *Pollux; the Dolphin*

985. Martianus Capella's *De Nuptiis Philologiae et Mercurii* (composed c. 410–39) describes an allegorical journey by Philology to heaven, to find and marry Mercury, god of eloquence (see also Bennett 1968: 93).

986. The *Anticlaudianus* by Alanus of Lille (1125/30–1203) is another allegorical work involving an extra-terrestrial journey. It also includes descriptions of a 'House of Fortune' (Bk VIII), the creation of a 'New Man', and the return of the Golden Age (see also Stevenson 1978: 17).

998. 'And all the celestial signs [of the Zodiac] as well'.

1001–8. *poetrie* here means 'ancient fables, myths', of the sort that Ch found in Ovid's *Metamorphoses*, Book II, which refers to a number of the constellations and to the metamorphoses of the Raven (ll. 542f.) and the Great and Little Bears (ll. 466f.). Castor and Pollux (twin brothers of Helen) were associated with the constellation of Gemini (see Euripides, *Helen*, l. 140), whilst *Delphyne* (l. 1006) is the Dolphin (see Ovid, *Fasti* II, ll. 117–18).

1002. *stellifye*: 'turn into a constellation'. Cf. above, l. 586.

Or Athalantes doughtres sevene –
How al these arne set in hevene.   *are placed*
For, though thou have hem ofte on honde,   *deal with them*
1010   Yet nostow not wher that they stonde.'
'No fors,' quod y, 'hyt is no nede;
I leve as wel, so God me spede,   *God help me*
Hem that write of this matere
As though I knew her places here.   *their positions*
1015   And eke they shynen here so bryght,
Hyt shulde shenden al my syght   *would blind me*
To loke on hem.' 'That may wel be,'
Quod he. And so forth bare he me
A while, and than he gan to crye,
1020   That never herd I thing so hye:
'Now, up the hede, for alle ys wele!   *raise your head*
Seynt Julyane – lo, *bon hostele*!
Se her the House of Fame – lo,   *Behold*
Maistow not heren that I do?'   *Can't you hear what*
1025   'What?' quod I. 'The grete soun,'
Quod he, 'that rumbleth up and doun
In Fames house, ful of tydynges –
Bothe of feire speche and chidynges,   *quarrelling*
And of fals and soth compouned.   *combined*
1030   Herke wel – hyt is not rouned   *whispered*
Herestow not the grete swogh?'   *rushing sound*
'Yis, parde,' quod y, 'wel ynogh.'   *Yes indeed*

1007.   'Or the seven daughters of Atlas', who formed the constellation of the
        Pleiades (see *Met.* I, l. 670, XIII, l. 293 and *Fasti* V, ll. 83–4).
1012–13. Simpson (1986: 8) suggests that this refers specifically to Martianus
        Capella and Alanus of Lille, whose work has just been mentioned (above,
        ll. 985–6).
1015–17. Doob (1990: 334) relates the dreamer's anxiety here to *HF*'s larger
        concern with 'impaired vision'. Fyler (1979: 48) detects an ironic reference
        to bestiary lore, seeing the dreamer as 'a not very promising eaglet [who]
        risks a punishment recorded in the bestiaries' (i.e. being dropped).
1022.   'Look, by St Julian – a good place to stay'. The saint is mentioned in
        connection with hospitality in *Gen Prol*, l. 340. He was also the patron of
        ferrymen, so the eagle's appeal to him has additional aptness here.
1029.   In Ovid's House of Rumour (*Met.* XII, ll. 54–5) there are 'mingled (*mixta*)
        with truths . . . thousands of rumours'.

'And what soune is it lyke?' quod hee.
'Peter! – betynge of the see,'   *By St Peter*
1035   Quod y, 'ayen the roches holowe,   *hollow rocks*
Whan tempest doth the shippes swalowe –
And lat a man stond, out of doute,   *for sure*
A myle thens and here hyt route –   *away; roar*
Or elles lyke the last humblynge   *reverberation*
1040   After a clappe of oo thundringe,   *single thunderclap*
Whan Joves hath the aire ybete.
But yt doth me for fere swete.'   *sweat with fear*
'Nay, drede the not therof,' quod he.
'Hyt is no thinge will beten the;
1045   Thou shalt non harme have, truly.'
And with this worde both he and y
As nygh the place arryved were
As men may casten with a spere.
Y nyste how, but in a strete
1050   He sette me fayre on my fete   *gently*
And seyde: 'Walke forth apace   *steadily*
And take thyn aventure or case   *take your chance*
That thou shalt fynde in Fames place.'
'Now,' quod I, 'while we han space
1055   To speke, or that I goo fro the,   *before I leave you*
For the love of God, telle me –
In sooth that wil I of the lere –
Yf thys noyse that I here
Be, as I have herd the tellen,
1060   Of folke that doun in erthe duellen
And cometh here in the same wyse
As I the herde or this devyse,

1034–41. Both similes (the surging of the sea and the reverberation of thunder)
recall Ovid's House of Rumour again (*Met.* XII, ll. 50–2); cf. above, ll.
711–24 & n.
1041.   *the aire ybete*: 'made the air reverberate'.
1048.   'As (the length that) a spear could be thrown'.
1049.   The 'street' leading towards the 'palace' (l. 1090) may well recall Ovid's
description of the *via lactea* ('Milky Way') as 'a road . . . to the halls of the
great Thunderer (Jupiter)' in *Met.* I, l. 170.
1057.   'I really want to find out from you'.
1062.   'As I heard you say earlier'.

	And that there lives body nys	*is no living body*
	In al that hous that yonder ys	
1065	That maketh al this loude fare.'	*commotion*
	'Noo,' quod he, 'by Seynt Clare,	
	And also wis God rede me!	
	But o thinge y will warne the,	
	Of the whiche thou wolt have wonder:	
1070	Loo, to the House of Fame yonder	
	Thou wost now how cometh every speche –	
	Hyt nedeth noght eft the to teche;	*tell you again*
	But understond now ryght well this:	
	Whan eny spech ycomen ys	
1075	Up to the paleys, anonryght	
	Hyt wexeth lyke the same wight	*becomes; person*
	Which that the worde in erthe spake –	*Who spoke that*
	Be hyt clothed rede or blake –	
	And hath so verrey hys lyknesse	
1080	That spake the word, that thou wilt gesse	
	That it the same body be –	
	Man or woman, he or she.	
	And ys not this a wonder thynge?'	
	'Yis,' quod I tho, 'by heven kynge!'	*Heaven's*
1085	And with this word, 'Farewel,' quod he,	
	'And here I wol abyden the.	*wait for you*
	And God of heven sende the grace	
	Some goode to lerne in this place!'	*To learn something*

1066.   On the eagle's oaths, see above, l. 573 n.
1067.   'As God's my guide'.
1072.   'There's no need to tell you again'.
1073–83. Gellrich (1985: 193) notes that the idea of the identity of author and
   word goes back to Plato's *Cratylus*. Taylor (1989: 34) cites John of
   Salisbury (12th century) for writing as 'shapes indicating voice' and letters
   as media that 'speak voicelessly the utterances of the absent' (*Metalogicon*
   I, l. 13), and suggests that the *rede or blake* in which the words may be
   clothed (l. 1078) could allude to 'manuscripts with red capitals and
   rubrics'·(for further evidence about this see Carruthers 1990: 224–6). On
   the relationship between letter, sound and author in medieval grammatical
   theory, see Irvine 1985: 869.
1079.   'And shows so close a likeness to him'.
1084, 1087. Cf. the appeal to *Criste* and *hevene* in ll. 492–5.

              And I of him toke leve anon
1090   And gan forthe to the paleys gon.   *to walk*

              [BOOK 3]

              O god of science and of lyght –   *learning*
              Appollo, thurgh thy grete myght   *with your*
              This lytel laste boke thou gye!   *direct*
              Nat that I wilne for maistrye   *wish*
1095   Here art poetical be shewed –
              But, for the ryme ys lyght and lewed,
              Yit make hyt sumwhat agreable,
              Though some vers fayle in a syllable –
              And that I do no diligence
1100   To shew craft, but o sentence.
              And yif, devyne vertu, thow,   *power*
              Wilt helpe to shewe now
              That in myn hede ymarked ys –

1091–1109. The invocation to the final Book recalls the opening of Dante's *Par.*
        I, ll. 13–36, particularly through the phrases *devyne vertu* (l. 1101), *in
        myn hede ymarked* (l. 1103), and *entreth in my brest* (l. 1109), and
        through the allusion to the laurel, the tree sacred to Apollo, god of the sun,
        wisdom and poetry (ll. 1107–8; cf. also Ovid, *Met.* I, ll. 553–65). On the
        parallels and differences between Ch and Dante here, see Bennett 1968:
        100–3; Schless 1984: 68–70; Gellrich 1985: 179; and Wallace in Boitani &
        Mann 1986: 23.
1093.   For *boke* in the sense of 'division of a work', cf. *TC* III, l. 1818, and IV,
        l. 26. Stevenson (1978: 14) points out that *this lytel laste boke* is in fact
        'only slightly shorter than the first two books together'.
1094.   *for maistrye*: 'out of pride, to display skill'.
1095.   'That poetic craft should appear here'.
1096.   *lyght and lewed*: 'slight and unskilful'. For other disparaging remarks
        about 'Chaucer's' technical skill, see above, ll. 620–1; also *ML Intro*,
        ll. 47–8, and *Thop*, ll. 919–32. Lack of skill and the paucity of rhymes in
        English are mentioned in the *envoi* to *Complaint of Venus* (see Davis
        1974: 63).
1098.   *fayle in*: 'may lack'.
1099–1100. 'And since I am concerned not with displaying skill, but simply with
        sense'.
1103.   'What is engraved upon my memory' (*MED marken* v. 6).

	Loo, that is for to menen this,	*that is to say*
1105	The Hous of Fame for to discryve –	
	Thou shalt se me go as blyve	*at once*
	Unto the next laure y see	*laurel tree*
	And kysse yt, for hyt is thy tree.	
	Now entreth in my brest anoon!	
1110	Whan I was fro thys Egle goon	
	I gan beholde upon this place;	
	And certein, or I ferther pace,	*before; go on*
	I wol yow al the shap devyse	*describe the form*
	Of hous and citee and al the wyse	*citadel; manner*
1115	How I gan to this place aproche,	
	That stode upon so hygh a roche –	
	Hier stant ther non in Spayne.	*None higher is there*
	But up I clombe with alle payne	*climbed; great difficulty*
	And, though to clymbe it greved me,	*was hard for me*
1120	Yit I ententyf was to see	*eager*
	And for to powren wonder low	
	Yf I koude eny weyes know	*by any means*
	What maner stoon this roche was,	*kind of stone*
	For hyt was lyke alym de glas,	*alum crystals*
1125	But that hyt shone ful more clere.	*much more bright*
	But of what congeled matere	*frozen*
	Hyt was, nyste I never, redely.	*to be sure*
	But at the laste aspied I	*I perceived*
	And founde that hit was everydele	*entirely*
1130	A roche of yse and not of stele.	*ice*

1116. The site of Fame's house recalls the lofty position of Fortune's in *Anticlaudianus* VII, ll. 405f. and VIII, ll. 1–2 (tr. Sheridan 1973: 186, 189) and *RR*, ll. 5891–6058 (tr. Horgan 1994: 91–3), as also that of Ovid's Rumour 'at the top . . . in a citadel' (*Met.* XII, l. 43).

1121. *powren wonder lowe*: 'bend down and peer very low'.

1124. *alym de glas*: alum (used as a fixative in dyeing) was, as Ch would have known, exported to England by the Genoese; see Childs in Boitani 1983: 70.

1127. 'It was, I had no idea, for sure'.

1130. The House of Fortune in Nicole de Margival's *Dit de la panthère d'amours* is also said to be built upon ice (ed. Todd 1983: l. 1964, tr. Windeatt 1982: 130).

	Thought I: 'By Seynt Thomas of Kent,	*Thomas à Becket*
	This were a feble fundament	*poor foundation*
	To bilden on a place hye!	
	He ought him lytel glorifye	*scarcely be proud*
1135	That her-on bilt, God so me save!'	
	Tho sawgh I the halfe ygrave	*slope inscribed*
	With famouse folkes names fele	*With many names of*
	That had iben in mochel wele	*been; great prosperity*
	And her fames wide yblowe,	*widespread*
1140	But wel unnethes koude I knowe	*scarcely at all*
	Any lettres for to rede	
	Hir names by, for, out of drede,	
	They were almost ofthowed, so	*thawed away*
	That of the lettres oon or two	
1145	Was molte away of every name –	
	So unfamouse was wox hir fame.	*had become*
	But, men seyn, what may ever last?	
	Thoo gan I in myn herte cast	*consider*
	That they were molte awey with hete	
1150	And not awey with stormes bete,	*worn away by*
	For on that other syde I say	*saw*
	Of this hille, that northewarde lay,	
	How hit was writen ful of names	*all inscribed with*
	Of folkes that hadden grete fames	
1155	Of olde tyme, and yet they were	*Long ago; still*
	As fressh as men had writen hem here	
	The selfe day, ryght or that oure	*same*
	That I upon hem gan to poure.	*peer*

1131. The reference is to St Thomas à Becket of Canterbury, one of a number of saints invoked in *HF* who have particular associations with pilgrimage and travel (cf. ll. 117, 885, 1022, 1183). See also above, l. 573 n.

1136–46. Bennett (1968: 107) sees the melting away of the famous names as Ch's development of the traditional comparison between worldly vanity and 'letters written in ice'. For examples of the image, see Boitani 1984: 69.

1141–2. *for to rede / Hir names by*: 'by which to identify their names' (*MED* reden v.(1) 3(a)).

1152. The *northewarde* side of the hill would be shaded from the *hete* of the sun (see below, ll. 1160–4).

1157. *ryght or that oure*: 'just before the time'.

But wel I wiste what yt made:
1160 Hyt was conserved with the shade   *preserved by*
(Alle this writynge that I sigh)   *saw*
Of a castel stoode on high,   *castle that*
And stoode eke on so colde a place   *(the writing) was*
That hete myght hit not deface.
1165   Thoo gan I up the hille to goone
And fonde upon the cop a woone,
That al the men that ben on lyve   *alive*
Ne han the konnyng to descrive   *skill*
The beaute of that ylke place,
1170 Ne coude casten no compace   *devise no scheme*
Swich another for to make
That myght of beaute ben his make –   *its equal*
Ne so wonderlych ywrought
That hit astonyeth yit my thought
1175 And maketh alle my wyt to swynke,   *strain*
On this castel to bethynke,
So that the grete beaute,
The caste, the curiosite,   *shape; elegance*
Ne kan I not to yow devyse –
1180 My wit ne may me not suffise.   *skill*
      But, natheles, alle the substance   *main features*
I have yit in my remembrance:
Forwhi, me thought, be Seynt Gyle,   *St Giles*
Alle was of ston of beryle,   *It was all made*
1185 Bothe castel and the toure   *tower*
And eke the halle and every boure,   *chamber*

1159 *what yt made*: 'what caused this'.
1166. 'And found at the top a house'.
1170. 'Nor could they devise any clever scheme'. For the meaning of *compace* here, see *MED compas* n. 1 (a–b).
1181. Cf. above, l. 768.
1183. St Giles was another popular pilgrimage saint. On his shrine (nr. Arles), see Sumption 1975: 82, 104, 107–8.
1184. *of ston of beryle*: 'made of beryl'. This may allude to the (green or white) precious stone that forms the eighth foundation of the paradisal city (New Jerusalem) in Rev. 21:20. See also Koonce 1966: 195–6, and the further reference to *walles of berille* below, l. 1288 & n.

	Wythouten peces or joynynges.	*segments; joints*
	But many subtile compassinges,	*contrivances*
	Babewynnes and pynacles,	
1190	Ymageries and tabernacles	
	I say, and ful eke of wyndowes	
	As flakes falle in grete snowes.	
	And eke in ech of the pynacles	
	Weren sondry habitacles,	*various niches*
1195	In which stoden, alle withoute,	
	Ful the castel alle aboute,	
	Of al maner mynstralles	*musicians*
	And gestiours that tellen tales	*storytellers*
	Both of wepinge and of game,	*sorrow; joy*
1200	Of alle that longeth unto fame.	*has to do with*
	Ther herd I pleyen upon an harpe	
	That sowned bothe wel and sharpe,	*sounded; loudly*
	Orpheus, ful craftely.	*very skilfully*
	And on the syde, faste by,	*close by*
1205	Sat the harper, Orion,	*Arion*
	And Eaycides Chiron	*Achilles's Chiron*

1187–94. Cf. the attention to architectural detail (and use of some similar vocabulary) above, ll. 120–7, and below, in ll. 1299–1306. Braswell (1981: 107–8) notes that several of the architectural terms (*joynynges, compassinges, habitacles*) occur here for the first time in recorded usage.

1189–90. 'Grotesques and pinnacles, carvings and canopied niches'. Smalley (1960: 167 & n. 3) points out that Robert Holcot (an early 14th-century Oxford theologian) 'illustrates the vice of self-importance from the painted carving of a grotesque or "babwen" [*babbewynus*] on a corbel'. On Holcot's importance for *HF*, see Boitani 1984: 141–9.

1196. 'All around the castle'.

1197. On the role of minstrels in this period, see Olson 1941: 69–70; Wilkins 1979: ch. 5; and Southworth 1989: chs 1, 8.

1203. Delany (1972: 90) cites a number of sources, including Dante (*Conv.* II, ch. 1) and the *Ovide moralisé* (X, ll. 396–407), stressing Orpheus's 'divine inspiration', but there does not seem to be much in the context here to suggest he is more than a supremely *crafty* performer.

1205. For the story of Arion, the Greek harper, see Ovid, *Fasti* II, ll. 79–118.

1206. Chiron, the centaur, was famed for his skill in music. He taught Achilles, here referred to as *Eaycides* (= grandson of Aeacus). See Statius, *Achilleid* (ed. and tr. Mozley 1928) I, ll. 1, 109–97.

And other harpers many oon,
And the Bret Glascurion.   *Welsh*
And smale harpers with her gleës   *instruments*
1210   Sate under hem in divers seës   *in various seats*
And gonne on hem upwarde to gape   *gaze*
And countrefen hem as an ape,   *imitate; like*
Or as crafte countrefeteth kynde.   *art; nature*
Tho saugh I stonden hem behynde,
1215   Afer fro hem, al be hem selve,
Many a thousand tymes twelve
That maden lowde menstralcies   *music*
In cornemuse and shalmyes –   *bagpipes; shawms*
And many other maner pipe
1220   That craftely begonne to pipe   *skilfully*
Both in doucet and in rede,   *recorders; reeds*
That ben at festes with the brede –   *roast dishes*
And many flowte and liltyng horne   *flute; small trumpet*
And pipes made of grene corne,   *unripe corn*
1225   As han thise lytel herde gromes   *young herdsmen*
That kepen bestis in the bromes.   *on the heath*
Ther saugh I than Atiteris   *Tityrus(?)*
And of Athenes Daun Pseustis,

1208.   *Glascurion*, probably 'Gwydion' (a N. Welsh bard), may be further
evidence of oral tradition in *HF* (Breeze 1994: 68), and could be a kind of
'modern counterpart' to Orpheus (Bennett 1968: 122).
1211–13. On medieval views of art as the 'ape of nature', see especially Janson
1952: 287–93, and, on the metaphoric use of *simia* ('ape'), Curtius 1953:
538–40. Delany (1973: 4) compares *Inf.* XXIX, l. 139.
1214.   *hem behynde*: 'below them'.
1215.   'Far away from them, all by themselves'. For accounts of the musical
instruments described here, see Olson 1941: 73–4; Hayes 1960; and
Wilkins 1979: ch. 6.
1216.   The same expression recurs below, l. 2126, and there may in both cases be
a parodic allusion to the 12 times 12,000 servants of God in Rev. 7:4–8.
1227.   *Atiteris*: Norton-Smith (1974: 41) suggests that the name might mean
'Far-from-Tityrus' (the shepherd-singer of Virgil's first *Eclogue*), hence a
bad versifier.
1228–32. *Pseustis* represented pagan mythology in Theodulus's *Egloga*
(9th-century Latin poem). He challenges Alithia (Truth) to a poetry
contest which she wins (see Bennett 1968: 123). *Marcia* is Marsyas, the

	And Marcia that lost her skyn,	*Marsyas*
1230	Bothe in face, body and chyn,	
	For that she wolde envien, loo,	*Because*; *aspire*
	To pipen bet than Appolloo.	*Apollo*
	Ther saugh I famous, olde and yonge	
	Pipers of all the Duche tonge,	*German nation*
1235	To lerne love-daunces, sprynges,	
	Rens and these straunge thynges.	*Running dances*
	Tho saugh I in an other place	
	Stonden in a large space	
	Of hem that maken blody soun	*Those who*; *ferocious*
1240	In trumpe, beme and claryoun –	
	For in fyght and blodeshedynge	
	Ys used gladly clarionynge.	*Trumpeting*; *eagerly*
	Ther herd I trumpen Messenus	*Misenus*
	Of whom that speketh Virgilius;	

satyr who similarly challenged Apollo to a flute-playing competition, and having lost was flayed alive (see *Met.* VI, ll. 382–400, and *Par.* I, ll. 19–21). The allusions to rash challenges may thus contribute to the theme of pride and folly in *HF* (see above, ll. 915, 919–24, 940–59). On Ch's confusion about the gender of *Marcia* (a male satyr), see Bennett 1968: 123; David 1974.

1233–6. The reference to Dutch/German/Flemish pipers marks a return to the world of contemporary fashions after the group of classical allusions in ll. 1227–32. Several pipers in the 14th-century English court seem to be from this area (see Smith 1950: 524–5; Southworth 1989: 104).

1235.   '(Who could) teach dances for lovers, lively dances'.

1237–42. The 'other place' occupied by the trumpeters could perhaps be the battlements of the castle, which is often where such musicians appear in manuscripts and accounts of royal entrances (see, for example, many of the illustrations in MS Bodley 264 of the *Roman d'Alexandre* (facsimile edn James 1933)).

1240.   *trumpe, beme … claryoun*: kinds of trumpet (possibly here long, wooden or short; see Remnant 1989: 147; Wilkins 1979: 154–5; and Southworth 1989: 102–3). See also *Boece* II, met. 5, ll. 23–4, and *Kn T*, ll. 2599–2600.

1243–4. Misenus was the son of Aeolus, the god of the winds (*Aen.* VI, l. 164), whose *clariouns* are first mentioned below, ll. 1573–9. Like Pseustis and Marsyas above (ll. 1228–9), he also seems to represent the perils of overreaching, since his challenge to the gods ended badly (*Aen.* VI, ll. 171–4).

1245	Ther herd I trumpe Joab also,
	Theodomas and other mo,
	And al that used clarion
	In Cataloigne and Aragon,
	That in her tyme famous were
1250	To lerne, saugh I trumpe there.
	There saugh I sit in other seës,
	Pleyinge upon sondry gleës
	Which that I kan not nevene,
	Moo than sterres ben in hevene,
1255	Of whiche I nyl as now not ryme,
	For ese of yow and losse of tyme –
	For tyme ylost, this knowen ye,
	Be no way may recovered be.
	Ther saugh I pley jugelours,
1260	Magiciens and tregetours,
	And Phitonesses, charmeresses,
	Olde wyches and sorceresses
	That use exorsicacions
	And eke thes fumygacions –

Marginal glosses:
- *others as well* (1246)
- *Catalonia* (1248)
- *instruments* (1252)
- *name* (1253)
- *your convenience* (1256)
- *entertainers* (1259)
- *illusionists* (1260)
- *incantations* (1263)
- *fumigation* (1264)

1245. Joab, one of the leaders of King David's army, blew the trumpet after killing the king's rebellious son, Absalom (see 2 Sam. 18:16, 2:28 and 20:22).

1246. Theodomas, a Theban soothsayer, was not a trumpeter, but his prophecies are followed in Statius's *Thebaid* by the blowing of trumpets (see *Theb.* VIII, ll. 277f., 342–5).

1247–50. Spanish trumpeters (from Catalonia and Aragon) may well have been heard by Ch during his journey to Spain in 1366 and may have been employed in John of Gaunt's household (see Smith 1950: 526).

1255–8. Other abbreviating formulae (the *occupatio* figure) are at ll. 1282–4, 1329–35, 1505–6 and 1513.

1259–64. *Jugelours* and *tregetours* are elsewhere in Ch's work associated with deception and illusion on a larger scale (*Fri T*, l. 1467, *Sq T*, ll. 217–19, *Fkl T*, ll. 1141, 1143, 1265). For the activities of professional illusionists in this period, see Loomis 1958: 242–55 and Kieckhefer 1989: 98–100.

1261. 'And female conjurers and enchantresses'. *Phitonesses* are witches possessed by a spirit, like the Witch of Endor, consulted by Saul (see 1 Sam. 28:7–25 and 1 Chr. 10:13).

1264–70. *fumygacions* involve the use of aromatic smoke (from aloes, saffron, balsam or more bizarre material) and are often connected with 'astral

1265	And clerkes eke, which konne wel	*are learned in*
	Alle this magikes naturel,	*occult science*
	That craftely doon her ententes	*cunningly; designs*
	To maken in certeyn ascendentes	
	Ymages, lo, thrugh which magike	*effigies*
1270	To make a man ben hool or syke.	*well or ill*
	Ther saugh I the, quene Medea,	
	And Circes eke and Calipsa;	*Circe; Calypso*
	Ther saugh I Hermes Ballenus,	
	Limete and eke Symon Magus;	*Elymas(?)*
1275	There saugh I, and knew by name,	
	That be such arte don men han fame.	*Those who; cause*
	Ther saugh I Colle tregetour	*Colin the conjurer*
	Upon a table of sygamour	*block; sycamore*
	Pleye an uncouthe thynge to telle:	
1280	Y saugh him carien a wyndmelle	*windmill*
	Under a walshnote shale.	*walnut shell*
	What shuld I make lenger tale	*give; description*
	Of alle the peple y ther say	

magic' of the kind referred to here; see Thorndike 1923–58: II, 698, III, 431 and 606–7; Kieckhefer 1989: 166. Some forms of *magik naturel* involving the making of *ymages* during *ascendentes* (appropriate astrological moments) are practised by Ch's Physician (*Gen Prol*, ll. 415–18). On the making of effigies for both benign and malign purposes, see Kieckhefer 1989: 97, 131–3.

1271–4. Medea used her magical powers to help Jason win the Golden Fleece (see *Met*. VII, ll. 1–296, and *LGW*, ll. 1580–1650). Circe was the enchantress overcome by Odysseus/Ulysses (see *Odyssey* X and *Met*. XIV), and Ballenus was thought to be the author of several treatises on magic (see Thorndike 1923–58: II, 234–5). All three are included in a list of ultimately ineffectual exponents of sorcery in *RR*, ll. 14365–78 (tr. Horgan 1994: 222). Along with *Limete* ('Elymas' in Acts 13:8–11?) and Simon Magus (Acts 8:9–24), they could all be seen as examples of overreaching *craft* (cf. above, ll. 1227–32 & n., 1243–50 & n.).

1277–81. *Colle tregetour* was 'probably an English magician mentioned [as "Colin T."] in a French manual of conversation composed in 1396, and declared to have practised his art recently at Orléans' (Rob.).

1279. 'Create an effect that is strange to describe' (*MED pleien* v. (1) 6(b)). For other illusions and similar tricks, see *Fkl T*, ll. 1139–51, 1189–1204, and Southworth 1989: 14–15.

Fro hennes unto domes-day?
1285   Whan I had al this folk beholde
And fonde me louse and not iholde –   *free; confined*
And eft imused longe while
Upon these walles of berile
That shoone ful lyghter than a glas
1290   And made wel more than hit was   *much larger*
To semen every thinge ywis,
As kynde thynge of Fames is –
I gan forth romen til I fonde
The castel yate on my ryght honde,   *gate*
1295   Which that so wel corven was   *carved*
That never suche another nas –
And yit it was be aventure
Iwrought as often as be cure.
Hyt nedeth noght yow more to tellen –
1300   To make yow to longe duellen –   *delay too long*
Of these yates florisshinges,   *ornamentation*
Ne of compasses, ne of kervynges,   *contrivances*
Ne how they hate in masoneries –
As corbettes full of ymageryes.   *corbels; carvings*
1305   But lorde, so feyre yt was to showe!   *to see*
For hit was alle with gold behewe.   *inlaid with gold*
But in I went and that anoon;
Ther mette I cryinge many oon:
'A, larges, larges! holde up wel!

1284.   '(Which would last) from now until Judgment Day'.
1287.   'And having then gazed for a long time'.
1288–9. Cf. above, l. 1184 & n. The description here suggests that Ch is thinking
         of a form of rock-crystal also known as 'beryl' that was used for glazing
         and magnifying (e.g. in spectacles). The beryl as gem was also said in the
         lapidaries to 'magnify' the status of the wearer (Marbode, *De Lapidibus*,
         ed. Riddle 1977: 49, 199; Evans & Serjeantson 1933: 28, 48, 72).
1290–2. 'And made everything, indeed, seem much larger than it was, as is the
         usual effect of Fame'.
1297–8. 'And yet it was shaped as much by chance as by design'.
1303.   *hate in masoneries*: 'are termed in architecture'; cf. above, ll. 1187–94, and
         Braswell 1981: 108.
1309.   *A, larges*: be generous; *holde up wel*: support (us) well (*MED holden* v.(1)
         17(a)).

1310	God save the lady of thys pel,	*castle*
	Our owne gentil lady, Fame,	*noble*
	And hem that wilnen to have name	*want; reputation*
	Of us!' Thus herd y crien alle,	*Through us*
	And fast comen out of halle	*(they) came*
1315	And shoke nobles and sterlynges.	
	And some corouned wer as kynges,	*were crowned*
	With corounes wrought ful of losynges,	*diamond shapes*
	And many ryband and many frynges	*ribbons*
	Were on her clothes, trewly.	
1320	Thoo, attelast, aspyed y	
	That pursevantes and heraudes	
	That crien ryche folkes laudes	*proclaim; praises*
	Hyt weren alle, and every man	
	Of hem, as y yow tellen can,	
1325	Had on him throwen a vesture	*garment*
	Whiche that men clepen a cote armure,	*heraldic tunic*
	Enbrowded wonderliche ryche,	*Embroidered*
	Alle though they nere nought ylyche.	*not matching*
	But noght nyl I, so mote y thryve,	*as I hope to*
1330	Ben aboute to dyscryve	*Start describing*
	Al these armes that ther weren	
	That they thus on her cote beren –	
	For hyt to me were impossible;	
	Men myght make of hem a bible	*tome, treatise*
1335	XX^{ti} foote thykke, y trowe.	*Twenty feet*
	For, certeyn, who so koude iknowe,	*anyone; identify*

1315. 'And scattered nobles and silver pennies'. The noble (value 6 shillings and 8 pence) was England's own gold coin during the later Middle Ages, and there are particularly fine examples from the reign of Edward III (Baker 1961: 284–6).

1321–35. The attention to heralds here may reflect their literary importance. *Pursevants* ('pursuivants', junior heralds) 'continued to provide the aristocracy with literary publicity until well into the Tudor period' (Green 1980: 169).

1329–30. 'But I do not, so help me, / Mean to start describing'.

1334–5. The notion (even the 'impossible' one) of composing a 20-foot-thick book to describe just one feature of the dream perhaps reflects the theme of increase and multiplicity in *HF*. For other references to books, see above, ll. 385, 426, 429, 622, 657 and 712.

	Myght ther alle the armes seen	
	Of famouse folke that han ybeen	
	In Auffrike, Europe and Asye,	*Africa*; *Asia*
1340	Sith first began the chevalrie.	
	Loo, how shulde I now tel al thys?	
	Ne, of the halle eke, what nede is	
	To tellen yow that every walle	
	Of hit, and flore and roof and alle,	
1345	Was plated half a foote thikke	
	Of gold, and that nas no thynge wikke –	
	But for to prove, in alle wyse,	
	As fyne as ducat in Venyse,	*Venice*
	Of whiche to lytyl yn my pouche is?	*purse*
1350	And they wer set as thik of nouchis	
	Ful of the fynest stones faire	
	That men reden in the *Lapidaire*,	*read of*; De Lapidibus
	As greses growen in a mede –	*grass*; *meadow*
	But hit were alle to longe to rede	*tell*
1355	The names, and therfore I pace.	*let it pass*
	But in this lusty and ryche place	*pleasant*
	That Fames halle called was	
	Ful moche prees of folke ther nas,	*throng*; *was not*
	Ne crowdyng for to mochil prees –	*too great a*
1360	But al on hye, above a dees,	*upon a daïs*

1340.   *the chevalrie*: 'knighthood'.

1346.   *no thynge wikke*: 'certainly not poor quality'.

1347.   'But could be shown by any kind of test'.

1348.   The Venetian ducat was first coined in 1284 (see Baker 1961: 287).

1349.   The poet's complaint about lack of money could be a wry echo on his part of the courtiers' call for *larges* (above, l. 1309).

1350–1.   'And they [the walls] were as thickly adorned with bosses made of the finest gems'.

1352.   *De Lapidibus* by Marbode, Bishop of Rennes (c. 1035–1123) was a major source of medical and magical lore about the properties of precious and semi-precious stones (see Riddle 1977). For English lapidaries of the 14th and 15th centuries, see Evans & Serjeantson 1933 (EETS o.s. 190).

1360–94.   The images and allusions that introduce Fame seem to be a mixture of the imposing and the grotesque. The *ruby* of which her throne is made (ll. 1362–3) was traditionally associated with lordship (see Evans & Serjeantson 1933: 21). Her alterations of size (ll. 1368–76) recall the

	Satte in a see imperiall,	*Placed; throne of power*
	That made was of a rubee all	
	Which that a carbuncle ys ycalled,	
	Y saugh, perpetually ystalled,	*enthroned*
1365	A femynyne creature,	
	That never formed by Nature	
	Nas suche another thing yseye.	*to be seen*
	For, altherfirst, soth for to seye,	*first of all*
	Me thought she was so lyte	*small*
1370	That the lengthe of a cubite	
	Was lenger than she semed be.	
	This was gret marvaylle to me: [she]	
	Hir tho so wonderly streight	*stretched*
	That with hir fete she erthe reight	*reached*
1375	And with hir hed she touched hevene,	
	Ther as shynen sterres sevene.	
	And therto eke, as to my witte,	*way of thinking*
	I saugh a gretter wonder yitte,	
	Upon her eyen to biholde –	
1380	But, certeyn, y hem never tolde,	*could never count*
	For as feele yen had she	*many eyes*
	As fetheres upon foules be,	*birds*
	Or weren on the bestes foure	*four beasts*
	That Goddis trone gunne honoure,	*throne*
1385	As John writ in th' Apocalips.	*Apocalypse*

initial appearance of Boethius's Philosophy in *Cons.* I, pr. 1, as well as the
bizarre figure of Rumour (*Fama*) in Virgil's *Aeneid* (IV, ll. 175–7). Her
multiple eyes (ll. 1377–85) explicitly evoke the four beasts 'full of eyes'
(representing the four evangelists and symbolizing divine omniscience)
who appear before God's throne in Rev. 4:6, 8. They also, less auspi-
ciously, recall Virgil's Rumour again (*Aen.* IV, ll. 181–2), as does Fame's
multitude of pricked-up ears and tongues in ll. 1389–90 (cf. *Aen.* IV,
l. 183).

1370.   *cubite*: 'cubit', the length of a forearm (about 45–50 cm).

1383–4. See above, n. on ll. 1360–94. The representation of the Last Judgment
and the city of New Jerusalem in the Book of Revelation (*Apocalips*)
provided images of great influence on medieval art and literature. For
other evocations of apocalypse, judgment and the 'world's end' in *HF*, see
ll. 1284, 1640 and 1867 (see also *Pearl*, ed. Gordon 1953, ll. 973ff.;
Koonce 1966: 181–279; Kiser 1991: 33–4).

Hir heere, that oundye was and crips,
As burned gold hyt shoon to see –   *polished*
And, soth to tellen, also she
Had also fele upstondyng eres   *many; pricked-up*
1390   And tonges as on bestes heres –
And on hir fete waxen saugh y   *I saw growing*
Partriches wynges, redely.   *Partridge's*
But, lorde, the perry and the richesse   *jewelry*
I saugh sittyng on this godesse!
1395   And, lord, the hevenyssh melodye   *heavenly*
Of songes ful of armonye
I herd aboute her trone ysonge,
That al the paleys walles ronge.   *resounded*
So songe the myghty Muse, she
1400   That cleped ys Caliope,   *is called Calliope*
And hir eighte sustren eke   *sisters*
That in her face semen meke.
And ever mo, eternally,
They synge of Fame, as thoo herd y:
1405   'Heryed be thou and thy name,   *Be praised*
Goddesse of renoun or of Fame!'
Tho was I war, loo, atte laste,   *aware*
As I myn eyen gan up caste,
That thys ylke noble quene
1410   On her shuldres gan sustene   *was bearing*

1386.   'Her hair that was wavy and curly'.
1390.   'And (as many) tongues as hairs upon an animal'.
1392.   The partridge wings may derive from a misreading of *Aen.* IV, l. 180, but could allude to the bird's limited powers of flight (see Koonce 1966: 212 n. 76). For a possible allusion to Perdix (Daedalus's nephew and a supposedly superior craftsman), see Doob 1990: 324.
1395–1406. The Muses' song for Fame has been variously interpreted. Koonce (1966: 213) argues that their performance parodies the songs of praise before the throne of the Lamb (Rev. 5 and 7) and recalls the 'sweet poison' offered to the prisoner by the 'poetical Muses' (*Cons.* I, pr. 1), whilst Bennett (1968: 132) and Boitani (1984: 15) see a more positive connection between poetry and fame. On the sources and models for Ch's Muses, see Hardman 1986: esp. 482–91, Taylor & Bordier 1992: esp. 219, 223; see also above, ll. 520–2 & n.
1402.   'Whose expressions seem humble'.

Bothe armes and the name	*the (coat of) arms*
Of thoo that hadde large fame:	
Alexander and Hercules,	
That with a shert hys lyfe les.	*through; lost*
1415 And thus fonde y syttynge this goddes	
In nobley, honour and ryches,	
Of which I stynte a while now,	*cease*
Other thinge to tellen yow.	
Tho saugh I stonde on eyther syde,	
1420 Streight doun to the dores wide	
Fro the dees, many a peler	*column*
Of metal that shoon not ful clere;	
But though they nere of no rychesse,	
Yet they were made for gret noblesse	*as a sign of*
1425 And in hem gret sentence;	
And folkes of digne reverence	
(Of whiche I wil yow telle fonde)	*try to tell*
Upon a piler saugh I stonde.	
Alderfirste, loo, ther I sighe,	*First of all*
1430 Upon a piler stonde on highe	
That was of lede and yren fyne,	*lead; iron*
Hym of secte saturnyne,	

1412–14. Opposing views of Alexander's contemporary reputation – as 'a medieval overreacher who must be taught the lesson of humility', or as 'a model prince and ruler, one of the Nine Worthies' – are offered by Delany (1972: 92) and Boitani (1984: 166–7). Hercules is usually treated as both heroic and virtuous (Delany 1972: 92–3), although his infidelity to Deianira is alluded to here and above, ll. 402–4. Cf. also *LGW*, ll. 1454 and 1543–7, where he appears both as heroic Argonaut and as party to Jason's seduction of Hypsipyle.

1419–27. Various actual or fictional models have been proposed for the rows of columns in Fame's hall: from the images of famous figures in *Anti-claudianus* (I, ll. 131–83) to buildings in Paris and Gothic cathedrals (Bennett 1968: 134–5; Braswell 1981: 108–9; Kendrick 1984: 121–4). For images on columns in this period, see also Camille 1989: 199–200.

1425. *gret sentence*: '(signs of) serious subject-matter'.

1426. *of digne reverence*: 'of well-deserved status'.

1432. *secte saturnyne*: 'the Jewish race'.

The Ebrayke Josephus, the olde,	*Hebrew*
That of Jewes gestes tolde,	*wrote chronicles*
1435 And he bare on hys shuldres hye	
The fame up of the Jewrye.	*Jewish people*
And by hym stoden other sevene,	*seven more*
Wise and worthy for to nevene,	*be named*
To helpen hym bere up the charge –	*load*
1440 Hyt was so hevy and so large.	
And, for they writen of batayles	
As wel as other olde mervayles,	
Therfor was, loo, thys pilere	
Of whiche that I yow telle here	
1445 Of lede and yren bothe, ywys –	
For yren Martes metal ys,	*Mars's*
Which that god is of batayle,	*who is god*
And the lede, withouten faille,	*indeed*
Ys, loo, the metal of Saturne	
1450 That hath a ful large whele to turne.	
Thoo stoden forthe on every rowe	*appeared*
Of hem which that I koude knowe,	*recognize*
Though I hem noght be ordre telle,	
To make yow to longe to duelle	
1455 These of whiche I gonne rede.	*began to tell*
There saugh I stonde, out of drede,	
Upon an yren piler stronge	
That peynted was al endlonge	*its whole length*
With tigres blode in every place,	
1460 The Tholausan that hight Stace	*Statius*

1433. *Josephus* (b. AD 37/8) was author of works on Jewish history that were known in the Middle Ages through Latin translations (see Bennett 1968: 138).

1435. For the idea of writers bearing their subject matter on their shoulders, cf. Horace, *De Arte Poetica*, ll. 38–40 (Simpson 1986: 14–15).

1445ff. The material of the columns reflects some traditional links between metals and planets/gods. Cf. *Kn T*, l. 1983, and Boccaccio, *Tes.* VII, st. 32–3, 57.

1450. 'Whose orbit is very wide'. Cf. *Kn T*, ll. 2454–5.

1454. *make ... to duelle*: 'delay'. See above, ll. 1255–8 & n.

1457–9. Statius (c. 45–96), author of the *Thebaid*, was confused with a rhetorician of the same name who was born in Toulouse. He is also identified here with an unfinished epic (the *Achilleid*), as in *Purg.* XXI, l. 92.

That bare of Thebes up the fame
Upon his shuldres, and the name
Also of cruelle Achilles.
And by him stood, withouten les,   *to be sure*
1465   Ful wonder hye on a pilere
Of yren, he, the gret Omere,   *Homer*
And with him Dares and Tytus   *Dictys*
Before, and eke he, Lollius,
And Guydo eke de Columpnis,
1470   And Englyssh Gaunfride eke, ywis –   *Geoffrey of Monmouth*
And eche of these, as have I joye,
Was besye for to bere up Troye;
So hevy therof was the fame
That for to bere hyt was no game.   *no joke*
1475   But yet I gan ful wel espie,
Betwex hem was a litel envye:
Oon seyde Omere made lyes,
Feynynge in hys poetries,
And was to Grekes favorable –
1480   Therfor held he hyt but fable.

1464–74. With Homer (*Omere*, also cited as an authority in *TC* I, l. 146 and V, l. 1792) Ch turns to the multiplicity of texts about Troy. These include the supposed eye-witnesses, Dares and Dictys (*Tytus*) (possibly 1st-century AD); the author of a 13th-century Latin abridgement of the story, Guido de Columnis (delle Colonne); and the 12th-century British chronicler, Geoffrey of Monmouth (*Englyssh Gaunfride*). The enigmatic *Lollius* appears to be the same fictitious *auctour* for the matter of Troy who is invoked in *TC* I, l. 394 and V, l. 1653, and whose name may stem from a medieval misreading of a line in Horace (Pratt 1950).

1468.   *Before*: 'in front [of Homer]'.

1475–80. For an account of the long medieval tradition of casting doubt on Homer's accuracy, see Minnis & Scott 1991: 114–16. The *oon* who does so here could conceivably be Guido de Columnis (see above, l. 1469), who at the beginning and end of his *Historia Destructionis Troiae* accuses the Greek poet of making things up (ed. Griffin 1936: 4, 276; tr. Meek 1974: 1, 265). See also the discussion of Homer and fiction in Boccaccio, tr. Osgood 1956: 48–9. On truth, tradition and storytelling more generally in *HF*, see Shepherd 1979.

1478.   *Feynynge*: 'falsifying'; *poetries*: 'poetic fictions'.

1480.   'And so he thought it [Homer's version] was just a tale'.

Tho saugh I stonde on a pilere
That was of tynned yren clere   *tin-plated iron*
The Latyn poete Virgile
That bore hath up longe while
1485   The fame of Pius Eneas.
And next hym on a piler was
Of coper, Venus clerk, Ovide,
That hath ysowen wonder wide   *spread*
The grete god of loves name,
1490   And there he bare up wel hys fame
Upon this piler, also hye   *as high*
As I hyt myght se with myn yë –
For-why this halle of whiche I rede
Was woxen on highthe, length and brede   *Had grown; breadth*
1495   Wel more, be a thousand dele,   *a thousand times*
Than hyt was erst, that saugh I wel.   *had been before*
Thoo saugh I on a piler by,   *nearby*
Of yren, wroght ful sturnely,   *sturdily*

1481–5. Virgil, like Ch's other main *auctours* for *HF* (Ovid, Boethius and Dante), is credited by name, though more often than the rest (cf. ll. 378, 449, 1244). His hero Aeneas here makes his last appearance, with an epithet (*Pius*) that reflects his devotion to family and country rather than his role as *traytour* to Dido (see above, ll. 267, 294, etc.). *Poete* here (and in l. 1499) still carries its usual meaning of 'classical, illustrious author' (see Olson 1979: 272–90; Brownlee 1984: 7, 220–1); the only vernacular writers to whom Ch (later) gives the title are Dante and Petrarch. The material of which Virgil's column is made is more *clere* than those of the other pillars and is probably meant to reflect his pre-eminent status; it was also the metal of Jupiter, Aeneas's protector (Bennett 1968: 142).

1486–7. *on a piler was / Of coper*: 'on a copper column was'.

1486–92. The second reference to Ovid by name in *HF* (see above, l. 379). The copper of his column was the metal of Venus (as was lead of Saturn and tin of Jupiter), and his stance reflects the importance of his work (esp. *Her.*, *AA*, *Met.*) as a source of exemplary material about the power of love.

1490. *hys*: i.e. 'the God of Love's'.

1497–1502. Lucan (AD 39–65), author of an epic (the *Bellum Civile*) about the war between Julius Caesar and Pompey (l. 1502), was highly regarded as an epic poet in the Middle Ages; see *Inf.* IV, l. 90; Curtius 1953: 260; Minnis & Scott 1991: 38, 115, 155–8.

	The grete poete, Daun Lucan,	
1500	And on hys shuldres bare up than,	*then*
	As high as that y myght see,	
	The fame of Julius and Pompe;	*Caesar; Pompey*
	And by him stoden alle these clerkes	*scholars*
	That writen of Romes myghty werkes,	
1505	That, yf y wolde her names telle	
	Alle to longe most I dwelle.	
	And next him on a piler stoode	
	Of soulfre, lyke as he were woode,	*sulphur; mad*
	Daun Claudian, the sothe to telle,	
1510	That bare up al the fame of helle,	*furthered*
	Of Pluto and of Proserpyne	*Proserpina*
	That quene ys of the derke pyne.	*grim torments*
	What shulde y more telle of this?	
	The halle was al ful, ywys,	
1515	Of hem that writen of the olde gestes	*famous deeds*
	As ben on treës rokes nestes –	*rooks'*
	But hit a ful confus matere	*troublesome thing*
	Were al the gestes for to here	
	That they of write, or how they hight.	*are called*
1520	But, while that y beheld this sight,	
	I herd a noyse aprochen blyve	*rapidly*
	That ferde as been don in an hive	*sounded; bees do*

1507–12. Claudian (d. c. 404) describes hell in *De raptu Proserpinae*, an
    unfinished epic about the abduction of Proserpina, daughter of Ceres
    (goddess of agriculture), by Pluto, god of the underworld. Pratt (1947:
    425) suggests that the *soulfre* of the column alludes to the vivid description
    of sulphur at points in Claudian's poem and notes that the portrayal of
    Claudian as *woode* 'must have been prompted by the rhapsodic manner of
    the *De raptu*'. Cf. the earlier reference to Claudian, alongside Virgil and
    Dante, as an authority on hell (above, l. 449).

1513–19. The comparison of the illustrious writers to rooks seems to shift the
    tone from celebration to confusion (cf. *confus matere*, l. 1517) and to
    prefigure the *noyse* that is about to break out (l. 1521). Watts (1973: 98)
    suggests the image 'may apply only to minor poets', but that distinction is
    not apparent in ll. 1514–15.

1521.   Cf. the other kinds of *noyse* associated with Fame and Rumour above, ll.
    1024–42, and below, ll. 1927–44.

1522–3. 'That sounded like bees in a hive / When they are about to swarm out'.

Ayen her tyme of oute fleynge;
Ryght suche a maner murmuryng,
1525   For al the world, hyt semed me.
          Tho gan I loke aboute and see
That ther come entryng into the halle
A ryght grete companye withalle –
And that of sondry regiouns,
1530   Of alleskynnes condiciouns
That duelle in erthe under the mone,
Pore and ryche – and also sone
As they were come in to the halle,
They gonne doun on kneës falle
1535   Before this ilke noble quene
And seyde: 'Graunte us, lady shene,   *bright*
Eche of us, of thy grace a bone!'   *favour*
And some of hem she graunted sone,   *at once*
And some she werned wel and faire,   *courteously refused*
1540   And some she graunted the contraire   *opposite*
Of her axyng, outterly.
But thus I sey yow, trewly:
What her cause was y nyste,
For this folke, ful wel y wiste,
1545   They had good fame eche deserved,
Alle though they wer dyversly served –   *treated differently*
Ryght as her suster, Dame Fortune,

1530.   'Of all kinds and conditions'. For the form *alleskynnes*, cf. *noskynnes* (l. 1794), and see Burnley 1989: 73.
1531.   This refers to the belief that the power of Fortune (see below, l. 1547 & n.) affected beings and events below the sphere of the moon, which was the nearest 'planet' to the earth in the medieval cosmic system and was itself associated with mutability (cf. below, ll. 2115–16).
1540–1. 'And she granted some the complete opposite of what they had asked for'.
1543.   'I did not know what her reason was'.
1547.   This is the first direct reference to Fortune in *HF* and is emphasized by a *nota* sign in one of the MSS (F), but see also l. 1297 above as well as ll. 1631, 1982–4 and 2016 below. Fame's consistent inconsistency in the poem is very much akin to that of Boethius's *Fortuna*, who reflects 'hir propre stablenesse in the chaungynge of hirself' (*Boece* II, pr. 1, ll. 54–5). On the relationship between Fame and Fortune in *HF*, see also Bennett

Ys wonte to serven in comune.
    Now herkne how she gan to paye

1550 That gonne her of her grace praye –   *Those who*
And yet, lo, al this companye
Seyden sooth and noght a lye:
'Madame,' quod they, 'we be
Folke that here besechen the

1555 That thou graunte us now good fame
And let our werkes han that name;
In ful recompensacion
Of good werke yive us good renoun.'
'I werne yow hit,' quod she anon,   *I refuse*

1560 'Ye gete of me good fame non,
Be God – and therfore goo your wey!'
'Allas,' quod they, 'and welawey! –
Telle us what may your cause be.'
'For me lyst hyt noght,' quod she.

1565 'No wyght shal speke of yow, ywis,
Good ne harme, ne that ne this.'
    And with that worde she gan to calle
Her messangere that was in halle
And bad that he shuld fast goon,

1570 Upon peyn to be blynde anon,   *On pain of*
For Eolus, the god of wynde,   *Aeolus*

1968: 146–8 and Boitani 1984: 152–3.

1548. 'Usually treats everyone'.

1549. *paye*: 'please' *or* 'repay' (*MED paien* v. 1(a) or 6(a)).

1557–8. On the Ciceronian concept of fame as reward for virtue, see Boitani 1984: esp. 35–6, 137–9.

1564. '"Because I don't feel like it", said she'.

1570. 'On pain of being blinded at once'.

1571. The figure of Aeolus, controller of the winds, is based on descriptions in *Met.* (I, ll. 262–3, IV, l. 663, XIV, ll. 223–5, etc.) and in *Aen.* I, ll. 50–80, where he is summoned by Juno from Aeolia to raise a storm and wreck Aeneas's fleet. The latter passage has already been alluded to in *HF* (above, ll. 198–208), and there are parallels between Fame and *crwel Junoo* as obstreperous goddesses. On Aeolus's role in *HF*, see Koonce 1966: 229–43; Boitani 1984: 165.

'In Trace, ther ye shal hym fynde,
And bid him bring his clarioun
That is ful dyvers of his soun   *wide-ranging; its*
1575   And hyt is cleped Clere Laude,   *Resounding Praise*
With whiche he wonde is to hiraude   *usually proclaims*
Hem that me list ipreised be.   *I wish to be*
And also bid him how that he   *order him to*
Brynge his other clarioun
1580   That hight Sklaundre in every toun,   *Calumny; everywhere*
With whiche he wonte is to diffame   *usually dishonours*
Hem that me liste and do hem shame.'   *I wish; causes*
       This messanger gan fast goon
And founde where, in a cave of stoon
1585   In a contree hight Trace,   *was called Thrace*
This Eolus, with harde grace,
Helde the wyndes in distresse   *under constraint*
And gan hem under him to presse
That they gonne as beres rore,   *bears*
1590   He bonde and pressed hem so sore.   *bound*
       This messanger gan fast crie:
'Ryse up,' quod he, 'and fast hye   *hurry*
Til thou at my lady be,
And take thy clariouns eke with the
1595   And spede the forth!' – and he anon
Toke to a man that hight Triton   *Gave; was called*

1572. The identification of Aeolus's *contree* as Thrace here and in l. 1585 may
       derive from an early commentary on *Aen.* I (Bennett 1968: 150) or *AA* II,
       l. 431 (Sk.). See also Shannon 1929: 97, 341–3.
1573–82. At least one medieval commentator identifies Aeolus as 'glory' and gives
       him two trumpets (see Koonce 1966: 229–30; Bennett 1968: 151–4). Ch
       may also be recalling Fortune's twin trumpets in Gower's *Mirour de
       l'omme* (ll. 22141–56).
1586. *with harde grace*: 'with ill luck to him'.
1587. *in distresse*: 'under pressure, constraint'. Cf. *Aen.* I, ll. 52–63, and *Met.* I,
       ll. 262–3 and XIV, ll. 223–5.
1596. *Triton* is a name given to mermen in Greek and Roman myth, often
       portrayed playing conch-shells and hence associated both with the sea and
       with wind instruments. One of them, through jealousy, seized and
       drowned the trumpeter Misenus in *Aen.* VI, ll. 173–4 (see above, ll.
       1243–4 & n., and Boitani 1984: 165). The role of Triton as Neptune's

Hys clarions to bere thoo,
And lete a certeyn wynde to goo
That blew so hydously an hye   *aloft*
1600   That hyt ne lefte not a skye   *cloud*
In alle the welkene, longe and brode.
        This Eolus nowhere abode   *lingered*
Til he was come to Fames fete,
And eke the man that Triton hete,   *was called*
1605   And ther he stode, as stille as stoon.
        And herwithal ther come anoon   *And with that*
Another huge companye
Of good folke and gunne crie: *began to*
'Lady, graunte us good fame
1610   And lat oure werkes han that name
Now, in honour of gentilesse,   *nobility*
And also God your soule blesse!   *as God may*
For we han wel deserved hyt,
Therfore is ryght that we ben quyt.'   *rewarded*
1615   'As thryve I,' quod she, 'ye shal faylle!   *So help me*
Good werkes shal yow noght availle   *won't help you*
To have of me good fame as now.   *get from; just now*
But wete ye what? – y graunte yow   *do you know*
That ye shal have a shrewde fame   *evil renown*
1620   And wikkyd loos and worse name,   *bad reputation*
Though ye good loos have deserved.
Now goo your wey, for ye be served –
Have doon! Eolus! – let see –
Take forth thy trumpe anon,' quod she,
1625   'That is icleped Sklaundre lyght   *called Ready Slander*
And blow her loos, that every wight   *proclaim; person*
Speke of hem harme and shrewdenesse   *wickedness*
In stede of good and worthynesse –

trumpeter is vividly described in *Met.* I, ll. 330–47.
1601. 'Anywhere in the whole sky'.
1611. The claim for fame on grounds of *gentilesse* recalls the activities of the
       heralds of *ryche folke* (above, l. 1322) and their appeals to *our owne gentil
       lady Fame* in l. 1311 (Bennett 1968: 155–6). See also *Boece* III, pr. 6, ll.
       12–37.
1622. *ye be served*: 'you've had what you came for'.
1623. 'That's your lot. Aeolus! Look here –'.

For thou shalt trumpe alle the contrayre
1630 Of that they han don wel or fayre.'   *Of what*
            'Allas,' thought I, 'what aventures   *bad luck*
Han these sory creatures,   *wretched*
For they amonges al the pres   *before; this throng*
Shul thus be shamed gilteles!
1635 But, what! – hyt most nedes be.'
            What did this Eolus, but he
Toke out hys blake trumpe of bras
That fouler than the devel was
And gan this trumpe for to blow,
1640 As al the worlde shuld overthrowe.
Through out every regioun
Went this foule trumpes soun,
As swifte as pelet out of gonne   *ball; gun*
Whan fire is in the poudre ronne;
1645 And suche a smoke gan out wende   *drift*
Out of his foule trumpes ende –
Blak, bloo, grenyssh, swartisshe rede –   *bluish grey; dark*
As dothe where that men melte lede,
Loo, alle on high fro the tuelle.   *upwards; chimney*
1650 And therto oo thing saugh I welle,
That the ferther that hit ran
The gretter wexen hit began,   *began to grow*
As dooth the ryver from a welle,   *spring*
And hyt stank as the pitte of helle.

1631. Cf. the association of Fame with chance (*aventure*) above, l. 1297, and below, ll. 1982–4; see also above, l. 1547 & n.
1640. 'As if the whole world were to be destroyed'. On the apocalyptic imagery and allusions here and elsewhere in Book III of *HF*, see above, ll. 1383–4 n.
1644. 'When flame ignites the powder'. At this time it seems that the flame would literally 'run through' the charge in a cannon, since the kind of 'corned' gunpowder that gave a more uniform explosion was not invented until the 1420s (see White 1962: 101).
1648. On the kind of 'industrial chemistry' referred to here, see Crombie 1969: I, 219–22, and for an account of lead-mining and lead-smelting in 14th-century England, see Gimpel 1988: 74.
1651–2. The magnifying effect of calumny seems to correspond to that of Fame; cf. above, ll. 1290–2, 1493–6.

1655	Allas, thus was her shame yronge,	*proclaimed*
	And giltles, on every tonge!	
	Tho come the thridde companye	*third*
	And gunne up to the deës hye,	
	And doun on knes they fille anon	
1660	And seyden: 'We ben everychon	*We all are*
	Folke that han ful trew[e]ly	
	Deserved fame, rightfully,	
	And pray yow hit mot be knowe	*to let it be*
	Ryght as hit is, and forth yblowe.'	*trumpeted forth*
1665	'I graunte,' quod she, 'for me lyste	*as I wish*
	That now your good werkes be wiste –	*should be known*
	And yet ye shul have better loos,	*renown*
	In dispite of alle your foos,	*Despite; enemies*
	Than worthy is, and that anoon.	*is deserved*
1670	Late now,' quod she, 'thy trumpe goon,	*Put aside*
	Thou Eolus, that is so blake,	
	And out thyn other trumpe take,	
	That hight Laude, and blowe yt, soo	
	That thurgh the worlde her fame goo	
1675	Esely and not to faste,	*Gradually*
	That hyt be knowen atte laste.'	
	'Ful gladly, lady myn,' he seyde.	
	And oute hys trumpe of golde he brayde	*he flourished*
	Anon and set hyt to his mouthe	
1680	And blew it est and west and southe	
	And northe, as lowde as any thunder,	
	That every wight hath of hit wonder –	
	So brode hyt ran or than hyt stent.	*before it ceased*
	And certes, al the breth that went	*certainly*
1685	Out of his trumpes mouthe smelde	
	As men a potful of bawme helde	*balm were poured*
	Amonge a basket ful of roses.	
	This favour did he til her loses.	*for; reputations*
	And ryght with this, y gan aspye,	

1658. 'And started to hasten towards the daïs'.
1670–8. The colours of Aeolus's two trumpets (see above, ll. 1573–82 & n.) seem
         similar in significance to those of the two inscriptions over the gate in *PF*,
         l. 141.
1671. *blake*: 'black' (referring to *trumpe*, l. 1670).

1690	Ther come the ferthe companye –	*fourth*
	But, certeyn, they were wonder fewe –	
	And gunne stonde in a rewe	*row*
	And seyden: 'Certes, lady bryght,	
	We han don wel with al our myght,	
1695	But we ne kepen have no fame.	*don't care to*
	Hide our werkes and our name	
	For Goddys love – for, certes, we	
	Han certeyn doon hyt for bounte	*as a good deed*
	And for no maner other thinge.'	*reason*
1700	'I graunte yow alle your askynge,'	*request*
	Quod she, 'let your werkes be dede.'	
	With that about y clywe myn hede	*scratched*
	And saugh anoon the fyfte route	*group*
	That to this lady gunne loute	*bow*
1705	And doun on knes anoon to falle,	
	And to hir thoo besoughten alle	
	To hyden her goode werkes eke,	
	And seide they yeven noght a leke	*leek*
	For no fame, ne for suche renoun –	
1710	For they for contemplacioun	*through*
	And Goddes love hadde ywrought,	*acted*
	Ne of fame wolde they nought.	
	'What!' quod she, 'Be ye woode?	*Are you mad?*
	And wene ye for to doo goode	*do you expect*
1715	And for to have of that no fame?	*get for*
	Have ye dispite to have my name?	*Are you too proud*

1702. The dreamer's gesture contrasts with his more articulate expression of shock in ll. 1631–5 above, and is a vivid reminder of his presence and attitude (cf. *PF*, l. 500). *Riv.* p. 988, col. 2 notes that *clywe* is Ch's only use of this particular form of the verb.

1703–12. Bennett (1968: 159) suggests that Ch is recalling the portrayal of contemplative spirits in *Anticlaudianus* V, ll. 443–55 (tr. Sheridan 1973: 152); the repeated negatives in l. 1709 here indeed seem to echo those in ll. 448–52 of Alanus's text.

1708. *yeven noght a leke*: 'gave not a straw [lit.: "leek"]'. The tone of the exchanges on both sides now becomes increasingly colloquial; cf. below, ll. 1713, 1744, 1768, 1777–8, 1783–5, 1796–9.

Nay, ye shul lyen everychoon!
Blowe thy trompe, and that anon,'
Quod she, 'thou Eolus ihote,
1720   And rynge this folkes werkes be note,
That alle the worlde may of hyt here.'
And he gan blowe her loos so clere   *trumpet their praise*
In his golden clarioun
That thrugh the worlde went the soun
1725   Also kenely and eke so softe,
But attelast hyt was on lofte.   *at last; aloft*
          Thoo come the syxte companye
And gonne fast on Fame crie
Ryght verraly in this manere –   *Exactly*
1730   They seyden: 'Mercy, lady dere –
To tellen certeyn, as hyt is,
We han don neither that ne this,   *nothing at all*
But ydel al oure lyfe ybe.   *been*
But natheles, yet prey we   *nonetheless*
1735   That we mowe han as good a fame   *may*
And gret renoun and knowen name   *well-known*
As they that han doon noble gestes   *deeds*
And acheved alle her lestes,   *aims*
As wel of love as other thynge –   *in love as in*
1740   Alle was us never broche ne rynge,   *Although*
Ne elles noght, fro wymmen sent –
Ne ones in her hert iment
To make us oonly frendly chere,
But myghten temen us upon bere.
1745   Yet lat us to peple seme
Such as the worlde may of us deme   *everyone may think*
That wommen loven us for wode;   *madly*

1717. *ye shul lyen*: 'you'll be mistaken, proved wrong (about that)' (*MED lien* v.
       (2) 3; see also *RR* (Chaucerian translation), l. 7524). Most editors
       (including Sk., Rob. and *Riv.*) emend to *ly[v]en* (i.e., presumably, 'you
       shall live [in fame]').
1719. *Eolus ihote*: 'the person called Aeolus'.
1720. 'And proclaim these people's deeds out loud'.
1725. 'As piercingly and yet as softly (as before)'; see ll. 1672f.
1742–4. 'Nor did they [women] ever really intend even to give us a friendly
       glance, but would (gladly) have laid us upon a bier [i.e. seen us dead]'.

      Hyt shal doon us as muche goode
      And to oure herte as muche avaylle   *benefit*
1750 (To countrepese ese and travaylle)
      As we had wonne hyt with labour –   *As if*
      For that is dere boght honour
      At regard of oure gret ese.
      And yet thou most us more plese:
1755 Let us be holden eke therto   *also considered*
      Worthy, wise and goode also
      And riche and happy unto love,   *in love*
      For Goddes love, that sit above.
      Thogh we may not the body have
1760 Of wymmen, yet, so God yow save,
      Leet men gliwe on us the name –   *fasten*
      Sufficeth that we han the fame.'
      'I graunte,' quod she, 'be my trouthe.
      Now Eolus, withouten slouthe,   *no slacking*
1765 Take out thy trumpe of golde – now let se –
      And blowe as they han axed me,   *asked*
      That every man wene hem at ese,   *think them to be*
      Though they goon in ful bad lese.'
      This Eolus gan hit so blowe
1770 That thrugh the worlde hyt was yknowe.
        Thoo come the seventh route anoon

1748. *Hyt*: i.e. the fame.

1750. 'If one sets ease against effort'.

1752–3. 'For that honour is too dearly purchased, by comparison with the importance of our comfort'. Cf. *Inf.* XXIV, ll. 47–51 (for the opposite view).

1754. The petitioners here address Fame in the second person singular (according to two of the MSS). This might be the familiar form (as against the more polite (?) *yow* in l. 1760) or the normal form of address to a deity. As Davis points out (*Riv.* p. xxxv), the distinction between the 'you' forms in social usage is complex, and it is not always clear why Fame's petitioners use one form rather than the other (cf. l. 1555 against l. 1563, or l. 1835 against l. 1860).

1768. 'Though they are in a bad way' (lit.: 'in a very poor pasture'). The idiom, with its implied image of the horse grazing, is again used, by Criseyde, in an erotic context in *TC* II, l. 752, although the 'pasture' she envisages is *lusty*. Cf. a similar image relating to Troilus in *TC* I, ll. 218–24.

	And fel on kn: everychoon	
	And seyde: 'Lady, graunte us sone	*at once*
	The same thing, the same bone	*favour*
1775	That to this next folk han doon.'	*last; (you) have*
	'Fy on yow,' quod she, 'everychon,	
	Ye masty swyn, ye ydel wrechhes,	
	Ful of roten, slowe techches –	*sluggish faults*
	What, fals theves! wher ye wolde	
1780	Be famous good and no thing nolde	
	Deserve why, ne never ye rought?	
	Men rather yow hangen ought!	
	For ye be lyke the sweynte catte	*feeble*
	That wolde have fissh, but wostow whatte?	*do you know what?*
1785	He wolde no thinge wete his clowes.	*in no way; claws*
	Ywel thrift come to your jowes	
	And eke to myn, yif I hit graunte,	
	Or do yow favour, yow to avaunte!	*to praise you*
	Thou, Eolus, thou kynge of Trace,	
1790	Goo blowe this folke a sory grace,'	
	Quod she, 'anon, and wostow how?	*do you know*
	As I shal telle the ryght now:	
	Sey, these ben that wolden honour	*wanted*
	Have and do noskynnes labour,	*no sort of*
1795	Ne doo no good and yet han lawde,	
	And that men wende that bele Isawde	

1777. *masty swyn*: 'lazy swine' (*masty* = 'fattened upon beechmast').

1779–82. 'What, you crooks – do you want fame for doing well without deserving it or even caring how you get it? You ought to be hanged instead!'

1783. For the form *sweynte*, see *MED swenchen* v. 1 (d). The proverb about the lazy cat that wanted fish but would not wet its paws has several 14th-century parallels, such as *CA* II, ll. 1108–11 (Whiting 1968: C 93).

1786. 'May you be cursed' (lit.: 'ill luck to your jaws').

1790. 'Trumpet these people's disgrace'.

1794. *noskynnes*: 'no sort of, no kind of'. For the form (preserving a possessive inflexion for the adjective as well as the noun, as in OE *nanes cynnes*), see Burnley 1989: 73, and cf. *alleskynnes* above, l. 1530.

1796–7. 'And would like people to think that (even) fair Yseult / Could not refuse them her love'. A mocking allusion to one of the most illustrious lovers in medieval romance: the mistress of Tristan. Yseult is also mentioned (as a victim of Venus) in *PF*, l. 290 and as a paragon of beauty in *LGW*, l. 208.

Ne coude hem noght of love werne –
And yet she that grynt at a querne   *grinds; handmill*
Ys alle to good to ese her hert.'   *their desire*
1800   This Eolus anon up stert,   *leapt up*
And with his blake clarioun
He gan to blasen out a soun   *blare*
As lowde as beloweth wynde in helle.   *the wind roars*
And eke therwith, sothe to telle,
1805   This soune was so ful of japes   *mockery*
As ever mowes were in apes;   *grimaces*
And that went al the worlde about
That every wight gan on hem shout   *person; hoot at them*
And for to lawgh as they were wode –   *as if; mad*
1810   Suche game fonde they in her hode.
   Tho come another companye
That had ydoon the trayterye,   *the most treachery*
The harme, the grete wikkednesse
That any hert kouthe gesse,   *could*
1815   And prayed her to han good fame
And that she nolde doon hem no shame,
But yeve hem loos and good renoun   *fame*
And do hyt blowe in a clarioun.   *have it proclaimed*
   'Nay, wis,' quod she, 'hyt were a vice –   *indeed*
1820   Al be ther in me no justice –   *Although there is*
Me liste not doo hyt nowe,
Ne this nyl I graunte yowe.'   *I will not*

1798–9. A peasant woman (who 'grinds at a handmill') is here contrasted with the aristocratic Yseult of ll. 1796–7.

1803. An ironic allusion to the roaring of the wind among the lustful in Dante's hell (*Inf.* V, ll. 28–33) seems probable here, particularly in view of this group's desire to have fame as lovers.

1805–9. The outburst of ridicule perhaps heralds the outbreak of folly that is about to occur (below, ll. 1823ff.). On apes and japes, see Janson 1952: 201–2, as also *Shipm–Pri link*, ll. 439–40 (same rhyme), and *Pars T*, ll. 651–4.

1810. 'That was the trick that was played on them' (lit.: 'such was the surprise they found in their hoods'). Similar idioms are in *TC* II, l. 1110 (cf. l. 1181), and *Shipm–Pri link*, l. 440. *Riv.* cites Whiting 1968: G 25.

1812. Perhaps recalls the preoccupation with treachery in Book I (see above, ll. 264, 266, 267).

	Tho come ther lepynge in a route	
	And gunne choppen al aboute	*slap*
1825	Every man upon the crowne,	*crown (of head)*
	That alle the halle gan to sowne,	*resound*
	And seide: 'Lady, leefe and dere,	*dearly beloved*
	We ben suche folkes as ye mowe here –	*may hear of*
	To telle al the tale aryght –	*properly*
1830	We ben shrewes, every wyght,	*rogues, all of us*
	And han delyte in wikkednes	
	As good folke han in godenes,	
	And joy to be knowen shrewes	*rejoice; known as*
	And ful of vices and wikked thewes.	*ways*
1835	Wherfor we pray yow arowe	*all together*
	That oure fame suche be knowe	*as such*
	In alle thing ryght as hit ys.'	
	'Y graunte hyt yow,' quod she, 'ywis.	
	But what art thow that seyst this tale,	*who; are telling*
1840	That werest on thy hose a pale	*strip, garter*
	And on thy tipet suche a belle?'	
	'Ma dame,' quod he, 'soth to telle,	
	I am that ylke shrewe, ywis,	*same*
	That brende the temple of Ysydis	*Isis*
1845	In Athenes, loo, that citee.'	
	'And wherfor didest thou so?' quod she.	*why*
	'By my thrift,' quod he, 'ma dame,	*As I hope to thrive*
	I wolde fayn han hadde a fame	

1824–6. The slapping of heads would probably have been done with a fool's 'bauble' or sceptre which might have a bladder on the end (see Welsford 1935: 121–2 and Willeford 1969: 11, 22, 37 (pl. 10)). This outbreak of mayhem might further support the view that *HF* is associated with festive foolery (as suggested by Billington in Williams 1979: 40).

1841. 'And a bell like that on your hood'. The costume appears to be that of a fool (cf. above, ll. 1824–6 & n.); this particular feature is common in MS illustrations of fools. Bells were also worn on a kind of garter around the hose, which could well be the *pale* referred to above, l. 1840 (see *MED pale* n. 4(a)).

1843–58. The name of the arsonist who burned the temple of Diana at Ephesus (not Isis at Athens) was subsequently condemned to remain unspoken – an ironic touch on Ch's part, as Bennett (1968: 162–3) points out.

1848. 'I was eager to get a reputation'.

          As other folke hadde in the toune,
1850   Allethough they were of grete renoune
          For her vertue and for her thewes.   *goodness*
          Thought y – as gret a fame han shrewes
          (Though hit be noght) for shrewdenesse
          As good folke han for godenesse.
1855   And sith y may not have that oon
          That other nyl y noght forgoon.   *fail to get*
          And for to gette of Fames hire   *Fame's reward*
          The temple sette y alle afire.
          Now doon our loos be blowen swithe,
1860   As wisly be thou ever blythe.'
          'Gladly,' quod she. 'Thow, Eolus –
          Herestow not what this folke prayen us?'
          'Ma dame, yis – ful wel,' quod he,
          'And I wil trumpen it, parde!'   *indeed*
1865   And toke his blake trumpe faste
          And gan to puffen and to blaste
          Til hyt was at the worldys ende.
                    With that y gan aboute wende,   *turn round*
          For oon that stoode ryght at my bake,
1870   Me thought, goodely to me spake   *politely*
          And seyde: 'Frende, what is thy name?
          Artow come hider to han fame?'
          'Nay, forsothe, frende,' quod y,   *indeed*
          'I cam noght hyder, graunt mercy,   *thanks very much*
1875   For no suche cause, by my hede!   *I swear*

1853.   *Though hit be noght*: 'although it is worthless'. The variant reading (in B, Cx) is easier: 'Though it be for shrewednesse'. However, the meaning of the adopted reading (from F, Th) is clarified by the use of brackets in Thynne's edition, and there are other such brief parenthetical statements in *HF* (e.g. ll. 621, 787, 1161).
1855–6.   *that oon ... that other*: 'the one [i.e. a reputation for goodness] ... the other [i.e. a reputation for villainy]'.
1859–60.   'Now get our fame proclaimed quickly / And may you indeed be happy forever.'
1867.   Perhaps a punning allusion to the Apocalypse (cf. above, ll. 1184 n., 1284, 1383–4 n., 1640 n., and below, l. 1905); this is, after all, the last judgment Fame delivers. On 'eschatological poetics' in *HF*, see Kiser 1991: ch. 2.

Sufficeth me, as I were dede,
That no wight have my name in honde.
I wote my self best how y stonde –
For, what I drye or what I thynke,
1880   I wol my selfe alle hyt drynke,
Certeyn, for the more parte,
As ferforthe as I kan myn arte.'
          'But what doost thou here thenne?' quod he.
Quod y: 'That wol y tellen the,
1885   The cause why y stonde here:
Some newe tydinges for to lere –   *to learn*
Some newe thinge – y not what –   *I know not*
Tydynges, other this or that,   *of some sort*
Of love, or suche thynges glade.
1890   For certeynly, he that me made
To come hyder seyde me
Y shulde bothe here and se   *see*
In this place wonder thynges.   *remarkable*
But these be no suche tydynges
1895   As I mene of.' 'Noo?' quod he.   *have in mind*
And I answered: 'Noo, parde!
For wel y wote, ever yit,   *always till now*
Sith that first y had wit,   *intelligence*
That some folke han desired fame
1900   Diversly, and loos and name.
But certeynly, y nyst howe

1876–82. 'All I ask is that, when I'm dead, no-one should have power over my reputation. I'm the best judge of my own situation – for, whatever I may feel or think, I'll certainly cope with all or most of it myself, as far as my skill allows.' The dreamer's reply here has been variously described as 'stoic and Christian' (Boitani 1984: 170) and 'huffy and evasive' (Wallace 1986: 22). The verb *drye* (l. 1879) primarily means 'endure, feel', but could also mean 'thirst' (*MED drien* v. 1 6(a)), thus relating to *drinke* in the following line (which has the figurative sense of 'experience, endure') and creating a kind of circular ambiguity that may reflect the dreamer's perplexed state. His way of talking about his *arte* here recalls the earlier protestations about lack of poetic skill (see above, l. 1096 n.).

1884–95. The dreamer seems (understandably) confused about what to expect in the way of *tydinges*. Heightened expectation is, however, generated by the increasing recurrence of the word from this point on.

Ne where that Fame duelled er nowe –
Ne eke of her descripcion,
Ne also her condicion,
1905 Ne the ordre of her dome,   *method of judging*
Unto tyme y hidder come.'   *Until; came here*
   'Why than – be, loo, these tydynges
That thou now hider brynges
That thou hast herde?' quod he to me.
1910 'But now no fors, for wel y se   *no matter now*
What thou desirest for to here.
Come forth, and stonde no lenger here,
And y wil the, withouten drede,
In suche another place lede
1915 Ther thou shalt here many oon.'
   Tho gan I forthe with hym to goon
Oute of the castel, sothe to seye.
Tho saugh y stond in a valeye,
Under the castel, fast by,
1920 An house – that Domus Dedaly,

1902–5. The reiteration of *Ne* at the start of each line here resembles repetitive patterns elsewhere in *HF* (in ll. 677–9, 685–9, 896–903, above, and, more extensively, below, ll. 1961–76). On 'cornucopic lists' in *HF* generally, see Ruffolo 1993.

1907–8. 'Why then – are *you* now bringing news here?' On the form *brynges*, see above, l. 426 & n. In the text adopted here, the anonymous questioner may be ironically implying that the dreamer himself is a self-important bringer of news. *These tydynges ... that thou hast herde* could thus refer to the dreamer's recent claim (in ll. 1897–1900) to have known about Fame all along.

1913–15. 'And I will, indeed, take you to another kind of place, where you will hear many such things.'

1918–19. The location of the House of Rumour in a 'valley' below the castle perhaps suggests a difference of status, like that between city and court (Knight 1986: 22).

1920–3. 'A house of such a kind that the House of Daedalus, which is called the Labyrinth, was never so strangely built nor half so intricate in its construction.' The comparison with the maze constructed by Daedalus (to contain the Minotaur in Crete) recalls the descriptions in *Met.* VIII, ll. 159–68, and *Aen.* V, ll. 588–91. An important intermediary source for the labyrinth as image of intellectual confusion is the complaint of Boethius's

	That Laboryntus ycleped ys,	
	Nas made so wondrlych, ywis,	
	Ne half so queyntlych ywrought.	
	And ever mo, so swyft as thought,	
1925	This queynt hous aboute went	*strange; spun round*
	That never mo stil hyt stent,	*did it stay still*
	And therout come so grete a noyse	
	That, had hyt stonde upon Oyse,	*the Oise*
	Men myght hyt han herd esely	
1930	To Rome, y trowe sikerly.	
	And the noyse which that I herde –	
	For alle the world, ryght so hyt ferde	*sounded*
	As dooth the rowtynge of the ston	*whizzing*
	That from th' engyne ys leten gon;	*siege engine*
1935	And al thys hous of whiche y rede	*speak*
	Was made of twigges – falwe, rede,	*brownish yellow*
	And grene eke, and some weren white –	
	Suche as men to these cages thwite,	
	Or maken of these panyers,	

prisoner that Philosophy has 'so woven me with ... resouns the hous of Didalus [*labyrinthum*], so entrelaced that it is unable to be unlaced' (*Boece* III, pr. 12, ll. 155–7). As a 'wonder', the structure may well have precedents in more popular traditions, such as romance and folktale (see Sypherd 1907: 213). It also looks like the kind of effect a *tregetour* (illusionist) might conjure up (see above, ll. 1277–81 & n.).

1928–30. The narrator's use of the distance between the River Oise (N. France) and Rome as a measure evokes again the idea of pilgrimage (cf. above, l. 1131, and below, l. 2122). The Oise flows into the Seine north of Paris, and all the main pilgrimage routes from England to Rome would have had to cross it (see Parks 1954: 180).

1930. 'All the way to Rome, I firmly believe'.

1933–4. A reference to *trébuchet* (stone-throwing) artillery (see Contamine 1984: 103–5, 194–5).

1935–40. The house of twigs recalls the poorer side of Fortune's house in *RR*, ll. 6076–84, which has a thatched roof and thin mud walls and is 'cracked wide open in more than five hundred thousand places' (tr. Horgan 1994: 93); cf. also *Anticlaudianus* VIII, ll. 1–15 (tr. Sheridan 1973: 189). In permeability it outdoes Ovid's House of Rumour in *Met.* XII, l. 44.

1938. 'Such as are whittled into things like cages'.

1940	Or elles h[o]ttes or dossers –	
	That, for the swough and for the twygges,	
	This house was also ful of gyges	*squeaking*
	And also ful eke of chirkynges,	*creaking*
	As ful this lo ...	
1945	And eke this hous hath of entrees	*entrances*
	As fele as of leves ben in trees	*many as there are leaves*
	In somer whan they grene been;	
	And on the rove men may yet seen	*roof*
	A thousand holes, and wel moo,	
1950	To leten wel the soune out goo;	
	And be day, in every tyde,	*at all times*
	Been al the dores opened wide,	
	And be nyght echon unshet –	*unlocked*
	Ne porter ther is noon to let	*hinder*
1955	No maner tydynges in to pace.	*Any kind; pass in*
	Ne never rest is in that place,	
	That hit nys filde ful of tydynges,	
	Other loude or of wisprynges.	
	And over alle the houses angles	*corners*
1960	Ys ful of rounynges and of jangles –	*whispering; gossip*
	Of werres, of pes, of mariages,	*wars; peace*

1940. *h[o]ttes*: 'wicker paniers'; *dossers*: 'baskets' (for carrying on the back).

1941. 'That, what with the swish of the air and the noise of the twigs'.

1944. Half of the line is missing in the MSS (see Notes on the Text).

1948–50. The *thousand holes* on the roof parallel those in Ovid's House of Rumour (*Met.* XII, l. 44). Cf. above, ll. 711–24 & n.

1951–60. The house's unrestricted opening hours and the restless noise within it again parallel Ovid's House of Rumour in *Met.* XII, ll. 46–8. Cf. above, ll. 1948–50 & n.

1957. '(Nor a time) when it is not crammed with reports'.

1961–76. The repeated *Of*'s make this the longest passage of such (anaphoric) patterning in *HF*; cf. above, ll. 1902–5 & n. The 16 initial O's could be mimetic of the holes through which the *tydynges* emerge – thus making these lines a kind of concrete poem. They certainly make a prominent impression on the pages of the two manuscripts (F and B) where they appear. Stevenson (1978: 23) argues that 'most of the passage is constructed of clearly related pairs or triplets of tidings'. Within it there appear to be continuing (and perhaps deliberately tantalizing) references to news about love: *mariages, love, jelousye* (cf. the eagle's list in ll. 672–98 above).

	Of restes and of labour – of viages,	*rest-times; travelling*
	Of abode – of deth, of lyfe –	*staying put*
	Of love, of hate – acorde or stryfe –	*harmony*
1965	Of loos, of lore and of wynnynges –	*renown; defeat; conquest*
	Of hele, of sekenesse, of bildynges –	*health*
	Of faire wyndes and eke of tempestes –	
	Of qwalme of folke and eke of bestes –	
	Of dyvers transmutacions	
1970	Of estates and eke of regions –	
	Of trust, of drede, of jelousye,	
	Of wit, of wynnynge, of folye –	*wisdom; profit*
	Of plente and of grete famyne –	
	Of chepe, of derthe and of ruyne –	*prices; scarcity*
1975	Of good or mys-governement –	
	Of fire and of dyvers accident.	
	And loo, thys hous of which I write –	
	Syker be ye, hit nas not lyte,	*Be sure; small*
	For hyt was sixty myle of lengthe.	
1980	Alle was the tymber of no strengthe,	*Although*
	Yet hit is founded to endure,	
	While that hit lyst to Aventure	
	That is the moder of tydynges,	
	As the see of welles and of sprynges –	*sea*
1985	And hyt was shapen lyke a cage.	
	'Certys,' quod y, 'in al myn age	*lifetime*
	Ne saugh y suche an hous as this.'	
	And, as y wondred me, ywys,	*I marvelled*
	Upon this hous, tho war was y	*I became aware*
1990	How that myn Egle, fast by,	

1968. 'Of pestilence among people, and animals also'.
1969–70. 'Of various alterations in classes and kingdoms'.
1982. 'As long as Fortune pleases'. Cf. the construction of the gate to Fame's palace above, ll. 1297–8. On the relationship of Fame to Fortune, see l. 1547 & n.
1985. Braswell (1981: 109–12) suggests that the structure of Ch's House of Rumour may be based on that of a medieval bird-cage. The bird-cage was also a metaphor for the memory at this time; see Carruthers 1990: 246–7 and pl. 27. The analogy may, however, still be with the imprisoning 'labyrinth': see above, ll. 1920–3 & n.; also Boitani 1984: 210; Doob 1990: 326–31.

Was perched hye upon a stoon.
And I gan streght to hym goon
And seyde thus: 'Y prey the
That thou a while abide me,   *wait for me*
1995   For Goddis love, and lete me seen
What wondres in this place been –
For yit, paraventure, y may lere   *perhaps; learn*
Some good therin, or sumwhat here
That leef me were, or that y wente.'
2000   'Petre! – that is myn entente,'   *St Peter; plan*
Quod he to me. 'Therfore y duelle.   *That's why; wait*
But, certeyn, oon thyng I the telle,   *will tell you*
That, but I bringe the therinne,   *unless*
Ne shaltow never konne gynne   *find a way*
2005   To come in to hyt, out of doute –   *for sure*
So faste hit whirleth, lo, aboute.
But – sithe that Jovys of his grace,
As I have seyde, wol the solace,   *wishes to comfort you*
Fynally, with these thinges
2010   (Unkouthe syght and tydynges,   *Strange sights*
To passe with thyn hevynesse) –   *To relieve; depression*
Suche routhe hath he of thy distresse   *pity; for*
That thou suffrest debonairly –   *patiently*
And wost thy selfen outtirly
2015   Disesperat of alle blys,
Syth that Fortune hath made amys

1996.   *wondres*: one of a number of recurrences of *wondre/wondrlych* (as noun, adjective, adverb and verb) at this late stage of the poem (ll. 1922, 1988, 2059, 2118).
1999.   'That would be good for me, before I left'.
2000.   *Petre*: an appropriate oath for a guide encountered at such a point of transition (St Peter being traditionally keeper of the gate of Heaven); cf. *PPl* (B-text) V, l. 537, and *Gawain & the Green Knight*, l. 813.
2007.   Cf. the initial promise of Jupiter's *grace* above, l. 661.
2011–13. For other, equally cryptic, indications of the dreamer's problems during his waking life, see above, ll. 115–18. Cf. also the descriptions of the narrator's *hevynesse* in *BD*, ll. 1–29 and *PF*, l. 89.
2014–17. 'Knowing yourself to be wholly without hope of any happiness, since Fortune has spoiled [lit.: "made defective the fruit of"] all you have set your heart upon.'

	The frot of al thy hertys reste.	
	Laughe! and eke in poynt to breste –	
	That he, thrugh hys myghty merite,	
2020	Wol do th' an ese, al be hyt lyte,	
	And yaf in expres commaundement,	*as special order*
	To which I am obedient,	
	To further the with al my myght	*assist you*
	And wisse and teche the aryght	*guide and instruct*
2025	Where thou maist most tidynges here.	*To where*
	Shaltow here anoon many oon lere.'	*You will; soon*
	With this worde he, ryght anoon,	
	[Hente me up bytwene his toon	*Snatched; claws*
	And] at a wyndowe yn me brought	
2030	That in this hous was, as me thought –	
	And therwithalle me thought hit stente	*with that; stopped*
	And no thinge hyt aboute wente –	*not at all*
	And me set in the flore adoun.	
	But which a congregacioun	*such; gathering*
2035	Of folke as I saugh rome aboute,	
	[Some wythin and some wythoute,]	
	Nas never seen, ne shal be eft –	*again*
	That certys in the worlde nys left	*certainly*
	So many formed be Nature,	*by*
2040	Ne dede so many a creature –	
	That wel unnethe in that place	*scarcely*
	Hadde y a fote-brede of space.	
	And every wight that I saugh there	*person*

2018. 'Laugh, just as if you were about to burst'.
2020. *do th' an ese*: 'give you some consolation'.
2028-9, 2036. On the status of these lines, see the Notes on the Text.
2039. *formed be Nature*: cf. the use of this phrase with regard to other creatures in ll. 490 and 1366 above.
2040. 'Nor so many of/among the dead'. A possible allusion to another confused crowd, in *Inf.* III, ll. 56-7.
2042. *a fote-brede*: 'a foot's breadth'. Stevenson (1978: 20) compares the crowded conditions in *PF*, ll. 309-15.
2043-75. Some features of the scene here again recall Ovid's House of Rumour (see above, ll. 1948-50 & n., 1951-60 & n.). The account of the whispering *in others ere* amplifies *Met.* XII, l. 56, and the description of the *encres* of each tiding here (ll. 2059-75) similarly elaborates on *Met.*

	Rouned in others ere,	*Was whispering*
2045	A newe tydynge, prevely,	*confidentially*
	Or elles tolde alle oppenly	*told it*
	Ryght thus, and seyde: 'Nost not thou	*Don't you know*
	That ys betydde, late or now?'	*just now*
	'No,' quod he, 'telle me what.'	
2050	And than he tolde hym this and that,	
	And swore therto that hit was sothe:	*as well; true*
	'Thus hath he sayde,' and 'Thus he dothe,'	
	And 'Thus shal hit be,' and 'Thus herde y seye,'	
	'That shal be founde, that dar I leye –'	*I guarantee*
2055	That alle the folke that ys alyve	
	Ne han the kunnynge to discryve	*skill*
	The thinges that I herde there,	
	What a-loude and what in ere.	
	But al the wondermost was this:	*most remarkable*
2060	Whan oon had herde a thinge, ywis,	*truly*
	He come forthright to another wight	*directly*
	And gan him tellen anonryght	
	The same that him was tolde,	
	Or hyt a forlonge way was olde –	
2065	But gan somwhat for to eche	
	To this tydinge in hys speche	
	More than hit ever was.	
	And nat so sone departed nas	
	Tho, he fro him, that he ne mette	
2070	With the thrid, and, or he lette	
	Any stounde, he told him als.	
	Were the tydynge sothe or fals,	
	Yit wolde he telle hyt natheles,	
	And evermo with more encres	*additions*
2075	Than yt was erst. Thus, north and southe	*before*

XII, ll. 57–8: 'the extent of what has been made up increases [*crescit*], and each new contributor [*auctor*] adds something to what has been heard'.

2058.   *in ere*: 'privately, in a whisper'.

2064.   'Before it was two minutes [lit.: "the space of a furlong"] old'.

2065.   *somwhat for to eche*: 'to add in some way'.

2068–71. 'And the one (who had heard the story) had hardly left the other (who told it) when he met a third person, and without losing any time told it him as well.'

	Went every [mote] fro mouthe to mouthe,	*scrap (of news)*
	And that encresing ever moo,	
	As fir ys wont to quyk and goo	*kindle and spread*
	From a sparke spronge amys,	*gone the wrong way*
2080	Till alle a citee brent up ys.	*is burnt down*
	And whan that was ful yspronge	*spread everywhere*
	And woxen more on every tonge	*amplified by*
	Than ever hit was, and went anoon	
	Up to a wyndowe out to goon –	
2085	Or, but hit myght oute there pace,	*Before it could*
	Hyt gan out crepe at some crevace	
	And flygh forth faste, for the nones.	
	And somtyme saugh I tho at ones	*together then*
	A lesyng and a sad sothe sawe	
2090	That gonne of aventure thrawe	
	Out to a wyndowe, for to pace,	
	And when they metten in that place	
	They wer acheked, bothe two,	*both checked*
	And neyther of hem most out goo	*could get out*
2095	For other, so they gonne crowde –	*Because of*
	Til eche of hem gan crien lowde:	*loudly*
	'Lat me go first!' 'Nay, but let me!	
	And here I wol ensuren the,	*promise you*
	With the nones that thou wolt do so,	*so long as*
2100	That I shal never fro the go,	
	But be thyn owne sworen brother.	
	We wil medle us eche with other,	*blend ourselves*

2076. *[mote]*: for the figurative sense of 'bit, scrap, trifle', see *MED mot* n. 1(c), and *OED mote* sb.[1] 1.c. The emendation adopted here was proposed in Willert's 1888 edition of *HF*. The readings in MSS F and B (*mothe* and *mouthe*) suggest how the hypothetical form *mote* could at some earlier stage have been corrupted by association with *mouthe* later in the line.

2078–80. *Riv.* compares James 3:5–8, and Bennett (1968: 179) parallels *Aen.* IV, ll. 666–71.

2086. *crevace* is also the word that describes the holes in Fortune's house in *RR*, l. 6083 (see above, ll. 1935–40 & n.).

2087. *for the nones*: 'indeed' *or* 'for a while'.

2089–91. 'A falsehood and a wholly true statement that by chance had flown up to pass through a window' (*OED throw* v.[1] B. I. 1).

2096–2107. For the personification of speech, cf. above, ll. 1073–83 & n.

That no man, be they never so wrothe,   *angry*
Shal have that oon, but bothe   *just one (of us)*
2105   At ones, al besyde his leve,   *against his will*
Come we amorwe or on eve,   *morning or evening*
Be we cried or stille yrouned.'   *shouted; whispered quietly*
Thus saugh I fals and sothe compouned   *combined*
Togeder fle for oo tydynge.   *as one story*
2110   Thus oute at holes gunne wringe   *squeeze*
Every tydynge, streght to Fame,
And she gan yeve eche hys name   *she would give*
After hir disposicion,   *As she chose*
And yaf hem eke duracion –   *lifespan*
2115   Some to wexe and wane sone   *wax and wane*
As doth the faire white mone –   *moon*
And lete hem goon. Ther myght y seen
Wynged wondres faste fleen,   *flying*
Twenti thousand in a route,   *flock*
2120   As Eolus hem blew aboute.
       And, lord! this hous, in al tymes,
Was ful of shipmen and pilgrimes,
With scrippes bretful of lesynges,
Entremedled with tydynges –   *Mingled*
2125   And eke allone, be hem selve,
O, many a thousand tymes twelve

2108.   *fals and sothe compouned*: the phrase (which recalls *Met.* XII, ll. 54–5) has occurred before, in *HF*, l. 1029.
2112–14.   Fame begins to seem like an alternative Nature here (cf. *PF*, ll. 379–81, 666–8).
2115–16.   A final allusion to the operations of Fortune in sublunary affairs (cf. l. 1531 & n.) and a further linking of Fame with her 'sister' (cf. l. 1547 & n.).
2118.   For winged creatures as images of thoughts and memory, see esp. Carruthers 1990: 35–7.
2122.   On the reputation of sailors (*shipmen*) for trickery, see *Gen Prol*, ll. 395–7, and Mann 1973: 171; and on the linking of pilgrims with lies, see *PPl* (B-text) *Prologue*, ll. 46–52, and Whiting 1968: P 18. On allusions to pilgrimage (of which this is the last in the poem), see above, ll. 115–18 n., 885, 1131 n., and 1183).
2123.   'With pouches crammed full of falsehoods'.
2126.   A possible allusion to Rev. 7: 4–8; see above, l. 1216 & n.

	Saugh I eke of these pardoners,	
	Currours and eke messangers,	*Couriers*
	With boystes crammed ful of lyes,	*cases*
2130	As ever vessel was with lyes.	*dregs*
	And, as I altherfastest wente	*quickest of all*
	About and did al myn entente,	*Around; and sought*
	Me for to pleyen and for to lere –	*To amuse myself; learn*
	And eke a tydynge for to here	
2135	That I had herd of some contre	*from some place*
	That shal not nowe be told for me	
	(For hit no nede is, redely;	*there's really no need*
	Folke kan synge hit bet than I –	*proclaim; better*
	For alle mote oute, other late or rathe,	
2140	Alle the sheves in the lathe) –	
	I herd a grete noyse, withalle,	*as well*
	In a corner of the halle	
	Ther men of love-tydynges tolde.	
	And I gan thiderwarde beholde,	*look that way*
2145	For I saugh rennynge every wight	
	As fast as that they hadden myght,	*they were able*
	And everyche cried: 'What thing is that?'	
	And some sayde: 'I not never what.'	*I've no idea*
	And whan they were alle on an hepe	*in a heap*
2150	Tho behynde begonne up lepe,	
	And clamben up on other faste	*climbed*
	And up the nose and yen caste	
	And troden fast on other heles	
	And stampen, as men doon aftir eles.	*when catching eels*

2127–30. Pardoners (official and often corrupt dispensers of 'indulgences' and relics) and *messagers* are also closely identified with lies in *PPl* (B-text) II, ll. 220–9. Cf. *Gen Prol*, ll. 686–700.

2136. *for me*: 'as far as I'm concerned'.

2139–40. 'For everything has to come out sooner or later – all the sheaves in the barn'. Goffin (1943: 44) compares *PF*, ll. 22–31 and *LGW*, ll. 61–4 and argues that 'the "sheaves" allusion is to the making of tales'. *Riv.* cites a proverbial parallel in Whiting 1968: S 199.

2152. 'And thrust up their faces' (lit.: 'noses and eyes').

2154. *eles*: refers to the practice of stamping along river-banks or river-beds to chase out eels (Rob.).

2155   Attelast, y saugh a man
      Whiche that y nat ne kan,   *can't identify*
      But he semed for to be
      A man of grete auctorite ...   *authority, status*

2155–8. The *man of grete auctorite* has been identified as Christ or a member of the clergy (Koonce 1966: 278); Boethius (Ruggiers 1953: 17, 28); or Boccaccio (Goffin 1943: 44). But most recent interpretations link him, as an anonymous figure, to various sceptical and ironic patterns of meaning in *HF* (see Delany 1972: 108; Gellrich 1985: 198; Miller 1986: 69). On the ending (or lack of one) more generally, see Brusendorff 1925: 155; Bennett 1968: 185; Burrow 1991: 33–6.

2158. It could well be that the poem's last word (as we have it) was influenced once again by Ovid's description of the House of Rumour (see above, ll. 2043–75 & n.) and specifically by the ironic use there (*Met.* XII, l. 58) of the term *auctor*, which simply refers to each new contributor to the ever-expanding story.

NOTES ON THE TEXT

Sources

The text of the *House of Fame* (*HF*) derives from five witnesses. Three of them are manuscripts of the 15th century; the other two are early prints (one of the late 15th, the other of the early 16th century), both of which have some textual authority.

The three manuscripts (preceded by the abbreviations that refer to them) are:

F MS Fairfax 16 (Bodleian Library, Oxford). For description, see above, p. 108. F's text of *HF* (on fols 154ᵛ–183ᵛ) takes the poem up to its present conclusion, in l. 2158. There are some omissions, notably of whole lines at 221, 280–3, 340, 504–7, 780, 911–12, 1275–6, 1546, 1572, 2028 and 2036.

B MS Bodley 638 (Bodleian Library, Oxford). For description, see above, p. 108. Like F, B takes the text of *HF* (on fols 141ᵛ–193ᵛ) up to the present conclusion. There are some omissions, notably at ll. 280–3, 504–7, 780, 911–12, 1546, 1572, 1944, 2028 and 2036.

P MS Pepys 2006 (Magdalene College, Cambridge) is also of the last quarter of the 15th century and could be later in date than B. Its first part contains (like F and B) a range of Chaucer's shorter poems – including *PF* and *LGW*, but not *BD* – as well as (once again) Lydgate's *Temple of Glas*. Its text of *HF* (on pp. 91–114) is in double columns except on the first page, and it takes the poem, with a large number of omissions, up to l. 1843 (the foot of p. 114), at which point two leaves have been cut out. For further details and facsimile, see Edwards 1985.

The two early prints which have some status as independent witnesses are:

Cx William Caxton's edition of *HF* (now extant in only four copies; see *STC* 5087) was probably printed in 1483, the year in which he also printed Gower's *Confessio Amantis*, the *Golden Legend* and (probably) the second edition of the *Canterbury Tales* and the *Troilus* (Blake 1976: 194). Caxton's text consists of a booklet of 30 leaves in folio (sig. a2ʳ–d5ʳ), headed: *The book of Fame made by Gefferey Chaucer*. His MS ended at l. 2094 (as he indicates in the endnote to his own text), and he provides a neat twelve-line conclusion of his own that was taken over by later editors, such as Thynne (for both the endnote and the conclusion, see the textual note on l. 2094 below). For further details, see Blades 1882: 292–5; De Ricci 1909: 24–5; Blake 1976: 194; Boyd 1978.

Th William Thynne included *HF* in his 1532 edition of *The workes of Geffray Chaucer* (on fols cccxiiᵛ–cccxxiiiᵛ). Thynne's edition also contains Usk's *Testament of Love*, a work of the mid-1380s which is the earliest text to show the influence of *HF* and which, in his text, follows directly after *HF*. Thynne's

214

version of *HF* is the most 'complete' of the five witnesses: he omits only one whole line (1291); his text (like those in MSS F and B) runs all the way to l. 2158; and he also includes a slightly modified version of Caxton's ending. His edition is also the only authority for ll. 280–3, and if these are genuine, they would indicate (along with other evidence) that Thynne had access to at least one MS of *HF* that has not survived. For further details see above, p. 108.

Although MS Fairfax 16 is probably the best of the extant witnesses and is used as the base manuscript by most editions of *HF*, it cannot be entirely relied upon. The present edition takes it as the base manuscript, whilst recognizing that there are frequent occasions where it is flawed or defective and where the choice between the F (or F, B) reading against that of P, Cx or Th is very finely balanced. Paragraphing often coincides with that in Thynne's 1532 edition (which is the only witness to set the text in paragraphs), but punctuation is almost wholly editorial.

Like Chaucer's *Troilus*, *HF* is divided into 'books'. Caxton and Thynne underline these divisions with Latin phrases, such as *Explicit liber secundus* ('Here ends the second book') after l. 1090. The three manuscripts indicate the divisions at ll. 509 and 1091 with large initial letters (F and B) or by leaving space for large initials (P). F and B also leave a space between the end of Book II and the start of Book III.

The following textual notes are very selective indeed: they are chiefly designed to indicate where emendations have been made or where there are notes or glosses in the manuscripts. For a full list of variant readings, see the Textual Notes in the separate edition of *HF* (Havely 1994: 101–33).

Selected textual notes

Titles: F, B, Th: 'The house of Fame' (heading and running title); P: 'The booke of ffame' (in later hand); Cx: 'The book of Fame made by Gefferey Chaucer'.
20. *Or why this more then that cause is* (emendation Rob., *Riv.*)] *Or why this is more then that cause is* P; *For why more then that cause is* F, B (various spellings); *Or why this is more than that is* Cx, Th.
71. All three MSS (F, B, P) cite Ovid, *Met.* XI, ll. 602–3 and 592 as a marginal gloss. This is the only such gloss in P.
111. F has *nota* ('note') in the margin here and on 19 other occasions in its text of *HF*. The significance of some of these pointers is fairly clear: they draw attention to the naming or appearance of certain important figures (as at ll. 217, 561, 663, 729, 1183, 1365 and 1546), or groups of Fame's clients (ll. 1607, 1661, 1689, 1703, 1727, 1771), and they underline several assertions about personal conduct (ll. 957, 1879). The purpose of others (at ll. 373, 1129, 1341) is not so immediately obvious.
280–3. These lines are missing in F, B, P, Cx, and are here supplied from Thynne. The original omission was presumably caused by 'eyeskip', in this

case from *fynde* in l. 279 to *fynde* in l. 283. Caxton solved the problem simply by changing *she* to *he* in l. 284. If the lines are genuinely Chaucerian, Thynne must have had access to a manuscript that has since been lost. See Edwards 1989: 85–6 and Phillips 1986: 121 n. 7.

305. F and B have the phrase *Cavete vos innocentes mulieres* ('Innocent women, beware') in the margin here.

329. *Agylte [I] yowe* (emendation Sk.)] *Agylte yow(e)* F, B, P, Cx, Th.

349–50. Virgil's description of *Fama* ('Rumour') in *Aen.* IV, l. 174, is cited in the margin by F and B: *Fama qua* [MSS *quo*] *non aliud velocius ullum* ('Rumour, which no other evil thing exceeds in speed').

351–2. F and B cite in the margin a shortened version in Latin of Matt. 10:26: *Nichil occultum quod non reveletur* ('For there is nothing hidden that shall not be revealed').

358–9. F and B cite in the margin the second half of a proverbial Latin couplet: *Cras poterunt turpia fieri sicut heri* ('scandal is as likely tomorrow as it was yesterday'). See *Riv.*, p. 980 col. 2. At 367 they cite *Aen.* IV, ll. 548–9.

388–407. F and B have six marginal glosses here:

against 388: *Nota of many untrewe lovers*;
against 390 both cite Ovid, *Her.* II, ll. 1–2;
against 397 both cite *Ovidius* and a slightly garbled version of *Her.* III, l. 1;
against 401 both cite *Her.* XII, l. 1 (with *ubi* for *at*);
against 403 both cite a very garbled version of *Her.* IX, l. 1;
against 407 both cite *Ovidius*, then *Her.* X, l. 1.

436. B adds *Palinurus* in the margin (to identify Aeneas's helmsman).

504–7. F and B omit these four lines, which are here supplied from P (there are versions of them too in Cx and Th). It seems likely that the repetition of *bryght* as a rhyme-word in ll. 503 and 507 caused 'eyeskip' in an ancestor of F and B.

561–2. The scribe of F is the first critic to record an interest in the identity of the person whose voice Chaucer refers to here, by adding a *nota* mark against l. 561.

755–6. F and B have an English note in the margin: *but be kept*. This presumably is meant to explain the meaning of *shuld not apaire* ('may not deteriorate') in the text.

794. *That sercle* (emendation)] *That whele sercle* F, B, Th; P Cx omit ll. 793–6.

912. *thow knowest yonde [a]doun* (emendation)] *thow knowest yonder down* P; *that in the world is of spoken* Cx; *that in this world is of spoken* Th. The emendation follows the use of the same phrase above, l. 889.

1287. *eft imused* (emendation Sk., Rob., *Riv.*)] *eft I mused* P, Cx; *oft I mused* F; *all I musyd*; *I amused* Th.

1372. *This was gret marvaylle to me*] *But thus sone in a while* P, Cx, Th (various spellings). *she* (P, Cx, Th)] F and B omit. Edwards (1989: 90) argues that the F, B reading makes good sense with the addition of *she*, which is already the rhyme-word in P, Cx, Th.

1569–70. F and B assume a missing line here and leave a gap after l. 1569.

1572. F, B and P omit the line. See Edwards 1989: 86.

1843. The text in P finishes at the end of this line (two leaves are missing at this point).

1944. *As ful this lo* . . .] Line incomplete in F, with note: *hic caret versus* ('here a verse is missing') in the margin; B omits the line entirely and leaves a gap; Cx, Th read: *And of many other werkynges* (various spellings). Caxton (followed by Th) appears to have put in a new piece of material here; for other occasions where he seems to have plugged a gap in the text, see the notes (below) on ll. 2028 and 2036.

2028–9. F and B omit the bracketed material, which may also be of Caxton's invention (see the textual note on l. 1944, above). F has a marginal note (*hic caret versus*, 'here a verse is missing') and leaves a gap; B simply leaves a gap.

2036. F and B both omit the line, which may well, again, be of Caxton's invention (see the textual notes on ll. 1944 and 2028–9, above). The line is added in F by a later (17th-century) hand.

2076. *mote* (emendation Willert)] *mothe* F; *mouthe* B; *tydyng* Cx, Th.

2094. Caxton's text appears to have run out at this point. His own conclusion, identified as *Caxton* in the margin, and his endnote follow thus (with modern punctuation and glosses):

> And wyth the noyse of them two
> I sodaynly awoke anon tho   *at once then*
> And remembryd what I had seen
> And how hye and ferre I had been
> In my ghoost, and had grete wonder   *spirit*
> Of that the god of thonder   *At what*
> Had lete me knowen, and began to wryte
> Lyke as ye have herd me endyte.   *describe*
> Wherfor to study and rede alway
> I purpose to do day by day;
> Thus in dremyng and in game
> Endeth thys lytyl book of Fame.
>   *Explicit* [The End]

I fynde nomore of thys werke to-fore-said. For, as fer as I can understonde, this noble man, Gefferey Chaucer, fynysshyd at the sayd conclusion of the metyng of lesyng and sothsawe, where-as yet they ben chekked and maye not departe. Whyche werke, as me semeth, is craftyly made and dygne [worthy] to be wreton [written] and knowen, for he towcheth [deals with] in it ryght grete wysedom and subtyll understondyng. And so in alle hys werkis he excellyth, in myn oppynyon, alle other wryters in ouir Englissh. For he wrytteth no voyde wordes, but alle hys mater is ful of hye and quycke sentence [deep and vivid meaning; cf. *Gen Prol*, l. 306]; to whom ought to be gyven laude and preysyng for hys noble makyng and wrytyng, for of hym

[from him] alle other have borowed syth [since] and taken, in alle theyr wel-
fareng and wrytyng [successful writing(?)]. And I humbly beseche and praye
yow, emonge your prayers to remembre hys soule, on whyche, and on alle
crysten soulis, I beseche almyghty god to have mercy. Amen.

Emprynted by Wyllyam Caxton

Blake 1991: 156–7 notes the resemblance between the verse part of Caxton's
ending and the actual ending of *PF*, which Caxton had printed a few years earlier.
2158. Thynne's edition follows this line with a version of Caxton's ending. The
first couplet is altered to fit the new context, thus:

And therwithal I abrayde
Out of my slepe halfe a frayde ...

The remaining ten lines follow Caxton. F has similar lines added in a 17th-century
hand. Originally in F two leaves were left blank (presumably in the hope that
Chaucer's own ending might be found), and in B the remainder of the final page
is left blank.

THE *PARLIAMENT OF FOWLS*

INTRODUCTION

Old books, new thoughts and troubled dreams

The *Parliament of Fowls* (PF) begins by viewing at close quarters a scene that has been described from a distance in another of Chaucer's dream poems. In Book II of the *House of Fame* (HF) the eagle has described the dreamer 'Geffrey' back home as a devotee of 'reckless Cupid'; as a follower who has no hope of real advancement in love; and as an indefatigable reader, sitting silently and blearily in front of yet 'another book'.[1] In the first few lines of PF these features once again come into focus, but this time through the dreamer's own words and voice. The uncertain expectations generated by the turbulent drift of the speaker's *felynge* and thinking about love in the first stanza seem, in the second, to converge upon the poem's first 'solid' image, that of *bookes*, and upon the authority that they appear to confer (ll. 10–12).

The words for *book* and *read* recur with incantatory frequency during the first thirty lines of PF.[2] The celebration of 'old books' as the seedbed of 'new learning' (ll. 22–5) has some affinity with the view of them as embodying ancient doctrine and giving access to the storehouse of collective memory in the *Prologue* to the *Legend of Good Women* (ll. 17–26 in this volume). Several of the writers to whom Chaucer is indebted here in PF themselves elevate the image of the book to mystical status. Alanus of Lille, who created the main model for the figure of Nature in the poem, claims that each created being is itself a kind of book; and Dante, whose journey Chaucer recalls at the start of his dream, makes the binding together of a volume one of the culminating images of his vision of Paradise.[3]

Another group of terms that carries some weight of meaning at this stage of PF is that which has to do with learning: the verbs *lerne* (ll. 1, 20) and *lere* (which in Chaucer's usage can mean 'learn' or 'teach', l. 25), and the noun *lore* ('instruction', l. 15). Instruction and learning figure largely in the action of dream poems of the thirteenth and fourteenth centuries.

219

The protagonist of the *Romance of the Rose*, for instance, is not only embarked upon a quest for love but also follows an extensive course of education at the hands of various personified guides and preceptors. And the dreamers in *Pearl* and *Piers Plowman* are engaged not only in encounters with marvels but also in protracted and often painful explorations of religious doctrine. One expectation, therefore, that Chaucer's reader might derive from this scene is that of authoritative instruction: 'a certeyn thing to lerne' (l. 20).

Such an expectation might, for the medieval reader at least, be further reinforced by the announcement of the title of the dreamer's book: Cicero's *Somnium Scipionis*, the 'Dream of Scipio' (l. 31), which had, we are soon to be reminded by Scipio himself (l. 111), been the subject of elaborate commentary by the late-Roman Neoplatonist Macrobius.[4] One possible function that the invocation of such a weighty *auctour* might serve is that of authentication: of conferring status upon the subsequent vision and thereby upon the poem. This seems to be the case in the *Book of the Duchess* (*BD*), where Macrobius is brought in, together with Pharaoh's dream-interpreter, Joseph (Gen. 41:25–36), to testify to the 'wonderful' complexity of the ensuing vision (*BD*, ll. 276–89); and biblical and classical dreamers, including *Cipion* (Scipio), are recruited for a similar purpose at the beginning of the second book of *HF* (ll. 512–17).

Yet the book that is held up at the start of *PF* doesn't seem to do a great deal either for the narrator's confidence or for the status of his own dream. After a day spent brooding over the cosmic scope and sombre ethos of the *Somnium*, the reader is left, it seems, none the wiser and considerably sadder (ll. 88–91). For, despite its prominent position in Chaucer's prologue and its rather perfunctory final attempt at encouragement ('god sende ech lover grace', l. 84), Cicero's text has not seemed to offer much hope of 'grace' to the lover or, indeed, much in the way of reliable guidance for the medieval Christian.[5] The ensuing dream, moreover, is introduced, not as a 'wonderful' vision whose status can be vouched for by reference to Macrobius and Joseph, but (initially at least) as the product of exhaustion and anxiety (ll. 89, 93, 99). Indeed, on the evidence of the analogies suggested in the stanza that Chaucer inserts as a kind of gloss at the start of his own narrative (ll. 99–105), the dream he is about to relate may not be of very high status at all.[6] On the strength of these lines, a medieval reader might well be led to expect the kind of dream that most models of traditional theory (including Macrobius) regarded as useless for conveying any significant degree of truth.[7]

At this point it is not yet clear whether *PF* is going to be the kind of vision that, as Macrobius puts it, will 'vanish into thin air' (*Commentary*

I, iii, 5). But the attitude towards books and dreams appears to be changing, and the atmosphere seems, after the weighty presence of learned authority, to be lightening up. There are several immediate signs of this change: one is the reappearance of the stern Africanus in lighter mood, making a genially disrespectful remark about his *olde booke*, not as a seed-bed of *science* but as a tattered tome (l. 110), and referring rather facetiously to the length of Macrobius's *Commentary* (l. 111).[8] Another is the narrator's blithe appeal to the anarchic power of Venus and her 'firebrand' (ll. 113–19), not all that long after the *Somnium*'s dire reports about the fate in store for 'lecherous folke' (ll. 79–80). Might all this suggest that an element of foolery is entering into and complicating the proceedings, as it has done especially in the final book of *HF*? It has been rightly noted that the solemn comparison of *olde bookes* to fields (ll. 22–5) had significantly ignored the act of labour required to make these *olde feldys* fruitful.[9] But it might also be noted that the narrator's own 'labour' upon Scipio's and Cicero's (and probably Macrobius's) *olde booke* (ll. 93, 112) itself quite quickly calls in question the ease of this process, and by the time the narrator's dream begins, the poem has begun to work upon and play with that earlier simplification.

The temple in the garden: Venus and Nature

A further means by which Chaucer tends to question an *olde booke* is through placing it in relation to another text. Already, in his rendering of Cicero's account of the souls who have been 'slaves of the body' and are thus condemned to 'fly' or 'hover' (*volutantur*) around the earth, Chaucer (ll. 79–80) may well have been particularly influenced by the particular *peyne* of Dante's lustful souls in Canto V of *Inferno*.[10] A few lines later (ll. 85–6), the movement away from the closed certainties of Cicero's cosmos is signalled by another, more obvious, allusion to Dante's uncertainties and anxieties at an equivalent moment in his journey (*Inf.* II, ll. 1–3). Both poets here express the sense of isolation and apprehension at the point of departure through the description of nightfall bringing rest to others, but Dante, as Chaucer probably knew (since he imitated later parts of the passage in *HF*, ll. 523–8), continues immediately: 'and I alone was preparing to face the stress of the journey and the suffering' (*Inf.* II, ll. 3–4).

Dante continues to provide *PF* with a vocabulary of departure or transition at the very point of entry into the dream's first landscape: the gate with its gold and black inscriptions. For those familiar with the uniformly grim message of Dante's inscription, Chaucer's 'translation' with its initial promise of a 'blysful place' would create a somewhat ominous impression.[11] Yet, despite the anxieties generated, the landscape the dreamer enters conforms in many ways to the traditional features of the earthly paradise or idealized garden that Dante himself had invoked in the last cantos of *Purgatorio*, or that Chaucer more literally translated from near the opening of the *Romance of the Rose*.[12] This landscape, as we shall see, continues to reveal occasional Dantean outcrops, but (from ll. 183 to 294) it is substantially shaped by another Italian textual stratum: that of Boccaccio's *Teseida*.

This passage, of a hundred or so lines describing both the garden and the temple it contains, is probably Chaucer's first close imitation of Boccaccio.[13] He may well at this time have been engaged in some more extensive version of Boccaccio's *Teseida*, the twelve-book classicized romance that was the narrative source for the *Knight's Tale*.[14] His reworking of stanzas from Book VII of the *Teseida* (st. 51–66) here incorporates Boccaccio's text into a narrative about rivalry in love, as the *Knight's Tale* does on a larger scale. That reworking, however, is not a simple process of translation, nor are the *Teseida* stanzas the only significant stratum in this part of *PF*'s landscape.

The *gardyn* that is experienced and explored by Chaucer's dreamer initially evokes not only the foreground of Boccaccio's scene but also the wider traditions of writing Paradise within the context of a quest, as is the case with the *Roman de la Rose* and Dante's *Purgatorio*. The situation of Chaucer's dreamer as he enters this landscape is somewhat closer to that of the lover in the *Roman* than it is to the personified prayer of Boccaccio's Palemone in *Teseida* VII; and it may possibly be a cue from *Purgatorio* XXVIII that leads Chaucer to make his first departure in this passage from the framework of Boccaccio's stanzas – a departure which leads (in ll. 204–10) to his most explicit evocations of the Earthly Paradise.[15]

The 'intensifying' effect of such departures from Boccaccio's text may also be felt when Chaucer's dreamer enters the next location within this landscape: the temple of Venus (ll. 246–94). Venus's power as *blysful lady* has already been acknowledged and invoked in this poem (ll. 113–19), as it was in *HF*,[16] and so has the 'lordship' of her son, Cupid, who has been seen attending to his instruments of power in the garden (ll. 10–14, 211–13). The temple that enshrines this power has prompted widely differing critical responses, and Boccaccio's portrayal of Venus herself, which is quite closely imitated by Chaucer (ll. 260–79), has been variously described as 'selfish, lustful, illicit, disastrous love . . . beautiful evil', or, on the other hand, as 'sexual appetite refined and beautified by legend, history and art'.[17]

A major difference between Boccaccio and Chaucer at this stage is that, whereas in *Teseida* VII the appearance of Venus herself follows the portraits of famous lovers, in *PF*, on the other hand, it precedes them. This change may carry some further consequences and implications. One effect is to bring Chaucer's Venus into closer proximity with the grotesque and frustrated figure of Priapus (ll. 253–9). Another is to turn the goddess's triumph into a different kind of event. In the *Teseida* Venus's victories over Diana and her followers and her exertion of her power over royal or noble figures, such as Semiramis and Hercules (VII, st. 61–2), have obvious relevance to a narrative in which Palemone (servant of Venus) is eventually to win Emilia (devotee of Diana), and it thus seems appropriate for such victories to go before her. In Chaucer's version the function of the examples seems less clear. In lines 281–94 the list of Venus's subjects is extended by the addition of a number of other famous lovers, most of whom (Dido, Tristan, Paris, Achilles, Helen, Cleopatra) had also appeared in the line of 'knights and ladies of antiquity' in *Inferno* V (ll. 61–72). Clearly, most of these (not quite all) can be regarded as tragic cases, perhaps even as victims rather than subjects of Venus; and Chaucer was to return to several of them (notably Troilus, Dido and Cleopatra) in later works. Perhaps, too, in their placing, after rather than before the appearance of Venus herself, we can read a phase in the experience of love that has led, in the dreamer's progress through the temple, from desire and frustration (sighs and donkeys braying) through fulfilment (Venus's *bed of golde*) to further yearning (the *two yonge folke*) and eventual extinction (the deaths of the famous lovers). But should such examples be read in the light, say, of Dante's second circle, as depicting 'the wretched end of those who spend themselves in passion', or should they be seen simply as 'an illustration, impressive both pictorially and poetically, of the wide-ranging power of love'?[18]

A further problem stems from the quite abrupt juxtaposition of these dead lovers' ghosts in the temple with the radiant figure of Nature in the garden (ll. 294–301). This figure shows, despite the evidence of Venus's power, more of an air of authority. She is described as a *quene* (l. 298) rather than a *lady* (l. 113); she is compared to the bright sun that outshines the star (ll. 299–300); and she is placed upon a 'hille of floures' (l. 302) rather than a bed. She also has ancestry in the only other text apart from the *Somnium Scipionis* to be invoked by name in *PF*: the *De Planctu Naturae* ('On the Complaint of Nature') by another, more recent, Neoplatonist, Alanus of Lille.

The reading of Alanus's book and the representation of Nature here is, like the rendering of Boccaccio's Venus, not a simple, immediate act of translation. Nature is portrayed, from her first appearance, in ways that recall her role not only in *De Planctu* but also in another work by Alanus, the *Anticlaudianus*, as well as in a wide range of earlier and subsequent sources, such as the *Roman de la Rose*.[19] Her activities as artificer and mediator of divine creativity are stressed here (l. 305) and later in *PF* (ll. 374, 379–81), as they are in the *Roman* and, less strikingly, in Chaucer's earlier dream poems, *BD* (ll. 908–12, 1195–8) and *HF* (ll. 490, 1366, 2039). The poem's placing of the authority of Nature in relation to the power of Venus is not solely a matter of reading one single book by Alanus after one by Boccaccio; for Alanus's *Anticlaudianus* (which Chaucer cites by name in *HF*, l. 986) also addresses the issue of the relationship between the two goddesses.[20]

Alanus's *De Planctu* is clearly an important model for ideas about Nature in *PF* and indeed for the representation of her presiding over an assembly of birds. It is a possible source for some specific features of birds mentioned in Chaucer's text – such as the 'gigantic' size of the crane, the adultery of the pheasant, and the swan heralding its own death. The lengthy account of the birds as they appear on Nature's mantle may also have influenced Chaucer, although in this case his response seems to have been a more sceptical one: to free them from that somewhat constraining symbolic structure and give them the kind of autonomy they have in several of the French debate poems of the thirteenth and fourteenth centuries.[21]

It is also possible that the didacticism of *De Planctu* may have encouraged Chaucer to explore in his own way an issue that relates Venus, Nature and the birds: that of *appetite*. Alanus's work, like Boccaccio's gloss on the temple of Venus, had heavily underlined the traditional moral wisdom about the link between gluttony and lust, and had done so at some considerable length as part of Nature's main message to humanity.[22] *PF*, on the other hand, seems more neutral in its representation of Bacchus and Ceres in attendance upon Venus; the references to *savours swoote* and *of hunger boote* ('relief from hunger') in this scene (ll. 274–6) could be metaphorical evocations of fulfilment rather than moralistic indications of lust. *Wille* ('Desire', 'Sexual Appetite'), the daughter of Cupid, appears early on in *PF* as the agent of his and Venus's power (ll. 214–17), and the noblest of the lovers in the subsequent debate frankly acknowledges the primacy of her prompting (l. 417). The further complexities of metaphors for appetite will also become apparent in the course of a debate in which noble predators will accuse lowly worm-eaters of 'gluttony'.

Noble pleading and low wretchedness

The birds assembled before Nature are initially defined mostly in terms of what they eat (ll. 323–9).[23] The diet of three of the four classes is a prominent feature which is recalled (sometimes unflatteringly) at a number of points throughout their eventual debate (ll. 505, 512, 527, 576, 604, 610, 613). The placing of the *fowles of ravyne*, led by the *royal egle*, at the highest point in the hierarchy, is as expected (ll. 323–4, 330), and the notion of preying upon other birds and beasts for a living would not of itself have been unduly disturbing to an audience familiar with falconry as an actual courtly pursuit and with the literary image of ducks cowering before hawks as an emblem of royal power (as in *Wynnere and Wastoure*, ll. 92–8). Yet the reappearance of the class-defining term, *ravyne*, within a very few lines (l. 336), qualified by the adjective *outrageouse* ('excessive, violent'), might well, in its new context, be somewhat unsettling. The stanza in which this reappearance occurs is the beginning of the specific descriptions of the birds, and within it the almost other-worldly authority of the royal eagle, whose 'sharpe looke perceth the sonne' (l. 331) gives place to the rapacity (*ravyne*) of a less glamorous predator, the goshawk, 'the tiraunte with his fethres donne / And grey' (ll. 334–6).[24] It seems that some elements among this class share the reputation of the cormorant and the cuckoo for avid gluttony.[25]

Conflicting and violent appetites within this assembly will demand further attention as the debate within *PF* progresses. Meanwhile, immediately after the description of the species in all their multiplicity and variety (ll. 330–68), ideas of harmony, nobility and hierarchical ordering are reasserted through Nature's identification with *accorde* (ll. 371, 381); through the placing of the female eagle 'of shappe the *gentileste*' upon her hand (the image both of creativity and of power, in ll. 372–8); and through the formal provision she makes for the choice of mate to be given first to the bird 'that most is worthy', the royal eagle (ll. 390–9).

Nature's reintroduction of the male royal eagle with epithets such as *worthy*, *secre* and *trewe* not only lends him status but also humanizes him in a specifically courtly 'guise', which is sustained by his own speech, expressing desire, pledging 'service' to his *sovereyne lady* (ll. 416–20), asserting his *trouthe* ('fidelity') and pleading for her *mercy, grace* and *routhe* (ll. 421–7).[26] In this intensely refined, courtly environment, birds do not only blush (ll. 442–5), they also bow, and the male eagle's gesture (l. 414) recalls the way that the knight in *BD* hangs his head before his lady (*BD*, ll. 1216–19). Similarly, the very deliberate devotion he displays (l. 417) recalls that of the knight (*BD*, ll. 789–96, 1092–1100), whilst his and his rivals' reiteration of the verb *serve* and the noun *servise* is paralleled in the earlier poem, as is the invocation of grim penalties for failure in such service.[27] Such parallels might suggest that, in this episode at least, one of the *olde bokes* that Chaucer is rewriting (alongside Cicero's, Boccaccio's and Alanus's) is his own *Book of the Duchess*.

Birds actually feature as lovers or debaters about love in various thirteenth- and fourteenth-century French poems that Chaucer might have known.[28] Some of the more interesting parallels and contrasts here are to be found in the *Messe des Oisiaus* ('Mass of the Birds') by Jean de Condé (c. 1275/80–1345) and the *Songe Saint Valentin* ('St Valentine's Day Dream') by Oton de Grandson (c. 1340–97).[29] The assembly in the *Messe des Oisiaus* is presided over by Venus, who explicitly acknowledges the authority she derives from Nature.[30] A disruptive presence in this assembly is the cuckoo, who is chased away but returns to mock the other birds and is condemned for, amongst other things, 'eating his foster mother'.[31] And the traditional metaphor of love as food or feeding (alluded to at several points in *PF*) is in the *Messe* developed into a fully blown allegorical scenario.[32] The *Songe Saint Valentin*, like *PF*, announces its occasion as St Valentine's Day and is thus linked to a number of Grandson's other poems.[33] It shows a feminine figure (a female eagle) presiding over the assembly, thus probably, like *PF*, sharing in the tradition whereby a 'queen' held the ring for deliberations about love.[34] Another lovelorn raptor (a peregrine falcon) also plays a prominent part, although he is ultimately a more excluded figure than Chaucer's male eagles, since not only does he dare say nothing to the female bird he loves, but he also flies off directly after telling his tale.[35] The other birds are generally a more harmonious company than is found in *PF*, and they resemble Chaucer's assembly only when embracing each other with their wings or pairing off as they disperse.[36]

Whether or not Chaucer knew these texts (or others like them), *PF* appears to differ significantly in developing the problematic and discordant elements in the situation. Harmony and hierarchy are affirmed at the beginning of the assembly in ways that might seem to recall the orderly structures and ideals of the 'Dream of Scipio', but noise and disruption are not far away. Words like *accorde*, *degree*, *royal*, *quene*, *sovereyne*, *gentil* and *noble* recur at this stage, but even here there are signs of strain in the high-toned idealism. The opening of the third eagle's intervention is worth some attention from this point of view. Within the space of six lines (ll. 464–9) it moves from a genial public-spiritedness of which Scipio might have approved ('Now, sirs, ye seen the lytel leyser here') to what seems like a rather desperate sort of self-advertisement: 'but I speke, I mote for sorwe dey'. The pressure of time and the need 'of foules for to ben delivered' (l. 491) is already apparent in the third eagle's speech, and it subsequently breaks out on a scale that shakes the surrounding landscape (l. 493) and shocks the dreamer to the core (l. 500).[37] Within ten lines *gentil plee* (l. 485) has become *cursed pledynge* (l. 495).

The stylistic change at this point is also striking. The colloquial expressions of the impatient birds (*Have doon*; *Com of*) recall some of the more churlish utterances in Book III of *HF*.[38] The *noyse* and onomatopoeic mayhem take over to such a degree that the 'fool' cuckoo can claim 'authority' to speak for the 'common good' (ll. 505–8), and Nature is constrained to accept the idea of wider consultation so as to maintain some semblance of order (ll. 521–5). The force of this challenge to Nature's authority and to the privilege of the *gentil* birds may perhaps reflect contemporary 'loss of plebeian respect for traditional elites'.[39] It may also make it rather more difficult to accept that the debate, the assembly and the poem as a whole have anything much to do with the progress of the betrothal of Richard II to Anne of Bohemia in the early 1380s.[40] There is of course no need to provide a single contemporary model for the behaviour of Chaucer's noble birds – but perhaps the founding (in the period 1377–85) of the 'Order of the *Tiercelet*' by a group of French provincial knights 'activated by ideas borrowed from the romances' might provide a more appropriate frame of reference for the embattled and slightly quixotic idealism of the male eagles, who by the end of the poem are being referred to as *terceletys* (l. 659).[41]

There may be further social, political or literary contexts within which the widening debate in the later stages of *PF* could be read. Parliamentary usage and procedure are invoked at several points in this part of the poem, and there was a tradition of associating the classes of birds with the various 'estates' of the realm.[42] The early 1380s were a troublesome time for the English government – with domestic unrest leading to the revolt of 1381, and high taxation for the unsuccessful war with France causing the Parliaments of 1381 and 1382 to refuse subsidies.[43] The voices of *so low a wrechednesse* in the later stages of *PF* – the comic and self-interested challenges to courtly and chivalric idealism by Chaucer's goose, duck and cuckoo – could thus be read in relation to the more sombre concerns about social and political leadership that were being voiced at the time by Langland, Gower and other writers of 'complaint'.[44]

Silence, harmony and the end of the work

The still centre of the increasingly raucous and vituperative conflict in *PF* is the epitome of Nature's *werkes*: the female eagle. She remains silent throughout the 'noble pleading' of the male eagles and the 'verdicts' of the lower fowl, and her voice is heard only at the end of the debate, postponing a decision and rejecting 'as yet' the notion of 'serving' in love that has meant so much to her suitors (ll. 648–9, 652–3). Such features and actions give her some affinity to the lady ('White') who is pursued by the man in black in *BD*, initially rejects him (*BD*, ll. 1240–4) and grants him 'mercy' 'another yere' (*BD*, ll. 1258, 1270). The silence of the *formel* may thus, like the portrayal of the *tercels*, represent in some ways a rewriting of Chaucer's earlier book. The similarities here, however, are not limited to *BD*: another of the books that *PF* draws upon, Boccaccio's *Teseida*, shows the heroine near the end attempting (less successfully) to resist this kind of pressure and asking to be left to 'serve' not Venus but Diana.[45] The voice and position of the *formel* are also more broadly characteristic of the heroine's role within the cult of 'courtly love' – whether one defines that ethos as 'based on a primal fear of women and a determination to treat them as objects', or (less sombrely) 'an arena in which negotiations can take place, even if we almost always only hear the male side of the argument'.[46]

The male eagles themselves are given for the moment no further opportunity for pleading, noble or otherwise. The vocabulary of courtly service and chivalric status (*degre*) is still evident in Nature's parting instructions to them (ll. 660–2). But her final words to them and to all her audience are a further (and slightly subversive) allusion to the sexual appetite of these *fowles of ravyne* and the metaphor of love as food or feeding (l. 665). She here presents the delay granted to the female eagle as an *entremesse* – a dish served between main courses, or an entertainment – and Chaucer may thus be making a final ironic revision of one of his *olde bokes*: the *Messe des Oisiaus*, where the three *entremés* served up in an allegorical feast of love consist of ingredients like sighs, complaints, favours and games.[47]

This period of suspense for the noble birds is immediately contrasted with the harmonious completion of the *werke* of mating for the assembly in general (ll. 666–8). The *acorde* by which each bird receives its *make* (l. 667) seems to be reflected by a punning rhyme, in the 'joye that they *make*' (l. 669). Consciousness of the poet's own role as traditional 'maker' in drawing this work 'to an ende' may be reflected in his subsequent reference to the birds' closing music as '*maked . . . in Fraunce*', and such consciousness is certainly evident in the attention he then draws to his own 'wordes' and 'vers' (ll. 678–9).

But the text (or gap) that then follows makes the poem in the end less neatly reflexive than this pattern might suggest. The birds' promised roundel, according to the textual evidence, is something of a makeshift.[48] Their *showtynge* that awakens the dreamer in the final stanza (l. 688) may perhaps recall the kinds of *noyse* heard earlier in the proceedings and suggest a possible threat to the precarious *acorde* (ll. 491, 500).[49] And the dreamer on waking turns not to the writing of the dream, as in the closing lines of *BD*, but to the continuing scrutiny of *other bookes* (l. 690). In their various ways, then, the dreamer and the writer seem, like the female eagle and Nature, to be indicating that, for the moment, 'Ye gete no more … here ys no more to sey'.

Nick Havely

1. See *HF*, ll. 614–68.
2. *PF*, ll. 10, 12, 16, 19, 21, 24, 27, 29.
3. Alanus in *PL* CCX, col. 579[A], cited in Curtius 1953: 319; and *Par.* XXXIII, ll. 85–90. On the idea and image of the book in the period and in Chaucer's work, see Neuss 1981 and Gellrich 1985.
4. For an easily accessible text of the *Dream* alone, see Miller 1977: 96–105; for a complete translation, see Stahl 1952. On Macrobius's dream theory and its reception in the Middle Ages, see Peden 1985 and Kruger 1992: 21–4, 62–4.
5. Aers (1981:6) emphasizes the unChristian features of the doctrine of the *Somnium*, as represented here.
6. For the source of this stanza, see the note on ll. 99–105, below.
7. Within Macrobius's fivefold classification of dreams, the kind of dream described in *PF*, ll. 99–105 would fall into the category of *insomnium* ('nightmare'), which 'may be caused by mental or physical distress' and is 'not worth interpreting'; see *Commentary*, tr. Ştahl 1952: I, iii, 2–5; also in Miller 1977: 49–52. Macrobius's was not the only or even the dominant scheme of classification; for other major models, especially those of Augustine and Gregory, see Kruger 1992: 35–56, 58–69.
8. Frank 1956: 534 notes among the surprises here the role of Africanus as the 'porter in a garden of love'.
9. See Aers (1981: 2), who also sees this passage as representing 'an attitude to knowledge and authority the poem will discredit'.
10. See Bennett 1957: 42, and for further details see the note on ll. 71–84, below.
11. A similar effect of unease is more recently created by Gloria Naylor's rewriting of Dante's inscription as the motto, on 'three bronze plaques', over the gate of a school in an upwardly mobile black American community: 'I am the way out of the city of woe / I am the way to a

prosperous people' (*Linden Hills* (British edn, 1992), p. 44).

12. For specific references, see the notes on ll. 183–210 and 201–3, below.

13. The influence of Boccaccio is, however, clearly apparent in *A&A* and is arguably evident in *HF* (see, for instance, Wallace 1985: 5–22).

14. Excerpts from the *Teseida* are translated in Havely 1992: 103–52, and there is a complete but not very reliable translation, *The Book of Theseus*, by B.M. McCoy (Sea Cliff, NY, 1974). McCoy's translation of Boccaccio's 'gloss' to his description of the temple of Venus (which Chaucer probably did not know) is reprinted in Miller 1977: 336–43.

15. See the note on ll. 201–3, below.

16. See esp. *HF*, ll. 130–9, 465–7, 518–19.

17. Brewer 1960: 31, 44, against Salter 1983: 132.

18. Contrast Bennett 1957: 105 and Salter 1983: 137.

19. For instance, she appears on a hill surrounded by a grove in *Anti-claudianus*, ed. Bossuat (1955: I, 107–9, tr. Sheridan 1973: 48). For her portrayal in general, see *RR*, ll. 15861ff., tr. Horgan 1994: 246ff., and, for surveys of the sources, Curtius 1953: 106–27 and Economou 1972.

20. See *Anticlaudianus*, ed. Bossuat 1955: I, 179–206, tr. Sheridan 1973: 52–3.

21. For examples of these in translation, see Windeatt 1982: 86ff.

22. See Alanus, *De Planctu*, Pr. 6.

23. For the possible sources of the fourfold classification Chaucer adopts here, see the endnote on 'Chaucer's birds' on pp. 270–1.

24. *Ravyne* at this time could mean simply 'prey' or 'quarry' (*MED ravin(e* n. 3), but it could also mean 'robbery', 'abduction' or 'greed' (*MED ravin(e* n. 1). A satirical poem of the end of Richard II's reign, *Richard the Redeless*, uses the word in this latter sense to describe the activities of rapacious kites (Passus II, l. 159) who there clearly symbolize exploitative nobles. For the legal definition of the term as 'robbery with violence', see also *Dives & Pauper* II, ed. P. Barnum, EETS (o.s.) CCLXXX (1980), p. 135, ll. 13–15.

25. See below, ll. 362, 613.

26. On the meanings of these terms, see the notes on ll. 412, 421 and 427, below.

27. For *serve*, *servise* and *servage* in the two texts, see *PF*, ll. 419, 440, 453, 459, 474, 478, 660, and *BD*, ll. 769 (with related terms in 764–74), 844, 1098, 1265. For the penalties for failure in *servise* or lack of *trouthe* in both texts, see the note on ll. 431–2, below.

28. For excerpts in translation, see Windeatt 1982: 86ff.

29. For translations, see Windeatt 1982: 104ff. and 121ff., and for the texts in the original, see *Jean de Condé: La Messe des Oiseaux*, ed. Ribard 1970:

13ff., and *Oton de Grandson: sa vie et ses poésies*, ed. Piaget 1941: 309ff.

30. *Messe*, ed. Ribard 1970: ll. 956–72, tr. Windeatt 1982: 113. Cf. also here the emphasis on Nature's command over Venus in Alanus's *De Planctu*, Pr. 5, tr. Sheridan 1980: 155–65.

31. See *Messe*, ed. Ribard 1970: ll. 381–92, tr. Windeatt 1982: 108.

32. *Messe*, ed. Ribard 1970: ll. 417–646, tr. Windeatt 1982: 108–10.

33. On Grandson and the traditions of St Valentine, see Piaget 1941: 132–4, 139; Brewer 1960: 131–2; Kelly 1986: 64–9.

34. For instance, in Boccaccio's *Filocolo* IV, chs 19–70.

35. *Songe*, in de Grandson, ed. Piaget 1941: ll. 130ff., 238–42 and 304, tr. Windeatt 1982: 121–3.

36. *Songe*, in de Grandson, ed. Piaget 1941: ll. 45–9, 312–14, tr. Windeatt 1982: 121, 123; cf. *PF*, ll. 667–71.

37. On the sense of time here and elsewhere in *PF*, see Strohm 1989: 125–30.

38. See *HF*, e.g. ll. 1622–3, 1713, 1776, etc.

39. Aers 1981:12, citing Hilton 1976: 8.

40. For a survey of attempts to link *PF* to these negotiations, see *Riv.*, p. 994 col. 1, and for a more sceptical approach to the question, Brewer 1960: 33–4.

41. The Order of the *Tiercelet* was founded partly to support the campaign against the English in south-western France. Its chief was a former vassal of the Black Prince who had returned to French obedience in 1372. On its history, see Vale 1967: 332–9. Connections between it and avian chivalry in *PF* have not, so far as I know, been considered before, and the present suggestion is mere speculation.

42. For parliamentary terms in *PF*, see the notes on ll. 507–8, 525–30, 545–6, below. On the possible associations between the birds and the social 'estates', see Brewer 1960: 34–5; Olson 1980: 61–5; Knight 1986: 29.

43. On the revolt of 1381 as context for *PF*, see Cowgill 1975: 332, and on attitudes to the war with France, see Coleman 1981: 76–7, 84–5.

44. Langland's B-text of *Piers Plowman* is usually dated between about 1377 and 1379 and the C-text around 1385–6. Gower's Latin complaint poem, the *Vox Clamantis*, is of about 1378–80. For a useful survey of the 'literature of unrest' in this period, see Coleman 1981: 58–156.

45. *Tes.* XII, st. 42, ll. 7–8.

46. The first of these views of 'courtly love' is that of G. Duby (tr. B. Bray), *The Knight, the Lady and the Priest* (Harmondsworth, 1983), p. 218; the second is that of L.M. Paterson, *The World of the Troubadours* (Cambridge, 1993), p. 259.

47. *Messe des Oiseaux*, ed. Ribard 1970: ll. 474–5, 517–23 and 621–3, tr. Windeatt 1982: 108–10.

48. See the note on ll. 680–7, below.
49. For this view, see McCall 1970: 30 and Cowgill 1975: 333; and for a contrary opinion, see Olson 1980: 57 n. 8.

	The lyf so short, the crafte so longe to lerne,	
	Th'assay so harde, so sharpe the conquerynge	
	The dredful joy alwey that slyd so yerne:	*fearful; soon*
	Al this meene I be Love, that my felynge	*by; emotion*
5	Astonyeth with his wondyrful worchyng	
	So soore, ywis, that, whan I on hym thynke,	*deeply; it [love]*
	Nat wote I wel wher that I flete or synke.	

	For, al be that I knowe not Love in dede,	*although*
	Ne wote how he quyteth folke her hire,	*know; rewards them*
10	Yet hapeth me ful ofte in bokis rede	*I often chance*
	Of hys miracles and of his cruelle yre.	*anger*
	There rede I wel he wol be lorde and sire.	*clearly*
	I dar nat seyn – hys strokes ben so sore –	*are*
	But 'God save suche a lorde!' I kan no more.	

15	Of usage, what for luste, what for lore,	
	On bookes rede I ofte as I yow tolde.	
	But why that I speke al this? – nat yore	*long (ago)*
	Agon hit happed me for to beholde	
	Upon a booke was write wyth lettres olde,	
20	And therupon, a certeyn thing to lerne,	
	The longe day ful fast I rad and yerne.	*closely and eagerly*

	For out of olde feldys, as men seyth,	*say*
	Cometh al this new corne fro yere to yere,	*from*
	And oute of olde bokes, in good feyth,	
25	Cometh al thys new science that men lere.	

1–7. The opening line is based on a proverb ('art is long but life is short') that goes back to Hippocrates (5th century BC); see Manzaloui 1962: 221–4. On the stylistic contrast between the whole stanza and the opening of *BD*, see Anderson 1992: 223.

2. 'The assault so fierce, the conquest so painful'.

5. 'Confuses (me) with its strange effects'.

7. 'I don't really know if I'm swimming or sinking'. Several MSS read *wake or wynke* ('am awake or asleep').

13–14. *I dar nat seyn . . . / But*: 'I dare say nothing but'.

15. 'Habitually, both for pleasure [*luste*] and for instruction [*lore*]'.

25. 'Comes all this new learning that is taught'. For the praise of *olde bokes*, cf. *LGW*, ll. 25–8.

But now, to purpose as of this matere:
To rede forth hit gan me so delyte
That al the day thought me but a lyte.   *seemed; short time*

This booke of which I make mension
30   Entitled was al, theras I shal yow telle,   *as*
'Tullius: of the Dreme of Cipion'.   *Cicero; Scipio*
Chapitres sevene it hadde, of hevene and
   helle   *seven chapters on*
And erthe and soules that theryn duelle –
Of which, as shortly as I kan trete,   *deal with it*
35   Of his sentence I wol yow tel the grete.

First telleth hyt, whan Scipion was come   *Scipio*
In to Aufryke, how he metyth Massynysse   *Africa; Masinissa*
That hym for joy in armes hath ynome.   *taken*
Than telleth he hir speche and al the blysse   *their talk*
40   That was betwixt hem til the day gan mysse,   *began to fade*
And how his auncestre, Aufrikan so dere,   *Africanus*
Gan in his slepe that nyght to hym appere.

26. 'But now, back to the subject of this discussion'. On Ch's terms for describing
     his subject-matter, see Burnley 1989: 221–3.

27. 'It so pleased me to go on reading'.

29–84. The *booke* summarized here is the *Somnium Scipionis* ('Dream of Scipio')
     by Cicero (106–43 BC), the final section of his *De re publica* which was the
     subject of a lengthy *Commentary* by Macrobius (c. 354–c. 430). For transla-
     tions, see Stahl 1952: 69–77; Brewer 1960: 133–7; Miller 1977: 96–105.

31, 36. *Cipion/Scipion*: Scipio was the name of an illustrious family of Republican
     Rome. Publius Cornelius Scipio the Younger (185/4–129 BC) was awarded the
     title 'Africanus' in recognition of his victory in the war with Carthage. So was
     his ancestor, Publius Cornelius Scipio the Elder (236–184/3 BC), who is the
     Aufrikan referred to below (ll. 41, 44, etc.).

35. 'I shall give you the gist of its argument'.

36–42. Summarizes ch. 1 of the *Dream of Scipio* (in the numbering of Macro-
     bius's *Commentary*). In ll. 36 and 43 *hyt/it* refers to the book, and in l. 39 *he*
     could be either the narrator or the book (personalized).

37. Masinissa (c. 240–148 BC) was a ruler of Numidia who had originally been
     allied to Carthage but had, through his friendship with the elder Scipio
     Africanus, become an ally of Rome. He is mentioned at the start of Cicero's
     Dream of Scipio.

41. *Aufrikan*: see note on ll. 31, 36, above.

Than tellith it that, fro a sterry place,   *starry sphere*
How Aufrikan hath hym Cartage yshewed   *shown Carthage*
45 And warned hym before of al hys grace
And seyde hym what man, lered or lewed,
That loveth comune profyt, wel ythewede,
He shal unto a blysful place wende   *go*
There joy is that lasteth without ende.   *where*

50 Than asked he, yf folke that here be dede
Han lyfe and dwellynge in another place.   *Have*
And Aufrikan seyde: 'Ye, withoute drede.   *Yes; doubt*
And oure present worldes lyves space   *life in the world*
Meneth but a maner dethe, what wey we trace;
55 And ryghtfull folke shul goo, whan they dye,   *righteous people*
To hevene', and shewed hym the Galoxye.   *Milky Way*

Than shewede he hym the lytel erthe that here
is   *the smallness of*
At regarde of the hevenes quantyte.   *compared with; size*

43–9. Summarizes ch. 2 and ch. 3, par. 1 of the *Dream of Scipio*. Cicero's
Africanus emphasizes that Scipio will destroy Carthage (*Cartage*, l. 44), and
his equivalents for Chaucer's *comune profyt* (l. 47) are 'serving the com-
monwealth' (*tutandam rem publicam*) and 'defending, aiding or enlarging
one's country' (*patriam*).

45–7. 'And prophesied to him about all his good fortune, and told him that any
person, learned or ignorant, who pursues the common good and is well-
disposed'. On the notion of *comune profyte* (l. 47), see Bennett 1957: 33–5.

50–6. Summarizes the rest of ch. 3 of the *Dream of Scipio*.

54. 'Amounts only to a kind of death, whatever path we follow'.

56. *Galoxye*: in the *Dream of Scipio* (ch. 3, par. 6), the Milky Way is described
as 'a circle of surpassing brilliance' inhabited by the souls of 'those who have
finished their lives on earth'. See also Ovid, *Met.* I, l. 170 and *HF*, ll. 935–9.

57–63. Summarizes chs 4–5 of the *Dream of Scipio*. The notion that the planets
as they moved made sounds that harmonized goes back to Pythagoras (5th
century BC), and the 'music of the spheres' features frequently in medieval and
Renaissance literature. See *Par.* I, ll. 78, 82, and Lewis 1964: 112. The belief
that such music was *cause of armonye* in the world is expressed in, for
instance, *RR*, ll. 16919–24 (tr. Horgan 1994: 262), and in the 13th-century
encyclopaedia, *De proprietatibus rerum*, by Bartholomaeus Anglicus
(14th-century English tr., ed. Seymour 1975: I, 458).

And aftir shewed he hym the nyne speris,   *spheres*
60 And aftir that the melodye herd he
That cometh of thilke speres thries thre,
That welle ys of musyke and melodye   *source*
In this world here, and cause of armonye.

Than bad he hym, syn the erthe was so lite   *since; was so petty*
65 And was somedel fulle of harde grace,
That he ne shuld hym in the worlde delyte.   *take pleasure*
Than tolde he hym, in certeyn yeres space,
That every sterre shulde come into his place   *its position*
There hit was first, and al shal oute of   *Where it;*
mynde   *be forgotten*
70 That in this worlde is doon of al mankynde.   *done by*

Than prayed hym Scipioun to tel hym alle   *Scipio begged him*
The wey to come into that hevene blysse.   *way; heaven's*
And he seyde: 'knowe thy selfe firste
immortalle   *(to be) immortal*
And loke ay besely thou werke and wysse

59. *the nyne speris*: 'the nine spheres'. In the medieval geocentric model of the
cosmos these were (moving outwards from the Earth): the Moon, Mercury,
Venus, the Sun, Mars, Jupiter, Saturn, the Fixed Stars, and the *Primum
Mobile* ('first moving thing').

61. *of thilke*: 'from those'; *thries thre*: 'nine' (lit.: 'thrice three').

64–70. Summarizes chs 6–7 of the *Dream of Scipio*. The smallness of the Earth
when seen in this perspective is also stressed in *HF*, ll. 904–7 (cf. *Cons.* II, pr.
7, and III, pr. 6).

65. 'And was in part full of hardship'. This could refer to the inhabited 'part' of
the world (*Boece* II, pr. 7).

67. *in certeyn yeres space*: '(that) after a certain number of years'. This (and
ll. 68–9) refers to the early astronomers' 'Platonic cycle' or 'Great Year', at the
end of which 'all the stars will have returned to the same places from which
they started out' (*Dream of Scipio*, ch. 7, par. 1).

71–84. Summarizes chs 8–9 of the *Dream of Scipio*. Cicero's equivalent to Ch's
comune profyte (l. 75, cf. l. 47) is *salute patriae* ('the well-being of your
country', *Dream of Scipio*, ch. 9, par. 1). The notion that the soul that has
been 'slave of the body' will be bound to the earth is Platonic (*Phaedo*, section
81), but Ch may have been influenced here by *Inf.* V, ll. 31–3, 43–5.

74–5. 'And be sure that you always actively work for and guide others towards
the common good, and you will never fail'.

75	To comune profyte, and thou shalt not mysse	
	To come swiftely unto that place dere	*worthy place*
	That ful of blysse ys and soules clere.	*pure souls*
	'But brekers of the lawe, soth to seyne,	*indeed*
	And lecherous folke, after that they be dede,	*after they are*
80	Shul whirle aboute th'erthe, alwey in peyne,	
	Til many a worlde be passed, out of drede;	*age; no doubt*
	And than, foryeven al hir wikked dede,	
	Than shal they come unto that blysful place,	
	To which to come, god sende ech lover grace.'	*grant; the favour*
85	The day gan faile, and the derke nyght	*began to fade*
	That reveth bestes from her besynesse	*deprives; concerns*
	Berefte me my boke for lake of lyght,	
	And to my bed I gan me for to dresse,	*turn*
	Fulfilled of thought and besy hevenesse;	
90	For bothe I had thinge which that I nolde,	
	And eke I ne had thyng that I wolde.	
	But fynally my spiryte, at the laste,	
	Forwery of my labour al the day,	*worn out by*
	Tooke reste, that made me to slepe faste,	*deeply*
95	And in my slepe I mette, as I lay,	*dreamed*
	How Aufrikan, ryght in that self aray	*the very same guise*
	That Scipion hym sawe before that tyde,	*time*
	Was comen and stoode ryght at my beddys side.	*Had come*
	The wery hunter, slepynge in hys bed,	

82. 'And then, with all their evil deeds forgiven'.

85–9. The contrast between the anxious seeker and the resting animals at nightfall recalls the opening of *Inf.* II, a scene to which Ch had already alluded in *HF*, ll. 523–8. Cf. also the allusion to the start of Dante's journey below (see ll. 123–40 & n.).

89. 'Filled with anxiety and restless depression'. The dreamer's waking state is also described as *hevynesse* in *BD*, l. 25 and *HF*, l. 2011.

90. *thinge which that I nolde*: 'the thing I didn't want'.

91. 'And furthermore, I didn't have what I wanted' – i.e., perhaps, 'love-doctrine' (Bennett 1957: 44–5).

99–105. These examples of dreams are modelled on a poem by Claudian (d. c. 404; see Pratt 1947: 421–3), although Ch's choice and ordering are slightly different.

100   To woode ayeine hys mynde gooth anoon;
       The juge dremeth how hys plees ben sped;   *lawsuits; have fared*
       The cartar dremeth how his carte is gon;
       The ryche of golde; the knyght fyght with his fone;   *foes*
       The seke met he drynketh of the tonne;
105   The lover meteth he hath hys lady wonne.

       Can I not seyne, yf that the cause were   *I can't tell*
       For I redde had of Aufrikan beforne
       That made me to mette that he stood there,   *to dream*
       But thus seyde he: 'Thou hast the so wel borne
110   In lokynge of myn olde booke totorne,   *studying; tattered*
       Of which Macrobye roughte nat a lyte,   *thought; little*
       That somedel of thy labour wolde I the quyte.'

       Cytherea, thou blysful lady swete   *Venus; sweet and joyful*
       That with thy fyrbrond dauntest whom the lest
115   And madest me thys swevene for to mete,   *dream this dream*
       Be thou myn helpe in this, for thou maist
           best –   *helper; are best able*
       As wisly as I sawe the, north north west,
       When I beganne my swevene for to   *to write down my*
           write,   *dream*

100. 'His thoughts straight away return to the woods'.
102. 'The charioteer dreams of how his chariot runs' (cf. *HF*, ll. 943, 956, and Claudian, ed. Platnauer 1922: II, 70).
104. 'The sick person dreams of drinking from the barrel'.
107. 'Because I had earlier read about Africanus'.
109. *the so wel borne:* 'conducted yourself so well'.
111. Macrobius (see above, ll. 29–84 n.) wrote a long commentary on the *Dream of Scipio*, hence he must have 'cared not a little' for it (i.e. rated it highly).
112. 'That I should like to repay you for some part of your labour'.
113–19. Venus (*Cytherea*, named after the island of Cythera, off the Peloponnese, supposed to have been her birthplace) is invoked both as the power of love and as a kind of Muse (cf. *HF*, ll. 518–19; *TC* III, ll. 1–44). Her fiery *brond* is also mentioned in *Merch T*, l. 1777.
114. 'Who tame with your torch anyone you wish'.
117. 'As surely as I saw you in the north-north-west'. The meaning could be ironic, since Venus is never seen in this precise position. Alternatively, two MSS read *northewest*, and Manzaloui (1974: 234) suggests this 'could be a straightforward description of the most northerly evening position of the planet'.

	So yeve me myght to ryme and to endyte!	*give; compose*
120	This forseyde Aufrikan me hent anoon	*aforementioned; grabbed*
	And forth with hym unto a gate broght	
	Ryght, of a parke, walled with grene stoon.	
	And over the gate, with letres large ywrought,	
	There were vers ywriten, as me thought,	*inscribed;* *it seemed to me*
125	On eyther halfe, of ful grete difference,	
	Of which I shal yow sey the pleyn sentence:	

'Thorgh me men goon into that blysful place   *people go*
Of hertes hele and dedely woundes   *hearts' healing; mortal*
   cure;
Thorgh me men goon unto the welle of grace   *source; joy*
130   There grene and lusty May shal ever endure.   *Where; pleasant*
This is the wey to al good aventure.   *fortune*
Be glad, thou reder, and thy sorwe ofcaste;   *cast away*
Al open am I, passe in, and spede the faste!'   *prosper greatly*

'Thorgh me men goon', than spake that other side,
135   'Unto the mortal stroke of the spere   *blow; spear*

121–2. 'And took me along with him straight to the gate of a park whose walls were of green stone'. *Grene* here 'may denote emerald or simply moss' (Bennett 1957: 62). It recurs in ll. 130, 174, 184, 202, etc.

123–40. The inscriptions over the gate in some ways recall that above the entrance to Dante's Hell (*Inf.* III, ll. 1–9), especially in their threefold repetition of *Thorgh me men goon* (which is a literal translation of Dante's *Per me si va*). But Dante's inscription is uniformly baleful and is placed at the apex (*sommo*) of his gate, not 'on either side'. Several of the images in Ch's inscriptions (*welle, tree, leves, streme, fyssh*) recur in altered form within the park (see below, ll. 173, 187–8).

123. *with letres large ywrought*: 'carved in large letters'.

125. 'On either side, and each differing greatly from the other'.

126. 'And I shall now tell you all they said'. *Sentence* in Ch can signify 'meaning', 'utterance' or 'judgement'.

134. '"Through me people go", the other side said'. The words over the gate here are thus given more of a 'voice' than they are in *Inf.* III, ll. 10–11, where Dante says he saw them 'written' (*scritte*).

Of which Disdayne and Daunger is the gyde;
There tree shal never frute ne leves
    bere.   *Where the*; *bear fruit or*
This streme yow ledeth unto the sorwful
    were   *leads you to*; *trap*
Ther as the fyssh in prison is al drye.   *Where*
140   Th'eschewyng is only the remedye.'

These vers of golde and blak ywriten were
Of which I gan astoned to beholde,
For with that oon encresed ay my fere,
And with that other gan myn hert to bolde;
145   That oon me hette, that other did me colde.
No wytte had I, for errour, for to chese
To entre or flee, or me to save or lese.   *abandon (myself)*

Ryght as betwix adamauntes twoo,   *loadstones*
Of evene myght, a pece of iren ysette   *equal strength*; *placed*

136. 'Which is wielded by Disdain and Aloofness'.
138–9. A *were* is an enclosure in a river for catching or keeping fish (cf. *TC* III, l. 35).
140. 'Avoidance is the only cure'.
141–7. The gold and black of the hopeful and ominous inscriptions (ll. 127–33 and 134–40) parallel the colours of Aeolus's contrasting trumpets in *HF*, ll. 1637, 1678. The dreamer's attitude to them may 'dramatize the confusion he feels as he writes the poem's opening stanza' (Kiser 1991: 46), and Gilbert (1978: 296) compares Boethius's dumbstruck and lethargic state as described by Lady Philosophy in *Cons.* I, pr. 2.
142. 'At which I began to gaze in bewilderment'.
143. *that oon*: 'the one'; *encresed ay*: 'continued to increase'.
144. *gan ... to bolde*: 'began to grow brave'.
145. 'The one encouraged [lit.: 'warmed'] me, the other gave me a chill'.
146. 'Because of this confusion [*errour*, also in l. 156], I lacked the sense to choose'. For the various meanings of *wit*, see Glossary, and for discussion, see Lewis 1960: 86–110.
148–51. The adamant or lodestone was said to be even stronger in attracting iron than the ordinary magnet (see Bartholomaeus, ed. Seymour 1975: II, 833, 849). On the theory and technology of magnetism at this time, see Crombie 1969: I, 131–3.

150   That hath no myght to meve to ne froo
       (For what that on may hale, that other lette),
       Ferde I, that nyste whether me was bette
       To entre or leve, til Affrikan, my gyde,
       Me hente and shoofe in at the gates wyde,

155   And seyde: 'hyt stondeth writen in thy face,   *it shows clearly*
       Thyn errour, though thou tel hyt not to me.   *confusion*
       But drede the not to come in to this place,   *have no fear*
       For this writynge ys no thing ment be the,
       Ne be noon, but he Loves servant be.   *Nor to anyone; unless*
160   For thou of love hast lost thy taste, y gesse,
       As seke man hath of swete and bitternesse.   *sick*

       'But natheles, al though thou be dulle,   *nonetheless*
       Yit that thou canst not do, yit mayst thow se.   *what*
       For many a man that may not stonde a pulle,
165   It lyketh hym at the wrastelynge to be   *he enjoys*
       And demeth yit whethir he do bet or he.   *still judges; does better*
       And yf thou haddest kunnynge for to endite,   *skill in composing*
       I shal the shewen mater of to wryte.'   *show you; to write of*

       With that my honde in hys he toke anoon,   *at once*
170   Of which I comfort kaught and went in faste.
       But, lorde, so I was glad and wel   *how glad and happy*
              begoon!   *I was*
       For, overal where I myn eyen   *everywhere; turned*
              caste,   *my gaze*

150–1. 'That has no power to move one way or the other / For whilst the one pulls
       the other resists'.
152.   'So behaved I, not knowing if it was better for me'.
154.   'Seized me and pushed me in at the wide entrance'.
158.   *ys no thing ment be the*: 'doesn't apply to you at all'.
160.   'For I imagine you have lost your taste for love'.
164.   *stonde a pulle*: 'get out of a hold' (in wrestling).
168.   Africanus's promise of material for the writer is more direct than is the eagle's
       in *HF*, ll. 661–99. The verb (*wryten*) has also occurred in ll. 141 and 155.
169.   Africanus's gesture and its reassuring effect recall how Dante is comforted
       (*mi confortai*) when Virgil takes his hand at the gate of Hell (*Inf.* III,
       ll. 19–21).
170.   'From which I gained comfort and went in quickly'.

Weren trees claad with levys that ay shal laste,
Eche in his kynde, with coloure fressh and
  grene   *its natural state*
175 As emeraude, that joye was to sene.

  The bylder oke and eke the hardy asshe, *oak for building*; *also*
  The pilere elme, the cofre unto careyne;
  The box-tre pipere, holm to whippes lasshe,
  The saylynge firre, the cipresse, deth to pleyne;
180 The sheter Ewe, the aspe for shaftes pleyne,
  The olyve of pes, and eke the dronken vyne;   *peace*
  The victor palme, the laurere to devyne.

  A gardyn sawe I, ful of blossomed bowis, *blossoming boughs*
  Upon a ryver, in a grene mede   *By*; *meadow*
185 Ther as swetnes ever mo ynow is,   *Where*; *in plenty*
  With floures white, blew, yelow and rede *flowers*; *blue*
  And colde well stremes, no thing dede
  That swymmyn ful of smale fisshes   *That abound in*;
   lyght,   *darting*

176–82. The list has been seen as 'the focus of the poet's delight in his own erudition' (Leicester 1974: 22), and Kiser (1991: 47–8) argues that the trees themselves 'seem to have been created with art in mind'. Many of the characteristics mentioned also appear in Book I, ll. 517–20 of the *Ilias* of Joseph of Exeter, a 12th-century work which Ch knew.

177–80. 'The elm for making posts and coffins for corpses; / The box-tree for flutes, the holm-oak for whips, / The fir for ships' masts, the cypress for grief; / The yew for bows, the aspen for smooth arrow-shafts'.

182. *the laurere to devyne*: 'the laurel for divination'. The tree is closely associated with Apollo and hence with both prophecy and poetry (see *Par.* I, ll. 15, 25, and *HF*, ll. 1106–8).

183–210. Details like the eternal present (l. 185: *evermo . . . is*), harmonious sounds, especially birdsong (ll. 191, 197–203), temperate climate (ll. 204–5), perfect health (ll. 206–7) and everlasting daylight (ll. 209–10) traditionally form part of earthly Paradises. Cf. *RR* (Chaucerian tr.), ll. 645–720, and *Purg.* XXVIII, ll. 1–33; and see Curtius 1953: 195–200 and Pearsall & Salter 1973: 56–118. At this point, especially with the description of birds and animals in ll. 190–6, the garden begins specifically to resemble the landscape around the Temple of Venus in *Tes.* VII (st. 51–66).

187. 'And cool fast-flowing [lit.: 'not at all stagnant'] springs'. Cf. *Tes.* VII, st. 51.

With fynnes rede and scales sylver bryght.

190 On every bowgh the briddes herde I synge,   *birds*
    With voys of aungel in her armonye,   *angelic voices; their*
    That besyed hem her briddes forthe to brynge.
    The lytel conyes to her pley gunnen hye;
    And further, al aboute, y gan espye   *around; perceive*
195 The dredful roo, the buk, the hert and hynde,   *timid roe-deer*
    Squerel, and bestis smale of gentil kynde.   *animals; best sort*

    On instrumentes of strynges in acorde   *in harmony*
    Herde I so pley, and ravysshinge swetnesse,   *playing with such*
    That god, that maker ys of al and lorde,
200 Ne herde never bettir, as I gesse.
    Therewith a wynde – unnethe hyt myght be
       lesse –   *scarcely; gentler*
    Made in the leves grene a noyse softe,
    Accordant to the foulys songe on lofte.   *in harmony with; birds'*

    The eire of that place so attempre was   *air; temperate*
205 That never was grevance ther of hoot   *discomfort;*
       ne colde.   *because of*
    Ther wex eke every holsome spice and   *grew; healthful;*
       gras.   *herb*
    No man may there waxe seke ne olde.   *grow ill nor*
    Yet was there joye more a thousande folde
    Than man kan telle; never wolde hyt nyght,   *(be) dark*
210 But ay clere day to any mannys syght.   *it (was) always*

192–3. 'Which were busy looking after their young. / The little rabbits ran about in play'. Birds make their first appearance in the poem here and, along with rabbits and other small furry animals (cf. *Tes.* VII, st. 52), are associated with erotic and procreative activity.

195. The hunting of the deer, particularly the *hert* (cf. the pun in *BD*, l. 1313), was traditionally linked to erotic pursuit. See Thiébaux 1974: 115–27.

199. On God as *maker* (also the word for 'poet'), cf. *HF,* ll. 470, 584, 646 and 970; also *Purg.* X, l. 99, and Curtius 1953: 544–6.

201–3. The harmonizing of birdsong with the rustling of leaves in the breeze is also a feature of Dante's earthly paradise in *Purg.* XXVIII, ll. 7–18. See Bennett 1957: 76–8.

210. Mustanoja (1960: 510) suggests that 'absence of the verb adds a fresh, impressionistic touch to the static, landscape-like picture'.

Under a tree, besyde a welle, I say   *saw*
Cupide, our lorde, hys arwes forge and fyle;
And at hys fete hys bowe al redy lay.
And Wille, hys doghtre, tempred al the   *was tempering;*
    while   *time*
215   The hedes in the welle, and with hir wile   *arrow-heads; cunning*
She couched hem, after as they shulde serve   *fixed*
Some for to slee, and some to wounde and kerve.   *to kill; pierce*

Thoo was I war of Plesaunce anon ryght,
And of Array and Lust and Curtesye,   *Display; Delight*
220   And of the Crafte that kan and hath the myght   *Cunning*
To doon by force a wyght to do folye –
Dysfigured was she, I shal not lye –
And by hem self, under an oke, I gesse,   *by themselves*
Saugh I Delyte, that stoode with Gentilesse.   *Charm; Nobility*

225   I sawgh Beaute, withoute any atire,   *clothing*
And Yowthe, ful of game and jolite;   *merriment; high spirits*
Foolhardynesse, Flatery and Desire,
Messagery, Mede, and other thre –
Her names shul not here be tolde for me.   *by me*

211–17. The sequence of personifications relating to the experience and pursuit of
    love is quite close to that in *Tes.* VII, st. 54ff., but already in this stanza there
    are some differences (see Bennett 1957: 85).
218–24. The figures in the corresponding lines of *Tes.* VII, st. 55 are Grace,
    Elegance, Friendliness, Courtesy, Magic Arts, Imaginary Delight and Nobil-
    ity. *Lust* (l. 219) in Ch has a range of meanings, from 'delight' to 'lust'; and
    Crafte (ll. 220–1) can be used of honest skills or (as here) of occult and
    disreputable arts (cf. *HF*, ll. 1259–74). The *oke* ('oak') in l. 223 is a detail
    added by Ch, who may have associated it with nobility (*Gentilesse*); it is the
    tree against which the knight in *BD* is sitting (*BD*, ll. 445–7).
218. 'Then, all at once, I noticed Pleasure'.
221. 'To force a person to act foolishly'.
225. Boccaccio's Beauty is more narcissistically 'gazing at herself' and engaged in
    mutual admiration with Charm.
228. 'Mediation, Payment, and three others'. Ch's *Messagery* and *Mede* corre-
    spond to the more brutal *Ruffiania* (Procuring) in *Tes.* VII, st. 56. The *other
    thre*, whose names Ch refuses to disclose, do not feature in *Tes.* and may be
    a gratuitously sinister (or facetious) touch.

230   And, upon pilers grete of jasper longe,
      I sawgh a temple of bras ifounded stronge.   *strongly built*

      Aboute the temple daunced alway
      Wommen ynow, of which some were   *Many women*
      Faire of hem self, and some of hem were gay.   *in themselves*
235   In kirtels, al disshevele, went they there;
      That was hir office alwey, yer by yere.   *behaviour*
      And, on the temple, of dowves white and faire
      Sawe I syttynge many a hundred paire.

      Before the temple dore, ful soberly,   *very*
240   Dame Pes sate, a curtyne in hir honde,   *Peace*
      And, hir beside, wonder discretly,   *most modestly*
      Dame Pacience sittynge ther I fonde,
      With face pale, upon an hille of sonde;   *sand*
      And aldernext, within and ek withoute,   *straight after; also*
245   Behest and Arte, and of her folke a rowte.

230. 'And, with tall, stout columns of jasper'. The temple in *Tes*. VII, st. 57 has
     columns of copper (the metal associated with Venus). Ch's jasper (then
     thought of as a green stone speckled with black or red) perhaps recalls the
     first foundation of the walls of the paradisal city of New Jerusalem (Rev.
     21:19), though it is also the stone on which Criseyde sits in *TC* II, l. 1229.
     Bennett (1957: 90) notes that the temple-threshold in Claudian's *Epithala-
     mium Honorii* (l. 90) is of jasper.
232–6. In *Tes*. VII, st. 57 the dancers also include 'young men'.
235. *disshevele*: 'with hair loose'. The 'kirtle' was 'an outer garment, sometimes
     worn over a smock or under a mantle' (*MED kirtel* n. 2(a)).
237–8. Doves (*dowves*) are often associated with Venus (cf. *HF*, l. 137 and *Kn T*,
     l. 1962). *Tes*. VII, st. 57 also includes a flock of sparrows (cf. the reference
     to the sparrow as *Venus sone* below, l. 351).
239–40. The representation of Peace at the entrance makes rather more sense in
     Tes. VII, where it sharpens the contrast between the temples of Venus (love)
     and Mars (war). The *curtyne* presumably shields the open entrance from
     light and dust.
243. Patience's hill of sand is another detail not found in *Tes*. Bennett (1957: 91)
     thinks it signifies sterility; cf. also the desert outside the temple of Venus in
     HF, ll. 480–8. It may, though, merely allude to the lover's endurance of the
     passing of time as measured in a sandglass (a timepiece that was in common
     use and illustrated in manuscripts and painting by this time).
245. 'Promises and Craft and a crowd of their followers'.

Withyn the temple, of syghes hoote as fire
I herde a swogh that gan aboute renne –
Which syghes were engendred with desire   *created by*
That maden every auter for to brenne   *altar; burn*
250   Of newe flawme, and aspyed I thenne   *with new flames*
That al the cause of sorwes that they drye   *endure*
Come of the bitter goddys, Jalousye.   *Was caused by*

The god Priapus saugh I, as I wente,   *I saw*
Withyn the temple in soverayne place   *standing in the*
stonde,   highest place
255   In suche array as whan the asse hym shente   *state; upset*
With crie be nyght, and with his ceptre in
honde.   *at night; sceptre*
Ful besely men gunne assay and fonde,
Upon his hede to sette, of sondry hewe,   *various colours*
Garlondes ful of fresshe floures newe.

260   And in a pryvy corner in disporte   *secret; amusing themselves*
Fond I Venus and hir porter   *I found; doorkeeper,*
Rychesse,   *Wealth*
That was ful noble and hawteyn of hir porte.   *proud in bearing*
Derke was that place, but afterward lyghtnesse   *brightness*
I saw a lyte – unnethe hyt myght be lesse –   *a little; scarcely*

247. 'I heard a rushing sound that ran all around'.
253–9. *Priapus* was the Roman god of fertility and gardens whose attempt to
    seduce the nymph Lotis was interrupted by the braying of an ass (l. 255; cf.
    Ovid, *Fasti* I, ll. 415–40; *Tes.* VII, st. 60). The 'sceptre' with which Ch
    endows him here (l. 256) is another detail not in *Tes.* Brown (1975: 260–1)
    points out that it is a common feature of the iconographic tradition and
    could here be royal or phallic.
257. 'People were busily and eagerly seeking'. Brown (1975: 261–2) stresses the
    'conative' function of the verbs here ('they tried and *tried*') as part of the
    pattern of frustration at this stage in the text.
260–79. The equivalent description of Venus herself is in st. 63–6 of *Tes.* VII. The
    reference to sunset (l. 266) is not in *Tes.*, and Gilbert (1978: 298) suggests
    that it alludes to Venus as evening star.
261–2. Boccaccio says that Wealth, as Venus's doorkeeper, has to be 'treated with
    great respect' (*Tes.* VII, st. 64), recalling the Friend's description of her as a
    necessary 'escort' for the Lover seeking to enter the Castle of the Rose in
    RR, ll. 7913–30 (tr. Horgan 1994: 122).

265	And on a bed of golde she lay to reste,	*at rest*
	Til that the hoote sonne gan to weste.	*to set*

	Hir gilte heeres with a golde threde	*golden hair*
	Ybounden were, untressed as she lay,	*with hair loose*
	And naked fro the brest unto the hede	
270	Men myght hir see; and, sothely for to say,	*indeed*
	The remenaunt was well keverede, to	
	my pay,	*concealed pleasingly*
	Ryght with a subtil keverchefe of valence.	
	There was no thikker clothe of no defence.	

	The place yafe a thousande savours	
	swoote,	*breathed; fragrances*
275	And Bachus, god of wyne, sate hir beside,	*Bacchus*
	And Ceres next, that dooth of hunger boote;	*appeases hunger*
	And, as I seide, amyddis lay Cipride,	*at the centre*
	To whom on knes two yonge folk there cryede	*kneeling*
	To ben hir helpe. But thus I late hir lye	*help them*
280	And, ferther in the temple, I gan espye	*perceive*

	That, in dyspite of Diane the chaste,	*defiance*

272. 'Just with a fine, draped veil'. *Valence* is probably cloth from the town of that name (on the Rhône between Lyon and Avignon), but coverchiefs from Valenciennes (N.E. France) are recorded as a luxury item in London shops in the 14th century (Thrupp 1948: 7).

273. *of no defence*: 'to protect her at all'.

276. *that dooth of hunger boote*: 'who helps appease hunger'. Ch and Boccaccio (*Tes.* VII, st. 66) seem to be alluding to the proverb: 'Without Ceres [food] and Bacchus [wine], Venus [libido] remains cold' (Terence, *Eunuchus*, l. 732).

277. *Cipride*: the cult of Aphrodite is associated with Cyprus in Homer; cf. the use of the term as a name for Venus in Alanus of Lille, *De Planctu Naturae* 18.87 and by Ch in *HF*, l. 518 and *TC* III, l. 725, IV, l. 1216 and V, l. 208.

278–9. The unresolved appeal from the two young devotees of Venus is not part of the scene in *Tes.* VII.

280–1. The most striking example in *PF* of *enjambement* between stanzas.

281–7. The Roman goddess Diana is associated with female chastity, forests, childbirth and the moon. The first two are particularly relevant to the stories of her two 'servants' here. Callisto (*Calixte*) was seduced by Jupiter and transformed into a bear and then a constellation (*Ursa maior*; see *Met.* II, ll. 409–507); whilst Atalanta (*Athalante*) was a huntress of Arcadia or

Ful many a bowe ybroke henge on the walle	*hung*
Of maydens suche as gonne hyr tymes	
waste	*were wasting their lives*
In hir servise – and, peynted overal,	*everywhere*

285 Ful many a story of which I touche shalle — *shall mention*
A fewe – as of Calixte and Athalante, — *Callisto; Atalanta*
And many a mayde of which the name — *whose name;*
I wante. — *lack*

Semyramus, Candace and Hercules; — *Semiramis*
Biblys, Dido, Tesbe and Piramus; — *Thisbe*
290 Tristram, Isaude, Paris and Achilles; — *Yseult*
Eleyne, Cleopatre and Troilus; — *Helen*
Silla and eke the moder of Romulus; — *Scylla*
Alle these were peynted on that other syde — *elsewhere*
And al her love, and in what plite they dide. — *circumstances; died*

295 Whan I was comen ayen into the place — *again*
That I of spake, that was so swoote and
grene, — *spoke of; pleasant*
Forth welke I tho, my selven to solace.
Tho was I war where ther sate a quene — *aware*
That, as of lyght the somer sonne shene — *in brightness; bright*
300 Passeth the sterre – ryght so, over — *Exceeds;*
mesure, — *immeasurably*

Boeotia who was (according to different versions) loved by (1) Meleager, which produced fatal jealousy (*Met.* VIII, ll. 260–444), or (2) Melanion or Hippomenes, who cheated her in a race which was a trial for winning her hand (*Met.* X, ll. 560–680).

284–6. In *Tes.* VII, st. 62, the stories of Venus's victims are said to be 'depicted everywhere', and they appear before Boccaccio's description of Venus, not after (as here). In this passage, as in *BD*, ll. 332–5 and *HF*, ll. 209–11, etc., Ch specifically envisages wall-painting as the medium for exemplary narrative.

288–94. For further information about the figures mentioned in this passage, see Endnote (i): 'Chaucer's lovers', on pp. 269–70.

299–301. Nature's head in *De Planctu Naturae* (see below, l. 316 & n.) is crowned with stars and planets (tr. Sheridan 1980: 76–85), and her appearance is signalled by an increase in light (ibid.: 109). Gilbert (1978: 299) suggests that the contrast between *sonne* and *sterre* also specifically relates to that between Nature and Venus.

She fairer was than any creature.

	And in a launde, upon an hille of floures,	glade
	Was set this noble goddesse, Nature.	placed
	Of braunches were hir halles and hir boures	chambers
305	Ywrought, aftir hir crafte and hir mesure;	
	Ne ther nas foule that cometh of engendrure	
	That thei ne were prest in hir presence	Who was not eager
	To take hir dome and yeve hir audience.	

	For this was on seynt Valentynes day,	
310	Whan every foule cometh there to chese his make,	choose; mate
	Of every kynde that men thynke may,	species; can think of
	And that so huge a noyse gan they make	And when
	That erthe and eyr and tree and every lake	
	So ful was that unnethe was ther space	hardly
315	For me to stonde, so ful was al the place.	

	And ryght as Alayne, in *The Pleynt of Kynde*,	
	Devyseth Nature of array and face,	Describes; appearance
	In suche array men myght hir there fynde.	
	This noble emperesse, ful of grace,	

303–5. *Nature* is here portrayed in ways that recall her appearance in sources such as Alanus of Lille's *De Planctu Naturae* (see also below, l. 316).

305. 'Constructed according to her skill and measurements'.

306. 'Nor was there any bird that is bred'.

308. 'To receive her [Nature's] judgement and wait on her words'.

309–10. *seynt Valentynes day*: possibly the present occasion on 14 Feb., the feast day of St Valentine Martyr of Terni. Oruch (1981: 556) suggests that Ch's poem is itself the source of 'the majority of the customs and literary expressions connected with Valentine's Day'. Kelly (1986: 157) agrees that 'it was Chaucer who first introduced the love-cult of St Valentine', but argues that 'he connected it with the Maytime feastday [2 May] of the Genoese saint of that name'.

316. 'And, just as Alanus, in *The Complaint of Nature*'. For the relationship between the terms *Nature* and *Kynde*, see Lewis 1960: 24–74. The allegorical Latin works, *De Planctu Naturae* and *Anticlaudianus*, by the Neoplatonist Alanus of Lille (1125/30–1203), were both influential upon Ch (see also *HF*, l. 986 & n.). The three lines devoted to Nature's appearance here contrast with the exhaustive description in Alanus's work (tr. Sheridan 1980: 73–107).

320	Bad every foule to take her owen place	
	As they were wont alwey fro yere to yere,	*used to*
	Seynt Valentynes day, to stonden there.	
	That ys to sey, the fowles of ravyne	*birds of prey*
	Were hyest sette, and than the foules smale	*placed highest*
325	That eten as hem Nature wolde enclyne –	*disposed them*
	As worm or thynge of which I tel no tale.	*say nothing*
	And watir foule sate lowest in the dale,	*valley*
	But foule that lyveth by seede sate on the grene,	*live on seeds*
	And that so fele that wonder was to sene.	
330	There myght men the royal egle fynde	
	That with his sharpe looke perceth the sonne,	
	And other egles of a lower kynde	*breed*
	Of which that clerkes wel devysen konne.	
	There was the tiraunte with his fethres	*tyrant;*
	donne	*greyish-brown*
335	And grey – I mene the goshauke that	*goshawk;*
	doth pyne	*who torments*
	To briddes for his outrageouse ravyne;	*birds; rapacity*
	The gentil faucoune that with his fete	*noble falcon;*
	distreyneth	*grips*
	The kynges honde, the hardy sperhauke	*bold sparrow-hawk*
	eke,	
	The quayles fo; the merlyon that peyneth	*merlin; strives*
340	Hym self ful ofte the larke for to seke.	
	There was the dowve, with hir eyen meke,	*dove; eyes*
	The jalouse swanne ayens his deth that syngeth;	
	The owle, eke, that of dethe the bode bryngeth;	*omen*
	The crane, the geante, with his trompes	*giant; trumpeting*
	soune,	*sound*

323–64. For further information about the birds mentioned in this passage, see
Endnote (ii): 'Chaucer's birds', on pp. 270–3.

329. 'And so many of them that it was astonishing to behold'.

331. 'Who with his sharp gaze penetrates the sun'.

333. 'Which scholars can properly describe'; referring to the encyclopaedias and
bestiaries (see, for instance, Bartholomaeus, ed. Seymour 1975; White
1954).

342. *ayens his deth that singeth*: 'that sings at the point of death'.

345   The thefe, the choghe, and eke the   *chough*;
           janglynge pye;   *gossiping magpie*
       The scornynge jay, the eles foo, heroune,   *mocking; eel's foe*
       The fals lapwynge, ful of trecherye;
       The stare that the counseylle kan bewrye,
       The tame ruddok and the coward kyte,   *robin; kite*
350   The cok that orlogge ys of thropes lyte;

       The sparow, Venus sone; the nyghtyngale
       That clepeth forth the grene leves newe,   *calls*
       The swalow, morthrer of the foules   *murderer*;
           smale   *small creatures*
       That maken hony of floures, fressh of hewe;
355   The wedded turtel with hir herte trewe,   *turtle-dove*
       The pecok with his aungels fethers bryght,
       The fesaunt, scorner of the cok by nyght;   *pheasant, cuckolder*

       The waker goos, the cukkow ever unkynde,   *vigilant; unnatural*
       The papiay, ful of delycacye;   *parrot; wantonness*
360   The drake, stroyer of his owne kynde,   *killer*
       The storke, wreker of avouterye,   *avenger of adultery*
       The hoote cormoraunte of glotonye;
       The ravenes and the crowes with her voys of care,
       The throstel olde, the frosty feldefare.   *mistle-thrush; fieldfare*

365 ✗ What shulde I seyn? – of foules every kynde   *can I say*
       That in this worlde han fetheres and stature   *have*
       Men myghte in that place assembled fynde
       Be fore that noble goddesse of Nature;
       And eche of hem did his besy cure   *eagerly sought*
370   Benygnely to chese or for to take,   *With good will*

348.   'The starling that will betray every secret'.
350.   'The cock that serves as timepiece for small villages'. Cf. *NPT*, ll. 2853–8
       and 3187–99, and Alanus, tr. Sheridan 1980: 89.
362.   'The fiercely gluttonous cormorant'.
363.   Or possibly: *The raven wys; the crowe wit[h] vois of care*, as in MS Gg
       alone. Brewer (1960: 60), following Gg, thinks it unlikely that Ch would
       change from singular to plural in this line only; on the other hand, such a
       change could be seen as creating a grimly choric effect. Members of the
       corvidae family (ravens, crows, rooks, etc.) were often grouped together,
       then as now; see Yapp 1981: 56–7.

By hir accorde, hys formel or hys   *agreement*;
    make.   *female*; *mate*

But to the poynte: Nature helde on hir honde
A formel egle, of shappe the gentileste   *the noblest form*
That ever she amonge hir werkes   *found among*
    fonde,   *her creations*
375 The moste benigne, and the goodlyeste;   *gracious*
In hir was every vertu at his reste
So ferforthe that Nature hir selfe had blysse *utterly*
To looke on hir and ofte hir beke to kysse.   *to kiss her beak*

Nature, the vyker of th'almyghty lorde   *representative*
380 That hoot, colde, hevy, lyght, moist and drye
Hath knyt be evene nombre of accorde,
In esy vois began to speke and seye: *pleasant*
'Foules, take hede of my sentence, I preye,   *speech*
And for youre ese, in furtherynge of youre nede,

371. Use of the word *accorde* appears to link the idea of agreement in the assembly with that of harmony in nature (cf. below, l. 381).

372–4. *hir hond ... the gentileste ... amonge hir werkes*: 'craftsmanship' is stressed here again, as in ll. 305, 379–81, 636. The idealized female is often represented as the epitome of Nature's handiwork; cf. below, l. 418, also *BD*, ll. 870–3, 908–11, *A & A*, ll. 79–80, *Comp d'Am*, ll. 51–4, and *Phys T*, ll. 9–29 (see also Bennett 1957: 201; Economou 1972: 26–7).

375. *benigne* ('gracious') is also an epithet applied to the idealized lady in *BD*, l. 918, *LGW*, l. 175, and *Comp d'Am*, l. 53.

376. 'Every noble quality found its perfect form in her'.

379–81. On the idea and figure of Nature in pagan antiquity, see Curtius 1953: 106–7. She is described as God's 'vicar' (deputy) by Alanus (tr. Sheridan 1980: 146); also in *RR*, ll. 16752, 19477 (tr. Horgan 1994: 259, 301) and in *Phys T*, l. 20. The properties Nature controls (l. 380) are those of the elements and the related 'humours' (fluids) constituting the human body; a similar process of binding them harmoniously together is ascribed to God as Creator by Boethius: see *Boece* III, met. 9, esp. ll. 18–32; also Alanus's account of this harmony in *De Planctu* (tr. Sheridan 1980: 145). The phrase *by evene acorde* recurs near the end of the poem (below, l. 668), where it refers to Nature's matching of males to females.

381. 'Has blended in exact and harmonious proportions'.

384–5. 'And, to comfort you and fulfil your desires, / I will help you as speedily as my speech allows'.

385   As faste as I may speke I wol yow spede.

Authority

'Ye knowe wel how that, seynt Valentynes day,
Be my statute and thorgh my governaunce,   *By*; *guidance*
Ye come for to chese and flee youre way   *to choose*; *fly away*
With youre makes, as I prik yow with plesaunce.   *urge*; *desire*
390   But natheles, my ryghtful ordenaunce
May I not let, for al this worlde to wynne:
That he that most ys worthy shal begynne.   *who is worthiest*

TERCEL-Male   ✳ Patriarchal

'The tercel egle, as that ye knowen
        wele,   *male*; *as you well know*
The foule royal aboven yow in degree,   *royal bird*; *in rank*
395   The wyse and worthy, secre, trewe as stele,   *discreet*
The whiche I have formed, as ye may see,
In every parte as hit best lyketh me –   *pleases*
Hyt nedeth noght hys shape yow to devyse,
He shal first chese and speken in his gyse.   *as he pleases*

400   'And aftir hym, by order, shul ye chese,
Aftir youre kynde, everyche as yow lyketh,   *By rank*
And, as your happe ys, shul ye wynne or lese.   *luck*; *lose*
But whiche of yow that love most entriketh,   *has ensnared*

387–90. Terms like *statute*, *governaunce* and *ordenaunce* suggest parliamentary language. According to Brewer (1960: 119), 'Nature's *statute* has the sacred character of law . . . her *ordenaunce* is a particular act or decision within the scope of the *statute*'. *Ordenaunce* is, however, more flexible than Brewer implies, and could here mean 'regulation' or 'prescribed custom, due procedure' or 'provision' (see *MED ordinaunce* n. 3(c), 5(a) or 10 (a)).

390–1. 'But nonetheless, I cannot, for the whole world, / Abandon my proper procedure (according to which)'.

395. To be *secre* ('discreet') is regarded as a male lover's virtue in *TC* I, l. 744, *Merch T*, l. 1909, and *NPT*, l. 2915.

396–7. Cf. the description of the female eagle in ll. 372–5. The idealized male is also seen as the epitome of Nature's work, e.g. in Alanus of Lille's *Anticlaudianus* (tr. Sheridan 1973: 173–5).

398. 'There is no need to describe his form to you'.

403. *entriketh*: Nature may be ironically alluding to the trapping of birds with nets, which was itself a metaphor for the power of love (cf. *TC* III, ll. 1355, 1730–6). The word also occurs in the Chaucerian tr. of *RR* (l. 1642).

254 The *Parliament of Fowls*

God sende hym hyr that sorest for hym syketh!'

405 And therwythalle the tercel gan she calle   *therewith*
And seyde: 'My sone, the choys is to the falle.   *falls to you*

But natheles, in thys condicion
Mote be the choys of everych that ys here: *everyone*
That she agree to hys eleccion,   *choice*
410 Who so he be that shulde ben hir fere.   *Whoever; be her mate*
This is oure usage alwey, fro yere to yere,   *custom*
And who so may at this tyme have hys grace,   *find favour*
In blisful tyme he come in to this place!'   *came*

With hed enclyned and with ful humble   *bowed;*
   chere,   *expression*
415 This real tercel spake, and taried noght: *royal; did not delay*
'Unto my sovereyne lady, and noght my fere,   *As*
I chese – and chese with wille and hert and thought –
The formel on youre honde, so wel ywrought,   *female; formed*
Whos I am alle and ever wol hir serve,   *completely*
420 Doo what hir lyste: to doo me lyve or sterve.

'Besechynge hir of mercy and of   *for acceptance*
   grace,   *and favour*
As she that ys my lady soverayne –   *sovereign lady*
Or let me dye present in thys place,   *at once*
For certes, longe may I not lyve in peyne,   *certainly I cannot*
425 For in myn herte ys korven every veyne.   *severed; vein*
Having rewarde oonly to my trouthe,   *regard; fidelity*

404. *that sorest for hym syketh*: 'that desires [lit.: 'sighs for'] him most fiercely'.
406. On Nature's modes of address, see n. on l. 633, below.
407–8. *in thys condicion / Mote be*: 'these conditions must apply to'.
412. *grace* can mean 'favour' very generally, but may here signify a divine or quasi-divine gift dispensed to the lover by the lady. Cf. the royal tercel's use of the term below, l. 421, and *BD*, l. 810.
414–16. The submission of the 'humble' yet 'royal' eagle to his 'sovereign' is part of the courtly posture of devotion and 'service' to love and the lady.
420. 'Let her do as she pleases – let me live or die'.
421. The plea for *mercy* can be for the lady's acceptance of the lover's 'service' (as in *BD*, l. 867 and *TC* III, l. 98), or it can be more clearly a bid for sexual favour (as in *TC* III, l. 1173, and *Mil T*, l. 3288), or a claim to possession, as below, l. 437.

My dere herte, have on my woo some
    routhe!   *pity for my sorrow*

'And yf I be founde to hir untrewe,   *disloyal to her*
Dysobeysaunt, or wilful negligent,
430   Avauntour or, in processe, love a newe –
I pray to yow, thys be my jugement: *let this be; sentence*
That with these foules y be al torent,   *by; torn apart*
That ylke day that ever she me fynde   *same; when*
To hir untrewe, or in my gylte unkynde.   *guilty of ingratitude*

435   'And syn that noon loveth hir so wel as I –   *since no-one*
Al be she never of love me behette –   *pledged me love*
Than oght she be myn thourgh hir mercy,   *mine; pity*
For other bonde kan I noon on hir knette;
For never, for no woo, ne shal I lette   *any sorrow; cease*
440   To serven hir, how ferre so that she wende.   *wherever; may go*
Sey what yow lyste, my tale ys at an ende.'   *you please; speech*

Ryght as the fressh, rede rose newe
Ayene the somer sonne coloured ys,
Ryght so, for shame, al wexen gan the hewe
445   Of thys formel whan she herde al thys.
She neyther answerde wel ne seyde amys,   No decision

427. *routhe* seems to have a range of meaning similar to that of *mercy*; cf. *TC* II,
l. 349. For a more ironic view of female *routhe* and male 'service', see Dido
in *HF*, ll. 332–40.
429–30. 'Disobedient or deliberately neglectful, / A boaster or (if), in the course of
time I love another'. To be an *avauntour* (l. 430) would contravene the ideal
of discretion for which the royal tercel is praised in l. 395.
431–2. This recalls the punishment for treachery suffered by Ganelon in the
Chanson de Roland, ll. 3964ff. His fate is explicitly invoked by lovers
protesting loyalty in *BD*, ll. 1121–3 and *Shipm T*, l. 136.
438. 'For I can lay no other obligation on her'.
442–5. The lyrical flourish here may perhaps derive from Boccaccio, *Filostrato* II,
st. 38, where Criseida, hearing about her lover, blushes 'like a morning
rose'.
443. 'Takes colour from the summer sun'.
444. *al wexen gan the hewe*: 'did the whole complexion (of this female eagle)
become'.
446. 'She answered neither favourably nor unfavourably'.

Nature assures her

rival.

So sore abasshed was she, til that Nature   *deeply embarrassed*
Seyde: 'Doghter, drede yow noght, I yow assure.'   *fear*

Another tercel egle spake anon,   *at once*
450   Of lower kynde, and seyde: 'That shulde not be.   *rank*
I love hir bet than ye do, by seynt John!   *better*
Or, atte lest, I love hyr as wel as ye,
And lenger have served hir in my degre.   *my own way*
And yf she shulde have loved for long lovyng,   *in return for*
455   To me allone had ben the guerdonynge.

'I dar eke seye, yf she me fynde fals,   *extreme*   *also say*
Unkynde, jangler, or rebel any wyse,   *indiscreet*
Or jalouse – do me hongen by the hals!   *have me hanged; neck*
And, but I bere me in hir servise   *unless I acquit myself*
460   As well as my wytte kan me suffise,
Fro poynt to poynt, hir honour for to save –
Take she my lyfe and al the good I have!'   *wealth*

The thridde tercel egle answerde thoo: *then*
'Now, sirs, ye seen the lytel leyser here;
465   For every foule cryeth out to ben agoo
Forth with his make, or with his lady dere,
And eke Nature hir selfe ne wol nought here,
For taryinge here, noght half that I wolde sey –
And, but I speke, I mote for sorwe dey.   *unless; may die of grief*

extreme.

451.   The second male eagle's oath seems appropriate, since St John was the 'disciple whom Jesus loved' (John 13:23; 19:26) and the symbol of St John as evangelist is the eagle. Oaths are relatively infrequent in the poem, by comparison with *HF*, for instance (see Elliott 1974: 242).

455.   'The reward should have been mine alone'.

456–8.   Cf. the extravagance of the royal tercel's protestation above (ll. 428–34 & n.) – though hanging for disloyalty in love (l. 458) is perhaps a less extreme penalty than dismemberment (l. 432).

460.   'As well as I know how'. On *wytte*, see above, l. 146 & n. The terms of devotion again recall those in *BD* (l. 1094); cf. above, ll. 414–16 & n.

461.   'To preserve her honour in every respect'.

464.   'Now, sirs, you can see how little time we have here'.

465–6.   *cryeth out to ben agoo / Forth*: 'is impatient to be on his way'.

468.   'For fear of delay, even half of what I want to say'.

470 'Of long servise avaunte I me no thinge.
     But as possible ys, me to dye to day
     For woo, as he that hath ben langwysshynge
     These twenty wynter; and well happen may,   *years; may well be*
     A man may serven bette and more to pay   *more deservingly*
475 In half a yere, al though hyt were no more,
     Than some man dooth that hath served ful yore.   *for very long*

     'I ne say nat this be me, for I ne kan   *on my behalf*
     Do no servise that may my lady plese,
     But I dar say I am hir trewest man,
480 As to my dome, and faynest wolde hir ese.
     At shorte wordes – til that deth me sese
     I wol ben hires, whethir I wake or wynke,   *day and night*
     And trew in al that herte may bethynke.'

     Of al my lyfe, syn that day I was borne,   *In; since*
485 So gentil plee in love or other thinge
     Ne herde never no man me beforne –
     Who that had leyser and kunnynge
     For to rehersen hir chere and her spekynge.
     And from the morwe gan this speche last,   *morning; talking*
490 Til dounwarde went the sonne wonder fast.   *very quickly*

     The noyse of foules for to ben delyvered   *to be set free*
     So loude rong: 'Have doon, and let us   *resounded; Finish;*
          wende!'   *go*
     That wel wende I the woode had al   *thought;*
          toshyvered.   *shattered*

470–1. 'I make no boast at all about length of service, / But it is just as possible
     for someone to die in a day'.
480. 'In my judgement, and am the most eager to please her'.
481. 'In brief, till Death takes hold of me'.
483. 'And loyal in every way a heart could desire'.
484–6. *I ... me*: the first of several reminders of the dreamer-narrator's presence
     at this stage of the assembly (see also below, ll. 493, 500).
485–8. '(Neither I) nor anyone before me ever heard / Such a noble dispute about
     love or other matters / – If anyone had the time or skill / To describe their
     expressions and their speeches'.
493. The *woode* presumably surrounds the *launde* (l. 302) and *grene* (l. 328) on
     which the birds and Nature have gathered.

'Com of!' they cride, 'allas, ye wol us shende!
495   Whan shal youre cursed pledynge have   *wretched wrangling*
      an ende?
      How shulde a juge eyther party leve,   *trust*
      For ye or nay, withouten any preve?'

      The goos, the duk, and the cukkowe also
      So criden: 'Kek! kek!','Kukkowe!','Quek! quek!' hye   *loudly*
500   That thorgh myn eres the noyse went tho.
      The goos seyde: 'Al thys nys worthe a flye!   *is not worth*
      But I kan shape herof a remedye   *devise; for this*
      And wol sey my veyrdit faire and swythe
      For watir foule, who so be wrothe or blythe!'

505   'And I for wormefoule,' seyde the foole cukkowe,   *foolish*
      'For I wol, of myn owne auctorite,   *by; authority*
      For comune spede, take on me the charge   *good; responsibility*
      nowe –
      For to delyveren us ys grete charite!'
      'Ye may abyde awhile yet, parde,'   *should wait; indeed*
510   Quod the turtel, 'yf hyt be youre wille!   *if you please*
      A wyght may speke, hym were as fayr be stille.

      'I am a sede foule oon the unworthieste,   *one of the*
      That wot I wel, and lytel of kunnynge.   *know; knowledge*

494. *Com of*: 'Get on with it'; *us shende*: 'spoil our plans'.
497. 'In what they affirm or deny, without any proof'.
500. *thorgh myn eres*: 'straight through my head'.
503–4. 'And I will give my verdict nice and quick, / on behalf of waterfowl,
      regardless of whom it may please or offend'.
506. The solemn term, *auctorite*, occurs only here in *PF* and, rather ironically, in
      the context of the cuckoo's folly. Cf. *HF*, l. 2158 and *NPT*, l. 2975.
507–8. *comune spede* seems to be a debasement by the cuckoo of the exalted
      concept of *comune profyt* (l. 47). *charge* may carry the parliamentary sense
      of 'matter to be discussed' (Brewer 1960: 123). *delyveren* (l. 508) can refer
      to the dissolution of Parliament (cf. ll. 491, 523, and Brewer 1960: 122).
511. 'A person may speak when he might as well be silent'. A characteristically
      polite rebuke from the turtle-dove.
512. The seed-eating birds (including the humble and pious turtle-dove) could
      perhaps be identified with the 'estate' of the clergy (see Olson 1980: 61 n.
      13, 63 n. 17).

But better ys that a wightys tonge reste
515 Than entremete hym of suche doynge
Of which he neyther rede kan ne synge.
And who so hyt dothe ful foule hym self acloyeth,
For office uncomytted ofte anoyeth.'

Nature, which that alway had an ere   *kept an ear (on)*
520 To murmour of the lewdenesse behynde,
With facound voys seyde: 'Holde youre tonges there!   *eloquent*
And I shal soone, I hope, a counseylle fynde   *plan*
Yow for to delyveren and from this noyse   *to free;*
  unbynde.   *release (you)*
I jugge, of every folke, men shal one calle,   *class*
525 To seyne the veirdit for yow foules alle.'   *give the opinion*

Assented were to thys conclusyon   *They agreed*
The briddes alle, and the foules of ravyne
Han chosen first, by pleyn eleccion,
The tercelet of the faucon, to dyffyne
530 Al her sentence and, as him list, termyne,
And to Nature hym gonnen to presente;   *proceeded to*
And she accepteth hym wyth glad entente.   *happily*

514–16. 'But it's better that a person's tongue should keep still / Than meddle in the kind of business / he knows nothing whatsoever about' (lit.: 'of which he can neither read/speak(?) nor sing'). On the ambiguity of the verb *rede* here, see Leicester 1974: 29; and cf. *HF*, l. 590.

517. *ful foule hym self acloyeth*: 'can get into deep trouble'.

518. 'Unwanted help is often a hindrance'. The line sounds proverbial, though the nearest verbal resemblance is to the warning about *officio non commesso* in *Purg*. X, l. 57. If the latter is Ch's source, it would suggest that his knowledge of Dante by this time was quite wide-ranging (cf. *A & A*, ll. 211, 350, citing *Purg*. XII, l. 20).

520. 'Upon the ignorant murmurings at the back'.

523. On *delyveren*, see l. 508 & n., and on *noyse*, ll. 491–500 & n.

525–30. The formal vocabulary may derive from that of the parliamentary procedure for electing a Speaker and 'presenting' him to the King (Bennett 1957: 140 & n. 2).

528. *by pleyn eleccion*: 'as their duly elected spokesman'.

529–30. 'The young male [*tercelet*] falcon, to declare / their opinion and draw a conclusion as he saw fit' (cf. l. 337 & n.).

The tercelet seyde thanne in this manere: *spoke*
'Ful harde were hyt to preven by resoun   *prove logically*
535   Who loveth best this gentil formel here,   *noble female*
For everych hath suche replicacioun
That by skylles may non be broght adoun.
I kan not seen that argumentys avaylle;   *are of any use*
Than semeth hit ther moste be bataylle.'   *has to be*

540   'Al redy!' quod these egles tercels thoo –   *then*
'Nay, sirs,' quod he, 'yf that I dorst hyt say,
Ye doon me wrong; my tale ys not ydoo.   *I've not finished*
For, sirs, taketh noght agrefe, I pray: *don't be offended*
Hyt may nought gon as ye wolde, in this wey.   *cannot be; thus*
545   Oures ys the voys that han the charge in honde,
And to the juges doome ye moten stonde.

'And therfore, pes! I say, as to my witte,
Me wolde think how that the worthieste   *One would think*
Of knyghthode, and lengest had used hitte,
550   Moste of estaate, of blode the   *highest in rank;*
         gentyleste,   *noblest*
Were syttynge for hir, yf that hir leste.
And, of these three, she woote hir selfe, I trowe,   *knows; believe*
Which that he be, for hyt is lyght to knowe.'   *easy to decide*

The watir foules han her hedes leyde   *have put their heads*
555   Togedir and, of shorte avysement,   *after; consultation*

536–7. 'For each (of the contestants) has made such a good case / that none can
be caught out in argument'.

539–40. For the resolution of lovers' rivalry through battle, see *Tes*. VII, st. 4–13,
and *Kn T*, ll. 1845–69. On actual 'judicial duels' as a last resort when
settling disputes in which both parties were of noble birth, see Keen 1984:
87, 204, 208.

544–6. 'It cannot be thus as you wish. / We who are dealing with this case have
the right to speak, / And you must await the judges' opinion.' For *vois* in the
sense of 'right to speak or vote', see *OED voice* sb. 2b (citing a parliamentary usage of 1433).

547–9. 'So hold your peace. It would seem, in my view, / That the one who was
most distinguished / In chivalry and had practised it longest'. On *witte*, see
above, l. 146 & n.

551. 'Would be suitable for her, if she so desired'.

Whan everych had his large golee seyde,   *each*; *bellyful*
They seyden sothely, al by on assent,   *indeed, unanimously*
How that 'the goos, with her facounde gent,   *noble eloquence*
That soo desireth to pronounce oure nede,   *deliver*; *judgement*
560   Shal telle oure tale', and preyde to God hir spede.   *help*

And for these watir foules tho began   *then*
The goos to speke, and in hir kakelynge
She seyde: 'Pes! now take kepe, every man,   *pay heed*
And herkeneth which a reson I shal forth brynge!   *what sort of*
565   My wytte ys sharpe – I love no taryinge: *intelligence*; *delay*
I sey, y rede hym, though he were my brother,   *I advise*
But she wol love hym, lat hym love another!'   *Unless*

'Loo here, a parfyt reson of a goos!'
Quod the sperhauke, 'never mote she   *may she never*
    thee!   *prosper*
570   Loo, suche hyt ys to have a tonge loos!
Now, parde, foole – yet were hit bet for the
Have holde thy pes than shewede thy nycete.
Hyt lyth not in hys wytte ne in hys wille,

556. For the idea of gluttony in words, cf. *PPl* B Prologue, l. 139.

558. *facounde* here is a noun (it is used as an adjective for Nature's voice in l. 521). *gent* ('noble') may be a stylistically banal word, used ironically here, as in *Mil T*, l. 3234 and *Thop*, l. 715; see Brewer 1960: 124; Burnley 1989: 142, 197.

564–5. The goose's admiration for her own argument is more intense, though more concise, than is the eagle's in, for instance, *HF*, ll. 853–69. On *wytte*, see above, l. 146 & n.

566–7. Cf. Pandarus's pragmatic advice to Troilus in *TC* IV, l. 406: *If she be lost, we shal recovere an other.*

568. 'Behold, a perfectly goosish argument!' The phrase *reson of a goos* seems intended to be oxymoronic. Ch elsewhere uses *goosish* to mean 'loose-tongued' (*TC* III, l. 584), and 'goose' can mean 'fool' in 14th- and 15th-century usage (*MED gos* n. 3). See Endnote (ii) on p. 272.

570–2. 'See – this is what it means to have a wagging tongue / Now indeed, fool, it would have been better for you / To have kept quiet than shown how stupid you are'.

573. 'He [the fool, l. 574] has neither the intelligence nor the wish to do so'. On *wytte*, see above, l. 146 & n.

But sooth ys seyde: "a foole kan noght be stille".'

575   The laughtre aroose of gentil foules alle;   *from all the noble birds*
And ryght anoone the sede foules chosen hadde   *straight away*
The turtel trewe, and gan hir to hem calle,   *loyal turtle-dove*
And prayden hir to sey the sothe sadde   *the real truth*
Of thys matere, and asked what she radde.   *Regarding; advised*
580   And she ansuerde that pleynly hyr entente
She wolde shewe and sothely what she mente.

'Nay – god forbede a lover sholde chaunge!'
The turtel seyde, and wexe for shame al rede.   *grew*
'Though that hys lady ever more be straunge,   *distant*
585   Yet let hym serve hir ever tyl he be dede.
For soth, I preyse noght the gooses rede:
For, thogh she deyed, I wolde noon other make.
I wol ben hirs til that the deth me take.'   *till Death takes me*

'Wel bourded,' quod the duk, 'by my hatte!   *That's a good one*
590   That men shulde alwey loven causeles –   *for ever without cause*

574. 'But it is rightly said: "A fool cannot keep quiet"'. Brewer (1960: 125)
compares *RR* (Chaucerian tr.), l. 5265, and there are several proverbs of
this sort (Whiting 1968: F 397, 413, 436).

578. For *sadde* in the sense of 'steady, serious', see *BD*, ll. 860, 918, and for the
meaning 'real' (applied to *sothe*), see *HF*, l. 2089. The meanings are
discussed by Lewis 1960: 75–85.

580–1. *pleynly hyr entente / She wolde shewe*: 'she would speak her mind fully'.

582–8. See Endnote (ii) on p. 272 (on l. 355). The turtle-dove's view is in line with
her reputation for fidelity, already noted in ll. 355 and 577.

586. 'Indeed, I do not value the goose's opinion'.

587. *she* – i.e. the lover's lady (l. 584); *wolde noon other make*: 'would want no
other lover'. Muscatine (in *Riv.*, p. 1001) finds a 'puzzling shift in person
and gender' in ll. 587–88, but the idea that the turtle-dove should imagine
being a male lover is surely no more puzzling than that birds should blush
(ll. 442–5, 583).

589. Cf. the colloquial effect of Arcite's swearing *by my pan* (skull) in *Kn T*,
l. 1165; also *Kn T*, l. 2670 (head) and *Rv T*, l. 4041 (crown) – but the idea
of a duck's *hatte* is pleasantly surreal as well. On oaths in *PF*, see above,
l. 451 & n. (and Elliott 1974: 242, 247–8).

Who kan a reson fynde or wytte in that?	*sense*
Daunceth he murye that ys murtheles?	
Who shulde rechche of that ys rechcheles?'	
'Ye queke,' seyde the goos, 'ful wel and faire;	
595 Ther ben moo sterres, god woot, than a paire!'	

'Now fye, cherle!' quod the gentil tercelet.   *Shame; oaf*
'Out of the dung hille come that word ful ryght!   *came; for sure*
Thou kanst noght see which thing is wel beset.   *for the best*
Thou farest be love as owles doon by lyght: *behave towards*
600 The day hem blent; ful wel they see by nyght.   *blinds*
Thy kynde ys of so lowe a wrechednesse
That what love is, thou kanst neyther see ne gesse!'

Thoo gan the cukkow put hym forth in pres   *push forward*
For foule that eteth worme, and seyde   *On behalf of;*
      blyve: *promptly*
605 'So I,' quod he, 'may have my make in pes,   *So long as*
I reche not how longe that ye stryve.   *care not; argue*
Lat eche of hem be soleyne al her lyve –   *single; their lives*
This ys my rede – syn they may not acorde!   *can't agree*
This shorte lesson nedeth noght recorde.'

610 'Yee – have the gloton filde ynogh hys paunche,
Than ar we wel!' seyde the emerlyon.   *merlin*

591. For *wytte* in the sense of 'wisdom' or '(good) sense' (*OED wit* sb. 6), cf.
      above, l. 146 & n.
592. 'Can a mirthless man dance merrily?'
593. 'Why should we care about someone who doesn't care?'
594–5. ' "You're quacking," said the goose, "very finely indeed / (for) God knows
      – there's more than a couple of stars (in the sky)!" ' The goose concludes the
      stanza on a resoundingly proverbial note (see Whiting 1968: 680). Many of
      the MSS (including F and Gg) ascribe these lines to the duck (for further
      discussion, see *Riv.*, p. 1150).
596. *tercelet*: the falcon, who is addressing the goose.
601. 'Your nature is so utterly debased'.
605–6. See Endnote (ii) on p. 272 (on l. 358).
609. 'There's no need to go over this again' (see *MED recorden* v. 6, and *TC* III,
      l. 51).
610. 'Yes, so long as the glutton's filled *his* paunch'.

'Thou mortherer of the heysogge on the   *hedge-sparrow*
   braunche
That broght the forth, thou rewfull gloton!   *contemptible*
Lyve *thou* soleyn, wormes corrupcion –
615   For no fors ys of lakke of thy nature.
Goo – lewde be thou while the worlde may dure!'

'Now, pes,' quod Nature, 'I comaunde here!   *now decree*
For I have herde al youre opynyon,
And, in effecte, yet be we never the nere.
620   But, fynally, this ys my conclusyon:
That she hir selfe shal have hir eleccion   *her own choice*
Of whom hir lyste – who so be wrooth or blythe,
Hym that she cheest, he shal hire han as   *chooses;*
   swithe.   *at once*

'For, syn hyt may not here discussed be   *since*
625   Who loveth hir best – as seyde the tercelet –
Than wol I doon thys favour to her: that she
Shal have ryght hym on whom hir herte is sette,   *simply*
And he hir that hys hert hath on hir knette.
This juge I, Nature, for I may not lye;

612–13.   The merlin's moral high ground is somewhat undermined by the poem's
      previous description of the noble birds' own predatory habits (ll. 334–6,
      339–40; see Aers 1981: 13). However, the cuckoo's murder of its 'parent'
      would be regarded as more 'unnatural' (*unkynde*); see above, l. 358, and
      Alanus, tr. Sheridan 1980: 92–3. The reading *rewfull* in l. 613 (as opposed
      to *reufulles* in MS Gg) creates an irregular line, but throws extra emphasis
      on the adjective in a way that seems appropriate to the merlin's sombre
      tone.
614.   *wormes corrupcion*: the merlin's insult has several senses: the cuckoo is seen
      as generally 'corrupt' and is literally a 'corrupter' (devourer) of worms (see
      Bennett 1957: 173).
615–16.   'For it doesn't matter if *you* fail to reproduce. / Just go on being stupid
      all the time!'
619.   'And in the end we are no nearer a decision'. The day-long debate parallels
      the narrator's day of reading, above, ll. 27–8 and 85–93 (see Bennett 1957:
      174; Kiser 1991: 54).
622.   'Of whom she wishes – whoever that may annoy or please'.
628.   'And he that has fixed his heart on her shall have her'.

630   To noon estaat I have noon other eye.

       'But – as for counseylle, for to chese   *advice about choosing*
         a make –
       Yf I were Reson, than wolde y
       Counseylle yow the royal tercel take –
       As seyde the tercelet ful skilfully –   *very reasonably*
635   As for the gentilest and moste worthy,   *Being the noblest*
       Whiche I have wroght so wel to my plesaunce
       That to yow hyt ought to ben a suffisaunce.'

       With dredeful vois, the formel hir answerde: *timid*
       'My ryghtful lady, goddesse of Nature –   *true*
640   Sooth ys that I am ever under youre yerde,   *Truly; control*
       As ys everych other creature,
       And moste be youres while my lyf may dure –   *last*
       And therfore, grauntyth me my firste boone,   *grant me; request*
       And myn entent yow wol I sey ryght soone.'

645   'I graunte hyt yow,' quod she, and ryght anoon   *straight away*
       This formel egle spake in thys degre: *in this way*
       'Almyghty quene, unto this yere be doon,   *until; is over*

630. 'I have no other regard for any (person's) rank'.
632. Some MSS (not F or Gg) read: *If hit* ['it'] *were reson* (see Knight 1986: 30). *If I were Reson* could, however, be a quite appropriate intertextual joke on Nature's part, since Reson, like herself, is a traditionally personified figure (e.g. in Alanus's *Anticlaudianus* (tr. Sheridan 1973: 62–72, 172) and in *RR*, ll. 2959ff., 4196ff. (tr. Horgan 1994: 46–8, 64–110)).
633. *yow*: Nature here (and in ll. 637 and 645) uses the 'courtly', second person plural form of address to the female eagle. This appears to contrast with the singular, 'parental' form she uses to the male eagle (according to most of the MSS) in l. 460, above; though on the complexities of such usage, see *Riv.*, p. xxxv.
636–7. 'Whom I have created in a way that so pleases me / that it surely ought to be good enough for you'. Cf. above, ll. 396–7 & n.
640. *under youre yerde*: the phrase can refer generally to subjection to authority (as in *TC* III, l. 137, and *Cl T*, l. 22). It derives from the Latin legal term, *sub virga* (literally 'beneath the rod'), which had applied, since at least the reign of Henry I, to the status of wards in relation to guardians, as perhaps in *Shipm T*, l. 97 (see Niermeyer 1984: *s.v. virga* 7).
644. 'And straight away I will tell you what I think'.

I aske respite, for to avysen me,
And after that to have my choyse al fre.
650 Thys al and some that I wol speke and seye;   *absolutely all*
Ye gete no more, al though ye do me deye.   *have me killed*

'I wolle noght serven Venus ne Cupide,
For sothe, as yet, by no maner wey.'
'Now, syn hyt may noon other weyes betide,'
655 Quod Nature, 'here ys no more to sey.
Than wolde I that these foules were awey,   *wish; might go*
Eche with his make, for taryinge lenger here!'
And seyde hem thus, as ye shal after here: *spoke to; hear now*

'To yow speke I, ye terceletys,' quod Nature.
660 'Beth of good hert, and serveth alle thre –   *Be; serve (well)*
A yere ys not so longe to endure!
And eche of yow peyne hym in hys degre   *strive; own way*
For to do wel – for, god wote, quyte ys she   *she is free*
Fro yow thys yere, what after so befalle. *whatever then happens*
665 This entremesse ys dressed for yow alle!'

And whan thys werke al wroght was to an
ende,   *action; completed*

648. 'I ask for a delay, to think about it'. For similar uses of *respite* in this
context, see *MED respit(e)* n. 1 (a), and Bennett 1979: 142–3.
650. Non-expression of the verb (*is*) in exclamations is common in ME (cf. *TC*
V, ll. 1849–52; Mustanoja 1960: 510).
652. Cf. the reference to those who choose to serve Diana rather than Venus,
above, ll. 281–4. Ch may also be recollecting Emilia's wish to continue
serving Diana in *Tes.* VII, st. 81, and her replying to Theseus, as the female
eagle replies to Nature, in *Tes.* XII, st. 42, ll. 5–8.
653. 'For certain, yet – in no way at all'.
654. 'Now, since things can take no other course'.
657. 'Each with its mate, to avoid further delay'.
665. *This entremesse ys dressed*: 'This interlude is provided'. The word initially
applied to 'a dish or group of dishes served between the main courses of a
meal' (as in *RR*, Chaucerian tr., l. 6831), then to 'entertainment between
courses' (see *MED entermes* n. (a) & (b)). It is also used metaphorically in
Jean de Condé's *Messe des Oisiaus* (ed. Ribard 1970: ll. 474, 517, 622).
666. The reading *wroght* is in F (as against *brought* in Gg); cf. *ywrought*
describing Nature's 'work' in l. 305.

To every foule Nature yafe hys make,
By evene acorde, and on her wey they   *as was fitting*; their;
    wende.   *go*
And, lorde, the blysse and joye that they make!
670   For eche of hem gan other in wynges take,
And with her nekkes eche gan other wynde,   *embrace*
Thankyng alway the noble goddesse of Kynde.   *Nature*

But firste were chosen foules for to synge,
As, yere by yere, was alwey hir usaunce,   *custom*
675   To synge a roundel at her departynge,
To do Nature honour and plesaunce.   *delight*
The note, I trowe, maked was in Fraunce;   *music; believe*
The wordes were suche as ye may here fynde,
The nexte vers, as I now have in mynde: *recall*

680   ['Nowe, welcome somer, with thy sonne softe,
That hast thes wintres wedres overshake   *storms; dispelled*

668. *By evene acorde*: cf. above, ll. 379–81 & n.
672. *Kynde*: see above, l. 316 & n.
675. *roundel*: 'song with refrain'; *departynge*: 'departure'. On the roundel as a French verse form (with two rhymes and a refrain recurring two or three times), see Ch's *Merciles Beaute* (where threefold repetition of the refrain is indicated) and Brewer 1960: 57.
676. The 'roundel' (see below, ll. 680–7, and Note on the Text, p. 279) addresses 'Summer/Spring' (l. 680) and 'St Valentine' (l. 683), but does not seem to be specifically 'in honour of' Nature.
677. Various French tunes have been proposed to replace or accompany the 'roundel'. Five of the MSS that omit the roundel itself include, after l. 679, a French phrase: *Que/Qui bien ayme [a] tarde oublie* ('One who loves well is slow to forget'), which occurs in a number of French lyrics (including several with music) and could thus be the cue for a song. For a French tune to fit the existing roundel, see Wilkins 1979: 29.
680–7. The textual status of the roundel is problematic. *Riv.* (p. 1002) suggests it 'may possibly have been first composed for another occasion', and Hanna (1991: 29–35) argues that, while it may be Chaucerian, it is not part of this poem (p. 34). For further discussion of the evidence, see the Notes on the Text. In ll. 680–2 there is some thematic resemblance to *BD*, ll. 410–15 and *LGW*, ll. 113–30, and ll. 683–4 are quite similar to *Compl Mars*, ll. 13–14. In l. 686 *recovered* may mean 'found again' or simply 'found' (*MED recoveren* v. (4) or (8)).

And drevyn awey the longe nyghtes blake!   *driven*
Seynt Valentyne, that art ful hye on lofte,   *above*
Thus syngen smale foules for thy sake.
685   Wel han they cause for to gladen ofte;   *have; be glad*
Sith eche of hem recovered hath his make,   *has gained*
Ful blisseful mowe they synge when they wake!']   *may*

And with the showtynge whan hir song was do,   *was finished*
That foules made at her flyght away,   *during their*
690   I wooke, and other bookes toke me to,   *I turned to*
To rede upon, and yet I rede alway.
I hope, iwis, to rede so, somday,   *indeed; so much*
That I shal mete some thyng for to fare   *find/dream*
The bet, and thus to rede I nyl not spare.   *will not cease*

691–4. The fourfold repetition of the verb *rede* here emphasizes the return of the
       narrator to his books (see above, ll. 15–25). Cf. the ending of *BD*
       (ll. 1326–9) and the eagle's comments about the narrator in *HF*
       (ll. 652–60).
693.   *mete* could mean 'find, meet' (<OE *metan*), as in l. 37, or possibly 'dream'
       (<OE *maetan*), as in ll. 95, 104, 105, 108 and 115.
693–4. *for to fare / The bet*: 'to do me some good'.

ENDNOTES

(i) Chaucer's lovers, lines 288–92

Boccaccio, in *Tes.* VII, st. 62, also includes Semiramis, Pyramus, Thisbe, Hercules and Byblis as examples of Venus's power, but makes no mention of the other figures in Ch's list here, most of whom (Dido, Tristan, Paris, Achilles, Helen and Cleopatra) also appear in the second circle of Dante's Hell (*Inf.* V, ll. 61–7). The following notes give information and references for which there was not enough space in the on-page annotation.

The figures mentioned in Ch's list mostly derive from Greek and Roman mythology, although Semiramis (l. 288) was queen of Babylon (810–805 BC; see *Inf.* V, ll. 52–60), and Tristan and Yseult (*Isaude*, l. 290) first appear as lovers in 12th-century romance (see also *HF*, l. 1796 and *LGW*, l. 208).

288. *Candace* is either the Ethiopian or Indian queen who (according to the medieval romances) fell in love with Alexander the Great, or the tragic figure of Canace who fell in love with her brother (Ovid, *Her.* XI). *Hercules*, the Greek hero, was the husband of Deianira who unintentionally poisoned him because of his love for Iole (*Her.* IX; *Met.* IX, ll. 134–272; *HF*, ll. 402–4).

289. Byblis (*Met.* IX, ll. 454–665) fell in love with her brother; Dido (*Aen.* IV; *HF*, ll. 241ff.) was the lover abandoned by Aeneas. Pyramus (*Met.* IV, ll. 55–166) was the lover of Thisbe and killed himself when he thought she had been devoured by a lion (she then killed herself with the same sword).

290–1. Tristan and Yseult were, along with Lancelot and Guinevere, the most famous lovers in medieval romance. *Paris* eloped with Helen (*Eleyne*), wife of Menelaus, King of Sparta, thus causing the Trojan War, in which *Achilles* was the foremost Greek warrior. Achilles's love for the Trojan princess Polyxena is one of the tragic subjects in Benoît de Sainte-Maure's *Roman de Troie* (c. 1155–60, ll. 17489–18472, 21838–22500); so also is the love of *Troilus* the Trojan for Briseida (later Criseida), which was to be the theme of Boccaccio's *Filostrato* and Ch's own *Troilus*. Cleopatra (69–30 BC) was ruler of Egypt and lover of Julius Caesar and Mark Antony; she followed the latter in committing suicide. Hers is the first of Ch's 'legends of good women' (*LGW*, ll. 580–705).

292. Scylla (*Silla*) fell in love with the Cretan Minos and betrayed her father's city to him, but was rejected by him and transformed into a lark (*Met.* VIII, ll. 6–151; *LGW*, ll. 1900–21). The 'mother of Romulus' was Rhea Silvia who was raped by Mars and gave birth to twins (Romulus and Remus). She was imprisoned by her uncle; the twins were thrown into the Tiber but later rescued (Livy, *Ab urbe condita* I, iii, 10 – iv, 9).

(ii) Chaucer's birds, lines 323–64

A rich variety of sources may have influenced Chaucer's representations of birds in *PF*. The idea of assembling these before Nature could have come from reading the description of birds on the goddess's mantle in Alanus's *De Planctu Naturae* (tr. Sheridan 1980), which is a source also for some specific features of avian appearance and behaviour in Chaucer's poem. Beyond Alanus, a well-known source for an assembly of this sort is the striking biblical description of the 'Call of the Birds' in the Apocalypse (Rev. 19:17–18), which, like Chaucer, stresses the appetite for flesh, and which was frequently a subject in MS illustrations (see Yapp 1981: fig. 1 and plates 14–15).

Encyclopaedias, such as those of Vincent of Beauvais and Bartholomaeus Anglicus, also provide parallels and models for classification that may have been drawn upon in *PF* (see the note on ll. 323–9, below). French romances and debate poems of the 13th and 14th centuries often give birds courtly or angelic voices, as do the *Roman de la Rose* (ll. 641–706, tr. Horgan 1994: 11–12) and the *Messe des Oisiaus* and the *Songe Saint Valentin* (tr. Windeatt 1982). The humanized accounts of animal behaviour in the bestiaries may provide reference points for the birds in *PF* on some occasions (see, for instance, White 1954 and the notes on ll. 331, 342–3 and 355, below).

The influence of popular belief and practical observation (for instance in falconry) should not be underrated (see Armstrong 1970); and another possibly neglected source is the visual culture of the period. Birds are frequently depicted in MSS, not only in illustrations of the 'Call of the Birds' (see above), but also in marginal decoration, particularly in English texts such as the late 13th- and early 14th-century East Anglian psalters and the late 14th-century Sherborne Missal (see Yapp 1981: 9 and plates 21–30, 34, 36–7).

The following notes give information and references for which there was not enough space in the on-page annotation. They chiefly relate to the descriptions of the birds in ll. 323–64, but they also include some discussion of bird-lore later in the poem (ll. 505, 568–74, 582–8, 599–600).

323–9.   The fourfold classification of the birds as raptors (*hyest*), worm-fowl, waterfowl (*lowest*) and seedfowl is found in Aristotle (Bennett 1957: 149), but Ch could have derived it from the 13th-century encyclopedist, Vincent of Beauvais (*Speculum naturale* I, 16, xiv; see Brewer 1960: 114–15), or from the 14th-century encyclopaedia by Bartholomaeus Anglicus, *On the*

Properties of Things, ed. Seymour 1975: I, 596–602; see Olson 1980: 60–1). On the possible correspondences with social classes of the time (including groups represented in Parliament), see Brewer 1960: 34–5; Olson 1980: 61–5; Knight 1986: 29.

330.   Cf. ll. 394, 415, 633. On the various mythical traditions identifying the eagle as 'royal', see Armstrong 1970: 125–40; and for the association of birds of prey in general with royalty and lordship, see *Wynnere & Wastoure*, ll. 92–8, and Olson 1980: 63 n. 16. Descriptions and illustrations of the eagle in the medieval bestiaries show it flying up to the sun to revive its youth or eyesight. See: White 1954: 105–6; a mid-13th-century English bestiary, EETS o.s. 49 (1872), p. 3, ll. 55–76; Bartholomaeus, ed. Seymour 1975: I, 603; and Yapp 1981: plate 18A.

334–6.   The goshawk was often used for hunting ducks, and Bartholomaeus describes it as 'a raptour and ravyschere' (ed. Seymour 1975: I, 607, l. 7). For a vivid late 13th-century MS illustration of its rapacity, see Yapp 1981: 123. *tiraunte* (l. 334) is said by Brewer (1960: 165) to be 'a kind of hawk', but I can find no evidence for this, and the word probably means 'despot' or 'oppressor' (cf. *LGW*, ll. 354–8). *ravyne* (l. 336) is elsewhere used as a legal term for robbery with violence (Alford 1988: 126).

337.   *Falco (faucoune)* in medieval vocabularies is already used of long-winged birds of prey, such as the peregrine, which was and is used for hawking (Yapp 1981: 33, 175). According to Bartholomaeus (ed. Seymour 1975: I, 630) it is 'a real [royal] foule ... and usith to sitte on his hand that bereth him'. See also *Richard the Redeless* (c. 1400) II, ll. 157, 160, 166.

341.   The dove was associated with Venus (see above, ll. 237–8), also with the Holy Spirit, the Virgin Mary and the righteous soul (Yapp 1981: 44–6). On its mildness see Bartholomaeus, ed. Seymour 1975: I, 615, ll. 4–5; 616, l. 30.

342–3.   On the swan's song, cf. *A & A*, ll. 346–7; *LGW*, ll. 1355–6; Alanus, tr. Sheridan 1980: 87; and Bartholomaeus, ed. Seymour 1975: I, 623, ll. 13–15. For the folklore relating to the swan's song and the owl as prophet of death (l. 343), see Armstrong 1970: 61, 114–17. Ch later refers (ll. 599–600) to the erroneous belief that owls cannot see well by day (an idea that is given a moral application in the bestiaries and other texts; see White 1954: 134 and *The Owl and the Nightingale*, ll. 239–52).

344–5.   Alanus's *De Planctu* (tr. Sheridan 1980: 88–9, 90) refers to both the gigantic size of the crane (often illustrated in MSS) and the thievery of the chough. Alexander Neckam's *De naturis rerum* (ed. Wright 1863: 99, 109) mentions the *clangor* of the crane's voice and the garrulousness of the magpie (see also White 1954: 138).

347.   This could allude to a version of the Philomela story in which the rapist Tereus ('fals and ... forswore', *LGW*, l. 2235) was turned into a lapwing

(Bennett 1979: 140, citing *CA* V, ll. 6041–7). See also Bartholomaeus, ed. Seymour 1975: I, 644.

349.   The kite is described as 'coward and fereful among grete briddes' by Bartholomaeus (ed. Seymour 1975: I, 634, l. 31), and its inferiority to the falcon is stressed in *Richard the Redeless* II, ll. 157–61, 176–9.

351–2.   The association of the sparrow ('a ful hoot bridde and lecherous', Bartholomaeus, ed. Seymour 1975: I, 639, l. 7) with Venus and libido is very common. Cf. Juvenal, *Satire* IX, ll. 54ff.; Neckam, ed. Wright 1863: 109; and *Tes.* VII, st. 57. The nightingale features as the bringer of spring in a number of ME poems – e.g. *The Owl and the Nightingale* (esp. ll. 433–46) and 'When the nightegale singes' (Davies 1963: 62).

353–4.   Bees and other insects (as also bats) were classified as birds; see White 1954: 153–9 and Bartholomaeus, ed. Seymour 1975: I, 609–14.

355.   Cf. the turtle-dove's identification with fidelity below, ll. 577 and 582–8. See also Alanus, tr. Sheridan 1980: 92; Neckam, ed. Wright 1863: 108; and White 1954: 145–6. According to Trevisa's tr. of Bartholomaeus (ed. Seymour 1975: I, 641): 'yif he[o] lesith [she loses] hir make, he[o] sechith nought companye of othir but gooth alone and hath mynde of the feleschipe [companion] that is ilost'; this seems quite close to what Ch's turtle-dove says about fidelity in ll. 582–8.

357.   Alanus (tr. Sheridan 1980: 89) refers to the wild cock cuckolding the domestic one.

358.   The raucous vigilance of the goose (the sacred geese on the Capitol were believed to have saved Rome from invaders by cackling) is noted by Neckam (ed. Wright 1863: 117). Ch later in *PF* associates the goose with stupidity (ll. 568–74; cf. *TC* III, l. 584), and the bird is also made to look foolish in medieval portrayals of 'the fox preaching to the geese' (cf. Varty 1967: plates 73, 82 and 86, and *Towneley Plays*, EETS e.s. 71 (1897), p. 12, l. 84), though its reputation in legend and folklore is more complex and respectable (see above, l. 358; Varty 1967: 37; Armstrong 1970: 25–47).

The 'unnatural' behaviour of the cuckoo is referred to again in ll. 612–13. On the cuckoo's 'selfishness', see Bennett 1957: 172–3 and Neckam, ed. Wright 1863: 117–18; for related beliefs see Alanus, tr. Sheridan 1980: 92–3, and Armstrong 1970: 203. On the poem's later association of the cuckoo with folly (below, l. 505), see Armstrong 1970: 197. Along with the hare it is a symbol of ignorance in *Kn T*, l. 1810, and it is associated with human folly (*stultitia*) by Neckam (ed. Wright 1863: 118). *Foole* is also used (as a noun) of the goose in ll. 571 and 574.

359.   Neckam (ed. Wright 1863: 88) describes the wantonness of the parrot, which is said to 'adopt the poses of a lover' on seeing its own reflection in a mirror.

360.   The description of the drake 'destroying its own species' probably refers to the phenomenon known as 'mallard rape' (attacks by males on females at the end of the mating season).

361.   Refers to the belief that the male stork would kill an unfaithful mate (see Bartholomaeus, ed. Seymour 1975: I, 619, ll. 24–7).

362.   Associates the poem's recurrent theme of rapacity (cf. ll. 336, 556, 613) with the cormorant (swallowing fish).

363.   On the associations of ravens and crows with prophecy and foreboding, see Bartholomaeus, ed. Seymour 1975: I, 622, l. 4; 620, l. 21; Armstrong 1970: 77–8.

364.   The last two birds in the list are the grey-brown (hence 'old') thrush, probably the mistle-thrush, and the pale, winter-resident (hence 'frosty') fieldfare.

NOTES ON THE TEXT

Sources

The text of the *Parliament of Fowls* (*PF*) derives from 15 witnesses: 14 MSS and one early print which has some independent authority. These are (preceded by the abbreviations that refer to them and in the order proposed by Hammond 1902: 3–25) as follows:

Gg MS Gg. 4. 27 (CUL), an important early 15th-century collection of Chaucer's works, which also includes *LGW*, *Troilus* and the *Canterbury Tales*, but not *BD* or *HF*. Its text of *PF* is on folios 480ᵛ–490ᵛ. It is, like MS Fairfax 16 (see **F** below), a large and good-looking manuscript, written on vellum, and it was probably produced earlier (c. 1400–25; see Parkes & Beadle 1979–80: I, 6–7). For details, see Brewer 1960: 58–62 and Parkes & Beadle 1979–80 (facsimile).

Fi The Findern manuscript: MS Ff. 1. 6 (CUL), a collection by several scribes, written c. 1480–1520. Its text of *PF* is on fols 29ʳ–42ᵛ. For details and facsimile, see Beadle & Owen 1977.

Ha MS Harley 7333 (BL) of c. 1440. Its text of *PF* is on fols 29ʳ–42ᵛ.

Tr MS R. 3. 19 (Trinity College, Cambridge), of 1478–83. Its text of *PF* is on fols 17ʳ–24ᵛ. For details and facsimile, see Fletcher 1987.

Sel MS Arch. Seld. B. 24 (Bodleian Library, Oxford), of c. 1490–1500. Its version of *PF* (on fols 142ʳ–152ʳ) lacks ll. 1–14, and from l. 601 onwards it replaces Ch's text with its own conclusion (see Appendix (iii), below). For details, see Edwards & Boffey 1996.

Hh MS Hh. 4. 12 (CUL), of c. 1450 or later. Its text of *PF* (on fols 94ʳ–99ᵛ) ends at l. 365.

Cx Caxton's print of 1477–8, *STC* 5091. Only two copies (on 16 folios) are known to exist. For details see: De Ricci 1909: 29–30; Blake 1969: 235, esp. item 83; Boyd 1978: 1–19.

P MS Pepys 2006 (Magdalene College, Cambridge). For details, see above, p. 214. This also includes *HF* and *LGW*, but not *BD*. Its text of *PF* (on pp. 127–42) ends at l. 667.

Jo MS LVII (St John's College, Oxford), of 1440–50; see Hanna 1991: 31 n. 26. Its text of *PF* is on fols 226ʳ–237ᵛ, and its version of the 'roundel' is probably the earliest (see the note on ll. 680–7, below).

La MS Laud 416 (Bodleian Library, Oxford), of c. 1460 or shortly after. Its text of *PF* (on fols 288ʳ–289ᵛ) ends at l. 142.

F MS Fairfax 16 (Bodleian Library, Oxford). For details, see above, p. 108. Its text of *PF* (fols 120ʳ–129ᵛ) is in between those of *LGW* and *BD*.

B MS Bodley 638 (Bodleian Library, Oxford). For details, see above, p. 108. Its text of *PF* (on fols 96ʳ–109ʳ) lacks ll. 1–22 and 157–200.

T MS Tanner 346 (Bodleian Library, Oxford). For details, see above, p. 108. Its text of *PF* is on fols 120ʳ–131ʳ.

Lo MS Longleat 258 (Longleat House, Wilts.), of c. 1460. See Hammond 1905: 77–9. Its text of *PF* is on fols 85ʳ–101ʳ.

D MS Digby 181 (Bodleian Library, Oxford), of the 1480s (see Hanna 1991: 31 & n. 27, 32 n. 29). Its text of *PF* is on fols 44ʳ–52ʳ.

Th William Thynne's printed edition of the poem in his *workes of Geffray Chaucer* (1532), fols cclxxixʳ–cclxxxiiiʳ, is of some textual value, especially with regard to the 'roundel' (see the note on ll. 680–7, below, and Hanna 1991: 30–1). His readings mostly coincide with those of the Caxton print (via Pynson's edition of 1526). For details, see above, p. 108.

There are facsimile editions of nine of these witnesses (Gg, Fi, Tr, Sel, P, F, B, T and Th). Transcriptions are also available in Chaucer Society vols XXI–XXIII (ed. Furnivall 1871 and 1868–80).

From the number and diversity of the surviving MSS, *PF* appears, during the 15th century, to have had wider circulation than Chaucer's other dream poems. Copies were made not only in the metropolitan area but also in East Anglia (Gg), the North Midlands (Fi) and Scotland (Sel), and were owned not only by gentry readers but also by the merchant class (P) and nuns (La) (according to Boffey 1994).

Gg and F are of particular importance as the two earliest witnesses and the ones which contain the fewest errors and omissions. Of these, Gg is usually thought to be the earlier and to have had the better exemplar. There is evidence, though, that the scribe of Gg engaged in some 'editing' of the text, mostly to regularize the metre (e.g. in ll. 358, 363, 369, 428, 551, 564, 594 and 613). This feature, together with Gg's rather idiosyncratic spelling, makes it difficult to decide between it and F as the basis for an edition.

The text here is largely based upon F, and mostly follows its spellings, whilst punctuation is wholly editorial. As a base manuscript F does not, however, have the same degree of authority for *PF* that it has for *HF* or *BD*. Hence a relatively large number of readings (about 100) have been adopted from other witnesses. The following notes are chiefly designed to indicate such departures from F, giving, in those cases, *one* of the sources for the adopted reading (usually Gg), followed by the reading in F. They also indicate emendations and gaps in the MSS. For fuller lists of variant readings, see Brewer 1960: 57–64, 92–9, and *Riv.*, pp. 1147–50.

Selected textual notes

TITLES *(examples)*:

Gg: *Here begynneth the parlement of Fowlys*
Ha: *The Parlament of Foules*
Tr: *Here foloweth the parlement of Byrdes reducyd to love &c.*
P: *The parlament of fowles*
La: *Of the assemble of the byrdis on Seint Volantins day*
F: *The parlement of Briddes*
B: *The parlement of Fowlys*
Lo: *The Parlament of Foules*
D: *the parlement of fowlis*
Th: *The assemble of foules*

3. *dredful* (Gg)] *slyder* F.   *alwey that* (Gg)] *that alwey* F.
5. *Astonyeth with his wondyrful* (Gg)] *Astonyeth soo with a dredeful* F.
7. *flete or synke* (Fi)] *wake or wynke* F.
10. *ful ofte in bokis rede* (Gg)] *in bookes ofte to rede* F.
13. *I dar nat sey(n)* (Gg)] *Dar I not seyn* F.
24. *feyth* (B)] *feythe* F.
26. *as of this* (Gg)] *of my first* F.
30. *theras I* (Fi)] *there I* F.
31. *of Cipion* (Fi)] *of the Cipion* F.
32. *sevene it hadde* (Gg)] *hit had vii* F.
43. *tellith it* (Gg)] *tolde he hym* F.
50. *yf folke* (Gg)] *yf the folke* (F).
58. *of the hevenes* (Gg)] *of hevenes* F.
64. *syn* (Gg)] *see* F.   *erthe was* (Gg)] *erthe that is* F.
70. *is* (Gg)] *was* F.
71. *prayed hym Scipioun* (Gg)] *prayed he Scipion* F.   *to* (Gg)] F omits.
78. *soth to* (Gg)] *soth for to* F.
80. *Shul whirle* (Gg)] *Shul alwey whirle* F.   *alwey in* (Gg)] *in* F.
82. *foryeven al* (Fi)] *foryeven hem al* F.
85. The first of six marginal *nota* ('note') signs in F appears here. The rest are also at the start of stanzas (at ll. 99, 267, 435, 470, 631). This first example seems to highlight the start of a new episode, and those at ll. 99 and 267 may perhaps reflect readers' interest in the list of dreamers and the description of Venus, but the reasons for the others are not so clear.
102. *how his carte is gon* (Gg)] *how his cartes goone* F.
108. *made* (Gg)] F omits.
110. *booke totorne* (P)] *booke al to torne* F.
114. *fyrbrond* (D)] *firy bronde* F.
124. *ywriten* (P)] *writen* F.
133. *spede the faste* (Gg)] *hye the faste* F.

140. *Th'eschewyng* (emendation)] *The eschuyng* Fi, P; *Thesthewynge* B; *The shewyng* T, D; *Thesavynge* F.
142. *astoned* (Gg)] *astounde* F. The text in La comes to an end here.
150. *ne* (B)] *nor* F.
152. *that nyste* (Gg)] *that I ne wiste* F.
156. *to* (Gg)] F omits.
163. *yit mayst thow se* (Gg)] *yet thou maist hyt se* F.
169. *With that* (Gg)] *And with that* F.
172. *eyen* (Gg)] *eyn* F.
175. *joye* (Fi)] *joy* F.
178. *box-tre pipere* (Gg)] *box pipe tre* F.
188. *That swymmyn* (Gg)] *And swymmynge* F.
191. *armonye* (Gg)] *armony* F.
194. *al* (Gg)] F omits.
197. *strynges* (Gg [sp.: *strengis*])] *strynge* F.
198. *so* (Gg)] F omits.
201. *be* (Gg)] F omits.
206. *Ther wex* (Gg)] *Ther growen* F.
207. *waxe* (Gg)] *wexe* F.
208. *joye more* (Gg)] *more joy* F.
209. *Than* (Gg)] *No* F.
215. *hir wile* (Gg)] *harde file* F.
221. *doon by force* (P)] *goo before* F.
229. *here* (Gg)] F omits.
231. *bras* (Gg)] *glas* F.
234. *some of hem were* (Gg)] *some of hem* F.
236. *yer by yere* (T)] *fro yere to yere* F.
237. *of dowves* (Gg [sp.: *dowis*])] *saugh I* F.
238. *Sawe I syttynge* (Gg)] *Of dowves white* F.
240. *honde* (Gg)] *hande* F.
244. *and ek withoute* (Gg)] *and withoute* F.
271. *was* (Gg)] F omits.   *well keverede* (Gg)] *kevered wel* F.
273. *no* (Gg)] F omits.
278. *two yonge folk there cryede* (Gg)] *the yonge folkes criede* F.
284. *peynted* (B)] *peyted* F.
285. *Ful* (Gg)] *Of* F.
295. *the* (Gg)] *that* F.
303. *goddesse, Nature* (Gg)] *goddesse of Nature* F.
313. *eyr* (Gg)] *see* F.
317. *of array* (Fi)] *of suche array* F.
319. *grace* (B)] *gace* F.
325. *hem* (Gg)] *that* F.
327. *And* (Gg)] *But* F.
328. *But* (Gg)] *And* F.

338. *hardy* (Gg)] F omits.
346. *eles* (Fi)] *Egles* F.
352. *grene* (Gg)] *fressh* F.
355. *hir* (Fi)] *hys* F.
358. *the cukkow ever unkynde* (B)] *cukkow ever unkynde* F.
365. The text in Hh comes to an end here.
370. *Benygnely* (Gg)] *Benyngly* F.
375. *the²* (Gg)] F omits.
381. *Hath* (Gg)] *halfe* F.
383. *hede* (Gg)] F omits.
390. *ordenaunce* (Gg)] *governaunce* F.
402. *lese* (Gg)] *lesse* F.
420. *or* (Gg)] *of* F.
436. *Al be she* (Fi)] *As thogh she* F.
467. *Nature* (Gg)] F omits.
476. *ful* (Gg)] F omits.
480. *ese* (Gg)] *plese* F.
482. *hires* (T)] *hirse* F.
508. *For to* (Gg)] *Fore for to* F.
511. *as fayr be stille* (Gg)] *as good be* F.
530. *list, termyne* (Fi)] *lyst to termyne* F.
534. *by* (Gg)] *hyt by* F.
544. *may nought gon as* (Gg)] *may nought as* F.
556. *golee* (B)] *goler* F.
573. *ne* (Gg)] *nor* F.
594. *seyde the goos* (Ha)] *quod the duk* F.
601. The text in Sel is from here on replaced by a 15th-century conclusion. For an account of this, see Appendix (iii) below.
612. *the¹* (Gg)] F omits.
623. *hire han* (Gg)] *han hir* F.
643. *grauntyth* (Gg)] *graunte* F.
650. *wol* (Fi)] *wolde* F.
660. *alle* (Gg)] *al* F.
665. *for* (Gg)] *fro* F.
667. The text in P comes to an end here.
669. *joye* (Gg)] *joy* F.
680–7. On the 'roundel' here, see Appendix (i) below. The main variants here are as follows:
 680. *thy* (D)] Gg omits.   *sonne* (Gg, D)] *sonnes* Th.
 681. *thes* (Gg)] *this* D.
 682. *longe* (Jo, D)] *large* Gg.
 683. *that art* (Jo, Gg, D)] *thou arte* Th.   *on lofte* (Jo, D, Th)] *o lofte* Gg.
 686. *recovered* (Jo, D, Th)] *recodede* Gg.
 687. *synge when they wake* (Jo)] *syng when they awake* Th; *ben when they*

wake Gg; *synge and endles joy thei make* D.
692. *iwis* (Gg)] *ywyse* F.
694. *nyl not* (Fi)] *wol not* F.

Appendix (i): The 'roundel' in lines 680–7

Only three of the witnesses (Gg, Jo, D) include versions of this 'roundel', although it also appears in William Thynne's *workes of Geffray Chaucer* (1532), which may here have some independent textual authority. The Gg version is in a later hand, dated 'no earlier than circa 1460–1470 and likely later still' (Hanna 1991: 30), and the dates of the versions in Jo and D are, respectively, mid-15th century and the 1480s. Of the other witnesses, five (F, B, Tr, Cx and Th) follow l. 679 with versions of the French phrase *Que/Qui bien ayme (a) tarde oublie*, and Thynne then includes the roundel as well. Two (Gg, before the addition, and Ha) leave a space sufficient for another stanza. Three (Fi, T, Lo) simply continue to the poem's final stanza without leaving or indicating a gap in the text.

Thus, as Hanna points out, there is no textual evidence at all for the roundel 'before something like the 1440s' (i.e. at least 60 years after the poem's probable date of composition), and Hanna also notes that it 'does not look as if it were ever intended for feathered singers' (1991: 31, 34). He concludes that the roundel is 'a mid-fifteenth-century intrusion, Chaucerian perhaps but not part of *PF*'.

Of the four versions of the roundel, the earliest, that in Jo, has only five lines (omitting the first three of the text printed here). The version added later in Gg runs to eight lines (in the order printed here). The versions in D and Th are of seven and eight lines respectively (D omits l. 685 of the text printed here and transposes ll. 682–3). The roundel form adopted by Skeat, Rob., Brewer, *Riv.*, etc. involves the repetition of the first two lines of the lyric after l. 684 and of the first three lines at the end. Their texts thus contain five more lines than this edition.

Appendix (ii): Endings

A number of witnesses give a title or tail-piece at the end. Examples are:

Gg: *Explicit parliamentum avium in die sancti valentini tentum secundum Galfridum Chaucer. Deo gracias.* ('Here ends the Parliament of Birds held on St Valentine's Day according to Geoffrey Chaucer. Thanks be to God.')

Fi: *Explicit Parliamentum Avium Quod W. Calverley* ('Here ends the Parliament of Birds Said W. Calverley [the scribe]')

Cx: *Explicit the temple of bras*

F, B and T: *Explicit tractatus de congregacione volucrum die Sancti Valentini*
('Here ends the treatise about the Assembly of Birds on St Valentine's Day')

Ha and Tr add a further stanza identifying the poem as Chaucer's and praising
his eloquence in terms that in some ways resemble those of Caxton's prose
endnote to *HF*. The stanza in Ha (modern punctuation) is as follows:

> Maister Gefferey Chauucer's, that now lith grave,
> The noble Rethor, poete of grete Bretayne,
> That worthi was the laurer to have
> Of poyetry and the palme atain;
> That furst made to still & to rain
> The gold dew Dropes of speche in eloquence
> In to English tonge thorow his excellence.

Appendix (iii): A more conclusive conclusion?

Sel replaces the text from l. 601 onwards with a 79-line conclusion of its own,
which is of some interest as late 15th-century Scots 'Chaucerian' writing
(possible reasons for this substitution have been suggested in Boffey 1994). In
this version brief speaking parts are provided for some of the birds who in
Chaucer's version are silent (the cock, nightingale, robin, parrot and peacock).
The peacock proposes, as a solution to the dispute, that each bird should
choose and woo in hierarchical order, beginning with the eagle (presumably
the royal tercel) as 'worthiest foule'. Nature agrees to this, and when she has
seen 'that al was ryght wel done' she takes her leave and the birds disperse,
except for an owl who is left behind to hoot. The poem then comes full circle,
with the narrator returning pensively to his 'old book' and quoting several of
the lines with which Chaucer began (modern punctuation):

> For out of olde feildis as men seis   (cf. *PF*, ll. 22ff.)
> Cummys all this new corn fro yere to yere,
> And out of olde bookis, quho thame uiseis   *for those who*
> Cummys all this new science that men now lere.   *use them*
> Thus beginnis and endis this matere.
> The lyf so schort, the craft so long to lere: (cf. *PF*, l. 1)
> To full connyng I can noght cum, suppose I rede all yere.

Here endis the parliament of foulis. Quod Galfride Chaucere.

THE *PROLOGUE* TO THE
LEGEND OF GOOD WOMEN

INTRODUCTION

The *Legend of Good Women* (*LGW*), apparently never finished, consists of a dream prologue and nine short narratives celebrating tragic heroines from classical legend, who died faithful in love and, in most cases, betrayed by the men they loved: Cleopatra, Thisbe, Dido, Hypsipyle and Medea (together in one narrative), Lucrece, Ariadne, Philomela, Phyllis, and Hypermnestra. Hypermnestra's story is incomplete, ending with the tantalizing line (l. 2723)

> This tale is seyd for this conclusioun

Like the *Canterbury Tales*, the *Legend* is a collection of stories: *Legend* meant a saint's life or a collection of saints' lives (see Strohm 1975). Chaucer's heroines are, as it were, saints and martyrs of the world of love, faithful unto death. The language and genres of Christianity were frequently used for writing about love in medieval literature, but Chaucer's handling of it here, in a defence of women, creates for most readers a degree of ambiguity about the enterprise.[1] Whether this amounts to deliberate satire is a question I shall return to later.

The two prologues

The *Prologue* exists in two forms. The so-called F Prologue, generally believed to date from about 1386, is called F after Oxford Bodleian Library MS Fairfax 16, one of the sources for that version.[2] The G version, presented in this edition, found only in Cambridge University Library MS Gg.4.27, after which it is named, was probably composed after 1394.[3] G has a clearer sequence of thought. It lacks much of the quasi-philosophical or religious language of F, its kaleidoscopic shifts of theme, and the sometimes startlingly reverential and also erotic style in which its narrator praises the *Prologue*'s central symbol, the daisy. Not all critics consider these differences to be improvements, and greater clarity is not proof that G was later.[4] Some verbal differences suggest that F's wording came first: see, for example, the notes to lines 244 and 258–63. G three times describes the narrator as old, though that is a motif also found in Machaut, Clanvowe and Gower, and it also functions as a favourite Chaucerian narratorial structure, the detachment of the narrator from his subject, here love poetry.[5] G adds to the list of Chaucer's writings in lines 405–20 a reference to his translation of *De miseria humanae condicionis*, now lost. This influenced some *Canterbury Tales*, including the *Man of Law's Tale*, whose Prologue refers to *LGW* as already in existence, in some form. The most sensible critical approach is not to see G simply as a revised version of F, and certainly not to use elements from either prologue indiscriminately in forming a critical reading, but to treat G as a new, separate prologue with its own unity and thematic priorities. The legends themselves were not altered in G. This edition presents the *Prologue* and the *Legend of Dido* from G.

The good women, Cupid's saints

The usual modern title, *Legend of Good Women*, comes from lines 473–4, and appears in Thynne's 1532 edition and rubrics to two manuscripts.[6] Chaucer also calls the work the 'Seintes Legende of Cupide' ('legend of Cupid's saints') in the *Man of Law's Prologue*, and 'book of the xxv. Ladies' in the Retraction to the *Canterbury Tales*.[7] In Hoccleve's *Lepistre de Cupide* ('Letter of Cupid'), line 316, the God of Love calls it 'our legende of martirs'. See below, p. 292 on dangers inherent in the modern title.

It is unclear how many legends Chaucer intended: the *balade*, G lines 203–23, names nineteen women: Esther, Penelope, Marcia, Isolde, Helen, Lavinia, Lucrece, Polixena, Cleopatra, Thisbe, Hero, Dido, Laodamia, Phyllis, Canace, Hypsipyle, Hypermnestra, Ariadne and Alceste, together with two men, Absalom and Jonathan. The *Prologue* also describes a procession of nineteen unnamed ladies who revere the daisy and exemplify fidelity in love.[8] The F Prologue says these women will be in the legend and are the ones in the *balade* (ll. 554–8), but G omits that, and they only partly correspond to the extant legends' heroines. The *Man of Law's Prologue* names eight women who are in the *Legend*: Lucrece, Thisbe, Dido, Phyllis, Ariadne, Hypsipyle, Medea and Hypermnestra, together with Alceste, who was apparently to be its final subject (ll. 532–40), and Deianira, Hermione, Hero, Helen, Briseida, Laodamia and Penelope, who are not in the extant *Legend*. He also says Chaucer did not write of incestuous Canace, who *is* in the *balade*. These discrepancies presumably reflect Chaucer's changing plans for the work. Perhaps by the time he wrote the G Prologue, figures in the *balade* like Helen, Isolde and Canace no longer fitted the moral parameters that had emerged as he worked on the legends.

All the lists include characters who cannot be called wholly 'good': Medea, who killed her children in an attempt to regain her lover, is the obvious example. The concept of 'Cupid's saints' in the *Man of Law's Prologue* is closer to Chaucer's own subject and tone than the 'good women' of the title preferred today: these are women whom passion has led to suffering or tragedy – including, for the *Man of Law's Prologue*, the 'crueltee' Medea committed (l. 72).

The *Prologue* is linked to the legends by a fiction that Chaucer's previous writings have caused offence: the God of Love accuses the dreamer of having, in *Troilus* and in his translation of the *Roman de la Rose*, led men to distrust love as folly, and women as faithless, and demands why he did not write rather of women who were 'goode and trewe' (l. 272).[9] Queen Alceste pleads for mercy for the narrator and he is handed over to her for judgement. She decrees his penance will be to compose 'a gloryous legende' of faithful women and men who betrayed them (ll. 469–80).

Alceste

Alceste is based on the legendary Greek queen Alcestis, who agreed to die in place of her husband Admetus but was brought back to life by the gods (ll. 530–40). Alceste may be in part a compliment to Richard II's first wife, Anne of Bohemia, daughter of the Holy Roman Emperor, Charles IV.[10] The fifteenth-century poet Lydgate said Chaucer wrote 'at request off the queen, / A legende off parfit hoolynesse / Off Goode Women' (*Fall of Princes*, ll. 330–2). He might have surmised that from the poem itself, but it may be true. In the F Prologue Alceste commands (ll. 496–7):

> And whan this book ys maad, yive it to the quene,
> On my byhalf, at Eltham or at Sheene.

Anne died in 1394 and Richard partially demolished Shene manor in 1395, though the story that he did this through grief at her death seems to be a chronicler's fabrication.[11]

Chaucer would have found Alcestis's fidelity and wifehood celebrated particularly by three authors he mentions in lines 280–1: Jerome, in *Against Jovinian* (c. 393), I, col. 45, Claudian, in *Praise of Serena* (*Laus Serenae*, c. 404), lines 238–57 – also a source for his *balade* – and Valerius

Maximus, in his widely read *Memorabilia* (c. 31). The last was probably known from Simon de Hesdin's French translation, c. 1376. As McCall shows, Valerius in his chapter on conjugal love contrasted Tiberius Gracchus, who gave his life for his wife's, with Admetus, who selfishly let Alcestis die for him, but Simon's translation switches the emphasis to Alcestis, presenting Tiberius and Alcestis as parallel examples of self-sacrificing spouses.[12] Other possible sources include Boccaccio's *De genealogia deorum* (1350–75), XIII, 1, the Prologue to Bersuire's *Reductorium morale*, Fulgentius's *Mythologies* I, 19, or Hyginus's *Fabulae* 51.[13] The *balade* 'Hyd Absalon' praises Alceste in its refrain (in the F version it is 'my lady'): perhaps it begins with Absalom in order to make an alliterative link with the name Anne, just as *Troilus* I, line 171 says 'oure firste lettre is now an A', presumably in compliment to the Queen. Absalom was already established as a type of beauty in the *Roman de la Rose* and several French *balades* praising women.[14] In the twelfth century Absalom's beauty and Jonathan's friendliness had been regularly listed in texts about transience,[15] and there is a wistful air to Chaucer's *balade* with its conceit of bright beauty which must hide or depart. The *balade* elevates Alceste above all others (including most of Chaucer's 'good women') celebrated for beauty, virtue or self-sacrifice.

Alceste, with her dignity and moral authority, beauty and benevolence, resembles other female authority figures in literary visions: Dante's Beatrice, Grace Dieu in de Deguileville's *Pèlerinage de vie humaine*, or Philosophy in Boethius's *Consolation of Philosophy*. Like Lady Leësce in Le Fèvre's *Livre de Leësce* ('Book of Delight', c. 1373–87?), she and Love defend women against misogynist writing and translation.

The daisy is Chaucer's emblem of Alceste's regality, goodness and constancy, through its symbolic colours, its heliotropism, and the fact that it is unchanged by the seasons (ll. 57–8). Both are honoured and both – even more overtly in F than in G – are associated with potentially religious imagery: darkness and the sun, descent and ascent. Alceste and the daisy are, like White in the *Book of the Duchess* (*BD*), described in terms which are reminiscent of literature and liturgy in honour of Mary: the crown, the white and gold symbolizing purity and royalty, Alceste's assumption into heaven, and the Marian phrase 'of alle flouris flour' (l. 55).[16] Interceding for the narrator with the God of Love, Alceste resembles the late medieval image of Mary as queen of heaven, pleading with God's justice for mercy for humanity.[17] Chroniclers sometimes depict real-life fourteenth-century queens mirroring this intercessory role: Queen Anne interceded with Richard II on behalf of Simon Burley during the 1388 parliament and on behalf of the citizens of London in 1392, and in the social mythology of the period, queens were associated with powers of intercession, wise counsel and mediation.[18]

Alceste is arrayed like a daisy and helps the dreamer because he is devoted to 'hire flour' (l. 512). This identification of Alceste with the daisy may owe something to Froissart's pseudo-Ovidian story of Héros, whose tears over her lover's death were turned into daisies by the gods. It appears in Froissart's seventeenth *Pastourelle*, his *Joli buisson de jonece*, lines 3216–41, and *Dittié de la flour de la Marguerite*, lines 67–82.[19] Froissart, who was at the English court as secretary to Queen Philippa in 1361–6 and 1367–8, often invented Greek names and tales which resembled legends from Ovid's *Metamorphoses*, or modified genuine names and legends. Wimsatt 1991: 192–3 suggests that Chaucer similarly modified the Alcestis legend and invented Cibella. Cibella may, however, not be an invented name, but Cybele, a goddess of fertility who was also, in several Roman sources – including Claudian's *Praise of Serena*, which Chaucer knew – a champion of women's chastity.[20]

Chaucer's myth of Alceste (ll. 498–522) turns out to be a fascinatingly complex mixture of existing legend, invention, and adaptation of other Ovidian myths. Chaucer says Cibella made the daisy (l. 519; an invention): by implication it is a symbolic embodiment of Alceste's virtues, and a memorial to her wifely purity and her ascent from darkness to light. Hercules raised her 'out of helle ageyn to blys' (ll. 503–4; this is in the legend); Jove made her, with her crown, into a star in heaven (l. 513; Chaucer's invention, probably influenced by Ovid's legend of the elevation of Ariadne's crown into a constellation in *Fasti* V, ll. 345–6, VIII, ll. 459–516; see also *Met*. VIII, ll. 176–82, and the legend of Ariadne in *LGW*, ll. 2221–4); Mars, whose planet is red, gave her a red crown, combined with the white: an invention, perhaps influenced by the flower-myth of Mars's birth (*Fasti* V, ll. 251–4). Chaucer may have been influenced, generally, by the set of flower-myths in the May section of Ovid's *Fasti* (V, ll. 183–378), which includes legends about people like Adonis and Attis turned into flowers after death. Red is the colour of martyrs' crowns. Thus Chaucer's daisy acquires some associations of the rose, the symbol both of love and of martyrs' glorification upon their ascent to heaven after death; compare the rose and lily crowns in *Second Nun's Tale* of St Cecilia, VIII, lines 220–1, which line 416 of the *Prologue* shows Chaucer had already written, in some form, before the *Legend*. That red and white colouring is multivalent symbolism: either purity and martyrdom, or the conventional compliment to feminine beauty, or the colours of St George and England (as in the banner and the rose crowns of the angels in the Wilton Diptych). It typifies the way in which the presentation of the daisy seems to inhabit several different discourses simultaneously: amatory, religious, and national.

The F Prologue (l. 110) uses 'resureccioun' of the daisy unfolding in the morning, and, as with Seys and Alcyone in *BD*, some critics have seen Alceste and the daisy as full Christian allegories: Kiser (1983: 61), for example, sees Alceste as 'the embodiment of Christian art'. In view of Chaucer's respectful remarks about purely pagan virtue (ll. 296–304), such an approach seems over-narrow. Chaucer mentions 'Agaton' (Plato's *Symposium*) as a source (l. 514) and may have known Plato's praise of Alcestis and contrast of her with Orpheus, whose failure to raise Eurydice from Hades represents attachment to lower, earthly, concerns.[21]

Literature and experience

The *Legend* begins by asserting that books can be invaluable reports of truths otherwise unavailable to us, taking as examples first the knowledge of heaven and hell and second the experiences of people in the past, which would be lost without the record of texts. The rest of the poem has two main subjects. It offers a series of accounts of faithful women (*story ... geste*, l. 87 – historical records), and it constantly returns to the issue of how and whether texts can faithfully present their subject: literary tradition provides us with the spectacle of misogynist texts which misrepresent women's real experience of fidelity and feminist texts that vindicate them; questions of intentionality and interpretation make the content and meaning of texts problematic (these two themes come to the fore in the G Prologue). Chaucer talks provocatively of creating a 'nakede tixt', but, as the *Legend* shows, there is no such thing as a text that directly represents reality, that is, the experience of people in the past; there is no unmediated text freed from issues of intentionality and interpretation. Within human culture there is also no unmediated Nature: although the narrator declares his intention of throwing aside his books and turning to nature, walking out into the *mede*, in fact the landscape he walks out into turns into a field of literary references: Maytime; the daisy; literature and its interpretation as *corn*; making one's bed outside instead of indoors. These are all images with extensive literary traditions behind them for late fourteenth-century readers. The image of corn goes back to St Augustine (see below), and sleeping out is an image of Golden Age innocence from Boethius (see p. 299). Poems praising the daisy, often in honour of women called Marguerite, were fashionable in contemporary French poetry. Latin *margarita* means 'pearl' and, by extension, 'daisy'; French *marguerite* means 'daisy'.

Daisy poems and the Flower and the Leaf

Fourteenth-century marguerite poems include: Guillaume de Machaut, *Dit de la Marguerite*, c. 1364;[22] Jean Froissart, *Dittié de la flour de la Marguerite*, c. 1364;[23] Machaut, *Dit de la Fleur de lis et de la Marguerite* (after 1369?);[24] Eustache Deschamps, *Lai de Franchise*, c. 1385;[25] and in Froissart's *Paradis d'Amour* (c. 1362–4), a source for *BD*, the unhappy lover, reproved for complaining against his liege-lord Love, encounters Love hunting and, comforted by Love's retainers Hope and Pleasure, he composes lyrics, including one in honour of the marguerite. Chaucer's *Prologue* obviously belongs with these marguerite poems, several of which may have influenced it.[26] Other English works which also use the symbols of pearl and/or daisy include Usk's *Testament of Love* (1386?), *Pearl* (c. 1390), and the *Boke of Cupide* (1380s?), attributed to Clanvowe, a dream poem using daisy symbolism which may have been influenced by the *Legend*.

Contemporary French texts refer to nobles declaring allegiance to the parties of the Flower and the Leaf, but the only extant English poem on the subject is the *Floure and the Leafe*, c. 1460–80.[27] In it, the company of the Flower are lovers who care above all for pleasure and idleness, which, like flowers, are very subject to mutability, symbolized in the poem by scorching sun followed by storm. The company of the Leaf are devoted to virtue and chaste love, which like leaves are more enduring. An allegorical scheme of the Flower and the Leaf must have been familiar in Chaucer's England, either through poetry or some kind of courtly game or device, and his unchanging daisy (ll. 57–8) may echo praise of the constancy of the Leaf in lyrics by Deschamps.[28] Chaucer's nineteen ladies who dance in honour of the daisy are all faithful lovers (l. 193), and he says his reverence for the daisy has nothing to do with the Company of the Flower: his subject is older than that conflict (ll. 71–80), implying that for him virtue and love's pleasures are not antithetical, just as Alceste epitomizes both virtuous 'wifhod' and 'fyn lovynge' (ll. 533–6). Chaucer also links the image cluster centred on the flower with the long-established metaphor of virtuous literature as 'corn'. Saint Augustine, *On Christian Doctrine* III, cols 7–12, contrasted the moral good that could be discerned in a text, its kernel or corn, and its valueless aspects, its husk. Augustine is talking about interpretation and about the moral status of literature, both concepts of central relevance to Chaucer's exploration of how literature has presented women.[29]

The God of Love, the defence of women and the *Roman de la Rose*

The *Legend* is part of a long medieval debate about women and marriage. Misogyny is age-old, but controversy about marriage in western Christian culture arose in particular with a fourth-century dispute over the relative status within the church of the celibate clergy and married laity. Jerome's *Against Jovinian* (393), sometimes regarded today simply as an anti-feminist work, was in the church politics of its era part of the propaganda of the clerical party against writers like Jovinian, who asserted that marriage and the life of lay people were not in themselves morally or spiritually inferior to the celibate priest's life.[30] In the history of the Church it was the celibate party which won, leaving a legacy of antipathy and anxiety with regard to marriage.[31] This bias towards virginity and the powerful tradition of literature and biblical exegesis in praise of virginity and chastity mean that even though works written in defence of women against misogyny are common in the Middle Ages, the defenders often base their arguments narrowly on women's chastity or wifely fidelity.

Women were widely believed, partly as a result of erroneous Greek biology, to be innately less rational, more sensual and changeable than men, and a central charge by anti-feminists against women was that they were unfaithful and deceptive. Misogynist tradition therefore faced medieval defenders with the task of presenting women as capable of constancy.[32] Modern readers may feel the medieval defenders of women do them no great service by so often insisting on women's faithfulness, chastity and obedience, but the attacks medieval feminists had to rebut differed from those faced by post-Victorian feminists. Though some defenders, like Christine de Pizan, raised other issues, like women's aptitude for learning, many works – like the *Legend* – took the chief battleground to be the issues of women's fidelity or chastity.

The daisy functions as a chaste alternative to the rose of the *Roman de la Rose*, which is a symbol of sensuality. The *Legend* must be viewed in the context of controversy about books which to many seemed to be in the forefront of the anti-feminist attack – above all the *Rose*. Its imperious God of Love, with his wings and arrows and giving orders to the dreamer, is a figure from the *Rose* (*RR*, ll. 863–983, 1679–2748), where he shot the lover with arrows representing desire for a beautiful woman, then demanded homage from him and gave him a set of orders which amount to prescribing a life of total subjugation of mind and body to passion and obsessive desire. It may therefore seem odd that in the *Legend* it is the God of Love who condemns the *Rose* and champions the cause of female virtue, but the *Legend* is one of several late-medieval works in which figures from the *Rose*, like the God of Love or Nature, who had been identified, justly or not, by readers with promoting sexual licence and contempt for women, are reformulated and used to promote chastity and pro-feminist arguments. They include Christine de Pizan's *Epistre au dieu d'Amours* (1399) and Hoccleve's English version, *Lepistre de Cupide* (1402), Martin le Franc's *Champion de Dames* (1440–2), and the *Chevalier des Dames* (c. 1460).[33] Le Fèvre's *Livre de Leësce* is a defence of women against the attacks in Mathéolus's anti-feminist *Lamentations of Mathéolus* (c. 1295). Le Fèvre himself had translated Mathéolus into French (c. 1370–3 or c. 1380–7) and presents *Leësce* as an apology to women for that, perhaps inspiring Chaucer's fiction that the *Legend* was a penance for his *Troilus* and translation of the *Rose*.

Penance and the writer's intention

During the Middle Ages, the doctrines and practice of penance changed.[34] By Chaucer's time the sacrament of penance was a private spiritual matter between individuals and their priest, centred on true contrition and confession, sincerity of intention, change of heart, absolution, and the performance of penance – usually extra prayers, charity or abstinence. Penance was regarded as spiritually therapeutic as well as a punishment or reparation for sin. Public penance had become extremely rare, but remained a motif popular with writers.[35] To some extent Chaucer, like Gower in *Confessio Amantis* or Pierre de Hauteville in his *Confession et testament de l'amant trespassé de deuil*, is using the motifs of contrition and 'penaunce' with elegant wit, as part of a literary game of talking about love in religious terms. How far does the *Prologue* suggest also a genuine desire to make restitution to women for any harm his works might have done? In fact, the *Legend* and *Troilus* are similar, rather than opposed, in their complex presentation of passion. Chaucer's dramatization of criticisms of his own writings in Love's speech (ll. 246–316) and his treatment of the question of his own intentionality as author – presenting himself merely as passive translator or servant of others (ll. 340–52) – are self-evidentially ingenuous. They cannot adequately represent his own view of the issues. Elsewhere in his writings, most strikingly in *Troilus*, *Venus* and the *Legend of Dido*, we find this pose as a passive receptor of other men's creations in cases where he has actually radically recast a source, particularly from the point of view of issues of gender.[36] Chaucer also depicts his narrator as a passive translator in some narratives whose protagonists undergo suffering, as if matching narrator to hero(ine). This is a development from the deferential observer-narrator found in several

French *dits amoureux*. In the *Canterbury Tales*, where it is transmuted into a narrator who has no choice but to repeat what his characters says, it is very clearly a structure for multiple viewpoints.

The *Legend* is a poem about literature as well as women and love. The F Prologue presented the daisy as the poet's divine muse. Chaucer's constant references to 'olde bokys', and to the sources of individual legends, paradoxically alert us to the problem that each narrative of a plot in fact reformulates the *experience*. Throughout the *Legend* runs an awareness that literary tradition, mostly written by men, is often unjust to women's experience. Chaucer seems to become gradually more aware during his career that there is what we would call a feminist aspect to that preoccupation with the relationship of *experience* to *auctorite* which underlies much of his writing.[37] The *Wife of Bath's Prologue* voiced it clearly: 'By God, if wommen hadde writen stories, / As clerkes han withinne hire oratories, / They wolde han writen of men moore wikkednesse ...' (ll. 693–5).

'A gloryous legende of goode women ... that were trewe in lovynge'

The form the 'penaunce' takes, a collection of stories about faithful women, employs a literary device with a long history, the catalogue of women. Virgil's *Aeneid*, Book VI, for example, contains a group of women destroyed by passion, including Dido. Claudian's *Praise of Serena*, composed – as the *Legend* may be – in honour of an emperor's daughter and the wife of the poet's ruler, has a catalogue of chaste wives celebrated by ancient poets, beginning with Alcestis. There is also Jerome's catalogue of chaste women in *Against Jovinian* I, 41–6. Despite the anti-matrimonial purpose of *Against Jovinian*, and the misogyny of material by both Jerome and Theophrastus in it, Chaucer possibly perceived Jerome himself, or at least Jerome in his catalogue of women, as defending women: see notes to lines 280–1. Both misogynists and pro-feminist writers used catalogues of women: Mathéolus's *Lamentations* has several catalogues which it claims show women are evil, and Le Fèvre's *Leësce*, in reply, offers catalogues to show women as good, sometimes citing the same heroines but in a positive light. Boccaccio's *De claris mulieribus* focuses on famous women, whether good or not; it is not certain that Chaucer knew it.

Chaucer's main inspiration for his legends was Ovid's *Epistles* (alternative title *Heroides*), a set of fictional letters purporting to have been penned by famous literary lovers, including all Chaucer's heroines except Cleopatra, Thisbe and Philomela, at tragic moments in their love stories. Ovid did not take a moral standpoint: he is concerned with the psychological interest of the individual emotional crisis. Chaucer's *Prologue* creates multiple expectations about the ensuing legends: his reference in lines 280–300 to Jerome and Claudian, and to chaste virgins, wives and widows (Jerome's categories), sets a solemn, pious tone, but the reference in lines 301–6 to Ovid's *Epistles*, and to 'trowe and kynde' women, shifts the ground to women who were faithful and generous in love. The latter values turn out to be the criteria by which most of Chaucer's heroines will be celebrated, even if they were not all chaste, pious or even married to the men in question.

The genre of the collection of saints' lives, another source of inspiration, provided narratives celebrating women's goodness, wisdom, courage and leadership. Recent criticism has recognized that for women, hagiography could be one of the most empowering of medieval genres. We might see Chaucer's use of 'legende', suggesting sainthood, like the quasi-religious aura cast by references such as that to Jerome (ll. 281–300), as introducing an air of spirituality to the topic of secular human passion. Just as religious language in *Troilus* suggests Troilus's experience of love contains something higher and more holy than mere obsessive passion, so also the intermittently solemn terms of the *Prologue* also encourage us to set the human sexual dramas which follow in a disconcertingly reverent light.[38] An alternative view of this project of treating figures like Medea and Dido as metaphorical saints – a view held by many critics – is that the uneven and contradictory tone of the *Prologue* signals a satirical view of human sexual passion, as it will be unfolded in the rest of the *Legend*.

How serious is the *Legend of Good Women*?

There is clearly some mock-seriousness in Chaucer's use of religious terms like heresy, penance, hymns for Love's holy days, the angry God of Love, and a 'glorious legende', but is there a deeper mockery running throughout the whole poem? Some critics, including Fyler 1979, Kiser 1983, McMillan 1987, Rowe 1988, Hansen 1992 and Delany 1994, whose approaches otherwise differ greatly, all find radical ironies throughout the poem which effectively, they believe, prevent readers from taking completely seriously the enterprise of defending women through a series of heroines of tragedies of passion. Ironical readings of this kind tend to be based either on the poem's use of Christian terms, or its attitude to women, or its treatment of past literature and sources. They are encouraged by the critical tradition of assuming that Chaucer characterizes his dream poem narrators as naively blind to the meaning or moral standpoint of what they see and report to us, in order to prompt us to find irony or religious warnings concealed in the texts. This approach to interpretation tends, however, to reduce the complexities within the text to a single polarity between the apparent sincerity and seriousness of the surface and the real irony, and in this case the anti-feminist frivolity, of the content, as revealed to the reader who gets behind the 'persona' of the narrator. Some ironical inter-pretations take on trust assumptions about Chaucer's sources which do not, in fact, stand up to investigation: the books he mentions as praising women, in G lines 280–1, which many critics believe include anti-feminist satires, are actually all respectable, and to medieval eyes reliably historical, texts that included praise of Alcestis or Lucretia (see notes to these lines).

Ironic interpretations often depend on passages found in F but not in G. Both Prologues have a typically Chaucerian variety of tones and levels of seriousness, but F's more extravagant expressions of worship and adoration of the daisy raise expectations of a Christian perspective, which can seem at odds with the celebration of secular love affairs in the extant legends. This religious and erotic language is replaced by anodyne alternatives in G (see notes to ll. 50, 81–2, 234, 242). Had they been misunderstood or caused offence? Were they compliments to Queen Anne and removed after her death? Did Chaucer make the themes of spiritual quest and ascent, linked to Alceste's quasi-apotheosis, an important strand in the *Prologue* when he wrote F, but reduced this in the G Prologue? Dante's Beatrice and Petrarch's Laura provided models for the trans-formation of a real woman into an icon, in life and after death, of all that humans strive towards (ll. 505–10). Did Chaucer plan that in the completed work disparate concepts – sacred and secular, courtly and philosophical – would be finally harmonized, perhaps through the culminating legend of Alceste?[39] Alceste in the G Prologue has become a more general inspirational figure of supreme goodness, especially the *gentil* virtue of mercy. If there was a royal event that discouraged Chaucer from completing the poem – though one can imagine many reasons for his leaving it as yet another of his incomplete works – it might have been Richard II's marriage in 1397 to a seven-year-old French princess, which might complicate readers' responses to an adult queen Alceste as the climax.

We should not let the standard use of the title *Legend of Good Women* by modern editors and critics lead us into concluding that it must be ironical simply because Chaucer's women do not exemplify 'goodness' in its fullest sense. His subject is the narrower one of women's 'trouthe': faithfulness. That said, the modern reader may still feel that the concentra-tion on fidelity and suffering women, together with literary games like the use of 'courtly love' language and religious metaphors, threaten the exercise of defending women. However, we must remember how prominent the charge of inconstancy was in medieval anti-feminism,[40] and also that 'courtly' language, like religious imagery, used of love can be a vehicle for greater seriousness as well as trivialization. Moreover, the world of private sexual relationships is, as feminist theory has reminded us, not a politically negligible one: it can be a site for oppression, as well as for serious moral action and judgement.[41] That seems to be Chaucer's view. Chaucer's heroines are, of course, losers in love affairs with men, a fact which might, consciously or unconsciously, underlie some of the contempt of an older – mostly male – critical establishment.[42]

In real saints' legends, death and suffering for the sake of faith are presented as a triumph. Transferring this genre to faithful lovers raises the issue of whether Chaucer's design ends up celebrating female abjectness and victimization.[43] If Chaucer avoids this, it is partly by incorporating moral condemnation of their male persecutors,[44] and by making the women's martyrdom a demonstration of the strength of their 'trouthe'. His own political *balade*, 'Lak of Stedfastnesse', after all, presents fidelity or steadfastness as a crucial power on the political stage and, indeed, as the definition of strong government.[45] Since Chaucer says it is in *gentil* hearts that pity arises, his pity-arousing stories – whether *Troilus* or the *Legend* – can hardly be offered to their (implicitly *gentil*) readers as lowly topics, ironic mockery or disgusting abjectness.

Many medieval writers composed palinodes, writings which reverse the point of view of a previous work, or apologies, often allegedly to women readers. Examples close to the *Legend* are Machaut's *Jugement dou roy de Navarre* and Le Fèvre's *Leësce*. Irrespective of how sincerely Chaucer opposed misogynist literature in general, there was also a literary game – and opportunity for literary self-promotion – in presenting the *Legend* as a palinode to *Troilus*. In reality, both poems gave him the opportunity to write of the pains of love and faithful hearts, while setting these themes amid an intriguing variety of viewpoints, serious and humorous. As with Machaut's *Behaigne* and *Navarre*, he follows a tale of love and suffering biased towards the man's point of view with one on the female side.

'Olde bokys': *experience* versus *autorite*?

The Wife of Bath famously set 'experience' against 'auctorite', and declared that *clerkes*' books present women in a bad light. Yet her *Prologue* is a dramatization of material from anti-feminist books. The *Legend* claims paradoxically that books – the right books – can be faithful to *experience*, the lives of 'trewe' women. Its narrator is on the side of books, as the preservers of humanity's history (ll. 17–31) and as defenders of women's reputation: because historians like Valerius Maximus and Livy, and *clerkes* who study them thoroughly, know – as God knows – the truth that chaste and faithful women outnumber bad women (ll. 273–87). These books are, I suggest, the 'aprovede storyis', histories which bear witness reliably to the truth about women's 'trouthe'. They are equivalent to 'preve', experiential knowledge, in matters where we have no direct experience. Chaucer's intention is to compose that impossible thing, a 'nakede tixt', one which, as it were, gets behind the interpretative and intentionalist bias found in previous texts, to re-establish the truth about his heroines' fidelity. Henryson focuses on the same challenge when, in his turn, he enquires 'Quha wait gif all that Chaucer wrait was trew?', as he prepares to embark on his own narrative of Criseyde's experience.[46]

The narrator's impulse to abandon books and adore the daisy may seem a Wordsworthian preference for Nature over Literature, but the Nature he presents to us is, we have seen, itself filled with imagery whose power comes from literary associations – the daisy, the fields of literature, St Valentine's Day birds, and birds escaping from 'sophistries'. Instead of prefacing this dream with a book, the *Prologue* poses as its issue the general relationship of allegedly misogynist books to women's reputation: Delany 1986 applies the term 'anxiety of influence' illuminatingly to this problem, the problem for women of a male literary tradition. The poem begins solemnly, with a reference not to Alceste's mythical descent and ascension but to heaven and hell themselves, and to questions of truth and the sources of truth. Perhaps, as the planned poem progressed, reaching its climax in Alceste's apotheosis, these religious terms with which it opens would have seemed more fitting than they do with the uncompleted work we have.

The political passage, lines 318–401: love and power

Chaucer's mature poetry does not so much shift between different registers as seem to inhabit different registers and levels of seriousness simultaneously. Alceste's speech of advice on kingship illustrates this. It may indirectly reflect contemporary anxieties about Richard II's tendencies towards arbitrary rule, and his clashes with many great lords, between c. 1385 and 1399, but we can also choose to read it non-politically, as merely using traditional platitudes about kingship to conduct a witty extended metaphor about love as a tyrannical power, and exemplify that quality of mercy, *routhe*, which is a central theme of the *Legend*. The question of interpretation arises not only from the way Chaucer characteristically writes but from the fact that resentment against government tended to be phrased in terms of themes (like tyrants and true kings) which had long been familiar in medieval political theory.[47] This passage urges a king to be wary of self-serving flatterers at court, not to use 'tyrannye' and 'wilfulhed', not to act like a mere 'fermour' (raiser of money) but a 'naturel' king, bound to his liege subjects by duties and oaths. He must attend to petitions and give accused persons the chance to reply; he should rule with mercy as well as justice, be equally just to rich and poor, maintain his lords in their 'degre' and eschew vengefulness.[48] If these points relate to political concerns at specific periods, the two most likely periods are the late 1380s and c. 1396-7. Though couched as generalizations – of advice to a prince – applicable to any period, they are also generalizations which match specific grievances against Richard by Lords and Commons in the parliaments of 1386 and 1388, associated particularly with the lords appellant, and they tally also with criticisms in the last three years of his reign, when his 'tyranny', irregular financial expedients and vengefulness against the lords who had opposed him, created opposition which led to his deposition in 1399.[49]

The G Prologue adds the reference to 'wilfulhed' (l. 355), perhaps an English equivalent to the increasingly frequent complaints against Richard's unbridled *voluntas*.[50] G also adds a reference, apparently, to the coronation oath (ll. 368-9), which like the 'old books' is presented as a text of age-old venerability. But the oath did not really have a fixed form: its wording could always offer an opportunity for attempts by magnates to curtail royal power (notably with Edward II).[51] It looks as if the oath became a reference point for critics of Richard: in 1388 Parliament forced him to reiterate his coronation oath, and in 1399 a text of his oath was prefaced to the *Record and Process* of charges against him. Interestingly, a work presumably favourable to Richard's self-image, the Wilton Diptych, c. 1396-7, seems to show Richard retrospectively at his coronation, as if rededicating himself or reuniting himself and his kingdom to heaven. In the same context of political symbolism, Alceste appears to represent both supreme virtue and faithfulness, and Queen Anne. After Anne's death she could still represent both virtue and Anglia, to which Richard is united.[52] Being familiar only with 'petition' as an archaic, romantic concept, and not with a political system where petitions are crucial tools for access to justice and power, we may miss the urgency with which the G text urges that personal sovereignty should be balanced by attention to 'excusacyouns ... conpleyntys and petyciouns' (ll. 362-3). All these had legal meanings.[53] The statements about flatterers and requests that kings should maintain and promote the position of lords (l. 370) might suggest the nobles' opposition to royal favourites like de Vere in the late 1380s (though Chaucer apparently lost his own job at the Customs in the ensuing purge). They might also refer to later conflicts over Richard's revenge against Gloucester, Arundel and Warwick in 1397 and attacks on Bolingbroke; also perhaps the financial grievances felt in the 1390s by the Duke of Gloucester, as well as the Beauforts, or lords punished by Richard for opposing him.[54] If we ignore the hypothesis linking the G Prologue specifically to Queen Anne's death in 1394 as no more than a guess, then G (indeed both prologues) could date from anywhere between c. 1385 and c. 1397. Against a later 1390s date for G is perhaps the fact that only two *Canterbury Tales* are mentioned in lines 403–20, and it is usually assumed Chaucer was writing them from the late 1380s, but a late date for G is supported by its references to the dreamer's age.

Chaucer cleverly turns on its head the view, apparently dear to Richard II, that he was God's anointed and therefore had absolute power above the law by declaring instead that it is precisely a 'naturel' king, unlike upstarts, who will act with 'benignity' towards his 'lige-men', his subjects (the parliament that confirmed his deposition in 1399 attributed to Richard the absolutist statement that his lieges' lives and property belonged to him).[55] Chaucer may have been trying to hint that the logic of Richard's image of his own role was that he must eschew arbitrary acts, accept the restraint of the law and his own coronation oaths (ll. 368–72): the king appointed by God is all the more bound, by his superior nobility of nature, to act mercifully to all and honour 'his lordys' – for they similarly are 'half goddys'. Chaucer seems to invoke a theory of divinely blessed kingship to encourage the king to treat his magnates with something of the same God-given respect he deemed due to himself. The whole passage may be an attempt to flatter a king into accepting restraints on his power – an attempt rendered the more flattering by the implied parallel between an English king and the God of Love. Like other attempts to curb kings, before and after, Chaucer invokes the convenient notion that it is sycophantic but false counsellors who are the dangerous source of trouble, not the monarch himself (ll. 326–38). In contrast, the advice within the poem to submit to the rule of law and benevolence comes not from a lowly subject like the author Geoffrey Chaucer, but from the celestial Alceste and the 'sentens of the philyosofre' (l. 365). Chaucer may be using the whole quaint superstructure of the God of Love, the daisy-Alceste and the rehabilitation of the female lovers for a potentially political end: male oppression, whether by lovers or writers, is confronted and its values overturned as a male poet is rebuked by Love and made to perform penance, while a king is rebuked by a lovely lady who seems an aspect of his own royal identity and is made to convert domination into mercy.

Even if it had topical resonances, this passage is not solely political. It has other significances. It is also a mock-heroic joke about love: a God of Love, being the personification of sexual passion, *is*, of course, metaphorically a tyrant, arbitrary and cruel, and it is natural to feel he should favour his devoted 'liegemen' – like love-poets. The mock-heroic fear resembles the bewildered awe at Love's power in the first two stanzas of the *Parliament of Fowls*. Secondly, there is covert self-flattery in Chaucer's attack on envious slanderers (ll. 319–37). Dante's name here (ll. 335–6) encourages us to read this as as much about literature as politics: it is Chaucer's only serious attack on critics of his own writings.[56] It contains a kind of critical discussion: the God of Love is a literary critic, albeit a narrow and tyrannical one, interpreting *Troilus* as an exemplum of infidelity; the dreamer replies with manifestly ingenuous claims about authorial intentionality. Thirdly, the warning about discerning false 'losengers' (ll. 326–31) is a variant on the poem's central themes of truth and falsehood, fidelity and treachery, and of discerning reliable sources for belief. The themes of this passage, then, are themes found throughout the whole work. The importance of mercy, stability and steadfastness, and fidelity to oaths, are recurrent motifs of the *Legend*; Love and Alceste represent Justice and Mercy respectively; and the legends depict heroines whose pity and benevolence was met by broken oaths. In his *Legend of Dido*, Chaucer shows pity, sincerity, benevolence and fidelity as the essence of true queenliness and *gentillesse* – attributes of royal strength, not weakness. This view is akin to the *Prologue*'s image of the lion whose royal nature and 'gentyl kynde' eschews vengefulness (ll. 377–85), and its contrast between the dutiful benevolence of a 'naturel' king and the selfish aggression of the money-grubbing 'fermour' (Chaucer's greedy, cynical Aeneas in the Dido legend will display the attitude more of a 'fermour' than a *gentil*).[57]

The *Legend* is not just a pretty fantasy. The period 1386–99 was dangerous and depressing for anyone close to government (Chaucer was a member of the 1386 parliament, Clerk of the King's Works from 1389 to 1391, and owed his livelihood to service to the royal household and the house of Lancaster). He saw important political figures, including earls and dukes, face financial ruin or execution for angering an increasingly arbitrary Richard II. If we believe that the arena of personal life is also a political area, then a poem such as this – an unfinished poem which seems to have continued to occupy his mind during a long period – which celebrates the jurisdiction of Love and the virtues of faithfulness, which sympathizes with those harmed by ruthless princes who cloak their lack of true noble principle under a cloak of *gentillesse*, a poem where a woman warns a monarch against unbecoming tyranny, arbitrary condemnations and behaving like a tax-gatherer, may have seemed a poem for its times as well as a text about classical lovers. In a fourteenth-century kingdom, for an artist to address its leader's *gentil* self-image had as much chance of political impact as more direct and dangerous comment. Chaucer's dictum that 'pete rennyth sone in gentil herte' (l. 491) sees no difference between the personal and the political. Patterson 1991: 237 reads the *Legend* as 'Chaucer's desire to escape from subjection to a court, and to aristocratic values generally, that are felt as increasingly tyrannical', the same tendency that led to the ambiguous tension in the *Canterbury Tales* between hierarchical design and subverting of order. Minnis 1995: 324 describes the *Legend* as a work of 'inversion, as it turns the world upside-down to present a regiment of good women and bad men', but the inversion, an attempt to empower gentleness and disparage aggression, applies beyond the world of lovers into the world of contemporary politics. In the *Legend* the political and the personal are expressed in terms of each other: the *Legend of Lucrece* compares women's fidelity in love directly with the 'tyrannye' men commit (ll. 1868–1884), presenting sexual and political 'oppressyoun' as one and the same.[58] Far from being a shallow, frivolous design, a false direction Chaucer had to reject to embark on the *Canterbury Tales*, the *Legend* was probably a work whose composition and themes continued to occupy him as he worked on his *Tales*: the *Man of Law's Prologue* suggests its design remained fluid.[59] Rather than being abandoned because it was too boring, the *Legend* may have proved too complex and paradoxical, too full of tensions.

The 'political' passage (ll. 318–401) is significant not because it makes the text a covert manifesto but because it brings momentarily closer to the surface what seem to be important aspects in Chaucer's apprehension of tenderness, passionate obsession and pain in love affairs. He always tends to apprehend such experiences with an *ethical* intensity which gives them (frequently to critical consternation) affinity to religious experience, and to the (political) principles by which powerful people should act. Chaucer's Boethian-political *balade*, 'Lak of Stedfastnesse', incorporates into a list of 'evils of the time' the characteristically Chaucerian protest 'Pite is exyled, no man is merciable' (l. 15).[60] Correspondingly, Chaucer's introduction of terms more suited to religion or advice to princes into the discourse of love in the *Prologue* is a literary joke, but not just a joke. Like its own symbol of the daisy, the *Legend of Good Women* or *Legende of Cupides Seintes* looks simple but has a rich complexity of meaning and reference. As Delany says, taking another deceptively simple image, that of the *Legend* as a 'naked text':

Chaucer ... chose a minimalism of topos (the women faithful in love) but went on to clothe this bare plot in as varied a costume as he could, producing a many-layered meditation on many things: on sex and gender, on language and nature, on philosophy and theology, on reading and writing, on hagiography and classical literature, on English intellectual life and English foreign policy.[61]

As always, Chaucer's characteristically multivalent vision of life problematizes the themes he offers us. Not only does he not come down on one side or the other of dichotomies; the way he writes shows that there are no simple dichotomies. Nature and interpretation, books and experience, love and tyranny: these are terms which turn out, in his exposition, all to interpenetrate each other paradoxically. There is no text or translation which nakedly transmits its subject-matter or is free of interpretative bias and its author's *entente*, just as there is no unmediated experience of nature. As already stated, though Chaucer's narrator turns away briefly from books, the vernal nature Chaucer depicts is a springtime formed by literary allusions. Although the God of Love, traditional representative of masculine passion, here speaks in defence of women and virtue and against misogynist authors and male lovers who betray and exploit ladies, that god is himself reproved for oppression just after he has reproved the narrator. And the *Prologue* does not come down on the side of either books or experience. Though writers have betrayed women of the past, some *aprovede* books bear true witness to their experience. Books, like lovers, betray experience, and books are faithful to experience. No wonder this writer jokes at the end of his *Legend of Phyllis* that his women readers should trust no-one but himself: 'And trusteth, as in love, no man but me'.

What may seem merely innocuously charming elements in Chaucer's prologue, like the narrator's Maytime enjoyment of Nature, can hold firm political and philosophical implications. When the narrator decides to sleep out of doors, Chaucer is evoking Golden Age associations. In his *Former Age*, a *balade* about the Golden Age of ancient peace and harmony, based loosely on a Boethian metrum, he says the innocent people of that era slept out of doors, and associates it with a society where bonds of fidelity are still observed:

Slepten this blissed folk withoute walles
On gras or leves in parfit quiete ...

Hir hertes were al oon withoute galle;
Everich of hem his feith to other kepte.   (ll. 43–4, 47–8)[62]

Chaucer links this idyllic world to a society without taxation, extravagant gourmandizing or tyrannical kingship, before Nimrod, the first tyrant, conceived the desire for power. It is a world unlike the present one:

> Allas, allas, now may men wepe and crye!
> For in oure dayes nis but covetyse,
> Doublenesse, and tresoun, and envye,
> Poyson, manslawhtre, and mordre in sondry wyse.   (ll. 60–3)[63]

These, we should note, are civil ills, not just personal or moral ones. *LGW* also contrasts an ideal world with the present: 'these olde women', the virtuous, 'trewe' women who lived 'in that tyde' (ll. 301–6), are exemplars to men in the present world, just as Alceste speaks from a purer realm to people 'in youre world' (l. 479), the poet's own world.[64] What Chaucer does, in these two very different works, the *balade* and the *Legend*, is to use antique legends to advocate the importance, for personal and political life, of the principles of kindness, generosity and 'feith'. This tends to be the solution he offers generally in his works for the ills of society as well as for the miseries of the individual.[65] It is the sanguine concluding message of both the *Wife of Bath's Tale* and the *Franklin's Tale*, yet within those of his longer narratives that proffer such a lesson, the text also reveals to the reader discordances based on disparities in power and freedom – in the *Legend* it is the greater power and autonomy of men in relation to women – which render that conclusion problematic.

Helen Phillips

1. For instance, Genius in *RR* promises a place in paradise for those who 'do the works of Nature' and help to multiply the human race; those who do not copulate will be 'excommunicated' (ll. 19475–512). He calls those who are not sexually active 'renegades', a notion to which Chaucer probably makes self-deprecating allusion in the *Prologue*, l. 401.
2. The *Prologue*, l. 265, says Chaucer had already written *Troilus and Criseyde*, and that is usually dated to c. 1385. Clanvowe, whose *Boke of Cupide* seems to echo the *Legend*, died in 1391.
3. See Lowes 1904 and 1905; Kane 1983; Cowen & Kane 1995: 124–39; and the survey in Kiser 1983: 18 n. 2.
4. See Delany 1994: 34–43.
5. Cowen & Kane 1995 analyse what they believe to be the G-scribe's own errors and then argue that the G alterations that still remain must be authorial revisions (pp. 132–3).

6. See Brusendorff 1925: 137–48, which reveals many variations in MS titles and rubrics.
7. Three MSS read 'xix', either scribal error or indication of Chaucer's changing plan.
8. The G *balade* adds Alceste. It seems impossible the list, partly biblical, partly classical, would have corresponded exactly to legends of 'trewe' women, because it includes Helen, who, even by the unconventional criteria of the *Legend*, was not a model of fidelity, and also two men, and it singles out its figures for qualities besides fidelity, like beauty. Ovid's *Remedia Amoris* (ll. 11–22), like Claudian's *Praise of Serena* (ll. 140–88), contrasted faithless Helen with faithful women like Penelope, Laodamia, Alcestis or Evadne. The Man of Law explicitly excludes Canace from Chaucer's plan (though this may be a later decision, and *Her.* treats her sympathetically). Fisher 1977: 620 cites a suggestion by Witlieb that the numbers relate to the number of women admitted to the Order of the Garter, nineteen in 1386, twenty-five by 1390.
9. Three fragments of ME translation of *RR* exist (the *Romaunt of the Rose*, *Riv.*, pp. 686–767), of which the first, at least, seems to be part of Chaucer's translation.
10. See summary of views in Kiser 1983: 18–19 n. 3.
11. In Adam of Usk's *Chronicon* (ed. Thomson 1904: 8). I am grateful to Alison McHardy for help on this and other aspects of the possible historical context for the poem.
12. McCall 1979: 178 n. 40. See Valerius Maximus, *Factorum et Dictorum Memorabilium*, IV. ch. 6, 197 (ll. 5–18); the French translation has not been published.
13. None of these possible sources looks particularly influential. Delany 1994: 108–12 discusses Bersuire and other possible sources.
14. See Phillips 1995a. Richard of Maidstone complimented Richard II by comparing his beauty to Absalom's.
15. See Shepherd 1956.
16. See, for example, Chaucer's *ABC*, l. 4. See also, on the figure of Alceste, Kolvé 1981.
17. Duffy 1988; Strohm 1992: 95–119 surveys the general theme of queens as intercessors.
18. Strohm 1992: 105–111. Here, as in many respects, the *Wife of Bath's Tale Prologue and Tale* provide parallels with *LGW*.
19. The *Pastourelle* is in Scheler's edn, I, pp. 57–60. See Wimsatt 1991: 190–3.
20. Cybele only allowed chaste women to pull her statue; when it got stuck while being brought in procession along the Tiber, Claudia pulled it to

shore with her belt (alternatively her hair), and thus the goddess vindicated her against false accusations of unchastity (*Fasti* VI, ll. 291–348; Claudian's *Praise of Serena*, ll. 15–18, 28–30). Claudia is also celebrated in Jerome's catalogue of chaste women, I, col. 41.

21.   *Symposium* 179B–180B; see O'Daly 1990: 207. See also Kiser 1983: 40–2.

22.   In Froissart, *Dits* (ed. Fourrier 1979), ll. 277–88; tr. Windeatt 1982: 145–7. The poet loves the flower which follows the sun all day and closes when it sets. She is white and pink, on a green stem, with sweet fragrance which cures love's pains. Her gold centre can raise the dead to life. She bows to the sun, symbolizing modesty. He has given her his whole heart and when far away he thinks of her and he serves her. She is his sun, his bright moon, his star guiding him in the sea, his ship, steersman, oar, mast and sail, his food and drink. She is called *marguerite*. (The marguerite poems vary in the symbolic meaning they attach to the daisy's colours, heliotropism, etc.)

23.   Froissart, *Dits* (ed. Fourrier 1979), ll. 147–53; tr. Windeatt 1982: 149–51. The poet honours and loves the daisy. She is the sovereign of goodness and beauty, weather does not harm her, each planet obeys her. She bows to the sun all day. He tells the story of Héros, whose tears for her lover were turned into daisies, whose white and red are bright even in January. Mercury at all seasons wears a chaplet of daisy because she helped him win Ceres's love. The poet wishes he could keep her somewhere where no-one else comes: he thinks no rough, unworthy person should touch her. He likes to gaze at the daisy all day, as it follows the sun, and prays to the God of Love to heal him of the wound her petals make in his heart.

24.   In Froissart, *Dits* (ed. Fourrier 1979), ll. 289–301; summary in Windeatt 1982: 147–8. The poet praises the lily, which is masculine, and the daisy, which is feminine. The daisy's red signifies modesty, her white signifies joy. He describes the daisy's crown which she hides at night to avoid violation. She worships the sun, bowing to him all through the day. Marguerite can mean a flower, a jewel, the saint or a woman's name. His marguerite symbolizes his lady (perhaps Marguerite of Flanders). Wimsatt 1991: 324 n. 27 points out that *Lis et Margeurite* associates the daisy with a pearl, as does Chaucer, *Prologue*, l. 153, and might therefore be a source.

25.   Deschamps, *Oeuvres* II, pp. 203–14; tr. Windeatt 1982: 152–5. The poet goes into woods on May morning, thinking of the daisy: her green symbolizes constancy, her white purity, her red timidity, green constancy, and gold her worthiness and unfailing purity. She follows the sun and closes at night to avoid slander or baseness. She is modest, universally beloved. He comes to a palace and sees noble young people celebrating

May and honouring their sixteen-year-old king. At the Castle of Beauty the flower tells them love must rule both prowess and riches. Vices flee and Honour instructs them. As they feast the narrator goes on his way and sees the shepherds living their simple life in contentment and criticizing the perils of life at court. The poem was perhaps written in honour of the visit of Marguerite of Boulogne to the sixteen-year-old Dauphin at the Château of Beauté, 1385.

26. For a variety of views about possible influence and dates, see Lowes 1904; Lossing 1942; Wimsatt 1991: 165–7, 324 n. 27.

27. In Speght's edition of Chaucer, 1598. See *The Floure and the Leafe*, ed. Pearsall 1962: 2–9.

28. See Deschamps, *Oeuvres* IV, ll. 257–64; *The Floure and the Leafe*, ed. Pearsall 1962: 22–9. Deschamps (c. 1340–c. 1406) refers to allegorizations of the Flower and the Leaf, and to noble women declaring allegiance to one or the other 'order' in several poems, one of which mentions Philippa, daughter of John of Gaunt, as leader of the Flower faction (p. 24).

29. The birdsnarers' sophistries, ll. 117–25; the 'eresye' of the *Rose* and *Troilus*, ll. 246–66; the 'draf of storyis', l. 312, all represent writings that rob women of their true reputation (the 'thevys dede' of misogyny, l. 455).

30. See Hunter 1987; Orpel 1993.

31. See Mann 1991: 48–55.

32. Blamires *et al.* 1993 contains a useful anthology of misogynist texts.

33. See Le Franc, ed. Piaget 1968; Fenster & Erler 1990. Le Franc's god Amours shines radiantly like the sun, like Chaucer's Love.

34. See the excellent brief account in Hopkins 1990: 32–69.

35. Ibid.: 58–69.

36. Chaucer's *Troilus* does not blame Criseyde in the misogynistic fashion of *Il Filostrato*; *Venus* changes the sex of its speaker (see Phillips 1993b). See the introduction to *Dido* in this volume on Chaucer's presentation of Dido and Aeneas.

37. The classic critical exploration of *experience* and *auctorite* is Lawlor 1968.

38. Vincent of Beauvais's *Speculum Historiale* contains accounts of many Christian saints and martyrs, as well as men and women of classical and medieval history; Chaucer mentions it in l. 307.

39. Pure speculation, but *Troilus* provides a precedent for a work of morally complex perspectives, culminating in an ascent to heaven. Additionally, Dante's *Divine Comedy* possibly provides a precedent for a structure which ends with spiritual ascent being also identified with a woman for whom the poet expresses an adoration which is partly courtly, partly ecstatic and mystical. Beatrice perhaps inspired the extravagant language

with which Alceste and the daisy are presented in the F Prologue?

40.   See Mann 1991: 5–47.

41.   On recent feminist approaches to heterosexual relationships, see Segal 1994.

42.   See Frank 1972: 189–210 on earlier dismissive criticism. Contemporary misogynist sneering can be seen in Lydgate's joke that Chaucer could not finish the work because he could not find even nineteen good women: *Fall of Princes* Prologue, ll. 330–6.

43.   See Green 1988.

44.   See Meale 1992.

45.   This differs from the suggestion in Overbeck 1967 that the references to broken pledges are bourgeois.

46.   *Testament of Cresseid*, l. 64.

47.   Schlauch 1945, though it makes assumptions that would now be questioned, is a useful short introduction; see also Nederman & Forhan 1993.

48.   Tuck 1971: 1–20 shows the importance in the period both of petitions to the king and of grants to individuals to 'farm' and receive revenues.

49.   For the later period, see Given-Wilson 1993, also Sayles 1981 and Barron 1990.

50.   The theme of the tyrant was a commonplace of medieval treatises on kingship; nevertheless, the accusation of tyranny became a kingpin of Lancastrian condemnation of Richard, but had its beginnings in the late 1380s (Given-Wilson 1993: 4–5). The items in the *Record and Process* of charges drawn up at the deposition (ibid: 169–84) include refusal to grant pardons, in contradiction of the coronation oath to rule with mercy and justice (item 9); rapacious and unjust methods of raising money (7, 14, 15, 21, 22); attacks on lords (1, 3, 4, 12, 30, etc.); lack of stability or reliability (25); claims to autonomous power above the law: the king said his laws were in his own mouth (16).

51.   See Walsingham 1866: I, 333 for Richard's oath; on Edward II's oath, see Fryde 1979: 16–19.

52.   On the Diptych see Gordon 1993: esp. 22–59. The *Lak of Stedfastnesse* ends with the subtly expressed image of the king *wedding* again his people, 'to stedfastnesse': a marriage and a pledge of mutual fidelity.

53.   See the notes on the text; 'the importance of petitions in medieval government can hardly be over-emphasised' (Tuck 1971: 4).

54.   See Walsingham 1866: I, 160 and 219 on de Vere; 223–5 on Warwick, Arundel and Gloucester; 172–4 on the Merciless Parliament (also *English Historical Documents*: 150–63).

55.   The *Record and Process* makes frequent use of the term 'liegemen' to

protest at Richard's disregard for law and subjects' rights (Given-Wilson 1993: 169–89, e.g. item 16).

56. Pier delle Vigne (c. 1190–1249), whose soul makes the accusation against Envy as harlot in Caesar's court, *Inf.* XIII, ll. 55–78, was both a politician (chancellor of Frederick II, who fell from power in 1249) and a poet.

57. For theories which have an interesting bearing on the argument here, see Hansen 1992: 1–25 on the 'feminization' of Chaucer's men, and Strohm 1992: 95–120 on the mingling of power and submissiveness in the image of the queen as intercessor.

58. Lucretia's story had, of course, from Livy on, been specifically linked to the issue of kings and tyrants.

59. Affinities can be seen between *LGW* and *WB Prol* and *T*, *Phys T* and *MLT* particularly.

60. One MS has an envoy addressing it to Richard II: perhaps an indication of Chaucer's readiness to recycle his works, and also their multivalency. Scattergood 1995: 490–1 plausibly suggests a political context around 1386–7 for the version with the envoy.

61. Delany 1994: 2. His speculations about 'orientalist' attitudes in the legends propose links with English foreign policy.

62. Boethius, *Cons.* II., met. 5, l. 10: 'Grass gave then wholesome slumbers'. Chaucer adds the themes of bygone safety and fidelity. The previous prose, talking of the inability of riches and grandeur to give lasting happiness, contrasts pleasure in fields, spring flowers and beautiful natural scenes.

63. Nimrod (Gen. 10:8–12) was believed to have built Babel (Gen. 11). Boethius's conclusion contrasted the Golden Age with later ages' riches and avarice, whereas Chaucer alters the reference to social aggression: 'If only those ancient manners would return to our times ... Alas, who was he who first dug up the expensive perils, the heavy weights of gold covered over with earth, and jewels that wanted to lie hidden?', *Cons.* II, met. 5, ll. 23, 27–30. The most recent critic to tie the *balade* firmly to contemporary political anxieties is J. Scattergood, in Minnis 1995: 489.

64. They seem to belong to that world described at the beginning of *BD*, the era when men 'loved the lawe of Kynde' (l. 56).

65. It is, of course, an essentially conservative solution, since it proposes personal rather than structural change as the key to resolving oppression, discontent and conflict.

THE *PROLOGUE* TO THE *LEGEND OF GOOD WOMEN*

	A thous[and] sythis have I herd men telle	*times*
	That there is joye in hevene and peyne in helle,	
	And I acorde wel that it be so.	*agree; it is so*
	But natheles, [yit] w[o]t I wel also,	*nevertheless; know*
5	That there ne is non that dwellyth in this cuntre	*no-one*
	That eythir hath in helle or hevene ibe,	*been*
	Ne may of it non othere weyis wytyn	
	But as he hath herd seyd or founde it wrytyn.	*according as*
	For by asay there may no man it preve.	*can no-one*

title: no title in G.

1–16. These lines set up a polarity central to *LGW*: between experience and reports of it, i.e. experience and the world of signs or literature; this preface problematizes that polarity.

1–2. Introduces themes of religion and the question of sources of reliable knowledge; also the issue of reliance on other people's statements, which will recur in several forms, e.g. the question of the responsibility of the poet as translator, ll. 340–50. Le Fèvre's *Leësce* also begins its defence of women with themes of truth and literature, alluding to conflict between Alithia (scriptural truth) and Pseustis (literary 'fable') from Theodulus's *Ecloga*. Froissart, *Joli buisson de jeunesse*, ll. 786–96 (ed. Fourrier 1975), contrasts disbelief in a fountain of Youth or stones of invisibility: he has heard of them but never seen them, with his faith in the resurrection which the gospels describe.

6–8. Hell and heaven, man's salvation and the scriptures, may seem odd topics to introduce, but the text is full of echoes of contemporary (Wycliffite) controversies about texts of scripture and their importance in matters of faith – another aspect of the theme of fidelity (see e.g. ll. 81–8, 250–7).

7. 'Nor can come to know it by any other means'.

8. Literature was performed orally as well as read: *herd seyd* can refer to literature as much as *wrytyn* does. It does not just mean talking.

9. *asay*: 'testing' (i.e. finding out by experience); *preve*: to prove through practical experience or testing. This line might seem to attack the value of experiential knowledge, but it must be read in context; it does not deny the value of experience *per se* but takes an example, salvation, where scripture is the pre-eminent source for belief, in preparation for Ch's claim (l. 20) that certain books can record truth. Cf. ll. 27–8.

306

10	But God forbode but men schulde leve	*believe*
	Wel more thyng than men [hath] seyn with eye!	
	Men schal nat wenyn everythyng a lye	
	For that he say it nat of yore ago.	
	God wot, a thyng is nevere the lesse so	
15	Thow every wyght ne may it nat ise.	
	Bernard the monk ne say nat al, parde.	*saw; everything*
	Thanne motyn we to bokys that we fynde,	
	Thurow whiche that olde thyngis ben in mynde,	
	And to the doctryne of these olde wyse	
20	Yevyn credence, in every skylful wyse,	
	And trowyn on these olde aprovede storyis	
	Of holynesse, of regnys, of victoryis,	*kingdoms*

10–11. 'But God forbade people not to believe far more than anyone has seen with his eye'. This gives a further religious dimension to the experience/truth issue: see John 20:29: 'blessed are they that have not seen and yet have believed'; Heb. 11:1: 'faith is ... the evidence of things not seen'. *Men* has an indefinite sense: 'people', 'anyone'.

12–13. 'A person should not suppose everything a lie because he himself did not see it a long time ago'. Ch associates the *preve* of experience (see l. 28) with the past, because his heroines' fidelity will be hidden in history and misrepresented by some later writers.

15. *wyght*: 'creature', 'person'; *may it nat ise*: 'cannot perceive it'.

16. *Bernard the monk*: probably Bernard of Clairvaux (1091–1153), founder of the Cistercian order. Like all mysticism, his contemplative works claim direct knowledge of divine truth. His *Sermons on the Song of Songs* explore the themes of the spiritual Bride and Bridegroom. Perhaps Ch alludes to Bernard's role in *Par.* XXXII–XXXIII, where he shows the narrator Beatrice (an analogue and perhaps source for Alceste) enthroned and a vision of the Virgin in heavenly glory. Perhaps it is a proverb; a Latin translation, *Bernardus non vidit omnia*, appears in MS margin. *parde*: from Fr. *par Dieu*, 'by God', used as mildly emphatic. Would contemporary readers feel a slight satirical edge to the protest that *monks* do not necessarily see everything, in the context of lines like 254?

17. 'Then we must turn to the books we can find'. ME can omit a verb of motion (here *to go* or *to turn*) if the sense is clear.

18–21. 'Through which old things are kept in memory, and give our belief to the teaching of these wise people of old, in every reasonable respect, and trust these ancient histories, proved to be reliable'; *aprovede*: 'proven', confirmed by experience to be trustworthy; Ch's word plays paradoxically on *preve*.

	Of love, of hate, of othere sundery thyngis,	*varied subjects*
	Of whiche I may nat make rehersyngys.	*cannot; repetition*
25	And if that olde bokis weryn aweye,	*were gone*
	Iloryn were of remembrance the keye.	
	Wel oughte us thanne on olde bokys leve,	*then; believe*
	Thereas there is non othyr asay be preve.	
	And, as for me, thow that my wit be lite,	
30	On bokys for to rede I me delyte	*delight*
	And in myn herte have hem in reverence,	*hold them*
	And to hem yeve swich lust and swich credence,	*such pleasure*
	That there is wel onethe game non	
	That from my bokys make me to gon,	*might make*
35	But it be other upon the halyday	*unless; either*
	Or ellis in the joly tyme of May,	*else; splendid*
	Whan that I here the smale foulys synge	*little birds*
	And that the flouris gynne for to sprynge –	*begin to spring*
	Farwel my stodye, as lastynge that sesoun!	*studying*
40	Now have I therto this condycyoun,	
	That of alle the flouris in the mede	*meadow*
	Thanne love I most these flourys white and rede,	*then; red*
	Swyche as men calle dayesyis in oure toun.	*such*
	To hem have I so gret affeccioun,	*them; inclination*
45	As I seyde erst, whan comyn is the May,	*earlier; come*
	That in my bed there dawith me no day	*dawns for me*

26. *Iloryn were*: 'would be lost'. Books can unlock otherwise inaccessible past experience.
28–30. 'In cases where there is no alternative proof through experience. And, as for me, although my understanding is slight, I delight in reading books'. For Ch's familiar pose of 'remote but ineffectual bookish little man', see Lawlor 1968: 96.
33. 'That there is certainly scarcely any amusement'.
39. *as lastynge*: 'for the duration of'.
40. 'Now also it is a habit of mine'.
42–95. On echoes of the French marguerite poems, see pp. 285–7.
42. Chaucer refers to the kind of daisies that have rosy tips and undersides to the white petals: the detail links the flower with a traditional formula for describing female beauty – white and red (on red and white, see p. 285). References to May, the traditional time for love in medieval poetry, and *love* (l. 42) further this lexical set. Cf. Froissart's *balade* with the refrain 'Sur toutes fleurs j'aimme la marguerite', *Paradis d'Amours*, ll. 1627–53.

That I ne am up and walkynge in the mede,   *am not*
To sen th[i]s flour agen the sunne sprede,
Whan it upryseth be the morwe schene,
50   The longe day thus walkynge in the grene.   *on the grass*
And whan the sunne begynny[th] for to
          weste,   *decline westwards*
Thanne closeth it and drawith it to reste,
So sore it is aferid of the nyght,
Til on the morwe that it is dayis lyght.   *when it is daylight*
55   This dayeseye, of alle flouris flour,   *flower of all flowers*
Fulfyld of vertu and of alle honour,   *filled with virtue*
And evere ilike fayr and frosch of hewe,
As wel in wyntyr as in somyr newe,   *new just as much*
Fayn wolde I preysyn, if I coude aryht.
60   But wo is me, it lyth nat in my myght,   *alas, it lies*
For wel I wot that folk han, herebeforn,   *have, before now*
Of makynge ropyn and lad awey the corn.

48–9. 'To see this flower open up towards the sun, when it rises in the bright morning'.
50. Replaces F ll. 50–60, which describe the narrator's intense 'reverence' and love for the daisy. This looks like an empty replacement line, following the theme of l. 47 rather than fitting well with the preceding l. 49.
52–3. 'Then it closes and retreats to its rest, so terribly afraid it is of the night'.
55. *of alle flouris flour*: a Marian image or merely an imitation of a French marguerite poem, Froissart's *Dittié de la marguerite*, l. 2. See p. 285.
56. *vertu*; *honour*: the diction associating the daisy with human attributes, up to now feminine beauty, now includes ethical and spiritual symbolism.
58. 'And ever beautiful in the same way and fresh in colour'; cf. Froissart, *Paradis d'Amours*, ll. 1636–9, *Dittié*, ll. 96–8. The unchanging flower suggests the theme of constancy.
59. 'I would gladly like to praise if I knew how'; *Fayn*: 'gladly'; *coude*: 'knew how to'.
59–70. A complex passage begins here which presents the narrator's literary enterprise (poetry praising the daisy) as both new and part of tradition; images of freshness and oldness are interwoven, often paradoxically.
62. 'Have reaped poetry and carried away the corn'. ME *makynge* often = 'poetry' (from the Gk *poiesis* = 'making'); perhaps it refers specifically to vernacular composition (Kiser 1983: 136). The metaphor of corn from fields for poets' creation of literature out of language and tradition ('old fields') occurs also in *PF*, ll. 22–5. On the corn/literature imagery, see Martin 1991.

I come aftyr, glenynge here and ther,   *gleaning*
And am ful glad if I may fynde an er   *can find; ear*
65   Of ony goodly word that they han laft.   *any; have left*
And [thow] it happe me reherse eft
That they han in here frosche songis said,
I hope that they wele nat ben evele apayed;
Sithe it is seyd in fortheryng and honour   *since; promotion*
70   Of hem that eythir servyn lef or flour.   *them; serve either*
          For trustyth wel, I ne have nat undyrtake
As of the lef agayn the flour to make,
Ne of the flour to make ageyn the lef –
No more than of the corn agen the shef.
75   For, as to me, is lefere non ne lothere:
I am witholde yit with never nothire.
I not [w]ho servyth lef ne who the flour: *do not know*

64. *er*: perhaps a pun: a metaphorical ear of poetic corn and a listening audience.

66–7. 'And even if it should happen to me that I tell again subsequently stories that they have narrated in their unfading songs'. *frosche* = 'lovely', 'gay', 'unfaded', 'new': continuing the contrasts of old and new, tradition and nature, and linking with the lexical sets of feminine beauty and bountiful fields. Is it a reference to the marguerite poets or to writers about Ch's heroines, like Virgil and Ovid, or more general: to the eternal newness of old texts?

68. *evele apayed*: 'dissatisfied', 'displeased'. A hint that, despite apparent deference, Ch's versions of the legends may go against some earlier poets' versions?

70. I.e. he writes as the servant of *all* lovers, a motif found also in *TC* I, l. 15; III, l. 41.

71–4. 'For trust me completely: I have not undertaken this as someone setting out to write on behalf of the leaf against the flower, nor on behalf of the flower against the leaf – any more than for the corn against the sheaf'; *trustyth*: a plural command, to readers or audience. Picking up the corn metaphor, Chaucer implies that, just as sheaf and corn are the same substance, he does not see pleasure and virtue ('Flower' and 'Leaf') as separable, conflicting values. On Flower and Leaf, see p. 287.

75–6. 'For to me neither of them is better or worse; up to now, I have not yet been taken on as a retainer of either of them'. Quasi-feudal imagery of service to lord or lady is common in love poetry; here it strengthens the pose of the passive narrator.

That nys nothyng the entent of my labour,
For this werk is al of anothyr tunne,
80   Of old story, er swich strif was begunne.   *before such conflict*
        But wherfore that I spak – to yeve credence
    To bokys olde and don hem reverence –
    Is for men schulde autoriteis beleve,   *in order that*
    Thereas there lyth non othyr asay be preve.
85   For myn entent is, or I fro yow fare,   *before; depart*
    The nakede tixt in Englis to declare
    Of manye a story or ellis of manye a geste,   *else; history*
    As autourys seyn (and levyth hem if yow leste).
        Whan passed was almost the monyth of May,
90   And I hadde romed al the somerys day   *roamed; summer's*
    The grene medewe of which that I yow tolde,
    Upon the frosche dayseie to beholde,   *to look upon*
    And that the sonne out of the sou[th] gan   *when;*
        weste   *to sink westwards*
    And clo[s]ede was the flour and gon to reste,   *gone to his rest*
95   For derknesse of the nyht, of which sche dradde,   *was afraid*
    Hom to my hous ful swiftly I me spadde,   *I sped*

78. 'That is not at all the intention of my work'. The 'penance' theme of the poet's good or bad intention recurs at ll. 340–52.

79. *of anothyr tunne*: 'out of a different barrel', i.e. of a quite different kind.

81–2. 'But the reason for what I said, about trusting in ancient books and giving them reverence'. G here omits praise (F ll. 83–96) of the daisy as the narrator's 'lady sovereyn' and 'erthly god'.

83. *autoriteis*: revered works of ancient literature. ME *au[c]torite* means both 'authors' and the authority books have, especially classical and learned books, sometimes contrasted with the evidence of experience (Lawlor 1968; Minnis 1995: 227–51).

84. 'In cases where there exists ('lies') no other proof from experience'.

86. 'To reveal the plain narrative in English'. *nakede tixt* (a concept unique to G): narrative without glosses, here tales without the interpretations imposed by earlier writers; *declare*: has legal associations, 'to establish publically', 'explain', 'narrate'. On possible echoes of Wycliffite advocacy of plain scripture, in English, without the Church's exegetical glosses, see Delany 1994: 119–23; Desmond 1994: 152–5. Ch provocatively claims his own narratives will have no slant, impose no *sens* on his *matière*.

87–8. *story, geste*: 'historical writings'; *autourys*: 'learned Latin writers'.

88. 'As learned authors tell (and believe them if you please)'.

	And in a lytyl erber that I have,	*garden*
	Ibenchede newe with turwis frosche igrawe,	
	I bad men schulde me my couche make.	
100	For deynte of the newe somerys sake,	*in honour*
	I bad hem strowe flouris on my bed.	*to strew*
	Whan I was layd and hadde myn eyen hid,	*hidden my eyes*
	I fel aslepe withinne an our or two.	*hour*
	Me mette how I was in the medewe tho,	*I dreamed; then*
105	And that I romede in that same gyse	*fashion*
	To sen that flour, as ye han herd devyse.	*heard described*
	Fayr was this medewe, as thoughte me, overal;	
	With flouris sote enbroudit was it al.	*sweet; embroidered*
	As for to speke of gomme or erbe or tre,	
110	Comparisoun may non imakede be,	
	For it surmountede pleynly alle odours	*surpassed fully*
	And of ryche beute alle flourys.	*in rich beauty*
	Forgetyn hadde the erthe his pore estat	*forgotten*
	Of wyntyr, that hym nakede made and mat,	*defeated*
115	And with his swerd of cold so sore hadde grevyd.	*bitterly hurt*
	Now hadde the [a]tempre sonne al that relevyd	*gentle; relieved*
	And clothede hym in grene al newe ageyn.	*newly*
	The smale foulis, of the seson fayn,	*glad at*

98. *Ibenchede*: 'provided with benches'; *turwis frosche igrawe*: 'turves freshly cut' (the *w* stands for a *v*): presumably squares of turf. This describes the practice of raising benches, made of earth and covered with turf, against garden walls or fences or between beds, where in hot weather people could sit or lie. On Golden Age connotations, see pp. 299–300.

99. 'I asked people [i.e. servants] to make up my bed for me'.

102. The narrator is 'hiding' his eyes just as the daisy hides her sun-like 'day's eye' with her petals at night. The sun-eye complex continues at ll. 163–5 (see Kiser 1983: 28–49).

104. In F the dream occurs later and does not end with the Prologue.

107. 'This meadow was beautiful everywhere, it seemed to me'.

109–10. 'And if we are speaking about balsam, plant or tree, no comparison can be made'. *gomme*: gum, i.e. aromatic sap or balsam emanating from the trees; *erbe*: plant.

110–18. This is the classic, paradise-like garden of love visions: see *RR*, ll. 1315–1414, 199970–20006; *BD*, ll. 398–443; *PF*, ll. 171–210. Balsam and fragrances add typical exotic, eastern touches.

113. *pore estat*: state of poverty. Cf. *BD*, ll. 410–15 & n.

	That from the panter and the net ben skapid,	*rope; are escaped*
120	Upon the foulere, that hem made awapid	
	In wyntyr and distroyed hadde hire brod,	
	In his dispit, hem thoughte it dede hem good	
	To synge of hym, and in here song despise	*despise in their song*
	The foule cherl that, for his coveytyse,	*hateful peasant; greed*
125	Hadde hem betrayed with his sophistrye.	
	This was here song: 'The foulere we defye.'	*their*
	Some songyn on the braunchis clere	*sang*
	[Layes] of love, that joye it was to here,	*songs; so that*
	In worschepe and in preysyng of hire make	*honour; mate*
130	And of the newe blysful somerys sake.	
	Th[ey] sungyn 'Blyssede be Seynt Volentyn,	*sang; blessed*

120–1. They compose (l. 123) a contemptuous song 'against the birdsnarer, who had made them terrified in winter and had destroyed their brood of young'. Birds were caught for fresh meat in winter. Their spring song has the newness of defences of women springing up after the long tradition of misogynist tradition.

122. 'In contempt of him, it seemed to them it did them good'.

124. *cherl* implies social and moral lowness: *cherls'* stereotyped avarice and hardheartedness are the opposite of stereotypical *gentil* qualities like generosity and pity. See Burnley 1979: 164–5.

125. Sophistry is the use of subtle academic logic to create arguments that are apparently sound but in fact are deceptive or empty of moral significance. It is an amusing metaphor for fowlers' devices to lure and trap birds, doubly witty because sometimes university 'sophistry' was compared to bird-catchers' tricks. Do these deceptions prefigure the deceptions practised by men to control women, either as wooers or misogynist writers? See *RR*, ll. 21467–70; Kiser 1983: 63–6; Delany 1994: 75–82.

126. Did Ch mean to insert the song's whole text here?

128–38. The MS is clearly corrupt in places. See Kane 1983: 54–6 and the Notes on the Text, p. 338.

130. 'And in celebration of the new joyful summer'.

131. *Volentyn*: St Valentine, Roman martyr whose feast day, 14 Feb., was believed to be when birds mate. Some 14th-century poems, incl. *PF* (see ll. 309, 322, 386–92, 683) and *Mars*, may have been written for celebrations of St Valentine's Day.

[For] at his day I ches yow to be myn,   *chose*
Withoute repentynge, myn herte swete'.   *without regrets*
And therwithal here bekys gunne mete,
135   [Yeldyng] honour and humble obeysaunce,   *giving*
And after dedyn othere observaunc[e],   *they did; ritual*
Ryht [longyng] onto Love and to Nature,   *properly belonging*
[That formed] eche of hem to cryatur[e].
This song to herkenyn I dede al myn entent,
140   Forwhy I mette I wiste what they ment.   *Because I dreamed*
         Tyl at the laste a larke song above: *sang*
'I se,' quod she, 'the myghty God of Love!   *see; said*
Lo, yond he comyth. I se hise wyngis   *there he comes;*
   sprede.'   *outstretched*
Tho gan I loke endelong the mede   *across*
145   And saw hym come, and in his hond a quene,
Clothid in ryal abyte, al of grene.   *royal array, entirely*
A frette of goold sche hadde next hyre her,   *over her hair*
And upon that a whit corone sche ber,   *on top of; bore*
With flour[ouns smale] – and I schal nat lye,   *if*

132–3. *repentynge*: can have a sense of 'regrets' or 'change of mind'; Ch echoes real Valentine lyrics like Oton de Granson's 'Je vous choisy, noble loyal amour' (in idem, ed. Piaget 1941: 226–7). The birds' unchanging love prefigures the poem's theme of human fidelity, cf. *Mars*, ll. 15–22.

134. 'At that their beaks then met'.

135–6. *obeysaunce*: expression of respect and obedience; *observaunce*: performance of a ritual or duty in accordance with rules. In *Sq T*, l. 516, *observaunces* (with the same rhyme) are signs of the chaste *gentillesse of love*. The description of mating (presumably) as *observaunces* may sound coy or sniggering to the modern reader, but the divine office vested in Nature makes birds' mating a quasi-holy, exemplary obedience to the Creator's plan.

138. 'Who formed each of them as a created being'. This emendation assumes an original line resembling *BD*, l. 716.

139–40. 'I gave all my attention to listening to this song, because I dreamed that I understood what they meant'.

145. As they advance, Love is holding the queen by the hand. They may resemble Richard II and Anne of Bohemia (see pp. 294–5 and Rowe 1988: 4–7, 162).

147. *frette*: band or net worn over hair. Ornamental hair-nets were fashionable.

149–51. 'With many flourons, as I speak true, just exactly as the daisy is crowned with small white petals'. *flourons*: petals or ornamental motifs shaped like

150	For al the world, riht as the dayseye	*exactly as*
	Icorounede is with white levys lite.	*crowned; petals*
	Swiche were the flour[ouns]s of her corene white.	*Just like that*
	For of o perle fyn oryental	*one; fine*
	Hyre white coroun was imakyd al.	*constructed entirely*
155	For whiche the white coroun, above the grene,	*In consequence,*
	Made hire lyk a dayseye for to sene,	*to appear like*
	Considerede ek the fret of gold above.	
	Iclothede was this myhty God of Love	*dressed*
	[In] silk, ibroudede ful of grene grevys,	*embroidered; sprigs*
160	A garlond on his hed of rose levys,	*petals*
	Stekid al with lylye flourys newe.	*alternating with*
	But of his face I can not seyn the hewe,	*describe the complexion*
	For sekyrly his face schon so bryhte	*certainly*
	That with the glem astonede was the syhte:	
165	A furlongwey I myhte hym not beholde,	
	But at the laste in hande I saw hym holde	*finally*
	[Two] fery dartis, as the gleedys rede,	*as red as coals*
	And aungellych hyse wengis gan he sprede.	*like an angel; wings*

petals or fleurs-de-lis or petals. Rob.'s n. suggests Ch knew this rare word from Froissart, *Dittié*, ll. 166, 187, where it means the daisy's petals raised to the sun, and the petals which pierce his heart like a dart.

154. On the association of pearls with daisies, see pp. 286–7. Sk.'s n. explains that *oriental* was used of specially fine gems.

157. 'Taking into consideration also the net of gold on her head'.

159–61. Roses and lilies symbolize female beauty, or martyrdom and purity, or passion and chastity in harmony. Heraldically, the rose = England, the lily = France, to which English kings laid claim (Rob.'s n. on F l. 161). In F the God is crowned with the sun – like the rose, a motif associated with Richard II. Rosemary sprigs were Q. Anne's badge.

164. 'So that eyesight was dazzled by the radiance'. Faces which gleamed with light, dazzling sight, symbolize divinity or divine grace; God, Mary, angels and Moses are on occasion so described by the Bible and medieval writers. Gilded faces or masks were used in mystery plays (Twycross 1990).

165. *A furlongwey*: 'for two or three minutes'. The idiom is derived from the length of time it takes to walk a furlong (one-eighth of a mile).

167. From his first appearance, the God of Love induces fear in the narrator (see also ll. 172–3).

	And al be that men seyn that blynd is he,	*although men say*
170	Algate me thoughte he myghte wel ise.	*all the same*
	For sternely on me he gan beholde,	*began to glare*
	So that his lokynge doth myn herte colde.	*made; grow cold*
	And be the hond he held the noble quene,	
	Corouned with whit and clothede al in grene,	
175	So womanly, so benygne and so meke,	*gentle*
	That in this world, thow that men wolde seke,	*even though*
	Half hire beute schulde men nat fynde	*beauty; would*
	In on cryature that formede is be Kynde.	*one; by Nature*
	Hire name was Alceste the [d]ebon[a]yre.	*gracious*
180	I preye to God that evere falle [hire] fayre,	
	For, ne hadde confort been of hire presense,	
	I hadde be ded, withoutyn ony defence,	*would have been*
	For dred of Lovys wordys and his chere,	*expression*
	As, whan tyme is, hereaftyr ye schal here.	
185	Byhynde this God of Love, upon this grene,	
	I saw comynge of ladyis nynetene,	
	In ryal abyte, a ful esy pas.	
	And aftyr hem come of wemen swich a tras	*throng*

169–70. 'And though it may be that people say he is blind, nonetheless it seemed to me he could see well'. On the classical motif of blind Cupid, see Panofsky 1939: 110–1282. Cf. *PF*, ll. 1–14 on the dazed sense of intimidation at the God of Love's power.

175. ME *womanly*, *womanhede*, are positive terms, connoting the virtues of women.

176. 'That in this world, even though men might wish to seek'.

178. 'In one single being who is created by Nature'.

180–1. 'I pray to God that good may ever befall her, for had there not been comfort from her presence'. If Ch originally intended Alceste as a compliment to Queen Anne, and the G Prologue is after her death, then either he is indirectly praying for her soul, or Alceste here has become a more general figure of moral authority. The juxtaposition of the God's condemnation and Alceste's kindness in G expresses the theme of justice and mercy.

187. 'In royal dress, with calm step'. These ladies may be the heroines of the ensuing legends, which Ch does not seem to have finalized: three *CT* MSS call *LGW* 'the book of the XIX ladies' (others have XXV). See Minnis 1995: 326–7.

That, syn that God Adam [hadde] made of erthe,   *since God*
190   The,thredde part of wemen ne the ferthe
    Ne wende I not by possibilite
    Haddyn evere in this [wyde] world ibe.
    And trewe of love these wemen were echon.   *faithful*; *each one*
        Now whether was that a wondyr thyng or non,   *marvel*
195   That, ryht anon as that they gunne espye   *as soon as they saw*
    This flour whiche that I clepe the dayseye,   *call*
    Ful sodeynly they styntyn alle atonys   *stopped all at once*
    And knelede adoun, as it were for the nonys.
    And aftyr that they wentyn in cumpas,   *circle*
200   Daunsynge aboute this flour an esy pas,   *with calm step*
    And songyn, as it were in carole wyse,
    This balade, whiche that I schal yow devyse.   *describe*

    'Hyd, Absalon, thy gilte tressis clere;   *bright golden tresses*

189–91. 'That I do not think it possible that all the women who had ever existed in this world, ever since God made Adam of earth, would make up more than a third or quarter of them'. Does the throng include women of the future as well as the past? If the 19 are his heroines, Ch is stressing that the number of faithful women is not that limited. God made Adam from dust and Eve from Adam's rib (Gen 2:18–22) – a famous topos, because used by both anti-feminists and pro-feminists, to argue that woman was either inferior or superior to man (Blamires *et al.* 1993: 79, 86, 145, 284).

195. By the norms of modern idiom, both *thats* in this line are redundant: 'immediately, as soon as they caught sight of'.

198. 'And knelt down, apparently because of that event' (i.e. seeing the daisy).

201–2. *in carole wyse*: 'in the style of a *carole*', a circular dance accompanied by a song with a refrain; *balade*: a Fr. lyric form, often three stanzas with refrain, introduced by Ch into English.

203–23. Perhaps inspired by *balades* by Thomas Paien, Machaut (*Voir-Dit*, ll. 6753–800), and Froissart's sixth *balade*; see Wimsatt 1991: 181–4, Phillips 1995a. Its main motif – that Alceste surpasses legendary figures famous for a virtue – occurs in Claudian, *Praise of Serena* (Phillips 1995a: 142). Ch's 'catalogue *balade*' reflects Jerome's catalogue in *Against Jovinian* and the series of heroines in Ovid's *Heroides*.

203. Paien's *balade* begins *Ne quier veoir la biauté d'Absalon*, 'I do not seek to gaze at the beauty of Absalom'; after listing other heroes, the refrain is 'I see enough when I see my lady'; *RR*, l. 13845, refers to Absalom's golden hair

Ester, ley thow thy meknesse al adoun;   *lay down*
205   Hyde, Jonathas, al thy frendely manere;
Penolope and Marcia Catoun,
Mak of youre wyfhod no comparisoun;   *wifely virtue*
Hyde ye youre beuteis, Ysoude and Elene.   *beauties*
Alceste is here that al that may destene.   *can make dim*

210   Thy fayre body lat it nat apeere,
Laveyne, and thow Lucresse of Rome toun,

(see 2 Sam. 13–19). His beauty and Jonathan's friendliness occur in *Ubi Sunt* texts: see Shepherd 1956.

204. Esther, heroine of the apocryphal Book of Esther, Jewish queen of Ahasuerus, saved her people from persecution. In medieval literature she is the type of the perfect queen: meek, kind, and wise in advice; she is praised for *debonairyete* in *BD*, ll. 986–7, meekness in *Merch T* IV, ll. 1744–5. See Strohm 1992: 97–9.

205. Jonathan, son of King Saul, devoted friend of David (1 Sam. 17–20): type of ideal friendship.

206–7. *Penelope*: the loyal wife of Ulysses, she waited for the ten years it took him to return from the (ten-year-long) war of Troy, refusing to remarry. Like Lucretia and Griselda, she is often cited as a perfect wife in late medieval and Renaissance literature: see *Her.* V; Jerome, *Against Jovinian*, I, col. 45; Claudian, *Serena*, ll. 25–8. *Marcia*: wife of Cato, agreed to be divorced from him and marry his friend, then remarried Cato. Listed by Jerome in *Against Jovinian* I, col. 46. Dante, in *Purg.* I, ll. 78–90, and *Conv.* IV, l. 28, takes Marcia, like Piramus and Thisbe, as a symbol of the soul's search for God. *Catoun*: Jerome and Ch confuse Marcia with Marcia Catonis (= 'of Cato'), Cato's chaste and devoted daughter. *wyfhod*: Marcia wants above all the title 'wife of Cato' on her tomb (Lucan, *Pharsalia* II, ll. 342–4).

208. Two tragic, adulterous loves: *Ysoude*: heroine of Arthurian romances. After innocently drinking a love-potion, she and Tristan, nephew of her husband King Mark, fell into an irresistible love affair; *Elene*: Venus promised Paris, a Trojan prince, the world's most beautiful woman; he eloped with Helen, wife of the Spartan King Agamemnon, causing the Trojan War.

209. The *balades* by Paien, Machaut and Froissart have the refrain 'I see enough when I see my lady'; the F refrain is 'My lady cometh ...'. G is here more Alceste-centred.

210–12. *Laveyne ... Lucresse ... Pollexene*: Lavinia and Polyxena were known to medieval readers more from their romantic roles in romances like the *Roman de Troie* or *Roman d'Éneas* than their part in classical sources.

      And Pollexene, that boughte love so dere;   *paid so dearly*
      Ek Cleopatre, with al thy passioun,
      Hide ye youre trouth in love and youre renoun;   *fidelity*
215   And thow Tysbe, that hast for love swich peyne.   *pain*
      Alceste is here that al that may desteyne.

      Herro, Dido, Laodomya, alle in fere,   *in companionship*
      Ek Phillis, hangynge for thy Demophoun,   *also*

Lavinia, a Latian princess, falls in love with Aeneas and shows herself to
him (*Éneas*, ll. 8890–99, 9230–52). Lucretia, the chaste Roman wife of
Tarquinius Collatinus (6th century BC), committed suicide after being raped
by Sextus Tarquinius (Livy I 57–9; Claudian, *Serena*, ll. 153–5; Jerome,
Against Jovinian I, col. 45; *RR*, ll. 8608–42). Polyxena, a Trojan princess,
loved the Greek Achilles (*Roman de Troie*, ll. 5521–57, 17489–18472,
26471–590); her family killed him and executed her over his tomb.

213.   Cleopatra (69–30 BC), Queen of Egypt, loved Mark Antony and followed
       him in committing suicide. Ch's Legend of Cleopatra is sympathetic, though
       some medieval writers presented her negatively: see Kolvé 1981: 130–78,
       who finds Ch's handling ironic. *passioun*: like *lyf* and *legend*, meant a
       saint's life, especially one who was martyred. ME *passioun* usually meant
       'suffering' or 'endurance', though the usual sense of modern English may
       also be present.

215.   *swich peyne*: Thisbe killed herself with a sword after Piramus's death. Their
       tragic love was well known to medieval readers: *peyne* probably recalls the
       12th-century *Piramus et Tisbé*, incorporated into *Ovide moralisé*: the theme
       of pain (metaphorical wounds of love, literal wounding of the lovers)
       dominates this erotic and sensational poem, filled with plangent lyric
       laments.

217.   *Herro*: Hero loved Leander, who swam the Hellespont every night to be
       with her; after he drowned she killed herself (*Her.* XVIII, XIX; Machaut,
       Navarre, ll. 3221–310); *Dido*: Queen of Carthage, killed herself after
       Aeneas deserted her (*Aen.* I–IV; *Her.* VII); *Laodomya*: Laodamia killed
       herself after her husband Protesilaus failed to return from the Trojan War
       (*Her.* XIII; Jerome, *Against Jovinian* I, col. 45; Claudian, *Serena*, ll. 150–1).

218.   Phyllis, a Thracian princess, killed herself when her lover Demophon failed
       to return on time from Athens (*Her.* II); *RR*, ll. 13211–14 says she hanged
       herself.

	And Canace, espied be thy chere,	*recognized; face*
220	Ysiphile, bytrayed with Jasoun:	*by*
	Mak of youre trouthe in love no bost ne soun.	*boast or noise*
	Nor Ypermystre or Adriane ne pleyne.	*do not mourn*
	Alceste is here that al that may disteyne.'	
	Whan that this balade al isongyn was,	*sung*
225	Upon the softe, sote, [smale] gras	*sweet, fine*
	They settyn hem ful softely adoun,	*sat*
	By ordere alle, in cumpas inveroun.	
	Fyrst sat the God of Love, and thanne this queene	*then*
	With the white corone, clad in grene,	
230	And sithyn al the remenant, by and by,	
	As they were of degre ful curteysly.	
	Ne nat a word was spokyn in th[e] place,	*nor*
	The mountaunce of a furlongwey of space.	

219. Canace, daughter of the wind-god Aeolus, loved her brother and was killed by her father. *MLT* II, ll. 78–9, insists that Ch did not write about this incestuous love; perhaps he changed his mind about including her among his 'trewe' heroines, though Ovid (*Her.* XI) treats her compassionately and Gower tells her tale in *CA* III, ll. 147–360. *espied ... thy chere*: Ovid focuses on her paleness, blushing and other tell-tale signs of anguish, when in love and when her crime is discovered. She is a pathetic innocent who seems to express her feelings only through silent facial signs. Ch obviously noticed this Ovidian device.

220. Hypsipyle, Queen of Lemnos, was abandoned, like Medea, by Jason (*Her.* VI).

222. *Ypermystre*: Hypermnestra's father ordered his daughters to slay their bridegrooms on their wedding night; she saved her husband but was killed by her father (*Her.* XIV); *Adriane*: Ariadne helped Theseus kill the Minotaur and escape, but he abandoned her on Naxos (Dionysus rescued her) (*Her.* X).

225. Rather than G's *grene*, Kane 1983 suggests *smale*, as in some other MSS, which would make ll. 224–6 onomatopoeic.

227. 'In order of rank, everyone in a circle, all around'.

230–1. 'And after that all the rest, one by one, according to their rank, with full courtly decorum'.

233. 'For as much as several minutes'. See note on l. 165, above.

I, lenynge faste by, undyr a bente,

235 Abod to knowe what this peple mente,   *waited to find out*

As stille as ony ston, til, at the laste,   *any stone*

The God of Love on me his eye caste,

And seyde, '[W]ho restith there?' And I answerde *who is waiting*

Unto his axsynge, whan that I [it] herde,   *question*

240 And seyde, 'Sere, it am I', and cam hym ner,   *Sire; closer to him*

And salewede hym. Quod he, 'What dost thow

her   *greeted; here*

In my presence and that so boldely?   *so boldly too*

For it were bettere worthi, trewely,   *more fitting*

A werm to come in my syht than thow.'   *for a worm*

245 'And why, Sere,' quod I, 'And it lyke yow?'

'For thow,' quod he, 'Art therto nothyng able. *not at all suitable*

My servauntis ben alle wyse and honourable;   *are all*

Thow art my mortal fo and me warreyest,   *war against me*

And of mynne olde servauntis thow mysseyst,   *say evil*

250 And hynderyst hem with thy translacyoun.   *harm; translating*

And lettist folk to han devocyoun   *prevent; from having*

To servyn me, and haldist it folye   *you consider*

To troste on me. Thow mayst it nat denye,   *cannot*

For in pleyn tixt – it nedyth nat to glose –

234–42. G omits F's description of the dreamer standing near the daisy and being criticized for it by Love.

234. *lenyng*: resting or standing in reverie; *bente*: grassy area, here a grassy slope.

236. For the narrator as hidden onlooker or eavesdropper, see *BD*, ll. 458–74, and pp. 39–41.

237. Love's fear-inducing stare and aggression towards the abject dreamer may just possibly resemble Richard II's intimidating habit of demanding that when his eye fell on a courtier they must kneel (McKisack 1959: 490).

244. *werm*: G, typically, cuts F's reference to the dreamer kneeling close to the daisy, thereby losing F's 'worm in the bud' joke, 'It wer bettre ... A worm to neghen neer my flour than thou' (F ll. 317–18): evidence that F is earlier?

245. ' "And why, sir," I said, "If it please you?" '

250–7. These complex lines are reminiscent of contemporary controversy over Wycliffites' advocacy of translations into English of the Bible, free from the Church's traditional exegesis.

254. *pleyn tixt* (cf. l. 86): a clear piece of writing, unglossed, whose meaning is unequivocal; *to glose* = to provide an interpretation, especially a scholarly exegesis.

255   Thow hast translatid the Romauns of the Rose,
       That is an eresye ageyns my lawe,   *heresy*
       And makyst wise folk fro me withdrawe,   *thou makest; desert*
       And thynkist in thy wit, that is ful cole,
       That he nys but a verray propre fole
260   That lovyth paramouris to harde and hote.
       Wel wot I therby thow begynnyst dote,   *become senile*
       As olde folis whan here sp[i]ryt faylyth: *bodily vigour weakens*
       Thanne blame they folk and wete nat what hem ealyth.
                  Hast thow nat mad in Englys ek the   *composed*
                  bok   *in English*
265   How that Crisseyde Troyl[u]s forsok,
       In schewynge how that wemen han don mis?
       B[u]t natheles answere me now to this: *nevertheless*
       Why noldist thow as wel a seyd goodnes
       Of wemen, as thow hast seyd wekedenes?

255–6. On *Roman de la Rose*, see pp. 288–9. *eresye*: picks up the religious
    connotations of *devocyoun*, l. 251, perhaps reflects the growing English
    concern about heresy and authority, the condemnation of Wycliff (1382) for
    heresies, and contemporary fears that biblical translation undermines the
    Church's authority of interpretation. It also carries the idea of a false record,
    misleading text.

258–60. 'And you think in your brain – which is very dull – that he is nothing but
    a real fool who is passionately in love, too fierce and ardent'. *paramouris*:
    an adverb, from Fr. *par amour*. De Meun attacked love as madness and
    illness in a famous passage, *RR*, ll. 4263–390. The motif of the incompetent
    narrator recurs in *CT* (e.g. VII, ll. 919–35); for the poet's old, dull brain, see
    Ch, *Venus*, ll. 77–8 (early 1390s?). References to old age in ll. 258–63, 315,
    400–1, only in G, suggest a date after F.

263.   'Then they criticize people and do not know what is wrong with them-
    selves'. Defenders of women often assert that impotence plays a part in
    misogynists' malice, e.g. *WB Prol*, ll. 700–10.

266.   'As an illustration of how women have done wrong'. Ames 1986 discusses
    Love's charges against *TC* and *RR*. The terms of this attack on Ch's works
    may seem self-evidentially absurd, but in an era when *exemplary* use of
    narratives was common, writing about the 'matyr' of unfaithful women
    might be read as anti-feminist *per se*.

267–312. This passage about books is only in G. Payne 1963: ch. III discusses it.

268–9. 'Why did you not want to have reported goodness about women, just as
    much as you have reported wickedness?'

270	Was there no good matyr in thy mynde,	*subject-matter; memory*
	Ne in alle thy bokys ne coudist thow nat fynde	*Nor*
	Sum story of wemen that were goode and trewe?	*faithful*
	Yis, God wot, lx bokys olde and newe	*knows; sixty*
	Hast thow thyself, alle ful of storyis grete,	*you possess*
275	That bothe Romaynys and ek Grekis trete	*which; write*
	Of sundery wemen: whiche lyf that they ledde,	
	And evere an hunderede goode ageyn on badde.	
	This knowith God, and alle clerkis ek	
	That usyn sweche materis for to sek.	
280	What seith Valerye, Titus or Claudyan?	*says*
	What seith Jerome agayns Jovynyan?	*against*
	How clene maydenys and how trewe wyvys,	*what pure*
	How stedefaste wedewys durynge alle here lyvys,	*what constant*
	Tellyth Jerome and that nat of a fewe,	*tells; not*

270. *matyr*: basic subject, material for a work of literature.

276–7. 'Of various women and what sort of life they led, and for one bad one there are always a hundred good ones'. See similar line in *Mil T* I, l. 3155, in the context of the parodic use of *legende* and *lyf* to refer to wifely infidelity.

278–9. 'God knows this, and so also do all scholars who have made a study of investigating such subjects'. McMillan 1987: 9 suspects irony because so many *clerkis* wrote anti-feminist works; see pp. 291–4. But see next n.

280–1. There have been various explanations of the books referred to here, and the import of the references. *Titus* (Titus Livius, c. 59 BC–AD 17): Livy's *Ab urbe condita*, primary source for the story of Lucrece. It has been suggested (e.g. Lawlor 1968: 100; *Riv* n.) that *Valerye* is Walter Map's anti-marriage satire *In Rufinum* (c. 1180?), written under the pseudonym Valerius, or Valerius Flaccus's epic *Argonautica* (AD 70?), a source for the story of Medea; also that *Claudyan* means Claudian's *De raptu Proserpinae* (c. 397), and *Jerome* refers to anti-feminist parts of *Against Jovinian*. But probably *Valerye* = Valerius Maximus, whose *Memorabilia* tells the story of Alcestis; *Claudyan* = Claudian's *Praise of Serena* (403?), which celebrates women, including Alcestis and Lucretia; and *Jerome* refers specifically to his catalogue of faithful women in *Against Jovinian* I, cols 41–6. The unifying principles are: all four writers are historians, presenting reliable accounts of women's *trouthe* in contrast to the *fables* favoured by misogynists; all four works celebrate Alcestis or Lucretia, or both. So it is not ironical.

282–304. Summarizes Jerome's account of chaste and faithful Greek and Roman women.

285   But I dar seyn an hunderede on a rewe,   *in a row*
       That it is pete for to rede, and routhe,   *so that*
       The wo that they endure for here trouthe.   *endured*
       For to hyre love were they so trewe   *their*
       That, rathere than they wol[d]e take a newe,   *new (lover)*
290   They chose to be ded in sundery wyse
       And deiedyn, as the story wele devyse: *died; will reveal*
       And some were brend and some were cut the hals,
       And some dreynkt for th[e]y woldyn not   *drowned;*
          be fals.   *refused to be*
       For alle kepid they here maydynhed   *preserved; virginity*
295   Or ellis wedlek or here wedewehed.   *their widowhood*
       And this thing was nat kept for holynesse   *religious motives*
       But al for verray vertu and clennesse,   *true virtue; purity*
       And for men schulde sette on hem no   *impute to them;*
          lak.   *criticism*
       And yit they were hethene, al the pak,   *all of them*
300   That were so sore adrad of alle schame.   *afraid; dishonour*
       These olde wemen kepte so here name,   *ancient; guarded*
       That in this world I trowe men schal nat fynde   *believe*
       A man that coude be so trowe and kynde
       As was the leste woman in that tyde.   *least; era*
305   What seyth also the Epistelle of Ovyde

286.   *pete, routhe*: both mean 'pity'; *pete* is the stronger term. Jerome's catalogue
        of women who died rather than accept violation or second marriage
        includes the forms of death summarized in ll. 293–4. They are quasi-martyrs
        to fidelity and purity.

292.   'And some were burned and some had their throats cut'.

296–301. This stress on the women's pagan state and pagan virtue comes from
        Jerome. Without the benefit of Christian revelation, their moral principles
        were based on virtue and purity in their own right and on concern for
        honour and good name.

305–8. Ovid's *Heroides*, then usually known as his 'Epistles': faithful lovers' letters.
        Vincent of Beauvais (c. 1190–1264), *Speculum Historiale*, tells of historical
        men and women, pagan and Christian, including Cleopatra, with several
        chapters on saints and martyrs. Possibly, *Her.* here represents the 'hethene'
        contribution and the *Speculum* saints' lives represent the 'Cristene' contribu-
        tion. Ll. 296–300 have already established the separate validity of pagan
        examples of virtue. For a contrary reading, that the mingling of Christian and
        pagan values reveals the God as misguided, see Kiser 1983: 82–94.

Of trewe wyvys and of here labour?   *about; trials*
What Vincent in his Estoryal Myrour?
Ek, al te world of autourys maysttow here,
Cristene and hethene, trete of swich matere: *treat this subject*
310   It nedyth nat al day thus for to endite.   *record it*
But yit I seye, what eylyth the to wryte   *ails thee*
The draf of storyis and forgete the corn?   *ignore*
Be Seynt Venus, of whom that I was born,   *By; from whom*
Althow thow reney[ed] hast my lay   *rejected; law*
315   As othere olde folys, manye a day,   *like*
Thow schalt repente it so that it schal be sene.'   *public*
           Thanne spak Alceste the worthy queene,   *noble*
And seyde, 'God, ryght of youre   *because of your*
      curteysye,   *nobility*
Ye motyn herkenyn if he can replye   *must listen whether*

306.   *wyvys* = 'women' in a general sense, or it refers to *Her.* wives like Penelope.
308.   'Also, you can listen to a whole world full of authors'. *autourys* is a term
       almost as dignified as the Lat. *auctores*, which means revered classical or
       learned Latin writers like Ovid, or the historian Vincent.
312.   *draf*: leftover bran (used for horses) after winnowing; *corn*: the kernel. From
       Augustine on, kernel and husk symbolized the spiritually profitable (allegor-
       ical) meaning of writings contrasted with their valueless literal surface; here
       Ch contrasts reliable records of female virtue with meretricious anti-
       feminist fictions. Again we have the metaphorical cluster, literature as corn/
       flower (cf. ll. 61–5).
313.   Venus, the classical goddess of love, Cupid's mother; wittily called a saint,
       she matches the pagan 'martyrs' of love and the metaphor of Christian
       penance.
315.   *manye a day*: implies that renouncing love is something old people
       commonly do. See p. 282. See the note to ll. 258–60 on the theme of the
       aged poet, also Gower's conclusion to *CA* VIII, l. 2941. Burnley 1979:
       162–6 discusses the detached stance of Ch's narrators.
316.   A public penance was rare in real life at the period; see p. 289. Clearly Love
       is about to announce what the penance will be when Alceste makes her plea.
318.   *curteysye*: flattering reminders that merciful government typifies the truly
       noble king recur, e.g. *deite* (l. 322), *naturel* (l. 356), *gentyl, genterye*
       (ll. 377–80), *noble corage* (l. 383), *maystrye, lord, honour* (ll. 386–94).
319–25. Cf. 355–64, 387–96. These lines press the point that kings should attend
       to petitions and not punish without hearing the accused's defence.

320	Ageyns these poyntys that ye han to hym	*have stated*
	mevid.	*against*
	A god ne schulde not thus been agrevyd,	*be resentful*
	But of his de[it]e he schal be stable	*divine nature; constant*
	And therto ryghtful and ek mercyable.	*just*
	He schal nat ryghtfully his yre wreke	*avenge his anger*
325	Or he have herd the tothyr partye speke.	*before; other party*
	Al ne is nat gospel that is to yow pleynyd.	*said in complaint*
	The God of Love heryth manye a tale ifeynyd.	*pretended story*
	For in youre court is manye a losenger	*flattering counsellor*
	And manye a queynte totulour	*subtle, tale-bearing*
	acusour,	*defamer*
330	That tabourryn in youre eres manye a thyng	*who drum*
	For hate or for jelous ymagynyng,	*out of hatred*
	And for to han with you sum dalyaunce.	*conversation*
	Envye – I pre[y]e to God yeve hire	*give her*
	myschaunce –	*misfortune*
	Is lavender in the grete court alway;	*laundress*
335	For she ne partyth, neythir nygh[t] ne day,	*never departs*
	Out of the hous of Cesar, thus seyth Dante.	

320. *poyntys*: 'accusations'; *mevid*: 'argued in court' are both legal terms.

320–97. On the possible topical relevance of this passage, see pp. 294–9.

321. Reflects the idea that the higher things are in the Chain of Being, the less subject to mutability and movement they are.

323–37. Both a witty allegory of how lovers (whose versions of situations are often untrustworthy: *ifeynyd*) would like to get Love on their side, and a satire on how self-advancement in real-life courts encourages false accusations: self-advancement trying to beat down its rivals (= *Envye*, l. 333) is always looking for other people's dirty linen to wash in public. Writers on kingship commonly warned of the dangers from flatterers and unreliable counsellors, e.g. John of Salisbury, *Policraticus* III, 4 and 6.

328–9. Uses words with a wealth of senses relevant to *LGW*: *losenger* (a favourite word with political satirists): 'flatterer', 'calumniator', 'deceiver of women', 'treacherous counsellor'; *acusour*: 'accusor', 'defamer'; *totulour*: 'gossip', 'tale-bearer'; *queynte*: 'subtle', 'ingenious', 'elegant', 'wily'.

331–2. *ymagynyng*: 'mental fantasies', also 'scheming'; *dalyaunce*: 'conversation', 'elegant conversation', 'love-talk'; ambitious courtiers are always anxious to get into intimate conversation with a ruler.

336. *Cesar* stands generically for 'the emperor', any ruler. In *Inf.* XIII, ll. 64–5, Pier delle Vigne, a poet and royal servant (like Ch) who rose to great

Whoso that goth, alwey sche [wol nat] wante.

This man to yow may wrongly ben acused   *be falsely*

Thereas, be ryght, hym oughte ben excusid,   *whereas, by right*

340   Or ellis, Sere, for that this man is nyce,   *sir, because; silly*

He may translate a thyng in no malyce   *without evil intent*

But for he usyth bokis for to make,   *is used*

And takyth non hed of what matere he take.   *no need*

Therfore he wrot the Rose and ek Crisseyde   *that is why*

345   Of innocence, and nyste what he seyde;   *did not know*

Or hym was bodyn make thilke tweye

Of sum persone, and durste it not withseye,   *dared not refuse*

For he hath wrete manye a bok er this.   *before this*

He ne hath not don so grevosly amys   *amiss*

350   To translate that olde clerkis wryte,   *what; scholars*

As thow that he, of maleys, wolde endyte

Despit of love and hadde hymself iwrouht.

This schulde a ryghtwys lord have in   *bear*

      his thought,   *in mind*

And not ben lyk tyrauntis of Lumbardye,   *be like*

eminence as Chancellor to the Emperor Frederick II, complains of his fall from power, calling Envy a harlot of the court who has slandered him: he did not spare himself in his fidelity to his master, but Envy accused him of treason (I am grateful to Nick Havely for help on this allusion). Ch's image introduces the proverbial motif of 'washing dirty linen': envious people criticize others to a person in authority. Laundresses had a reputation for being prostitutes, e.g. 'Lecherie my lavendere' in *The Harley Lyrics* 1956: 47; John of Garland's drama about two laundresses who are whores to a garrison (*Parisiana Poëtria*, 1974).

337. 'Whoever goes away, at all events she is not going to be absent'; cf. *Inf.* XIII, l. 65.

339. 'In a case where, by right, he should be excused'.

346–7. 'Or a command was given to him to compose those two by some person and he dared not say anything against it'. Ch likes the pose of passive translator; cf. *TC* II, ll. 8–21.

347. ME *persone* can imply higher rank than, say, *man*.

351–2. 'As he would have done if he had decided, out of malicious intention, to write something despising Love and had created it himself'.

328 The *Prologue* to the *Legend of Good Women*

355	That usyn wilfulhed and tyrannye.	
	For he that kyng or lord is naturel	*born ruler*
	Hym oughte nat be tyraunt [ne] crewel –	
	As is a fermour, to don the harm he can.	
	He muste thynke it is his lige-man,	*true retainer*
360	And that hym owith o[f] verry duetee	
	Schewyn his peple pleyn benygnete,	*to show; true*
	And wel to heryn here excusacyouns	*hear carefully their*
	And here conpleyntys and petyciouns	*their*
	In duewe tyme, whan they schal it profre.	*due*
365	This is the sentens of the philysophre:	*judgement*
	A kyng to kepe hise lygis in justise	*maintain; loyal subjects*
	[Withoutyn] doute, that is his offise.	*duty of his position*

355. Reference to *wilfulhed* is only in G: 'Who habitually act with unbridled arrogance and tyranny'. Treatises on kingship commonly contrasted just kingship with tyranny, e.g. *Policraticus* IV, 1. ME *tyraunt* can mean 'usurper' as well as oppressive ruler: contrast with a true king (l. 356), and see Burnley 1979: 11–43 on the network of ideas surrounding the concept in Ch and the use of 'tyranny' and 'cruel' in Lancastrian criticisms of Richard II. The Visconti ruled Milan and other cities of Lombardy with brutal tyranny. Ch visited Bernabò Visconti on royal business in 1380; see Pearsall 1992: 107–9. See *Mk T* VII, ll. 2399–406, on Bernarbò, as a warning of the fall of a powerful ruler.

358. *fermour*: someone to whom right is granted to draw revenue or taxes from an estate or region: an important feature of 14th-century patronage and administration. Unlike a true king, who recognizes his duty to govern in the interests of all because he and his subjects are bound together by oaths, a *fermour* is only interested in using territory or power to serve his own interests.

360. 'And that there is a profound duty on him'.

360–4. Only in G: see p. 295. Brunetto Latini, *Livre dou Trésor* 3.90–1, stresses the importance of rulers listening to defences. Technical legal terms abound: *excusacyouns*: not 'excuses' but 'pleas for acquittal'; *conpleyntys*: lawsuits, accusations; *petyciouns*: legal applications for redress of wrongs, etc.

365. *the philysophre*: usually means Aristotle. Medieval writers on kingship and political theory often cite Aristotle's *Politics*, e.g. Giles of Rome, *De regimine principium*. Fisher's n. suggests that Ch remembered here generally a passage about kingship in the *Secreta secretorum*, sometimes attributed to Aristotle.

	And therto is a kyng ful depe isworn,	
	Ful manye an hunderede wyntyr herebeforn,	*years*
370	And for to kepe his lordys hir degre,	
	As it is ryght and skylful that they be	
	Enhaunsede and honoured [and] most dere.	
	For they ben half-goddys in this world here.	
	This schal he don bothe to pore [and] ryche,	*must do thus*
375	Al be that here [e]stat be nat alyche,	*although; their rank*
	And han of pore folk compassioun.	*on poor people*
	For, lo, the gentyl kynde of the lyoun:	*noble nature*
	For whan a flye offendyth hym or bytith,	*bites*
	He with his tayl awey the flye smytyth	*knocks*
380	Al esyly, for of his genterye	*very gently; nobility*
	Hym deynyth nat to wreke hym on a flye,	*deigns; avenge himself*
	As doth a curre or ellis anothir beste.	*cur; animal*
	In noble corage oughte ben areste	*to be cautiousness*
	And weyen everyth[ing] by equite,	*to assess; justice*
385	And evere han reward to his owen degre.	*regard; honour*
	For, Sire, it is no maystrye for a lord	*triumph*
	To dampne a man withoute answere or	*convict; right*
	word,	*of reply*
	And for a lord that is w[e]l foul to use.	*truly vile to do*
	And if so be he may hym nat ascuse,	

368–74. 'A king takes a profound oath concerning this, going back a full hundred
years. And to protect the authority of his nobles, as it is right and prudent
that they should be benefited and honoured and most dear to him, because
they are demi-gods in this world of ours.' Actually, coronation oaths had
not remained unchanged for centuries, but they did include a promise to
rule with justice and mercy. *half-goddys*: may refer to kings or to lords, or
to people in authority, generally; cf. *Measure for Measure* I. ii, l. 112: did
Shakespeare, in that play about authority, tyrannous use of it, and the
oppression of women, recall the political passage in *LGW*? The concept of
kings as the image of God recurs in medieval discussions of kingship: e.g.
John of Salisbury, *Policraticus* IV, 1 and VIII, 17 (compares true kings, like
God, with mere tyrants, like Lucifer); Bracton 1968: I, x. 5, pp. 38–40.

368–9. Only in G.

377–82. A lion, as king of the beasts, is an apt natural parallel to a true monarch.
Skeat cites similar examples in Martial, *Epigrams* XII, 61, ll. 5–6, and Pliny,
Natural History VIII, l. 16.

389. 'And, if it be the case that he cannot exculpate himself'.

390   [But] axith mercy with a sorweful herte,   *asks for*
       And proferyth hym, ryght in his bare scherte,   *offers himself*
       To been rygh[t] at youre owene jugement,   *to be totally*
       Than ought a god, by schort avisement,
       Considere his owene honour and his   *offence*
         trespace,   *against him*
395   For, sythe no cause of deth lyth in this cace,   *since no reason for*
       Yow oughte to ben the lyghtere merciable.   *more readily*
       Letith youre yre and beth sumwhat tretable:
       The man hath servyd yow of his konny[n]g   *abilities*
       And fortheryd youre lawe with his makyng.   *promoted; poetry*
400   Whil he was yong he kepte youre estat.   *defended your honour*
       I not where he be now a renagat,
       But wel I wot with that he can endyte   *with what; compose*
       He hath makid lewede folk to delyte   *unlettered*
       To servyn yow, in preysynge of youre name.
405   He made the bok that highte the Hous of Fame,   *is called*
       And ek the Deth of Blaunche the Duchesse,
       And the Parlement of Foulis, as I gesse,   *believe*
       And al the love of Palamon and Arcite
       Of Thebes, thow the storye is knowe lite,   *little known*
410   And manye an ympne for [y]our haly dayis,   *hymn*
       That hightyn baladis, roundelys, vyrelayes.   *are called*

393. *schort avisement*: 'without too long deliberation'? Perhaps this means
      prompt justice, as in l. 364.
397. 'Put aside your anger and be somewhat amenable to reason'.
401. 'I don't know whether he is now a traitor to your cause': older men serve
      love less actively.
403–4. A parallel to English religious poets' writing in the vernacular to make
      uneducated and lay people (*lewede* meant both) delight in serving and
      praising the Christian God. As with *nakede tixt*, l. 86, the literary defence of
      women adopts terms used for the vernacular in religious contexts.
405–20. The dreamer is here identified with the poet Ch. Is this a list of all his
      works at the time of writing, or just those deemed to be in praise of Love?
      They are either about virtuous women, or morality generally, or courtly,
      idealistic lovers – no *Miller's Tale*; does that suggest a date early in the
      1390s or merely that this list is selective?
406. The *Book of the Duchess*.
408–9. Either the *Knight's Tale* or an early version of it.
411. '*balades*, roundels, virelays'.

	And for to speke of othyr besynesse,	*activities*
	He hath in prose translatid Boece,	
	And of the Wrechede Engendrynge of Mankynde,	
415	As man may in Pope Innocent ifynde,	*discover*
	And made the lyf also of Seynt Cecile.	
	He made also, gon is a gret while,	*a long time past*
	Orygenes upon the Maudeleyne:	
	Hym ouughte now to have the lesse peyne.	*suffering*
420	He hath mad manye a lay and manye a thyng.	*poem*
	Now, as ye ben a god and ek a kyng,	*are*
	I, youre Alceste, whilom queen of Trace,	*formerly*
	I axe yow this man, rygh[t] of youre grace,	
	That ye hym nevere hurte in al his lyve,	*life*
425	And he schal swere to yow, and that as	*and that*
	blyve,	*immediately*
	He schal no more agiltyn in this wyse,	*offend; fashion*
	But he schal makyn, as ye wele devyse,	*write; will ordain*
	Of wemen trewe in lovynge al here lyve,	*about; their life*
	Wherso ye wele, of maydyn or of wyve.	*however you wish*
430	And fortheryn yow as meche as he	*exalt; much;*
	mysseyde	*slandered*
	Or in the Rose or ellis in Crisseyde.'	*either; or*

412. *besynesse*: F has *holynesse* – another instance of G toning down the extent of the quasi-religious diction.
413. Ch's translation of Boethius, *Consolation of Philosophy*.
414–15. G adds this reference to Ch's lost translation of *De miseria condicionis humanae*, attributed to Innocent III; it influenced some *Canterbury Tales*, incl. *MLT*: perhaps it was written close to G?
416. Either the *Second Nun's Tale*, about martyred St Cecilia, or an earlier version. Like the *Physician's Tale* of Virginia, the *Man of Law's Tale* of Constance, and the *Clerk's Tale* of Griselda, it illustrates Ch's continuing interest in virtuous, martyred and tested heroines, outside *LGW*.
417–18. Ch's lost translation of the Sermon on St Mary Magdalen, attributed to Origen. Another loving, virtuous and suffering saintly woman.
419. 'It is right for him to receive all the less punishment'.
422. Alcestis was queen not of Thrace but of Thessaly in other versions, e.g. Claudian, *Serena*, l. 13 (could Thrace stand for Bohemia?).
423. 'I make a request concerning this man that, by exercise of your royal mercy'. On the tradition of intercessory queens in life and literature, see Strohm 1992: 95–119.

The God of Love answerede hire thus anon:
'Madame,' quod he, 'It is so longe agon
That I yow knew so charytable and trewe,

435   That nevere yit, sithe that the world was newe,   *since*
To me ne fond I nevere non betere than the.   *no-one better*
That, if that I wele save my degre,
I may ne w[o]l not warne youre requeste.
Al lyth in yow: doth with hym [as] yow leste,

440   And al foryeve, withoute lengere space.   *forgiven; delay*
For whoso yevyth a yifte or doth a grace,   *gives; gift; kindness*
Do it betyme, his thank is wel te more.
And demyth ye what he shal don therfore.
Go thanke now my lady here,' quod he.   *go to thank*

445   I ros and doun I sette me on my kne
And seyde thus, 'Madame, the God above   *may the God above*
Foryelde yow, that ye the God of Love   *reward*
Han makyd me his wrethe to foryeve,   *towards me; forgo*
And yeve me grace so longe for to leve   *the gift; live*

450   That I may knowe sothly what ye be   *truly*
That han me holpyn and put in swich   *have helped;*
    degre.   *honour*
But trewely, I wende, as in this cas,
Naught have agilt ne don to Love trespas,
Forwhy a trewe man, withoute drede,

455   Hath nat to parte with a thevys dede,
Ne a trewe lovere [oght] me nat [to] blame   *Nor*
Thaw that I speke a fals lovere sum schame.   *even though*
They aughte rathere with me for to holde   *to support me*
For that I of Criseyde wrot or tolde,   *because I wrote*

433–4. '"Madame," he said, "For a long time now I have known you to be so
    charitable and faithful"'.

437–9. 'So that, if I want to keep my own honour, I neither can nor wish to reject
    your request. Everything lies in your hands: do whatever pleases you with
    him'.

442. 'If he does it promptly, the thanks are all the greater'. Sk.'s n. shows this was
    proverbial.

443. 'And you make the judgement about what he must do for this'.

452–5. 'But truly I believed in this matter I had not committed any crime nor done
    any injury to Love, because, without doubt, an honest man has no part in
    a thief's deed'.

460	Or of the Rose, whatso myn aughtour mente.	*about the Rose*
	Algate, God wot, it was myn entente	*At any event*
	To forthere trouthe in love and it cheryse,	*promote fidelity*
	And to be war from falsenesse and from vice,	*to warn away from*
	By swich ensaumple: this was my menynge.'	*such example*
465	And sche answerde, 'Lat be thyn arguynge,	*cease arguing your case*
	For Love ne wele nat countyrpletyd be	*be argued against*
	In ryght ne wrong. And lerne this at me:	*from me*
	Thow hast thy grace and holde the ryght therto.	*favour; hold on to it*
	Now wole I seyn what penaunce thow scha[l]t do	*must perform*
470	For thy trespace, and undyrstonde it here.	*offence*
	Thow schalt whil thow levyst, yer be yere,	*as long as; by*
	The moste partye of thy lyf spende	*greater part*
	In makynge of a gloryous legende	*composition*
	Of goode wemen, maydenys and wyves,	*virgins*
475	That were trewe in l[o]vynge al here lyvys.	*their lives*
	And telle of false men that hem betrayen,	*betrayed them*
	That in here lyf ne don nat but asayen	*nothing but attempt*
	How manye wemen they may don a schame.	*cause; dishonour*
	For in youre world that is now holdyn game.	*considered a game*
480	And, thow the lestyth nat a lovere be,	*though you do not choose*
	Spek wel of Love. This penaunce yeve I the,	*I give you*

460. *whatso myn aughtour mente*: 'whatever the original author meant'. Ch distances himself as author and translator here from both his characters' morality and the intentions of the original authors, without stating unequivocally what his own attitude to his material was, apart from encouraging faithfulness and exposing falseness and evil.

463-4. *to be war from*: 'to be aware/wary of'. It seems to mean making people aware of the dangers of falseness, rather than *warning* them against them.

477-9. A criticism, directed out of the perfect world of Alceste and the dream, to the degenerate world of the narrator – by implication, the real world of the audience. The text is preaching a lesson from the fidelity of good women to men in the audience. Cf. *Dido*, ll. 1254-89, a warning to women in the audience on men's trickery and the exploitation of women in love.

482-4. A hint (also at ll. 511-12) that the poet might be rewarded for the poem

And to the God of Love I schal so preye
That he schal charge hise servauntys, by *command;*
   ony weye, *by all methods*
To fortheryn the and wel thy labour quite. *aid; reward*
485 Go now thy wey: thy penaunce is but lyte.' *but little*
      The God of Love gan smyle and thanne he seyde,
'Wostow,' quod he, 'Wher this be wif *do you know; whether*
   or mayde,
Or queen or cuntesse, or of what degre, *countess; rank*
That hath so lytil penaunce yevyn the, *given thee*
490 That hast deservyd sore for to smerte? *to suffer painfully*
But pete rennyth sone in gentil herte. *except that; runs*
That mayst thow sen: she kytheth what sche is.' *see; shows thee*
And I answerde, 'Nay, Sere, so have I blys, *by my salvation*
No more but that I se wel sche is good.'
495 'That is a trewe tale, by myn hod,' *true statement*
Quod Love, 'And that thow knowist wel, parde. *you know that*
Yif it be so that thow avise the, *think it over*
Hast thow nat, in a bok lyth in thy cheste, *which lies*
The grete goodnesse of the queene Alceste
500 That turnede was into a dayesye? *was transformed*
Sche that for hire husbonde ches to deye, *chose to die*
And ek to gon to helle rathere than he; *in his place*
And Ercules rescued hire, parde,

by servants of Love (i.e. aristocratic readers/patrons). Such hints, quite common towards the end of medieval poems, operate partly as elegant literary conceit but also express the real-life economics of 'publication' before printing.

491. A favourite theme with Ch; see Gray 1979; Burnley 1979: 153–61.

497–522. On this device of the fictional source, and Chaucer's Froissartian modifications of the Alcestis myth, see p. 285.

495. 'That is an accurate statement, by my hood' (i.e. 'I swear'); *hod* stands for 'head'. The theme of reliable statements again.

498–510, 518. The rival *auctorite* of books and experience is reconciled in the figure of Alceste: after death a book records the 'renoun' of her goodness in life, and the daisy is created as a non-verbal memorial.

502. ME *helle* is often used for the classical Hades (Spencer 1927), but may also play a part in the intermittently religious diction of the Prologue (the F version, l. 110, refers to the daisy's *resureccioun* each dawn).

507.

	And broughte hyre out of helle ageyn to blys.'	*back to bliss*
505	And I answerde ayen and seyde 'Yis.	*replied back*
	Now knowe I hire and is this goode Alceste	
	The dayes eye and myn owene herteis reste.	*day's eye*
	Now fele I wel the goodnesse of this wif,	*perceive*
	That bothe aftyr hire deth and [in] hire lyf,	
510	Hire grete bounte doubelyth hire	*generosity doubles;*
	renoun.	*fame*
	Wel hath sche quit me myn affeccioun	*rewarded me for*
	That I have to hire flour the dayesye.	
	No wondyr is thow Jove hire stellefye,	*though*
	As tellyth Agaton, for hyre goodnesse.	*tells; because of*
515	Hire white coroun beryth of it witnesse,	*bears witness*
	For also manye vertuys hath sche	*just as many*
	As smale flour[oun]s in hyre coroun be.	*are*
	Of remembrauns of hire and in honour,	
	Cibella made the dayesye and the flour	
520	Icoroned al with whit, as men ma se.	*crowned; can*

507. *dayes eye*: the etymology of *daisy*; it associates Alcestis and the flower with images of light, dawn, ascent and the sun (cf. ll. 48–9). 'Heart's resting place' (cf. *TC* V, l. 1349): what the heart desires as the goal of its restless desire and seeking, stillness beyond movement and instability (the phrase suggests *Heartsease*, a flower-name since the Renaissance at least, esp. for the wild pansy).

509. Like a saint or martyr, through the power of her virtues she helps others after her death.

513. *stellefye*: 'make into a star'. Mythical heroes and heroines were often turned into stars, cf. *HF*, l. 586. Ariadne's crown became part of the constellation Taurus (see Ovid, *Met*.VIII, ll. 176–82; *Fasti* V, ll. 345–6; VIII, ll. 459–516). See also pp. 283–6.

514. *Agaton*: 'Agatho's Feast', a name for Plato's *Symposium*, which mentions Alcestis (179c). Peck 1986: 40–2 speculates that Ch may have known it from visiting Bernabò Visconti, who had a great library.

519–22. The crown image forms a climax, uniting Alceste's ascent to heaven as a star-crown with the daisy's crown-like face raised towards the sun. It is divine recognition of the triumph of female *vertuys* (in contrast to male writers' blindness?); the white and red hues have suggested female beauty, chastity and passion, and now the harmony of male and female – gifts of Cybele and Mars – and also eternity, for the rubies may suggest a martyr's crown, as white pearl at l. 153 suggests purity.

	And Mars yaf to hire corone red, parde,	*gave; a red crown*
	Instede of rubeis, set among the white.'	*rubies*
	Therwith this queene wex red for schame a lyte,	*grew; modesty*
	Whan sche was preysid so in hire presence.	
525	'Thanne,' seyde Love, 'A ful gret neglygence	*then*
	Was it [in] the to write onstedefastnesse	*write of inconstancy*
	Of women, sithe thow knowist here goodnesse,	*since; their*
	By pref and ek by storyis	*experience; histories*
	herebyforn;	*already*
	Let be the chaf and writ wel of the corn.	*leave the chaff*
530	Why noldist thow han writyn of Alceste	
	And latyn Criseide ben aslepe and reste?	*let*
	For of Alceste schulde thy wrytynge be	*about*
	Syn that thow wist that calandier is she	*know; guide*
	Of goodnesse, for sche taughte of fyn lovynge,	*true love*
535	And namely of wifhod the lyvynge,	
	And alle the boundys that sche	*restraints;*
	aughte kepe;	*to observe*
	Thy lityl wit was thilke tyme aslepe!	*at that time*
	But now I charge the, upon thy lyf,	*command*
	That in thy legende thow make of this wif,	*write about*
540	Whan thow hast othere smale mad byfore.	*written lesser ones*
	And fare now wel, I charge the no more.	*command thee*
	At Cliopatre I wele that thow begynne,	*I wish*

528. *pref, storyis*: experience and literary *auctorite* unite.

529. *chaf* and *corn* (husk and kernel): 'worthless topics' and 'solid, real statements of the truth', or enlightened and unenlightened reading (cf. *NPT* VII, l. 3443, and *Riv.* n.). The image of corn from ll. 61–4 has come full circle.

530. 'Why did you not choose to have written of Alceste?' See *TC* V, ll. 1772–8, which suggest that Ch was planning a palinode about Alceste, in apology to women readers, when he finished *Troilus*.

533. The calendar was the guide to saints' days and holy days prefaced to books of prayers, often decorated with red letters and illumination. The image has multiple implications: an epitome; celebration of saints; a guide to holiness and reverence; something which comes first.

534. *fyn lovynge*: probably the English equivalent of Fr. *fine amour*, 'perfect love' (often translated 'Courtly Love').

535. 'And especially the kind of life a wife should follow'.

536. *sche*: presumably generically any wife.

And so forth, and my love so shalttow   *then so on; thou shalt*
  wynne.'
And, with that word, of slep I gan awake,   *from sleep*
545 And right thus on my legende gan I make.   *just like this*

Explicit prohemium

545. In F the fictional dream continues into the legends. Ch gives the G Prologue
a variant on the 'self-creating fiction': the dream represents the literary
inspiration which will result in new writing: cf. *BD*, ll. 1330–4. The first
legend, that of Cleopatra, follows.
rubric. 'Here ends the prologue'.

NOTES ON THE TEXT

Sources

The text is in CUL MS Gg. 4. 27, fols 445ʳ–52ʳ (see p. 274). On the F and G versions, see p. 000. On the text, see Amy 1918; Kane 1983; Hanna 1991; Cowen & Kane 1995. Substantial emendations, unless otherwise indicated, are based on Oxford Bodleian Library MS Fairfax 16 (not necessarily with F's spelling). Minor emendations, such as the alteration of forms like *myn*, before a consonant, to *my* are not noted. Punctuation is editorial. It looks as if the G scribe introduced fairly frequent and characteristic alterations to the texts he copied; many of Cowen & Kane's emendations have been accepted. *Abbreviations*: scribes do not use abbreviations wholly systematically; where they have been expanded, it has been with regard to the necessity for readability in a text of this kind. For fuller textual readings, see Cowen & Kane.

Selected textual notes

title: see Seymour 1995: 79–82.
1. *thousand*] *thousent* G.
4. *yit wot*] *this wit* G.
10. *God*] *goddis* G.
11. *hath*] *han* G.
16. in margin: *Bernardus non vidit omnia*
48. *this flour*] *these flouris* G.   *sprede*] *to sprede* G.
51. *begynnyth*] *be gynnys* G.
58. Added in MS at bottom of page after l. 76.
66. *thow*] *if* G.
77. *who*[1]] *ho* G. Also at l. 238.
93. *south*] *souht* G.
94. *closede*] *clothede* G.
98. *frosche*] *frorsche* G.
106. in margin: *daieseye*
116. *atempre*] *tempre* G.
128–38. This passage is clearly corrupt.
128. *Layes*] G omits.   *that*] *& that* G.
131. *They*] *That* G; *And* F.
132. *For*] G omits.
135. *Yeldyng*] *The* G.   *humble*] *the humble* G.
136. *observaunce*] *observauncys* G.
137. *longyng*] emendation G omits.   *Nature*] *natures* G.
138. Emendation on basis of BD, l. 716] *So eche of hem to cryaturys* G.
149. *flourouns smale*] *mane flourys* G.
152. *flourouns*] *flourys* G.

153. *oryental*] *& oryental* G.
159. *In*] *Of* G.
167. *Two*] *Tho* G.
179. *debonayre*] *thebonoyre* G.
180. *hire*] *sche* G.
189. *hadde*] G omits.
192. *wyde*] G omits.
225. *sote, smale*] emendation; *& sote grene* G.
227. *inveroun*] *alle inveroun* G.
232. *the*] *that* G.
233. *mountaunce*] *mountenaunce* G.
239. *it*] *hym* G.
262. *spiryt*] *spryt* G.
265. *Troylus*] *Troylis* G.
267. *but*] *bit* G.
289. *wolde*] *wole* G.
293. *they*] *thy* G.
314. *reneyed*] *reneyist* G.
317. *worthy*] emendation; *worthyere* G.
322. *deite*] *dede* G.
333. *preye*] emendation; *prere* G.
335. *nyght*] *nygh* G.
337. *wol nat*] *mote* G.
357. *ne*] *&* G.
358–93. Misplaced in the MS after l. 429.
360. *of*] emendation; *o* G.
367. *Withoutyn*] *Which oughtyn* G.
372. *and²*] G omits.
374. *and*] G omits.
375. *estat*] *stat* G.
384. *everything*] *everyth* G.
388. *wel*] *wol* G.
390. *But*] G omits.
392. *ryght*] *rygh* G.
398. *konnyng*] *konnyg* G.
410. *your*] *thour* G.
411. *roundelys*] *roundelys &* G.
423. *ryght*] *rygh* G.
438. *wol*] *wel* G.
439. *as*] *what* G.
451. *put*] *put me* G.
456. *oght*] *may* (corrected) G.   *to*] G omits.
469. *schalt*] *schat* G.
475. *lovynge*] *levynge* G.

490. *sore*] *sorere* G.
509. *in*] *ek* G.
517. *flourouns*] *flourys* G.
526. *in*] *to* G.

THE *LEGEND OF DIDO*

INTRODUCTION

Shannon (1929: 196) observed that, though Chaucer's material in *Dido* was mainly from the *Aeneid*, his approach, sympathetic to Dido and hostile to Aeneas, is closer to the Letter of Dido in Ovid's *Heroides* VII, but the latter point is true only in a general sense. Chaucer's Dido and Aeneas are personalities of his own making as much as they are legacies from either Virgil or Ovid, and the sympathy Chaucer's text shows to Dido differs in quality from Ovid's, presenting her in a more dignified light. It is clear that the selection, omission, alteration and addition of material by Chaucer was carefully managed to produce a narrative design with its own structure and meanings. Readers will find it illuminating to compare Chaucer's narrative with *Aeneid* Books I–IV for themselves, and different readers may come to different conclusions about the overall effect of Chaucer's changes. Comparison with Chaucer's earlier version in the *House of Fame* (*HF*) shows him departing here more radically and purposively from Virgil: this *Legend* version is far more tightly moulded and designed, in both its wording and its selection of details, to adumbrate a certain group of themes.[1] Those themes are the ideas and morality that shape the *Legend* as a whole rather than those of Virgil or Ovid.[2]

Gods and humans, truth and falsehood

Virgil's figures of Dido and Aeneas are overshadowed by the quarrels and purposes of the gods, and by their own respective national destinies (which become quasi-cosmic because of the involvement of various gods in the fates of Rome and Carthage). Virgil's Dido is, like Aeneas, a royal exile and founder of cities: a king's daughter, she leaves Tyre with a fleet of political supporters after the murder of her husband Sychaeus and, after coming to Libya, cleverly secures territory and founds the city that is to become Carthage. Carthage is destined, centuries hence, to be defeated by Rome: Juno loves Carthage, and in the *Aeneid* it is Juno's determination to hinder Aeneas in his progress towards Italy that causes his shipwreck and sojourn with Dido. Chaucer does not describe Juno's anger, the details of Aeneas's journey and the storm, nor the discussions between the gods, which occupy much of *Aeneid* I.[3] He also presents events chronologically, whereas Virgil narrates the fall of Troy and Aeneas's voyage retrospectively in books II and III, as a tale told by Aeneas at Dido's feast. Chaucer 'medievalizes' some details: examples include the feast and his references to Fortune.[4] Chaucer and his readers would be familiar with Dido (and also Aeneas and Lavinia) not only as they appear in classical texts like the *Aeneid* and *Heroides* but also in medieval romances, above all the great twelfth-century version of their story, the *Roman d'Éneas*. Its author emphasizes Dido's greatness and ability as a ruler, though one whose judgement and happiness are overthrown by her love for Aeneas.[5] As in his other legends, Chaucer often refers to his need to abridge or omit material from his sources. Early critics took these comments literally, as pedantic acknowledgements of procedure or signs of Chaucer's boredom with writing legends of faithful women. Frank (1972: 189–210) surveys and dismisses the latter view, discussing more sophisticated possible reasons for Chaucer's use of *occupatio*, and suggests that he was attempting a new type of brief narrative, without the amplitude of *Troilus* (c. 1385). Throughout his career, Chaucer's references to sources, ostensibly deferential, tend in fact to alert the reader to his own separateness from them in overall effect.

He reduces the role of the gods, and even when he records that Virgil says Aeneas was made invisible or Cupid substituted for Ascanius (ll. 1020–2, 1139–45), he conveys an attitude of distrust and distaste. He omits the gods' role in the storm and cave episodes (ll. 1219–39), instead showing Aeneas accompanying Dido once she has entered the cave. The gods may have seemed dispensable because they were pagan or because they make the story less believable, but the major results of Chaucer's minimizing of the supernatural are: first, to reduce the national importance of the lovers, and concentrate on his own *matere* of their love story and Aeneas's treachery (ll. 927, 955–7), and secondly to contribute to altering the character and moral status of Aeneas.[6] The policy of substituting the characters' personal volition for the gods' intervention goes together with Chaucer's almost complete excision of Virgil's central theme of Aeneas's duty to his destiny as future founder of Rome. Consequently, Chaucer's Aeneas leaves Dido because he is false, shallow and selfish. He is repeatedly presented as deceptive and calculating, and enjoying the material advantages that come to him as a result of Dido's love. Even his attractions are dubiously phrased: he is 'lyk ... a verray gentil man' at lines 1066–8, and 'wel a lord he semede for to be', line 1074.

Throughout the text he is characterized by his facility with words, and when Chaucer puts Mercury's message and the warning from Anchises's ghost, which are factual events in Virgil's narrative, into a speech by Aeneas, they seem merely excuses.

Virgil's Aeneas gives presents (*Aeneid*, I, ll. 643–56, 695–711), but Chaucer precedes these with a passage (ll. 1114–25) describing Dido's magnificent gifts. Aeneas's gifts (ll. 1130–5) now seem less impressive and merely a prudent response to hers. His own little courtesies and signs of affection to her are presented as the 'crafte' of a calculating deceiver. Chaucer's additions create a Dido who is characterized by generosity and magnanimity and an Aeneas who is false and ungrateful.[7] Chaucer presents Aeneas, directly and indirectly, as deceitful, and his Dido, in her role of one of the *Legend*'s women 'trewe in lovynge', appears all the more 'trewe' in contrast.[8] There was already a tradition going back to early writers, including Jerome, of Dido as an exemplum of marital faithfulness, but this was based on her long fidelity to the memory of her murdered husband for years before the advent of Aeneas.[9] Chaucer ignores this ready-made tradition of her exemplary constancy and omits references to her earlier history almost entirely, to concentrate on a single relationship, and her behaviour towards Aeneas and her death. What is admirable about Dido's character in Chaucer's *Legend* is the attitude she brings to a passionate and extra-marital love affair. His concept of what makes her a moral exemplum is thus unconventional. A hint for the twin themes of generosity and treachery, the polarities of Chaucer's narrative, may have come from *Heroides* VII, line 27, where Dido castigates Aeneas for ingratitude, but this pattern of contrast between female generosity and male treachery, on which *Dido* is constructed, appears elsewhere in his legends: those of Cleopatra, Hypsipyle, Medea, Ariadne, Phyllis, Hypermnestra. Another inspiration was perhaps the protest at Aeneas's treachery in the *Roman de la Rose*, lines 13157–67, and Le Fèvre's *Livre de Leësce* which, in its defence of women, claims that women's generosity to men is often repaid with ingratitude and betrayal, giving a catalogue of examples including Dido and Medea.[10] To see disloyalty as a kind of ingratitude was perhaps more obvious in an age in which 'feudal' cultural images were still current. Note furthermore how fidelity is presented in the *Prologue* to the *Legend* as central to the morality both of books (the fidelity with which their authors preserve past events) and to kingship, as well as to sexual relationships.

Generosity, falseness and *gentilesse*

Chaucer's Dido is impressive.[11] His sympathy is with her, but that does not entail presenting her as weak or pathetic, except momentarily in her pleas to Aeneas (ll. 1312–16) – though even these are given a weighty political justification in lines 1317–18. Chaucer's Dido is 'flour' of all queens (l. 1009), and in the next line her generosity is, together with other virtues, associated with this royal, 'gentil' nature. In the most striking elevation of all, Chaucer calls her fit to be a divine consort (ll. 1039–43; compare the Marian imagery used of Alceste in the *Prologue*, and of White in the *Book of the Duchess*: ways of elevating the earthly noblewoman above earthliness and earthly love). Chaucer stresses Dido's regality and magnanimity, her nobility, honour, *fredom* and *gentilesse*. These are presented as qualities of her personality and central elements in the moral imbalance of the relationship between her and Aeneas, a different emphasis from that of Virgil: his Dido has queenly power and splendour as manifestations of her political position as a great ruler.[12]

Her gifts in lines 1114–25 intriguingly resemble those presented by the City of London to Richard II and Queen Anne in 1392: two 'coursers' with silver-gilt saddles for Richard, a palfrey with a gold saddle for Anne, gold, silver, sacks of gold, coins, bowls, jewels and brooches, jewels, all of great beauty and value.[13] In his apostrophe to 'sely wemen' (ll. 1254–63), which reverses traditional misogynist strategy by presenting *exempla* to women of men's vice and infidelity, Chaucer also presents Dido's munificence and benevolence as typical of women's unguarded trust of men, who are liable to rob, exploit and betray them. Dido's goodness is already famous (ll. 1053–4); Chaucer repeatedly mentions her pity. Compassion and love operate together in her personality (ll. 1078–80). Her motives are uncalculating: she is 'sely' and acts 'with good entente', in contrast to Aeneas's 'crafte'. Like several other men aided by other *Legend* heroines (Jason, ll. 1473–1510, 1560–70, 1629–59, 1662–66; Theseus, ll. 1945–61; Demophon, ll. 2409–40), Aeneas is depicted as a man reduced by peril and need or destitution, not the equal of his lover in the relationship, but rather her dependant and beneficiary (this is also one effect of Chaucer's use of the motif of Fortune's wheel). In contrast to his stress on the nobility of Dido's attitudes and actions, Chaucer's phrasing at line 1264 pours scorn on Aeneas's adoption of the outward airs of a *gentil man* (Jason is similarly a false 'gentil man': *LGW*, ll. 1368–82, 1524–56, 1603–8). Aeneas's triumphing over his rival Yarbis is described (ll. 1250–1) in a style resembling Chaucer's description of Nicholas triumphing over Absalon in the far from gentlemanly *ambiance* of the *Miller's Tale*, lines 3386–98.

Untypically, Chaucer does retain a scene involving a god's intervention when Aeneas meets a huntress who is Venus in disguise, though Chaucer dispenses for the most part with its original *raison d'être* in the *Aeneid*, which was the opportunity to tell Dido's previous life history at length. Perhaps he kept his own version of the scene to present images of female freedom and power: because Libya has a female ruler, its young women have the liberty to move freely about in the woods, far from the restraints of home and city, carrying weapons and killing beasts. These themes of female strength and freedom both enhance Chaucer's subsequent portrait of the queen (ll. 1004–14) and provide a tragic parallel to the later hunt, where the woman is transformed more into prey than pursuer, and where her ensnarement and destruction begin.

Frank (1972: 66–73) and Desmond (1994: 157–62) explore Chaucer's presentation of Dido's perceptions of events. Frank also shows how Chaucer has mastered the narrative arts of brevity and of an objective style that can represent noble and tragic emotion, and how he creates a portrait of Dido in love which is independent of Virgil. Virgil's Dido, once abandoned, is presented as furious, insane and savage, a device which aids the rehabilitation, in the reader's eyes, of Aeneas her abandoner, who is characterized by duty to the gods, his people and his destiny. In Ovid, although events are presented from Dido's emotional point of view, she is frequently irate, undignified and ranting, her stature fatally reduced by emotion, and she swings inconsistently from one rhetorical argument or attack to another. Ovid's sympathy is a psychological exercise: he presents the situation as it might be seen through Dido's biased eyes. Chaucer's narrative, in contrast, is morally on Dido's side, and it shows her to be right, Aeneas wrong. She is noble, he is ignoble; she is a queen, he an ungrateful wanderer. Chaucer can also make Carthage the centre, the fixed base for his story; Aeneas becomes the exotic foreigner, 'this newe Troyan' (l. 1172), the wanderer who floats to the shores and in due time, true to his shallow inconstancy, wanders away again simply because he has become bored with playing the lover (ll. 1286–7).[14] He 'steals' away furtively during the night (ll. 1289, 1333, 1335).

Curiously, many critics have ignored the queenly power and splendour that accompany Dido's benevolence and sincerity in Chaucer, and seen her as weak, or even as a bourgeois girl naively falling for a handsome stranger. Sanderlin 1986 surveys this line of interpretation, while not in fact freeing himself from it: he goes on to propose – in the name of feminism – that Chaucer presents Dido as an example of how weak and easily destroyed women are in relationships with men. This is a misreading: not only does Chaucer amply assert Dido's nobility and magnificence, he presents her kindness and emotional sincerity themselves as part of true *gentilesse*. For Chaucer it was in truly *gentil* hearts that 'pete rennyth sone' (*Prologue*, l. 491).

Though Chaucer used *Heroides* VII, lines 1–9, for his Dido's final letter, comparison reveals how even then he avoids the phrasing that presented Ovid's Dido as weak or emotional. His Dido is now strong, disillusioned and disdainful; she may be dying in despair because of Aeneas, but she speaks *de haut en bas* to him. Chaucer's lines, superficially close to Ovid's, are significantly different. Aeneas's departure is in the past tense (ll. 1364–5) as Dido looks back judgementally on what she now sees coldly and clearly as his falseness, whereas Ovid's Dido used constructions which have a future reference, as if she still imagined she could clutch him back by pleadings:

> Certus es ire tamen miseramque relinquere Dido,
>   atque idem venti vela fidemque ferent?
> certus es, Aenea, cum foedere solvere naves. . . ?   (ll. 7–9)

> (Are you resolved to depart, nonetheless, and abandon unhappy Dido, and shall the same winds carry away your sails and your fidelity? Are you resolved, Aeneas, to untie your promise when you untie your ships?)

Ovid's Dido, even at this point, talks of pleading with Aeneas, of her dwindling hope that he 'can be moved by my prayer' (l. 3), whereas Chaucer's Dido says rather (ll. 1358–9) that she does not have expectations of *getting* him back. She 'wel ... wot that it is al in veyn' – wording perhaps implying a perception of an emptiness at the heart of the whole affair. Chaucer's letter concludes at line 1365, at a point corresponding to Ovid's lines 8–9 quoted above, so that he ends appropriately on the central theme of his own *matere*: fidelity and Aeneas's treachery:

> 'That same wynd hath blowe awey youre *fey*.'   (my italics)

He does not go on to Ovid's next lines, where Dido rails disparagingly about the unlikeliness of Aeneas finding anything better in the next land he sails to, a passage which, through an ironic reminder of Aeneas's great Virgilian destiny in Italy, fatally weakens in our eyes Ovid's Dido and her capacity to comprehend or control events.

Chaucer's narrative has the advantage, for his purposes in this *Legend* of faithful women, of being able to create a self-contained world of Carthage. In contrast, Ovid's emotionally biased Dido is a portrait which cannot erase, and is not meant to erase, the reader's memories of Virgil's royal and dutiful 'pius Aeneas', with his destiny and his great journey to Rome. Ovid's *Heroides* VII is thus parasitic, creatively and deliberately parasitic, on Virgil's larger narrative of Aeneas's virtues, and exploits our knowledge of it, referring obliquely backwards and forwards to events the reader of the *Aeneid* knows in another context and another moral perspective. Chaucer's *Dido*, like his whole *Legend*, with its curiously obtrusive and teasing reminders of his ancient sources (ll. 1002, 1352, 1367), makes its own intertextuality also quite clear, but with very different effect: as in *HF*, we become aware of the instability of literary *fama*, the disparity there can be between different literary versions of the same events, and between an experience and its recording in 'olde bokys'. Perhaps indeed we might say that, ultimately, Chaucer's *Dido* restores Dido's reputation for *trouthe*, and her honour and dignity, in the face not just of Aeneas's infidelity, but of the less than fair representation of her by her ancient male reporters and *auctours*, Ovid and Virgil. Chaucer's text does not, if we believe his own propaganda in the *Prologue* to the *Legend*, betray her: it presents a 'nakede tixt' which reliably records her virtue.

Chaucer, Virgil, Dante: the poet and the great tradition

Chaucer begins with these disingenuous words:

> Glorye and honour, Virgile Mantoan,
> Be to thy name, and I shal as I can
> Folwe thy lanterne as thow gost byforn,
> How Eneas to Dido was forsworn   (ll. 924–7)

There seem to be three reasons for this opening apostrophe to Virgil. First, though, as we have seen, Chaucer does not dutifully 'folwe' Virgil, but departs in many respects from his work, this apostrophe appropriately hails Virgil's importance as the primary and supreme source for the whole subject of Aeneas and Dido in European literature.[15]

Secondly, the wording of these lines associates Chaucer's own enterprise as a poet in the English vernacular with Dante's presentation of his own role as poet of Italy in the *Divine Comedy*. There, in the *Inferno*, Dante's expressions of homage to an earlier poet, Virgil, mingle in equal degrees respect and self-confidence. Dante, as a Christian writer on the next world, can go beyond what Virgil could know (his Beatrice can show him Paradise), yet he takes Virgil as his 'master', guide and inspiration not only to the next world but also to the whole business of composing a national epic for the Christian era. Chaucer may eschew the grandeur of Dante's self-vision, yet in his own way here he also boldly simultaneously follows and overturns Virgil. In the *Divine Comedy*, the narrator literally walks behind Virgil, following his footsteps through the dark and difficult tracks of Hell and Purgatory. Chaucer makes the 'following' only metaphorical, in lines 924–7 quoted above, and his 'lanterne' image echoes lines from the outset of the *Divine Comedy*, where Dante presents Virgil as the leader of other poets, beginning 'O honour and light of other poets . . .' (*Inferno* I, ll. 82–6).

Thirdly, Chaucer's reference to Mantua may recall passages in the *Divine Comedy* where Dante expresses a confidence that poetry can be reborn in the vernacular to match classical Latin. Virgil had been born in Mantua and Dante refers to this several times.[16] In *Purgatorio* VI, lines 72–151, the fourteenth-century Italian vernacular poet Sordello hails Virgil as a fellow-Mantuan, and then Dante laments the strife-ridden state of modern Italy. In VII, lines 16–18, Sordello again addresses Virgil, in an apostrophe echoing Dante's first one quoted above, referring again to Mantua as a link between the classical and modern poet: 'O glory of the Latins... through whom our tongue showed forth its power, O eternal honour of the place whence I sprang'. Chaucer's own apostrophe, 'Glorye and honour ...', echoes both these Italian apostrophes, with their confidence that modern vernacular art can provide worthy successors to Virgil. Thereby he implicitly places his own enterprise as a modern poet in the English tongue, with his own modern moral ideology, confidently into the line of great poets.

A reference to Mantua perhaps also seemed specially apt as preface to the tale of Dido, a female city-founder. For Dante had changed Virgil's account of the origins of Mantua, giving it a female rather than a male legendary founder: Dante claimed that the Theban prophetess Manto, fleeing the slaughter of the Thebans, established the city and is commemorated in its name (*Purg.* XX, ll. 52–99), whereas Virgil had said that Mantua was founded by a man, Orcnus (*Aen.* X, ll. 198–200).[17] If Chaucer, especially in view of his interest in the Thebes story, recalled Dante's revision of Virgil's legend, the reminder of Mantua might have seemed specially appropriate both for his heroine, Queen Dido, and also for himself, rewriting the Virgilian material to his own revisionary feminist moral agenda, in order to reinstate female histories to which ancient *autourys* have not always been faithful. Chaucer's apostrophe to Virgil is wittily blatant about his intention of rewriting Virgil's original ethos: directly after his words about following Virgil, he announces his own *matere*, and whereas Virgil's *matere* had actually been 'arms and the man' – the heroic triumph of Aeneas – Chaucer's will be 'How Eneas to Dido was forsworn'. This is hardly following Virgil. Yet the mingling of reverence and autonomy in Chaucer's apostrophe is not mere impudence; like Dante, he knows that the only way to equal the great poets, to take one's place in the line of the great tradition, is to be new: to use the past and be present. In the *Prologue* to the *Legend*, after all, he insisted that his programme of depicting the virtue of his heroines, his *nakede tixt*, is both new and a restoration of the truth of the past. Images like the daisy opening up again fresh each morning, the birds singing in the new season after escaping the winter birdcatcher, and the new corn gleaned out of old fields (*Prologue*, ll. 55–70; *PF*, ll. 22–5), all express this complex vision of his inspiration as both new and old.

The *Legend* never attempts the task of reconsidering the subject-matter of *Troilus* or the *Roman de la Rose* in the light of their alleged injustice to women, but we could see Chaucer's *Dido* as not only redressing the balance on the question of fidelity, by presenting a 'trewe' woman and 'fals' man, but also restoring to Dido the queenly dignity and strength (the truth of her past) which had been undermined by the sympathetic but essentially weakening style of portrayal of her by Virgil and Ovid. The issues underlying Chaucer's enterprise of writing about Dido come down to the same issues, about texts and truth, and about interpretation, which were found to be central to the *Prologue*. This sort of narrative, stripped of the misogynistic and other moral biases of previous writers' versions (to be shaped anew, of course, to Chaucer's own bias), is what Chaucer had meant by the 'naked text' in the *Prologue* (l. 86) and his references to corn without chaff (see pp. 286–7). Such a text then becomes one that can stand with 'olde aprovede' histories (l. 21) like Claudian, Valerius Maximus and Livy, *trustable* accounts of women's 'trouthe', bearing witness to what the reality of women in history was.[18] Delany 1994: 120–3 observed (drawing on Deanesly's research) that 'naked' or 'bare' text was used by Lollards of accurate vernacular biblical translation uncontaminated by the Church's traditional glossing and interpretation, and it is a 'nakede tixt in Englis' that is Chaucer's aim: a vernacular work to stand in the tradition of great *autoriteis* (*Prologue*, l. 83). While the literary tradition must always be, for writers defending women, an anxious and problematic medium, Chaucer's positioning of himself as a morally innovative poet in relation to earlier male *autourys* on the subject shows that a searching anxiety about the issues and a willingness to be a revisionist are the only ways of joining the great tradition of literary lantern-bearers.

Helen Phillips

1.   In contrast, the *HF* version seems almost loose and rambling: there is less sense that a guiding *sens* or thematic dynamic decides why some Virgilian episodes are included, like the loss of Creusa, and some omitted, like the hunt and the cave, though the basic effect is to spread the balance of sympathy between Dido and Aeneas in a two-part narrative and, of course, to stress the role of Venus. Its narrative is general, with little specific detail and no dialogue; it is rather clumsy in the narrative presentation of moral viewpoint. Rather than integrating intimations of Aeneas's weaknesses into the whole narrative texture, as in *LGW*, Ch simply gives his narrator a passage of sudden diatribe against Aeneas (ll. 265–95), and then puts accusations into a long tirade by Dido against him as he leaves (ll. 300–60).

2.   See also Hall 1963; Desmond 1994: 155–62. Desmond 1994: 267 n. 63 lists studies of the sources of the story.

3.   Virgil's emphasis on the dominating influence of the gods' will is part of his design of the *Aeneid* as political epic prefiguring Roman history.

4.   This appears also in Benoît de Ste Maure, *Roman d'Éneas*, e.g. ll. 663–92.

5.   Ibid., ll. 1391–1432; see Nolan 1992 and Desmond 1994: 99–127.

6.   He might have heeded Le Fèvre's view that the gods' intervention rendered some classical tales unbelievable: *Leësce*, ll. 2463–530.

7.   Note 'pryvyly', l. 1018 (and 1288); 'devys', l. 1102; 'fals', l. 1236; 'feynede', 'feynyth', ll. 1257, 1266; 'craft', l. 1286; 'stele', 'stal', ll. 1289, 1327, 1333, 1335; 'traytour', l. 1328. Ch mentions superficial attractions, e.g. at ll. 1070–7, 1173, and his skill with words, ll. 1069, 1177, 1234–7.

8.   There was a medieval tradition going back to Dares, Dictys and Benoît de Ste Maure that saw Aeneas as false and treacherous, notably the belief that he helped to betray Troy (see *Gawain and the Green Knight*, ll. 1–5).

9.   See Jerome, *Against Jovinian* I, cols 41–6; Desmond 1994: 55–9.

10.   *Leësce*, ll. 2369–464. The *RR* protest is voiced by the misogynistically conceived Old Bawd, the *Vieille*, but Ch was never one to be put off by paradoxes. His own *Wife of Bath's Tale* voices protests about the ungratefulness of a *gentil* bridegroom, generously saved by his wife, which are very much in the spirit of *LGW*. See Phillips 1995a.

11.   See Frank 1972: 68–73.

12.   For a diametrically opposite interpretation, see Delany 1994: 197: she suggests Ch's audience might have found Dido's gifts of gold coins distasteful.

13.   Higden 1865–86: *Polychronicon*: IX, 272–6; Walsingham 1866: II, 210–11 (who adds that they gave these and then Richard deceived them – a parallel to Aeneas?).

14. Delany 1994: 164–86 finds 'orientalism' (the prejudice – outlined by Said 1978 – that leads Western writers, in the course of creating an identity for Western culture, to depict Eastern culture as exotic, excessive, luxurious and irrational) in the legends generally, and in the portrait of Dido. An opposite view is offered here, that it is the Trojans who are presented as foreign. She rightly (p. 180) observes that Trojans were sometimes associated with homosexuality (an example is *Éneas*). This is not found in Ch (of course, it might have been complicated for British authors by the legend that Trojans founded Britain).

15. Ch pioneered the apostrophe in English literature; see Minnis 1995: 172–9.

16. E.g. *Inf.* I, ll. 63–9; II, ll. 58–9; XX, ll. 52–99; *Purg.* VI, ll. 72–4; VII, l. 86; XVIII, ll. 83–4.

17. Boccaccio also celebrated Manto's achievements, as one of the heroines in his *De claris mulieribus*. His version of the Mantua link is that her son in filial piety built it near her grave and named it after Manto.

18. See Haas 1990 for an analogous argument in relation to the development of a tradition of female tragedy. Perhaps the phrasing of 'clene maydenes … trewe wyves … stedefaste widewes durynge alle here lyves' (ll. 281–3), 'goode women … That were trewe in lovynge al here lyves' (l. 475), has something to do with this idea of real life recorded in literature, as well as the need for a rhyme for *wyves*.

THE *LEGEND OF DIDO*

[Incipit Legenda Didonis martiris Cartaginis Regine &c.]

	Glorye and honour, Virgile Mantoan,	
925	Be to thy name, and I shal as I can	
	Folwe thy lanterne as thow gost byforn,	
	How Enea[s] to Dido was forsworn;	*treacherous*
	In [thyn Eneyde and Naso] wele I take	
	The tenor, and the grete effectis make.	
930	Whan Troye brought was to distruccioun	
	By Grekis sleyghte, and namely by Synoun,	*trickery; especially*
	Feynynge the hors iofferede to Mynerve,	

Rubic: 'Here begins the legend of Dido, martyr, queen of Carthage, etc.' Such headings give the legends the style of a *legendary*, a collection of saints' lives (Brusendorff 1925: 144 compares headings in Boccaccio's *De claris mulieribus*; a closer parallel is Vincent of Beauvais's chapter headings in *Speculum historiale*). They occur in seven MSS and may be by Ch.

924–9. See pp. 347–9 on these lines.

925. *be* is subjunctive: 'may they be (given)'; *can* = 'know'; *as I can*: 'as far as I know how'.

926. 'Follow your guiding light as you walk ahead'. ME *lanterne* often has the senses 'guide', 'inspiration'.

927. Ch does not make clear how this line relates to the lines before or after it: it provocatively diverges from Virgil (see p. 348). Perhaps it is a free-standing line, a summary of Ch's own theme: '[My subject being] how Aeneas was a traitor to Dido'. A statement of subject is usual early in an epic. Ch's statement of his subject here is a subversive equivalent to Virgil's Aeneas-centred statement, 'Arms and the man I sing' (*Aen.* I, l. 1).

928–9. 'From your *Aeneid* and from Ovid I intend to take the essence of the story, and portray the main events'. Ch further defines his own 'matere' at ll. 955–7. *Naso* = Ovid (Publius Ovidius Naso): see letter of Dido, *Her.* VII.

930–41. The list of events, with the main verb delayed until l. 941, is awkward in modern English but was probably designed as a neat, classical-sounding way of summarizing the mighty events leading up to Aeneas's voyage.

932–3. 'Inventing the trick of the horse offered to Minerva, because of which many a Trojan had to die'. The Greek Sinon let himself be captured by the Trojans and deceived them into letting into their city the huge wooden horse which caused the fall of Troy: he said it was an offering to the goddess of

Thour which that many Troyan muste sterve,
And Ector hadde, aftyr his deth, apiered,   *appeared*
935   And fyr so wod it myghte nat been steerid,
In al the noble toure of Ylioun,   *tower*
That of the cete was the chif dongeoun,
And al the cuntre was so lowe brought,   *cast down*
And Priamus the kyng fordon and nought,
940   And Enyas was chargit by Venus   *commanded*
To fleen awey, he tok Ascanius,   *flee*
That was his sone, in his rygh[t] hand and fledde.   *who was*
And on his bak he bar and wit[h] hym ledde,   *bore; took away*
His [olde] fadyr, clepid Anchises,   *called*
945   And by the weye his wif Crusa he les,   *lost*
And meche sorwe hadde he in his mynde   *great*
Or that he coude his felaueschepe fynde;   *before; company*
But at the laste, whan he hadde hem founde,   *them*
He made hym redy in a certeyn stounde,   *time*
950   And to the se [ful] faste he gan h[i]m hye.   *proceeded to hurry*
And saylyth forth [with] al his cumpaynye   *embarks*

wisdom, Athena (Latin name Minerva), but it was filled with Greeks who emerged at night and sacked the city; see *Aen.* II, ll. 57–198, *HF*, ll. 150–6.

934.   Hector's ghost warned Aeneas to leave Troy: *Aen.* II, ll. 268–97.

935.   'And fire so out of control it could not be directed away [from the city]' – a recurrent motif in Virgil's long description of the fall of Troy: *Aen.* II, ll. 304–17, 329–30, 431–4, 624–5. The fire, falseness and destruction perhaps prefigure the effects of love on Dido.

936-7.   *Ylioun*: Ilium, the central citadel of Troy; *dongeoun*: a fortified strong-hold, not merely a prison as in modern English.

939.   *Priamus*: the Trojan king; 'And Priam the king was destroyed and brought to nothing'.

940-5.   *Anchises*: Aeneas was the offspring of Anchises's love affair with Venus, the goddess of love.

945.   'And on his journey he lost his wife Creusa'. Ch ignores Virgil's account of Aeneas's anguished search for Creusa and her ghost's loving message (*Aen.* II, ll. 735–95). Ch includes this episode and the gods' interventions in *HF*, ll. 174–220.

949.   'He made himself ready at a certain hour'.

Toward Ytayle, as wolde his destene.
But of hise aventourys in the se   *about his adventures*
Nis nat to purpos for to speke of heyre,
955   For it acordyth nat to my matere,
But, as I seyde, of hym and of Dido   *about him*
Schal be my tale, til that I have do.   *is to be; finished*
      So longe he saylede in the salte se
Tyl in Libie onethe aryvede he,
960   With schepis vii and with no more navye.   *no larger fleet*
And glad was he to londe for to hye   *to hasten to land*
So was he with the tempest al toshake.   *completely buffeted*
And whan that he the havene hadde take   *harbour; entered*
He hadde a knyght was [called] Achates,   *who was*
965   And hym of al his felaushepe he ches   *out of all*
To gon with hym, the cuntre for t'espie.   *to spy out*
He tok with hym no more cumpaynye,   *larger group*
But forth they gon and lafte hise schepis   *go;*
    ryde,   *riding at anchor*
His fere and he, withoutyn any gyde.   *companion; guide*
970   So longe he walkyth in this wildyrnesse,
Til at the laste he mette an hunteresse.
A bowe in hande and arwis hadde sche,   *arrows*
Hire clothis cutte were unto the kne,   *cut short to*
But she was yit the fayreste creature   *nevertheless; loveliest*

952. 'Towards Italy, as his fate willed it' – a rare acknowledgement of Virgil's theme of fate. For Virgil, Aeneas's highest duty is to his destiny as founder of Rome, and Dido, representing passion and being also the founder of the city which later warred against Rome, is presented as a distraction that he must have the moral strength to reject.

954–5. 'It is not part of my plan to speak here, for it does not belong to my subject'. Aeneas's travels between Troy and Carthage are told, in flashback, in *Aen*. III.

959. 'Till with difficulty he came to land in Libya'. Libya: a N. African kingdom; Dido had won land for founding Carthage from Iarbas its king.

962. It is his ships, and their sails, etc., that have been battered by the storm.

963. 'And when he had arrived in the harbour'.

964. *Achates*: Aeneas's faithful companion.

971–1001. See *Aen*. I, ll. 314–417, *HF*, l. 229.

973, 982. *Aen*. I, ll. 320, 323, describes short skirts, knotted up to leave the knees bare, for speed and freedom while hunting.

975 That evere was iformyd by Nature.   *formed*
    And Eneas and Achates sche grette,   *greeted*
    And thus sche to hem spak, whan sche hem mette: *met them*
    'Saw ye,' quod sche, 'As ye han walkid wyde,   *did you see; about*
    Onye of my susteryn walke yow besyde,
980 With ony wilde bor or othir beste,   *other animal*
    That they han huntid to, in this foreste,   *have been hunting*
    Itukkid up, with arwis in hire cas?'
        'Nay, sothly, lady,' quod this Enyas,   *truly; said*
    'But by thy beute, as it thynkyt me,   *seems to me*
985 Thow myghtyst nevere erthely woman be,
    But Phebus' systyr art thow, as I gesse.   *you are; surmise*
    And, if so be that thow be a goddesse,   *if it be*
    Have mercy on oure labour and oure   *struggles;*
        wo.'   *unhappiness*
    'I ne am no goddesse, sothly,' quod sche tho,   *am no; then*
990 'For maydenys walkyn in this cuntre here,   *girls walk*
    With arwis and with bowe in this manere.
    This is the reyne of Libie there ye ben,
    Of [which] that Dido lady is and queen.'
    And schortely tolde hym al te occasyoun
995 Whi Dido cam into that regioun,
    Of whiche as now me lestyth nat to ryme:
    It nedyth nat, it were but los of tyme;
    For this is al and som: it was Venus,
    His owene modyr, that spak [with him]   *who was speaking*
        thus.   *thus*

979. 'Any of my sisters walking near you'.
982. 'With skirt tucked up, and arrows in her quiver?'
985. 'You could never be an earthly woman'.
986. *Aen.* I, l. 329. Phoebus = Apollo the sun-god. His sister is Diana, the moon-
    goddess and goddess of hunting. Aeneas's speech prefigures the 'mercy' he
    will receive from Dido.
992-3. 'This is the kingdom of Libya, where you are, of which Dido is mistress
    and queen'. Virgil's huntress (*Aen.* I, ll. 331–68) narrates here Dido's
    previous adventures and achievements.
994-8. 'And briefly she told him all the causes that had led to Dido arriving in that
    region, about which I have no wish at the moment to write. It is not
    necessary, it would be but loss of time; for this is the essential fact: it was
    Venus'.

| 1000 | And to Cartage [s]he had he schulde hym dighte, | *direct his path* |

1000   And to Cartage [s]he had he schulde hym dighte,   *direct his path*
        And vanyschid anon out of his syghte.   *straightaway*
            I coude folwe word for word Virgile,
        But it schul[d]e lastyn al t[o] longe while.   *take far too long time*
        This noble queen, that clepid was Dido,
1005   That whilom was the wif of Sytheo,   *who formerly had been*
        That fayrere was than is the bryghte sunne,
        This noble toun of Cartage hath bygunne,   *founded*
        In which sche regnyth in so gret honour
        That sche was hold[e of] alle queenys flour,
1010   Of gentillesse, of fredom, of beute,
        That wel was hym that myghte hire onys se:
        Of kyngis and of lordis so desyred,
        That al the world hire beute hadde ifyred,
        Sche stod so wel in every wightis grace.   *everyone's admiration*
1015   Whan Enya[s] was come onto that place,   *to that place*
        Unto the maystir temple of al the toun,   *chief*

1002. *word for word*: medieval theories about translation often distinguish two
    types of translation: literal glossing, *word for word*, and paraphrase, *sense
    for sense* (though most non-biblical translation was very free by modern
    standards). Here, however, the phrase means not 'literally' but 'in all his
    detail'; Ch draws covert attention to his departures from Virgil.

1005–7. *Sytheo*: Sychaeus. Before Virgil's epic narrative of her love affair with
    Aeneas, Dido was primarily renowned as a Phoenician princess who, after
    her husband Sichaeus's murder, escaped from Phoenicia with many
    followers and established Carthage in Libya, where, as a chaste widow,
    she refused to remarry, burning herself on a pyre. Jerome praised her for
    this fidelity in *Against Jovinian* I, col. 43. Ch cuts Virgil's references to
    Sichaeus, eschewing this tradition of her conventional wifely fidelity in
    favour of his own more daring concept of fidelity within extra-marital
    passion. Jerome said she 'preferred to burn rather than to marry'; Ch
    rephrases: her beauty set the world alight (l. 1013).

1009–13. 'So that she was considered to be the greatest of queens, in noble
    actions, in generosity, in beauty, so that he who could see her even once
    was fortunate: so desired in marriage by kings and lords, that her beauty
    had set alight the whole world'.

1016–17. Virgil's Dido is first seen engaged in administration and judgement
    outside the mighty temple; Ch has her first seen at prayer. ME *large*
    has the senses 'generous', 'ample' and 'wide' as well as 'big': fitting
    connotations here and at l. 1118. In *HF*, ll. 239–64 Ch briefly records

Ther Dido was in hire devocyoun,   *engaged in prayers*
Ful pryvyly his weye thus hath he nome.
Whan he was in the large temple come,   *spacious; had come*
1020   I can nat seyn if that it be possible,   *say; might be possible*
But Venus hadde hym makid invysible,   *made him*
Thus seyt[h] the bok withoutyn ony les.
And whan this Enyas and Achates
Haddyn in this temple ben overal,   *had gone everywhere*
1025   Thanne founde they, depeyntid on the wal   *painted*
How Troye and al the lond distroyed was.
'Allas that I was born,' quod Enyas,
'Thourout the worl[d] oure shame is kid   *throughout;*
  so wyde   *made known*
Now it is peyntid upon every syde.   *everywhere*
1030   We that weryn in prosperite   *who were*
Been now disclanderyd, and in swich degre   *dishonoured; state*
No lengere [for to] lyvyn I ne kepe.'   *have no care*
And with that word he brast out for to wepe,   *burst out weeping*
So tendyrly that routhe it was to sene.   *poignantly; pitiful; see*
1035   This frosche lady, of the cete queene,   *lovely; city*
Stod in the temple in hire estat ryal   *royal power*
So rychely, and ek so fayr withal,

Dido's love for Aeneas during his stay in Carthage, omitting all details, like the feast, presents or hunt.

1018. *nome*: 'taken'; 'Quite inconspicuously he has picked his way like this'. Ch replaces the magic cloud of invisibility given by Venus in Virgil (l. 1021), to make Aeneas's unnoticed approach wholly mortal; yet by choosing the stealthy-sounding *ful pryvyly*, he introduces his own theme of Aeneas's deceitfulness even to this innocuous action.

1022. 'That is what the book says, in truth': Ch is ambiguous. In *Aen.* I, ll. 412, 516, Venus surrounds Aeneas and Achates with cloud.

1030. Ch alters *Aen.* I, ll. 453–95, where Aeneas is impressed and heartened by the fact that Troy's tragedy is so widely known: his Aeneas is distressed by their loss of honour and fall from prosperity. He seems weaker, and the motif of Dido's *pite* is again prefigured. There is also a suggestion of the medieval theme of Fortune (see ll. 1044–5).

1031. *degre*, like *estat* (l. 1036), means 'rank' or 'level in society': they have fallen to such a low state he no longer cares whether he lives. Compare Dido's *estat ryal*.

1037. 'So sumptuously and also so beautiful as well'.

So yong, so lusty with hire eyen glad,   *cheerful; happy eyes*
That, if that God that hevene and erte made,   *who made; earth*
1040   Wolde han a love, for beute and goodnesse,   *wanted to have*
And womanhod, and trouthe and semelyness,
Whom shulde he lovyn but this lady swete?   *love; sweet*
Ther nys no woman to hym half so mete.   *suitable for him*
Fortune, that hath the world in
governaunce,   *under her control*
1045   Hath sodeynly brough[t] in so newe a chaunce   *event*
That nevere [was ther yit so] fremde a cas.
For al the cumpaynye of Enyas,
[Which] that he wende a lorn in the se,
Aryvyd is, nat fer fram that cete.   *come to shore*
1050   For which the gretteste of hise lordis some
By aventure ben to the cete come,   *by chance are*
Unto that same temple, for to seke   *to seek*
The queene, and of hire socour to beyseke,   *ask for help from her*
Swich renoun was there sprongyn of hire   *fame; had sprung up*
goodnesse,
1055   And whan they hadden told al here distresse,   *their*

1039–43. The idea that, if the Creator wanted to love a woman, Dido would be
the only suitable one, may strike modern ears as grotesque, but (because
the Beloved in the Song of Songs was identified with her) many lyrics
describe Mary in such a fashion: Ch, as with Alceste and White, is praising
a woman in heavenly terms.

1041.   'And all the virtues of women, and constancy and graciousness'.

1044–6. Ch introduces Fortune imagery: just as Aeneas's company fell from
prosperity (ll. 1030–2), so now Fortune brings about the meeting of Dido
and Aeneas and his happy reunion with the rest of his fleet. Fortune is
appointed by the Creator to rule over change, transience and unpredict-
ability in this world. *cas* (Latin *casus*) = 'a fall', as well as 'situation'; like
chaunce and *aventure* (l. 1051), it is a word associated with Fortune.
newe: used elsewhere of Aeneas and the Trojans, e.g. l. 1151.

1046.   The line's wording and order vary in the MSS without altering the sense:
'that never before had there fallen so strange a coincidence'.

1048.   *a* (variant *ha*): an unstressed form of the infinitive *have(n)*, *han*: 'whom he
had believed to have lost at sea'.

1050.   'Because of which several of the most important of his nobles'.

1052–6. Ch stresses Dido's compassion and generosity here, as at ll. 1063,
1078–89.

	And al here tempest and here harde cas,	*harsh fate*
	Unto the quyen apiered Enyas	
	And opynly [b]eknew that it was he.	*revealed*
	[W]ho hadde joye thanne, but his meyne,	*who; retainers*
1060	That hadde founde here lord, here gouvernour?	*their leader*
	The quyen saugh that they dede hym swych honour,	*paid; such*
	And hadde herd ofte of Eneas er tho,	*before then*
	And in hire herte she hadde routhe and wo	*pity and sorrow*
	That evere swich a noble man as he	
1065	Schal ben diserityd in swich degre.	
	And saw the man, that he was lyk a knyght,	
	And sufficiaunt, of persone and of mygh[t],	*able, in body; strength*
	And lyk to been a verray gentil man,	
	And wel hise wordis he besette can,	
1070	And hadde a noble visage, for the nonys,	*face; also*
	And formed wel of braun[es] and of bonys.	*muscles; bones*
	For, aftyr Venus, hadde he swich fayrnesse	*taking after; beauty*
	That no man myghte be half so fayr, I gesse,	*could; believe*
	And wel a lord he semede for to be.	*every inch a lord*
1075	And, for he was a staunger, sumwhat sche	
	Likede hym the bet, as – God do bote –	
	To sum folk ofte newe thyng is sote.	
	Anon hire herte hath pite of his wo,	*immediately; pity for*
	And with that pete love come in also.	
1080	And thus, for pete and for gentillesse,	*because of her noble nature*
	Refreschede muste he been of his distresse.	*must be recuperated*
	[Sche] seyde, certis, that sche sory was	*certainly; distressed*
	That he hath had swych peryl and swich cas,	*such; misfortune*
	And in hire frendely speche in this manere	

1065. 'Should have been thrown out of his inheritance to such a degree'.
1066. 'And saw the man, that he looked like a knight'.
1068–9. 'And the image of a truly noble man, and he knows how to deploy his words well'.
1075–7. 'And because he was a stranger, she to some extent liked him all the better, as, God give us help, to some people often a new thing is sweet.' Cf. *HF*, ll. 287–92, which warn of the folly of loving the unfamiliar too readily.

1085	Sche to hym spak and seyde, as ye may here:	*can hear*
	'Be ye nat Venus' sone and Anchises'?	*are you not*
	In good fey, al the worshepe and encres	*faith; honour and aid*
	That I may goodly don yow ye schal have.	
	Youre shepis and youre meyne shal I save.'	*retinue*
1090	And manye a gentil word sche spak hym to,	*noble*
	And comaunded hire massangerys for to go	
	The same day withoutyn any fayle,	
	Hise shippis for to seke and hem vitayle,	*provision them*
	[Ful] manye a beste sche to the shippis sente,	*animal*
1095	And with the wyn sche gan h[e]m to presente,	
	And to hire real paleys she hire spedde,	*royal; hastened*
	And Enyas alwey with hire she ledde.	*constantly*
	What nedyth yow the feste to descrive?	*What need is there*
	He nevere [beter at ese was in] hese lyve.	*never happier*
1100	Ful was the feste of deynteis and rychesse,	*luxuries; profusion*
	Of instrumentis, of song and of gladnesse,	
	And manye an amerous lokyng and devys.	*glance; strategem*
	This Enyas is come to paradys	
	Out of the swolw of helle, and thus in joye	*abyss*
1105	Remembrith hym of his estat in Troye.	*he recalls; high rank*
	To daunsynge chaumberys full of paramentys,	*tapestries*
	Of riche beddis and of ornementis	*sumptuous couches*

1088. 'Which I can do to help you, you shall receive'.

1094. The animals are for fresh food on the next voyage.

1095. 'She provided them with wine'.

1098. 'What need is there to describe the feast to you?': the rhetorical device of *occupatio*. The poet says he will omit a full description, but see Frank 1972: 202–3 on its artistic uses; for example, it often emphasizes the splendour of feasts and luxuries.

1099. Frank 1972: 75 comments that this line and ll. 1103–5 create 'an overall impression of Aeneas as a fellow who has fallen on a cushy spot and is enjoying it to the full'.

1100. *deynteis*: etymologically connected to 'dignity', this retains a grander sense than modern English *dainties*; it has more the meaning of 'magnificent foods', 'luxuries'.

1102. *devys*: 'trick' or 'strategem'. Though it can innocently describe the little games, secret strategems and element of secrecy in the early stages of a flirtation, it is also a word which ominously prefigures Aeneas's subsequent deceitfulness.

	This Enyas is led, aftyr the mete.	*food*
	And with the quene whan he hadde sete,	*had sat*
1110	And spicis partid and the wyn agon,	*the spices were removed*
	Unto hise chambris was he led anon,	*rooms; straightaway*
	[To take] his ese and for to [have] his reste,	
	With al his folk, to don whatso hem	*whatever pleased*
	leste.	*them*
	There nas courser wel ibrydelid non,	
1115	Ne stede for [the justyng] wel to gon,	
	Ne large palfrey, esy for the nonys,	
	Ne jewel frettid ful of ryche stonys	
	Ne sakkis ful of gold, of large weyghte,	*lavish weight*
	No rubye non, that shynede by nyghte,	*not one*
1120	Ne gentil hawtein faucoun heroner,	
	Ne hound, for hert or wilde bor or der,	*boar; deer*
	Ne coupe of gold, with floreynys newe ibete,	
	That in the land of Libie may be gete,	*can; obtained*
	That Dido [ne] hath it Enyas isent.	
1125	And al is payed, what that he hath spent.	
	This can this honurable quene hire gestis calle,	
	As sche that can in fredom passyn alle.	*generosity surpass*
	Eneas sothly ek, withoute les,	*truly also; doubt*
	Ha[th] sent onto his schip, by Achates,	*sent a message to*
1130	Aftyr his sone and aftyr riche thyngis,	*for his son*
	Bothe septre, clothis, [brochis, and ek] ryngis,	*brooches*

1109–10. 'And after he had sat [at dessert] with the queen, and the spices and wines had been removed'. After dinner guests might be entertained with a dessert of sweet wines, spiced wines, fruit, spiced cakes and sweets (partly for pleasure, partly to aid digestion). Now, later on, the spices and wines have been taken away.

1114–17. 'There was no racehorse whatsoever, splendidly bridled, no steed excellent for performing in a joust, no large riding horse, comfortable for that purpose, no jewel decorated all over with costly stones'.

1120.   'Nor any noble, proud falcon for hunting herons'.

1122–5. 'No basket of gold, with florins newly struck, that can be obtained in the land of Libya, that Dido has not sent to Aeneas. And she pays off all he has spent'. *floreynys*: florins, gold coins originally made in Florence.

1126–7. *calle*: to treat or make welcome. 'Thus this honourable queen knows how to make her guests welcome, being a woman who knows how to surpass everyone in generosity.'

	Some to were and some [for] to presente	*wear*
	To hy[re] that alle [thise noble] thyngis hym sente.	
	And bad his sone how that he schulde	*instructed;*
	make	*must make*
1135	The presenti[ng], and to the quyen it take.	*presentation*
	Repeyrid is this Achates agayn,	*returned*
	And Enyas ful blysful is and fayn	*eager*
	To sen [his yonge] sone Ascanyus.	*to see*
	But, natheles, oure autour tellith us	*nevertheless; author*
1140	That Cupido, that is the God of Love,	*who*
	At preyere of his modyr, hye above,	*at the request*
	Hadde the liknesse of the child itake,	*taken the likeness*
	This [noble] queen enamorede to make	*in love*
	On Eneas, but as of that scripture,	*with Aeneas; text*
1145	Be as be may, I take of it no cure.	
	But soth is this: the queen hath mad swich chere	*such kindly welcome*
	Unto this child that wondir is to here.	*amazing; hear*
	And of the present, that his fadyr sente,	*For*
	Sche thank[ed] hym ful ofte [in] good entente.	*great sincerity*
1150	Thus is this quyen in plesaunce and in joye,	
	With alle these newe lusti folk of Troye.	*lively*
	And of the dedis hath she more enquyrid	*adventures*
	Of Enyas, and al the story lerid	*learnt*
	Of Troye; and al the longe day they tweye	*the two of them*
1155	Entendedyn to spekyn and to pleye.	
	Of whiche ther gan to bredyn swich a fyer	*began to breed*
	That sely Dido hath now swich desyr	*innocent*
	With Enyas hire newe geste to dele,	*to be with*
	That she hath lost hire hewe and ek hire hele.	*colour; health*
1160	Now to th'effect: now [to] the freut of al,	*result; fruit*

1140–1. *Cupido*: Cupid, the god of desire and love, Venus's son; here, unlike Love in the *Prologue*, a child-god. *modyr*: i.e. Venus.

1145–6. 'But, to that statement, whatever the truth of it, I do not pay much attention. The truth is this: the queen has given such a kindly welcome'; the theme of reliable texts again. Ch downplays the gods' role; cf. *Aen.* I, ll. 657–722, where Venus and Cupid make Dido fall in love by supernatural arts and the charms of Cupid, disguised as Ascanius.

1151.   *newe, of Troye*: stresses the exotic novelty of the Trojans to Dido.

1155.   'They gave all their attention to talking and amusing themselves'.

Whi I have told this story and telle schal.

Thus I begynne: it fil upon a nyght,   *came about*

Whan that the mone upreysed hadde hi[r]   *raised up her*
    lyght,   *light*

This noble queene onto hire reste wente.   *unto*

1165 Sche sikyth sore and gan hyreself turmente;   *sighs painfully*

Sche [wakith, walwith], makith manye a breyde,

As don these loveris, as I have herd seyde.   *do*

And at the laste, unto hire systr Anne

Sche made hire mone and ryght thus spak sche   *lament*;
    thanne: *then*

1170 'Now [dere] sistyr myn, what may it be   *my dear sister*

That me agastith in my [dreme]?' quod she.   *frightens me*

'This newe Troyan is so in my thought,

Me thynkith that he is so wel iwrought   *splendidly formed*

And [ek so likli] to ben a man,

1175 And [therwithall] so mech good he can,

That al my love and lyf lyth in his cure.   *lie in his power*

Have ye nat herd [him telle] his aventure?

Now, certis, Anne, if that ye rede me   *certainly; advise*

I wolde fayn to hym iweddit be;

1180 This is th'effect: what schulde I more seye?

In hym lyth al: to do me leve or deye.'

    Hyre systir Anne, as she that coude hire good,

Seyde as hire thoughte, and sumdel it withstod.

But herof was so long a sarmounnyng   *about it; conversation*

1185 It were to longe to make rehersyng.   *would be; repetition*

But finaly it may nat ben withstande.   *in the end*

1161. 'The reason why I have told this story and shall tell further'.

1166. 'She lies awake, is restless, makes many a sudden turn'; see *Aen*. IV, ll. 1–8.

1174–5. 'And also so like what a man should be, and in addition he has so much
ability'.

1179–81. 'I would dearly like to be married to him. That sums it up: what more
should I say? Everything lies in his hands: to make me live or die'. In *Aen*.
IV, ll. 9–29, Dido's speech is dominated by the issue of her fidelity to her
dead husband.

1182. *coude hire goode*: 'knew the course that was best for her'.

1183. 'Said how it seemed to her, and to some extent she opposed it'. This is Ch's
invention: Virgil's Anna is encouraging (*Aen*. IV, ll. 31–53; see also *HF*,
ll. 366–70).

	Love wil love: for nothing wele it wande.	*will it desist*
	The dawenyng uprist out of the se;	*dawning*
	This amerous quien chargith [hi]re	*commands;*
	meyne	*household*
1190	The nettis dresse and speris brode and kene.	*to prepare; sharp*
	An huntyng wol[e] this lusti frosche queene,	*vivacious, lovely*
	So prikyth hire this newe jolye wo.	*spurs her on*
	To hors is al hi[r] lusty folk igo.	*vigorous; gone*
	Into the court the houndis been ibrought,	*courtyard; are fetched*
1195	And upon courseris, swift as ony thought,	*fast horses*
	Hire yonge knyghtis hovyn al aboute,	*hang around waiting*
	And of hire wemen ek an huge route.	*crowd*
	Upon a thikke palfrey, paper-whit,	*sturdy riding-horse*
	With sadyl red, enbroudit with delyt,	*embroidered delightfully*
1200	Of gold the barris up-enbosede hye,	
	Sit Dido, al in gold and perre wrye,	*sits; jewellery; covered*
	And she as [faire] as is the bryght morwe	*morning*
	That helith syke [folk] of nyghtis sorwe.	*heals sick; night's*
	Upon a courser, stertelynge as the fyr –	*lively*
1205	Men myghte turne hym with a litil wyr –	
	Sit Enyas, lik Phebus to devyse,	*sits; describe*
	So was he frosch arayed in his wyse.	*style of apparel*
	The fomy brydil, with the bit of gold,	*foamy*

1191. *An huntyng*: 'on a hunt', also in l. 1211 (*huntyng* = noun). Cf. the hunt in *Aen*. IV, ll. 129–59. Virgil prefaces the hunt with a long negotiation between Juno and Venus: Juno, by bringing them together, hopes to prevent Aeneas moving on to found Rome.

1192. 'So this new happy misery spurs her on'. *jolye wo*: an oxymoron, a typically Petrarchan style of describing love (cf.*TC* I, ll. 400–20).

1196. *hovyn*: to hover, wait expectantly. Their temporary, enforced inaction enhances our sense of their youth and their *coursers'* swiftness. Many verbal details in this passage create the sense of impetus, expectation and eagerness.

1200. 'The stripes of gold embossed to stand up high'.

1205. 'People could turn him with just a slender wire': the horse is so responsive that a delicate wire bit (ME *wire* = often decorative gold wire) will control him.

1207. 'He was so attractively dressed up in his style of clothing'. Ch cuts Virgil's complimentary epic simile elevating Aeneas by comparing him at length to Phoebus the sun-god.

Governyth he ryght as hymself hath wold.
1210 And forth this noble queen [thus lat I] ride   *I leave to ride*
On huntynge, with this Troyan by hyre side.
        The hirde of hertis [founden ys] anon;   *herd; harts*
With 'Hay!', '[G]o bet!', 'Pryke thow!', 'Lat gon,
    lat gon!'
'Why nyl the lioun comyn or the bere   *why won't*
1215 That I myghte [onys mete hym] with this   *so I could just*
    spere?'   .   *once*
Thus sey these yonge folk, and up they kylle
These [wilde hertes], and han hem at here   *have them;*
    wille.   *their will*
Among al this to rumbelyn gan the hevene.   *rumble*
The thundyr rorede, with a gresely stevene.   *grisly voice*
1220 Doun cam the reyn, with hayl and slet so faste,   *powerfully*
With hevenys fer, that it so sore agaste
This noble quien, and also hire meyne,   *retinue*
That iche of hem was glad awey to fle.   *each*
        And, schortely, from the tempest hire   *briefly; herself*
    to save,
1225 Sche fledde hireself into a litil cave.

1209. 'He controls, exactly according to his own will'. In these twin mounted por-
    traits, Dido is portrayed as gloriously attractive and Aeneas as wielding the
    power to manipulate (a horse, Dido or events) to his own pleasure and with
    minimum effort on his part – because Dido has provided him with so willing
    and superior a mount. Cf. the motif of Aeneas's power at ll. 1176, 1181; at
    l. 1217 the hunters have noble harts in their power. In *Aen.* IV, ll. 134–5, it is
    Dido whose horse is lively and foaming at the bit; Ch gives her a sedate pal-
    frey, Aeneas the energetic *courser*. Virgil does not describe Aeneas's horse.
1210. 'Thus I leave this noble queen to ride forth'.
1213. 'With "Hey!", "Go faster!", "Use your spurs!", "Let go! Let go!"'.
1214–16. In *Aen.* IV, l. 159, Ascanius expresses a wish like this. Ch generalizes it,
    focusing on no individual apart from the lovers, stressing motifs of energy
    and eagerness for capture, potential sexual symbols.
1221. Ch's rhetorical *hevenys fer*, for lightning, is the only phrase suggesting the
    divine intervention that dominates this scene in Virgil.
1225–6. Ch's wording, 'She took herself, to escape, into a little cave', suggests that,
    Dido having entered solely for her own weather protection, Aeneas then
    opportunistically follows her; *Aen.* IV, l. 165 unites their entry in one
    statement: 'Into the same cave Dido and the Trojan leader make their way'.

And with hire wente this Enyas also.
I not with hem if there wente any mo: *do not know*
The autour makyth of it no mencioun.
And here began the depe affeccioun   *passion*
1230   Betwixe hem two; this was the ferste morwe
Of hire gladnesse and gynn[ynge] of hire sorwe. *beginning; their*
For there hath Enyas ikneled so,
And told hire al his erte and al his wo,   *revealed; heart*
And swore so depe to hire to be trewe,   *deeply*
1235   For wel or wo, and chaunge hire for no newe,
And, as a fals lovere, so wel can pleyne   *lament*
That sely Dido rewede on his peyne.   *innocent; had pity*
And tok hym for husbonde, and become his wyf
For everemo, whil that h[e]m lefte lyf.
1240   And aftyr [this, whan] that the tempest stynt,   *ceased*
With myrthe out as they comyn, hom they wente.

1232–7. In *Aen*. IV, ll. 90–130, 166–8, the goddesses preside over the cave
episode; Ch makes it entirely human. Ch adds Aeneas's oath, soon to be
broken, perhaps imitating Le Fèvre's *Leësce*, l. 2448. Aeneas's ready
tongue is mentioned at ll. 1069, 1155, 1177, 1265–6. *Aen*. IV, ll. 166–72
focus on Dido and her responsibility; Aeneas's attitude is not mentioned.
Here the moral issues are his, not Dido's.

1235–6. 'For better or worse, and never change her for a new lover. And, like a
false lover, he knows so well how to present his sufferings'.

1236.   In medieval law it was consent that made a marriage. Here there is consent
on Dido's part, though no marriage rite, and ll. 1236, 1238–9 echo
marriage vows still familiar in Christian wedding services. *Aen*. IV,
ll. 166–72 ambiguously suggests quasi-marriage: Juno, the goddess of
marriage, is present, yet Virgil condemns Dido: 'Neither reputation nor
the impression she gave restrained her; it was no longer a secret love she
meditated in her heart: she calls it marriage; with this name she hides her
fault'. Ch uses language which encourages the reader to feel that, in Dido's
moral and emotional perception (like Troilus's), the union has the
essentials of committed, faithful union. Given the binding power of pre-
marriage consent and betrothal in medieval attitudes to marriage, it is
probably a mistake for critics to become exercised about whether a legal
marriage has or has not occurred (Rowe 1988: 58 n. 20 summarizes
Kelly's views and his own condemnation of Dido).

1239.   'For evermore, as long as life may last for them'.

1241.   'With cheerfulness, just as they set out, they went home'.

The wikke fame [up]ros, and that anon,
How Enias hath with the queen igon   *gone*
Into the cave, and demede as hem leste.   *judged as they liked*
1245   And whan the kyng that Yarbis highte it
            w[i]ste,
        As he that hadde [hire] lovyd evere his lyf
        And wowede hyre, to han hire [to] his wyf,   *wooed; have*
        Swich sorwe as he makede and swich cheere   *such reaction*
        It is a routhe and pite for to here.
1250   But [as] in love alday it happith so,
        That on schal layghyn [at] anotherys wo,
        Now layhith Enias and is in joye,   *laughs*
        And more richesse than evere was in Troye.   *in more wealth*
            O sely wemen, ful of innocence,   *unsuspecting*
1255   Ful of pite, of trouthe [and] conscience,
        What makyth yow to men to truste so?
        Have ye swych routhe upon hyre feynede wo   *pretended*
        And han swich olde ensaumplis yow beforn?   *when you have*
        Se ye nat alle how [they] ben forsworn?   *perjured*
1260   Where sen ye on that he ne hath laft his lief,
        Or ben onkynde or don hire sum myschief,   *harm*

1242. 'Unpleasant rumour rose up, and that happened immediately'. *Aen.* IV,
       ll. 173–95 has a famous description of personified Fame here; cf. *HF*,
       ll. 1360–92.
1245–6. *Yarbis*: the king of the neighbouring land who had wooed Virgil's Dido
       unsuccessfully (*Aen.* IV, ll. 196–218); 'When the king who was called
       Iarbas learned of it, being a man who had loved her all his life'.
1251. 'That one is destined to laugh at another's misery'. ME *schal* has a sense
       of 'obligation': what must be, ought to be, or is destined to be.
1253. 'And in more prosperity than ever was in Troy'.
1255. *conscience*: = both 'conscience' and 'consciousness' or 'sensitivity'; per-
       haps 'sensitivity to moral priorities'.
1256. 'What makes you put such trust in men?' The accusation that men use
       rhetoric (*feynede wo*, l. 1257) to seduce unwary women is common in
       man–woman dialogues from Andreas Capellanus to *La belle dame sans
       merci*, but Ch goes much further in his picture of ruthless exploitation,
       treachery and injury.
1260. 'Where do you see one who has not abandoned his dear one'.

Or pilid hire, or bostid of hise dede?
Ye may as wel it sen as ye may rede.
Tak hede now, of this grete gentil man,   *notice now*
1265   This Troyan, that so wel hire plesyn can,   *knows how to please*
That feynyth hym so trewe and   *falsely presents;*
    obeysynge,   *obedient*
So gentil and so [privy] of his doinge,   *discreet*
And can so wel don alle hise obeysauncis,
And waytyn hire at festis and at dauncis,
1270   And whan sche goth to temple, and hom ageyn.
And fastyn til he hath his lady seyn,
And beryn in hise devysis for hire sake
Not I not what. And songis wolde he make,
Justyn and don of armys manye thyngis,   *joust, in arms*
1275   Synde hire letteres, tokenys, brochis, ryngis.   *keepsakes*
        Now herkith how he shal his lady serve. *listen; recompense*
Thereas he was in peril for to sterve,
For hungyr and for myschif in the se,   *disaster at sea*
And desolat and fled from his cuntre,   *alone; escaped*
1280   And al his folk with tempest al todryvyn,   *driven to harm*
Sche hath hire body and ek hire reame yevyn   *kingdom given*
Into his hand, thereas she myghte have been
Of othere landys than of Cartage [a] quien,

1262–3. 'Or robbed her, or boasted of what he has done? You can see it as easily as you can read about it': offences showing male ingratitude and aggression, robbing a woman materially by exploiting her generosity, and robbing her reputation by boasting to male friends.

1268. 'And knows so well how to make all sorts of signs of respect, and be attentive to her at banquets and dances'.

1271–3. 'And not to eat until he has seen his lady, and wear I don't know what, for her sake [as a symbol of devotion], in his badges. And he would compose songs'. A medievalization: retainers wear a lord's badge (increasingly common and unpopular in Richard II's reign: Sherborne 1994: 234–43); lovers wear badges to symbolize emotional 'allegiance' to their ladies.

1276. *he*: Aeneas; *serve*: ironic pun: on the (pretence) of lover's 'service' to his lady and the non-existent *recompence* he will make for her generosity.

1277. 'Whereas he had been in danger of dying'.

1283–4. Other MSS have *lande*: does Chaucer mean Iarbas's kingdom?

	And lyvyd in joye inow – what wele ye more?	*abundant happiness*
1285	This Enyas, that hath so depe iswore,	
	Is wery of his craft withinne a throwe,	*strategy; short spell*
	The hote ernest is al overblowe,	*eagerness; blown away*
	And pryvyly he doth hise shepis dyghte	*makes ready his ships*
	And shapith hym to stele awey be nyghte.	*makes his plan; by*
1290	This Dido hath suspescioun of this,	
	And thoughte wel that it was al amys,	
	For in hire bed [he] lyth anyght and sykyth.	*at night; sighs*
	Sche axeth hym anon what hym myslykyth.	*causes him displeasure*
	'My dere herte, whiche that I love most,	*most of all*
1295	Sertis,' quod he, 'This nyght my faderys gost	*in truth; spirit*
	Hath in my slep so sore me tormentid,	
	And ek Mercurye his massage hath presentid,	*also; message*
	That nedis to the conquest of Ytayle	*necessarily*
	My destene is sone for to sayle.	*it is my destiny*
1300	For which me thynkyth brostyn is myn herte.'	*broken*
	Therwith hise false terys out they sterte,	*pour*
	And takith hire withinne hise armys two.	*he takes*
	'Is that in ernest?' quod sche, 'Wele ye so?	*Do you intend that?*
	Have ye nat sworn to wyve me to take?	*as wife*
1305	Allas, what w[o]man wele ye of me make?	
	I am a gentil woman and a quien.	*noble; queen*

1284. Ch addresses the audience: do they need him to say more? It is followed by a summary of Aeneas's total lack of stability or gratitude.

1292. MS variation suggests that scribes were confused as to whether *he or she* was sighing in *his or her* bed.

1292–4. Ch's wording conveys Dido's loving concern for *Aeneas*, rather than herself.

1297–1304. Mercury, the messenger-god. It is presented as a factual event in *Aen.* IV, ll. 205–95; Ch makes it merely what Aeneas says, adding *false terys* (l. 1301). Dido's reply continues the theme of words and oaths: were they in earnest or pretended? *nedis*: 'necessarily'; the adverbial ending *-s/-ce* goes back to OE.

1305. Dido protests at the kind of reputation (according to the standards against which women are judged) he is creating for her; cf. *Aen.* IV, l. 322. Virgil weakens Dido's case, in at least male readers' eyes, by giving her furious speeches, while his Aeneas tries tenderly but dutifully to explain.

Ye wele nat from youre wif thus foule fleen?   *do not wish*
That I was born, allas! What schal I do?'   *alas that*
   To telle in schort, this noble quen Dydo
1310   Sche sekith halwis and doth sacryfise,
Sche knelyth, cryeth, that routhe is to devyse,   *appeals; describe*
Conjurith hym, and proferyth hym to be   *appeals to; offers*
His thral, his servant in the leste [de]gre.   *of the lowest rank*
Sche fallith hym to-fore and swounnyth ther,   *before him; faints*
1315   Dischevele with her bryghte gilte hair,
And seyth, '[Have] mercy, let me with yow ryde.
These lordis whiche that wonyn me besyde
Wele me distroyen, only for youre sake.   *will*
And so ye wele now to wive take,   *if, as wife*
1320   As ye han sworn, thanne wele I yeve yow leve   *give permission*
To slen me with youre swerd now, sone at eve.   *evening*
For thanne yit shal I deye as youre wif.   *then, notwithstanding*
I am with childe: and yeve my child his lyf!
Mercy, lord, have pete in youre thought!'
1325   But al this thing avaylith hire rygh[t] nought,
For on a nyght, slepynge he let hire lye

1307. 'You are not intending to run away despicably from your wife like this?'

1310–11. 'She goes to saints' shrines and performs sacrifices, she kneels, cries, so that it is pity to describe'. The *halwis* are Ch's medievalization and spiritualization of Dido's reaction. The writer feels *routhe* is absent from Aeneas's feelings. The theme of pity begins and ends her speech (ll. 1316, 1324).

1315. *dischevele*: not 'dishevelled' but unbound from its normal arrangement: 'With her bright golden hair loose'. Cf. *Her.* VII, l. 70.

1317–18. 'These rulers who inhabit the neighbouring regions will destroy me, solely because of you'; he puts her in danger, presumably because the African kings resent Aeneas as a foreign prince, as Dido claims in *Her.* VII, ll. 123–4. Dido thinks to herself of neighbouring kings' derision while sleepless, *Aen.* IV, l. 534.

1323. 'I am pregnant: let my child have his life!' Like *Leësce*, ll. 2446–7, and Machaut's *Jugement dou Roy de Navarre*, l. 2121, Chaucer's Dido says she was pregnant; Ovid's Dido protests that she *might* be pregnant (*Her.* VII, ll. 133–8); *Aen.* IV, ll. 327–9 is clear she was not pregnant.

1325–6. 'But all this does her absolutely no good, for one night he left her lying sleeping': another detail added by Ch to the *Aeneid* story.

And stal awey onto his cumpaynye,
And as a traytour forth he gan to sayle,
Toward the large cuntre of Ytayle.   *mighty*
1330 Thus [hath he] laft Dido in wo and peyne,
And weddede ther a lady hyghte Lavyne.   *called*
        A cloth he lafte, and ek his swerd stondynge,   *propped up*
Whan he from Dido stal in hire slepynge,   *stole*
Ryght at hire beddys hed, so gan he hie
1335 Whan that he stal awey to his navye.   *fleet*
Which cloth, whan sely Dido gan awake,   *innocent*
Sche hath it kyst ful ofte for his sake,
And seyde, 'O swete cloth – whil Juppiter it leste!
Tak now my soule, [unbynde me] of this onreste.
1340 I have fulfild of Fortune al the cours.'
And thus, [allas,] withoutyn his socours   *comfort*
Twenti tyme iswounyd hath sche thanne.   *swooned; then*

1327, 1333. Note the repeated *stal*; he is also secretive in the *Roman d'Éneas*,
ll. 1645–64. Virgil's Aeneas makes an anguished and loving reply; Jove
compels him, against his love for Dido, to fulfil his destiny to found Rome
(*Aen.* IV, ll. 333–61).

1331. *Lavyne*: Lavinia, princess of Latium, site of the future city of Rome. She
was a famous romantic heroine for medieval readers from her bold
passion for Aeneas in the *Roman d'Éneas*, as well as her role in the second
half of the *Aeneid*.

1334. 'Just by her bed's head, he was in such a hurry'; Ch introduces irresponsi-
ble habits and cowardly haste. *Aen.* IV, ll. 646, 651–3 has a different view
of the equipment left behind: he had given her a Trojan sword as a present;
she addresses the 'sweet remnants' of his clothes on their bed.

1338. 'And said, "O precious cloth – as long as it pleased Jupiter"', i.e. as long
as Jupiter allowed her to be happy with Aeneas. Perhaps this reflects the
long lament Dido makes in the *Roman d'Éneas* as she lies stabbed on top
of Aeneas's clothes on their bed: she lies dying, kissing the bed and his
clothes, ll. 2038–2074.

1339. This line refers to the belief that the soul is in the breath and kissing can
transfer one's soul to what is kissed. *unbynde*: release it out of this
torment; 'exsolvite curis', *Aen.* IV, l. 652.

1340. 'I have gone through the whole revolution of Fortune's wheel': this
medievalizes *Aen.* IV, l. 653: 'I have lived and travelled the route that
Fortune gave to me'.

1341. He leaves her to suffer, without the *socours* he as husband should give.

And whanne that sche unto hire systyr Anne
Compleynede hadde, of which I may nat wryte: *lamented; can*
1345   So gret a reuthe I have [it] for t'endite,   *pity; to compose*
And bad hire norice and hire sistir gon   *asked her nurse*
To fechyn fyr and othyr thyng anon,   *things*
And seyde that sche wolde sacryfye,   *wanted to*
And whan she myghte hire tyme wel espie   *opportunity*
1350   Upon the fir of sacryfise she sterte;   *leaped*
And with his swerd she rof hyre [to the] herte.   *stabbed herself*
But yit, as myn autour [seythe], thus sche seyde;
Or she was hurt, byforn or she deyede,
Sche wrot a lettere anon, that thus began:
1355   'Ryght so,' quod she, 'As that the white swan   *exactly as*
Ayens his deth begynnyth for to synge,   *just before*
Right so to yow make I my compleynynge.   *lament*
Not that I trowe to getyn yow ageyn,
For wel I wot that it is al in veyn,
1360   Syn that the goddis been contrarye to me.   *are opposed*
But, syn my name is lost thour yow,' quod she,
'I may wel lese on yow a word or lettere,
Al be it that I shal ben nevere the bettere.   *even though*
For thilke wynd that blew youre schip awey,   *that same*

1346.   For the nurse, see *Aen.* IV, ll. 630–41.

1352.   *myn auctour*: Ovid here; Ch poses as a mere translator, follower of a Latin
auctor; *yit* means 'still': she still had time to write something before she
finally expired. By moving the opening lines of the Ovidian text to his
narrative's conclusion, Ch graphically shows a written text issuing from
experience, a record of it.

1353.   'Before she was hurt, first before she died'. The idea of the reproachful
letter comes from *Her.* VII; ll. 1355–65 are based on *Her.* VII, ll. 1–8.

1355-6.   *Her.* VII, ll. 1–4 open with the swansong simile; see *PF*, l. 342. In legend,
swans were supposed to sing once, before dying; *Met.* II, ll. 267–80 tell the
myth of Cycnus, turned into a swan while lamenting his friend's death.

1358.   'Not because I have any belief that I shall win you back'.

1360.   Based on *Her.* VII, l. 3: see *Riv.* n. for possible intermediary sources and
influences.

1361-2.   '"But since my reputation is lost through you," she said, "I can perfectly
lose a word or letter on you"'. This disdainful word-play on 'lost' is based
on *Her.* VII, ll. 5–6.

1364-5.   The word-play on 'winds' comes from *Her.* VII, l. 8 (see p. 346).

1365   The same wynd hath blowe awey youre fey,'   *faith*
       But [w]hoso wele al this lettere havyn in   *whoever wishes to*
            mynde,
       Rede Ovyde, and in hym he shal it fynde.

NOTES ON THE TEXT

Sources

The text is based on CUL MS Gg.4.27, known as G (fols 456^v–462^v). Substantial emendations, unless otherwise indicated, are on the basis of F (Oxford Bodleian Library MS Fairfax 16). Many of the emendations proposed by Cowen & Kane 1995 have been adopted. Certain minor emendations are regularly made without reference in the notes, including the emendation of *thyn, myn*, etc. before a consonant to *thy, my*, etc. *Abbreviations*: scribes do not use abbreviations wholly systematically; where these have been expanded it has been with regard for the necessity for readability in a text of this kind.

The other authorities are: Magdalene College Cambridge MS Pepys 2006 (P), Trinity College Cambridge MS R.3.19 (Tr), Oxford Bodleian MS Tanner 346 (T), Oxford Bodleian MS Bodley 638 (B), Oxford Bodleian MS Arch. Selden B.24 (Sel), BL MS Additional 9832 (A^1), BL MS Additional 28617(A^3), Oxford Bodleian MS Rawlinson C.86 (R), Thynne 1532 (Th). Only G, P, R and A^3 have ll. 960–1. Although the G scribe seems to make characteristic changes and errors (see Kane 1983; Cowen & Kane 1995; Hanna 1991: 27–30), he appears to preserve good readings lost in many or all other texts in ll. 960–1, 1102, 1107, 1126 and perhaps 1269 and 1292. Punctuation is editorial. For fuller readings see Cowen & Kane 1995.

Selected textual notes

Rubric: F; similar rubrics are found in B, T, A^3 (Latin), P, R, Sel (English). G leaves a space for a heading.

927. *Eneas*] F etc.; *Enea* G (also *Enya* in l. 1015).
928. *thyn Eneyde and Naso*] *Naso & Eneydos* G; *t. supporte ovide and naso* R; *t. Ovide and Naso* Sel.
932. *Feynynge*] *Feyned* Tr, P, A^1, R.   *iofferede to*] *offerede to* P; *offered unto* F, B, T, A^1.
941. *he*] *& he* G.
942. *ryght*] *rygh* G.
943. *with hym*] *withym* G.
944. *olde*] *owene* G.   *clepid*] *iclepid* G.
950. *ful*] *wol* G.   *him*] *hem* G.
951. *with*] G omits.
964. *called*] *clepid* G.
973. *cutte*] *knytte* F, B.
993. *which*] G, R omit.
999. *with him*] G omits.
1000. *she*] *he^1* G.
1003. *schulde*] P, A^1, R; *schule* G; *wolde* rest.   *to*] *the* G.
1009. *holde of*] *holdyn* (*of* added in later hand) G.

374

1032. *for to*] G omits.

1046. *was ther yit so*] Tr, Th; *yit was so* G; *w.y.s.* F, B, T; variants.

1048. *Which*] *With* G.

1055. *whan*] *whan that* G.   *al*] *of al* G.

1058. *beknew*] *he knew* G; *they knew* P, R; *tho knew* A¹, Tr.

1059. *Who*] *Ho* G.

1071. *braunes*] *braun* G, Th; *browes* Tr.

1082. *Sche¹*] *And* G.

1094. *Ful*] *Sche* G.   *sche²*] erased in G.

1095. *hem*] *hym* G, A¹, A³, Sel; T omits.

1099. *beter at ese was in*] P, Tr; *a. e. w. b. i. al* G; *b. a. e. w.* F, B, Sel; variants.

1112. *To take*] *For* erasure G.   *have*] *take* G, A¹, R.

1115. *the justyng*] F etc.; *to iuste* G; *the iuste* P; *the Iustis* R; *Iustynge* A¹.

1124. *ne*] G omits.

1126. *hire gestis calle*] *her gyftes calle* P; *her gyftes all* R; *his gestes calle* T.

1129. *Hath*] *Hadde* G.

1131. *brochis, and ek*] *& ek brochis* G.

1132. *for*] G, Th omit.

1133. *hyre*] F etc.; *hym* G, A¹.   *thise noble*] G omits.

1135. *presenting*] *presentis* G.

1138. *his yonge*] *this blysful* G.

1143. *noble*] *holy* G.

1149. *thanked*] *thankyth* G.   *in*] *with* G, A¹.

1160. *Now to¹*] *And to* P.   *now to²*] F, B, T, Sel, Th; *now² comyth* G; *and to* Tr; *and* P.

1163. *hir*] *his* G.

1165. *turmente*] *turnement* G.

1166. *wakith, walwith*] T, F; *waylith & sche* G; *waileth she waketh* P; variants.

1170. *dere*] *leve* G.

1171. *dreme*] *slep* G.

1174. *ek so likli*] *likli for* G.

1175. *therwithall*] Tr, Sel, P, A¹; *ek thereto* G; *withal* F, B, T.

1177. *him telle*] G omits.

1178. *rede*] *rede it* G.

1187. *nothing*] G, P, R; *no wight* rest.

1189. *hire*] *oure* G.

1191. *wole*] *wolde* G, P, R, A¹.

1193. *hir*] *his* G.

1202. *as faire*] P, A¹, R, Tr, Sel; *as bright* G; *is faire* F, B, T, Th.

1203. *folk*] P, B, Sel, R, A³; *men* G; *folkes* F, T, Tr, A¹, Th.

1210. *thus lat I*] Tr, A¹; *this lady* G, F, B, T, Sel, Th.

1212. *founden ys*] *Is I founde* G.

1213. *Go bet*] *bobet* G.

1215. *onys mete hym*] *h. o. m.* G; *hym ones meten* F, B, T, Th.
1217. *wilde hertes*] *bestys wilde* G.
1231. *gynnynge*] *gynnere* G.
1239. *hem*] *hym* G, Sel, Tr, A¹.
1240. *this, whan*] *whil* G.
1242. *upros*] *aros* G.
1245. *wiste*] *woste* G.
1246. *hire lovyd evere*] emendation, *hadde I louyd evere* G; *had hir loved* F;
      various others.
1247. *to²*] *as* G.
1250. *as*] G, P, R omit.
1251. *at*] *of* G.
1253. *was*] G, F, B, T, Th; *he was* P, R, Sel, Tr, A¹.
1255. *and*] *of* G, Tr.
1259. *they*] *that ye* G.
1263. *may²*] *may it* G.
1267. *privy*] *trewe* G; *besy* Sel.
1269. *And waytyn*] *And plesyn* Tr, A¹; *To* rest.
1283. *landys*] *land* rest.   *a*] G omits.
1292. *hire*] *his* rest.   *he*] *sche* G.
1305. *woman*] *weman* G.
1313. *degre*] *gre* G.
1316. *Have*] *Havyth* G, also at 1324.   *let*] *& let* G, P, R.
1325. *ryght*] *rygh* G.
1330. *hath he*] *he hath* G.
1337. *ful*] *& ful* G.
1339. *unbynde me*] *& brynge it* G.
1341. *allas*] G omits.
1345. *it*] G, Tr, A¹, R omit.
1351. *to the*] G omits.
1352. *seythe*] *right* G, Sel.
1367. *Rede*] *Rede he* G.

BIBLIOGRAPHY

Adam of Usk (1904), *Chronicon Adae de Usk*, ed. E.M. Thomson (4 vols), Rolls Series, London.

Aers, D. (1981), '*The Parliament of Fowls*: Authority, the Knower and the Known', *Chau R* XVI, pp. 1–17.

(ed.) (1992), *Culture and History 1350–1600*, New York.

Alanus of Lille/Alain de Lille (1955), *Anticlaudianus*, ed. R. Bossuat, Paris.

(1973), *Anticlaudianus* or *The Good and Perfect Man*, tr. J. Sheridan, Toronto.

(1979), *De Planctu Naturae*, ed. N. Häring, *Studi mediaevali* (3rd series) XIX; (1980), *The Plaint of Nature*, tr. J. Sheridan, Toronto.

Alexander Neckam (1863), *De naturis rerum,* ed. T. Wright, Rolls Series, London.

Alford, J.A. (1988), *Piers Plowman: A Glossary of Legal Diction*, Cambridge.

Allen, R.J. (1956), 'A Recurring Motif in Chaucer's *House of Fame*', *JEGP* LV, pp. 393–405.

Allen, V. (1992), 'Blaunche on Top and Alisoun on Bottom', in J. Dor (ed.), *A Wyf Ther Was*, Liège.

Almansi, G. & Beguin, C. (1986), *Theatre of Sleep: An Anthology of Dream Poems*, London.

Ames, R.M. (1986), 'The Feminist Connections of Chaucer's *Legend of Good Women*', in Wasserman & Blanch 1986: 57–74.

Amy, E.F. (1918, repr. 1965), *The Text of Chaucer's 'Legend of Good Women'*, New York.

Ancrene Wisse (1962), ed. J.R.R. Tolkien, EETS no. 249, London.

Anderson, J.J. (1992), 'The Narrators in the *Book of the Duchess* and the *Parliament of Fowls*', *Chau R* XXVI, pp. 219–35.

Aquinas, Thomas (1964), *Summa Theologiae*, ed. T. Gilby (60 vols), London and New York.

Armitage-Smith, S. (1904), *John of Gaunt*, London.

Armstrong, E.A. (1970), *The Folklore of Birds*, New York.

Augustine (1955), *De civitate Dei*, ed. B. Dombart and E. Kalb (2 vols), *Aurelii Augustini opera, XIV*, Corpus Christianorum, Ser. Latina, XLVII, XLVIII, Turnholt; (1945) *City of God*, tr. J. Healey, London.

(1958), *On Christian Doctrine*, New York.

Badel, P.-Y. (1980), *Le Roman de la Rose au XIVe siècle: étude de la réception de l'oeuvre*, Geneva.

Baird, J.L. & Kane, J.R. (1978) (eds), *La Querelle de la Rose: Letters and Documents*, Chapel Hill, NC.

Baker, D.C. (1961), 'Gold Coins in Medieval English Literature', *Spec* XXXVI, pp. 282–7.

Barr, H. (1993): see *Richard the Redeless*.

Barron, C.M. (1968), 'The Tyranny of Richard II', *BIHR*, pp. 1–18.

(1990), 'The Deposition of Richard II', in *Politics and Crisis in Fourteenth-Century England*, ed. J. Taylor and W. Childs, Gloucester, pp. 132–49.

Bartholomaeus Anglicus (1975–88), *On the Properties of Things: John of Trevisa's translation of Bartholomaeus Anglicus, 'De Proprietatibus Rerum'*, ed. M.C. Seymour *et al.* (3 vols), Oxford.

Baswell, C. (1995), *Virgil in Medieval England: Figuring the 'Aeneid' from the Twelfth Century to Chaucer*, Cambridge.

Beadle, R. & Owen, A.E.B. (1977) (eds), *The Findern Manuscript (Cambridge University Library MS Ff. 1. 6.)*, London.

Bech, M. (1882), 'Quellen und Plan der "Legende of Goode Women" und ihr Verhältniss zur *Confessio Amantis*', *Anglia* V, pp. 314–18.

Beichner, P.E. (1954), *The Medieval Representatives of Music: Jubal or Tubalcain*, Notre Dame.

Bennett, J.A.W. (1957), *The Parlement of Foules*, Oxford.

(1968), *Chaucer's Book of Fame: An Exposition of the 'House of Fame'*, Oxford.

(1979), 'Some Second Thoughts on the *Parlement of Fowls*', in *Chaucerian Problems and Perspectives: Essays Presented to Paul E. Beichner C.S.C.*, ed. E. Vasta and Z.P. Thundy, Notre Dame.

Benoît de Ste Maure (1904–12), *Le roman de Troie*, ed. L. Constans (6 vols), SATF, Paris.

(attrib.) (1925–29), *Le roman d'Éneas*, ed. J.J. Salverda de Grave (2 vols), CFMA XL, LXXII, Paris.

Benson, C.D. (1980), *The History of Troy in Middle English Literature*, Cambridge and Totowa, NJ.

Benson, L.D. (1986), 'The "Love-Tydynges" in Chaucer's *House of Fame*', in Wasserman & Blanch 1986.

Bersuire, Pierre (1960–66), *Reductorium morale (Book XV), Ovidius moralizatus*, ed. J. Engels, Utrecht.

Bethurum, D. (1959), 'Chaucer's Point of View as Narrator in the Love Poems', *PMLA* LXXIV, pp. 511–20.

Bevington, D.M. (1961), 'The Obtuse Narrator in Chaucer's *House of Fame*', *Spec* XXXVI, pp. 288–98.

Billington, S. (1979): see Williams 1979.

Blades, W. (1882), *The Biography and Typography of William Caxton, England's First Printer*, London.

Blake, N.F. (1969), *Caxton and His World*, London.

(1976), *Caxton: England's First Publisher*, London.

(1981), 'The Textual Tradition of the *Book of the Duchess*', *E S* LXII, pp. 237–48.

(1984), 'Geoffrey Chaucer: The Critics and the Canon', *Archiv* CCXXI, pp. 65–79.

(1986), '*The Book of the Duchess* Again', *E S* LXVII, pp. 122–5.

(1991), *William Caxton and English Literary Culture*, London and Rio Grande.

Blamires, A. *et al.* (1993), *Woman Defamed and Woman Defended: An Anthology of Medieval Texts*, Oxford.

Blodgett, J.E. (1984), 'William Thynne (d. 1546)', in *Editing Chaucer: The Great Tradition*, ed. P.G. Ruggiers, Norman, Okla.

Boccaccio (1951), *Genealogie deorum gentilium libri*, ed. V. Romano (2 vols), *Opere*, X, XI, Scrittori d'Italia CC, CCI, Bari.

(1956), *Boccaccio on Poetry*, tr. C.G. Osgood, Indianapolis and New York.

(1964–) *Tutte le opere di Giovanni di Boccaccio*, gen. ed. V. Branca, vols: I (*Filocolo*), II (*Filostrato* and *Teseida*); III (*Amorosa Visione*); IV (*Decameron*), Florence.

(1972), *Decameron*, tr. G.H. McWilliam, Harmondsworth.

(1992), *Chaucer's Boccaccio: Sources for 'Troilus' and the 'Knight's' and 'Franklin's Tales'*, tr. N.R. Havely, rev. edn, Cambridge.

Boethius (1918, repr. 1968), *Tractates, De consolatione Philosophiae*, ed. and tr. H.F. Stewart and E.K. Rand, London and Cambridge, Mass.

Boffey, J. (1993), 'The Lyrics in Chaucer's Longer Poems', *Poetica J* XXXVII, pp. 15–37.

(1994), 'Manuscript Evidence for Chaucer's Early Readers', paper for the New Chaucer Society Conference.

Boitani, P. (1982), *English Medieval Narrative in the 13th and 14th Centuries*, tr. J.K. Hall, Cambridge.

(1983) (ed.), *Chaucer and the Italian Trecento*, Cambridge.

(1984), *Chaucer and the Imaginary World of Fame*, Cambridge.

Boitani, P. & Mann, J. (1986) (eds), *The Cambridge Chaucer Companion*, Cambridge.

'Boke of Cupide' (1979), in *The Works of Sir John Clanvowe*, ed. V.J. Scattergood, Totowa, NJ.

Boyd, B. (1978), *Chaucer according to William Caxton: Minor Poems and 'Boece'*, Lexington, Ky.

Bracton, Henry de (1878–83), *De legibus et consuetudinibus Angliae*, ed. Sir T. Twiss, Rolls Series, London.

Braswell, M.F. (1981), 'Architectural Portraiture in Chaucer's *House of Fame*', *JMRS* XI, pp. 101–12.

Breeze, A. (1994), 'The Bret Glascurion and Chaucer's *House of Fame*', *RES* (new series) XLV, pp. 63–9.

Brewer, D.S. (1960, repr. 1972) (ed.), *The Parlement of Foulys*, Manchester.

(1966) (ed.), *Chaucer and Chaucerians: Critical Studies in Middle English Literature*, London.

(1969, repr. 1976) (ed.), *Geoffrey Chaucer, The Works, 1532: With Supplementary Materials from the editions of 1542, 1561, 1598, and 1602*, Menston.

(1974) (ed.), *Geoffrey Chaucer (The Writer and his Background)*, London (repr. Cambridge, 1990).

(1978) (ed.), *Chaucer: The Critical Heritage, vol. I: 1395–1837*, London, Henley and Boston.

Bridges, M. (1984), 'The Sense of an Ending: The Case of the Dream-Vision', *Dutch Quarterly Review XIV*, pp. 81–96.

Bronson, B.H. (1952), '*The Book of the Duchess* Re-Opened', *PMLA* LXVII, pp. 263–81.

Brook, S. (1983), *The Oxford Book of Dreams*, Oxford.

Brown, C.J. (1995), *Poets, Patrons, and Printers: Crisis of Authority in Late Medieval France*, Ithaca, NY, and London.

Brown, E. (1975), 'Priapus and the *Parlement of Foulys*', *SP* LXXII, pp. 258–74.

Brownlee, K. (1984), *Poetic Identity in Guillaume de Machaut*, Madison, Wis.

Brusendorff, A. (1925), *The Chaucer Tradition*, Oxford.

Burnley, J.D. (1979), *Chaucer's Language and the Philosophers' Tradition*, Cambridge.

(1986a), 'Some Terminology of Perception in the *Book of the Duchess*', *ELN* XXIII, pp. 15–22.

(1986b), 'Courtly Speech in Chaucer', *Poetica J* XXIV, pp. 16–38.

(1989), *The Language of Chaucer*, Basingstoke and London.

Burrow, J.A. (1971), *Ricardian Poetry: Chaucer, Gower, Langland and the Gawain-Poet*, London.

(1982), *Medieval Writers and Their Work: Middle English Literature and Its Background, 1100–1500*, Oxford.

(1991), 'Poems Without Endings', *SAC* XIII, pp. 17–37.

Burrow, J.A. & Turville-Petre, T. (1996), *A Book of Middle English* (2nd edn), Oxford.

Butterfield, A. (1991), 'Lyric and Elegy in *The Book of the Duchess*', *M Ae* LX, pp. 33–60.

Calcidius (1876), *Platonis Timaeus interprete Chalcidio cum eiusdem commentario*, ed. I. Wrobel, Leipzig.

Calin, W. (1974), *The Poet at the Fountain: Essays on the Narrative Verse of Guillaume de Machaut*, Lexington, Ky.

(1994), *The French Tradition and the Literature of Medieval England*, Toronto.

Camille, M. (1989), *The Gothic Idol*, Cambridge.

Carruthers, M.J. (1987), 'Italy, *Ars Memorativa*, and Fame's House', *SAC (Proceedings, no. 2)*, pp. 179–88.

(1990), *The Book of Memory: A Study of Memory in Medieval Culture*, Cambridge.

Cartier, N.R. (1964), 'Froissart, Chaucer and *Enclimpostair*', *Revue de littérature comparée* XXXVIII, pp. 18–34.

Cerquiglini, J. (1985), '*Un engin si soutil': Guillaume de Machaut et l'écriture au XIVᵉ siècle*, Paris.

Chamberlain, D. (1970), 'The Music of the Spheres and the *Parlement of Foules*', *Chau R* V, pp. 32–56.

Chanson de Roland (1946), ed. F. Whitehead, Oxford.

Chartier, Alain (1974), *The Poetical Works of Alain Chartier*, ed. J.C. Laidlaw, London.

Chartier, R. (1989), 'The Practical Impact of Writing', in *Passions of the Renaissance*, ed. R. Chartier, Cambridge, Mass., and London.

Chaucer, Geoffrey (1868–80), *Odd Texts of Chaucer's Minor Poems*, ed. F.J. Furnivall (Chaucer Society XXIII), London.

(1871), *Supplementary Parallel-Texts of Chaucer's Minor Poems*, ed. F.J. Furnivall (Chaucer Society XXII), London.

(1871), *A Parallel-Text Edition of Chaucer's Minor Poems*, ed. F.J. Furnivall (Chaucer Society XXI), London.

(1888), *G Chaucer, The Hous of Fame*, ed. H. Willert, Berlin.

(1889), *The Legend of Good Women*, ed. W.W. Skeat, Oxford.

(1896), *The Minor Poems*, ed. W.W. Skeat, Oxford.

(1904), *Versuch einer kritischen Textausgabe von Chaucers Parlement of Foules*, ed. J. Koch, Berlin.

(1928), *Geoffrey Chaucer's Kleinere Dichtungen*, ed. J. Koch, Heidelberg.

(1957), *The Complete Works of Geoffrey Chaucer*, ed. F.N. Robinson (2nd edn), Oxford.

(1960), *The Parlement of Foulys*, ed. D.S. Brewer, London (repr. Manchester, 1972).

(1977), *The Complete Poetry and Prose of Geoffrey Chaucer*, ed. J.H. Fisher, New York.

(1984), *Troilus and Criseyde*, ed. B. Windeatt, London.

(1987), *The Legend of Good Women*, tr. with an Introd. by A. McMillan, Houston, Tex.

(1987, UK edn 1988), *The Riverside Chaucer* (3rd edn), gen. ed. L.D. Benson, New York and Oxford.

(1983, rev. edn 1993), *The Book of the Duchess*, ed. H. Phillips, Durham.

(1994), *The House of Fame*, ed. N.R. Havely, Durham.

(1995), *The Legend of Good Women*, ed. J. Cowen and G. Kane, London.

Le Chevalier des Dames du Dolant Fortuné (1990), ed. J. Micquet, Ottawa.

Childs, W. (1983), 'Anglo-Italian Contacts in the Fourteenth Century', in Boitani 1983.

Christine de Pizan (1990), *Epistre au Dieu d'Amours*, in Fenster & Erler 1990: 3–155.

Cicero (1928), *De re publica*, ed. C.W. Keyes, London.

(1968) *De inventione*, ed. H.M. Hubbell, London.

Claudian (1922), *Works*, ed. M. Platnauer (2 vols), London and New York.

Clemen, W. (1963), *Chaucer's Early Poetry*, tr. C.A.M. Sim, London.

Coleman, J. (1981), *English Literature in History, 1350–1400: Medieval Readers and Writers*, London.

Conlee, J.W. (1991), *Middle English Debate Poetry: A Critical Anthology*, East Lansing, Michigan.

Connolly, M. (1994), 'Chaucer and Chess', *Chau R* XXIX, pp. 40–4.

Contamine, P. (1984), *War in the Middle Ages*, tr. M. Jones, Oxford.

Cooley, F.D. (1948), 'Two Notes on the Chess Terms in *The Book of the Duchess*', *MLN* LXIII, pp. 30–5.

Cooper, H. (1988): see Martindale 1988.

Cowen, J.M. (1985), 'Chaucer's *Legend of Good Women*: Structure and Tone', *SP* LXXXII, pp. 416–36.

Cowen J.M. & Kane, G. (1995): see Chaucer 1995.

Cowgill, B.K. (1975), 'The *Parlement of Foules* and the Body Politic', *JEGP* LXXIV, pp. 315–35.

Crane, S. (1993), 'Froissart's *Dit dou Bleu Chavalier* as a Source for Chaucer's *Book of the Duchess*', *M Ae* LXI, pp. 59–74.

Crombie, A.C. (1969), *Augustine to Galileo* (2 vols), Harmondsworth.

Crow, M.M. & Olsen, C.C. (1966) (eds), *Chaucer Life-Records*, Oxford.

Curry, W.C. (1926, enlarged edn 1960), *Chaucer and the Medieval Sciences*, New York and London.

Curtius, E.R. (1953), *European Literature and the Latin Middle Ages*, tr. W.R. Trask, London.

Dane, J.A. (1981), 'Chaucer's Eagle's Ovid's Phaëton: A Study in Literary Reception', *JMRS* XI, pp. 71–82.

Dante Alighieri (1966), *Il Convivio*, ed. M. Simonelli, Bologna.

(1973), *The Literary Criticism of Dante Alighieri*, ed. and tr. R.S. Haller, Lincoln, Nebr.

(1979–88), *La Divina Commedia*, ed. U. Bosco and G. Reggio (3 vols), Florence.

David, A. (1960), 'Literary Satire in the House of Fame', *PMLA* LXXV, pp. 333–9.

(1974), 'How Marcia Lost Her Skin', in *The Learned and the Lewd*, ed. L.D. Benson, Cambridge, Mass.

(1976), *The Strumpet Muse: Art and Morals in Chaucer's Poetry*, Bloomington, Ind.

(1993), 'Chaucer's Edwardian Poetry', in *The Idea of Medieval Poetry: New Essays on Chaucer and Medieval Culture in Honor of Donald R. Howard*, ed. J.M. Dean and C.K. Zacher, Newark, NJ, pp. 35–54.

David, H. (1947), *Philippe le Hardi*, Dijon.

Davidoff, J.M. (1988), *Beginning Well: Framing Fictions in Late Middle English Poetry*, London and Toronto.

Davies, R.T. (1963) (ed.), *Medieval English Lyrics*, London.

Davis, N. (1974), 'Chaucer and Fourteenth-century English', in Brewer 1974.

De Condé: see Jean de Condé.

De Deguileville, Guillaume (1893), *Pèlerinage de vie humaine*, ed. J.J. Stürzinger, Roxburghe Club, London.

De Lorris, Guillaume: see *Roman de la Rose*.

De Meun, Jean: see *Roman de la Rose*.

De Ricci, S. (1909), *A Census of Caxtons*, Oxford.

Delany, S. (1968), 'Chaucer's *House of Fame* and the *Ovide moralisé*', *CL* XX, pp. 254–64.

    (1972), *Chaucer's 'House of Fame': The Poetics of Skeptical Fideism*, Chicago and London.

    (1973), '"Ars Simia Naturae" and Chaucer's *House of Fame*', *ELN* XI, pp. 1–5.

    (1986), 'Rewriting Women Good. Gender and the Anxiety of Influence in Two Medieval Texts', in Wasserman & Blanch 1986.

    (1994), *The Naked Text: Chaucer's 'Legend of Good Women'*, Berkeley, Calif.

Delasanta, R. (1969), 'Christian Affirmation in the *Book of the Duchess*', *PMLA* LXXXIV, pp. 245–51.

Delle Colonne: see Guido de Columnis.

Deschamps, Eustache (1878–1904), *Oeuvres complètes*, ed. le Marquis de Queux de Saint-Hilaire and G. Raynaud (11 vols), SATF, Paris.

Desmond, M. (1994), *Reading Dido: Gender, Textuality and the 'Aeneid' in the Middle Ages*, Minneapolis, Minn.

Dickerson, J.I. (1968), *Chaucer's Book of the Duchess: A Critical Edition*, Ph.D. thesis, Univ. of N. Carolina, Chapel Hill, NC.

Diekstra, F. (1981), 'Chaucer's Way with his Sources: Accident into Substance and Substance into Accident', *E S* LXII, pp. 215–36.

Dillon, J. (1993), *Geoffrey Chaucer*, Basingstoke.

Donaldson, E.T. (1980), 'Venus and the Mother of Romulus: *The Parliament of Fowls* and the *Pervigilium Veneris*', *Chau R* XIV, pp. 313–17.

Doob, P.R. (1990), *The Idea of the Labyrinth, from Classical Antiquity through the Middle Ages*, Ithaca, NY, and London.

Dubois, P. (1983), *History, Rhetorical Description and the Epic*, Cambridge.

Duffy, E. (1988), 'Mater Dolorosa, Mater Misericordiae', Aquinas Lecture, *New Blackfriars*, Oxford.

Economou, G.D. (1972), *The Goddess Natura in Medieval Literature*, Cambridge, Mass.

Edwards, A.S.G. (1985) (ed.), *MS Pepys 2006, Magdalene College, Cambridge: A Facsimile*, Norman, Okla.

    (1986), 'Chaucer's *House of Fame* [line 143]', *Explicator* XLIV (No. 2), pp. 4–5.

    (1988), 'Chaucer's *House of Fame*: Lines 1709, 1907', *ELN* XXVI, pp. 1–3.

(1989), 'The Text of Chaucer's *House of Fame*: Editing and Authority', *Poetica J* XXIX–XXX, pp. 80–92.

(1990), '*House of Fame* 2018: An Unnecessary Emendation', *Chau R* XXV, pp. 78–9.

Edwards, A.S.G. & Boffey, J. (1996) (eds), *Chaucer: Works. Bodleian Library MS Arch Selden B.24. A Facsimile Edition*, Woodbridge and Rochester, NY.

Edwards, R.R. (1989), *The Dream of Chaucer*, Durham, NC, and London.

Eldredge, L. (1970), 'Chaucer's *Hous of Fame* and the *Via Moderna*', *NM* LXXI, pp. 105–19.

Elliott, R.W.V. (1974), *Chaucer's English*, London.

Ellis, S. (1988), 'Chaucer, Dante and Damnation', *Chau R* XXII, pp. 282–94.

(1995), 'The Death of the *Book of the Duchess*', *Chau R* XXIX, pp. 249–58.

Ellman, M. (1984), 'Blanche', in *Criticism and Critical Theory*, ed. Jeremy Hawthorn, London, pp. 98–110.

Emerson, O.F. (1922), 'Chaucer and Medieval Hunting', *Rom R* XIII, pp. 115–50.

Erickson, C. (1976), *The Medieval Vision: Essays in History and Perception*, New York.

Evans, J. & Serjeantson, M.J. (1933), *English Medieval Lapidaries*, EETS (o.s.) CXC, London.

Fenster, T.S. & Erler, M.C. (1990) (eds), *Poems of Cupid, God of Love*, Leiden.

Ferris, S. (1983), 'John Stow and the Tomb of Blanche the Duchess', *Chau R* XVIII, pp. 92–3.

Fichte, J.O. (1973), '*The Book of the Duchess* – A Consolation?', *SN* XLV, pp. 53–67.

(1980), *Chaucer's 'Art Poetical': A Study in Chaucerian Poetics*, Tübingen.

Fischer, S.R. (1978), *The Dream in Middle High German Epic*, Bern.

Fisher, J.H. (1977): see Chaucer 1977.

(1979), 'The *Legend of Good Women*', in Rowland 1979.

Fletcher, B.Y. (1987) (ed.), *MS R.3.19, Trinity College, Cambridge: A Facsimile*, Norman, Okla.

The Floure and the Leafe (1962, repr. 1980), ed. D.A. Pearsall, Manchester.

Frank, R.W. Jr (1956), 'Structure and Meaning in the *Parlement of Foules*', *PMLA* LXXI, pp. 530–9.

(1972), *Chaucer and 'The Legend of Good Women'*, Cambridge, Mass.

French, W.H. (1949), 'Medieval Chess and the *Book of the Duchess*', *MLN* LXIV, pp. 261–4.

Friend, A.C. (1953), 'Chaucer's Version of the *Aeneid*', *Spec* XXVIII, pp. 317–23.

Froissart, Jean (1870–72), *Poésies*, ed. A. Scheler (3 vols), Brussels.

(1963), *L'espinette amoureuse*, ed. A. Fourrier, Paris.

(1975), *Le joli buisson de jonece*, ed. A. Fourrier, TLF, Geneva.

(1979), *Dits et débats*, ed. A. Fourrier, TLF, Geneva.

Fryde, N. (1979), *The Tyranny and Fall of Edward II, 1321–6*, Cambridge.

Fulgentius (1898), *Opera*, ed. R. Helm, Leipzig.

(1971), *Fulgentius the Mythographer*, tr. L.G. Whitbread, Columbus, Ohio.

Fyler, J.M. (1979), *Chaucer and Ovid*, New Haven, Conn.

Gardner, J. (1977), *The Poetry of Chaucer*, Carbondale and Evansville, Ill.

Gawain and the Green Knight (1967), ed. J.R.R. Tolkien and E.V. Gordon (2nd edn N. Davis), Oxford.

Gellrich, J.M. (1985), *The Idea of the Book in the Middle Ages*, Ithaca, NY.

Genette, G. (1980), *Narrative Discourse: An Essay in Method*, tr. Jane E. Lewin, Ithaca, NY.

Gilbert, A.J. (1978), 'The Influence of Boethius on the *Parlement of Foulys*', *M Ae* XLVII, pp. 292–303.

Gimpel, J. (1988), *The Medieval Machine* (2nd edn), London.

Given-Wilson, C. (1986), *The Royal Household and the King's Affinity: Service, Politics and Finance in England 1360–1413*, New Haven, Conn.

(1993), *The Chronicles of the Revolution, 1397–1400: The Reign of Richard II*, Manchester.

Goffin, R.C. (1943), 'Quiting by Tidings in the *Hous of Fame*', *M Ae* XII, pp. 40–4.

Goodman, A.E. (1992), *John of Gaunt: The Exercise of Princely Power in the Fourteenth Century*, Harlow.

Gordon, D. (1993) (ed.), *The Wilton Diptych, Making and Meaning*, London.

Gower, John (1899–1902), *The Complete Works of John Gower*, ed. G.C. Macaulay (4 vols), Oxford.

(1961), *The Major Latin Works of John Gower*, ed. and tr. E.W. Stockton, Seattle.

Grant, E. (1977), *Physical Science in the Middle Ages*, Cambridge.

Gray, D. (1972), *Themes and Images in the Medieval English Religious Lyric*, London.

(1979), 'Chaucer and "Pite"', in *J.R.R. Tolkien, Scholar and Storyteller: Essays In Memoriam*, ed. M. Salu and R.T. Farrell, Ithaca, NY, and London.

Gray, D. & Stanley, E.G. (1983) (eds), *Middle English Studies Presented to Norman Davis in Honour of his Seventieth Birthday*, Oxford.

Green, D.H. (1979), *Irony and the Medieval Romance*, Cambridge.

Green, R.F. (1980), *Poets and Princepleasers: Literature and the English Court in the Late Middle Ages*, Toronto, Buffalo and London.

(1988), 'Chaucer's Victimized Women', *SAC* X, pp. 3–21.

Grennen, J.E. (1964), '"Hert-huntyng" in the *Book of the Duchess*', *MLQ* XXV, pp. 131–9.

(1967), 'Science and Poetry in Chaucer's *House of Fame*', *An M* VIII, pp. 38–45.

(1984), 'Chaucer and Chalcidius: The Platonic Origins of the *House of Fame*', *Viator* XV, pp. 237–62.

Guido de Columnis (delle Colonne) (1936), *Historia Destructionis Troiae*, ed. N.E. Griffin, Cambridge, Mass.

(1974), *Historia Destructionis Troiae*, tr. M.E. Meek, Bloomington, Ind., and London.

Guillaume de Machaut (1908–21), *Oeuvres*, ed. E. Hoepffner (3 vols), SATF, Paris.

Haas, R. (1990), ' "Kissing the Steppes of Uirgile, Ouide etc." and the *Legend of Good Women*', in *Anglistentag 1989 Würzburg*, ed. R. Ahrens, Tübingen.

Hall, D.J. (1965), *English Medieval Pilgrimage*, London.

Hall, L.B. (1963), 'Chaucer and the Dido-and-Aeneas Story', *Med St* XXV, pp. 148–59.

Hammond, E.P. (1902), 'On the Text of the *Parlement*', *University of Chicago Decennial Publications*, First Series, VII, pp. 3–25.

(1905), 'MS Longleat 258 – A Chaucerian Codex', *MLN* XX, pp. 77–9.

Hanawalt, B.A. (1992) (ed.), *Chaucer's England: Literature in Historical Context*, Minneapolis, Minn.

Hanna, R. III (1991), 'Presenting Chaucer as an Author', in *Medieval Literature: Texts and Interpretations*, ed. T.W. Machan, Binghamton, NY.

Hansen, E.T. (1992), *Chaucer and the Fictions of Gender*, Berkeley, Los Angeles and Oxford.

Hardman, P. (1986), 'Chaucer's Muses and his "Art Poetical"', *RES* (n.s.) XXXVII, pp. 478–94.

(1993), '*Ars celare artem*: Interpreting the Black Knight's "Lay"', *Poetica J* XXXVII, pp. 49 57.

(1994), '*The Book of the Duchess* as a Memorial Monument', *Chau R* XXVIII, pp. 205–17.

The Harley Lyrics (1956), ed. G.L. Brook, Manchester.

Harwood, B.J. (1992), 'Chaucer on "Speche": *House of Fame*, the *Friar's Tale* and the *Summoner's Tale*', *Chau R* XXVI, pp. 343–9.

Havely, N.R. (1992): see Boccaccio 1992.

(1994): see Chaucer 1994.

Hayes, G. (1960), 'Musical Instruments', in *The New Oxford History of Music: 'Ars\Nova' and the Renaissance, 1300–1540*, ed. A. Hughes and G. Abraham, Oxford.

Hicks, E. (1977), *Le Débat sur le 'Roman de la Rose'*, Paris.

Hieatt, C.B. (1967), *The Realism of Dream Visions: The Poetic Exploitation of the Dream-Experience in Chaucer and his Contemporaries*, The Hague.

Higden, Ranulf (1865–86), *Polychronicon*, ed. C. Babington and J.R. Lumby, Rolls Series, London.

Hill, J.M.L. (1993), *The Medieval Debate on Jean de Meung's 'Roman de la Rose': Morality versus Art* (Studies in Medieval Literature IV), Lampeter.

Hilton, R.H. (1976), *Peasants, Knights and Heretics*, Cambridge.

Hoccleve, Thomas (1990), *Lepistre de Cupide*, in Fenster & Erler 1990.

Hopkins, A. (1990), *The Sinful Knights: A Study of the Middle English Penitential Romance*, Oxford.

Horgan, F. (1994): see *Roman de la Rose*.

Howard, D.R. (1976), 'Chaucer's Idea of an Idea', *E & S* (n.s.) XXIX, pp. 39–55.

—— (1987) *Chaucer: His Life, His Works, His World*, New York.

Hunter, D.G. (1987), 'Resistance to the Virginal Ideal in Late-Fourth-Century Rome: The Case of Jovinian', *Theological Studies* XLVIII, pp. 45–64.

Huot, S. (1987), *From Song to Book: The Poetics of Writing in Old French Lyric and Lyrical Narrative Poetry*, Ithaca, NY.

Huppé, B.F. & Robertson, D.W. Jr (1963), *Fruyt and Chaf: Studies in Chaucer's Allegories*, Princeton, NJ.

Hutchinson, J. (1977), 'The *Parliament of Fowls*: A Literary Entertainment?', *Neophilologus* LXI, pp. 143–51.

Hyginus (1993), *Fabulae*, ed. P.K. Marshall, Stuttgart and Leipzig.

Innocent III, Pope (1978), *De miseria condicionis humanae*, ed. and tr. R.E. Lewis, Chaucer Library, Athens, Ga.

Irvine, M. (1985), 'Medieval Grammatical Theory and Chaucer's *House of Fame*', *Spec* LX, pp. 850–76.

Isidore of Seville, *Etymologiae*, PL 82, Paris.

James, M.R. (1933), Introd., *The Romance of Alexander: a collotype facsimile of MS Bodley 264*, Oxford.

Janson, H.W. (1952), *Apes and Ape Lore in the Middle Ages and the Renaissance* (Studies of the Warburg Institute XX), London.

Jean de Condé (1970), *La messe des oiseaux et le dit des Jacobins et des Fremeneurs*, ed. J. Ribard, TLF, Geneva.

Jean [Jehan] de la Mote (1882), *Le Regret Guillaume, comte de Hainault*, ed. A. Scheler, Brussels.

Jerome, *Against Jovinian* (*Adversus Jovinianum*), in *Opera*, PL XXIII, Paris.

John of Garland (1974), *Parisiana Poetria*, ed. and tr. T. Lawler, New Haven, Conn.

John of Salisbury (1990), *Policraticus*, ed. and tr. C.J. Nederman, Cambridge.

Jordan, R.M. (1987), *Chaucer's Poetics and the Modern Reader*, Berkeley, Calif.

Joseph of Exeter (Josephus Iscanus) (1970), *Daretis Phrygii Ilias*, in *Briefe und Werke*, ed. L. Gompf, Leiden and Cologne.

—— (1970), *The Iliad of Dares Phrygius*, tr. G. Roberts, Cape Town.

Juvenal (1940), *Satires*, in *Juvenal and Persius*, ed. and tr. G.G. Ramsay, London.

Kane, G. (1965), *The Autobiographical Fallacy in Chaucer and Langland Studies*, Chambers Memorial Lecture 1965, London.

(1983), 'The Text of the *Legend of Good Women* in CUL MS Gg.4.27', in Gray & Stanley, 1983: 39–58.

Kantorowicz, E. (1954), 'Inalienability: A Note on Canonical Practice and the English Coronation Oath in the Thirteenth Century', *Spec* XXIX, pp. 488–502.

Kean, P.M. (1972), *Chaucer and the Making of English Poetry I: Love Vision and Debate*, London.

Keen, M. (1984), *Chivalry*, New Haven, Conn., and London.

Kellman, S.G. (1976), 'The Fiction of Self-Begetting', *MLN* 91, pp. 1243–56.

Kelly, H.A. (1986), *Chaucer and the Cult of St Valentine* (Davis Medieval Texts and Studies V), Leiden.

Kendrick, L. (1984), 'Chaucer's *House of Fame* and the French Palais de Justice', *SAC* VI, pp. 121–33.

Kermode, F. (1967), *The Sense of an Ending*, London.

Kieckhefer, R. (1989), *Magic in the Middle Ages*, Cambridge.

Kiser, L.J. (1983), *Telling Classical Tales: Chaucer and the 'Legend of Good Women'*, Ithaca, NY.

(1991), *Truth and Textuality in Chaucer's Poetry*, Hanover, NH, and London.

Kittredge, G.L. (1899), 'Chaucer and Froissart', *E St* XXVI, pp. 321–36.

(1915a), 'Chaucer and the *Book of the Duchess*', *PMLA* XXX, pp. 1–24.

(1915b), *Chaucer and his Poetry*, Cambridge, Mass.

Knight, S. (1986), *Geoffrey Chaucer*, Oxford.

Kolvé, V.A. (1981), 'From Cleopatra to Alceste: An Iconographical Study of the *Legend of Good Women*', in *Signs and Symbols in Chaucer's Poetry*, ed. J.P. Hermann and J.J. Burke, University, Ala.

(1984), *Chaucer and the Imagery of Narrative*, London.

Koonce, B.G. (1966), *Chaucer and the Tradition of Fame*, Princeton, NJ.

Kruger, S.F. (1992), *Dreaming in the Middle Ages*, Cambridge.

Kurman, G. (1974), 'Ecphrasis in Epic Poetry', *Comparative Literature* XXVI, pp. 1–13.

Ladd, C.A. (1988), 'Look Out for the Little Words', in *Medieval Studies Presented to George Kane*, ed. E.D. Kennedy *et al.*, Wolfboro, NH, and Woodbridge, pp. 163–6.

Langland, William (1978), *The Vision of Piers Plowman: A Complete Edition of the B-Text*, ed. A.V.C. Schmidt, London and New York.

(1978), *Piers Plowman by William Langland: An Edition of the C-Text*, ed. D.A. Pearsall, London.

Lawlor, J. (1968), *Chaucer*, London.

Lawton, D. (1985), *Chaucer's Narrators*, Cambridge.

Le Couter, J.D. (1978), *English Medieval Painted Glass* (2nd edn), Oxford.

Le Fèvre, Jean (1882 and 1905), *Les Lamentations de Mathéolus et le Livre de Leësce de Jehan Le Fèvre*, ed. A.-G. Van Hamel (2 vols), Paris.

Le Franc, Martin (1968), *Le Champion des Dames*, Book I, ed. A. Piaget, Lausanne.

Le Goff, J. (1984), *The Birth of Purgatory*, tr. A. Goldhammer, Chicago.

Leicester, H.M. (1974), 'The Harmony of Chaucer's *Parlement*: A Dissonant Voice', *Chau R* IX, pp. 15–34.

Lewis, C.S. (1960), *Studies in Words*, Cambridge.

(1964), *The Discarded Image: An Introduction to Medieval and Renaissance Literature*, Cambridge.

Leyerle, J. (1971), 'Chaucer's Windy Eagle', *UTQ* XL, pp. 247–65.

Livy (1919–59), *Ab urbe condita*, ed. B.O. Foster *et al.* (14 vols), London and Cambridge, Mass.

Loomis, L.H. (1941), 'Chaucer and the Breton Lays of the Auchinleck MS', *SP* XXXVIII, pp. 14–33.

(1958), 'Secular Dramatics in the Royal Palace. Paris, 1378, 1389, and Chaucer's "tregetoures"', *Spec* XXXIII, pp. 242–55.

Lord, M.L. (1969), 'Dido as an Example of Chastity: The Influence of Example Literature', *Harvard Library Bulletin* XVII, pp. 22–44, 216–32.

Lossing, M. (1942), 'The Prologue to the *Legend of Good Women* and the *Lai de Franchise*', *SP* XXXIX, pp. 15–35.

Lottin, O. (1931), *Le droit naturel chez saint Thomas d'Aquin et ses prédécesseurs* (2nd edn), Bruges.

Lounsbury, T.R. (1892), *Studies in Chaucer, III*, New York.

Lowes, J.L. (1904), 'The Prologue to the *Legend of Good Women* as Related to the French *Marguerite* Poems and the *Filostrato*', *PMLA* XIX, pp. 593–683.

(1905),'The Prologue to the *Legend of Good Women* Considered in its Chronological Relations', *PMLA* XX, pp. 749–864.

(1905–6), 'The Dry Sea and the Carrenare', *MP* 3, pp. 1–46.

Lucan (1926), *Pharsalia: The Civil War*, ed. and tr. J.D. Duff, London and Cambridge, Mass.

Lynch, K.L. (1988), *The High Medieval Dream Vision*, Stanford, Calif.

Macrobius (1952), *Commentary on the Dream of Scipio*, tr. W.H. Stahl, New York.

Mann, J. (1973), *Chaucer and Medieval Estates Satire*, Cambridge.

(1991), *Geoffrey Chaucer*, Feminist Readings, New York and London.

Manzaloui, M.A. (1962), 'Ars longa, vita brevis', *EC* XII, pp. 221–4.

(1974), 'Chaucer and Science', in Brewer 1974/1990.

Marbode of Rennes (1977), *De Lapidibus*, ed. and tr. J.M. Riddle (*Sudhoffs Archiv* Beiheft XX), Wiesbaden.

Margherita, G.R. (1994), *The Romance of Origins*, Philadelphia.

Martianus Capella (1977), *The Marriage of Philology and Mercury*, tr. Stahl *et al*.

Martin, J.B. III (1972), *The Sources of Chaucer's 'Ceyx and Alcyone'*, Ph.D. thesis, Duke University, NC.

Martin, E.E. (1983), 'The Interpretation of Chaucer's Alcyone', *Chau R* XVIII, pp. 18–22.

(1991), 'Chaucer's Ruth: An Exegetical Poetic in the Prologue to the *Legend of Good Women*', *Exemplaria* III (1991), pp. 467–90.

Martindale, C. (1988), *Ovid Renewed: Ovidian Influence on Literature and Art from the Middle Ages to the Twentieth Century*, Cambridge.

McCall, J.P. (1970), 'The Harmony of Chaucer's *Parliament*', *Chau R* V, pp. 22–31.

(1979), *Chaucer Among the Gods: The Poetics of Classical Myth*, University Park, Pa.

McDonald, C.O. (1955), 'An Interpretation of Chaucer's *Parliament of Foules*', *Spec* XXX, pp. 444–57.

McGerr, R.P. (1989), 'Medieval Concepts of Closure: Theory and Practice', *Exemplaria* I, pp. 144–79.

McKisack, M. (1959),*The Fourteenth Century*, Oxford and New York.

McMillan (1987): see Chaucer 1987.

Meale, C.M. (1992), 'Legends of Good Women in the European Middle Ages', *Archiv* CCXCIX, pp. 55–70.

(1993)(ed.), *Women and Literature in Britain, 1150–1500,* Cambridge.

Miller, J.T. (1982), 'The Writing on the Wall: Authority and Authorship in Chaucer's *House of Fame*', *Chau R* XVII, pp. 95–115.

(1986), *Poetic License: Authority and Authorship in Medieval and Renaissance Contexts*, New York and Oxford.

Miller, R.P. (1977), *Chaucer: Sources and Backgrounds*, New York and Oxford.

Minnis, A.J. (1995), *Chaucer's Shorter Poems* (Oxford Guide to Chaucer), Oxford.

Minnis, A.J. & Scott, A.B. (1991) (eds), *Medieval Literary Theory and Criticism, c. 1100–c. 1375: The Commentary Tradition* (rev. edn), Oxford.

Montaiglon, A. (1855–78) (ed.), *Recueil des poésies francoises des XVe et XVIe siècles: morales, facetieuses, historiques* (13 vols), Paris.

Morse, R. (1981), 'Understanding the Man in Black', *Chau R* XV, pp. 204–8.

Murray, H.H.R. (1913), *A History of Chess*, Oxford.

Mustanoja, T.F. (1960), *A Middle English Syntax, Part I*, Helsinki.

Nederman, C.J. & Forhan, K.L. (1993), *Medieval Political Theory: The Quest for the Body Politic*, New York and London.

Neuss, P. (1981), 'Images of Writing and the Book in Chaucer's Poetry', *RES* (n.s.) XXXII, pp. 385–97.

Nicolas, Sir J. (1845), 'Expenses of the Great Wardrobe of Edward III', *Archaeologia* XXXI, pp. 1–163.

Nicole de Margival (1983), *Le dit de la panthère d'amours*, ed. H.A. Todd, Paris.

Niermeyer, J.F. (1984) (ed.), *Mediae Latinitatis Lexicon Minus*, Leiden.

Nolan, B. (1992), *Chaucer and the Tradition of the Roman Antique*, Cambridge.

Norton-Smith, J. (1974), *Geoffrey Chaucer*, London.
(1979) (ed.), *MS Fairfax 16: A Facsimile*, London.

O'Daly, G. (1990), *The Poetry of Boethius*, Oxford.
Olson, C. (1941), 'Chaucer and the Music of the Fourteenth Century', *Spec* XVI, pp. 64–92.
Olson, G. (1979), 'Making and Poetry in the Age of Chaucer', *CL* XXXI, pp. 272–90.
Olson, P.A. (1980), '*The Parlement of Foules*: Aristotle's *Poetics* and the Foundations of Human Society', *SAC* II, pp. 53–69.
Orme, N. (1992), 'Medieval Hunting: Fact and Fancy', in Hanawalt 1992: 133–53.
Orpel, J. (1993), 'St Jerome and the History of Sex', *Viator* XXIV, pp. 1–22.
Oruch, J.B. (1981), 'St Valentine, Chaucer and Spring in February', *Spec* LVI, pp. 534–65.
Oton de Graunson (1941), *Oton de Grandson: sa vie et ses poésies,* ed. A. Piaget, Lausanne.
Overbeck, P.T. (1967), 'Chaucer's Good Women', *Chau R* II, pp. 75–94.
Ovid (1914), '*Heroides*' and '*Amores*', ed. and tr. G. Showerman, London and Cambridge, Mass.
(1916), *Metamorphoses*, ed. and tr. F.J. Miller, London and Cambridge, Mass.
(1931), *Fasti*, ed. and tr. J.G. Frazer, London and Cambridge, Mass.
(1939, 2nd edn 1979), *The Art of Love and Other Poems*, ed. and tr. J.H. Mozley, rev. G.P. Gould, London and Cambridge, Mass.
Ovide moralisé: Poème de commencement du quatorzième siècle (1915–38), ed. C. de Boer (5 vols), Amsterdam.
The Owl and the Nightingale (1960, rev. edn 1972), ed. E.G. Stanley, London (rev. edn, Manchester).

Palmer, J.J.N. (1974), 'The Historical Context of the *Book of the Duchess*: A Revision', *Chau R* VIII, pp. 253–61.
Panofsky, E. (1939), 'Blind Cupid', in *Studies in Iconology: Humanistic Themes in the Art of the Renaissance*, New York, pp. 95–128, 110ff.
Parkes, M.B. & Beadle, R. (1979–80) (eds), *Geoffrey Chaucer, Poetical Works: A Facsimile of Cambridge University Library MS Gg 4.27* (3 vols), Cambridge.
Parks, G.B. (1954), *The English Traveller in Italy, I: The Middle Ages*, Rome.
Patch, H.R. (1919), 'Chaucer's Desert', *MLN* XXXIV, pp. 321–8.
(1927), *The Goddess Fortuna in Medieval Literature*, Cambridge, Mass.
Patterson, L. (1991), *Chaucer and the Subject of History*, London.
Payne, R.O. (1963), *The Key of Remembrance: A Study of Chaucer's Poetics*, New Haven, Conn.
Pearl (1953), ed. E.V. Gordon, Oxford.

Pearsall, D.A. (1992), *The Life of Geoffrey Chaucer: A Critical Biography*, Oxford and Cambridge, Mass.

Pearsall, D.A. & Salter, E. (1973), *Landscapes and Seasons of the Medieval World*, London.

Peden, A. (1985), 'Macrobius and Medieval Dream Literature', *M Ae* LIV, pp. 59–73.

Petrarch (1988), *Triumphi*, ed. M. Ariani, Milan.

Phillips, H. (1981), 'Structure and Consolation in the *Book of the Duchess*', *Chau R* XVI, pp. 107–18.

(1986), '*The Book of the Duchess*, ll. 31–96: Are they a Forgery?', *E S* LXVII, pp. 113–21.

(1993a): see Chaucer 1983/1993.

(1993b), '*The Complaint of Venus*: Chaucer and Oton de Graunson', in *The Medieval Translator 4*, ed. R. Ellis and R. Evans, Exeter.

(1995a), 'Literary Allusion in Chaucer's "Hyd, Absalon, Thy Gilte Tresses Clere"', *Chau R* XXX, pp. 134–49.

(1995b), 'Chaucer and Jean Le Fèvre', *Archiv* CCXXXII, pp. 23–36.

Pierre de Hauteville (1982), *Confession et testament de l'amant trespassé de deuil*, ed. R.M. Bidler, Montreal.

Plant, M. (1987), 'Patronage in the Circle of the Carrara Family: Padua 1337–1405', in *Patronage, Art and Society in Renaissance Italy*, ed. F.W. Kent and P. Simons, Canberra and Oxford.

Plato (1930), *Lysis, Symposium, Gorgias*, ed. W.R.M. Lamb, Cambridge, Mass.

(1975), *Phaedo*, tr. M.J. Woods, Oxford.

Poirion, D. (1965), *Le Poète et le Prince: l'évolution du lyrisme courtois de Guillaume de Machaut à Charles d'Orléans*, Grenoble.

Policraticus: see John of Salisbury.

Pratt, R.A. (1947), 'Chaucer's Claudian', *Spec* XXII, pp. 419–29.

(1950), 'A Note on Chaucer's Lollius', *MLN* LXV, pp. 183–7.

Pritchard, R.T. (1986): see Walter of Chatillon 1986.

Rand, E.K. (1926), 'Chaucer in Error', *Spec* I, pp. 222–5.

Redwine, B. (1988), 'Chaucer's Representations of Posture', *NM* LXXXIX, pp. 312–19.

Remnant, M. (1989), *Musical Instruments: An Illustrated History from Antiquity to the Present*, London.

Richard the Redeless: in *The Piers Plowman Tradition*, ed. H. Barr, London, 1993.

Riddle 1977: see Marbode of Rennes.

Riddy, F. (1993), '"Women Talking about the Things of God": A Late Medieval Sub-culture', in Meale 1993: 104–27.

Rigg, A.G. (1966), '*Gregory's Garden*: A Latin Dream Allegory', *M Ae* 35, pp. 29–37.

(1993), *A History of Anglo-Latin Literature, 1066–1422*, Cambridge.

Robertson, D.W. Jr (1962), *A Preface to Chaucer*, Princeton,NJ.

(1965), 'The Historical Setting of Chaucer's *Book of the Duchess*', in *Medieval Studies in Honor of U.T. Holmes*, ed. J. Mahoney and J.E. Keller, Chapel Hill, NC.

Robinson, F.N. (1957): see Chaucer 1957.

Robinson, P. (1980), *Minor Poems: Bodleian Library MS Tanner 346: A Facsimile*, Norman, Okla.

(1981), *MS Bodley 638: A Facsimile*, Norman, Okla.

Roman d'Alexandre: see James 1933.

Roman d'Éneas: see Benoît de Ste Maure.

Roman de la Rose (1965–70), ed. F. Lecoy (3 vols), CFMA, Paris.

(1994), *The Romance of the Rose*, tr. F. Horgan, Oxford.

Rooney, A. (1987), *The Tretyse off Huntyng* (Mediaeval and Renaissance Texts and Studies XIX), Brussels.

(1993), *Hunting in Middle English Literature*, Woodbridge.

Rosenthal, C.L. (1933), 'A Possible Source for Chaucer's *Book of the Duchess – Li Regret de Guillaume*, by Jehan de la Mote', *MLN* XLVIII, pp. 511–14.

Ross, D.J.A. (1971), *Illustrated Medieval Alexander Books*, Cambridge.

Rowe, D. (1988), *Through Nature to Eternity: Chaucer's Legend of Good Women*, Lincoln, Nebr.

Rowland, B. (1968, rev. edn 1979), *Companion to Chaucer Studies*, New York and Oxford.

Ruffolo, L. (1993), 'Literary Authority and the Lists in Chaucer's *House of Fame*', *Chau R* XXVII, pp. 325–41.

Ruggiers, P.G. (1953), 'The Unity of Chaucer's *House of Fame*', *SPL*, pp. 16–29.

Russell, J.S. (1988), *The English Dream Vision: Anatomy of a Form*, Columbus, Ohio.

Said, E.W. (1978), *Orientalism*, New York.

Salter, E. (1983), *Fourteenth-Century English Poetry: Contexts and Readings*, Oxford.

Salter, E. & Pearsall, D.A. (1973): see Pearsall & Salter 1973.

Sanderlin, G. (1986), 'Chaucer's *Legend of Dido*: A Feminist Exemplum', *Chau R* XX, pp. 331–40.

Saul, N. (1992), 'Chaucer and Gentility', in Hanawalt 1992: 41–55.

Sayles, G.O. (1981), 'The Deposition of Richard II: Three Lancastrian Narratives', *BIHR* LIV, pp. 240–70.

Scattergood, V.J. (1995), 'The Short Poems', in Minnis 1995: 455–512.

Scheler: see Froissart, Jean (1870–72).

Schlauch, M. (1945), 'Chaucer's Doctrine of Kings and Tyrants', *Spec* XX, pp. 133–56.

Schless, H. (1984), *Chaucer and Dante: A Revaluation*, Norman, Okla.

(1985), 'A Dating for the *Book of the Duchess*: Line 1314', *Chau R* XIX, pp. 273–6.

Schoeck, R.J. (1953–4), 'A Legal Reading of Chaucer *Hous of Fame*', *UTQ* XXIII, pp. 185–92.

Scott-McNab, D. (1988), 'A Re-Examination of Octavian's Hunt in *The Book of the Duchess*', *M Ae* LVI, pp. 183–99.

Seaton, E. (1950), '*Le songe vert*: Its Occasion, Writing and Author', *M Ae* XIX, pp. 1–16.

Segal, L. (1994), *Straight Sex*, London.

Seymour, M.C. (1995), *A Catalogue of Chaucer Manuscripts*, vol. 1, Aldershot.

Shannon, E.F. (1913), 'Chaucer's Use of Octosyllabic Verse in the *Book of the Duchess* and *The House of Fame*', *JEGP* XII, pp. 277–94.

——— (1929, repr. 1964), *Chaucer and the Roman Poets*, Cambridge, Mass., and New York.

Shepherd, G.T. (1956), '"All the wealth of Croesus ...": A Topic in the *Ancrene Wisse*', *MLR* LI.

——— (1979), 'Make Believe: Chaucer's Rationale of Story-Telling in the *House of Fame*', in *J.R.R. Tolkien, Scholar and Storyteller: Essays in Memoriam*, ed. M. Salu and R.T. Farrell, Ithaca, NY, and London.

Sherborne, J. (ed.) A. Tuck (1994), *War, Politics and Culture in Fourteenth-Century England*, London.

Sherwood, M. (1947), 'Magic and Mechanics in Medieval Fiction', *SP* XLIV, pp. 567–92.

Shook, L.K. (1979), '*The House of Fame*', in Rowland 1968/1979.

Simmons, J.L. (1966), 'The Place of the Poet in Chaucer's *House of Fame*', *MLQ* XXVII, pp. 125–35.

Simpson, J. (1986), 'Dante's "Astripetam Aquilam" and the Theme of Poetic Discretion in the "House of Fame"', *E & S* (n.s.) XXXIX, pp. 1–18.

Sklute, L. (1981), 'The Inconclusive Form of the *Parliament of Fowls*', *Chau R* XVI, pp. 119–28.

——— (1984), *Virtue of Necessity: Inconclusiveness and Narrative Form in Chaucer's Poetry*, Columbus, Ohio.

Smalley, B. (1960), *English Friars and Antiquity in the Early XIVth Century*, Oxford.

Smith, J.J. (1995), 'Chaucer's Language', in Minnis 1995: 513–27.

Smith, R.M. (1950), '"Minstralcie and Noyse" in the *House of Fame*', *MLN* LXV, pp. 521–30.

Smithers, G.V. (1983), 'The Scansion of *Havelok* and the Use of M.E. *-en* and *-e* in *Havelok* and Chaucer', in Gray & Stanley 1983.

Smyser, H.M. (1941), 'Chaucer's Two-Mile Pilgrimage', *MLN* LVI, pp. 205–7.

Songe vert (anon.) (1904), ed. L. Constans, *Romania* XXXIII, pp. 490–539.

Southworth, J. (1989), *The English Medieval Minstrel*, Woodbridge.

Spearing, A.C. (1976), *Medieval Dream Poetry*, Cambridge.

——— (1993), *The Medieval Poet as Voyeur. Looking and Listening in Medieval Love Narratives*, Cambridge.

Spencer, T. (1927), 'Chaucer's Hell: A Study in Mediaeval Convention', *Spec* II, pp. 177–200.

Spitzer, L. (1946), 'Note on the Poetic and Empirical "I" in Medieval Authors', *Traditio* IV, pp. 415–16.

Stahl 1952: see Macrobius 1952.

(1977): see Martianus Capella 1977.

Statius (1928), *Achilleid*, in *Statius* (vol. 2), ed. and tr. J.H. Mozley, London.

(1955–7, rev. edn 1971–5), *Thebaid*, ed. and tr. J.H. Mozley and J.B. Poynton (3 vols), London and Cambridge, Mass.

Steadman, J.M. (1960), 'Chaucer's Eagle: A Contemplative Symbol', *PMLA* LXXV, pp. 153–9.

Steneck, N.H. (1976), *Science and Creation in the Middle Ages: Henry of Langenstein (d. 1397) on Genesis*, Notre Dame and London.

Stevens, M. (1966), 'Narrative Focus in the *Book of the Duchess*: A Critical Revaluation', *An M* VII, pp. 16–32.

Stevenson, K.G. (1978), 'The Endings of Chaucer's *House of Fame*', *E St* LIX, pp. 10–26.

(1989), 'Readers, Poets, and Poems within the Poem', *Chau R* XIV, pp. 1–19.

Stillwell, G. (1950), 'Unity and Comedy in Chaucer's *Parlement of Foules*', *JEGP* XLIX, pp. 482–92.

(1956), 'Chaucer's "o sentence" in the *Hous of Fame*', *E S* XXXVII, pp. 149–57.

Strohm, P. (1975), '*Passioun, Lyf, Miracle, Legende*: Some Generic Terms in Middle English Hagiographical Narrative', *Chau R* X, pp. 62–75, 154–71.

(1983), 'Chaucer's Audience(s): Fictional, Implied, Intended, Actual', *Chau R* XVIII, pp. 137–45.

(1989), *Social Chaucer*, Cambridge, Mass.

(1992), *Huchon's Arrow: The Historical Imagination in Fourteenth Century Texts*, Princeton, NJ.

Sumption, J. (1975), *Pilgrimage: An Image of Medieval Religion*, London.

Sypherd, W.O. (1907), *Studies in Chaucer's 'Hous of Fame'* (Chaucer Society XXXIX), London.

Taylor, B. (1977), 'The Medieval Cleopatra: The Classical and Medieval Tradition of Chaucer's *Legend of Cleopatra*', *JMRS* VII, pp. 249–69.

Taylor, K. (1989), *Chaucer Reads 'The Divine Comedy'*, Stanford, Calif.

Taylor, P.B. & Bordier, S. (1992), 'Chaucer and the Latin Muses', *Traditio* XLVII, pp. 215–32.

Teager, F.E. (1932), 'Chaucer's Eagle and the Rhetorical Colours', *PMLA* XLVII, pp. 410–18.

Thiébaux, M. (1974), *The Stag of Love: The Chase in Medieval Literature*, Ithaca, NY.

Thomson, W.G. (1906), *History of Tapestry from Earliest Times to the Present Day*, London.

Thorndike, L. (1923–58), *The History of Magic and Experimental Science* (8 vols), New York.

Thrupp, S. (1948, repr. 1962), *The Merchant Class of Medieval London*, Ann Arbor, Mich.

Tkacz, C.B. (1983), 'Chaucer's Beard-Making', *Chau R* XVIII, pp. 127–36.

Tristram, P. (1976), *Figures of Life and Death in Medieval Literature and Art*, London.

Tuck, J.A. (1971), 'Richard II's System of Patronage', in *The Reign of Richard II: Essays in Honour of May McKisack*, ed. F.R.H. du Boulay and C.M. Barron, London, pp. 1–20.

(1973), *Richard II and the English Nobility*, London.

Turville-Petre, T. (1989) (ed.), *Alliterative Poetry of the Later Middle Ages*, London.

Twycross, M.A. (1972), *The Medieval Anadyomene: A Study in Chaucer's Mythography*, Oxford.

(1990), '"As the Sun with his Beams When He is Most Bright"', *METh* XII, pp. 34–79.

Usk, Thomas (1971), 'Thomas Usk, "The Testament of Love": A New Edition', ed. V.B. Jellich, Ph.D. thesis, Washington University.

Vale, M.G.A. (1967), 'A Fourteenth-Century Order of Chivalry: The "Tiercelet"', *EHR* LXXXII, pp. 332–9.

Valerius Maximus (1888, repr. 1982), *Factorum et dictorum memorabilium*, ed. C. Kempf, Stuttgart.

Varty, K. (1967), *Reynard the Fox: A Study of the Fox in Medieval English Art*, Leicester.

Vincent of Beauvais (Vincentius Bellovacensis) (1964), *Speculum naturale* (facsimile of 1624 edn), Graz, Austria.

Virgil (1935), *Aeneid I–VI*, in *Virgil* (vol.1), ed. and tr. H.R. Fairclough, London.

Wallace, D. (1983), 'Chaucer and Boccaccio's Early Writings', in Boitani 1983.

(1985), *Chaucer and the Early Writings of Boccaccio*, Cambridge.

(1986), 'Chaucer's Continental Inheritance', in the *Cambridge Chaucer Companion*, ed. P. Boitani and J. Mann, Cambridge.

Walsingham, T. (1866), *Chronica Major* in *Annales Ricardi Secondi*, ed. H.T. Riley, Rolls Series, London; extracts in Given-Wilson 1993.

Walter of Chatillon (1986), *The Alexandreis*, tr. R.T. Pritchard, Toronto.

Wasserman, J.N. & Blanch, R.J. (1986) (eds), *Chaucer in the Eighties*, Syracuse, NY.

Watts, A.C. (1970), 'Chaucerian Selves – Especially Two Serious Ones', *Chau R* IV, pp. 229–41.

(1973), '"Amor Gloriae" in Chaucer's *House of Fame*', *JMRS* III, pp. 87–113.

Welsford, E. (1935), *The Fool: His Social and Literary History*, London.

Whitbread 1971: see Fulgentius 1971.

White, L. (1962), *Medieval Technology and Social Change*, Oxford.

White, T.H. (1954), *The Book of Beasts, being a Translation from the Latin Bestiary from the Twelfth Century*, London.

Whiting, B.J. & H.W. (1968) (eds), *Proverbs, Mainly Before 1500*, Cambridge, Mass., and London.

Whitman, F.H. (1969), 'Exegesis and Chaucer's Dream Visions', *Chau R* III, pp. 229–38.

Wilkins, N. (1979), *Music in the Age of Chaucer*, Woodbridge and Totowa, NJ.

Willeford, W. (1969), *The Fool and his Sceptre: A Study in Clowns and Jesters and their Audience*, London.

Williams, G.G. (1957), 'The *Hous of Fame* and the House of the Musicians', *MLN* LXXII, pp. 6–9.

Williams, P.V.A. (1979) (ed.), *The Fool and the Trickster: Studies in Honour of Enid Welsford*, Cambridge.

Wilson, W.S. (1964), 'Exegetical Grammar in the *House of Fame*', *ELN* I, pp. 244–8.

Wimsatt, J.I. (1967a), 'The Apotheosis of Blanche in the *Book of the Duchess*', *JEGP* LXVI, pp. 26–44.

(1967b), 'The Sources of Chaucer's "Seys and Alcyone"', *M Ae* XXXVI, pp. 231–41.

(1968), *Chaucer and the French Love Poets: The Literary Background to the 'Book of the Duchess'*, Chapel Hill, NC.

(1970), *The Marguerite Poetry of Guillaume de Machaut*, Chapel Hill, NC.

(1979), 'Chaucer, Fortune, and Machaut's "Il m'est avis"', in *Chaucerian Problems and Perspectives: Essays presented to Paul E. Beichner, C.S.E.*, ed. E. Vasta and Z.P. Thundy, Notre Dame, Ind.

(1982), *Chaucer and the Poems of 'Ch'*, Cambridge.

(1993), *Chaucer and his French Contemporaries: Natural Music in the Fourteenth Century*, Toronto.

Windeatt, B. (1982) (ed.), *Chaucer's Dream Poetry: Sources and Analogues*, Cambridge and Totowa, NJ.

(1992), *Troilus and Criseyde*, Oxford Guides to Chaucer, Oxford.

Winny, J. (1973), *Chaucer's Dream Poems*, New York.

Wolff, W. (1952), *The Dream: Mirror of Conscience*, New York.

Wood, M. (1965), *The English Medieval House*, London.

Woolf, R. (1968), *The English Religious Lyric in the Middle Ages*, Oxford.

Wynnere & Wastoure: in Conlee 1991.

Yapp, B. (1981), *Birds in Medieval Manuscripts*, London.

Young, K. (1937), 'Chaucer and Peter of Riga', *Spec* XII, pp. 299–303.

SELECTIVE GLOSSARY

This glossary offers fuller information than can be provided in the on-page glossing. It deals chiefly with obsolete or unfamiliar words, forms and meanings, although it also includes some examples of familiar words that are of particular thematic interest in these poems (e.g. **bo[o]ke**, 'book').

Where several senses of a single word (e.g. the noun **wit[t]e**) are listed, they should be approached as branches of meaning, rather than rigidly demarcated categories. The glossary does not give all spelling variants.

Past participles with the *i-* or *y-* prefix usually appear with the verbs of which they are part: if the verb appears in more than one form, the infinitive is given first (thus: *yblowe* appears after *blowe(n)*; *ybrent* after *brenne(n)*, etc.). Where *y* represents a vowel (e.g. *blyve* or *yf*) it appears alphabetically with *i*; where it represents a consonant (e.g. *yate* or *yere*) it appears in the modern alphabetical order. Very common words are only selectively glossed.

Additional abbreviations used in the glossary

adj.	adjective	*pa.*	past tense
adv.	adverb	*pl.*	plural
comp.	comparative	*poss.*	possessive
conj.	conjunction	*p.p.*	past participle
demonstr.	demonstrative	*prep.*	preposition
emph.	emphatic	*pres.*	present tense
imper.	imperative	*pres. part.*	present participle
impers.	impersonal	*pron.*	pronoun
infin.	infinitive	*sg.*	singular
interj.	interjection	*subj.*	subjunctive
interrog.	interrogative	*v.*	verb
n.	noun		

The numbers quoted throughout refer to the lines where the words occur.

a *v. see* **have(n)**
a *prep.* **on a Goddys halfe** for God's sake *BD* 370, 758.
abawed *p.p.* disconcerted, cast down *BD* 614.
abyden *v.* wait for *HF* 1086, 1994, *PF* 509; **abode** (*pa. 3 sg.*) waited, lingered *HF* 1602, *LGWP* 235; experienced, received *BD* 247.

able *adj.* predisposed, receptive *BD* 779; capable *BD* 786.

abode *n.* staying put (see **abyden**) *HF* 1963.

abreyde(n) *v.* awaken, be roused *HF* 110, 559; **abrayede** (*pa. 3 sg.*) *BD* 192.

accident *n.* occurrences *HF* 1976.

accordant *adj.* in agreement *PF* 203.

a-cheked *p.p.* brought to a halt *HF* 2093.

acloyeth *v.* (*pres. 3 sg.*) overburdens *PF* 517.

acorde *n.* agreement, settlement, reconciliation *HF* 695, 1964, *PF* 371, 381, 668; harmony *BD* 305, 316, *PF* 197; (*pl.*) harmonic intervals *HF* 696.

acorde(n) *v.* agree *PF* 608, *LGWP* 3.

acustumaunce *n.* habit, custom *HF* 28.

adamaunt *n.* lodestone, magnet *PF* 148.

adrad/adred *p.p.* daunted, frightened *BD* 493, 879, 1190, *HF* 928.

advertence *n.* attention *HF* 709.

affeccion *n.* inclination, attraction *LGWD* 1229.

affrayed *p.p.* alerted, aroused *BD* 296.

after/aftir *adv.* afterwards *BD* 100, *HF* 256, *PF* 59; *prep.* for *BD* 83; according to *BD* 1095, *HF* 2113, *PF* 305, 401; *conj.* according (to how) *PF* 216.

agaynes/agen/ayen *prep.* against, contrary to *BD* 16, *HF* 1035, *LGWP* 73, 74, etc.; towards *HF* 1523, *LGWP* 48.

ageyn(e) *adv.* in reply *BD* 367; back again *BD* 1032, 1222, *HF* 564.

agrefe *adv.* amiss *PF* 543.

ay *adv.* always, ever *BD* 643, *HF* 74, 467, etc.

ayerissh/eyryssh *adj.* made of air *HF* 932, 965.

alday/al day *adv.* all the time, commonly *HF* 386, 737.

alder- (*intensive prefix with superlative*) of all *BD* 246, 907, 1050, 1279, *PF* 244.

alegge(n) *v.* cite *HF* 314.

algate/algatis *adv.* anyway, at all events *BD* 887, 1087, *HF* 943, *LGWP* 170; nonetheless *BD* 1171.

al(le) *adv.* although *HF* 1740, 1820, 1980.

alther-, alder- (*intensive prefix with superlative*) of all *BD* 1173, *HF* 2131, etc.

amys *adv.* wrongly, mistakenly, astray *BD* 1141, *HF* 269, 596, 2016, 2079, *PF* 446.

amorwe/a-morwe *adv.* in the morning *BD* 1103, *HF* 2106.

and *conj.* if, supposing that *HF* 740, 807, 1037, *LGWP* 245.

ano(o)n *adv.* at once *BD* 80, 88, 106, etc., *HF* 69, 149, 339, 366, etc., *PF* 100, 120, 169, etc.

anoonryght/anoon-ryght *adv.* straightaway *BD* 354, 450, 536, etc., *HF* 132, 1075, 2062, *PF* 218.

apaire *v.* deteriorate *HF* 756.

apayed *p.p.* pleased; **evel apayed** displeased *LGWP* 68.

apparence *n.* outward appearance *HF* 265.

aprovede *p.p.* proved true *LGWP* 21.

aqueynten *v.* come to know *HF* 250 (*pa. 3 pl.*); make oneself known *BD* 532 (*reflexive*).

arede *v.* interpret *BD* 289.

areste *n.* hesitation, cautiousness *LGWP* 383.

art(e) *n.* skill, craft *BD* 788, 1161, 1163, 1169, *HF* 335, 627, 1095, 1276, 1882; **Arte Craft,** Cunning (personified) *PF* 245.

aryved(e) (*pa. 3 sg.*) came to shore *LGWD* 959, 1049.

as *conj.* as if *BD* 530, *HF* 229, 530, 546, 1156, 1751; (*pleonastic*) *BD* 216, 248, *HF* 1617, *PF* 26, 547.

ascuse *see* **excuse**

askyng *n.* question *BD* 33.

aspe *n.* aspen (tree) *PF* 180.

aspie(n)/espye(n)/espie *v.* perceive *BD* 836, *HF* 594, 706, 944, etc., *PF* 194, 250, 280; seek to discover *LGWD* 966 (possibly also next sense); **espyed** (*pa. 3 sg.*) spy on *BD* 836.

as(s)ay *n.* test, trial, proof *BD* 552, *LGWP* 28; assault *PF* 2.

as(s)aye(n) *v.* try, test *BD* 346, 574, *PF* 257, *LGWP* 477.

astert *v.* break away, leave *BD* 1154.

aston(y)ed(e) *p.p.* stunned *HF* 549, *LGWP* 164.

asweved *p.p.* dazed *HF* 549.

at(t)empre/atempry *adj.* temperate, mild *BD* 341, 1008, *PF* 204, *LGWP* 116.

au(c)torite *n.* authority *HF* 2158, *PF* 506; trustworthy writer *LGWP* 83 (*pl.*).

au(c)tour *n.* source, author *HF* 314, *LGWP* 88 (*pl.*), *LGWD* 1139, 1228, etc.

audience *n.* hearing *PF* 308.

autentyke *adj.* trustworthy *BD* 1086.

avayl(l)e(n) *v.* be of use, help, benefit *HF* 363, 1616, 1749, *PF* 538, *LGWD* 1325.

avaunte(n) *v.* boast *PF* 470.

avauntour *n.* boaster *PF* 430.

aventure *n.* luck, chance, fortune *HF* 1052, 1297, 2090, *PF* 131; quest *HF* 463; **Aventure,** Fortune (personified) *HF* 1982; events, occurrences *HF* 47, 1631.

avysement/avisement *n.* deliberation *PF* 555, *LGWP* 393.

avisen/avysen *v.* (*reflexive*) think over *BD* 697; *PF* 648.

avision *n.* precognitive dream *BD* 285, *HF* 7, 48; enigmatic dream *HF* 104, 513; dream reflecting waking concerns *HF* 40.

avouterye *n.* adultery *PF* 361.

awapid *p.p.* terrified *LGWP* 120.

bad *see* **bede(n)**

baggeth *v.* (*pres. 3 sg.*) squints *BD* 623.

bale *n.* trouble, misery *BD* 535; **for bote ne bale** for good or ill *BD* 227.

bane *n.* destroyer *HF* 408.

be/bi/by *prep.* by *BD* 1, etc.; about *HF* 742; in *LGWP* 49; **by and by** in order *LGWP* 230.

beare/bere(n) *v.* bear, carry, hold up *BD* 196, etc., *HF* 568, 947, 1439, etc., *PF* 137; behave *PF* 459; **beare lyfe** live *BD* 64; **bere charge** merit consideration *BD* 894; **bore/born(e)** (*p.p.*) *BD* 566, 686, 1301, *PF* 109, 484.

bede(n) *v.* offer *HF* 32.

bede(n)/bidde(n) *v.* tell, propose, order *HF* 32; **bade** (*pa. 1 sg.*) *BD* 47; **bad** (*pa. 3 sg.*) *BD* 135, 187, *HF* 165, 186, 236, 430, 1569, 1578, *PF* 64, 320; **byd/bid** (*imper.*) *BD* 141, 144, *HF* 808, 1573; **bede** (*p.p.*) *BD* 194; **bodyn** (*p.p.*) *LGWP* 346.

befalle *v.* happen *HF* 101, *PF* 664; **befel/befyl** (*pa. 3 sg.*) *BD* 66, 1258.

begoon *p.p.* contented *PF* 171.

Behest *n.* Promises (personified) *PF* 245.

behoteth *v.* (*pres. 3 sg.*) promises *BD* 621; **behette** (*pa. 3 sg.*) *PF* 436.

bele *adj.* beautiful *HF* 1796.

be(n) *v.* be *note esp.* are *BD* 28, 409, *LGWP* 18, *LGWD* 1051, 1086, etc.; (*p.p.*) been *LGWD* 1261; **wern/were** (*pa.*) were *BD* 52, etc.; **were** (*subjunct.*) would be *LGWD* 997, etc.

bere *n.* pillow-case *BD* 254.

beryl/berile *n.* crystalline stone *HF* 1184, 1288.

beseche(n) *v.* entreat, beseech *BD* 1132, 1224, *HF* 1554; **besechynge** (*pres. part.*) *PF* 421; **besoughten** (*pa. 3 pl.*) *HF* 1706.

besey *p.p.* -looking (with adv.); **wel besey** good-looking *BD* 829.

besette *v.* bestow *BD* 772; **besette hytte** (*pa. 1 sg.*) applied it *BD* 1096; (*p.p.*) *BD* 863, 1043; provided for *PF* 598.

beste *n.* animal *HF* 900, 932, 965, 1003, 1226, 1383, 1390, *PF* 86, 196.

beten *v.* beat; **ibete** (*p.p.*) beaten, struck *LGWD* 1121.

bethenke/bethynke *v.* reflect, consider *HF* 1176; (*pres. 1 sg.*) *BD* 698; (*imper.*) *BD* 1304; **bethoght(e)** (*pa. 1 sg.*) *BD* 1183, 1195; imagine, desire *PF* 483.

bette *adj.* better *BD* 672; *adv.* better *BD* 668, 669, 1044, 1045, *HF* 13, 559, 1232, *PF* 166, 451, 474, etc.; **go bet** go quickly *BD* 136.

betyde(n)/betide(n) *v.* happen, occur *HF* 680, *PF* 654; **betyd(d)e** (*p.p.*) *HF* 384, 578, 2048.

bewrye *v.* reveal, betray *PF* 348.

bi/by *see* be

bidde(n) *see* bede(n)

blasen *v.* blow a blast *HF* 1866.

blenden *v.* blind, deceive; **blent** (*pres. 3 sg.*) *PF* 600; **yblent** (*p.p.*) *BD* 647.

blyve *adv.* quickly, promptly *BD* 152, *HF* 1106, 1521, *PF* 604; **as blyve** immediately *BD* 248, 1277, *HF* 1106, *LGWP* 425.

blowe(n) *v.* spread *HF* 1859; **yblowe** (*p.p.*) *HF* 1139, 1664; proclaim *HF* 1769, 1790; **blowen** (*p.p.*) *HF* 1859.

bodyn *see* bede(n)

boystes *n.* (*pl.*) boxes *HF* 2129.

bo(o)ke *n.* book *BD* 47, 52, 57, 96, 274, 1326, *HF* 385, 426, 429, 622, 657, 712, *PF* 10, 16, 19, 24, 29, 87, 110, *LGWP* 17, 25, 27, 30, 34, 264, 271, 273, 405, 498; part of poem *HF* 1093.

boon *n.* bone *BD* 940, 943.

bo(o)ne *n.* favour, request, prayer *BD* 129, 835, *HF* 1537, 1774, *PF* 643.

bo(o)te *n.* remedy *BD* 38, *HF* 32, *PF* 276; **bote ne bale** *BD* 227 see **bale**; **do bote** bring about healing, save *LGWD* 1076.

bost *n.* noise, boast *LGWP* 221.

bounte *n.* goodness *BD* 1198, *HF* 1698, *LGWP* 510.

bourded *p.p.* jested *PF* 589.

boure *n.* chamber, private room *HF* 1186, *PF* 304.

brede *n.* breadth *BD* 956, *HF* 1494, 2042.

breyde *n.* pull, tug, turn *LGWD* 1166.

brekke *n.* fault, flaw *BD* 940.

browke *v.* enjoy the use of *HF* 273.

but *conj.* but *BD* 12, etc., *HF* 12, etc., *PF* 14, etc.; except *PF* 49, 500, 1636, *LGWP* 8; unless *BD* 94, etc., *HF* 2003, *PF* 159, 459, 469, 567; but if *HF* 505; **nevir but** never more than *BD* 983; **nolde but** would not give up the chance to *BD* 311; (*as adv.*) just, only *BD* 39, 456, 674, etc., *HF* 482; simply, nothing but *BD* 204; rather *BD* 811.

ca(a)s/case *n.* event, occurrence *HF* 254, 578; situation *BD* 725; chance *HF* 1052, *LGWD* 1046, 1056; legal case *LGWP* 395.

cachche/cache *v.* take, receive, acquire *BD* 781, 969; **kaught** (*pa. 1 sg., 3 sg. & pl.*) *BD* 124, 681, *PF* 170; **ycaught** (*p.p.*) *BD* 395, 838; **cache his deth** die *HF* 404.

calle *v.* make welcome, treat *LGWD* 1126.

can *see* **konne**

careyne *n.* carcass, corpse *PF* 177.

carole *v.* dance a carole *BD* 849.

cartar *n.* charioteer *PF* 102.

cart(e) *n.* chariot *HF* 943, 956; (*pl.*) *PF* 102.

caste *n.* shape, design *HF* 1178.

caste(n) *v.* throw, lift *HF* 495, 935, 956; cast *PF* 172; consider, decide *HF* 1148; devise *HF* 1170.

charge *n.* load, weight *HF* 746, 1439; significance *BD* 894.

charite/charyte *n.* generosity, benevolence *BD* 642, *HF* 108, *PF* 508.

chaunce *n.* **suche a chaunce** as much hope as of *BD* 1113; **in al chaunce** in every situation *BD* 1285.

chere *n.* face, expression *BD* 545, *HF* 179, 214, *PF* 414, 488, *LGWP* 219; pleasant appearance *HF* 154, 277; spirits, mood, reaction *HF* 671, *LGWD* 1248; presentation of a pleasant welcome *LGWD* 1146.

cherl(e) *n.* boor, low-born person *PF* 596, *LGWP* 124.

chyde *v.* reprove, scold, grumble *BD* 937.

choghe *n.* chough, jackdaw (not distinguished at this time) *PF* 345.

citee, cete *n.* city *HF* 901, 1845, 2080, etc.; citadel *HF* 1114.

clefte *pa. 3 sg.* split, broke up *BD* 72.

clepe(n) *v.* call, name *BD* 185, 512, 810, 814, *HF* 73, 937, 1326, 1400, etc.;

icleped/ycleped/clepid (*p.p.*) *HF* 1625, 1921, *LGWD* 944, etc.; **clepeth forth** summons *PF* 352.

clerk(e) *n.* scholar, authoritative writer *BD* 53, *HF* 53, 760, 1487, 1503, *PF* 333, *LGWP* 278, 350; scientist/magician *HF* 1265.

colours *n. (pl.)* rhetorical figures, ornaments of style *HF* 859.

comelely *adv.* gracefully, becomingly *BD* 848.

comlynesse *n.* beauty *BD* 827, 966.

compas/compace/cumpas *n.* contrivance, scheme *HF* 462, 1170, 1302; circumference *HF* 798; circle *LGWP* 228.

compleynt/complaynt *n.* lament *BD* 464, 487, *HF* 362, 924; **conpleyntys** legal complaints, lawsuits *LGWP* 363

complexion *n.* temperament *HF* 21.

compoune(n) *v.* combine *HF* 1029, 2108.

comune *adj.* common, general *PF* 47, 75, 507; **accustomed ful comune** most inveterate *BD* 812; **in comune** generally *HF* 1548.

conclusion/conclusyon *n.* result, outcome *HF* 103, 342; decision, opinion *PF* 526, 620; inference, demonstration *HF* 848, 871.

condicioun/condycyoun *n.* condition *BD* 750, *PF* 407; nature *HF* 1904; characteristic *LGWP* 40; *(pl.)* ranks of society *HF* 1530.

conjuren *v.* call upon; **conjurith** (*pres. 3 sg.*) calls upon *LGWD* 1312.

conscience *n.* consciousness, conscience, sensitivity *LGWD* 1255.

conserve(n) *v.* preserve *HF* 732, 1160.

contraire/contrayre *n.* opposite *HF* 1540, 1629; contrary *HF* 808.

contrayre *adj.* at odds (with) *BD* 1290.

cop *n.* top, summit *HF* 1166.

corbettes *n. (pl.)* corbels, ornamental roof-supports *HF* 1304.

corn *n.* kernel *LGWP* 529.

corseynt *n.* body of a saint *HF* 117.

cote armure *n.* coat of arms or garment embroidered with heraldic arms *HF* 1326.

coude *see* konne(n)

counseyl(le) *n.* advice, instruction, guidance *BD* 840, *PF* 631; plan *PF* 522; secret *PF* 348.

counseylle(n) *v.* advise *HF* 371, *PF* 633.

countenaunce *n.* demeanour, manner *BD* 833; self-possession *BD* 613; look, behaviour *BD* 1022.

countrefete(n) *v.* imitate *HF* 1212, 1213.

countrepese(n) *v.* balance, set against *HF* 1750.

couthe *see* konne(n)

coward *adj.* cowardly *PF* 349.

craft(e) *n.* skill, art *BD* 791, *HF* 1100, 1213, *PF* 1; cunning *LGWP* 127, (personified) *PF* 220; strategy *LGWD* 1286.

craftely *adv.* skilfully *HF* 1203, 1220; cunningly *HF* 1267.

crips *adj.* curly *HF* 1386.

croppes *n.* foliage, treetops *BD* 424.

cubite *n.* length of the forearm *HF* 1370.

cure *n.* care, responsibility *HF* 464, *LGWD* 1176; **be cure** by design *HF* 1298; **did his ... cure** was concerned *PF* 369; remedy, cure *PF* 128; **take cure** pay attention *LGWD* 1145.

curiosite *n.* elegance *HF* 1178.

curiouse *adj.* painstaking *HF* 29; exquisite *HF* 125.

currours *n. (pl.)* couriers *HF* 2128.

curteysye *n.* noble behaviour, courtly behaviour, nobility *LGWP* 318; (personified) Courtesy, Courtly Behaviour *PF* 219.

dasewyd *adj. p.p.* dazed, stupefied *HF* 658.

daun *n.* lord (foll. by name) *HF* 137, 161, 175, 199, 434, 591, 759, 916 (< Latin *dominus*).

Daunger *n.* (personified) Aloofness, Rebuff (< late Latin *dominiarium;* see *RR,* tr. Horgan 1994: 44) *PF* 136.

daunte(n) *v.* tame, subdue *PF* 114.

dawen *v.* to dawn; **dawith** *(pres. 3 sg.) LGWP* 46.

debonaire *adj.* gracious, gentle *BD* 860; *(as n.)* benefactress *BD* 624 (see note).

debonairly *adv.* graciously *BD* 851, 1284; politely, gently *BD* 518; meekly *HF* 2013.

debonairyete *n.* gentleness, patience *BD* 986.

declare *v.* explain, reveal *LGWP* 86.

ded(e)/deed *adj.* dead *BD* 91, 121, 204, *HF* 184, 1701, 1876, etc., *PF* 50, 79, 585; lifeless *BD* 127, 489; stagnant *PF* 187; deadly, mortal *BD* 1211.

dede(n) *v.* be lifeless or numb *HF* 552.

dedely *adj.* deathlike *BD* 462; soporific *BD* 162.

deynte *n.* value, pleasure *LGWP* 100; **deinteis** delicacies *LGWD* 1100.

dele *n.* bit, scrap *HF* 331; times *HF* 1495.

delyte *v. (reflexive)* am delighted *LGWP* 30.

delyvere(n) *v.* set free, dissolve (assembly) *PF* 491, 508, 523.

demeyne(n) *v.* drive, control, manage *HF* 959.

departed *p.p.* separated *HF* 2068.

depeynted *p.p.* decorated with painting *BD* 322, *LGWD* 1025.

descryve(n)/discryve(n)/diskryve *v.* describe *BD* 897, 916, *HF* 1105, 1168, 1330, 2056.

deserte *adj.* abandoned, solitary *HF* 417.

destroubled *p.p.* disturbed *BD* 524.

devyne(n) *v.* guess *HF* 14.

devys *n.* scheme, strategem *LGWD* 1102; *(pl.)* badges, heraldic badges worn to show allegiance *LGWD* 1272.

devyse(n) *v.* describe *BD* 901, *HF* 772, 1062, 1113, 1179, *PF* 317, 333, 398, *LGWD* 1206; ordain *LGWP* 427.

dighte *v.* prepare *LGWD* 1000.

digne *adj.* worthy, honorable *HF* 1426.

dynt *n.* stroke, clap (of thunder) *HF* 534.

discryve(n) *see* **descryve(n)**

discure *v.* disclose, reveal *BD* 549.

disesperat *adj.* hopeless, despairing *HF* 2015.

dysfigured *adj.* disfigured, deformed *PF* 222.

dispite *n.* spite *HF* 96, 1668; resentment *HF* 1716; **in dyspite of** in defiance of *PF* 281.

dispitously *adv.* cruelly, ruthlessly *HF* 161.

disport(e) *n.* amusement, fun *HF* 664, *PF* 260.

disporte(n) *v.* cheer, amuse *HF* 571.

disshevele *adj.* with hair loose (unbound, unplaited) *PF* 235.

distreyne(n) *v.* grasp, grip *PF* 337.

ditees *n. (pl.)* poems (to be said or sung) *HF* 622.

dyvers *adj.* different, various *HF* 1969, 1976; variable *HF* 1574; opposed, hostile *BD* 653.

doynge *n.* business, affair *PF* 515.

dolven *p.p.* buried *BD* 222.

do(on) *v.* (1) do, act, perform *BD* 29, 188, 194, etc., *HF* 261, 320, 603, 611, etc., *PF* 163, 478, etc.; **dost** (*pres. 2 sg.*) *LGWP* 241; **doo(n) ... entente** do all one can *BD* 752, *HF* 1267, 2132; (2) carry out, bring about *BD* 134, 562, 680, 719, 868; (3) (as substitute for other verb or verb phrase) *BD* 150, 264, 268, 892, 1047, *HF* 261; (4) finish, achieve *BD* 40, etc., *HF* 372; **have doon** finish! *HF* 1623, *PF* 492; (5) give, devote *BD* 554; **do ... some disport** give some fun *HF* 664; **do ... an ese** give consolation *HF* 2020; **do ... worshippe** honour *BD* 1098; **do no fors** pay no heed *BD* 542; **did my besynesse** devoted all my efforts *BD* 1156; **dooth ... bote** allays, appeases *PF* 276; (6) cause (usually with infin.) *BD* 145, 149, 259, 713, 1017, *HF* 610, 1276, 1582, 1818, *PF* 221, 458, *LGWD* 1076, 1181; (7) put, take; **did of** took off *BD* 516; (8) (*emph. with infin.*) *BD* 754.

do(o)me *n.* judgement *HF* 1905, *PF* 308, 480, 546.

dosser *n.* basket (for carrying on back) *HF* 1940.

dote(n) *v.* grow senile, become foolish *LGWP* 261.

double *adj.* duplicitous, unfaithful *HF* 285.

draf *n.* husks (left after threshing), residue, (metaphoric) something worthless *LGWP* 312.

drede *n.* fear, anxiety, uncertainty, doubt *BD* 24, 490, 608, 1212, *HF* 31, 551, 723, 1971; **withoute(n) drede** doubtless, for sure *BD* 280, 1073, 1096, *HF* 292, 830, 1913, *PF* 52, *LGWP* 454; **out of drede** to be sure, indeed *HF* 1142, 1456, *PF* 81.

dreden *v.* fear *HF* 38, *LGWP* 95; **drede the not** (*reflexive*) don't be afraid *HF* 1043, *PF* 157, 448; abhor *BD* 1264.

dred(e)ful *adj.* fearful *PF* 3; timid *PF* 195, 638.

drenche(n) *v.* drown, sink *HF* 205; **dreynt** (*pa. 3 sg.*) *BD* 72 (*transitive*), *HF* 923 (*intransitive*); **dreynt(e)** (*p.p.*) *BD* 148, 195, 229, *HF* 233, *LGWP* 293.

drye(n) *v.* endure, bear, suffer *HF* 1879, *PF* 251.
dure(n) *v.* last, endure *HF* 303, *PF* 616, 642; go on living *HF* 352.

echon *pron.* each of them, every one *BD* 335, 695, 817, *HF* 150, 1953, *LGWP* 193.
effecte *n.* actuality *HF* 5; **in effecte** in the end, actually *PF* 619; **effect (is)** substance, essential elements *LGWD* 929, 1180.
efte *adv.* afterwards, later *BD* 41, *HF* 401.
eyryssh *see* **ayerissh**
ek(e) *adv.* also *BD* 330, etc., *HF* 179, etc., *PF* 91, etc.
eleccion *n.* choice *PF* 409, 621; election *PF* 528.
embosed *p.p.* driven into the wood *BD* 353.
empryse *n.* chivalric exploit or undertaking *BD* 1093.
enbrowde(n) *v.* embroider; **enbrowded** (*p.p.*) *HF* 1327.
enclyne(n) *v.* incline, dispose *BD* 991, *HF* 749, 825, 828, *PF* 325; bow, bend (head) *PF* 414.
enclynynge *n.* propensity, disposition *HF* 734.
endelong *prep.* along, across *LGWP* 144.
endite(n)/endyte(n) *v.* compose, write *HF* 381, 520, 634, *PF* 119, 167, *LGWP* 351.
endlonge *adv.* lengthways, from end to end *HF* 1458.
endure(n) *v.* last *HF* 1981, *PF* 130; endure *BD* 20, *PF* 661.
engendred *p.p.* produced (by) *PF* 248.
engendrynge *n.* production, source *HF* 968; conception (of children) *LGWP* 414.
engendrure *n.* conception (of offspring) *PF* 306.
engyne *n.* skill *HF* 528; siege engine *HF* 1934.
Englis/Englissh/Englyssh *n.* English language *HF* 510, *LGWP* 86; **bothe Englyssh and wit** both the words and the skill *BD* 898.
Englyssh *adj.* English *HF* 1470.
enhaunsede *p.p.* advanced, strengthened *LGWP* 372.
ensaumple *n.* model, exemplar, exemplum (story which illustrates a general truth) *BD* 911, 1258; (*pl.*) *LGWD* 1258.
ensure(n) *v.* promise *HF* 2098.
entenden *v.* intend, incline, apply oneself to; **entendedyn** (*pa. pl.*) they gave their attention to; *LGWD* 1155.
entent(e) *n.* intention *HF* 2000, *LGWP* 85; desire *PF* 644; purpose, design *HF* 1267, 2000, 2132; mind, thoughts *PF* 580; **wyth glad entente** happily *PF* 532; **with goode entente** with good will *BD* 766; **doo(n) ... entente** do all one can *BD* 752, *HF* 1267, 2132.
entewnes *n.* (*pl.*) melodies, perhaps 'chants' *BD* 309.
entremete(n) *v.* meddle *PF* 515.
envie(n)/envye(n) *v.* compete *BD* 173; strive, contend *BD* 406, *HF* 1231.
er *see* **or**
errour *n.* confusion *PF* 146, 156.

erst(e) *adv.* first, before *HF* 1496, 2075, *LGWP* 45; **at erste** for the first time *HF* 512.

eschewyng *n.* avoidance *PF* 140.

ese *n.* pleasure, rest, benefit *PF* 384, *LGWD* 1112.

ese(n) *v.* relieve, comfort, please *BD* 556, *HF* 1799, *PF* 480.

esely *adv.* gradually *HF* 1675; easily *HF* 1929.

espye(n), espie *see* aspie(n)

esta(a)t(e) *n.* class, rank, state *HF* 1970, *PF* 550, 630, *LGWP* 113; grandeur *LGWD* 1036, 1105.

evel *adv.* badly, imperfectly *BD* 1204; **me lyst evel** I am ill-disposed (to) *BD* 239; **ferde ... evel** was in a bad state, suffered *BD* 501.

evene *adj.* exact, equal *BD* 1289.

evene *adv.* exactly *BD* 198, 289, 441; definitely, for certain *BD* 120; promptly *BD* 275; right *BD* 458, 1329; **evene upryght** upright *BD* 451; **lyche evene** exactly the same *HF* 10; **ryght even** exactly *HF* 714.

everych(e) *adj.* each (separate) *HF* 817, 975, *PF* 641.

everych(e) *pron.* each one *BD* 301, *HF* 47, *PF* 401, 408.

everycho(o)n(e) *pron.* each one *HF* 337, 1660, 1717, 1772.

everydel(l)e/everedel *adv.* wholly, completely *BD* 222, *HF* 65, 880; in all things *BD* 1014; in every way, in all respects *BD* 698, 1041, *HF* 1129.

excusacyouns *n.* pleas for acquittal *LGWP* 362.

excuse(n) *v.* make excuse for, forgive *BD* 678, *HF* 427; (legal) offer a defence *LGWP* 389.

exorsicacions *n. (pl.)* conjuring up of spirits, incantations *HF* 1263.

fable *n.* story *BD* 52; fiction, untruth *HF* 1480.

facound(e) *adj.* full, harmonious, eloquent *BD* 926, *PF* 521.

facounde *n.* eloquence *PF* 558.

faille/fayle *n.* **sauns faille /fayle** without doubt *HF* 188, 429.

fayl(l)e(n)/faile(n) *v.* lack, fall short *HF* 297, 1098; grow less *PF* 85; fail *BD* 441, *HF* 1615.

fayn *adv.* eagerly *LGWP* 59; **I wolde fayn** I very much wanted *HF* 1848; **faynest** most eagerly *PF* 480.

faire/fayre *adv.* gently *HF* 1050; courteously *HF* 1539; well *PF* 511; clearly *PF* 503; finely *PF* 594.

falle(n) *v.* fall *BD* 13, 71, *HF* 741, 1192, 1534, 1705, etc.; **fille** *(pa. 1 sg.)* *HF* 114; **felle/fil(le)/fyll** *(pa. 3 sg.)* *BD* 123, 128, 275, *HF* 922; **fel** *(pa. 3 pl.)* *HF* 1772; **fille** *(pa. 3 pl.)* *HF* 1659; **yfalle** *(p.p.)* *BD* 384; ebb, drain away *BD* 564; enter, come into *BD* 706; befit, be provided or given *BD* 257, *PF* 406; happen *BD* 1320; **fille to doon** was appropriate to do *BD* 374.

fame *n.* fame, reputation *HF* 305, 1139, 1146, 1154, 1200, 1555, 1609, 1619, 1662, 1674, 1695, 1715, 1735, 1762, 1815, 1848, 1852, 1872.

fantasye *n.* image, imagining *BD* 28, *HF* 593; delusion *HF* 992.

fanto(u)me *n.* delusion *HF* 11, 493.

fare *n.* well-being *HF* 682; commotion *HF* 1065.

fare(n) *v. (pa. 3 sg.* **ferde**) go *LGWP* 85; happen *HF* 271; fare, get on *BD* 113, 616, 785, *PF* 693; feel *BD* 99, *HF* 887; behave, act, seem, sound *BD* 967, *HF* 1522, 1932, *PF* 152, 599, etc.; **wel farynge** handsome, prosperous-looking *BD* 452.

fast *adj.*; **fastest** (*superlative adv.*) quickest *HF* 2131.

faste *adv.* quickly *BD* 140, *HF* 1675, 1865, 2087, *PF* 133, 170, etc.; eagerly, attentively, closely *BD* 505, *HF* 481, 1728, *PF* 21; seriously, deeply *BD* 488, *PF* 94; loudly, powerfully *BD* 385; **faste be/by** close by *BD* 369, *HF* 497, 1919, 1990.

fauned *pa. 3 sg.* wagged tail, crouched, displayed fondness *BD* 389.

fedme *n. (pl.)* fathoms (measurement of six feet/two metres) *BD* 422.

fe(e)le *adj.* many *BD* 400, *HF* 1137, 1381, 1389, 1946, *PF* 329.

feyne(n) *v.* pretend *BD* 317; make up stories *HF* 1478; **feynynge** (*pres. part as verbal noun*) pretence *BD* 1100; **feyned** (*p.p. as adj.*) pretended, insincere *HF* 688.

ferde *n.* fear *BD* 1214, *HF* 950.

ferde *see* **fare(n)**

fere *n.* mate, companion *PF* 410, 416, *LGWD* 969.

ferforth(e) *adv.* far *HF* 328, 1882; **so ferforthe** so utterly, to such an extent *PF* 377.

fermour *n.* person to whom the government grants the right to take revenue from land or other source of money, collector of taxes *LGWP* 358.

fers *n.* (chess) queen *BD* 654, etc.; *(pl.)* pieces *BD* 723.

fest(e) *n.* feast *BD* 974, *(pl.)* 433, *HF* 1222; **maketh feste** welcomes *BD* 638.

fy(e) *interj.* not at all! for shame! (expresses indignation at what has been said) *BD* 1115, *HF* 1776, *PF* 596.

figure *n.* image, portrait *HF* 126, 132; *(pl.)* symbols *HF* 48; tropes, rhetorical figures *HF* 858; *(pl.)* numerals *BD* 437, 438.

fil(le)/fyll *see* **falle(n)**

fynde(n) *v.* find, discover *BD* 102, 208, *HF* 237, 279, etc., *PF* 318, 330, etc.; learn *HF* 44; deduce *HF* 750; invent *HF* 283; manage *BD* 916; **fynde out** invent *BD* 319, 1163; **fynde a tale** try to find a topic (for conversation); **fonde/founde** (*pa. 1 sg.*) *BD* 60, 451, 533, etc., *HF* 141, 1166, 1293, *PF* 242, 261; *(pa. 3 sg.)* *HF* 443, *PF* 374; *(pa. 3 pl.)* *BD* 89, *HF* 1810; **(y)founde(n)** (*p.p.*) *BD* 73, 378, 916, 925, *HF* 1286, 2054, *PF* 428.

fynder *n.* discoverer *BD* 1168.

flee(n) *v.*1 flee *HF* 165, 186, *PF* 147; **fled** (*pa. 3 sg.*) *HF* 166; **fleden** (*pa. 3 pl.*) *HF* 179.

flee(n) *v.*2 fly *HF* 610, 934, 973, 2109, 2118, *PF* 388; **fleynge** (*pres. part.*) *BD* 178, *HF* 543; **fleegh** (*pa. 3 sg.*) *HF* 921; **fledde hireself** fled to save herself *LGWD* 1225; **flowen** (*p.p.*) *HF* 905.

flesshy *adj.* plump, rounded *BD* 954.

flyttynge *pres. part.* variable, flitting here and there *BD* 801.

floode *n.* river *HF* 72, 751.

florisshinges *n. (pl.)* ornamentation *HF* 1301.

flour *n.* flower *BD* 400 etc., *PF* 186, 259, 302, etc.; (fig.) achievement *BD* 630, highest example, paragon *LGWP* 55, *LGWD* 1009.

folye *n.* folly *HF* 1972, *PF* 221.

fonde *see* **fynde(n)**

fonde(n) *v.* try *BD* 1020, 1259, 1332, *HF* 1427, *PF* 257.

fo(o) *n.* enemy *BD* 583, *HF* 1668, *PF* 339, 346; **fone** (*pl.*) *PF* 103.

fool(e) *n.* fool *BD* 734, 867, *HF* 958, *PF* 571, 574.

foole *adj.* foolish *PF* 505.

for *conj.* for *BD* 2, etc., *HF* 2, etc.; because *BD* 730, etc., *HF* 24, 51, 395, 412 etc., *PF* 107; in order that *HF* 559; **for that** because, since *BD* 81, *HF* 1231; **for to** (in order) to *BD* 24, etc., *HF* 180, 189, 563, etc.; **for-whi/y** because *HF* 553, 725, 1183, 1493.

for *prep.* (1) because of *BD* 5, etc., *HF* 277, 278, etc., *PF* 87, 146, 336; as a result of *HF* 24, 384, 1359, etc.; for the sake of *BD* 87, 741, 1185, *HF* 1094; (2) in order to gain *BD* 1110, 1150, *HF* 579, 1256; in return for *BD* 310, *PF* 454, *LGWD* 1235, etc.; **for noght** in vain, for no reward *BD* 180, 844; **for bote ne bale** for good or ill *BD* 227; **for al the worlde** entirely *BD* 825; (3) as regards *BD* 932, 1313; (4) as, to serve as *BD* 1179, *HF* 1424; as for as *BD* 1079; (5) in spite of *BD* 535, *HF* 462; (6) **for evermore** always *BD* 1233; (7) **for me** by me, as far as I'm concerned *HF* 2136; (8) **for sothe/forsothe** truly, indeed *BD* 341, 1292, *HF* 1873, *PF* 586, 653; (9) **for tary(i)ng** because of delay *PF* 468; to prevent delay *PF* 657; (10) **for wode** (adverbial phrase) madly *HF* 1747.

forleten *p.p. adj.* neglected, abandoned *HF* 694.

formel *adj. (as n.)* female bird *PF* 371; female (eagle) *PF* 373, (*as n.*) 418, 445, 535, 638.

formest *adj. (superlative)* first, foremost *BD* 890.

fors *n.* **no fors** no matter *BD* 522, 1170, *HF* 999, 1011, 1910, *PF* 615; **do no fors** care nothing *BD* 542.

forsweren *v.* swear to a falsehood; **forsworn** (*p.p.*) perjured, treacherous *LGWD* 927.

forswerynge *n.* perjury *HF* 153.

fortheryng/furtherynge *n.* advancement, assistance *HF* 636, *LGWP* 69; fulfilment *PF* 384.

forwery *adj.* very tired, worn out *PF* 93.

foule *adj.* ugly, nasty *HF* 767, 833, 1642, 1646, (*comp.*) 1638.

foule *adv.* hideously *BD* 623; deeply, seriously *PF* 517.

founde(n) *v.* found, establish; **founded/ifounded/yfounded** (*p.p.*) *BD* 922, *HF* 1981, *PF* 231.

fre(e) *adj.* generous, noble, gracious *BD* 484, 1055, *HF* 442; free *PF* 649.

fresh/fressh/fros(c)h(e) *adj.* joyous, gay *BD* 484; fresh, delicate *BD* 905, *PF* 174, 259, 354, 442, *LGWP* 57; new *HF* 1156, *LGWP* 67.

fresshly *adv.* afresh *BD* 1228.

frette *n.* ornamental net over hair *LGWP* 147.

frettid *v.* (*p.p.*) decorated *LGWD* 1117.

frot *n.* fruit, outcome *HF* 2017.
ful *adv. (intensifier with adj.)* very *BD* 103, etc., *HF* 139, etc., *PF* 10, etc.; wholly, altogether *BD* 143, etc., *HF* 102, etc.; **ful evene** just exactly, right there *BD* 1329; **ful moche** a very great deal *HF* 147; **ful nygh** very nearly *BD* 104; **ful sone** immediately *BD* 837.
furlongwey *see* **forlonge way**

gabbe *v. (pres. 1 sg.)* talk nonsense *BD* 1075.
game *n.* amusement, entertainment, fun *HF* 664, 886, 1199, *LGWP* 33; sport *BD* 539; game *BD* 618, 663; joke, trick *BD* 238, 1220, *HF* 822, 1474, 1810; playfulness *HF* 226.
gan see **ginne(n)**
gape(n) *v.* gaze, stare *HF* 1211.
gendres *n. (pl.)* classes, types *HF* 18.
gentil *adj.* high born, noble *HF* 1311, *PF* 337, 485, 535, *LGWP* 491, *LGWD* 1068, 1090, etc.; excellent, fine *PF* 196; **gentilest(e)/gentylesyte** *(superlative)* noblest *PF* 550, 635; most excellent *PF* 373.
gentilesse *n.* nobility *HF* 1611, *LGWD* 1080; (personified) *PF* 224.
gere *n.* clothes, equipment, behaviour; changeable fashion *BD* 1257.
gesse *v.* suppose, imagine *HF* 1080, 1814, *PF* 160, 200, 223, 602; believe *BD* 35.
geste *n.* historical account *LGWP* 87; *(pl.)* famous deeds *HF* 1515, 1518, 1737; chronicles *HF* 1434.
gestiour *n.* storyteller, entertainer *HF* 1198.
gye(n) *v.* direct *HF* 943, 1093.
ginne(n) *v.* begin to, proceed to (often with little or no independent meaning); **gan** *(pa. 1 sg.)* *PF* 88, 142, 194, etc. *(pa. 3 sg.)* *BD* 371, etc., *HF* 190, 231, 299 etc., *PF* 27, 40, 42 etc.; **gonne/gunne** *(pa. 3 pl.)* *HF* 944, 953, 1658, *PF* 193, 257, 283, etc., *LGWP* 134.
gyse *n.* way, manner *PF* 399, *LGWP* 105.
glareth *pres. 3 sg.* shines brightly, glitters *HF* 272.
glees *n.* musical instruments *HF* 1209, 1252.
gonne *v. see* **ginne(n)**
go(o)n *v.* go on foot, walk *HF* 934; **gost** *(pres. 2 sg.)* walkest *LGWD* 926.
gouvernaunce/governaunce *n.* conduct, behaviour *BD* 1008; control *BD* 1286, *HF* 945, 958, *LGWD* 1044.
gouvernour *n.* leader *LGWD* 1060.
governe *v.* governith *pa. 3 sg.* controls *LGWD* 1209.
grace *n.* grace *BD* 111, 118, *PF* 319; favour *HF* 85, 240, 1550, *PF* 84, 129, *LGWD* 1014, etc.; benevolence *HF* 661, 1537, 2007; endowment *BD* 1006; future destiny *PF* 45; good fortune *HF* 1087; **harde grace** ill-fortune *PF* 65; **with harde grace** ill luck to him *HF* 1586; **sory grace** disgrace *HF* 1790.
graunt *(French) adj.* great; **graunt mercy** many thanks *BD* 560, *HF* 1874.
grave(n) *v.* dig; **igrawe** *p.p.* dug out of the earth, *LGWP* 98; carve, inscribe,

portray; **grave(n)** *(p.p.)* HF 157, 193, 212, 253, 256, 433, 451, 473; **ygrave** *(p.p.)* BD 165, HF 1136.

grete *n.* major part, essence BD 1242, PF 35.

grete *adj.* dominant, important LGWD 929.

grette *v. pa. 1 sg.* greeted BD 503; **ygret** *(p.p.)* BD 517.

greven *v.* be unhappy BD 1106; cause trouble HF 1119.

grome *n.* boy HF 206, 1225.

gunne *see* **ginne(n)**

ha *see* **have(n)/han**

habitacle *n.* canopied niche HF 1194 (see commentary).

hale *v.* pull, attract PF 151.

hals *n.* neck HF 394, PF 458, LGWP 292.

halt *see* **holde(n)**

halte(n) *v.* limp BD 622.

halwes *n. (pl.)* saints BD 831, shrines of saints LGWD 1310.

han *see* **have(n)/han**.

happe *n.* chance, fortune BD 810, PF 402; good fortune BD 1039; *(pl.)* chance events BD 1279.

happen *v.* happen, chance BD 805, PF 10, 18, 473; **happe me** *(subj. pres. 3 sg.)* it may chance for me LGWP 66.

hardely *adv.* surely BD 1043, HF 359.

hate *see* **hote(n)**

have(n)/han/ha /a *v.* (1) *(as auxiliary)* BD 26, 27, 53, 222, 228, 308, 395, etc., HF 100, etc., PF 38, 44, etc., LGWP 61 etc.; **hath** *(pres. 3 pl.)* have LGWP 11; (2) have, get, possess BD 1, etc., HF 41, etc., PF 32, etc.; (3) **have doon** *(imper.)* enough! finish! HF 1623, PF 492.

hawteyn *adj.* proud, haughty PF 262; noble, excellent LGWD 1120.

he/hym/him/his *masc. personal pronoun;* **his** his *or* its (see **hit**).

hed *see* **hyd/yhedde**

held(e) *see* **holde(n)**

helde(n) *v.* pour HF 1686.

hem *see* **they**

hente(n) *v.* take, catch, grab HF 543, 2028, PF 120, 154.

hepe *n.* throng BD 295.

her/hir(e)/hyr *poss. adj.* her BD 80, etc.; their HF 24; **hires** *(poss. pron.)* hers BD 1041, PF 482.

her(e)/hir(e)/hyre *pron.* see **she** *and* **they**.

hereto *adv.* to this BD 754.

herke(ne) *v.* listen *(imper.)* HF 109, 509, 613, 725, 764, 1030, etc.; attend to, listen BD 752, LGWP 318; **herkith** *(pl. imper.)* listen LGWD 1276.

hete *see* **hote(n)**

hyd/yhedde/hed *p.p.* hidden BD 175, 932, LGWP 102.

hye(n) *v.* hasten, hurry HF 1592, 1658, PF 193; *(reflexive)* BD 152, 363.

hight(en) *see* **hote(n)**

hynde *n.* hind (female deer of three or more years) *BD* 427, *PF* 195.

hire *n.* reward *PF* 9.

hit/hyt/yt/it *pron.* B 7, etc., *HF* 2, 6, etc. *PF* 18, etc.; **hym** (*direct and indirect object*) *BD* 383, etc.; **his/hys** (*poss.*) *BD* 310, etc., *HF* 734, 745, 754, 768, 784, 834, etc.

ho = who

holde(n) *v.* (1) hold, keep *PF* 372; **holde in balaunce** keep in uncertainty *BD* 1021; **holde thy pes** keep quiet *PF* 572; **holde up** support *HF* 1309; **holde ... in honde/holdynge in hondes** string(ing) along *BD* 1019, *HF* 692; (2) keep, confine, restrain *HF* 324, *PF* 521; **helde** (*pa. 3 sg.*)*HF* 1587; **i-holde** (*p.p.*)*HF* 1286; (3) keep (promise); **halte** (*pres. 3 sg.*) *BD* 621; **holde** (*imper.*) *BD* 754; (4) consider *BD* 36, 269, 540, 671; **halt** (*pres. 3 sg.*) *HF* 630; **held** (pa. 3 sg.) *HF* 1480; **holden** (*p.p.*) *HF* 1755; **holde for** accept as, regard as *BD* 1179.

hool *adj.* whole *BD* 554; **with hool herte** with all my heart *BD* 1224; well, healthy *BD* 553, *HF* 1270.

hoole/ho(o)ly/holly *adv.* entirely *BD* 991.

hote(n) *v.* be called; **hight** (*pres. 3 sg.*) *HF* 663, 942, etc.; **hightyn** (*pres. 3 pl.*) *LGWP* 411; **hate** (*pres. 3 pl.*) *HF* 1303; **highte** (*pa. 3 sg.*) *HF* 226; **hete** (*pa. 3 sg.*) *BD* 200, 948, *HF* 1604; **i-hote** (*p.p.*) *HF* 1719; promise *BD* 1226.

h[o]tte *n.* wicker panier for carrying earth *HF* 1940.

humblesse *n.* humility *HF* 630.

humblynge *verbal n.* rumbling, reverberation *HF* 1039.

[*Words beginning with the consonant 'y-' follow 'w-'*]

ibe been, *see* **be(n)** *LGWP* 6.

ycrased *p.p.* cracked; **nat an hoole ycrased** not flawed by a single crack *BD* 324.

ydel *adj.* empty, pointless *BD* 4; worthless *HF* 1777; idle *HF* 1733.

ydelnesse *n.* leisure, inactivity *BD* 602, etc.

if/yf/yif *conj.* if *BD* 224, 233, 249, etc. *HF* 21, 43, 80, 143 etc., *PF* 50, 167, 456, etc., *LGWP* 59, 64, etc.; **if/yf that** if *HF* 788, *PF* 106, 541, *LGWP* 25; **but yif** unless *BD* 1023.

yfounded/ifounded *p.p.* founded *BD* 922; established, set *PF* 231

ygrounded *p.p.;* **wel ygrounded** learned *BD* 921.

ihalowed *p.p.* chased with shouts *BD* 379.

ylyche, ilike *adv.* equally *BD* 9, 803; in the same way *BD* 1292, 1294, *LGWP* 57; **ever ylyche** continually *BD* 1288.

ilke/ylke *adj.* same *BD* 265, *HF* 37, 1169, 1409, 1535, 1843, *PF* 433.

impression *n.* emotional reaction *HF* 39.

in fere *adv.* together *LGWP* 217.

yse(e), ise *v.* see *BD* 205, *HF* 804, *LGWP* 15.

iwis/ywis *adv.* indeed, truly *BD* 657, etc., *HF* 326, 641, 809, etc., *PF* 6, 692; **wis** *HF* 1819.

jangler *n.* gossip *PF* 457.

jangles *n.* (*pl.*) chattering, gossip *HF* 1960.

janglynge *pres. part. as adj.* gossiping, chattering *PF* 345.

jape *n.* frivolity, mockery *HF* 96, 1805 (*pl.*); trick *HF* 414.

jeupardyes *n.* (*pl.*) chess stratagems *BD* 666.

jolye *adj.* joyous *LGWD* 1192.

juste *adj.* suitable, well-situated *HF* 719.

kan *see* **konne(n)**

kepe *n.* **take kepe** pay attention *BD* 6, etc., *HF* 437, *PF* 563.

kepe(n) *v.* keep, cherish, guard *BD* 669, 1155, 1263, *HF* 192, 216, 1226; keep to *BD* 43; care *HF* 1695.

kynde *n.* kind, species *PF* 174, 311, 360, etc.; nature, natural characteristics, disposition *BD* 512, *HF* 43, 204, 280, 824, *PF* 196, 401, 601, *LGWP* 377; Nature, Creation *BD* 16, 56, *HF* 584, *LGWP* 178, (personified) *PF* 316, 672; **kyndes** natural properties *HF* 968; **be/by kynde** naturally *BD* 494, *HF* 749; **of (his) pure kynde** by his/its very nature *HF* 208, 824; **oute of alle kyndes** with unnatural ferocity *HF* 204.

kynde *adj.* natural *HF* 834, 836; usual *HF* 1292.

kyndely *adv.* naturally *BD* 778, *HF* 831, 841, 852.

kyndely(ch) *adj.* natural, proper *HF* 730, 731, 734, 829, 842.

kythe(n) *v.* show, make known *HF* 528, *LGWP* 492.

konne(n) *v.* (1) know, understand, find out *HF* 2004; **kan** (*pres. 1 & 3 sg.*) *BD* 1187, 673, *HF* 15, 248, 1882, 2156; know how to *LGWD* 1069, etc.; **konne** (*pres. 1 pl.*) *HF* 335; **koude/kowde/coude/couthe** (*pa. 1 & 3 sg.*) *BD* 105, 1099, etc., *HF* 945; **koud(e)/ykoud** (*p.p.*) *BD* 666, 777, 998; **konne wel** are expert in *HF* 1265; **goode . . . couthe, coude/koude** good knew what to do for the best *LGWD* 1182, knew what was right to do *BD* 800, etc; (2) (*as auxiliary*) know how to, be able to *BD* 279; **kan/can** (*pres. 1 & 3 sg.*) *BD* 34, 263, 575, 902, etc., *HF* 64, 143, 334, 450, 510, etc., *PF* 34, 106, 209, 220, 348, 438, etc., (*pres. 3 pl.*) *BD* 674; **kanst/canst** (*pres. 2 sg.*) *PF* 163, 598, 602; **konne** (*pres. 2 pl.*) *HF* 338; (*pres. 3 pl.*) *PF* 333; **kouthe** (*pres. subj. 3 sg.*) could *HF* 1814; **koud(e)/kouthe** (*pa. 1 & 3 sg.*) *BD* 656, etc., 101, etc., (*pa. 3 pl.*) *BD* 235, 976; **kan no more** can say no more *PF* 14.

konnyng/kunnynge *n.* skill *HF* 1168, 2056, *PF* 167, 487; knowledge *PF* 513.

kouthe *adv.* familiarly, well *HF* 757.

lak(ke) *n.* defect, fault *BD* 958; lack, want *PF* 87, 615; blame, criticism *LGWP* 298.

lakketh *impers. v.* **me lakketh** I lack *BD* 898.

large *adj.* large, wide *HF* 482, 926, 1238, *LGWD* 1019, etc., *PF* 123; big, sizeable, spacious *HF* 1440, *PF* 556, *LGWD* 1329; widespread *HF* 1412; generous *BD* 893.

large *n.* **at his large** at its liberty, unobstructed *HF* 745.

larges *n.* gift, handout *HF* 1309.

lathe *n.* barn *HF* 2140.

laude/lawde *n.* praise, fame *HF* 1322, 1795.

leche *n.* physician, healer *BD* 920.

leef(e)/leve *adj.* dear *HF* 816, 1827; pleasing *BD* 8; **lefere** *(comp.)* dearer *LGWP* 75; **leef me were** I would prefer *HF* 1999; **hem were levest** they would most prefer *HF* 87.

leie(n) *v.* lay, apply *BD* 394, *HF* 291, *PF* 554; set, devote, spend *BD* 1036, 1146, *HF* 260 (**leyde**, *pa. 3 sg. & p.p.*); wager, guarantee *HF* 674, 2054.

lere(n) *v.* learn *HF* 511, 993, 1057, *PF* 25 (? or 'teach'); teach *HF* 764.

lerne(n) *v.* learn *BD* 786, 1091, *HF* 1088, *PF* 1, 20; teach *HF* 1235, 1250.

les *n.* lie *HF* 1464, *LGWD* 1022.

lese *n.* meadow, pasture *HF* 1768.

lese(n) *v.* lose *BD* 33, *PF* 147, 402; **les** *(pa. 3 sg.)* 1414, *LGWD* 945; **lorn(e)/lore** *(p.p.)* *BD* 685, 748, 1135, *HF* 346, *LGWD* 1048, etc.; destroyed **(lorne)** *BD* 565.

lesyng(e) *n.* lie, falsehood *HF* 154, 676, 2089, 2123.

lest(e), *see* **list(e)/lyst(e)/lest(e)**

leste, *see* **lust(e)**

lete(n) *v.*1 allow, let *BD* 576, *HF* 243, etc., *PF* 279, 423, 492, etc.; cease, abandon *PF* 391, 439, *LGWP* 397; **lette** *(pa. 3 sg.)* delayed *HF* 2070; **lat be/let** be stop, leave off *BD* 202, *HF* 992.

lete(n) *v.*2 hinder, obstruct, prevent *HF* 1954, *PF* 151, *LGWP* 251.

leve(n) *v.* believe *BD* 691, 1047, 1048, 1148, *HF* 708, 875, 1012, *PF* 496, *LGWP* 10, 27.

levest, *see* **leef(e)**

lewde *adj.* plain, lay, unlearned *HF* 866, *PF* 46, *LGWP* 403; unskilful *HF* 1096; ignorant, stupid *PF* 616.

lewdely *adv.* plainly *HF* 866.

lewdenesse *n.* ignorance, (hence) ignorant persons *PF* 520.

lige *n.* vassal; **lige-man** one who has sworn allegiance to a lord, loyal subject *LGWP* 359; **lygis** *(pl.)* *LGWP* 366.

lymere *n.* hound kept on leash *(liam)* and trained to scent out and start the game *BD* 365; **lymerys** *(pl.)* *BD* 362.

lysse *n.* relief, calming, lull *HF* 220.

lysse *v.* relieve *BD* 210.

list(e)/lyst(e)/lest(e)/lestyth *impers. v.* please *(pres. & pa., with indirect object pron.)* wish *BD* 239, 878, 962, 1019, *HF* 282, 640, 844, 1564, etc., *PF* 114, 420, 441, 530, 551.

lyth *n.* limb *BD* 953.

lythe *adj.* soft, easy *HF* 118.

longe(n) *v.* belong, have to do with *HF* 244, 1200; belonging *LGWP* 137.

lo(o)s *n.* fame, reputation *HF* 1620, 1621, 1626, 1667, 1722, 1817, 1900, 1965; **loses** (pl.) *HF* 1688.

looth(e) *adj.* distasteful *BD* 8, 581; **lothere** *(comp. adj.)* more hated *LGWP* 75.

lore *n.* teaching, instruction *HF* 579, *PF* 15.

lorn(e), *see* **lese(n)**

losengeour *n.* flatterer, backbiter, deceiver of women, false counsellor *LGWP* 328.

lust(e)/lest(e) *n.* wish, desire *BD* 273, *HF* 287, 1738; delight, pleasure *BD* 581, 688, 908, 1038, *HF* 258, *PF* 15; (personified) *PF* 219, *LGWP* 32.

lusty *adj.* handsome, pleasant *HF* 1356, *PF* 130, happy *LGWD* 1038; lively *LGWD* 1151, 1191.

lustyhede *n.* liveliness, zest *BD* 27.

may, *see* **mowe(n)**

maistrye/maystrie *n.* domination, high skill; **for maistrye** to display skill, for show *HF* 1094; **no maystrye** no great achievement *LGWP* 386.

make *n.* equal *HF* 1172; mate *PF* 310, 371, 389, 466, etc.

make(n) *v.* (1) make, perform *BD* 114, etc., *HF* 56, 67, etc., *PF* 29, 202, 312, etc.; portray *BD* 782; compose, write *BD* 96, 1157, 1159, 1160, 1171, *HF* 622, *PF* 677, *LGWP* 72, *LGWD* 929; invent *BD* 663; **made/maked** (*p.p.*) *BD* 404, etc.; (2) make, cause to be *BD* 491, 510, 577, *HF* 155, 240, 1159; (3) (*as auxiliary*) cause to, make *BD* 71, 235, 412, etc., *HF* 42, 413, 1290, etc., *PF* 94, 108, 249.

makynge *n.* composition, making of poetry *LGWP* 62, 399.

malyce *n.* sin *BD* 794, 993; evil intention *LGWP* 341, 351.

maner *n.* residence *BD* 1004.

maner(e) *n.* kind, sort *BD* 471, etc., *HF* 126, 489, 509, 1123, *PF* 54, 653; way, method *BD* 433, etc., *HF* 249, 1729, *PF* 533; conduct, behaviour *BD* 453, etc., *HF* 278; **maners** (*pl.*) customary conduct, habits *BD* 1014.

masty *adj.* fed (like pigs) on beech-mast, acorns or chestnuts, (hence) fat, bloated, lazy *HF* 1777.

mat *adj.* 'mate' in chess. Also has sense of 'total defeat' in ME, from orig. Arabic meaning of checkmate: 'the king is dead' *BD* 660.

matere *n.* affair, business *HF* 1517, *PF* 579; subject, subject-matter, topic *BD* 43, 218, *HF* 637, 861, 1013, *PF* 26, 168, *LGWP* 343; material, substance *HF* 1126.

mawgree *prep.* in spite of *HF* 461; **mawgree my hede** in spite of everything *BD* 1201.

Mede *n.* (personified) payment, bribery *PF* 228.

meyne(e) *n.* household, retinue *LGWD* 1059, 1089, 1189, 1222; company *HF* 194, 933.

meyntenaunce *n.* behaviour, conduct *BD* 834.

melancolye *n.* melancholy *BD* 23.

melancolyouse *adj.* melancholic *HF* 30.

Messagery *n.* (personified) mediation, sending messages *PF* 228.

met(t)e(n) *v.* dream *BD* 118, *PF* 108, 115, 693(?); **met(te)/metten** (*pa. 1 & 3 sg., 3 pl.*) *BD* 286, *HF* 61, 110, 119, 313, 517, 523, 560, *PF* 95; **me mette** I dreamt *BD* 276, etc., *HF* 119, etc., *LGWP* 104.

metynge *n.* dream *BD* 282.

might/myght(e), *see* **mowe(n)**

mynde *n.* mind, thoughts *BD* 15? (see next sense), 511, *HF* 583, *PF* 100, *LGWD* 946; memory *BD* 55, *PF* 69; consciousness *HF* 564; **have in mynde** recall *HF* 823, *PF* 679.

mysdeme(n) *v.* think badly of, despise *HF* 92, 97.

myssatte *pa. 3 sg.* was badly placed *BD* 941.

myssette *p.p.* misplaced, badly set out *BD* 1210.

mochel *n.* stature *BD* 454; dimensions *BD* 861.

mochel/mochil/moch(e) *adj. BD* 713, etc., *HF* 147, etc.; (*as n.*) **thus moche** this much *BD* 221, 904.

mochel/moche *adv.* much, greatly *BD* 353, 1001, 1102, *HF* 500, 600, 1749.

moder *n.* mother *PF* 292, *LGWD* 999; origin, source *HF* 1983.

moo *adj.* more *BD* 266, *HF* 121, 123, 124, etc.

mot(e) *v.* must *BD* 42, *HF* 720, 2139, *PF* 469, 546; may *HF* 102, 786, 1329, 1663, *PF* 569; **motyn** (*pa. 1 & 2 pl.*) *LGWP* 17, 319.

mote *n.* scrap, trifle *HF* 2076 (see Textual Note).

mote *n. (pl.)* notes (of a hunting horn) *BD* 376.

mountaunce *n.* quantity, extent *LGWP* 233.

moustre *n.* pattern *BD* 912.

movynge *verbal n.* motion *HF* 812.

mowe(n) *v.* can, be able; may (*pres. 1 sg.*) *BD* 3, etc., *HF* 1855, 1997, *PF* 385, 391, 424, etc., *LGWP* 24 etc.; **maist(e)/mayst(e)** (*pres. 2 sg.*) *HF* 639, 737, 747, 826, etc., *PF* 116, 163; **maistow** can you *HF* 699, 1024; may (*pres. 3 sg.*) *BD* 266, etc., *HF* 32, etc., *PF* 151, etc., *LGWP* 7, etc.; may (*pres. 1 pl.*) *HF* 1759; (*pres. 2 pl.*) *PF* 396, etc.; (*pres. 3 pl.*) *HF* 385, etc., *PF* 311, etc.; **mowe** (*pres. 2 pl.*) *BD* 208, 552, *HF* 1828; (*pres. 3 pl.*) *PF* 687; (*pres. subj. 1 sg.*) *BD* 94; (*pres. subjunct. 1 pl.*) *HF* 1735; **might/myght(e)(n)** could, might (*pa. 1 sg.*) *BD* 44, etc., *HF* 483, etc.; (*pa. 2 sg.*) *LGWD* 985; (*pa. 3 sg.*) *BD* 64, etc., *HF* 210, etc., *PF* 201, etc.; (*pa. 2 pl.*) *BD* 1044; (*pa. 3 pl.*) *BD* 40, *HF* 197, 1744, 1929, *PF* 318, 367.

multiplicacioun *n.* expansion, amplification *HF* 784, 820.

multiplye(n) *v.* repeat *HF* 801.

muse(n) *v.;* **i-mused** (*p.p.*) gaze, consider *HF* 1287.

name *n.* name, reputation, honour *BD* 201, 664, 949, 951, 1018, 1263, *HF* 306 (see note), 346, 558, 997, 1137, 1142, 1145, 1153, 1275, 1312, 1355, 1405, 1411, 1462, 1489, 1505, 1556, 1610, 1620, 1696, 1716, 1736, 1761, 1871, 1877, 1900, 2112, *PF* 229, 287, *LGWP* 179, 404, *LGWD* 925, 1361.

namely *adv.* especially *LGWP* 545, *LGWD* 931, etc.

nas (*= ne + was*) was not *HF* 915, 1296, 1346, etc., *PF* 306.

nat, *see* **not**

nature *n.* species, offspring *PF* 615; divinely created nature, being *BD* 715;

disposition, character *BD* 631 (see also Nature (personified) in Index of Names).

ne *adv.* not (preceding verb) *BD* 22, etc., *HF* 49, etc., *PF* 66, etc.; (*as conj.*) nor *BD* 2, etc., *HF* 15, 19, etc., *PF* 9, etc.; **ne** (*adv.*) ... **ne** (*conj.*) neither ... nor *BD* 22.

nede/nedes/nedis *adv.* necessarily, inevitably *BD* 42, 1074, 1075, 1076, *HF* 724, 786, 1635, *LGWD* 1298.

nere (= *ne* + *were*) were not *BD* 959, *HF* 1423.

nevene *v.* mention, name *HF* 562, 1253, 1438.

nevermoo/never mo *adv.* never, not at all *BD* 1125, *HF* 1926.

nyce/nyse *adj.* foolish *HF* 276, 287, 920, *LGWP* 340.

nycete *n.* foolishness, naivete *BD* 613, *PF* 572.

nyl (= *ne* + *wyl*) (*pres. 1 sg.*) will not *BD* 92, 1125, 1235, *HF* 56, 1255, 1329, etc., *PF* 694. *See* **wyl/wil/wol**

nim(en) *v.* take; **(nim)en wey** make way; **(y)nome** (*p.p.*) taken *LGWD* 1018, *PF* 38.

nis/nys (= *ne* + *is*) is not *BD* 8, 693, *HF* 349, 913, 1063, etc., *PF* 501.

nyste, *see* note

noble *n.* English gold coin valued at 6 shillings and 8 pence *HF* 1315.

noght/nought *adv.* not (at all) *BD* 3, 460, 503, etc., *HF* 10, 15, 52 etc., *PF* 415, 448.

noyse *n.* noise *BD* 297, *HF* 783, 819, 1058, 1522, 1927, 1931, 2141, *PF* 202, 312, 491, 500; discord, disagreement *PF* 523.

nolde (= *ne* + *wolde*) would not (*pres. 2 pl.*) *HF* 1780; (*pa. 3 sg.*) *BD* 736, *HF* 1816; (*pa. subj. 1 sg.*) *BD* 1109; did not want (*pa. 1 sg.*) *PF* 90; **nolde but** would not have given up the chance to *BD* 311. *See also* **wil/wol**.

noldest (= *ne* + *woldest*) would not, refused to (*pa. 2 sg.*) *BD* 482.

non *pron.* no-one, none *LGWP* 5; no *LGWP* 7.

nones *n.* situation; **for the nones** indeed *HF* 2087, also, in that situation *LGWD* 1070; **with the nones** so long as, granted that *HF* 2099.

no(o)te *n.* tune *BD* 472, *PF* 677; **notys** (*pl.*) *BD* 319; **by/be no(o)te** with a tune *BD* 303; ringingly, out loud *HF* 1720.

nost (= *ne* + *wost*), *see* **not** (6)

nostow (= *ne* + *wost* + *thou*), *see* **not** (*v.*)

not *v.* not know (*see* **wete/witen**); **not** (*pres. 1 sg.*) *BD* 29, 353, 1044, etc., *HF* 12, 184, 982, etc.; **nost** (*pres. 2 sg.*) *BD* 1137, *HF* 2047; **nostow** (*pres. 2 sg., with suffixed pron.*) *HF* 1010; **nyste** (*pa. 1 & 3 sg.*) *BD* 272, 777, 1147, *HF* 234, 548, 1049, etc.

not/nat *adv.* not *BD* 3, 18, 20, etc., *HF* 247, 248, 307, etc., *PF* 8, 13, etc., *LGWP* 12, 13, 16, etc. (**nat** in, for example, *BD* 996, *HF* 1094, *PF* 7 is possibly more emphatic).

nothyng(e) *adv.* not at all, in no way *BD* 143, etc., *HF* 575, etc., *PF* 158, etc.

nouchis *n. pl.* jewelled bosses *HF* 1350.

nought *n.* nothing *BD* 89, *HF* 994, *LGWD* 939, etc.

of *adv.* off, away; **com of** get on with it *PF* 494; **take of lyght** take light from *BD* 964.

of *prep.* (1) of, about *BD* 5, 57, etc., *HF* 5, etc., *PF* 11, etc., *LGWP* 7, 19, etc; (2) because of *HF* 312, 666; (3) by *HF* 161, 241, 785, 812, *PF* 93; **of goode wille** willingly *BD* 1077; **of usage** habitually *PF* 15; (4) from *BD* 110, etc., *HF* 107, 146, 305, 758, 773, 807, 2135, *PF* 61, etc.; **of yore ago** formerly, previously *LGWP* 13; (5) for *BD* 1071, *HF* 428, 666, 1550, *PF* 421; (6) in, as regards *BD* 26, etc., *HF* 297, 816, 1172 etc., *PF* 234, 299, 317, etc.; (7) at *BD* 793, *HF* 607, 1069, 1682, *PF* 110, 142.

ofcaste *imper.* cast away *PF* 132.

office *n.* behaviour, allotted task *PF* 236; service *PF* 518 (see note).

onethe, *see* **unneth(es)**

or/er *conj.* before *BD* 128, etc., *HF* 101, 110, 437, etc.; **er that** *HF* 380; **or that** *BD* 776, 1032, *HF* 1055, 1999; **or than** *HF* 1683; **or but** *HF* 2085.

or *prep.* before *HF* 1062, 1157; **or nowe** before this *HF* 1902.

ought, *see* **aught**

o(u)ght(e) *pres. 3 sg.* ought to, should *BD* 678, *HF* 860, 1134, *PF* 437, 637; (*3 pl. pres.*) *HF* 1782.

oundye *adj.* wavy *HF* 1386.

o(u)ther *conj.* or *BD* 810, 1100; either *HF* 1888, 1958, 2139, *LGWP* 35.

pace(n)/passe(n) *v.* pass, proceed, pass over *BD* 41, *HF* 239, 392, 720, 841, 851, 1112, 1355, 1955, 2091, *PF* 133; elapse *PF* 81; exceed, surpass *PF* 300; **to passe with** to relieve *HF* 2011.

pay(e) *n.* pleasure *PF* 271; **to pay** deservingly, so as to deserve reward (*see* **paye(n)**) *PF* 474.

paye(n) *v.* reward *HF* 1549; **payede** (*p.p.*) paid *BD* 269.

panyer *n.* basket *HF* 1939.

paramouris *adv.* romantically *LGWP* 260.

paraventure/peraventure/paraunter *adv.* perhaps *BD* 556, etc., *HF* 304, 792, 1997.

parde(e) *interj.* indeed *BD* 721, etc., *HF* 134, 404, 575, 840, 860, *PF* 509, 571.

party(e) *n.* part *LGWP* 472; side *PF* 496.

patrone *n.* pattern *BD* 910.

peyne(n) *v.* (*reflexive*) strive, take pains *BD* 318, *HF* 246, 627, *PF* 339, 662.

peraventure, *see* **paraventure**

perré/perry *n.* precious stones, ornament *HF* 124, 1393.

perseveraunce *n.* constancy *BD* 1007.

pie/pye *n.* magpie *PF* 345; (*pl.*) magpies, informers *HF* 703.

pyne *n.* trouble, difficulty *HF* 147, 222; torment *HF* 1512, *PF* 335.

pipere *adj.* for making (musical) pipes *PF* 178.

pledynge *n.* argument *BD* 615, *PF* 495.

pley/play *n.* amusement *BD* 50, *PF* 193; enactment *BD* 648; (*pl.*) contrivances *BD* 570.

pley(en)/play *v.* (1) amuse oneself *BD* 850, 961, *HF* 2133; joke *BD* 239; (2) perform, play (game, trick or musical instrument) *BD* 51, 618, 652, 656, 668; **to pley at** playing (a game) *BD* 662.

pleyn(e) *adj.* smooth *PF* 180; open, proper, due *PF* 528.

pleyne(n) *v.* bewail, lament, complain *HF* 231, 311, *LGWP* 222; **pleynyd** (*p.p.*) *LGWP* 326.

pleynynge *n.* lamentation *BD* 599.

pleynt *n.* complaint *PF* 316.

plesa(u)nce *n.* happiness *BD* 704; pleasure *BD* 767, 773, *PF* 389, 636, 676; (personified) *PF* 218.

poete *n.* poet, classical author *HF* 1483, 1499, (*pl.*) *BD* 54.

poetical *adj.* of (high) poetry *HF* 1095.

poetrie *n.* (high) poetry *HF* 858; fables, myths *HF* 1001; fiction (*pl.*) *HF* 1478 (*see notes*).

poynt(e) *n.* point (at issue) *PF* 372; **myd poynt** centre *BD* 660; **at poynt devys** entirely, quite clearly *HF* 917; **in poynt to** even till, to/on the point of *BD* 13, *HF* 2018; **fro poynt to poynt** in every respect *PF* 461; legal charges, accusations *LGWP* 320.

porte *n.* bearing *BD* 834, *PF* 262.

poure/powren *v.* peer, scrutinize *HF* 1121, 1158.

prees/pres *n.* mêlee *HF* 167; crowd, assembly *HF* 1358, 1359, 1633; **in pres** from the crowd *PF* 603.

prest *adj.* ready, eager *PF* 307.

preve *n.* proof, demonstration *HF* 878, 989, *PF* 497.

prevely *adv.* secretly, quietly *HF* 223, 360, 2045.

preve(n)/proven *v.* test the truth of, prove *BD* 552, *HF* 707, 787, 808, etc., *PF* 534.

prik *v.* urge, spur *PF* 389; **prikyth** (*pres. 3 sg.*) *LGWD* 1192; **pryke** (*imper. sg.*) *LGWD* 1213.

prikke *n.* dot *HF* 907 (*see note*).

processe *n.* process, course *BD* 1331; **in processe** in the course of time *PF* 430; story *HF* 251.

profyt(e) *n.* benefit, good *PF* 47, 75.

propre *adj.* own *HF* 43, 754; fine, conclusive *HF* 726.

proven, *see* preve(n)

pure *adj.* pure *BD* 250, 259; very, sheer *BD* 490, 1209, 1212, etc.; **of (his) pure kynde** by his/its very nature *HF* 280, 824; **pure deeth** death itself *BD* 583; natural, unaffected *BD* 870.

purely *adv.* solely, simply, merely *BD* 5, 843, 934, *HF* 39.

queynt(e) *adj.* intricate, elaborate, elegant *BD* 784, *HF* 126, 228, 1925; ingenious, wily *LGWP* 329; remarkable *BD* 1330; **made hyt ... queynte** behaved in an affected way *BD* 531.

queynte *adv.* elaborately *HF* 245.

queyntlych *adv.* intricately *HF* 1923.

querne *n.* handmill 'consisting of two circular stones, the upper of which is turned by hand' (*OED quern* 1) *HF* 1798.

quyte *adj.* free *PF* 663.

quyte(n) *v.* reward *HF* 670, *PF* 9, 112; **quyt** (*p.p.*) *HF* 1614.

quod *pa. 1 & 3 sg., 3 pl.* said *BD* 367, etc., *HF* 605, etc., 300, etc., 1553, 1562, *PF* 510, etc., *LGWP* 142, etc.

qwalme *n.* pestilence, epidemic *HF* 1968.

rathe *adv.* soon, early *HF* 2139.

rather *adv.* the more readily; **never the rather** not at all readily *BD* 562, 868; sooner, rather *BD* 240, *HF* 1782.

ravyne *n.* prey *PF* 323, 527; greed, rapacity *PF* 336.

reason/reso(u)n *n.* reason *BD* 922, 1011, (personified) *PF* 632; logic *PF* 591; (logical) argument *HF* 708, 753, 761, *PF* 534, 564, 568.

rebel *adj.* disobedient *PF* 457.

recchiles/rechcheles *adj.* careless (about oneself) *PF* 593; uncaring, ungrateful *HF* 397, 668.

recche(n)/rekke(n) *v.* care, be concerned *PF* 593, 606; **ro(u)ght(e)** (*pa. 1 & 3 sg.*) cared, thought, rated *BD* 244, 887, *PF* 111; **rought** (*pa. 2 pl.*) cared *HF* 1781.

reche(n) *v.* reach down *BD* 47; **reight** (*pa. 3 sg.*) reached up to *HF* 1374.

recorde *v.* repeat, rehearse *PF* 609.

recovere(n)/rekever *v.* regain *HF* 354, 1258; regain or obtain (*see note*) *PF* 686.

rede *n.* advice, opinion *PF* 586, 608; solution, remedy *BD* 105, 203, 587, etc.

redely *adv.* to be sure, certainly *HF* 130, 313, 1127, 1392, 2137.

rede(n) *v.* (1) read *BD* 49, 55, 98, *HF* 378, 1352, *PF* 10, 27, etc., *LGWP* 30, etc.; **rad** (*pa. 1 sg.*) *PF* 21; **red(de)** (*p.p.*) *BD* 224, 228, 231, etc., *HF* 347, 722, *PF* 107; (2) read or tell, speak (?) *HF* 590, *PF* 516; (3) tell, speak *HF* 77, 1354, 1455, 1493, 1935; (4) interpret *BD* 279, 281; (5) advise, guide *HF* 491, 1067, *PF* 566, *LGWD* 1178; **radde** (*pa. 3 sg.*) *PF* 579.

reder *n.* reader *PF* 132.

reflexions *n.* (*pl.*) images *HF* 22 (*see note*).

reft, *see* **reve(n)**

regard/rewarde *n.* regard *PF* 426; **at regard of** by comparison with, set beside *HF* 1753, *PF* 58.

reight, *see* **reche(n)**

relayes *n.* (*pl.*) packs of fresh hounds *BD* 362.

renegat *n.* apostate from a faith, traitor *LGWP* 401.

renne(n) *v.* run *HF* 202, *PF* 247; **ronnen** (*pa. 3 pl.*) *BD* 163; **rennynge** (*pres. part.*) trickling *BD* 161; **ronne** (*p.p.*) *HF* 1644.

repaire(n) *v.* return *HF* 755.

respite *n.* delay *PF* 648 (*see note*).

reve(n) *v.* take away *PF* 86; **reft** (*pa. 3 sg.*) *HF* 457.

rewarde, *see* **regard**

richesse/rychesse/ryches *n.* wealth *BD* 1060, 1253; (personified) *PF* 261; profusion *HF* 472, *LGWD* 1100; costly appearance, rich ornamentation *HF* 1393, 1416, 1423.

ringe(n) *v.* ring, resound *BD* 312; **ronge** (*pa. 3 pl.*) *BD* 1164, *HF* 1398; proclaim (*imper. 2 sg.*) *HF* 1720; **y-ronge** (*p.p.*) *HF* 1655.

ryve(n) *v.* pierce, stab; **rofe** (*pa. 3 sg.*) *HF* 373.

Ro(o)de *n.* Cross *BD* 924, 992, *HF* 2, 57.

ropyn *p.p.* reaped *LGWP* 62.

rought, *see* **recche(n)**

roundel(l) *n.* circular shape, ring *HF* 791, 798; song with refrain (*see note*) *PF* 675.

roune(n) *v.* whisper; **rouned** (*pa. 3 sg.*) *HF* 2044; **(y)rouned** (*p.p.*) *HF* 722, 1030, 2107.

route/rowte *n.* group, crowd *BD* 360, 819, *HF* 1703, 1771, 1823, 2119, *PF* 245.

route(n) *v.* snore *BD* 172; roar *HF* 1038.

routhe/rowthe *n.* pity, compassion *BD* 97, 592, *HF* 332, 614, 2012, *PF* 427, *LGWP* 286, etc.; a pity, a piteous thing *BD* 465, 1310, *HF* 396; injury, mischief *HF* 383.

rowtynge *n.* whizzing, humming *HF* 1933.

rused *pa. 3 sg.* gave the hounds the slip (the stag doubled back and escaped from the hounds by making a detour from the original track) *BD* 381.

sad/sadde *adj.* steady, serious *BD* 860, 918, *HF* 2089, *PF* 578.

saylynge *pres. part.* for sailing, for making ships' masts *PF* 179.

sarmounnyng *n.* speaking *LGWD* 1184.

sauns *prep.* without; **sauns faille/fayle** without doubt, for sure *HF* 188, 429.

savacion *n.* rescue; **withoute any savacion** without anyone being rescued *HF* 208.

sawe *n.* saying, statement *HF* 676, 2089.

s(c)hene *adj.* bright, fair *HF* 1536, *PF* 299, *LGWP* 49.

science *n.* learning, knowledge *HF* 1091, *PF* 25.

scrippes *n. (pl.)* pouches *HF* 2123.

scripture *n.* writing, text *LGWD* 1144.

secre *adj.* discreet *PF* 395.

see *n.* seat *HF* 1210, 1251, 1361.

(i)see(n) *v.* see *BD* 111, *HF* 211, *PF* 163, *LGWP* 48, etc.; **seen** (*pres. 2 pl.*) *PF* 464; **sawe/sawgh** (*pa. 1 & 3 sg.*) *BD* 44, 500, etc., *HF* 127, 162, 163, etc.; **sey** *HF* 948, 989; **say** *HF* 1151, 1191, *PF* 211, *LGWP* 13; **sigh** *HF* 1161; **seen/seyne/yseye** (*p.p.*) *BD* 809, 854, *HF* 1367.

seke(n)/seche(n) *v.* seek out, look for *BD* 89, 1255, *HF* 626, *PF* 340; **soughte** (*pa. 3 sg.*) *HF* 185; **soght** (*p.p.*) *HF* 626; proceed, tend (*pres. 3 pl.*) *HF* 744; attempt (to do sthg.) *HF* 755 (*pres. 3 sg.*).

sely *adj.*1 poor, innocent *LGWD* 1237, 1254.

sely *adj.*2 remarkable, marvellous *HF* 513.

semelynesse *n.* pleasantness, every quality exactly as it should be, elegance, graciousness, *LGWD* 1041.

semynge *n.*; **be semynge** to all appearances *BD* 944.

sentence *n.* argument, theory *HF* 710, 757, 776, 877; speech, opinion, judgement *PF* 383, 530, *LGWP* 365; meaning, sense *HF* 1100, *PF* 126; subject-matter *HF* 1425, *PF* 35.

serve(n) *v.* serve *BD* 844, 1265, *PF* 216, etc.; **(y-)served** *(p.p.)* *HF* 616,678; treat, deal with *HF* 1548; **served** *(p.p.)* *HF* 337, 1546, 1622.

seson *n.* (a) while *HF* 341.

seweth *pres. 3 sg.* follows *HF* 840.

shal(le) *v.* (1) (expressing necessity or obligation) must, am to *(pres. 1 & 3 sg.)* *BD* 810, 830, 1191, *HF* 82, etc., *LGWP* 374; **shal** (with unexpressed verb of motion) must pass *PF* 69; **shalt** *(pres. 2 sg.)* *BD* 751, *LGWP* 469; (with unexpressed verb of motion) are to go, are bound *HF* 602; **shuld(e)/sholde** *(pa. 1 sg.)* ought *BD* 1116; *(pa. 3 sg.)* ought to *BD* 188, *PF* 66, 593, *LGWP* 353; *(pa. 2 pl.)* ought to *BD* 725; *(pa. 3 pl.)* were destined to *PF* 216; **shuldest** *(pa. 2 sg.)* must *BD* 187; (2) (expressing futurity, sometimes with a sense of volition) shall *(pres. 1 & 3 sg.)* *BD* 114, 261, etc., *HF* 6, 107, 150, etc., *PF* 30, 130, 137, 168, etc.; **shalt** *(pres. 2 sg.)* *HF* 577, 672, 711, etc., *PF* 75, *LGWP* 316, etc.; **shul** *(pres. 2 pl.)* *BD* 205, *PF* 400, 402; **shulde** *(pa. auxiliary, 1 & 3 sg., equivalent to subj.)* should *BD* 240, *PF* 496, 582; would (have) *BD* 668, 1200; were to *BD* 1266; would *BD* 441, 772; *(3 pl.)* should *PF* 590; would *BD* 916.

shame *n.* dishonour, disgrace *BD* 1017, 1264, *HF* 557, 1582, 1655, 1816; embarrassment, shyness *BD* 617, 1213, *PF* 444, 583, *LGWP* 523.

shap(pe) *n.* form *HF* 1113, *PF* 373, 398.

shape(n) *v.* shape *HF* 1985; devise *PF* 502.

she *pron.* she *BD* 83, etc., *HF* 163, etc., *PF* 216, etc.; **hir(e)/hyr/her** *(direct & indirect object)* *BD* 81, etc., *HF* 267, 295, etc. *PF* 270 etc., *(reflexive)* herself *BD* 269.

shende(n) *v.* damage, destroy *HF* 1016; spoil (someone's) plans *PF* 255, 494.

sheter *n.* as *adj.* for shooting, making bows *PF* 180.

sholde, *see* **shal(le)**

shonde *n.* harm, disgrace *HF* 88.

shoofe *pa. 3 sg.* pushed *PF* 154.

shrewde *adj.* wicked, evil *HF* 275, 1619.

shrewdenesse *n.* wickedness, villainy *HF* 1627, 1853.

shrewe *n.* villain *(pl.)* *HF* 1830, 1852.

shryfte *n.* absolution, forgiveness of sins granted after confession *BD* 1114.

shul/shulde/shuldest, *see* **shal(le)**

sygne *n.* sign, feature *BD* 917; (of the Zodiac) constellation *HF* 949, 998.

syketh, sikyth, sykyth *pres. 3 sg.* sighs *PF* 404, *LGWD* 1165, 1292.

symple *adj.* innocent, straightforward *BD* 861, 918; bare, plain *BD* 934.

syn *conj.* since *PF* 64, 608, 624, 654; **syn that** *PF* 435, *(as prep.)* *PF* 484.

syth/sith *conj.* since (of time) *BD* 759, *HF* 100, 1340; since (= because) *HF*

1855, PF 686, LGWP 69; **syth/sith that** since (of time) HF 59, 218, 1898, etc; since (= because) BD 1267.

sithyn adv. afterwards LGWP 230.

sythis n. (pl.) times LGWP 1.

sitte(n)/sytte v. sit BD 449, etc., HF 1251, etc.; **sytte** (pres. 3 sg.) remains BD 1108; be throned HF 1361, 1758; **sittyng** placed upon, adorning HF 1394; **syttynge** (pres. p. as adj.) suitable PF 551; **sate her/me** troubled, concerned her/me BD 884, 1220.

sywynge adj. similar, to match BD 959.

skylful adj. reasonable BD 534, LGWP 371.

skilfully adv. reasonably PF 634.

skil(le)/skylle n. argument HF 726; (pl.) reasons, proofs, logic HF 750, 867, PF 537.

slee(n) v. kill BD 351, HF 317, PF 217; **slough/slowgh/slowe** (pa. 3 sg.) BD 727, 733, 739, etc., HF 268, 956; **(y)slayn(e)/slain** (p.p.) BD 26 1067, 1069, HF 159.

slyd pres. 3 sg. slips away PF 3.

smert(e) adj. bitter, painful BD 507, 1107, HF 316; severe HF 374.

smyten v. strike HF 777; **smote** (pa. 3 sg.) HF 438, 536; **smyte** (p.p.) struck BD 1323.

so conj. provided that HF 423; so that HF 671, 709; so that BD 29; as BD 998.

solace(n) v. comfort, console HF 2008, PF 297.

somedel pron. some part PF 112; (as adv.) in part PF 65.

so(o)n(e) adv. quickly, soon BD 66, etc., HF 114, 288, 904, etc.; immediately BD 130, etc., HF 1538, 1773; **thus soone** straightaway at this point BD 836; **ful sone** absolutely immediately BD 837.

sooth/soth(e) n. truth BD 321, 520, HF 1057, 1552, PF 578, etc.; in phrases like **so(o)the to say(ne)/telle(n)** to tell the truth BD 460, 514, 818, 856, 989, 1090, 1181, 1189, 1194, 1221, HF 563, 960, 1368, 1388, 1509, 1804, 1842, PF 78, 574 (? **sooth** here may be an adv.), etc.

so(o)th(e) adj. true BD 846, HF 351, 502, 676, 987, 2051, 2072, 2089, PF 640; (as n.) truth HF 1029, 2108, etc.

sore adv. painfully, anxiously LGWP 53.

sory adj. wretched HF 1632, 1790; sorry BD 523.

sothely adv. for sure HF 364, PF 270, 557, 581, etc.

soun(e)/soon n. sound BD 162, etc., HF 720, 742, 762, etc., PF 344; boast, vaunt LGWP 221.

sours n. upward flight, soaring HF 544, 551.

sownynge n. sounding, sound BD 926.

spede(n) v. help HF 78, 1012, PF 385, 560; prosper, fare, go PF 101; hasten (reflexive) HF 1595; hasten or prosper (reflexive) PF 133.

speris/speres n. (pl.) spheres PF 59, 61.

sprede v. spread, open up towards LGWP 48; **sprad** (p.p.) dispersed BD 874.

springe(n) v. fly; **spronge** (p.p.) HF 2079; **yspronge** (p.p.) spread HF 2081.

stages *n. pl.* levels, layers *HF* 122 (*see note*).

stellefye(n)/stellifye(n) *v.* turn into a star or constellation *HF* 586, 1002, *LGWP* 513.

stent, *see* **stinte(n)**

stere(n) *v.* stir, move feebly *HF* 567; (*transitive*) set in motion *HF* 817; **any stiryng man** anyone around *HF* 478.

sterry *adj.* starry, celestial, amongst the stars *PF* 43.

sterte(n) *v.* leap (*pa. 3 sg.*) *HF* 1800; **stertelynge** (*p.p.*) jumping around, lively *LGWD* 1204; **stert** (*pres. 3 sg.*) disturb, flush out *HF* 681.

sterve(n) *v.* die *BD* 1266, *HF* 101, *PF* 420.

steven(e) *n.* tone, voice *BD* 307, *HF* 561.

stewe *n.* confinement *HF* 26 (*see note*).

stinte(n)/stynte *v.* stop, cease *HF* 1417; **stent(e)** (*pa. 3 sg.*) *BD* 358, etc., *HF* 221, 1683, 1926, 2031; **styntynge** (*pres. part.*) *BD* 1213.

stounde *n.* time, hour *LGWD* 949.

strake *v.* make their way *BD* 1312.

streight *pa. 3 sg. HF* 1373.

strowe(n) *v.* scatter, strew *LGWP* 101.

sturnely *adv.* strongly, sturdily *HF* 1498.

substance *n.* essential nature *HF* 768, 1181.

subtil(e) *adj.* ingenious *HF* 1188; fine-woven *PF* 272.

suerté *n.* confidence *HF* 723.

suffisa(u)nce *n.* contentment *BD* 703, 1038; **a suffisaunce** good enough *PF* 637.

suffise(n) *v.* be adequate, suffice *BD* 902, 1094, *HF* 1180; (*impers. pres. 3 sg.*) **sufficeth** it is enough that/for *HF* 1762, 1876; allow *BD* 18.

suffraunt *adj.* patient, tolerant *BD* 1010.

suffre(n) *v.* allow *BD* 468; endure, undergo, suffer *BD* 37, 1184, 1245, 1292, *HF* 2013.

surmountede *p.p.* surpassed *BD* 826.

sute *n.* pattern *BD* 261 (*see note on ll. 251–5*).

swartisshe *adj.* dark, dusky *HF* 1647.

sweynte *p.p.* tired, feeble *HF* 1783 (*see note*).

swevene *n.* dream *BD* 119, etc., *HF* 3, 9, 79, *PF* 115, 118.

swich(e)/such(e), swych(e) *adj.* such *BD* 28, etc., *HF* 35, 103, 209, etc., *PF* 14, 283, 515, etc., *LGWP* 32, 80, etc., *LGWD* 1064, etc.

swinke(n)/swynken *v.* labour, strain *HF* 16, 1175.

swithe/swythe *adv.* quickly *HF* 538, 1859, *PF* 503; **as swythe** at once *PF* 623.

swo(u)gh *n.* rushing sound *HF* 1031, 1941, *PF* 247.

swouned *pa. 3 sg.* swooned *BD* 103.

swowe *n.* swoon *BD* 215.

tabernacle *n.* canopied niche *HF* 123, 1190.

table *n.* table *BD* 646; tablet (surface for writing or drawing) *BD* 780; (metal) plate *HF* 142; block *HF* 1278; **tables** backgammon *BD* 51.

taylle *n.* tail; **toppe and taylle** from start to finish *HF* 880.

take(n) *v.* take *BD* 964, etc., *HF* 277, etc., *PF* 320, etc., *LGWP* 289, etc.; receive *BD* 95, 781; seize *BD* 273; take up *BD* 793; give *BD* 48, *HF* 1596; turn, go (to) (*reflexive*) *PF* 690; **take kepe** give attention, notice *BD* 6, etc.; **taketh ... agrefe** take amiss, be offended *PF* 543; **take ... wele** take in good part *HF* 91; **toke arryvage** made landfall *HF* 223.

tale *n.* tale, story *BD* 60, etc., *HF* 1198, 1829, 1839; talk, subject for conversation *BD* 536, etc.; speech, what one has to say *BD* 1199, *PF* 441, 542; **make lenger tale** give a longer account *HF* 1282; **tel no tale** say nothing *PF* 326; **telle oure tale** speak for us *PF* 560.

tapite *v.* hang with tapestries *BD* 260.

techche *n.* blemish *HF* 1778.

teche(n) *v.* teach, tell, instruct *HF* 782, 1072; guide *HF* 2024.

telle(n) *v.* tell, describe, determine *BD* 34, etc., *HF* 251, etc., *PF* 30, etc., *LGWP* 1, etc.; **telleth** (*pres. 3 sg.*) *BD* 1083, 1169, *HF* 406, etc., *PF* 36, etc.; **telles** (*pres. 3 sg.*) *BD* 73, *HF* 426; count *BD* 440, *HF* 1380.

teme(n) *v.* place, lay *HF* 1744.

tene *n.* distress *HF* 387.

tenor *n.* main point of a document *LGWD* 929.

tercel *adj.* male (eagle or falcon) *PF* 393, 449, 463; **tercels** (*pl.*) *PF* 540; (*as n.*) *PF* 405, 415.

tercelet *n.* male falcon *PF* 529, 533, 596, 625; **tercletys** (*pl.*) male eagles *PF* 659.

terme *n.* time, period of time *BD* 79; appointed, allotted period of time *HF* 392; **terme day** day appointed for return *BD* 730; **termes** (*pl.*) terminology *HF* 857.

thar *impers. v. pres. 3 sg.* **hym thar** not he need not *BD* 256.

that *definite article* the *BD* 634, 1290, 1291; (*demonstr. adj.*) that *BD* 122, *HF* 20, 216, 227, etc., *PF* 42, 72, etc.; **that oon ... that other** the one ... the other *HF* 1855–6; **that ylke** the very same *HF* 1169, 1843; **tho** (*pl.*) *BD* 438.

that *demonstr. pron.* that *BD* 40, 212, 354, etc., *HF* 7, 9, 162 etc., *PF* 60, 163, etc.; **with that** at that, thereupon *HF* 910, 991, 1702, *PF* 169; **tho(o)** (*pl.*) those *BD* 914, *HF* 1412, 2150.

that *conj.* that (introducing clauses of result, indirect statements, clauses after interjections, etc.) *BD* 6, etc., *HF* 39, 180, 184, 321, 332, 345, etc., *PF* 6, 28, etc.; when *LGWP* 54; **as that** as if *BD* 1200; **how that** how *BD* 2, etc.; **now that** now *BD* 477; **or that** before *BD* 776, 1032, *HF* 1055, 1999; **syth/ sith that** since *BD* 1267, *HF* 59, 218, 1898, etc.; **ther that** where *BD* 806; **wher that** where *HF* 129; **thogh that** although *BD* 875; **whan that** when *BD* 68, etc.; **for that** because *LGWP* 13; **wherfore that** for what reason *BD* 747, etc.; **wherthorgh that** by which *BD* 120; **why that** why *BD* 747, etc.; **yif/yf that** if *BD* 548, 969 972, *HF* 41, 788; (introducing a wish) *BD* 206.

that *relative pron.* that, which, who *BD* 37, etc., *HF* 38, 54, 70, etc., *PF* 3, 25, etc., *LGWP* 5, 6, etc.; whom *BD* 979; what *BD* 42.

the/th' *definite article* the *BD* 35, etc., *HF* 2, etc., *PF* 1, etc., *LGWP* 16, etc.; (equivalent to her, his, my) *BD* 122, 453, 1216.

th(e) *adv.* (*with comparatives*) by so much the *BD* 99, etc.; **the bet** (all) the better *BD* 668, 669, 672, *HF* 559, *PF* 694.

thee *v.* prosper *PF* 569.

they *pron.* they *BD* 89, etc., *HF* 84, 181, 197, etc., *PF* 55, 79, 83, etc., *LGWP* 67, 68, etc.; **hem/hym** (*direct & indirect object*) *BD* 72, etc., *HF* 15, 19, 22, etc., *PF* 40, 216, 234, etc., *LGWP* 32, 44, etc.; **her(e)/hir** (*poss.*) *BD* 71, etc., *HF* 17, 24, 39, etc., *PF* 9, 39, 82, etc., *LGWP* 67, 123, etc.

therby *adj.* thus, by that means *BD* 669.

therfro/ther-froo *adv.* from that place *HF* 736, 838, 895.

theryn/therinne *adv.* on it *BD* 782; into it *HF* 2003.

therof *adv.* of that, of it *BD* 1001, *HF* 101, 1043, 1473; from that *BD* 1166; about that *BD* 542, 1132, 1170.

therto(o) *adv.* to it *BD* 679, etc.; to do so, to this end *HF* 371; leading to it *HF* 718; in it *BD* 527, 704; for it *BD* 779; in addition, also, moreover *HF* 998, 1377, 1650, etc.

therwith/therwyth *adv.* with that, at this *BD* 275, etc., *HF* 582; in addition, moreover *BD* 878, *HF* 1804; and yet, at the same time *BD* 954.

therwithalle/therwythalle *adv.* at this *HF* 2031, *PF* 405; in addition *BD* 989.

thewes *n.* ways, qualities *HF* 1834, 1851.

thilke *demonstr. adj.* that *BD* 243, 785; those *HF* 173, *PF* 61.

thing(e)/thyng(e) *n.* thing *BD* 12, etc., *HF* 350, etc., *PF* 20, etc., (*pl.*) things *LGWP* 11, etc.; matter *HF* 53, 239; cause *H* 1699; effect, way *HF* 1292; **no thing/no thynge** not at all *HF* 1346, 1780, 2032; **in alle thing** exactly *HF* 1837; **on alle thynge** without fail *BD* 141.

thinketh/thynketh/thynkyth/thynkith/thenketh *impers. pres. 3 sg.* seems *BD* 545, 547, 913, etc., *HF* 684, 871; **me wolde think** one would think *PF* 548; **thought(e)** (*pa. 3 sg.*) seemed *BD* 50, *HF* 499, 1183, 1369, etc., *PF* 28, 124.

tho(o) *definite article, see* **that**

tho(o) *adv.* then *BD* 234, etc., *HF* 149, 235, 319, etc., *PF* 218, 297, 298, etc., *LGWP* 104, etc.

thow *conj.* though *LGWP* 15, 29, 66, 176, 351, 409, 513.

thralle *n.* thrall, bondsman *BD* 767.

thrawe *v.* fly up *HF* 2090.

thrift *n.* fortune *HF* 1786; **by my thrift** as I hope to prosper *HF* 1847.

thryve(n) *v.* prosper *HF* 1329, 1615.

thurow *prep.* through *LGWP* 18.

thwite(n) *v.* whittle *HF* 1938.

tyde(n) *v.* happen; **tyd** (*p.p.*) *HF* 255.

tydynge/tidynge/tidinge *n.* story, piece of news *HF* 2045, 2066, 2072, 2109, 2111, 2134; (*pl.*) news, stories *HF* 644, 648, 675, 1027, 1886, 1888, 1907, 1955, 1957, 1983, 2010, 2025, 2124; **love-tydynges** news about lovers *HF* 2143.

tipet *n.* point of cape or hood *HF* 1841.

to-breketh *pres. 3 sg.* splits apart, is shattered *HF* 779.

token *n.* sign; **tokenys** (*pl.*) gifts and other things which symbolize love *LGWD* 1275.

tonged *p.p.* **trewer tonged** truer spoken, more trustworthy *BD* 927.

toppe *n.* head; **toppe and taylle** from start to finish *HF* 880.

torent *p.p.* torn to pieces *PF* 432.

toshyvered *p.p.* shattered *PF* 493.

totorne *p.p.* tattered *PF* 110.

totulour *n.* tittle-tattler, tale-bearer *LGWP* 329.

trace *v.* go, follow *PF* 54.

trayterye *n.* treachery *HF* 1812.

travayl(l)e *n.* hard work, effort *BD* 602, *HF* 1750.

tregetour *n.* illusionist *HF* 1260, 1277 (*see note*).

tretable *adj.* accessible, easy to talk to *BD* 533; open *BD* 923.

trete(n) *v.* deal with, write about *HF* 54, *PF* 34, *LGWP* 309.

trewer, *see* **tonged**

trouthe/trowthe *n.* oath *BD* 753; promise, pledge *BD* 936, *HF* 297; fidelity *BD* 999, 1003, *HF* 331, *LGWP* 287; loyal service *PF* 426; **by my/thy trouthe** upon my/your honour *BD* 6, etc., *HF* 613, 889, 1763; truth *HF* 807.

trowe(n), trowyn *v.* believe, think *BD* 90, etc., *HF* 61, 699, 1335, 1930, *PF* 552, 677.

tuelle *n.* chimney, vent *HF* 1649.

twey(ne) *numeral* two *BD* 156, *LGWP* 346.

uncomytted *p.p.* unauthorized, unwanted *PF* 518.

uncouthe/unkouthe *adj.* strange, wonderful *HF* 1279, 2010.

undo *v.* reveal, show how it is *BD* 899.

unfamouse *adj.* obscure *HF* 1146.

unkynde *adj.* unnatural *PF* 358; ungrateful *PF* 434, 457; disdainful *HF* 284.

unkyndely *adv.* cruelly *HF* 295.

unmerie *adj.* dull *HF* 74.

unnethe(s) *adv.* scarcely, hardly, with difficulty *BD* 270, 712, *HF* 699, 900, 1140, 2041, *PF* 201, 264, 314.

unshet *adj.* unlocked, open *HF* 1953.

unsofte *adj.* hard, difficult *HF* 36.

unswete *adj.* bitter *HF* 72.

up *prep.* on, upon *BD* 750, 922.

upbere(n) *v.* carry upwards *HF* 818.

upper *adv.* higher *HF* 884, 961.

upstondyng *adj.* standing up, erect *HF* 1389.

usage *n.* custom, practice *PF* 411; **of usage** habitually *PF* 15.

use(n) *v.* use *BD* 401, *HF* 562; make use of, employ *HF* 1242, 1263; practise *PF* 549; play upon *HF* 1247; is accustomed *LGWP* 342.

utterly *adv., see* **outterly**

valence *n.* cloth made at Valence/Valenciennes (? *see note*) *PF* 272.
varye(n) *v.* differ, diverge from *HF* 807.
varyinge *pres. part. as adj.* changeable *BD* 802.
veyrdit/veirdit *n.* verdict, judgment *PF* 503, 525.
vers *n. (pl.)* verses, lines *BD* 463, *HF* 1098, *PF* 124, 141, 679.
vertu *n.* power, capacity *HF* 526, 1101; faculty *HF* 550; merit, moral virtue *HF* 631,1851, *PF* 376.
viages *n. (pl.)* travel, journeyings *HF* 1962.
victor *n. as adj.* associated with victory *PF* 182.
vyker *n.* deputy *PF* 379.
vilanye *n.* discourtesy, boorishness *HF* 96.
virelayes *n. (pl.)* lyric poems with refrain *LGWP* 411.

waker *adj.* watchful, vigilant *PF* 358.
wakynge *n.* insomnia *BD* 611.
wayte(n) *v.* look at, note, observe *HF* 342.
walkene, *see* **welken**
wande *v.* shrink from, hesitate, withdraw *LGWD* 1187.
wante(n) *v.* lack, be absent *PF* 287, *LGWP* 337.
war(e) *adj.* aware *BD* 445, 515, 1030, *HF* 496, 1407, 1989, *PF* 218, 298; wary of *LGWP* 462.
warysshed (*emendation*) *p.p.* cured *BD* 1104.
warne, *see* **werne(n)**
warne(n) *v.* warn *HF* 46, 51; inform *HF* 893, 1068, *PF* 45.
warreyest *pres. 2 sg.* fight *LGWP* 248.
waxe(n)/wexe(n) *v.* grow *BD* 415, *HF* 1391, 1652, 2115, *PF* 206; grow, become *HF* 979, 1076, *PF* 207, 444, 583; **waxen/iwaxe** (*p.p.*) *BD* 414, 1275; **wox** (*p.p.*) *HF* 1146; **woxen** (*p.p.*) *HF* 1494, 2082.
wedres *n. (pl.)* storms *PF* 681.
wel(e)away/weylaway *interj.* alas! *BD* 729, *HF* 170, 318, 345, 383.
wele *n.* happiness, good fortune *BD* 603, *HF* 1138
wele, *see* **wil**
welfare *n.* well-being, happiness *BD* 582, 1040.
welken(e)/walkene *n.* sky *BD* 339, etc., *HF* 1601.
wel(le) *adv.* well, fully, entirely *BD* 16, etc., *HF* 53, 129, 273, etc., *PF* 7, 47, 109, etc., *LGWP* 3, 4, etc.; certainly, clearly *PF* 12, 493, *LGWP* 452; (*emphatic with vbs.* **sey** *and* **swere**) *BD* 221, etc.; **wel moo/more** many more, much more *HF* 1495, 1949, *LGWP* 11; **wel and faire** nicely, courteously *HF* 1539.
wende(n) *v.* go, travel *BD* 67, *PF* 48, 440, 492; turn, depart *HF* 298, 1868; drift, flow *HF* 1645.
wene(n) *v.* think, believe, expect *BD* 744, 1138, 1306, *HF* 1714, 1767, *LGWP* 12; **wenynge** (*pres. part.*) *HF* 262; **wende** (*pa. subjunct. 3 pl. & pa.*

3 sg.) *HF* 1796, *PF* 493, *LGWP* 191, 450; **wenden** (*pa. 3 pl.*) *BD* 867.

werche(n)/wirche(n)/werke(n) *v.* make, construct, fashion *HF* 474; **wro(u)ght/ywro(u)ght** (*p.p.*) *BD* 90, 327, *HF* 1173, 1298, 1317, 1498, 1923, *PF* 123, 305, 418, 636, 666; **worcheth** (*pres. 3 sg.*) causes *BD* 815; **y-wrought** (*p.p.*) acted, performed (deeds) *HF* 1711.

were *n.*1 trap (in weir-pool) *PF* 138.

were *n.*2 doubt *BD* 1295, *HF* 979.

werke *n.* deed *HF* 1556, 1558, 1610, 1616; achievement *HF* 1504; matter, business *HF* 54, *PF* 666; work, labour *BD* 169; workmanship *HF* 127; Nature's creation(s) *BD* 911, (*pl.*) *PF* 374.

werne(n)/warne *v.* deny, refuse *HF* 1539, 1559, 1797, *LGWP* 438.

werre *adv.* (*comp.*) worse *BD* 616.

wers/worse *adj.* (*comp.*) worse *BD* 814, 1118, *HF* 1620; **worste/werst** worst *BD* 579, 1174.

wete(n), *see* **wite(n)/wete(n)**

wexe(n), *see* **waxe(n)**

what *adj. & pron.* what *BD* 29, etc., *HF* 3, 320, 475, etc., *PF* 294; (*adj. & pron.*) whatever *HF* 86, *PF* 54, 420, 441; (*interrog. pron.*) what *BD* 449, 481, 650, etc., *HF* 320, etc., *PF* 365, etc., *LGWP* 241, etc.; (*interj.*) well! *HF* 372, 1635; what? *HF* 1713.

what *adv.* as much as *PF* 151; **what ... what** partly ... partly *HF* 2058, *PF* 15.

wher(e), *see* **whether**

wherfore *adv. & conj.* why *BD* 219, etc., *HF* 1846; wherefore, and so *HF* 268, 629, 641, etc.

wher(e)so *adv.* wherever *BD* 10, etc.; where *BD* 112.

wherthorgh *conj.* through which *BD* 120.

wherto *interrog. adv.* to what purpose *BD* 670.

whether/whethir/wher(e) *conj.* whether *BD* 121, etc., *HF* 778, *PF* 152, 166, 482; **wher(e)** B 417, 1174, *HF* 981; **wher that** *HF* 890, *PF* 7; (introducing a speculation: 'could it be that ...?') *BD* 91, *HF* 586.

which(e) *adj & interrog.* what *BD* 893, etc., *HF* 733 etc.; (in exclamations) which a, what a *BD* 734, 895, *HF* 2034, *PF* 564.

which(e) *rel. pron.* who/whom *BD* 478, *HF* 1255, etc., *PF* 287, etc.; which, that *BD* 1131, 1317, *HF* 37, 121, 156, etc., *PF* 29, 34, 126, etc.; **which(e) that** who *HF* 1077, *PF* 519; he who *HF* 1447; whom *HF* 609, 931, *PF* 553; which *PF* 90, 333.

while *n.* (short) space of time, time *BD* 211, etc., *HF* 904, etc., *PF* 214; **a while** for a little while *HF* 1994, *PF* 509; **longe while** for a long time *HF* 1287, 1484; **withyn a while** after a (short) time *HF* 415.

whiles *conj.* as long as *BD* 177; **the whiles that** while *BD* 151.

who(o) *interrog. pron.* who? *BD* 181, etc., *HF* 474, *PF* 593.

(w)ho(o) *indefinite pron.* whoever *BD* 1154; **who that** if anyone *PF* 487; **who(o) so(o)** whoever, if anyone *BD* 574, etc., *HF* 12, 94, 377, etc., *PF* 410, 412, 504, etc.; **who aske** anyone who asks *BD* 32; **as who sayth** like someone who says *BD* 559.

wife/wyfe *n.* woman *BD* 1037; wife *BD* 63, etc., *HF* 175, 199, 424, etc.

wight/wyght *n.* person *BD* 530, *HF* 276, 1076, 1565, etc., *PF* 221, 511, 514; creature *BD* 597, 1176, 1281; **somme wight** someone *BD* 244; **every wight** everyone *BD* 968; **no wyght** no-one *BD* 1016 etc.

wikke *adj.* wicked, unpleasant *HF* 349, *LGWD* 1242; poor quality *HF* 1346.

wil/wyl/wol *v.* (1) want (to), mean to *BD* 67, etc., *HF* 728, 1094, *PF* 12, etc., *LGWP* 429; **wol not** refuses *BD* 584; **wolde** (*pa. 1 sg.*) attempted to *BD* 395, *HF* 1505; wanted to *HF* 1848; wanted to have *PF* 91; (*pres. 1 subj.*) would gladly, would like to *BD* 550, etc., *PF* 112, 468, 480, etc., *LGWP* 59; (*pres. 3 subj.*) may wish to *HF* 78, 302; (2) (*as auxiliary of future tense*) will, shall (*pres. 1 & 3 sg.*) *BD* 218, etc., *HF* 247, 281, 283, etc., *PF* 35, etc.; **wolde** (*pa. 3 sg.*) *BD* 18, *HF* 424, *PF* 581; (*pa. 3 pl.*) were going to *BD* 351, 355; (*pres. subj. 1 & 3 sg.*) would *BD* 242, etc., *PF* 548; (*pres. subj. 3 pl.*) were to *BD* 1023. See also **nyl, nolde.**

wile *n.* skill, cunning *PF* 215; wile *BD* 673.

wille *n.* wish *PF* 510; inclination *PF* 573; will *PF* 417; desire (personified) *PF* 214.

wis/wys(se) *adv.* certainly, indeed *HF* 1819; **as wys(se)** as surely as *BD* 550, 1235; **also wys** as surely as *BD* 683. *See also* **y-wis.**

wyse/wise *n.* fashion, way, manner *BD* 17, etc., *HF* 771, 1061, 1114, 1347.

wisly *adv.* surely *HF* 1860, *PF* 117.

wisse(n)/wysse(n) *v.* guide, instruct *HF* 491, 2024, *PF* 74.

wiste/wyst(e), *see* **wite(n)/weten**

wite(n)/wete(n) *v.* know *BD* 112, etc.; **wot(e)** (*pres. 1 sg.*) *HF* 52, 474, 980, *PF* 7, 9, 513; **wit** (*pres. 1 sg.*) *LGWP* 4; **wost(e)** (*pres. 2 sg.*) *BD* 743, 1152, 1305, *HF* 762, 790, 982; **wostow** (*pres. 2 sg., with suffixed pron.*) *HF* 781, 1000, 1784, 1791; **wo(o)te** (*pres. 3 sg.*) *BD* 1237, 1307, *HF* 680, *PF* 552, 595, 663; **wiste/wyst(e)** (*pa. 1 sg.*) *BD* 1009, *HF* 129, 1159, 1544; (*pa. 3 sg.*) *BD* 1185, *HF* 364, 393; **wyste** (*p.p.*) *HF* 351; **wiste** (*subj. 1 & 3 sg.*) were to know, knew *BD* 262, 591. *See also* **not** (*v.*).

withalle *adv.* alongside, as well *HF* 212, 1528, 2141; indeed *BD* 1205; **her-withal** with that *HF* 567, 1606.

wit(te)/wyt(te) *n.* mind, reason *BD* 505, 751, 763, etc., *HF* 950, 1175, 1898; intelligence, understanding *BD* 756, 990, 1094, etc., *HF* 16, 328, *PF* 146, 573; skill, talent *BD* 278, 610, 898, etc., *HF* 620, 1180, *PF* 460; wisdom *HF* 1972; **(as) to my wytte/witte** as far as I understand it, in my view *HF* 3, 702, 1377, *PF* 547.

wonder *n.* wonder *BD* 467, *HF* 533, 607, 913, 1069, 1682; strange thing *BD* 233, *HF* 806, 1378, 1996; (*pl.*) strange creatures *HF* 2118; **have wonder,** be amazed *BD* 1, 78, *HF* 607, 1069, 1682.

wonder *adj.* strange, remarkable, astonishing *BD* 61, *HF* 2, 674, 1083, 1893, *PF* 329; **wonder-most** (*superlative*) *HF* 2059.

wo(u)nder *adv.* astonishingly, extremely, very *BD* 165, 183, 344, etc., *HF* 114, 1121, 1465, 1488, 1691, *PF* 241, 490.

wonderful/wondyrful *adj.* strange, marvellous *BD* 277, *HF* 62, *PF* 5.

wond(e)rlich(e)/wonderly *adv.* marvellously, strangely *HF* 1173, 1327, 1373, 1922.

wondre(n) *v.* marvel *HF* 583; (*reflexive*) *HF* 1988.

wone *n.* way, habit *HF* 76.

wone(n) *v.* stay, dwell *BD* 889; **woned wonte/wonde** (*p.p. as adj.*) used, accustomed *BD* 150, *HF* 113, 566, 1548, 1581, etc.

wo(o)de *adj.* mad *BD* 104, *HF* 202, 1508, 1713, 1809; **for wode** madly *HF* 1747.

wo(o)ne *n.* provision, supply *BD* 475; house, dwelling *HF* 1166.

wo(o)te, *see* **wite(n)/wete(n)**

word(e) *n.* word *BD* 101, etc., *HF* 191, 246, 311, etc., *PF* 678; speech *BD* 933, *HF* 1077, 1080, *PF* 597; **at oo worde/at shorte wordes** to be brief *HF* 257, *PF* 481.

worshippe/worshyppe *n.* honour *BD* 630, etc.

worthe(n) *v.* become; **yworthe** (*p.p.*) *BD* 579; **well worth** good luck to, all very well for *HF* 53.

worthynesse *n.* greatness, prowess *BD* 1059; honour *HF* 1628.

wost(e), *see* **wite(n)/wete(n)**

wounde *n.* wound *HF* 374; (*pl.*) wounds, pains *BD* 1211; plagues *BD* 1207.

wrastelynge *n.* wrestling *PF* 165.

wraththed *p.p.* angered *BD* 1151.

wrechched/wrechede *adj.* wretched, miserable *HF* 335, *LGWP* 414.

wrechednesse *n.* vileness *PF* 601.

wreker *n.* avenger *PF* 361.

wrie(n) *v.*1 cover; **ywrien** (*p.p.*) covered over *BD* 628.

wrien (*emendation*) *v.*2 turn away *BD* 627.

wringe(n) *v.* wring *HF* 299; squeeze *HF* 2110.

[*For words beginning with the vowel 'y-' see under 'i'*]

yaf, *see* **yive(n)**

ye(e) *adv.* yes *BD* 1137, *PF* 52, 497, etc.

yerde *n.* rod; authority, control *PF* 640 (*see note*).

yer(e) *n.* year *BD* 775, 1258, 1296, *HF* 302, *PF* 23, 236, 321, etc.; (*pl.*) *BD* 37, 455, *PF* 67; **to yere** this year *HF* 84.

yerne *adv.* quickly *HF* 910, *PF* 3; eagerly *PF* 21.

yerne(n) *v.* long *BD* 1092.

yet/yit(te) *adv.* yet, still *BD* 1108, *HF* 386, 487, 580, etc., *PF* 10, 163, 208, etc., *LGWP* 14, 76, etc.; up to this time/moment *BD* 157, 277, 764, etc., *HF* 471; nonetheless *BD* 38, etc., *HF* 421, 705, 805, etc.; moreover, besides *BD* 679, 914, *HF* 1948; **ever yit(te)** so far *HF* 619, 1897; **never yit** not so far *HF* 327, 984; **as yet** just yet *HF* 599.

yive(n)/yeve(n) *v.* give *BD* 242, etc., *HF* 2112, *PF* 308; **yaf(e)** (*pa. 3 sg.*) *BD* 1269, 1273, *HF* 2021, 2114, *PF* 274, 667, *LGWP* 172; **yeve/yive** (*imper. sg.*) *BD* 111, *HF* 1558, *PF* 119; **yive(n)/yevyn** (*p.p.*) *BD* 765, *LGWP* 489.

yonder *adj.* over there *HF* 1064.

yore *adv.* long ago; **of yore ago** belonging to time gone by *LGWP* 13.

INDEX OF NAMES

Gyle (Seynt) St Giles *HF* 1183.
Glascurion Glasgwydion *HF* 1208.
God *BD* 210, 550, 665, etc., *HF* 1, 584, 700, etc., *PF* 14, 84, 199, etc., *LGWP*
    10, 14, 180, etc.
Grekes the Greeks *HF* 186, 1479, *LGWD* 931.
Guydo … de Columpnis Guido delle Colonne *HF* 1469.

Hercules *see* Ercules
Hermes Ballenus *HF* 1273.
Hero *LGWP* 217.

Yarbis Iarbas *LGWD* 1245.
Ihesus god Jesus Christ *HF* 97.
Ykarus Icarus *HF* 920.
Ilyo(u)n Ilium *BD* 1248, *HF* 158, *LGWD* 936.
Ynde India *BD* 889.
Innocent (Pope) *LGWP* 415.
Yole Iole *HF* 403.
Ypocras *see* Galyen
Isaye Isaiah *HF* 514.
Isaude/Isawde/Ysoude Yseult *HF* 1796, *PF* 290, *LGWP* 208.
Isydis Isis *HF* 1844.
Isiphile Hypsipyle *HF* 400, *LGWP* 220.
Itayl(l)e Italy *HF* 147, 187, 196, 298, 430, 433, 452, *LGWD* 952, 1298,
    1329.

Jame (Seynt) St James *HF* 885.
Jaso(u)n *BD* 330, 727, *HF* 400, 401, *LGWP* 220.
Jerome *LGWP* 281, 284.
Jewes the Jews *HF* 1434.
Jewrye the Jewish nation *HF* 1436.
Joab *HF* 1245.
Joh(a)n St John the evangelist *BD* 1319, *HF* 1385, *PF* 451.
Jonathas Jonathan *LGWP* 205.
Joseph *BD* 280.
Josephus *HF* 1433.
Jove(s)/Jovys Jupiter *HF* 219, 586, 597, 630, 661, 1041, 2007, *LGWP* 513.
Jovynyan Jovinian *LGWP* 281.
Julyane (Seynt) St Julian *HF* 1022.
Julius Julius Caesar *HF* 1502.
Julo Julus *HF* 177.
Juno(o) *BD* 109, 129, 132, 136, 187, 243, 267, *HF* 198, 461.
Ju(p)piter *HF* 199, 215, 464, 591, 609, 642, 955, *LGWD* 1338.

Kynde Nature (personified) *BD* 16, 56, *PF* 316, 672.

Laboryntus the Labyrinth (in Crete) *HF* 1921.
Laodamya Laodamia *LGWP* 217.
Lapidaire De Lapidibus HF 1352.
Latyne Latinus *HF* 453.
Laude Praise *HF* 1575, 1673.
Lavyna/Lavyne Lavinia *BD* 331, *HF* 458, *LGWP* 211, *LGWD* 1331.
Lavyne Lavinium *HF* 148.
Leonard (corseynt) St Leonard *HF* 117.
Lete Lethe *HF* 71.
Libie/Lybye Libya *HF* 488, *LGWD* 959, 992, 1123.
Lyde Lydia *HF* 105.
Limete Elymas (?) *HF* 1274.
Lollius *HF* 1468.
Love (personified: Amor, Cupid) *BD* 766, 835, *HF* 625, 634, 645, 675, *PF* 4,
    8, 159, *LGWP* 183, 466, etc.
Lucan *HF* 1499.
Lucresse Lucretia *BD* 1082, *LGWP* 211.
Lumbardye Lombardy *LGWP* 347.

Macrobeus/Macrobye Macrobius *BD* 284, *PF* 111.
Mantoan Mantuan *LGWD* 924.
Marcia[1] Marsyas *HF* 1229.
Marcia Catoun[2] Marcia *LGWP* 206.
Marcian Martianus Capella *HF* 985.
Mary (Seynt) *HF* 573.
Mars/Marte Mars *HF* 1446, *LGWP* 521.
Massynysse Masinissa *PF* 37.
Maudeleyne the Magdalen, St Mary Magdalen, *LGWP* 418.
May *BD* 291, *PF* 130, *LGWP* 36, 45, 89.
Mede Payment (personified) *PF* 228.
Medea *BD* 330, 726, *HF* 401, 1271.
Melky Weye the Milky Way (see **Galoxie** *HF* 937).
Mercuri/Mercurye Mercury *HF* 429, *LGWD* 1297.
Messenus Misenus *HF* 1243.
Mynerve Minerva *LGWD* 932.
Morpheus *BD* 136, 167, 242, 265.
Muse *HF* 1399.

Nabugodonosor Nebuchadnezzar *HF* 515.
Narcisus Narcissus *BD* 735.
Nature (personified) *BD* 18 (?), 467, 715 (?), 871, 908, 1195, *HF* 490, 1366,
    2039, *PF* 303, 317, 325, 368, 372, 377, 379, 447, 467, 519, 531, 617, 629,
    639, 659, 667, 676, *LGWP* 137, *LGWD* 975.

Octovyen Octavian *BD* 368.

Oyse the river Oise *HF* 1928.
Omere Homer *HF* 1466, 1477.
Orygenes Origen *LGWP* 418.
Orion *see* Arion.
Orpheus *BD* 569, *HF* 1203.
Owtermere the Holy Land (Fr. 'beyond the [Mediterranean] sea') *BD* 253.
Ovyde Ovid (Publius Ovidius Naso) *BD* 568, *HF* 379, 1487, *LGWD* 1367.

Palamon *LGWP* 420.
Palinurus *HF* 443.
Paris *BD* 331, *HF* 399, *PF* 290.
Parnaso Parnassus *HF* 521.
Penolope(e) Penelope *BD* 1081, *LGWP* 206.
Peter/Petre St Peter *HF* 1034, 2000.
Pharao/Pharoo Pharaoh *BD* 282, *HF* 516.
Phebus Phoebus *LGWD* 1206. *See* Apollo
Phedra Phaedra *HF* 419.
Pheton Phaëthon *HF* 942.
Phillis Phyllis *BD* 728, *HF* 390, *LGWP* 218.
Pictagoras Pythagoras *BD* 667 (*see note*).
Piramus Pyramus *PF* 289.
Pirrus Pyrrhus *HF* 161.
Plato(n) Plato *HF* 759, 931.
Pluto *HF* 1511.
Polite Polites *HF* 160.
Pollex Pollux *HF* 1006.
Pollexene Polyxena *BD* 1071, *LGWP* 212.
Pompe Pompey *HF* 1502.
Priam/Priamus *BD* 328, *HF* 159, *LGWD* 939.
Priapus *PF* 253.
Proserpyne Proserpina *HF* 1511.
Pseustis *HF* 1228.

Ravene Corvus (constellation) *HF* 1004.
Romauns of the Rose BD 334, *LGWP* 255, 431, 460.
Rome *BD* 1063, *HF* 1504, 1930, *LGWP* 211.
Romulus *HF* 589, *PF* 292.
Roode the Cross *BD* 924, 992, *HF* 2, 57.

Sampsoun Samson *BD* 738.
Saturne Saturn *HF* 1449.
Scipio(u)n *see* Cipio(n)
Scorpioun Scorpio (the constellation) *HF* 948.
Semyramus Semiramis *PF* 288.
Silla Scylla *PF* 292

32768915